COOK

THE AUSTRALIAN Women's Weekly

COOK

HOW TO COOK ABSOLUTELY EVERYTHING

acp books

Contents

Introduction	6
Terms & techniques	8
Kitchen equipment	14
Conversion charts	22
Breakfast	24
Drinks	46
Finger food	64
Soups	86
Starters	108
Salads	132
Seafood	154
Poultry & game birds	186
Beef & veal	216
Pork	250
Lamb	272
Vegetables	300
Eggs	324

Pasta & noodles	342
Rice	368
Pulses & grains	392
Sauces, dressings & salsas	410
Christmas & other festivities	432
Preserving	458
Breads & buns	476
Muffins, scones & friands	498
Biscuits & slices	516
Cakes	536
Pies & tarts	568
Desserts	594
After-dinner treats	624
Glossary	640
Index	664

SPECIAL FEATURES

Toast toppers	38
Garnishes for drinks	54
Fast finger food ideas	78
Soup accompaniments	96
Fast starters	118
Lettuces & other leaves	142
Herbs	168
Fast barbecued chicken recipes	202
Fast barbecue ideas	234
Unusual ingredients	260
Fast lamb cutlets	288
Asian greens	312
Cheeses	334
Noodles	352
Rice	380
Pulses & grains	402
Nuts & seeds	420
Christmas tree cookies	446
Spices	466
Pizza toppings	488
Butters & creams	506
Teas & coffees	526
Cupcakes	550
Quick puff pastry recipes	580
Tropical fruits	608
Truffles	632

I've wanted to do a cookbook like this for ages – a book that's a must-have; that reflects the way we eat today; that captures in one volume old favourites and contemporary recipes. Mind you, there are more than just recipes here. Hints and tips explain the unusual and give old favourites some new twists. There is also information on serving and storage, and every recipe comes with a nutrition count.

Selecting the recipes for this book was difficult: we were spoilt for choice. *The Australian Women's Weekly* Test Kitchen has been operating in one way or another since the 1930s and, as a result, we have many thousands of recipes, all triple-tested, from which to choose.

Hundreds of people have been responsible for creating, developing, testing, editing, styling and photographing the recipes that appear in this book, and the finished product is a credit to them all. The recipes don't come out of a filing cabinet or off a database; they weren't submitted by paid contributors or readers (with the exception of prize recipes that have appeared in our magazines). They were developed and made from scratch and cooked three times or more in our Test Kitchen, right in the heart of Sydney, before making their debut in our cookbooks.

I hope you enjoy this book as much as we've enjoyed putting it together.

Pamela Clark
Director,
The Australian Women's Weekly Test Kitchen

Terms & Techniques

For many of us, cooking is such a rewarding activity – not just for the edible end result, but the whole process of making something from scratch. For the uncertain cook, though, recipes can be dotted with unfamiliar words or instructions, and this can make the process quite daunting. Gaining a good understanding of commonly used terms and techniques will take the guesswork out of cooking. Use the following pages as a reference and soon you'll be able to disgorge, truss, macerate and make an emulsion without batting an eyelid. We've also included basic terms, such as fold, beat and whisk; after this quick refresher course, we promise your results will be even better.

BAIN-MARIE A hot-water "bath" into which dishes of food are placed for cooking either on top of the stove or in the oven. The hot water keeps the dishes at a constant, gentle temperature so that the food is not overheated, which is important for eggs, delicate custards and some fish dishes. The technique is also used for keeping cooked food hot without drying out. Bain-marie is French for "Mary's bath". Why Mary? We don't know.

BAKE BLIND To bake an empty tart, flan or pie shell/case, either partially (to colour and crisp the pastry before the filling is added) or completely if the filling is not to be cooked with it. It is necessary to guard against the empty shell puffing up or buckling as it cooks.

- To blind-bake small tarltet shells, prick all over but not quite all the way through with a fork, bake about half the cooking time, then check. If any have puffed up, press down gently with a spoon then finish baking.
- To blind-bake a larger shell, line it with foil or baking paper, fitting lightly into the corners, and fill with dried beans, peas or uncooked rice.
- For partial baking, cook until the sides are just coloured, then lift out the paper and beans and return the shell to the oven to dry and colour the base. Remove from the oven, add the filling and finish cooking as directed. If the sides start overbrowning, protect them with strips of foil.
- For baking completely, continue cooking after removing paper and beans until golden.

Note: To prevent a baked pastry shell from becoming soggy from the filling, brush the inside with beaten egg white or warm jam and place in the oven for a few minutes to set.

BASTE To spoon or brush liquid – usually pan juices, oil or melted butter – over meat, fish or vegetables as they roast or grill, to encourage browning and to stop them drying out.

BIND To hold together. Usually used to describe the way egg holds minced meat together in meat balls, hamburgers or a meatloaf as they cook.

BLANCH, REFRESH Blanch is French for "to whiten", but the term is used in cooking to mean the following:

- Cooking food briefly as a separate operation before proceeding with further cooking as the recipe directs.
  Delicate meats, such as brains, sweetbreads, rabbit or veal, may be blanched by simmering briefly to firm and whiten them. They are then plunged into cold water to stop the cooking immediately – this is called refreshing. Blanching also loosens the skin of brains and sweetbreads so that it can be removed.
  Fruits or vegetables may be blanched by plunging briefly into boiling water to brighten and set their colour before they are cooked further or frozen. They are then refreshed. Blanching can also mean par-cooking vegetables to be braised or stir-fried.
  Potato chips (french fries) are usually blanched by cooking first in 170°C oil until soft but not coloured. They are cooled, then placed in 190°C oil until brown and crisp.
- Removing the skins of nuts, tomatoes, fruits such as peaches, and organ meats such as tongue, liver or kidneys. Most are blanched by covering briefly with boiling water to loosen the skins, then peeling. Hazelnuts and pistachios, however, are "blanched" by roasting in a moderate oven for about 10 minutes, then rubbing off the skins in a cloth.

BRAISE To cook food slowly in a small amount of liquid, in a covered container on the stovetop or in the oven. Meat and poultry are usually browned first; vegetables may be blanched as a first step.

BRUISE To crush lightly, usually by rolling or pressing with an implement such as a rolling pin, heavy knife or pestle. Used to release the flavours of spices, citrus skin, lemon grass, aromatic leaves etc.

BUTTERFLY To cut a piece of meat so that it opens out flat. Used for large pieces such as a boned leg of lamb and also for small pieces such as a chicken breast.

CARAMELISE To brown food through the action of heat on sugar – either the invisible sugars contained in most foods, or sucrose (table sugar) itself. When sugar is heated, it first melts and then changes colour in stages from pale yellow to darker shades of brown. At the same time, its flavour and fragrance become richer and more intense. The process gives us the delicious brownness of familiar treats from roast meat to fried potatoes, piecrust to bread and cakes, marshmallows to meringue and hundreds more. When a recipe says to cook until caramelised, it means until it becomes a rich brown and fragrant.

CHAR-GRILL To brown food by a combination of hot air currents (convection) and contact with hot metal. When food is browned under an overhead grill or in an oven, its surface is browned by hot air. When it is browned on a ridged grill pan on top of the stove, or on barbecue bars, the parts of the food that touch metal become charred and smoky-flavoured, while the other parts are browned by convection.

CLARIFIED BUTTER/GHEE Butter which has had the water and non-fat solids removed. It can be heated to higher temperatures than ordinary butter without burning. You can buy it as ghee (its name in Indian and other Asian cooking), or you can make it yourself. Cut salted or unsalted butter into pieces, place in a saucepan, melt and heat slowly until hot but not browning. Remove from the heat and stand for a few minutes; a milky residue will sink to the bottom, leaving clear yellow liquid – the clarified butter – above. Pour off the butter slowly and allow to cool until solid. Store, covered, in the fridge. The milky solids left behind can be used to enrich soups or sauces.

CONFIT Food cooked very slowly in deep fat, then stored in the cooled and solidified fat which seals and preserves it until wanted. Making confit started as a way of preserving duck and goose parts for the winter. It is still mostly used for duck and goose, but other meats, fish and even vegetables can also be cooked by the confit method.

CRUMB To cover in a coating of breadcrumbs (or other crumbs such as crushed cereal) before frying or baking, to give a crisp, flavoursome finish. Used mainly for small pieces of food such as lamb cutlets or fish fillets. The pieces are first tossed in flour and the surplus shaken off, then dipped in beaten egg, drained, then tossed in crumbs. The coating is pressed on with the hands. The coating will adhere better during cooking if the food is first placed on lined oven trays and refrigerated for 20 minutes or more to allow the egg to set.

Moist, sticky foods such as croquettes or meatballs are sometimes crumbed; they do not need the flour and egg layers to make the crumbs adhere, but are simply tossed in crumbs and patted to firm on the coating.

DEGLAZE To simmer liquid (stock, wine, vegetable cooking water) in the pan after roasting or frying, having first poured off the fat slowly so as to leave the browned bits behind. Stir and scrape in the browned bits and coagulated juices from the pan while simmering until the liquid is somewhat reduced, then strain into a bowl. The liquid can be used as part of a sauce or reduced further and spooned over the food that was cooking in the pan.

DEGREASE To remove the fat from a liquid such as stock, clear soup or stew juices. Stand the liquid until the fat rises to the top, then spoon off as much as possible – if you can, tilt the container so that the fat collects at one side. The last traces of fat can be blotted off by placing absorbent paper directly on the surface, allowing to become soaked and then removing. An easier way, if there is time, is to chill the liquid so that the fat solidifies on top, then remove the fat layer.

DEVEIN To remove the intestinal vein from cooked prawns and other crustaceans before eating, or from uncooked prawns before cooking. See also page 157.

DISGORGE To draw out any bitter juices from vegetables such as eggplant, zucchini and cucumber. Slice the vegetables, sprinkle with coarse cooking salt and leave for 20 minutes to 1 hour in a colander or on a plate set at a tilt so that juices will drain away as the salt draws them out. Rinse and dry the vegetables before proceeding with the recipe.

DUST To decorate a cake or dessert with a fine, even coating of icing sugar or cocoa powder, etc by holding a fine sieve over food and sifting the sugar or powder through.

EMULSION In cooking, an emulsion sauce is one thickened by the emulsifying action of egg yolk, which acts to hold together ingredients that would usually separate – vinegar or lemon juice with butter or oil – to create a thick, creamy, stable texture. Mayonnaise is a cold emulsion sauce, béarnaise and hollandaise are warm ones.

FLAME/FLAMBE To flame food, that is, to set it alight briefly but spectacularly by pouring flaming high-alcohol liquor over it so that it is enrobed in blue flames. The food is described as flambé and the whole dish is called a flambé. Flaming is usually done as a final flourish and a final, heady flavouring just as the food – Crepes Suzette, for example – is served.

The safest way to flame food is to warm the alcohol – usually rum, brandy or whisky – in a small saucepan or metal ladle, take it to the food, set the liquor alight (with a long match if you're nervous) and pour immediately over the dish. You should, of course, be sure that you have turned off the exhaust fan first and once lighted, never leave the flaming food. You can do this at the table or just before taking the dish into the dining room.

FOLD, STIR, BEAT, CREAM, WHIP, WHISK These are all ways of combining ingredients, but each is performed differently and is different in its effect.

- **Fold** To combine ingredients lightly and delicately, usually because one ingredient contains air bubbles that are needed for rising and must not be lost.
  For folding, use a large metal spoon or a rubber or plastic spatula. Leading with the edge, cut down through the mixture, pick up some at the bottom, lift it to the surface, let it fall and cut down again. Turn the bowl as you go; stop as soon as the ingredients are loosely together but not thoroughly mixed. It is better to underfold than overfold.
- **Stir** To mix with a spoon in a circular or figure-of-eight motion, reaching right to the bottom, sides and corners of the bowl or saucepan. This may be done to combine ingredients completely or, if they are already combined, to keep the mixture moving so that it heats evenly as it cooks.
- **Beat** To mix foods vigorously and thoroughly, using a hitting motion with a spoon, fork, wire whisk, or a hand-operated or electric rotary beater at low to medium speed, or a flat electric beater at medium to high speed. The aim is to incorporate ingredients to a smooth consistency. Beating may also incorporate some air.
- **Cream** To beat ingredients, usually butter, or butter and sugar, to the consistency of heavy cream. The mixture becomes paler as it is beaten, as some air is incorporated.
- **Whip, whisk** To incorporate as much air as possible so the mixture puffs up into a light, airy mass. Use a wire whisk, fork, or hand-operated or electric rotary beater. If using a whisk or fork, keep the whole mixture moving up and over, and turn the bowl as you go. If using a rotary beater, move it round the bowl and turn the bowl so that you reach all of the mixture. Read the recipe carefully for directions about how long to whisk and how to tell when you should stop, as some ingredients collapse if overbeaten.

FRY: SAUTE/SAUTER, DRY-FRY, PAN-FRY, SHALLOW-FRY, DEEP-FRY, STIR-FRY To cook food in hot butter or oil. The word frying implies temperatures high enough to brown the food.

- **Sauté** To cook food at a high temperature with just enough butter to cover the base of the pan. Sauter is French for "to jump", and indicates the need to toss or turn the food so it colours evenly.
- **Dry-fry** To cook food in a dry frying pan, using only the fat or oil contained in the food to brown it. Used for high-fat foods such as nuts, seeds, sausages or bacon.
- **Pan-fry** To cook food in a small amount of butter or oil, some or all of which is usually used to make a sauce for the dish after the food is removed.
- **Shallow-fry** To cook small pieces of food such as fritters or cutlets in enough butter or oil to come halfway up the pieces, so that when they are turned to cook the other side they are evenly browned all over.
- **Deep-fry** To cook food in oil deep enough to float the pieces.
- **Stir-fry** To cook small pieces of food, cut to an even size, in a small amount of butter or oil over high heat while constantly tossing them.

INFUSE To steep ingredients in a liquid to flavour and/or colour it. For example, tea leaves are infused in hot water for tea.

KNEAD To work dough by folding over, pushing away, turning slightly and repeating the process. Bread dough is kneaded for 10 minutes or more to develop the gluten so that the dough is strong and elastic. Scone or pastry dough is kneaded gently and lightly only once or twice to make it smooth. Do not overknead or the scones or pastry will be tough.

MARINATE, MACERATE To marinate means to stand savoury food with flavoursome liquids and aromatics in order to flavour and sometimes to soften or lubricate it. To macerate means to stand sweet food, usually fruit, with flavoursome and aromatic ingredients in order to flavour it and sometimes to draw out the juices.
PAR-COOK, PAR-BOIL To half-cook or partially cook food, usually by boiling as a separate operation before proceeding with further cooking as the recipe directs – for example, to par-boil potatoes before roasting them or par-boil sausages before grilling them.
POACH, SIMMER, BOIL Three stages of heating a liquid in which food is to be cooked. It is important to use the right one – for instance, fish that is boiled when it should be poached will be tough and dry, while pasta not cooked at a brisk boil will stick together.

- Poach A liquid is at poaching temperature when the surface shivers but no bubbles appear. In clear liquid, you can see bubbles on the bottom of the pan but they don't rise.
- Simmer When the surface shudders and bubbles rise to the surface one at a time.
- Boil When bubbles rise briskly and continuously to the surface. It is at a full or rolling boil when the surface is rolling and seething with bubbles.

REDUCE, REDUCTION To reduce is to boil liquid in order to reduce the volume and so concentrate the flavour or produce a thicker consistency. Liquid which has been reduced is called a reduction.
RENDER To render is to melt the fat from meat by heating it slowly.
REST To rest roasted or grilled meat means to stand it, covered, in a warm place after cooking so that its juices settle, making it more succulent. This is an important part of the cooking process. A roast should be rested for 15 to 20 minutes, a steak for 5 minutes.
RICE COOKING METHODS The aim is to cook the rice grains until tender but separate rather than stuck together. There are two main methods of achieving this (boiling and the absorption method – see page 370). Rice cookers cook rice by the absorption method.
RUB IN, CUT IN To rub in is to coat flour grains with fat, usually butter, by mixing the chopped fat through the flour, then picking up a little mixture at a time in your fingers and rubbing it between the fingertips and thumbs, continuing until the mixture resembles coarse breadcrumbs. The technique is used to make scone dough, for example. The fat should be chilled so that it will not melt but remain in large particles; these particles melt during baking, leaving tiny pockets in the dough to help make the scones light.

To cut in is to incorporate flour and chilled fat in somewhat the same way as rubbing in but more coarsely, using a wire pastry cutter or two knives to cut the fat and flour together into smaller and smaller particles. This method works for pastry dough because it has a high proportion of fat compared with scone dough, which has so little fat that it can only be distributed throughout the flour by the rubbing-in method.

Both techniques can also be done in a food processor: put the flour in the processor, switch on and drop in chopped fat, a few pieces at a time, until it is all incorporated.
SCALD To scald has three distinct meanings.

- To heat a liquid almost to boiling point, a stage usually recognisable by bubbles beginning to appear round the edge.
- To make cloths or utensils hygienically clean by covering them with water and heating to scalding point.
- To make larger equipment hygienically clean by cleaning first with a brush or cloth then pouring very hot water over it.

SEASON To season means either of the following.

- To improve the flavour of food before, during or after cooking by adding salt, pepper and other flavourings; some foods should not be seasoned until after cooking.
- To prepare the surface of a new utensil such as a wok or cast-iron pan before using it. Seasoning helps to prevent food sticking.
  Before seasoning, the utensil should by washed in hot water with mild soap, rinsed, dried with a cloth then placed over low heat to dry thoroughly.
  A cast-iron pan is seasoned, while hot, by having the inside brushed or rubbed all over with cooking oil such as peanut oil (not a polyunsaturated oil) to coat very thinly, then being placed in a moderate oven for 1 hour. This process should be repeated several times before using.
  A wok is seasoned, while hot, by having the inside brushed or rubbed all over with cooking oil such as peanut oil (not a polyunsaturated oil) to coat very thinly, then being heated over high heat while being tilted and turned so that the oil does not run down and the entire surface is intensely heated for several minutes. After removing the wok from the heat and cooling, any excess oil that has run into the centre is mopped up with absorbent paper. The heating process is then repeated. The whole seasoning process should be repeated several times before using.
  To keep seasoned utensils in good order, they should be washed with hot water only, not with soap or detergent. If any food is stuck on, it should be rubbed off with a sponge or brush. The utensil should be placed over heat to dry thoroughly. If the surface begins to stick, seasoning should be repeated.

SWEAT To cook food slowly in a little butter or oil in a covered pan; the food should not colour. This is often the first step in making a soup or casserole.

TRUSS To tie a chicken or other bird into a neat, compact shape for cooking. There are various methods of trussing: a classic one is to lay the chicken on its back, cut a small hole in the skin at the base of the front and push the parson's nose (tail) through to close the vent. Pull the skin back over the neck and tuck the wings back so that the wingtips secure the skin. Take a piece of string, place the centre over the neck end, take it back across the wings and cross it underneath, then bring it up to tie the legs securely together, taking the string round the legs twice if necessary. This way of trussing does not mark the breast. Duck is trussed in the same way as chicken.

Turkey is not usually trussed, but prepared for roasting by having the neck flap tucked under and the legs tied together. The opening may be closed, if desired, by threading small skewers (sold in sets as poultry pins) across it then lacing string across and around the skewers and tying to close it.

Kitchen Equipment

You don't need a lot of utensils to cook well. You do need good, dependable utensils that do the job properly, hundreds of times over. The shops are full of temptations, but train your eye for quality by looking in the shops that supply professionals. If you haven't much to spend, put most of it into a few top-quality pieces rather than sets of second-raters. You can survive with no more than a knife, a steel to keep it sharp, a chopping board, a saucepan and a frying pan, to start with. If they are top quality, they will still be serving you well when the second-raters would be long-since discarded.

There is no need to spend a lot on the small essentials. While designer lemon squeezers, measuring cups and spoons, colanders and so on may be attractive, the more basic supermarket or chain-store equivalents will do exactly the same job. Add to the basics as you are able.

1. *Gratin dish*
2 & 3. *Fruit and vegetable knives*
4. *Roasting pan*
5. *Casserole*
6. *Measuring jug*
7. *Scales*
8. *Set of 4 measuring spoons*
9. *Steel*
10. *Nest of 4 measuring cups*
11. *Large serrated knife (breadknife)*
12. *Chef's knife*

KNIVES AND CHOPPING BOARDS

CHEF'S KNIFE large, heavy, expensive and worth every cent. It will have a forged blade (thick on the top side, tapering to a fine cutting edge) not a stamped-out one. Look for a tang (the metal that extends into the handle) that runs the entire length of the handle and is riveted in so that the constant impact of chopping won't loosen it. Or, there are excellent knives available that have the blade and handle moulded from one piece of metal. A 25cm blade is a good size, but hold several sizes to decide on the one whose size and weight suits your hand.

All good kitchen knives used to be carbon steel, which can be sharpened to razor sharpness but will stain and rust if not well cared for. Some modern knives are stainless steel, which is easy to look after but hard to sharpen to a fine edge. The best are made from a hybrid of these two materials, high-carbon stainless steel, which is very expensive but has the virtues of both carbon and stainless steel. Never wash these knives in a dishwasher; the detergent will damage and mark the metal.

PARING KNIFE a much smaller version of the chef's knife that fits the hand for peeling and close work.

LARGE SERRATED KNIFE (BREADKNIFE), with a blade at least 20cm long. A serrated (scalloped) edge is better than saw-teeth for cutting delicate cakes and pastries without squashing them.

FRUIT AND VEGETABLE KNIFE a small, pointed knife with a stainless-steel blade and a serrated edge. A cheap, light, chain-store one will do. It will cut tomatoes and other soft fruits and vegetables more cleanly and effortlessly than a plain blade.

1
2
3
4
LE CREUSET
5
6
7
not legal for commercial use
8
9
10
11
12

STEEL pick up the steel nearly every time you pick up a knife and just draw the edge, from heel to tip, down the front and then the back of the steel several times. Re-sharpen your knives as needed on a sharpening stone or electric wheel if you have the skill, or get them re-sharpened professionally once or twice a year.
CHOPPING BOARD perfectly flat, warp-resistant and large enough to hold the food that may fall from the knife and scatter. It may be nylon (or other man-made composition) or wood. Nylon can be scrubbed in hot water or even go into the dishwasher so that it is kept hygienically clean. Wood is kinder to your knives, ages better than nylon and, many cooks think, is more pleasant to use. If you choose wood, keep it hygienic and odour-free by wetting with cold water after use, then scrubbing with a handful of coarse salt, and rinsing quickly with hot water.

MEASURING UTENSILS

NEST OF 4 MEASURING CUPS chain-stores sell plastic measuring cups, which are fine.
SET OF 4 MEASURING SPOONS make sure the tablespoon is 20ml, not 15ml.
MEASURING JUGS 1 litre and 250ml sizes, marked strongly enough to show up clearly whether filled with pale or dark liquid.
SCALES the electronic kind that you can return to zero after you put a bowl on, but before you add the ingredients, is best. A portable one is more convenient than one that hangs on the wall.

BOWLS

LARGE, MEDIUM AND SMALL ceramic or heatproof glass, not plastic because it absorbs grease. The large or medium one should fit over one of your saucepans to make a double boiler. A few light, inexpensive stainless-steel bowls are a useful addition.

POTS AND PANS

This is what every kitchen needs in the way of pots and pans:

- small, medium and large saucepans with lids
- frying pan with a lid
- wok with a lid.

Judge a saucepan or frying pan by its weight and the material from which it is made. Ovenproof handles and knobs make it much more useful.
WEIGHT good pans are heavy; only a thick, heavy base will hold and distribute heat evenly. The sides should also be thick so that the food is surrounded by steady heat.
MATERIALS good conductors distribute heat evenly and respond quickly when heat is turned up or down; poor conductors develop hot spots and respond slowly.
HANDLES screwed-on handles can work loose and need the screw tightening, and the thread may eventually be too worn for effective tightening. Riveted handles stay steady much longer. Welded-on handles never wobble, though a catastrophic drop onto a hard surface could snap the weld.

ALUMINIUM is a superb conductor of heat but must be thick. It cannot be used for some foods, such as fruit, tomatoes and spinach, because it reacts with them, causing "off" flavours and discolouration of both pan and food.

STAINLESS STEEL is non-reactive but is a poor conductor. Bases are usually aluminium- or copper-clad, or a "sandwich" of one of these to help conduction.

ENAMELLED CAST-IRON is heavy, sometimes excessively so for comfortable use. Iron conducts heat well but the baked-enamel coating slows it down. The enamel must be thick enough and hard enough to resist scratching and chipping. Many cooks swear by top-quality enamelled iron utensils; others say that the lining does, in time, scratch and stick and that the pans respond slowly to heat changes.

BARE CAST-IRON is heavy, sometimes excessively so, and browns well but can impart a metallic taste to food. It must be well seasoned before use (see page 13) and will probably need re-seasoning quite often.

SHEET STEEL is familiar in cheap, thin woks – which are the exception to the heavy-is-best rule, because stir-frying calls for brief, high heat and the food is kept moving to cook by contact. They must be seasoned well before use (see page 13). These woks become more seasoned and non-stick with each use, but can rust if not washed promptly and dried properly. More expensive woks, often heavier with non-stick linings and sometimes electric, seldom perform as well as these inexpensive classics.

TITANIUM browns well, is an excellent conductor and is non-stick by virtue of its basic composition rather than a coating, so it is not damaged by metal tools and is non-stick for life. Look for saucepans and frying pans that have ovenproof handles and knobs.

OVEN DISHES AND CASSEROLES

GRATIN DISH shallow and open for food to be browned on top. More useful if flameproof as well as ovenproof.

CASSEROLE should be heavy, with a well-fitting lid. More useful if flameproof as well as ovenproof. This is where enamelled cast-iron is perfect.

ROASTING PAN heavy cast steel or other metal resists buckling better than thin sheet metal. Should have its own rack to hold the roast, or accommodate one of your cake racks. A lid is sometimes useful but not essential.

1 & 2. *Plastic and metal sieves*
3. *Colander*
4. *Rubber spatulas*
5. *Large metal spoon*
6. *Large slotted spoon*
7. *Ladle*
8. *Pastry brush*
9 & 10. *Wooden spoons*
11. *Heat-spreading mat*
12. *Grater*
13. *Tongs*
14. *Wire balloon whisk*
15. *Hand-turned rotary beater*
16. *Egg/fish slices*

STIRRERS, SCRAPERS, LIFTERS AND TURNERS

TWO WOODEN SPOONS, one with a hole so that sauces won't collect to a thick lump in the bowl or pan as you stir. Since wood absorbs flavours and fat, it's a good idea to keep one spoon for savoury recipes and one for sweet recipes.

LARGE METAL SPOON for serving and folding.

LARGE SLOTTED SPOON for draining food as you lift it.

TWO RUBBER SPATULAS, large and small for scraping bowls.

WIRE BALLOON WHISK in a size suitable for your hand and one of your bowls. A tiny one is a useful extra for making salad dressings.

HAND-TURNED ROTARY BEATER unless you have a hand-held electric mixer.

TWO EGG/FISH SLICES metal or reliably heatproof composition. Cheap flexible ones perform better than rigid ones.

OTHER BASIC ESSENTIALS

TWO SIEVES, one nylon for fruit, one metal for sifting flour, icing sugar etc.

COLANDER or large, strong sieve.

GRATER microplane graters, razor-sharp and non-clogging, are expensive but worth the investment. Medium-coarse is the most useful. Otherwise, a square or round stainless-steel conventional grater.

LEMON-SQUEEZER made mostly from plastic or glass.

ROLLING PIN plain, heavy, cylindrical; made mostly from wood or glass.

HEAT-SPREADING MAT to go on a gas stove burner to spread heat evenly over the base of the pan, making heat distribution more controllable.

KITCHEN SCISSORS are extremely useful for all sorts of odd jobs.

TONGS indispensible for turning and moving food.

LADLE for serving food; also good for measuring servings.

FINE METAL SKEWERS sold in various lengths and also in sets as poultry pins. For testing doneness of cakes, meat or vegetables, securing loin chops curled up for cooking, as well as for closing the opening in a chicken or turkey.

PASTRY BRUSH buy small paint brushes from hardware shops; they're cheap and effective.

EXTRAS FOR BAKING cake pans, cake racks, muffin pans, patty pans, oven trays, scone and other cutters.

1
2
3
4
5
6
7
8
9
10
11
12
13
14
15
16

1
2
3
4
5
6
7
8
9
10
11
12
13
14
15
16
17
18

NOT ESSENTIAL BUT USEFUL

GRILL PAN usually made from cast iron; great for meat – the excess fat drains away during cooking.

STOVETOP CHAR-GRILL usually square or rectangular to sit over one or two gas burners.

OMELETTE/CREPE PAN buy these only if you love to cook omelettes and crepes.

SALAD SPINNER for washing and drying salad leaves, herbs and shredded cabbage.

MANDOLINE OR V SLICER cheap ones are efficient though less versatile than the expensive mandoline.

CARVING KNIFE, HAM KNIFE long and flexible for negotiating the curves of a roast or ham.

ROTARY GRATER OR MOULI for cheese or nuts.

CHEESE PLANE for uniform, thin slices.

MEAT THERMOMETER makes cooking joints and roasts foolproof.

OVEN THERMOMETER to keep a check on your oven's thermostat.

CANDY THERMOMETER indispensible if you enjoy making confectionery.

POTATO MASHER makes short work of mashing cooked potatoes

PALETTE KNIFE small, thin, flexible, for loosening cakes from pans, and desserts from moulds. Look in art-supplies shops.

TIMER useful if your oven does not have an in-built timer.

BAR EQUIPMENT

CORKSCREW let price be your guide to quality; cheap ones can break easily.

INSULATED ICE CONTAINER for chilling wine or champagne.

LONG-HANDLED SPOON/STIRRER for cocktails and mixed drinks.

BAR MEASURE if you're serious about making cocktails.

BAR STRAINER (HAWTHORN STRAINER) a must for straining cocktails.

MUDDLER for crushing fruit and sugar together. A pestle can be used instead.

COCKTAIL SHAKER they work, and make you look like a professional.

JUG for measuring.

COCKTAIL PICKS to hold garnishes.

SMALL CUTTING BOARD AND KNIFE for slicing and chopping garnishes for glasses.

ELECTRICAL APPLIANCES

Fancy features and attachments don't count as much as strength. A powerful motor won't struggle to perform and will serve you for many years – there are plenty of 40-year-old food processors and mixers still going strong. Consider the extra features and try to be realistic about how much you would really use them. Look critically at both machine and attachments with an eye to flimsy versus well-made parts, and make your choice with a bias towards solid power.

1. *Palette knife*
2. *Cheese plane*
3. *Grill pan*
4. *Omelette/crepe pan*
5. *Salad spinner*
6 & 7. *Meat thermometer and candy thermometer*
8. *V slicer*
9. *Ricer*
10. *Muddler*
11. *Oven thermometer*
12. *Carving knife*
13. *Ham knife*
14. *Bar strainer (Hawthorn strainer)*
15. *Bar measure*
16. *Cocktail shaker*
17. *Stovetop char-grill*
18. *Rotary grater*

Conversion Charts

One Australian metric measuring cup or jug holds approximately 250ml; one Australian metric tablespoon holds 20ml; one Australian metric teaspoon holds 5ml.

The difference between one country's measuring cups and another's is within a two- or three-teaspoon variance, which is only 10 or 15ml and will not affect your cooking results. Most countries, including the US, the UK and New Zealand, use a 15ml tablespoon.

All cup and spoon measurements are level. The most accurate way of measuring dry ingredients is to weigh them. When measuring liquids, use a clear glass or plastic jug with metric markings at eye level.

In this book we used large eggs with an average weight of 60g each. Please note that those who might be at risk from the effects of salmonella poisoning (such as pregnant women, the elderly or young children) should consult their doctor before eating raw eggs.

OVEN TEMPERATURES

These oven temperatures are only a guide for conventional ovens. For fan-forced ovens, check the manufacturer's manual.

	°C (CELSIUS)	°F (FAHRENHEIT)	GAS MARK
Very slow	120	250	½
Slow	150	275-300	1-2
Moderately slow	170	325	3
Moderate	180	350-375	4-5
Moderately hot	200	400	6
Hot	220	425-450	7-8
Very hot	240	475	9

DRY MEASURES

METRIC	IMPERIAL
15g	½oz
30g	1oz
60g	2oz
90g	3oz
125g	4oz (¼lb)
155g	5oz
185g	6oz
220g	7oz
250g	8oz (½lb)
280g	9oz
315g	10oz
345g	11oz
375g	12oz (¾lb)
410g	13oz
440g	14oz
470g	15oz
500g	16oz (1lb)
750g	24oz (1½lb)
1kg	32oz (2lb)

LIQUID MEASURES

METRIC	IMPERIAL
30ml	1 fluid oz
60ml	2 fluid oz
100ml	3 fluid oz
125ml	4 fluid oz
150ml	5 fluid oz (¼ pint/1 gill)
190ml	6 fluid oz
250ml	8 fluid oz
300ml	10 fluid oz (½ pint)
500ml	16 fluid oz
600ml	20 fluid oz (1 pint)
1000ml (1 litre)	1¾ pints

LENGTH MEASURES

METRIC	IMPERIAL
3mm	⅛in
6mm	¼in
1cm	½in
2cm	¾in
2.5cm	1in
5cm	2in
6cm	2½in
8cm	3in
10cm	4in
13cm	5in
15cm	6in
18cm	7in
20cm	8in
23cm	9in
25cm	10in
28cm	11in
30cm	12in (1ft)

BREAKFAST

Breakfast

For many of us there are two kinds of breakfast: the speedy weekday one that gets us out the door on time, and the blissfully indulgent, take-your-time kind that drifts through two or three favourite treats, plus leisurely tea or coffee, on a lazy weekend morning. On occasion, you can call it brunch; ask some friends over and you're entertaining in a delightfully relaxed way that won't break the budget.

Living well includes eating well, both when you're in a tearing hurry and when you're not. It is well established that children and adults alike feel better and perform better during the day if they start it with a healthy and sustaining breakfast. Browse through this chapter and you'll find some wonderful quick-breakfast ideas as well as great slow-breakfast inspirations.

QUICK BREAKFASTS

CEREAL POWER The original muesli, also known as the Swiss Health Breakfast, was developed by a famous nutritionist Dr Bircher-Benner at his Swiss alpine sanatorium as the nearest possible approach to a perfect food. Thousands of Swiss and countless others throughout the world still thrive on it. Based on a mixture of raw cereal, dried fruit and sometimes nuts and raw sugar or honey, it can be eaten with milk and fresh fruit.True Bircher muesli doesn't come from a packet but takes only minutes to prepare, as our recipe shows (see page 40).

Today, muesli is prepared commercially in many variations, but making your own is easy, cheaper and gives you complete control over the amount of sugar and fat you're eating. Many families develop their own variations – start with our roasted muesli recipe (see page 30) and take it from there. Fresh fruit can be chopped or shredded over the cereal. Add milk or yogurt for a light but sustaining start that provides a significant part of the fibre, calcium and vitamins you should have every day for good health.

Nothing beats the comfort of hot, real porridge (see page 32) on a cold morning. It takes only a few minutes to get it going, and it will keep you feeling good all morning.

BREAKFAST IN A GLASS Egg-flip – an egg beaten up in hot or cold milk with honey or sugar and vanilla or another favourite flavouring – has been comforting and delighting all sorts of people for generations, from small children and those feeling a bit delicate to those who believe in a real breakfast but simply can't make the time for any other kind. Break an egg into a blender, add a cup of hot or cold milk, honey or sugar to taste and a good dash of vanilla, drinking chocolate, raspberry syrup or another favourite flavour, and whiz until smooth and frothy. If you don't have a blender, beat the egg in a bowl and add the other ingredients, beating until smooth. The protein, vitamin and calcium hit will keep your energy level up all morning. As a precaution, though, anyone who might be at risk from the effects of salmonella (such as pregnant women, the elderly or young children) should consult their doctor before eating raw eggs.

For other nutritious breakfasts-in-a-glass, try the mixed berry smoothie or the banana passionfruit soy smoothie in the Drinks chapter (see page 60).

SLOW BREAKFASTS

The joy of an indulgent weekend breakfast is that anything goes. You may opt for tradition with cereal and eggs, and then again, you may not. If you feel like sweet waffles followed by sweet pastries, or a hang-the-kilojoules fry-up, this is the time to revel in them.

The same non-rules apply if you're having friends over: simply choose a few things you would love to eat and they'll be happy too. If you want to have eggs, feed a crowd in style with the Spanish tortilla (see page 33); this can be made ahead of time and eaten just warm.

You may choose to offer alcohol, or not; a good way to manage is to have orange juice and bubbly on hand so that guests can have either one straight or mix them. The one rule that is unbreakable is that the tea and coffee must be real, hot and plentiful.

PERFECT TEA, GREAT COFFEE

Try the same blend and same brand of tea made from a teabag and from loose tea and you will find that the cup made with loose tea is perceptibly fresher and "brighter" in flavour. Even when you want to make only one cup, you will get a better result by using loose tea in one of those nifty little hinged infusers. When catering for several people, a teapot is the way to go. Heat both the teapot and a second pot by filling with hot water and standing for a few minutes. When the kettle is nearly boiling, empty both pots and put one teaspoon of tea per cupful, plus one extra, into the teapot. As soon as the water boils, fill both pots and put the lids on. Swirl the teapot gently and stand a few minutes before pouring, using a strainer. If the tea is too strong for anyone, adjust the strength with the hot water. Milk is added after the tea so that people can see when it looks the way they like it.

Purists buy their coffee as whole beans and grind it themselves for each brew, but you will still get good flavourful coffee if you buy it ground, in quantities you will use within a week or two, and keep it in an airtight jar away from heat and light. For a paper-filter pot or espresso machine, you need a fine grind, and for a jug, plunger or Italian stovetop coffee maker, a medium grind. The once-popular percolator is now out of favour because it vaporises some of the most delicious and ethereal flavour components, while continuing to extract other harsh-tasting components. For a jug, plunger or stovetop coffee maker, use a heaped dessertspoon of coffee per cup. For a filter pot, use a little less because it is finer. Preheat a jug, plunger or filter pot as for tea, and use water just before it reaches the boil; follow the maker's instructions for an espresso machine. For a plunger, allow the coffee to settle for 3 to 4 minutes before plunging. Serve with hot milk.

Serve these savoury little "puddings" and their tomato garnish with grilled Turkish bread or wholegrain toast. They would also be good as a vegetarian main course, or as a first course for a dinner party.

Baked ricotta with tomato

PREPARATION TIME 15 MINUTES **COOKING TIME** 15 MINUTES **SERVES** 4

2 teaspoons olive oil
1 tablespoon pine nuts
2 cloves garlic, crushed
100g baby spinach leaves
1¼ cups (300g) low-fat ricotta
1 egg, beaten lightly
2 tablespoons coarsely chopped fresh chives
500g baby vine-ripened truss tomatoes
1 tablespoon balsamic vinegar

1 Preheat oven to hot (220°C/200°C fan-forced). Oil 6-hole (⅓-cup/80ml) muffin pan.
2 Heat half of the oil in medium frying pan; cook nuts and garlic until fragrant. Add spinach; stir until wilted. Cool 10 minutes.
3 Combine spinach mixture in medium bowl with ricotta, egg and chives; divide among holes. Bake, uncovered, about 15 minutes or until browned.
4 Combine tomatoes and vinegar with remaining oil in small shallow baking dish. Roast, uncovered, 10 minutes.
5 Serve baked ricotta with tomatoes.

PER SERVING 12.9g total fat (5.1g saturated); 782kj (187 cal); 4.5g carbohydrate; 11.9g protein; 2.7g fibre

---

The correct pan is important for successful omelette-making. It should be shallow, with sloping sides to make it easier to slide the omelette onto a plate.

Smoked salmon omelette

PREPARATION TIME 10 MINUTES **COOKING TIME** 15 MINUTES **SERVES** 4

6 eggs
⅔ cup (160ml) cream
1 tablespoon warm water
⅔ cup (160g) sour cream
2 tablespoons coarsely chopped fresh dill
1 tablespoon lemon juice
220g thinly sliced smoked salmon
30g baby rocket leaves

You can use smoked trout instead of smoked salmon for this recipe.

1 Break eggs into medium bowl, whisk lightly; whisk in cream.
2 Pour a quarter of the egg mixture into heated lightly oiled 22cm frying pan; cook over medium heat, tilting pan, until omelette is almost set. Run spatula around edge of pan to loosen omelette, turn onto plate; cover to keep warm. Repeat process with remaining egg mixture to make four omelettes.
3 Combine the water, sour cream, dill and juice in small bowl. Fold omelettes into quarters; place on serving plates. Top each with equal amounts of salmon, sour cream mixture and rocket.

PER SERVING 43.6g total fat (24.8g saturated); 2077kj (497 cal); 2.8g carbohydrate; 24.6g protein; 0.1g fibre

French toast with berry compote

PREPARATION TIME 15 MINUTES **COOKING TIME** 10 MINUTES **SERVES** 4

For a delicious alternative to icing sugar, sprinkle French toast with vanilla or cinnamon sugar. Simply combine ¼ cup caster sugar with the seeds of half a vanilla pod or a good pinch of ground cinnamon.

4 eggs

½ cup (125ml) cream

¼ cup (60ml) milk

1 teaspoon finely grated orange rind

1 teaspoon ground cinnamon

¼ cup (90g) honey

100g butter, melted

8 thick slices sourdough bread (560g)

¼ cup (40g) icing sugar

BERRY COMPOTE

1 teaspoon arrowroot

⅓ cup (80ml) water

2 cups (300g) frozen mixed berries

2 tablespoons caster sugar

1 tablespoon finely grated orange rind

1 Whisk eggs, cream, milk, rind, cinnamon and honey in large bowl until combined.
2 Make berry compote.
3 Heat a quarter of the butter in medium frying pan. Dip two bread slices into egg mixture; cook, uncovered, until browned both sides. Remove french toast from pan; cover to keep warm. Repeat with remaining butter, bread slices and egg mixture.
4 Dust french toast with sifted icing sugar; serve with warm berry compote.

BERRY COMPOTE Blend arrowroot with the water in small saucepan until smooth. Stir in remaining ingredients; cook until mixture almost boils and thickens slightly.

PER SERVING 43.7g total fat (25g saturated); 3787kj (906cal); 104.8g carbohydrate; 20.9g protein; 9.9g fibre

Breakfast fry-up

PREPARATION TIME 10 MINUTES **COOKING TIME** 20 MINUTES **SERVES** 4

To speed up the cooking time of the tomatoes, preheat your grill to high and "roast" the tomatoes for about 10 minutes.

Serve the breakfast fry-up with thick slices of toasted sourdough.

4 medium egg tomatoes (300g), quartered

2 tablespoons balsamic vinegar

cooking-oil spray

300g mushrooms, sliced thickly

½ cup loosely packed fresh basil leaves, torn

¼ cup loosely packed fresh coriander leaves

¼ cup loosely packed fresh flat-leaf parsley leaves

200g shaved ham

1 Preheat oven to moderately hot (200°C/180°C fan-forced).
2 Combine tomato and half of the vinegar in medium shallow oiled baking dish; spray with oil. Roast, uncovered, 20 minutes.
3 Meanwhile, cook mushrooms and remaining vinegar in medium oiled frying pan until tender; stir in herbs. Transfer to serving dishes; cover to keep warm.
4 Heat ham in same pan. Serve ham with mushroom mixture and roasted tomatoes.

PER SERVING 2.6g total fat (0.7g saturated); 401kj (96 cal); 2.7g carbohydrate; 13.1g protein; 3.2g fibre

Oats have a tendency to go rancid more quickly than other grains, as they contain more oils. Therefore only make enough muesli to last a couple of weeks. Keep muesli in a sealed container in a cool place; it will keep longest if stored in the fridge.

Roasted muesli with dried fruit and honey

PREPARATION TIME 15 MINUTES **COOKING TIME** 15 MINUTES **SERVES** 6

2 cups (180g) rolled oats

1 cup (110g) rolled rice

¼ cup (15g) unprocessed wheat bran

¼ cup (50g) pepitas

1 teaspoon ground cinnamon

⅓ cup (115g) honey

1 tablespoon vegetable oil

¾ cup (35g) flaked coconut

⅓ cup (50g) coarsely chopped dried apricots

⅓ cup (20g) coarsely chopped dried apples

⅓ cup (55g) sultanas

¼ cup (35g) craisins, chopped coarsely

1 Preheat oven to moderate (180°C/160°C fan-forced).

2 Combine oats and rice in large bowl, then spread evenly on two oven trays. Roast, uncovered, in oven 5 minutes.

3 Stir bran, pepitas and cinnamon into oat mixtures, then drizzle evenly with combined honey and oil; stir to combine. Toast, uncovered, 5 minutes. Stir in coconut. Roast, uncovered, 5 minutes.

4 Remove trays from oven; place muesli mixture in same large bowl, stir in remaining ingredients. Serve with milk or yogurt.

PER SERVING 16.1g total fat (4.8g saturated); 1768kj (423 cal); 52.8g carbohydrate; 7.3g protein; 11.1g fibre

Strawberries, raspberries or sliced bananas can be used instead of the blueberries. The hotcakes can be kept warm on a tray in a slow oven.

Blueberry hotcakes with walnuts and maple syrup

PREPARATION TIME 10 MINUTES **COOKING TIME** 15 MINUTES **SERVES** 6

1 ½ cups (225g) self-raising flour

⅓ cup (75g) caster sugar

1 cup (240g) ricotta

1 cup (250ml) milk

6 eggs, separated

1 ½ cups (225g) blueberries

½ cup (50g) roasted walnuts, chopped coarsely

1 cup (250ml) pure maple syrup

1 Sift flour and sugar into medium bowl. Whisk in ricotta, milk and egg yolks; stir in blueberries.

2 Beat egg whites in medium bowl with electric mixer until soft peaks form. Fold into flour mixture in two batches.

3 Pour ¼ cups of the batter into heated oiled large frying pan; cook until bubbles appear on the surface. Turn hotcakes; cook until browned underneath. Remove hotcakes from pan; cover to keep warm. Repeat to make 18 hotcakes.

4 Serve hotcakes with nuts and syrup.

ROASTED MUESLI WITH DRIED FRUIT AND HONEY

For a creamier porridge, replace half the hot water with milk.

Porridge

PREPARATION TIME 5 MINUTES **COOKING TIME** 5 MINUTES **SERVES** 4

3½ cups (875ml) hot water
1½ cups (135g) rolled oats
½ cup (125ml) milk

1 Combine the water and oats in medium saucepan over medium heat; cook, stirring, about 5 minutes or until porridge is thick and creamy.
2 Stir in milk. Serve with the topping of your choice.

PER SERVING (WITHOUT TOPPING) 4.1g total fat (1.3g saturated); 627kj (150 cal); 22.4g carbohydrate; 4.7g protein; 2.3g fibre

You may like to serve a choice of toppings so breakfasters can help themselves. In that case, increase the quantities to make sure there is plenty to go around.

APPLE AND PEAR COMPOTE TOPPING Peel, core and coarsely chop 1 large apple and 1 medium pear. Combine fruit with ⅓ cup apple juice and 1 tablespoon lemon juice in medium saucepan over medium heat; bring to a boil. Reduce heat; simmer, covered, stirring occasionally, about 15 minutes or until fruit softens and liquid is absorbed.

PER SERVING (WITH PORRIDGE) 4.2g total fat (1.3g saturated); 899kj (215 cal); 37.5g carbohydrate; 5.0g protein; 4.2g fibre

CINNAMON SUGAR TOPPING Combine 1 teaspoon ground cinnamon with 2 tablespoons caster sugar in small bowl. Sprinkle over bowls of porridge. Any remaining cinnamon sugar can be sprinkled on hot buttered toast for an afternoon snack.

PER SERVING (WITH PORRIDGE) 4.1g total fat (1.3g saturated); 773kj (185 cal); 31.4g carbohydrate; 4.7g protein; 2.3g fibre

HONEY AND YOGURT TOPPING Divide ⅓ cup low-fat vanilla yogurt and 1 tablespoon honey among bowls of porridge.

PER SERVING (WITH PORRIDGE) 4.1g total fat (1.3g saturated); 790kj (189 cal); 30.8g carbohydrate; 5.9g protein; 2.3g fibre

---

Why store eggs in the fridge? The fact is, an egg will age more in one day at room temperature than in a whole week in the fridge.

Bacon and eggs

PREPARATION TIME 5 MINUTES **COOKING TIME** 10 MINUTES **SERVES** 2

4 bacon rashers (280g)
1 tablespoon vegetable oil
4 eggs
1 medium tomato (150g), halved

1 Cook bacon in medium frying pan until browned. Remove from pan; cover to keep warm.
2 Preheat grill.
3 Heat oil in same pan; break eggs into pan. Cook, uncovered, until egg white has set and yolk is cooked as desired.
4 Meanwhile, place tomato, cut-side up, onto oven tray. Place under grill until browned lightly and just tender.
5 Serve fried eggs, bacon and tomato with toast, if desired.

PER SERVING 38.4g total fat (11.2g saturated); 2157kj (516 cal); 2.3g carbohydrate; 41.4g protein; 0.9g fibre

Spanish tortilla

A Spanish tortilla is an omelette made predominantly with potato. It tastes great served warm or at room temperature, and makes an excellent breakfast, lunch, dinner or appetiser with drinks.

PREPARATION TIME 15 MINUTES **COOKING TIME** 30 MINUTES **SERVES** 4

800g potatoes, sliced thinly
1 tablespoon olive oil
1 large brown onion (200g), sliced thinly
200g chorizo sausage, sliced thinly
6 eggs, beaten lightly
300ml cream
4 green onions, sliced thickly
¼ cup (25g) coarsely grated mozzarella cheese
¼ cup (30g) coarsely grated cheddar

1 Boil, steam or microwave potato until just tender; drain.
2 Meanwhile, heat oil in medium frying pan; cook brown onion, stirring, until soft. Add chorizo; cook, stirring, until crisp. Drain chorizo mixture on absorbent paper.
3 Whisk eggs in large bowl with cream, green onion and cheeses; stir in potato and chorizo mixture.
4 Pour mixture into same heated lightly oiled pan; cook, covered, over low heat about 10 minutes or until tortilla is just set. Carefully invert tortilla onto plate, then slide back into pan; cook, uncovered, about 5 minutes or until cooked through.

PER SERVING 64g total fat (32.4g saturated); 3398kj (813 cal); 29.3g carbohydrate; 29.6g protein; 4.5g fibre

---

Mini muffin dampers

If you're a bit short of time, use bottled pesto. A sun-dried tomato pesto or olive tapenade can also be substituted.

PREPARATION TIME 10 MINUTES **COOKING TIME** 25 MINUTES **MAKES** 12

3 cups (450g) self-raising flour
40g butter, chopped coarsely
1¾ cups (430ml) buttermilk
2 tablespoons basil pesto
¾ cup (90g) coarsely grated cheddar
¼ teaspoon sweet paprika
1 tablespoon plain flour

1 Preheat oven to moderately hot (200°C/180°C fan-forced). Grease 12-hole (⅓-cup/80ml) muffin pan.
2 Place self-raising flour in large bowl; rub in butter. Using fork, stir in buttermilk to form a soft, sticky dough. Swirl pesto and cheese through; do not overmix.
3 Divide mixture among holes of pan. Sprinkle with combined paprika and plain flour. Bake, uncovered, about 25 minutes. Stand dampers in pan 5 minutes before turning out onto wire rack to cool.

PER DAMPER 7.8g total fat (4.3g saturated); 924kj (221 cal); 29.2g carbohydrate; 7.6g protein; 1.5g fibre

1

2

3

4

Fruit scrolls with spiced yogurt

PREPARATION TIME 10 MINUTES **COOKING TIME** 25 MINUTES **SERVES** 4

This recipe is best made close to serving time to prevent the pastry from going soggy.

40g butter

¼ teaspoon ground nutmeg

1½ tablespoons brown sugar

1 tablespoon ground cinnamon

1 small apple (130g), peeled, cored, grated coarsely

⅓ cup (50g) finely chopped dried apricots

½ cup (125ml) orange juice

1 sheet ready-rolled puff pastry

½ cup (140g) yogurt

1 tablespoon honey

1 Preheat oven to moderately hot (200°C/180°C fan-forced). Lightly grease oven tray.

2 Melt half of the butter in small saucepan; cook nutmeg, sugar and half of the cinnamon, stirring, over low heat, until sugar dissolves. Stir in apple, apricot and half of the juice; bring to a boil. Reduce heat; simmer, uncovered, 2 minutes. Remove from heat; stir in remaining juice. Cool.

3 Spread fruit mixture over pastry sheet; roll into log. Cut log into quarters; place 5cm apart on tray, brush with remaining melted butter. Bake, uncovered, about 20 minutes or until scrolls are cooked through.

4 Meanwhile, combine yogurt, honey and remaining cinnamon in small bowl.

5 Dust hot scrolls with sifted icing sugar, if desired; serve with spiced yogurt.

For extra crunch sprinkle 50g chopped roasted almonds over the fruit, before rolling the pastry into a log.

PER SERVING 9.5g total fat (6.2g saturated); 786kj (188 cal);23.0g carbohydrate; 2.5g protein; 1.6g fibre

---

Spiced plums with yogurt

PREPARATION TIME 10 MINUTES **COOKING TIME** 10 MINUTES (PLUS COOLING TIME) **SERVES** 4

Blood plums are of Japanese origin. Their flesh is red and tart – ideal for cooking.

1 litre (4 cups) water

½ cup (125ml) orange juice

⅓ cup (75g) caster sugar

5cm strip orange rind

2 star anise

4 cloves

1 teaspoon mixed spice

1 cinnamon stick

1 vanilla bean, halved lengthways

8 blood plums (900g), unpeeled

1⅓ cups (375g) yogurt

1 Place the water, juice, sugar, rind and spices in medium frying pan. Scrape vanilla seeds into pan then add pod; cook mixture, stirring, until sugar dissolves.

2 Add plums to pan; poach, uncovered, over low heat about 10 minutes or until just tender. Using slotted spoon, place two plums in each of four serving dishes (reserve 2 tablespoons of the poaching liquid). Cool plums 20 minutes.

3 Combine yogurt and reserved poaching liquid in small bowl; serve with plums.

Before adding the plums to the pan prick the skin with a fork, to prevent it from tearing.

PER SERVING 3.4g total fat (2.1g saturated); 949kj (227 cal); 39.5g carbohydrate; 5.7g protein; 4.1g fibre

1 FRUIT SCROLLS WITH SPICED YOGURT **2** SPICED PLUMS WITH YOGURT
3 POLENTA AND CORN FRITTERS [P 36] **4** PROSCIUTTO AND FONTINA CROISSANTS [P 36]

To add extra flavour to the polenta use boiling stock instead of the water.

Polenta and corn fritters

PREPARATION TIME 5 MINUTES (PLUS STANDING TIME) **COOKING TIME** 15 MINUTES **SERVES** 4

1 cup (250ml) boiling water
1 cup (170g) polenta
1 teaspoon salt
1 egg, beaten lightly
½ cup (125ml) milk
40g butter, melted
½ cup (75g) self-raising flour
125g can corn kernels, drained
½ cup (60g) coarsely grated cheddar
⅔ cup (170g) bottled chunky tomato salsa

1 Combine the water, polenta and salt in medium heatproof bowl, cover; stand 10 minutes.
2 Stir egg, milk and butter into polenta mixture, then add flour, corn and cheese; stir until batter is well combined.
3 Pour ¼ cup of the batter into large heated lightly oiled frying pan; using spatula, spread batter to shape into a round. Cook about 2 minutes each side or until fritter is browned lightly and cooked through, remove from pan; cover to keep warm. Repeat with remaining batter.
4 Serve fritters with salsa.

PER SERVING 17.2g total fat (10.0g saturated); 1743kj (417 cal); 50.8g carbohydrate; 13.1g protein; 3.3g fibre

---

Croissants are by far the most famous of all the French pastries and are made using a butter-rich flaky pastry. In France they usually eat them just with jam, while around the world they have become popular filled with both savoury and sweet fillings.

If you prefer, you can replace the fontina with a good-quality parmesan.

Prosciutto and fontina croissants

PREPARATION TIME 10 MINUTES **COOKING TIME** 10 MINUTES **SERVES** 4

4 croissants
2 teaspoons olive oil
8 slices prosciutto (120g)
½ cup (50g) coarsely grated fontina cheese
⅔ cup (100g) drained semi-dried tomatoes, sliced thinly
30g baby rocket leaves

1 Preheat oven to moderately slow (170°C/150°C fan-forced).
2 Split croissants in half horizontally, without separating; place on oven tray. Heat in oven about 5 minutes.
3 Meanwhile, heat oil in small frying pan; cook prosciutto about 5 minutes or until crisp. Drain on absorbent paper.
4 Place equal amounts of the cheese inside croissants; bake about 5 minutes or until cheese melts. Fill croissants with prosciutto, tomato and rocket.

PER SERVING 30.2g total fat (15.2g saturated); 2270kj (543 cal); 43.9g carbohydrate; 21.0g protein; 6.4g fibre

Minted fruit salad

PREPARATION TIME 25 MINUTES **COOKING TIME** 15 MINUTES (PLUS REFRIGERATION TIME) **SERVES** 4

The longer you allow the fruit to macerate in the syrup, the better the flavour will be.

1½ cups (375ml) water
1 tablespoon grated palm sugar
2 star anise
2 tablespoons lime juice
1 small pineapple (900g), chopped coarsely
1 small honeydew melon (1.3kg), chopped coarsely
500g fresh lychees, seeded
200g seedless red grapes
½ cup loosely packed fresh mint leaves, torn

1 Stir the water, sugar and star anise in small saucepan over heat until sugar dissolves. Simmer, uncovered, 10 minutes. Stir in juice. Cover; refrigerate 3 hours. Strain syrup into medium jug; discard star anise.
2 Combine fruit, mint and syrup in large bowl.

PER SERVING 1.0g total fat (0.0g saturated); 1007kj (241 cal); 50.4g carbohydrate; 4.4g protein; 6.9g fibre

---

Buttermilk pancakes with glazed strawberries

PREPARATION TIME 15 MINUTES **COOKING TIME** 15 MINUTES **SERVES** 4

Despite the implication of its name, buttermilk is actually low in fat, varying between 0.6g and 2.0g per 100ml. Originally the name given to the slightly sour liquid left after butter was churned from cream, today it is intentionally made from low-fat milk to which specific cultures are added. Not only can it be used as a substitute for higher-fat dairy products in cooking, it also makes a tasty and healthy drink, being low in fat, but high in calcium and "good" bacteria.

4 eggs
2 tablespoons caster sugar
1½ cups (375ml) buttermilk
100g butter, melted
1½ cups (225g) self-raising flour

GLAZED STRAWBERRIES
⅓ cup (80ml) water
½ cup (170g) marmalade
1 tablespoon caster sugar
2 tablespoons lemon juice
250g strawberries, quartered

1 Beat eggs and sugar in small bowl with electric mixer until thick; stir in buttermilk and half of the butter.
2 Sift flour into large bowl; whisk egg mixture gradually into flour until batter is smooth.
3 Heat medium heavy-based frying pan; brush pan with a little of the remaining butter. Pour ¼ cup of the batter into pan; cook, uncovered, until bubbles appear on surface of pancake. Turn pancake; cook until browned underneath. Remove from pan; cover to keep warm. Repeat with remaining butter and batter.
4 Meanwhile, make glazed strawberries.
5 Serve pancakes with glazed strawberries.

GLAZED STRAWBERRIES Place the water, marmalade, sugar and juice in small saucepan; bring to a boil. Add strawberries, reduce heat; simmer, uncovered, about 2 minutes or until strawberries are hot.

PER SERVING 28.5g total fat (16.5g saturated); 2851kj (682 cal); 88.5g carbohydrate; 17.6g protein; 3.9g fibre

Toast toppers

These toppings can also be used on ciabatta, sourdough, bagels, turkish rolls, crumpets or english muffins.

TOMATO, SPINACH AND CHEESE
Layer baby spinach leaves, thinly sliced tomato and grated cheddar on toast. Toast under a preheated grill until the tomato is warmed and the cheese is melted.

ANTIPASTO
Spread sun-dried tomato pesto over toast; top with drained marinated artichoke quarters, drained char-grilled capsicum and drained char-grilled eggplant slices. Sprinkle with baby basil leaves.

TUNA AND AVOCADO
Combine flaked tuna with lemon rind and chopped fresh chives in a bowl. Top toast with sliced avocado, tuna and grated cheddar. Toast under a preheated grill until the cheese melts.

RICOTTA, PEAR AND HONEY
Combine ½ cup ricotta, 1 teaspoon honey and 2 tablespoons finely chopped dried pears in a small bowl. Spread over toast; drizzle with a little more honey.

SMOKED SALMON AND CREAM CHEESE
Combine 25g cream cheese, 2 teaspoons lemon juice and 1 tablespoon drained, rinsed baby capers in a small bowl. Top toast with the cheese mixture, sliced smoked salmon and baby rocket leaves.

PANCETTA AND BOCCONCINI
Cook slices of pancetta under a preheated grill until crisp. Layer on toast with sliced bocconcini and thinly sliced semi-dried tomatoes. Sprinkle with finely chopped fresh chives.

CHEESE, TOMATO AND BACON
Coarsely chop cooked bacon rashers. Spread toast with mayonnaise. Top toast with sliced swiss cheese, baby spinach leaves, thinly sliced egg tomato and bacon.

BREAKFAST WITH THE LOT
Layer sliced smoked ham, trimmed baby spinach, rocket or lettuce leaves, one softly poached or fried egg and two quarters of grilled egg tomato on toast. Season with salt and pepper.

CINNAMON SUGAR
Toast bread slice on one side; spread untoasted side with butter. Sprinkle with combined 1 teaspoon ground cinnamon and 1 tablespoon caster sugar. Toast under a preheated grill until golden.

BANANA AND HAZELNUT
Melt a knob of butter in a frying pan; add sliced bananas, and sprinkle with coarsely chopped roasted hazelnuts and brown sugar. Cook 2 minutes or until the banana is caramelised slightly. Spoon over toast.

SAUTEED MUSHROOMS
Melt a small amount of butter in a small frying pan; add a crushed clove of garlic and thinly sliced mixed mushrooms. Cook, stirring, about 10 minutes or until the mushrooms are tender. Stir in coarsely chopped fresh flat-leaf parsley; spoon over toast.

MIXED BERRY
Combine raspberry jam with thawed mixed frozen berries. Stir over low heat in a small pan until warm. Spoon over toast; serve with yogurt. Top with baby mint leaves.

Try to find plain full-cream yogurt, sometimes called country-style or Greek-style yogurt, for this recipe. Other types, especially the low-fat kind, are not suitable. Additional milk can be added if the muesli is too thick.

Bircher muesli

PREPARATION TIME 15 MINUTES (PLUS REFRIGERATION TIME) **SERVES** 6

3 cups (270g) rolled oats
2 cups (500ml) fresh orange juice
400g yogurt
1 cup (140g) seeded dried dates, chopped coarsely
½ cup (75g) dried apricots, sliced thinly
½ cup (75g) raisins
⅓ cup (115g) honey
1 cup (250ml) milk
1 large apple (200g), peeled, grated coarsely
⅓ cup (45g) roasted slivered almonds

Use a tart, crisp green apple, such as a granny smith, for this recipe.

1 Combine oats, juice and yogurt in large bowl. Cover tightly; refrigerate overnight.
2 Stir dates, apricot, raisins, honey, milk and apple into oat mixture. Refrigerate 30 minutes.
3 Serve muesli in bowls; top with almonds and fresh mixed berries, if desired.

PER SERVING 12.2g total fat (3.5g saturated); 2203kj (527 cal); 88.4g carbohydrate; 12.7g protein; 8.4g fibre

---

To balance the sweetness of this recipe combine 300g Greek-style yogurt with 1 tablespoon brown sugar and ½ teaspoon vanilla extract, mixing well. Spoon over the waffles.

Caramelised banana and pecan waffles

PREPARATION TIME 10 MINUTES **COOKING TIME** 15 MINUTES **SERVES** 4

4 packaged waffles (320g)
40g butter
4 medium ripe bananas (800g), sliced thickly
2 tablespoons caster sugar
½ cup (60g) roasted pecans, chopped coarsely
⅓ cup (80ml) pure maple syrup

1 Preheat oven to moderately slow (170°C/150°C fan-forced).
2 Place waffles, in single layer, on oven tray; heat about 8 minutes.
3 Meanwhile, melt butter in medium frying pan; cook banana, stirring, about 2 minutes or until hot. Add sugar; cook, uncovered, over low heat, about 2 minutes or until banana is caramelised lightly.
4 Divide waffles among serving plates; top with banana mixture, nuts and syrup.

PER SERVING 33.9g total fat (12.0g saturated); 2939kj (703 cal); 85.6g carbohydrate; 13.1g protein; 6.4g fibre

Boiled eggs

PREPARATION TIME 5 MINUTES **COOKING TIME** 5 MINUTES

To make "soldiers" to dip in the soft egg yolk, butter some toast and cut it into fingers, removing the crusts if you wish.

1 Choose saucepan to suit the number of eggs you are boiling; one egg in small saucepan, up to four eggs in medium saucepan; more eggs in large saucepan (there should be enough room to move eggs around). Add enough cold water to cover eggs. Stir constantly using wooden spoon over high heat until water boils; this will centralise each yolk. Boil, uncovered, until yolks are as soft or as firm as you like. As a guide, 3 minutes will give you set egg white and soft yolk. After 5 minutes, the yolk will be set.
2 Serve boiled eggs with toast soldiers, if desired.

☐ **PER EGG** 5.3g total fat (1.6g saturated); 309kj (74 cal); 0.2 carbohydrate; 6.7g protein; 0.0g fibre

---

Chocolate banana bread

PREPARATION TIME 15 MINUTES **COOKING TIME** 1 HOUR **SERVES** 12

Left-over banana bread makes delicious French toast. Whisk two eggs with ¼ cup milk. Heat a little butter in a medium frying pan. Dip the banana bread slices into the egg mixture, one at a time; cook, uncovered, until browned on both sides.

1 cup mashed banana

¾ cup (165g) caster sugar

2 eggs, beaten lightly

¼ cup (60ml) light olive oil

¼ cup (60ml) milk

⅔ cup (100g) self-raising flour

⅔ cup (100g) wholemeal self-raising flour

¾ cup (80g) coarsely chopped roasted walnuts

¼ cup (45g) finely chopped dark eating chocolate

WHIPPED NUT BUTTER

100g butter

¼ cup (30g) finely chopped roasted walnuts

1 Preheat oven to moderate (180°C/160°C fan-forced). Grease 14cm x 21cm loaf pan; line base and long sides with baking paper.
2 Combine banana and sugar in medium bowl; stir in egg, oil and milk. Add remaining ingredients; stir until combined. Spread mixture into pan. Bake, uncovered, about 1 hour.
3 Make whipped nut butter.
4 Stand bread 5 minutes then turn onto wire rack; turn bread top-side up to cool. Serve bread warm with whipped nut butter.

WHIPPED NUT BUTTER Beat butter in small bowl with electric mixer until light and fluffy; stir in nuts.

☐ **PER SERVING** 20.2g total fat (7.0g saturated); 1367kj (327 cal); 31.4g carbohydrate; 5.0g protein; 2.4g fibre

Dried beans are soaked overnight to help them cook faster, improve their flavour and texture, and make them easier to digest. You can soak double or triple the quantity called for here then drain and freeze the extra beans in snap-lock bags for future use.

Baked beans with fried eggs

PREPARATION TIME 10 MINUTES (PLUS SOAKING TIME) **COOKING TIME** 2 HOURS 10 MINUTES **SERVES** 4

1 cup (200g) dried borlotti beans

3 bacon rashers (210g), rind removed, chopped coarsely

1 medium brown onion (150g), chopped finely

1 clove garlic, crushed

1 tablespoon tomato paste

400g can crushed tomatoes

1 ½ cups (375ml) water

1 tablespoon worcestershire sauce

2 teaspoons dijon mustard

1 tablespoon pure maple syrup

4 eggs

1 Place beans in medium bowl, cover with cold water; soak overnight, drain.

2 Cook bacon, onion and garlic in large saucepan, stirring, until onion softens. Add drained beans with paste, undrained tomatoes, the water, sauce and mustard; bring to a boil. Reduce heat; simmer, covered, about 1 ½ hours. Uncover; simmer about 15 minutes or until beans soften. Stir in syrup.

3 Fry eggs, uncovered, in heated oiled medium frying pan until white has set and yolk is cooked as desired. Serve beans with eggs.

PER SERVING 12.9g total fat (4.3g saturated); 1287kj (308 cal); 25.0g carbohydrate; 22.8g protein; 4g fibre

---

For a savoury alternative, replace the hazelnut spread and chocolate with a mixed-herb cream cheese and serve topped with about 50g sliced smoked salmon or trout.

Chocolate hazelnut croissants

PREPARATION TIME 15 MINUTES **COOKING TIME** 15 MINUTES **MAKES** 8

2 sheets ready-rolled puff pastry

⅓ cup (110g) chocolate hazelnut spread

30g dark eating chocolate, grated finely

25g butter, melted

1 tablespoon icing sugar

1 Preheat oven to hot (220°C/200°C fan-forced). Lightly grease two oven trays.

2 Cut pastry sheets diagonally to make four triangles. Spread hazelnut spread over triangles, leaving a 1cm border; sprinkle each evenly with chocolate.

3 Roll triangles, starting at one wide end; place 3cm apart on trays with the tips tucked under and the ends slightly curved in to form crescent shape. Brush croissants with melted butter. Bake, uncovered, about 12 minutes or until croissants are browned lightly and cooked through. Serve croissants dusted with sifted icing sugar.

PER CROISSANT 17.7g total fat (4.8g saturated); 1158kj (277 cal); 26.4g carbohydrate; 3.4g protein; 0.9g fibre

Prosciutto and roast capsicum rösti stacks

PREPARATION TIME 15 MINUTES **COOKING TIME** 30 MINUTES **SERVES** 4

Make sure you don't wash grated potato before squeezing excess moisture from it, as this removes the starch, which helps to bind the rösti together.

- 1 small red capsicum (150g)
- 1 small yellow capsicum (150g)
- ⅓ cup (90g) tomato relish
- 1kg potatoes
- 80g unsalted butter
- 2 teaspoons olive oil
- 8 slices prosciutto (120g)
- 20g baby spinach leaves
- 50g parmesan, shaved

1 Quarter capsicums; discard seeds and membranes. Roast capsicum under grill or in very hot oven, skin-side up, until skin blisters and blackens. Cover capsicum pieces with plastic or paper for 5 minutes; peel away skin, then slice capsicum thinly. Combine capsicum and relish in small bowl.

2 Meanwhile, grate potatoes coarsely; squeeze excess moisture from potato, transfer to large bowl. Divide into eight portions.

3 Heat 10g of the butter in 20cm frying pan; spread one portion of the potato mixture over base of pan, flatten with spatula to form a firm pancake. Cook, uncovered, over medium heat, until golden brown on underside; shake pan to loosen rösti, then invert onto large plate. Gently slide rösti back into pan; cook, uncovered, until other side is golden brown and potato centre is tender. Drain on absorbent paper; cover to keep warm. Repeat to make eight rösti.

4 Heat oil in same frying pan; cook prosciutto, stirring, until crisp. Place one rösti on each serving plate; top with spinach, prosciutto, capsicum mixture and cheese, then with a second rösti.

PER SERVING 25.1g total fat (14.5g saturated); 1835kj (439 cal); 34.4g carbohydrate; 16.8g protein; 4.4g fibre

---

Scrambled eggs with dill and smoked salmon

PREPARATION TIME 10 MINUTES **COOKING TIME** 5 MINUTES **SERVES** 4

The surface of an eggshell is made up of thousands of tiny pores so eggs can easily absorb the flavours and odours around them. Refrigerating them in their cardboard cartons will help keep them fresh.

- 8 eggs
- ½ cup (125ml) buttermilk
- 1 tablespoon finely chopped fresh dill
- 10g butter
- 300g sliced smoked salmon

1 Whisk eggs in medium bowl; add buttermilk and dill, whisking until mixture is frothy.

2 Melt butter in medium frying pan over low heat; cook egg mixture, stirring constantly, until egg mixture is just set.

3 Divide scrambled egg among serving plates; top with salmon.

PER SERVING 16.7g total fat (5.7g saturated); 1191kj (285 cal); 2.1g carbohydrate; 31.9g protein; 0.0g fibre

Blood plums, a favourite type readily available during the height of summer, include the sweet, juicy yet firm mariposa and satsuma among their plump, dark-fleshed varieties. Of Japanese origin, blood plums are the preferred fruit for use in cooking but they are equally good eaten fresh, as a snack or an ingenious breakfast idea as shown.

Blood plums with honey and cardamom yogurt

PREPARATION TIME 5 MINUTES **SERVES** 1

¼ cup (70g) sheep milk yogurt
2 teaspoons honey
¼ teaspoon ground cardamom
2 small blood plums (180g), quartered

1 Combine yogurt, honey and cardamom in small bowl.
2 Place plums on small serving plate; drizzle with yogurt mixture.

PER SERVING 4.4g total fat (0g saturated fat) 26.7g carbohydrate 732kJ (175 cal) 4.2g protein 3.6g fibre

Stewed prunes with orange

PREPARATION TIME 5 MINUTES **COOKING TIME** 15 MINUTES **SERVES** 1

½ cup (85g) seeded dessert prunes
¼ cup (60ml) fresh orange juice
¼ cup (60ml) water
5cm strip orange rind, sliced thinly
1 cinnamon stick
2 cardamom pods, bruised

1 Place ingredients in small saucepan; bring to a boil. Reduce heat; simmer, covered, 10 minutes. Serve stewed prunes with sheep milk yogurt, if desired.

PER SERVING 0.4g total fat (0g saturated fat) 42.2g carbohydrate 752kJ (180 cal) 2.3g protein 6.8g fibre

Why is pure maple syrup so much more expensive then maple-flavoured syrup? Pure maple syrup is produced only in North America and comes from the sap of a maple tree that is at least 40 years old. The season for collecting maple sap is just 4 to 6 weeks annually, and for every litre of sap collected, only 25ml of maple syrup is produced. Maple-flavoured syrup, on the other hand, is made in bulk from sugar cane.

Maple creamed rice with pecans and dates

PREPARATION TIME 10 MINUTES **COOKING TIME** 40 MINUTES **SERVES** 8

1.5 litres (6 cups) milk
2 cups (500ml) cream
⅔ cup (160ml) pure maple syrup
¼ teaspoon ground cinnamon
⅔ cup (130g) white medium-grain rice
½ cup (70g) coarsely chopped seeded dried dates
½ cup (60g) roasted pecans, chopped coarsely

1 Combine milk, cream, syrup and cinnamon in large saucepan; bring to a boil.
2 Gradually stir in rice; cook, uncovered, over low heat, stirring occasionally, about 40 minutes or until rice is tender.
3 Serve rice topped with dates and nuts; drizzle with extra maple syrup, if desired.

PER SERVING 39.9g total fat (23.0g saturated); 2429kj (581 cal); 47.8g carbohydrate; 9.6g protein; 1.6g fibre

BLOOD PLUMS WITH HONEY AND CARDAMOM YOGURT

DRINKS

Drinks

Drinks mean comfort and cheer. They can be as convivial as a martini, as refreshing as a frappé, as elegant as iced tea, as nourishing as a smoothie. Nothing beats the right drink for cheering the homecomer, fortifying friendship, giving a day or a party a good start or rounding it off with a glow. Here are drinks for every time of day from breakfast-on-the run to a soothing nightcap.

GLASSES AND BAR EQUIPMENT

Classic wine glasses, champagne flutes (long and stemmed), V-shaped, stemmed cocktail glasses (martini glasses) and straight-sided tumblers will cover most needs. The only special items needed are a bar measure, a cocktail shaker or bar jug and stirrer, and a bar strainer (Hawthorne strainer), which fits neatly over a glass. Chilling the glasses is a nice touch; put them in the fridge for half an hour or so, or in the freezer for 10 to 15 minutes.

COCKTAIL PARTY DRINKS

While you can have a perfectly good party serving only wine and beer, it does feel more special if you offer cocktails. Unless you have a barman, choose just one or two cocktails and practise them beforehand. A helper is an asset, especially if you are doing cocktails that need shaking. For a large party, you might feel more relaxed offering drinks such as sangria or punch, which still say "special occasion", but can be made ahead of time.

Many cocktails are quite powerful. A responsible host ensures that there is enough food to help absorb the alcohol being served. Many experienced hosts offer cocktails for only the first hour or so, then switch to wine, beer, mineral water and a soft drink with class, such as peach iced tea (see page 58).

ICE You will need plenty of ice. Fill a large container, such as a laundry tub, with ice and use it as a cooler for bottles and cans. Make room in the freezer for a bag or covered box of crushed ice (home-made or bought) to go in drinks. Shortly before the party, check that the ice is not stuck together – if it is, wrap it in a towel and whack with a hammer or rolling pin to separate it, then immediately return to the dried container and place in the freezer.

SUGAR SYRUP Bartenders freqently use sugar syrup instead of sugar to sweeten drinks because it blends instantly. To make it, combine 1 cup (220g) sugar and 1 cup (250ml) water in a small saucepan and stir over low heat until the sugar is dissolved. Bring to a boil, then reduce the heat and simmer for 5 minutes. Cool and store in a screwtop jar in the fridge. This recipe makes 350ml and will keep for up to 2 months.

WINE

Glasses for both still and sparkling wines should be filled only half-full so that the bouquet (aroma) will collect in the top of the glass for the drinker to enjoy before drinking.

If you are a wine enthusiast, you need no advice from us about which wines to serve. If you could do with some advice, ask a reliable wine merchant. Don't be afraid to mention your price limit; good wine merchants love to match wines to customers' needs, and can point you to good buys.

CHAMPAGNE

Champagne and other sparkling wines should be chilled in a tub of ice or in the fridge (not the freezer) until needed. Before opening, place a couple of glasses handy to catch any wine that may gush from the bottle, and be sure you have the bottle pointing away from yourself, your guests and anything breakable. To open, remove enough foil from the top of the bottle to reveal the cork and its wire cage. Pull the cage's little handle away from the bottle and, with one thumb firmly on the cork, use the other hand to untwist the wire and remove the cage. Still holding the cork with one hand, slowly twist the bottle round (not the cork) with the other. Once the cork begins to be pushed out by the pressure inside the bottle, ease it out slowly so that it comes out with a "sigh" or a gentle pop rather than a loud one. To pour champagne, add a little at a time to each glass so that they don't overflow.

FRUIT AND VEGETABLE JUICES

No bought drink can match the healthy charm of something long, cool and home-made from fresh fruit and vegetables. They can be made a few hours ahead and refrigerated until needed, but don't store them for too long as they will lose some of their vitamin content and fresh flavour.

FRAPPES

Frappés are made by blending or processing drink ingredients with ice until the texture is thick, smooth and frothy. Alteratively, fresh ingredients are processed then poured over crushed ice. Either way, they must be served immediately as they will subside on standing.

SMOOTHIES AND LASSIS

These are nutritional powerhouses, combining milk, soy milk or yogurt with fresh fruits to make a drink that is the equivalent of a light meal: they make great breakfasts-on-the-run. Lassi, which comes from Indian cuisine, is also the perfect cooler to serve with a curry.

TEAS

Fruit or herb teas are delicious hot or cold, and a calming and restorative pleasure for any time during the day or at bedtime. For crystal-clear iced tea, start ahead of time, using water that is only warm instead of boiling, and steep for several hours instead of minutes before straining. The reason for this is that boiling water dissolves more components, including tiny pigment molecules, from the tea leaves, and when the liquid is chilled, these come out of the solution and cloud the tea. The longer steeping is necessary with warm water as the infusion process is much slower.

This refreshingly tart concoction is a favourite summer cocktail. You can double the quantities to make two at a time.

Cosmopolitan

PREPARATION TIME 5 MINUTES **SERVES** 1

10ml citron vodka
20ml vodka
30ml Cointreau
60ml cranberry juice
10ml lime juice
1 cup ice cubes

1 Place ingredients in cocktail shaker; shake vigorously then strain into 150ml cocktail glass. Garnish with a twist of lime rind.

PER SERVING 0.2g total fat (0.0g saturated); 736kj (176 cal); 17.3g carbohydrate; 0.4g protein; 0.1g fibre

---

This contemporary take on the traditional Brazilian caipirinha is a blend of vodka, fresh limes, sugar and ice. In bars, it is often prepared using a wooden tool called a muddler, but it works just as well using a mortar and pestle or the end of a rolling pin.

Caipiroska

PREPARATION TIME 5 MINUTES **SERVES** 1

1 lime, cut into 8 wedges
1 tablespoon grated palm sugar or brown sugar
60ml vodka
10ml sugar syrup (page 48)
½ cup ice cubes
½ cup crushed ice

1 Using mortar and pestle (or muddler), crush six lime wedges with sugar.
2 Place lime mixture in a cocktail shaker with vodka, sugar syrup and ice cubes; shake vigorously then pour into 180ml old-fashioned glass with crushed ice; do not strain. Garnish with remaining lime wedges.

PER SERVING 0.1g total fat (0.0g saturated); 861kj (206 cal); 19.2g carbohydrate; 0.4g protein; 1.0g fibre

---

The spirits and other ingredients should be well mixed to blend the flavours.

Long island iced tea

PREPARATION TIME 5 MINUTES **SERVES** 1

1 cup ice cubes
30ml vodka
30ml tequila
30ml Bacardi
30ml gin
15ml Cointreau
15ml lemon juice
15ml sugar syrup (page 48)
30ml cola

1 Place ice in 300ml highball glass; add vodka, tequila, Bacardi, gin and Cointreau, one after the other.
2 Add juice and syrup, top with cola; stir. Garnish with mint and a twist of lemon rind.

PER SERVING 0.1g total fat (0.0g saturated); 1392kj (333 cal); 16.7g carbohydrate; 0.1g protein; 0.0g fibre

Dry martini

PREPARATION TIME 5 MINUTES **SERVES** 1

The are many differences of opinion regarding how the perfect martini should be made; this is one classic method.

45ml gin
15ml dry vermouth
1 cup ice cubes

1 Place ingredients in cocktail shaker; shake vigorously then strain into 90ml martini glass. Garnish with a rinsed caperberry.

PER SERVING 0.0g total fat (0.0g saturated); 451kj (108 cal); 0.4g carbohydrate; 0.0g protein; 0.0g fibre

---

Piña colada

PREPARATION TIME 5 MINUTES **SERVES** 1

This is one cocktail that lends itself to being made in bulk. Just for fun, you could freeze it in ice-block moulds, with wooden handles inserted, for grown-up paddle pops.

45ml Bacardi
120ml bottled pineapple juice
30ml coconut cream
15ml Malibu
15ml sugar syrup (page 48)
1 cup ice cubes

1 Blend ingredients until smooth; pour into 400ml tulip-shaped glass. Garnish with pineapple leaves.

PER SERVING 6.4g total fat (5.4g saturated); 1183kj (283 cal); 27.5g carbohydrate; 1.0g protein; 0.5g fibre

---

Daiquiri

PREPARATION TIME 5 MINUTES **SERVES** 1

The daiquiri was developed in Cuba by an American engineer, who combined the local spirit (rum) with native limes to make the ultimate pick-me-up after a hot day in the mines.

45ml Bacardi
30ml lime juice
15ml sugar syrup (page 48)
1 cup ice cubes

1 Place ingredients in cocktail shaker; shake then strain into 150ml cocktail glass.

PER SERVING 6.4g total fat (5.4g saturated); 1183kj (283 cal); 27.5g carbohydrate; 1.0g protein; 0.5g fibre

---

Champagne cocktail

PREPARATION TIME 5 MINUTES **SERVES** 1

One bottle of champagne will make five cocktails.

For a simple yet elegant combination mix guava juice with champagne.

1 sugar cube
5 drops angostura bitters
⅔ cup (160ml) chilled champagne
5cm strip orange rind, sliced thinly

1 Place sugar in champagne glass; top with bitters then champagne. Garnish with rind.

PER SERVING 0.0g total fat (0.0g saturated); 527kj (126 cal); 6.9g carbohydrate; 0.3g protein; 0.1g fibre

Punch is best served very cold. Try freezing some of the berries and lemonade together in shaped ice trays and add these to the punch instead of regular ice. This way, you won't dilute the flavour.

Mixed-berry punch

PREPARATION TIME 15 MINUTES (PLUS REFRIGERATION TIME) **SERVES** 8

- 1 teabag
- 1 cup (250ml) boiling water
- 120g raspberries
- 150g blueberries
- 125g strawberries, halved
- ¼ cup loosely packed fresh mint leaves
- 750ml chilled sparkling apple cider
- 2½ cups (625ml) chilled lemonade

1 Place teabag in mug, cover with the boiling water; stand 10 minutes. Squeeze teabag over mug, discard teabag. Cool 10 minutes.

2 Using fork, crush raspberries in punch bowl. Add blueberries, strawberries, mint and tea; stir to combine. Cover; refrigerate 1 hour. Stir cider and lemonade into punch just before serving; sprinkle with extra mint leaves, if desired.

PER SERVING 0.1g total fat (0.0g saturated); 435kj (104 cal); 18.5g carbohydrate; 0.6g protein; 1.6g fibre

---

Margaritas are often served in salt-rimmed glasses. Mexicans discovered that salt on the tongue calms down the fiery flavours in their food. Served with tequila, salt reduces the "burn".

Margarita

PREPARATION TIME 5 MINUTES **SERVES** 1

- 45ml tequila
- 30ml lime juice
- 30ml Cointreau
- 1 cup ice cubes

1 Place ingredients in cocktail shaker; shake vigorously then strain into a salt-rimmed 150ml margarita glass. Garnish with a slice of lemon.

PER SERVING 0.2g total fat (0.0g saturated); 794kj (190 cal); 12.4g carbohydrate; 0.3g protein; 0.1g fibre

---

Apple and melon lassi

PREPARATION TIME 15 MINUTES **SERVES** 4

- 700g honeydew melon, chopped coarsely
- 2 cups (500ml) clear apple juice
- 500g yogurt
- 2 cups crushed ice
- ½ cup firmly packed fresh mint leaves
- 4cm piece fresh ginger (20g), grated
- 1 cup (250ml) water

1 Blend or process ingredients, in batches, until almost smooth. Combine batches in large jug.

PER SERVING 5.1g total fat (2.8g saturated); 986kj (236 cal); 36.7g carbohydrate; 7.9g protein; 3.2g fibre

MIXED-BERRY PUNCH

Garnishes for drinks

The final flourishes that make drinks memorable. For a party, prepare ahead and refrigerate in covered containers.

CHERRIES
Choose pairs of ripe black, red or white cherries joined by their stalks. Hang over the rim of a tall glass of any fruity or creamy drink.

CITRUS SLICE
Cut a slit in a slice of lemon or lime (or both together) and place on the rim of a glass; for larger fruit, such as orange or blood orange, use half-slices, slit from the centre.

PINEAPPLE
Pull small leaves from a pineapple top, slit in half at the bottom end and place on the rim of a glass. A small wedge of pineapple can be placed alongside.

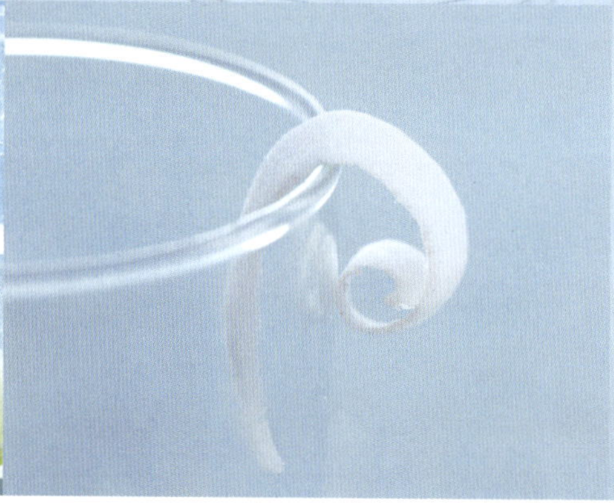

DECORATED ICE CUBES
Fill an ice-cube tray half-full of water and freeze. Dip herb leaves, citrus-slice segments, edible flowers etc in iced water, place on top of the cubes and freeze until firm. Top up with iced water and freeze.

COCONUT CURLS
Bake a whole coconut in a moderate oven for about 10 minutes, then split by hitting it with a hammer. Remove the flesh and, using a very sharp knife, pare off thin peelings to make curls to hang on the rim of a glass.

FROSTING
Hold a glass upside down and wipe the outside of the rim with a cut lemon until evenly moistened, then dip the rim into a saucer filled with salt or caster sugar. Shake away excess.

STRAWBERRY
Choose firm, ripe strawberries with fresh green calyxes; almost slit in half from the point, or make a few slits and fan out. Place on the glass rim.

CELERY STICK
Cut celery into sticks about 4cm longer than the glasses to be used, leaving the leafy tops on if fresh and undamaged. Place in a Bloody Mary or vegetable juice as a stirrer.

MELON BALLS
Use a melon-baller to cut balls from melons of different colours. Thread alternately onto cocktail sticks and place in drinks in short glasses.

CUCUMBER
Using Lebanese cucumbers, thinly slice the unpeeled cucumber. More than just a fresh garnish, these are also useful stirrers.

PEAR AND MINT
Cut a thin slice of pear and cut a slit from the bottom of the slice to the centre. Gently press a small fresh mint sprig into the pear and place in a drink.

CITRUS PEEL
Peel the rind from citrus fruit in a spiral. Place in a drink, hooking one end over the rim; or slice straight strips into narrow "strings", tie in knots and drop into drinks.

Sangria

PREPARATION TIME 5 MINUTES **MAKES** 1.25 LITRES

Originating in Spain where it was developed as a long, cool drink to combat the summer heat, sangria has become a popular punch at pubs and parties all over the world.

750ml bottle dry red wine

30ml Cointreau

30ml Bacardi

30ml brandy

½ cup (110g) caster sugar

2 cinnamon sticks

½ medium orange (120g), peeled, chopped coarsely

½ medium lemon (70g), peeled, chopped coarsely

125g medium strawberries, chopped coarsely

1 cup ice cubes

1 Place ingredients in large jug; stir until sugar dissolves.

PER 250ML 0.1g total fat (0.0g saturated); 1016kj (243 cal); 26.6g carbohydrate; 0.1g protein; 1.1g fibre

---

Cucumber, celery, apple and spinach juice

PREPARATION TIME 10 MINUTES (PLUS REFRIGERATION TIME) **MAKES** 1 LITRE

1 telegraph cucumber (400g), chopped coarsely

2 trimmed celery stalks (200g), chopped coarsely

2 large green apples (400g), cored, chopped coarsely

50g baby spinach leaves, stems removed

1 cup (250ml) water

⅓ cup firmly packed fresh mint leaves

1 Blend or process ingredients, in batches, until pureed; strain mixture through coarse sieve into large jug.

2 Refrigerate, covered, until chilled.

PER 250ML 0.2g total fat (0.0g saturated); 146kj (35 cal); 5.1g carbohydrate; 1.9g protein; 2.6g fibre

---

Fresh berry frappé

PREPARATION TIME 10 MINUTES **SERVES** 4

Another way to make this frappé is to freeze the berries first and then process with the juice until smooth. Stir in the ice and serve.

300g blueberries

250g raspberries

40 ice cubes, crushed

½ cup (125ml) fresh orange juice

1 Blend or process berries until just smooth. Push berry puree through fine sieve into large bowl; discard solids in sieve.

2 Stir in ice and juice.

PER SERVING 0.4g total fat (0.0g saturated); 330kj (79 cal); 14.6g carbohydrate; 1.4g protein; 4.8g fibre

SANGRIA

Lemon or vanilla biscuits are lovely eaten with this delicate infusion.

Peach iced tea

PREPARATION 10 MINUTES (PLUS REFRIGERATION TIME) **SERVES** 8

- 1 large orange (300g)
- ½ cup (125ml) water
- ½ cup (110g) caster sugar
- 1.25 litres (5 cups) boiling water
- 3 black tea bags
- 3 peach-flavoured herbal infusion bags
- 1⅔ cups (400ml) peach nectar
- ¼ cup loosely packed fresh mint leaves
- 1½ cups ice cubes

1 Peel rind thinly from half of the orange, avoiding white pith. Peel off pith, cut orange into thin slices.

2 Place the water and sugar in small saucepan; stir over low heat, without boiling, until sugar dissolves. Add rind; simmer, uncovered, without stirring, about 5 minutes or until thickened slightly. Discard rind, cool 15 minutes. Cover; refrigerate until required.

3 Place the boiling water in large heatproof jug, add black tea and peach tea bags; infuse for 5 minutes. Remove tea bags; cool 10 minutes. Cover; refrigerate until chilled.

4 Place sugar syrup, tea, orange slices, nectar, mint and ice in large jug; stir to combine.

PER SERVING 0.2g total fat (0.0g saturated); 418kj (100 cal); 24.0g carbohydrate; 0.8g protein; 0.9g fibre

---

Americans living in the tropical Deep South make "sun tea" to drink, iced, as a very refreshing beverage. Stand three or four tea bags in a 2-litre jug of cold water in the sun for several hours. Discard the bags and serve the tea in tall glasses over ice with a few mint leaves or a squeeze of lemon juice.

Minted lemon grass and ginger iced tea

PREPARATION TIME 10 MINUTES (PLUS REFRIGERATION TIME) **MAKES** 1 LITRE

- 6 lemon grass and ginger tea bags
- 1 litre (4 cups) boiling water
- 2 tablespoons grated palm sugar
- 10cm stick (20g) fresh lemon grass, chopped finely
- ½ small orange (90g), sliced thinly
- ½ medium lemon (70g), sliced thinly
- ¼ cup firmly packed fresh mint leaves, torn
- 1 cup ice cubes

1 Place tea bags and the boiling water in large heatproof jug; stand 5 minutes.

2 Discard tea bags. Add sugar, lemon grass, orange and lemon to jug; stir to combine. Refrigerate, covered, until chilled.

3 Stir in mint and ice to serve.

PER 250ML 0.3g total fat (0.0g saturated); 184kj (44 cal); 8.6g carbohydrate; 0.7g protein; 1.1g fibre

Mandarin apple juice with passionfruit ice

PREPARATION TIME 10 MINUTES (PLUS FREEZING TIME) **MAKES** 1.25 LITRES (5 CUPS)

Making fruit ice cubes prevents drinks from being diluted as the ice melts. Try freezing other juices and pulps such as mango, strawberry or watermelon.

¼ cup (60ml) passionfruit pulp
⅓ cup (80ml) cold water
6 large apples (1.2kg), chopped coarsely
6 large mandarins (1.5kg)

1 Using fork, combine pulp and the water in small bowl. Pour passionfruit mixture into ice-cube tray; freeze until set.

2 Push apple and mandarins through juice extractor into large jug. Divide juice among serving glasses; top with passionfruit ice cubes.

PER 250ML 0.7g total fat (0.0g saturated); 782kj (187 cal); 38.1g carbohydrate; 2.9g protein; 9.2g fibre

---

Bloody mary

PREPARATION TIME 5 MINUTES **SERVES** 1

For an extra flourish, dip the rims of the glasses in celery salt before serving.

1 cup ice cubes
60ml vodka
10ml lemon juice
150ml vegetable juice
¼ teaspoon Tabasco
½ teaspoon horseradish
dash worcestershire sauce
pinch celery salt
1 trimmed celery stalk (100g)

1 Place ice, vodka, juices, Tabasco, horseradish, sauce and celery salt in 340ml highball glass; stir to combine.

2 Garnish with celery stick and cracked black pepper, if desired.

For a delicious non-alcoholic alternative omit the vodka and you have a classic virgin mary.

PER SERVING 0.5g total fat (0.2g saturated); 732kj (175 cal); 8.4g carbohydrate; 2.0g protein; 2.5g fibre

---

Kiwifruit, orange and mint frappé

PREPARATION TIME 20 MINUTES **SERVES** 4

To make an alcoholic frappé, add a measure (30ml) each of orange and melon liqueur.

1 medium pineapple (1.25kg), coarsely chopped
6 kiwifruit (500g), halved
1 cup loosely packed fresh mint leaves
2 cups (500ml) orange juice
4 cups crushed ice
¼ cup finely shredded fresh mint

1 Blend or process pineapple, kiwifruit, mint leaves, juice and ice, in batches, until almost smooth. Combine batches in large jug. Top glasses with shredded mint.

PER SERVING 0.7g total fat (0.0g saturated); 744kj (178 cal); 33.7g carbohydrate; 4.3g protein; 8.3g fibre

Try adding a few spoonfuls of toasted muesli to create a healthy and satisfying breakfast smoothie.

Mixed-berry smoothie

PREPARATION TIME 5 MINUTES **MAKES** 1 LITRE

250ml frozen strawberry yogurt, softened slightly

1 ⅓ cups (200g) frozen mixed berries

3 cups (750ml) no-fat milk

1 Blend or process ingredients, in batches, until smooth. Combine batches in large jug.

PER 250ML 5.6g total fat (3.6g saturated); 982kj (235 cal); 34.8g carbohydrate; 11.6g protein; 1.8g fibre

---

For a colder, thicker smoothie freeze the passionfruit pulp in an ice-cube tray and freeze chopped pieces of banana on a tray lined with baking paper. Place the frozen fruit straight into the blender.

Banana-passionfruit soy smoothie

PREPARATION TIME 10 MINUTES (PLUS REFRIGERATION TIME) **MAKES** 1 LITRE

½ cup (125ml) passionfruit pulp

2 cups (500ml) soy milk

2 medium ripe bananas (400g), chopped coarsely

1 Strain pulp through sieve into small bowl; reserve liquid and seeds.

2 Blend or process passionfruit liquid, milk and banana, in batches, until smooth.

3 Pour smoothie into large jug; stir in reserved seeds. Refrigerate, covered, until chilled.

PER 250ML 0.6g total fat (0.0g saturated); 493kj (118 cal); 19.9g carbohydrate; 5.3g protein; 6.5g fibre

---

A frappé is best made shortly before serving as its thick, creamy texture will subside and separate if it stands for too long.

Pineapple-orange frappé

PREPARATION TIME 10 MINUTES **MAKES** 1 LITRE

1 medium pineapple (1.25kg), chopped coarsely

½ cup (125ml) orange juice

3 cups crushed ice

1 tablespoon finely grated orange rind

1 Blend or process pineapple and juice, in batches, until smooth.

2 Pour into large jug with crushed ice and rind; stir to combine.

PER 250ML 0.2g total fat (0.0g saturated); 334kj (80 cal); 15.7g carbohydrate; 1.8g protein; 3.6g fibre

1 MIXED-BERRY SMOOTHIE **2** BANANA-PASSIONFRUIT SOY SMOOTHIE
3 PINEAPPLE-ORANGE FRAPPE **4** TOMATO, CARROT AND RED CAPSICUM JUICE [P 62]

1

2

3

4

You may want to retain some or all of the vegetable pulp to make this drink even healthier; if so, strain through a colander or omit the straining altogether.

Tomato, carrot and red capsicum juice

PREPARATION TIME 10 MINUTES (PLUS REFRIGERATION TIME) **MAKES** 1 LITRE

1 medium red capsicum (200g), chopped coarsely

4 medium tomatoes (600g), chopped coarsely

2 medium carrots (240g), chopped

⅓ cup firmly packed fresh flat-leaf parsley leaves

1 cup (250ml) water

dash Tabasco

1 Blend or process capsicum, tomato, carrot, parsley and the water, in batches, until pureed; strain through coarse sieve into large jug.

2 Stir in Tabasco; refrigerate, covered, until chilled.

PER 250ML 0.3g total fat (0.0g saturated); 217kj (52 cal); 7.3g carbohydrate; 2.7g protein; 4.0g fibre

---

Grapefruit and blood orange juice

PREPARATION TIME 5 MINUTES **SERVES** 1

2 small blood oranges (360g)

1 small grapefruit (350g)

1 Juice oranges and grapefruit on citrus squeezer; pour into glass over ice.

PER SERVING 0.7g total fat (0.0g saturated); 652kj (156 cal); 31.2g carbohydrate; 4.6g protein; 6.5g fibre

---

Beetroot, carrot and spinach juice

PREPARATION TIME 20 MINUTES **SERVES** 4

6 medium beetroots (1kg), peeled, chopped coarsely

5 large carrots (900g), chopped

600g spinach, trimmed, chopped coarsely

1 Push ingredients through juice extractor. Stir to combine.

PER SERVING 0.9g total fat (0.0g saturated); 815kj (195 cal); 29.8g carbohydrate; 9.3g protein; 16.5g fibre

---

Tom Collins

PREPARATION TIME 5 MINUTES **SERVES** 1

60ml gin

80ml lemon juice

2 teaspoons icing sugar

80ml soda water

¼ cup ice cubes

1 Combine ingredients in chilled 340ml highball glass. Garnish with maraschino cherry.

PER SERVING 0.2g total fat (0.0g saturated); 694kj (166 cal); 7.7g carbohydrate; 0.6g protein; 0.1g fibre

Spiced iced coffee milkshake

PREPARATION TIME 10 MINUTES **MAKES** 1 LITRE

For an even bigger energy hit, add a banana to this milkshake. You may think this sounds odd; it actually tastes delicious.

- ¼ cup (20g) ground espresso coffee
- ¾ cup (180ml) boiling water
- 2 cardamom pods, bruised
- ¼ teaspoon ground cinnamon
- 1 tablespoon brown sugar
- 3 scoops (375ml) low-fat vanilla ice-cream
- 2½ cups (625ml) no-fat milk

1 Place coffee then the boiling water in coffee plunger; stand 4 minutes before plunging. Pour coffee into small heatproof bowl with cardamom, cinnamon and sugar; stir to dissolve sugar then cool 10 minutes.

2 Strain mixture through fine sieve into blender or processor; process with ice-cream and milk until smooth. Serve immediately.

PER 250ML 1.6g total fat (1.1g saturated); 535kj (128 cal); 20.4g carbohydrate; 8.6g protein; 0.8g fibre

---

Low-fat mocha smoothie

PREPARATION TIME 5 MINUTES **SERVES** 4

Milk is an excellent source of calcium, essential to the development of strong, healthy bones. The calcium content of no-fat milk is the same as for whole milk.

- 1 litre (4 cups) no-fat milk
- 1 cup (250g) low-fat chocolate mousse
- 1 cup (250g) low-fat chocolate ice-cream
- 1 tablespoon instant coffee granules
- ½ teaspoon vanilla extract

1 Blend or process ingredients, in batches, until smooth.

PER SERVING 6.9g total fat (4.6g saturated); 1166kj (279 cal); 39.1g carbohydrate; 16.7g protein; 0.2g fibre

---

Party punch

PREPARATION TIME 5 MINUTES (PLUS REFRIGERATION TIME) **SERVES** 8

Compared with some other alcoholic drinks punch is very easy to drink and people often consume more alcohol than they realise. Make sure there is a labelled non-alcoholic alternative, and always serve food.

- 2 x 750ml bottles chilled medium-dry white wine
- 1 tablespoon dark rum
- ⅓ cup (80ml) peach schnapps
- 2 tablespoons triple sec
- 1½ cups (375ml) apple and mandarin juice
- 3 starfruit (480g), sliced thickly
- 4 small peaches (460g), sliced thickly

1 Combine wine, rum, schnapps, triple sec and juice in large bowl. Stir in sliced fruit.

2 Refrigerate, covered, 1 hour before serving.

PER SERVING 0.2g total fat (0.0g saturated); 882kj (211 cal); 13.8g carbohydrate; 1.0g protein; 0.8g fibre

FINGER FOOD

Finger Food

There are times in most of our lives when we want to offer hospitality without seating our guests at a table. It may be a big party or a small one, or it may be as relaxed as a few friends gathered by the pool after a swim or around the television for a grand final. These are the times for serving appetising little somethings that can be eaten neatly, without a plate, in one or two mouthfuls.

The first rule for all these occasions is to be realistic about how much you can undertake without getting too frazzled to enjoy it all. Don't worry about striving for a large variety of offerings, just a few kinds will keep your guests happy. And don't think that you must make everything yourself: most supermarkets now have quality dips and pâtés as well as a variety of ready-made appetisers in the freezer cabinet. Look, too, in the local cake shop, fish shop and delicatessen for finger-food possibilities.

IMPROMPTU ENTERTAINING

If your entertaining tends to happen on the spur of the moment, it is wise to keep some provisions on hand. Most savoury pastries and items such as pizza or blini can be frozen and then half-thawed in the microwave, followed by a few minutes in a hot oven. Unopened supermarket packs of smoked salmon, dips, pâtés and salami will keep for weeks in the fridge and can be served with a sliced baguette from the freezer. Cheeses are great stand-bys with bread or crackers, and so are olives, salted nuts and the best potato crisps.

PRE-DINNER FINGER FOOD

If your guests have come to dinner, or you are going on to dinner, serve light nibbles and not too many of them, so as not to spoil your appetites. Serve foods that are easy to pick up, too – trying to cut and spread food from a platter held in mid-air is not comfortable.

PLANNING

A small, informal occasion doesn't need a lot of planning – all that is needed is to make or buy the food and grab a few bottles, get out your serving platters and check that you have plenty of ice and enough cups, glasses and napkins. The following advice applies mainly to parties big enough to need real planning.

QUANTITIES For a cocktail party, allow four to five pieces of food per person for the first hour and then four pieces for each hour after that. For a full afternoon or evening, allow 12 to 14 pieces of food per person for the duration of the whole party. It is good insurance to have one or two good breads and cheeses in case some guests linger. Just put these out with knives and a board and the stayers can help themselves.

Ten guests will consume about 20 drinks at a cocktail party. If it's a full afternoon or evening affair, this increases to 40 drinks. Have a modest extra reserve of wine and beer and a larger one of soft drink and mineral water; as the party proceeds, slow down the service of alcoholic drinks and keep the soft ones circulating.

CHECKLISTS A party calls for four checklists.

One is a detailed menu, listing all the food and drink plus all the incidentals – accompaniments such as dipping sauces for Asian appetisers and breads or other items to go with dips; garnishes; and ice and lemon slices or other items to go in drinks.

Second, go back over the first list and note what you will need in the way of bench space for putting final touches on the food and for filling serving platters, and how much time in the oven and/or space in the fridge and freezer each item on the menu will need. Make a list of the best order in which to serve them so that you won't be trying to heat several things in the oven, or grill or fry them, at the same time; make a big copy of this "running list" to be taped up in the kitchen on the day of the party, so that both you and any helpers will know what to do next. Decide where you will have the bar, whether behind the scenes or in the party space, and consider how to organise it.

The third checklist is of all the equipment you may need to assemble, borrow or hire, from extra forks and spoons to a marquee plus fans to cool it or heaters to warm it. Shop around before hiring; the variations in prices can be quite amazing. Here is a list to help you; insert your own numbers and change it as you need.

- forks and spoons
- serving platters, bowls, baskets and trays
- bowls for toothpicks, olive stones etc
- airtight food storage containers
- glasses
- cups and saucers
- plates for cake or dessert
- coasters
- tea and coffee-making equipment and serving pots, jugs and sugar bowls
- bar equipment and ice supply
- napkins – allow three times the number of guests
- oven trays
- extra appliances such as hotplates
- insulated boxes plus cold bricks to supplement the fridge in keeping food cold
- chairs
- music equipment
- flowers or decorations
- tea-towels
- disposable washcloths
- handtowels for the bathrooms
- garbage bins
- marquee
- fans or heaters

The fourth checklist is your plan of action, starting weeks before a big party and at least one week before a small one. It should list everything you have to do from inviting the guests to hiring equipment, shopping, cooking, setting up the bar, decorating and organising the party space, and last-minute chores on the day such as doing the flowers or collecting ice. Put the tasks in order and assign each one to a day, counting down to the day of the party. If it all looks too much, this is the time to consider it calmly and cut down, simplify or delegate to reliable helpers until it is manageable.

Soften rice papers, in warm water, one at a time for 15 to 20 seconds. Make sure you don't over-soak them as they will fall apart in your hands.

Vietnamese rice paper rolls

PREPARATION TIME 50 MINUTES **COOKING TIME** 15 MINUTES **MAKES** 24

1 tablespoon peanut oil

2 chicken breast fillets (400g)

24 x 17cm-square rice paper sheets

1 small red capsicum (150g), sliced thinly

1 ¼ cups (100g) bean sprouts

1 cup firmly packed fresh mint leaves

1 cup firmly packed fresh coriander leaves

DIPPING SAUCE

1 clove garlic, crushed

2 tablespoons fish sauce

¼ cup (60ml) lime juice

¼ cup (60ml) oyster sauce

¼ cup (65g) grated palm sugar

2 fresh small red thai chillies, chopped finely

The rolls can be made at the table or made ahead of time and stored in the fridge for up to 3 hours. Cover them with a damp clean tea-towel.

1 Make dipping sauce.

2 Meanwhile, heat oil in small frying pan; cook chicken until browned all over and cooked through. Stand 10 minutes; slice thinly into 24 pieces.

3 Place one sheet of rice paper in medium bowl of warm water until just softened; carefully lift from water. Place on board; pat dry with absorbent paper. Position rice paper in diamond shape; place chicken slice vertically down centre of rice paper, top with capsicum, sprouts and herbs. Fold bottom corner over filling; roll rice paper from side to side to enclose filling. Repeat with remaining rice paper sheets and filling.

4 Serve rice paper rolls cold with dipping sauce.

DIPPING SAUCE Combine ingredients in small saucepan; stir over medium heat until sugar dissolves. Refrigerate until cold.

PER ROLL (INCLUDING SAUCE) 1.7g total fat (0.4g saturated); 263kj (63 cal); 6.9g carbohydrate; 4.6g protein; 0.6g fibre

---

Uncooked scallops and lime wedges can be skewered up to 4 hours ahead. Cover and refrigerate until required. You need 24 bamboo skewers for this recipe; soak them in cold water for at least an hour before using to prevent splintering or scorching.

Tarragon and lime scallops

PREPARATION TIME 15 MINUTES **COOKING TIME** 10 MINUTES **MAKES** 24

24 scallops, without roe (600g)

2 tablespoons coarsely chopped fresh tarragon

1 tablespoon lime juice

1 tablespoon olive oil

3 limes

1 Rinse scallops under cold water; dry with absorbent paper. Combine tarragon, juice and oil in medium bowl, add scallops; toss to coat scallops in mixture.

2 Cut each lime into eight wedges. Thread one scallop and one lime wedge on each skewer. Cook, in batches, for 1 or 2 minutes on heated oiled grill plate (or grill or barbecue) until scallops are cooked through. Serve hot.

PER SKEWER 0.9g total fat (0.2g saturated); 92kj (22 cal); 0.2g carbohydrate; 3.0g protein; 0.1g fibre

Bloody mary oyster shots

PREPARATION TIME 10 MINUTES **MAKES** 16

The bloody mary mixture can be made a day ahead. Cover and refrigerate until ready to serve.

16 oysters
2 tablespoons vodka
2 tablespoons lemon juice
¾ cup (180ml) tomato juice
¼ teaspoon Tabasco
1 teaspoon worcestershire sauce

1 Place one oyster in each shot glass.
2 Combine remaining ingredients in medium jug; divide among glasses. Serve cold.

PER SHOT 0.2g total fat (0.1g saturated); 67kj (16 cal); 0.7g carbohydrate; 1.3g protein; 0.1g fibre

---

Mini pizzas

PREPARATION TIME 20 MINUTES **COOKING TIME** 10 MINUTES **MAKES** 24

Each of these pizza topping variations makes 24 mini pizzas. The pizzas can be assembled up to 2 hours ahead and refrigerated until ready to bake.

335g (30cm) ready-made pizza base

1 Preheat oven to moderately hot (200°C/180°C fan-forced).
2 Using 4.5cm cutter, cut rounds from pizza base; place on oven trays. Top with your choice of topping.

MASCARPONE AND HAM Spread 2 tablespoons tomato paste evenly over rounds; divide 100g shaved ham, 2 tablespoons mascarpone and 2 teaspoons finely chopped fresh chives among rounds. Bake, uncovered, about 5 minutes or until pizzas are heated through. Serve warm.

PER PIZZA 1.5g total fat (0.7g saturated); 226kj (54 cal); 7.7g carbohydrate; 2.2g protein; 0.6g fibre

LAMB AND ROCKET Spread 2 tablespoons tomato paste evenly over rounds; divide 70g thinly sliced firm goat cheese among rounds. Bake, uncovered, about 5 minutes or until pizzas are heated through. Top with 12 halved drained sun-dried tomatoes, 140g thinly sliced cooked lamb fillet and 40g thinly sliced baby rocket leaves. Serve warm.

PER PIZZA 1.6g total fat (0.6g saturated); 259kj (62 cal); 8.2g carbohydrate; 3.1g protein; 0.8g fibre

BLUE CHEESE AND GREEN ONION MINI PIZZAS Spread 2 tablespoons tomato paste evenly over rounds; top with 2 thinly sliced green onions and 75g coarsely chopped blue cheese. Bake, uncovered, about 5 minutes or until pizzas are heated through. Serve warm.

PER PIZZA 1.6g total fat (0.7g saturated); 226kj (54 cal); 7.6g carbohydrate; 2.0g protein; 0.6g fibre

CHAR-GRILLED VEGETABLE Spread 2 tablespoons tomato paste evenly over rounds; divide 150g drained, chopped char-grilled vegetables and 80g crumbled goat cheese among rounds. Bake, uncovered, about 5 minutes or until pizzas are heated through. Serve warm.

PER PIZZA 1.4g total fat (0.5g saturated); 217kj (52 cal); 7.8g carbohydrate; 1.8g protein; 0.6g fibre

Gyoza is the Japanese name for a wonton, gow gee or dumpling. They were introduced to Japan after the second world war and have become so popular that there are now gyoza restaurants.

Gyoza with soy vinegar sauce

PREPARATION TIME 40 MINUTES (PLUS REFRIGERATION TIME) **COOKING TIME** 15 MINUTES **MAKES** 40

300g pork mince
2 tablespoons kecap manis
1 teaspoon white sugar
1 tablespoon sake
1 egg
2 teaspoons sesame oil
3 cups (240g) finely shredded chinese cabbage
4 green onions, sliced thinly
40 gyoza or gow gee wrappers
1 tablespoon vegetable oil

SOY VINEGAR SAUCE
½ cup (125ml) light soy sauce
¼ cup (60ml) red wine vinegar
2 tablespoons white wine vinegar
2 tablespoons sweet chilli sauce

1 Combine pork, kecap manis, sugar, sake, egg, sesame oil, cabbage and onion in large bowl; refrigerate 1 hour.
2 Place a heaped teaspoon of the pork mixture in centre of one wrapper; brush around half of the wrapper's edge with a little water. Pleat damp side of wrapper only; pinch both sides together to seal. Repeat with remaining pork mixture and wrappers.
3 Cover base of large frying pan with water; bring to a boil. Add dumplings, in batches; reduce heat, simmer, covered, 3 minutes. Using slotted spoon, remove dumplings from pan. Drain pan; dry thoroughly.
4 Heat vegetable oil in same cleaned pan; cook dumplings, in batches, unpleated side and base only, until golden brown.
5 Meanwhile, make soy vinegar sauce. Serve with gyoza.

SOY VINEGAR SAUCE Combine ingredients in small bowl.

PER GYOZA (INCLUDING SAUCE) 1.5g total fat (0.4g saturated); 196kj (47 cal); 5.1g carbohydrate; 2.1g protein; 0.1g fibre

---

If you plan to make a lot of dumplings you can buy moulds in Asian supermarkets. These help press the edges together and shape the dumplings. Not only do they make life easier, they will give a far more professional result.

Prawn dumplings

PREPARATION TIME 40 MINUTES **COOKING TIME** 10 MINUTES **MAKES** 24

1kg uncooked prawns
¼ cup (50g) bamboo shoots, rinsed, drained, chopped finely
2 teaspoons sesame oil
1 tablespoon finely chopped fresh chives
2 teaspoons cornflour
24 gow gee wrappers

1 Shell and devein prawns; chop finely. Combine prawns in medium bowl with bamboo shoots, oil, chives and cornflour. Blend or process half of the prawn mixture until just smooth. Return to large bowl with remaining prawn mixture; stir to combine.
2 Place one wrapper on your hand; place a heaped teaspoon of the prawn filling into centre. Gently cup your hand and gather sides of wrapper to form pleats, leaving top open. Press base of wrapper on bench to flatten. Repeat with remaining wrappers and filling.

3 Place dumplings, without touching, in lightly oiled steamer; steam, in batches, over large saucepan of boiling water 10 minutes. Serve hot with light soy sauce if desired.

PER DUMPLING 0.6g total fat (0.1g saturated); 192kj (46 cal); 4.8g carbohydrate; 4.3g protein; 0.1g fibre

---

Tomato, leek and marinated fetta tartlets

The fetta can be marinated up to 2 weeks before making the tartlets; it will store well in an airtight jar in the fridge.

PREPARATION TIME 45 MINUTES (PLUS REFRIGERATION TIME) **COOKING TIME** 35 MINUTES **MAKES** 24

1 medium leek (350g)
20g butter
1 tablespoon olive oil
2 sheets ready-rolled puff pastry
250g cherry tomatoes, sliced thinly
½ teaspoon fresh thyme leaves
1 tablespoon red wine vinegar

MARINATED FETTA
1 teaspoon finely grated lemon rind
¼ teaspoon cracked black pepper
2 cloves garlic, crushed
2 teaspoons fresh thyme leaves
200g fetta, cut into 24 pieces
1¼ cups (310ml) olive oil

Work with one puff pastry sheet at a time, keeping the other in the freezer so that it doesn't become too soft.

1 Make marinated fetta.
2 Preheat oven to hot (220°C/200°C fan-forced). Lightly oil two oven trays.
3 Cut leek into 6cm pieces; cut pieces in half lengthways, slice halves lengthways into thin strips. Heat butter and oil in large frying pan; cook leek, stirring occasionally, about 20 minutes or until soft.
4 Meanwhile, cut each pastry sheet into twelve 6cm x 8cm rectangles; place on trays. Fold in each side to form a 2mm border; prick pastry pieces with fork. Bake, uncovered, about 10 minutes or until browned lightly. Remove from oven; using fork, immediately press pastry pieces down to flatten. Reduce oven temperature to moderately hot (200°C/180°C fan-forced).
5 Meanwhile, place tomato, thyme and vinegar in medium bowl; toss gently to combine.
6 Spread 1 tablespoon of the leek mixture over each pastry piece; crumble one piece of the cheese over each then top with tomato mixture. Bake, uncovered, about 5 minutes or until tomato just softens. Serve immediately.

MARINATED FETTA Combine rind, pepper, garlic and thyme in medium sterilised glass jar with a tight-fitting lid; add cheese. Seal jar then shake gently to coat cheese in mixture. Open jar and pour in enough of the oil to completely cover cheese mixture. Reseal; refrigerate overnight.

PER TARTLET 18.3g total fat (3.7g saturated); 823kj (197 cal); 5.6g carbohydrate; 2.5g protein; 0.7g fibre

Spring rolls

PREPARATION TIME 20 MINUTES **COOKING TIME** 20 MINUTES (PLUS REFRIGERATION TIME)
MAKES 12 ROLLS AND 1 ½ CUPS DIPPING SAUCE

20g rice vermicelli
100g cooked small king prawns
2 teaspoons peanut oil
100g pork mince
1 clove garlic, crushed
1 fresh small red thai chilli, chopped finely
1 green onion, chopped finely
1 small carrot (70g), grated finely
1 teaspoon finely chopped coriander root and stem mixture
1 teaspoon fish sauce
1 teaspoon cornflour
2 teaspoons water
12 x 12cm-square spring roll wrappers
vegetable oil, for deep-frying

CUCUMBER DIPPING SAUCE
1 lebanese cucumber (130g), seeded, sliced thinly
½ cup (110g) white sugar
1 cup (250ml) water
½ cup (125ml) white wine vinegar
4cm piece fresh ginger (20g), grated
1 teaspoon salt
2 fresh small red thai chillies, sliced thinly
3 green onions, sliced thinly
1 tablespoon coarsely chopped fresh coriander

To shell a prawn remove the head above the legs. Holding prawn firmly pull off the legs. Peel the shell away from the body. When you reach the tail, hold the body and pull away the tail; the shell will come off with it.

1 Place noodles in small heatproof bowl; cover with boiling water. Stand until just tender; drain. Using kitchen scissors, cut noodles into random lengths.
2 Shell and devein prawns; chop prawns finely.
3 Heat oil in wok; stir-fry pork, garlic and chilli until pork is changed in colour. Add onion, carrot, coriander mixture, fish sauce and prawns; stir-fry until vegetables just soften. Place pork mixture in small bowl with noodles; cool 10 minutes.
4 Blend cornflour with the water in small bowl. Place 1 level tablespoon of the filling near one corner of each wrapper. Lightly brush edges of each wrapper with cornflour mixture; roll to enclose filling, folding in ends.
5 Make cucumber dipping sauce (freeze excess for a future use).
6 Just before serving, heat vegetable oil in wok; deep-fry spring rolls, in batches, until golden brown. Drain on absorbent paper; serve spring rolls warm with dipping sauce.

CUCUMBER DIPPING SAUCE Place cucumber in heatproof serving bowl. Combine sugar, the water, vinegar, ginger and salt in small saucepan, stir over heat without boiling until sugar is dissolved; pour mixture over cucumber. Sprinkle with chilli, onion and coriander; refrigerate, covered, until chilled.

PER SPRING ROLL 3.4g total fat (0.6g saturated); 255kj (61 cal); 4.0g carbohydrate; 3.3g protein; 0.4g fibre
PER TABLESPOON DIPPING SAUCE 0.0g total fat (0.0g saturated); 109kj (26 cal); 6.4g carbohydrate; 0.1g protein; 0.2g fibre

SPRING ROLLS

An easy way to make sure that you get an equal amount of filling mixture in each sausage roll is to pipe it down the length of the pastry, using a piping bag fitted with a 2cm tube.

Sausage rolls

PREPARATION TIME 15 MINUTES **COOKING TIME** 20 MINUTES **MAKES** 72

1 medium brown onion (150g), chopped finely

½ cups (35g) stale breadcrumbs

500g sausage mince

500g beef mince

1 egg

1 tablespoon tomato paste

1 tablespoon barbecue sauce

2 tablespoons finely chopped fresh flat-leaf parsley

6 sheets ready-rolled puff pastry

1 egg, beaten lightly

2 tablespoons sesame seeds

Uncooked sausage rolls keep well in the freezer for up to 3 months.

1 Preheat oven to hot (220°C/200°C fan-forced). Line oven trays with baking paper.
2 Combine onion, breadcrumbs, minces, egg, paste, sauce and and parsley in large bowl.
3 Cut pastry sheets in half lengthways. Place equal amounts of filling mixture lengthways along centre of each pastry piece; roll each pastry piece, from one wide edge, to enclose filling. Cut each roll into six pieces; place rolls, seam-side down, on trays. Brush with egg, sprinkle with sesame seeds; cut small slit on top of each roll. Bake about 25 minutes.
4 Serve hot with tomato sauce, if desired.

PER ROLL 4.6g total fat (1.0g saturated); 293kj (70 cal); 4.4g carbohydrate; 2.7g protein; 0.4g fibre

---

The dipping sauce and uncooked fish cakes can be made a day ahead. Cover and refrigerate until required. We used redfish or flathead fillets.

Fish cakes with mirin dipping sauce

PREPARATION TIME 20 MINUTES (PLUS REFRIGERATION TIME) **COOKING TIME** 20 MINUTES **MAKES** 56

1kg boneless skinless fish fillets

5 green onions, chopped finely

2 cloves garlic, crushed

¼ cup coarsely chopped fresh coriander

2 tablespoons red curry paste

1 egg

¼ cup (60ml) coconut milk

100g green beans, trimmed, sliced thinly

peanut oil, for shallow-frying

⅔ cup (160ml) mirin

⅓ cup (80ml) soy sauce

When cooking the fish cakes make sure you don't overcook them or they will become rubbery and chewy.

1 Blend or process fish, half of the onion, garlic, coriander, paste, egg and coconut milk until just combined. Stir beans into mixture.
2 Shape level tablespoons of the fish mixture into cakes, cover; refrigerate 30 minutes.
3 Heat oil in large frying pan; shallow-fry fish cakes, in batches, about 3 minutes or until browned lightly both sides and cooked through. Drain on absorbent paper.
4 Combine mirin, soy sauce and remaining onion in small serving bowl. Serve with cakes.

PER FISH CAKE (INCLUDING SAUCE) 2.5g total fat (0.7g saturated); 176kj (42 cal); 0.3g carbohydrate; 4.0g protein; 0.2g fibre

1 SAUSAGE ROLLS **2** FISH CAKES WITH MIRIN DIPPING SAUCE
3 THAI COCONUT PRAWNS [P 76] **4** DUCK AND HOISIN CROSTINI [P 76]

1

2

3

4

To remove the fishy odour from your fingers after shelling uncooked prawns, rub lemon and salt on them or rub on a little toothpaste.

Thai coconut prawns

PREPARATION TIME 30 MINUTES **COOKING TIME** 15 MINUTES **MAKES** 24

- 24 uncooked medium king prawns (1kg)
- ¼ cup (35g) plain flour
- 2 eggs, beaten lightly
- 1½ cups (115g) shredded coconut
- ½ cup (125ml) sweet chilli sauce
- 2 tablespoons water
- 2 tablespoons coarsely chopped fresh coriander leaves

1 Preheat oven to moderate (180°C/160°C fan-forced). Lightly oil two oven trays.

2 Shell and devein prawns. Coat prawns in flour, shake away excess; dip into egg, then coat in coconut.

3 Thread one prawn on each skewer; place, in single layer, on trays. Cook, uncovered, about 15 minutes or until prawns are cooked through.

4 Meanwhile, combine remaining ingredients in small bowl.

5 Serve prawns hot with dipping sauce.

PER PRAWN (INCLUDING SAUCE) 3.8g total fat (2.9g saturated); 280kj (67 cal); 2.4g carbohydrate; 5.3g protein; 1.0g fibre

---

Crostini in Italian means "little toasts". The thin slices of bread are drizzled or sprayed with olive oil, toasted and served warm.

Duck and hoisin crostini

PREPARATION TIME 15 MINUTES (PLUS REFRIGERATION TIME) **COOKING TIME** 15 MINUTES **MAKES** 24

- 2 green onions
- 2 cups (250g) thinly sliced barbecued duck meat
- ½ lebanese cucumber (65g), seeded, sliced thinly
- ¼ cup (60ml) hoisin sauce

CROSTINI

- 1 small french bread stick
- vegetable oil, for drizzling

1 Preheat oven to moderately slow (170°C/150°C fan-forced). Make crostini.

2 Meanwhile, cut green section of onions into 8cm pieces; slice each piece lengthways into 12 thin strips (reserve white bulb sections of onions for another use). Place green onion strips in small bowl of iced water; refrigerate about 20 minutes or until curled.

3 Top crostini with duck, cucumber, sauce and onion curls. Serve immediately.

CROSTINI Discard ends of bread; cut into 1cm slices. Place slices, in single layer, on oven tray; drizzle with oil. Toast both sides in oven.

PER CROSTINI 2.4g total fat (0.7g saturated); 196kj (47 cal); 3.4g carbohydrate; 2.8g protein; 0.5g fibre

Peanut and chicken gow gees

PREPARATION TIME 30 MINUTES (PLUS STANDING TIME) **COOKING TIME** 20 MINUTES **MAKES** 40

Gow gees or wontons are the Chinese equivalent of Italian ravioli. You can make them up to 4 hours ahead and refrigerate until ready to cook, or freeze them, covered, for up to 3 months. They can then be cooked straight from the freezer, which will increase the cooking time slightly.

3 dried shiitake mushrooms

1 trimmed celery stalk (100g), chopped finely

1 tablespoon finely chopped roasted unsalted peanuts

1 clove garlic, crushed

1 green onion, chopped finely

2 teaspoons hoisin sauce

200g chicken mince

40 gow gee wrappers

DIPPING SAUCE

¼ cup (60ml) kecap manis

2 teaspoons red wine vinegar

1 Place mushrooms in medium heatproof bowl, cover with boiling water; stand about 20 minutes, drain. Discard stems; chop caps finely.

2 Combine mushrooms in bowl with celery, nuts, garlic, onion, sauce and chicken mince.

3 Place 1 heaped teaspoon of the chicken mixture in centre of one wrapper; brush around half of the wrapper's edge with a little water. Pleat damp side of wrapper only; pinch both sides together to seal. Repeat with remaining chicken mixture and wrappers.

4 Cook gow gees, in batches, in large saucepan of boiling water about 5 minutes.

5 Meanwhile, make dipping sauce. Serve with gow gees.

DIPPING SAUCE Combine ingredients in small bowl.

PER GOW GEE (INCLUDING SAUCE) 0.4g total fat (0.1g saturated); 134kj (32 cal); 4.9g carbohydrate; 1.2g protein; 0.1g fibre

---

Spicy teriyaki tuna

PREPARATION TIME 30 MINUTES (PLUS REFRIGERATION TIME) **COOKING TIME** 15 MINUTES **MAKES** 24

The word teriyaki is a combination of the Japanese words "teri", meaning shine, and "yaki", meaning grill or roast. To make a teriyaki dish, ingredients are grilled or roasted after being marinated or basted in teriyaki sauce. It's the teriyaki sauce that makes the food glossy.

¾ cup (180ml) japanese soy sauce

2 tablespoons honey

¼ cup (60ml) mirin

1 tablespoon wasabi paste

1 teaspoon sesame oil

300g sashimi tuna steak

2 tablespoons thinly sliced drained pickled ginger

1 Combine soy, honey, mirin, wasabi and oil in medium bowl; reserve ½ cup of marinade in small jug. Place tuna in bowl with remaining marinade. Cover; refrigerate 3 hours or overnight. Drain tuna; discard marinade.

2 Cook tuna in heated oiled medium frying pan until browned both sides and cooked as desired (do not overcook as tuna has a tendency to dry out).

3 Cut tuna into 24 similar-sized pieces (approximately 2cm each).

4 Place chinese spoons on serving platter. Place one piece of tuna on each spoon; top with 1 teaspoon of the reserved marinade and a little ginger.

PER SPOON 0.9g total fat (0.3g saturated); 134kj (32 cal); 2.2g carbohydrate; 3.6g protein; 0.0g fibre

Fast finger food ideas

These quick and easy finger food recipes are perfect to serve with a glass of something cold and fizzy.

TUNA SALAD ON PITTA CRISPS
Process 180g can drained tuna with 1 tablespoon each yogurt, mayonnaise and prepared horseradish; stir in sliced green onion. Serve on toasted pitta.

GREEK MINI PIZZAS
Cut 4.5cm rounds from a ready-made pizza base; place on an oven tray. Top with tomato paste, then halved olives, char-grilled capsicum slices and crumbled fetta. Bake in a hot oven until hot; top with basil leaves.

SALMON, AVOCADO ON CUCUMBER
Process 250g cream cheese with an avocado, lemon juice and sambal oelek to taste. Pipe or spoon onto slices of cucumber; top with drained canned salmon and green onion slices.

TURKEY, BRIE AND CRANBERRY
Slice brie thinly. Top pumpernickel rounds with brie, thinly sliced smoked turkey breast, whole-berry cranberry sauce and chopped fresh chives.

TOMATO AIOLI AND PRAWN CANAPES
Combine 1 cup mayonnaise with 2 cloves crushed garlic and 2 tablespoons sun-dried tomato pesto; spread over toasted baguette slices. Top each with 1 prawn and finely shredded lime rind.

MINI PRAWN COCKTAIL
Flavour mayonnaise with tomato and worcestershire sauces, Tabasco and horseradish cream. Fill baby lettuce leaves with shelled cooked prawns; top with sauce, chopped chives and finely grated lemon rind.

POTATO AND GOAT CHEESE PUFFS

Combine 2 cups mashed potato, 1 egg, ½ cup self-raising flour, crushed garlic, 3 rashers chopped bacon, 2 sliced green onions and 100g goat cheese. Roll into balls; deep-fry until browned.

SMOKED SALMON AND DILL CANAPES

Combine sour cream with finely chopped fresh dill, finely grated lemon rind, finely chopped red onion and chopped baby capers; spread onto mini toasts. Top with smoked salmon and dill sprigs.

BLT ON MINI TOASTS

Cut bacon rashers into 2cm pieces; cook in a lightly oiled frying pan until crisp. Spread mini toasts with mayonnaise; top each with lettuce, bacon and sliced grape tomatoes.

ASIAN SCALLOPS

Combine 2 teaspoons each lime juice, and fish sauce, 2 tablespoons coconut cream and 1 sliced green onion with chilli and coriander in a frying pan; bring to a boil. Add 24 scallops; serve immediately.

HALOUMI AND TAPENADE BRUSCHETTA

Cut haloumi into slices; cook in a lightly oiled frying pan until browned lightly on both sides. Spread tapenade over toasted baguette slices; top each with warm haloumi and fresh oregano leaves.

SMOKED CHICKEN WONTON CRISPS

Cut wonton wrappers into squares; deep-fry until crisp. Combine shredded smoked chicken with chopped apple and green onions, mayonnaise and mustard. Spoon onto the cooled wonton crisps.

A samosa is the Indian interpretation of a pastie or pie. It is a popular snack made with a savoury filling wrapped in pastry, then baked or deep-fried.

Samosas with tamarind sauce

PREPARATION TIME 40 MINUTES (PLUS COOLING TIME) **COOKING TIME** 30 MINUTES **MAKES** 48

1 small brown onion (80g), chopped finely
1 clove garlic, crushed
2 teaspoons ground cumin
1 tablespoon mild curry paste
300g lamb mince
2 tablespoons finely chopped fresh coriander
1 small kumara (250g), chopped finely
¼ cup (60ml) chicken stock
1 tablespoon lime juice
¼ cup (30g) frozen peas
3 sheets ready-rolled shortcrust pastry
1 egg, beaten lightly
2 tablespoons tamarind paste
10cm stick (20g) finely chopped fresh lemon grass
2 tablespoons grated palm sugar
⅓ cup (80ml) orange juice

For a lighter version, use spring roll wrappers or fillo pastry instead of the shortcrust pastry.

1 Cook onion, garlic, cumin and curry paste in medium frying pan, stirring, until onion softens. Add lamb; cook, stirring, until lamb changes colour. Stir in coriander, kumara, stock and lime juice; bring to a boil. Reduce heat; simmer, uncovered, until kumara softens. Stir in peas; simmer, uncovered, until most of the liquid has evaporated. Cool 10 minutes.
2 Preheat oven to moderately hot (200°C/180°C fan-forced). Lightly oil two oven trays.
3 Cut each pastry sheet into 16 squares. Divide lamb mixture among squares, brushing edges with a little egg. Bring four corners of each square together in centre, pressing together to enclose filling.
4 Place samosas on trays; brush tops with remaining egg. Bake, uncovered, about 15 minutes or until browned lightly.
5 Meanwhile, combine remaining ingredients in small saucepan; cook, stirring, over low heat until tamarind sauce is smooth.
6 Serve hot samosas with tamarind sauce.

PER SAMOSA (INCLUDING SAUCE) 3.7g total fat (1.8g saturated); 284kj (68 cal); 6.2g carbohydrate; 2.3g protein; 0.4g fibre

---

You can buy marinated fetta at most delicatessens or make your own (see page 71).

Fig and fetta canapés

PREPARATION TIME 10 MINUTES **MAKES** 24

125g marinated fetta
1 tablespoon finely chopped fresh chives
24 mini toasts
3 medium fresh figs (180g)

For a meaty option wrap each fig wedge in a thin slice of prosciutto.

1 Using fork, mash cheese with chives in small bowl; spread on one side of each toast.
2 Cut each fig into eight wedges; place one wedge on each toast. Serve canapés immediately sprinkled with cracked black pepper, if desired.

PER CANAPE 13.2g total fat (2.5g saturated); 594kj (142 cal); 4.3g carbohydrate; 1.7g protein; 0.4g fibre

Curry puffs with sweet chilli sauce

PREPARATION TIME 30 MINUTES **COOKING TIME** 35 MINUTES
MAKES 8 CURRY PUFFS AND 1½ CUPS DIPPING SAUCE

Make sure the oil is very hot before deep-frying the curry puffs, and don't crowd them in the pan or they will cook unevenly. Turn them constantly, using a metal slotted spoon.

2 teaspoons peanut oil
2 teaspoons finely chopped coriander root
2 green onions, chopped finely
1 clove garlic, crushed
100g beef mince
½ teaspoon ground turmeric
½ teaspoon ground cumin
¼ teaspoon ground coriander
2 teaspoons fish sauce
1 tablespoon water
½ cup (110g) mashed potato
2 sheets ready-rolled frozen puff pastry
1 egg, beaten lightly
vegetable oil, for deep-frying

SWEET CHILLI DIPPING SAUCE
12 fresh small red thai chillies, chopped coarsely
8 cloves garlic, quartered
2 cups (500ml) white vinegar
1 cup (220g) white sugar
2 teaspoons salt
2 teaspoons tamarind paste

1 Make sweet chilli dipping sauce (freeze excess for a future use).
2 Heat peanut oil in wok; stir-fry coriander root, onion, garlic and beef until beef is changed in colour. Add turmeric, cumin and ground coriander; stir-fry until fragrant. Add fish sauce and the water; simmer, uncovered, until mixture thickens. Stir in potato; cool 10 minutes.
3 Using 9cm cutter, cut four rounds from each pastry sheet. Place 1 level tablespoon of the filling in centre of each round; brush around edge lightly with egg. Fold pastry over to enclose filling, pressing edges together to seal.
4 Just before serving, heat vegetable oil in wok; deep-fry curry puffs, in batches, until crisp and browned lightly. Drain on absorbent paper; serve curry puffs warm with sweet chilli dipping sauce.

SWEET CHILLI DIPPING SAUCE Place ingredients in medium saucepan, stir over heat without boiling until sugar is dissolved; bring to a boil. Reduce heat; simmer, uncovered, 20 minutes or until slightly thickened. Cool 5 minutes; blend or process until pureed.

PER CURRY PUFF 16.5g total fat (2.0g saturated); 1012kj (242 cal); 16.8g carbohydrate; 6.3g protein; 0.9g fibre

PER TABLESPOON DIPPING SAUCE 0.0g total fat (0.0g saturated); 222kj (53 cal); 12.5g carbohydrate; 0.1g protein; 0.3g fibre

Once cooled, both the curry puffs and the samosas on these pages can be frozen for up to 3 months. Just before serving, place several, still frozen, in a single layer on a metal rack set over an oven tray, and cook in a moderate oven for about 10 minutes or until crisp and heated through.

This recipe also works well with uncooked prawns. Fillo pastry can be used instead of wonton wrappers, if preferred.

Coconut chicken salad in crisp wonton cups

PREPARATION TIME 25 MINUTES **COOKING TIME** 25 MINUTES (PLUS COOLING TIME) **MAKES** 40

- 350g chicken breast fillets
- ¾ cup (180ml) chicken stock
- 1 cup (250ml) coconut cream
- 4 fresh kaffir lime leaves, shredded finely
- 1 tablespoon brown sugar
- 1 tablespoon fish sauce
- 1 clove garlic, crushed
- 1 fresh small red thai chilli, chopped finely
- 40 square wonton wrappers
- cooking-oil spray
- 100g snow peas, trimmed, sliced thinly
- ½ cup finely chopped fresh coriander

1 Preheat oven to moderately hot (200°C/180°C fan-forced). Lightly oil four 12-hole mini (1-tablespoon/20ml) muffin pans.

2 Combine chicken, stock, coconut cream and lime leaves in medium saucepan; bring to a boil. Reduce heat; simmer, uncovered, about 10 minutes or until chicken is cooked through. Cool chicken in coconut mixture 10 minutes.

3 Remove chicken from coconut mixture; chop chicken finely. Bring coconut mixture to a boil. Reduce heat; simmer, uncovered, until mixture reduces by half. Strain into medium bowl; stir sugar, sauce, garlic and chilli into dressing. Cool to room temperature.

4 Meanwhile, push wrappers into pans; spray with oil. Bake about 7 minutes or until browned lightly. Stand in pans 2 minutes; turn onto wire racks to cool.

5 Stir chicken, snow peas and coriander into dressing in bowl; divide chicken mixture among wonton cups. Serve immediately.

PER CUP 1.8g total fat (1.3g saturated); 209kj (50 cal); 5.2g carbohydrate; 3.0g protein; 0.2g fibre

---

Rösti, the classic Swiss potato cakes, are best made with starchy potatoes, such as spunta or russet burbank. Perfect rösti have a thick crunchy crust and are moist and buttery inside.

Rösti with smoked trout and crème fraîche

PREPARATION TIME 30 MINUTES (PLUS COOLING TIME) **COOKING TIME** 25 MINUTES **MAKES** 32

- 1kg potatoes, unpeeled
- 20g butter, melted
- ¼ cup coarsely chopped fresh chives
- ½ cup (125ml) olive oil
- 1½ cups (260g) flaked smoked trout
- ⅓ cup (85g) crème fraîche

1 Boil, steam or microwave whole potatoes for 5 minutes; drain. Cool 20 minutes, peel; grate coarsely into medium bowl with butter and half of the chives.

2 Heat oil in medium frying pan. Shape level tablespoons of the potato mixture into patties; cook patties in batches until crisp both sides. Drain on absorbent paper.

3 Divide trout and crème fraîche among rösti; top with remaining chives.

PER ROSTI 5.6g total fat (1.6g saturated); 330kj (79 cal); 4.2g carbohydrate; 2.9g protein; 0.6g fibre

COCONUT CHICKEN SALAD IN CRISP WONTON CUPS

Originally from Russia, blini are small, leavened buckwheat pancakes that are traditionally served with sour cream and caviar. They make a perfect base for any number of canapé toppings.

Buckwheat blini

PREPARATION TIME 10 MINUTES **COOKING TIME** 20 MINUTES **MAKES** 48

½ cup (75g) buckwheat flour
¼ cup (35g) plain flour
1 ½ teaspoons baking powder
1 egg
¾ cup (180ml) buttermilk
30g butter, melted

1 Sift flours and baking powder into medium bowl, gradually whisk in combined egg and buttermilk; stir in butter.

2 Cook blini, in batches, by dropping 2-teaspoon portions of the batter into large heated frying pan until bubbles appear on surfaces of blini; turn blini, cook until browned on other side. Turn onto wire racks to cool. Serve blini with your choice of topping.

PER BLINI 0.8g total fat (0.4g saturated); 71kj (17 cal); 1.9g carbohydrate; 0.6g protein; 0.1g fibre

CREME FRAICHE WITH SALMON ROE

PREPARATION TIME 10 MINUTES **MAKES** 16

Divide ¼ cup crème fraîche, 50g salmon roe and 1 tablespoon coarsely chopped fresh chives among 16 blini.

PER BLINI 2.6g total fat (1.5g saturated); 150kj (36 cal); 2.0g carbohydrate; 1.3g protein; 0.1g fibre

Blend 50g cream cheese and 1 teaspoon horseradish cream with 75g wilted baby spinach. Divide among 16 blini and top with 100g smoked salmon, cut into strips; top with half a hard-boiled quail egg.

SMOKED CHICKEN AND MUSTARD

PREPARATION TIME 10 MINUTES **MAKES** 16

Mix together ¼ cup mayonnaise and 1 tablespoon mild english mustard in small bowl. Combine 200g thinly sliced smoked chicken with mayonnaise mixture and divide among 16 blini; top each with fresh oregano leaves.

PER BLINI 2.8g total fat (0.8g saturated); 213kj (51 cal); 2.7g carbohydrate; 3.7g protein; 0.1g fibre

ROAST BEEF AND HORSERADISH CREAM

PREPARATION TIME 10 MINUTES **MAKES** 16

Combine ¼ cup sour cream, 1 tablespoon horseradish cream, 2 teaspoons finely chopped fresh chives and ¼ teaspoon cracked black pepper in small bowl. Divide sour cream mixture and 100g coarsely chopped rare roast beef slices among 16 blini; top each with a piece of fresh chive.

PER BLINI 4.2g total fat (2.5g saturated); 322kj (77 cal); 6.0g carbohydrate; 3.5g protein; 0.2g fibre

Smoked salmon and sour cream crepe cakes

PREPARATION TIME 30 MINUTES (PLUS STANDING TIME)

COOKING TIME 30 MINUTES (PLUS REFRIGERATION TIME) **MAKES** 16

½ cup (75g) plain flour

2 eggs

2 teaspoons vegetable oil

1 cup (250ml) milk

2 tablespoons drained capers, rinsed, chopped coarsely

2 tablespoons finely chopped fresh dill

1 tablespoon finely grated lemon rind

2 teaspoons lemon juice

1 clove garlic, crushed

1 cup (240g) sour cream

500g sliced smoked salmon

1 Line base and side of deep 20cm-round cake pan with plastic wrap.

2 Place flour in medium bowl. Make well in centre; gradually whisk in combined eggs, oil and milk. Strain into large jug; stand 30 minutes.

3 Heat oiled 19cm frying pan; pour ¼ cup of the batter into pan, tilting pan to coat base. Cook over low heat, loosening around edge with spatula until browned lightly. Turn; brown other side. Remove from pan; repeat with remaining batter to make a total of five crepes.

4 Combine capers, dill, rind, juice, garlic and sour cream in small bowl. Place a crepe in cake pan; spread with ⅓ cup of sour cream mixture, cover with a quarter of the fish. Continue layering, finishing with a crepe. Cover; refrigerate overnight.

5 Turn cake onto chopping board; discard plastic wrap. Trim cake into a square; discard trimmings. Cut into 4cm squares; top squares with sour cream and dill, if desired.

PER PIECE 9.3g total fat (4.9g saturated); 589kj (141 cal); 4.8g carbohydrate; 9.4g protein; 0.3g fibre

For a vegetarian version, combine 250g spreadable fetta, 2 tablespoons chopped mint, 2 teaspoons finely grated lemon rind, 2 teaspoons lemon juice and 1 clove crushed garlic. Spread over crepes; top with thin slices of roasted red capsicum, char-grilled eggplant, 50g seeded chopped kalamata olives and 50g chopped semi-dried tomatoes.

Raclette parcels in vine leaves and prosciutto

PREPARATION TIME 25 MINUTES **COOKING TIME** 5 MINUTES **MAKES** 24

2 tablespoons finely chopped fresh basil

1 fresh small red thai chilli, chopped finely

2 teaspoons finely grated lemon rind

1 tablespoon lemon juice

2 teaspoons olive oil

500g piece raclette cheese, cut into 24 pieces

8 slices prosciutto (120g)

24 grapevine leaves in brine, rinsed, drained

1 Place basil, chilli, rind, juice and oil in medium bowl with cheese; toss gently to combine. Cut each prosciutto slice lengthways into three even strips.

2 Centre one cheese piece on each vine leaf; fold leaf over cheese to enclose completely. Wrap one strip of prosciutto around each vine-leaf parcel.

3 Heat large frying pan; cook parcels, uncovered, about 5 minutes or until prosciutto is crisp all over.

PER PARCEL 7.0g total fat (4.1g saturated); 368kj (88 cal); 0.1g carbohydrate; 6.3g protein; 0.2g fibre

If you cannot find raclette, you can use gruyère or emmental instead. Grapevine leaves, available in cans or cryovac-packed in brine, can be found in Greek and Middle Eastern food stores as well as good delicatessens.

SOUPS

Soups

Soup has changed roles. Now that the family cook probably holds down a job as well, we're more likely to serve soup as the main dish rather than a mere opener to a meal. It has to be proper soup, of course, robust, nourishing and real. Make it at the weekend and it's an insurance policy for the week. Serve it with worthy partners, such as those described below, and it's a great entertainer. This chapter gives you some of the world's best-loved meal-in-a-bowl soups, as well as some delicious lighter ones for times when you still want to serve soup in its traditional role as the first of several courses.

As matchlessly comforting as soup is in cold weather, don't give up its joys just because it's summer. Think light and refreshing with fresh tomato soup, ice-cold savour with gazpacho, cool and elegant with vichyssoise, spicy and restorative with tom yum goong. Like all soups, they can be made ahead (except for some finishing stages) and stored in the fridge.

STOCKS

Stocks are flavoursome liquids made by simmering meat, chicken or fish bones and trimmings with aromatic vegetables and herbs (or vegetables and herbs only) to extract their flavour. Though not all soups are made with stock, so many do depend on it that it is worthwhile joining the host of cooks who make it as a matter of course.

Stockmaking is easy and economical, and good stock is a kitchen treasure not only for soups but for gravies, sauces and casseroles. Though it does take time to simmer to perfection, it needs your attention only at the beginning and end of the process, and because all stocks freeze perfectly, you can pick times when it suits you to make a batch, and enjoy the satisfaction of having these beautiful basics always on hand.

Meat and chicken stocks are simmered for hours to extract the gelatine from the bones for richness, but vegetable and fish stocks are simmered for only a short time as lengthy cooking would not extract significantly more flavour and would blur their fresh character. Sometimes meat, chicken or vegetables are browned before simmering to give deeper colour and flavour.

After simmering, the solids are strained out, any fat is removed by chilling the stock and lifting off the solidified fat layer, and the stock is ready for use in soups, casseroles, gravies and sauces. You can store beef, veal, chicken and vegetable stocks in the fridge for 2 to 3 days, fish stock for 2 days, and all of them in the freezer for months. Since you usually make a big potful at a time, most cooks freeze it in batches: support plastic bags in straight-sized containers, fill with stock and, when frozen, lift out the bags, seal and label. See page 662 for our favourite stock recipes.

COMMERCIAL STOCKS Do bought stocks have a place in good cooking? In general, home-made is to be preferred to commercial stocks or stock cubes because its flavour is more subtle and complex. Also, because home-made stock is not salted, you have complete control over the saltiness of the finished dish. That said, the packaged liquid stocks now available in supermarkets are quality products and it is worth keeping a couple of packets on hand for times when you may not have home-made. Just be careful when seasoning, as commercial stock is often salty. Jars of concentrated stock or glacé (glaze) in the form of a stiff jelly, available from delicatessens, gourmet food stores and some butchers, are also high-quality products, but watch the salt level with these too. Stock cubes and powders tend to be strong but harsh in flavour, so they are not ideal to use alone for stock, but they can be useful as a flavour boost – for instance, to add to vegetable cooking water, or the water you've used to deglaze a pan, and then use this as stock. Dissolve the cube or powder first in a little hot water and add gradually, tasting as you go, so that it won't overwhelm the natural flavours.

FINISHING TOUCHES

However delicious they may be, many soups look worthy rather than wonderful until the right garnish brings them to life. The simplest garnish is a sprinkling of chopped parsley, chives or other fresh herb that suits the flavour – dill for borscht, fennel for a fish soup, basil for a tomato one (not too much, or the flavour will overwhelm the soup). Cream soups can be topped with a spoonful of cream swirled into a C with the point of the spoon, plus a sprig of parsley for colour. Tiny vegetable cubes or julienne (matchsticks), briefly simmered so that they are still a bit crisp, can go on clear or thick soups. One or two paper-thin lime or lemon slices, a little finely shredded lettuce or a tiny bouquet of watercress tips make a chilled soup inviting. A potato, pumpkin or other robust soup looks good with a few crisp croutons in the centre, with more croutons passed separately. To make them, remove the crusts from thickly sliced bread and cut into small cubes. Fry in a mixture of oil and butter until golden, drain on absorbent paper and store in an airtight container. When needed, reheat briefly in a moderate oven.

GOOD PARTNERS

Good bread, crisp crackers or toast are classic accompaniments that suit nearly all soups. Warm savoury muffins, savoury turnovers or other pastries, toast fingers topped with grilled cheese or anchovy paste, or finger sandwiches with appropriate fillings make a bowl of soup into a meal.

For an elegant soup served as a first course, melba toast is the right companion: lightly toast slices of white sandwich bread, cut off the crusts and, with a thin, sharp knife, split each slice of toast through the middle. Cut into small triangles and bake in a moderately hot oven until golden, checking often so that they don't get too brown. Store in an airtight container, and reheat as for croutons.

Mixed dried beans, lentils or potato make a nice addition to this hearty soup.

Lamb shank soup

PREPARATION TIME 30 MINUTES **COOKING TIME** 2 HOURS 30 MINUTES (PLUS COOLING AND REFRIGERATION TIME) **SERVES** 4

- 8 french-trimmed lamb shanks (2kg)
- 1 medium brown onion (150g), chopped finely
- 2 trimmed celery stalks (200g), sliced thinly
- 2 medium red capsicums (400g), chopped coarsely
- 2 cloves garlic, crushed
- 2 litres (8 cups) water
- 400g silverbeet, trimmed, chopped finely
- ⅓ cup (80ml) lemon juice

1 Heat large lightly oiled saucepan; cook lamb, in batches, until browned. Cook onion, celery, capsicum and garlic in same pan, stirring, about 5 minutes or until onion softens. Return lamb to pan with the water; bring to a boil. Reduce heat; simmer, covered, about 1¾ hours. Remove soup mixture from heat.

2 When lamb is cool enough to handle, remove meat from bones then chop coarsely. Refrigerate cooled soup and meat, covered separately, overnight.

3 Discard fat from surface of soup mixture. Place soup mixture and meat in large saucepan; bring to a boil. Reduce heat; simmer, covered, 30 minutes. Add silverbeet and juice; simmer, uncovered, until silverbeet just wilts.

PER SERVING 22.5g total fat (10.0g saturated); 1965kj (470 cal); 8.0g carbohydrate; 5.6g protein; 5.1g fibre

---

The key to this recipe is ripe tomatoes. Store your tomatoes at room temperature, allowing their flavours to really develop.

Fresh tomato soup

PREPARATION TIME 20 MINUTES **COOKING TIME** 35 MINUTES **SERVES** 4

- 700g medium tomatoes, seeded, chopped coarsely
- 1 large brown onion (200g), chopped coarsely
- 2 trimmed celery stalks (200g), chopped coarsely
- 1 clove garlic, crushed
- 1 litre (4 cups) chicken stock
- 400g can tomato puree

1 Place tomato, onion, celery, garlic and half of the stock in large saucepan; bring to a boil. Reduce heat; simmer, covered, about 15 minutes or until vegetables soften. Cool 10 minutes.

2 Blend or process soup, in batches, until smooth. Return soup mixture to same pan. Stir in remaining stock and tomato puree; bring to a boil. Reduce heat; simmer, uncovered, about 10 minutes.

PER SERVING 1.3g total fat (0.5g saturated); 385kj (92 cal); 12.0g carbohydrate; 5.9g protein; 4.2g fibre

Minestrone

PREPARATION TIME 25 MINUTES (PLUS SOAKING TIME) **COOKING TIME** 1 HOUR 10 MINUTES **SERVES** 6

This recipe is a typical example of a northern Italian minestrone, where the colder winters call out for hearty, warming fare. Ditalini or ditali are small hollow pasta tubes; tiny macaroni can be substituted. You can use canned white beans here instead of soaking dried beans but rinse and drain them first, and only add them towards the end of cooking time, just after you add the pasta.

½ cup (100g) dried cannellini beans

2 teaspoons olive oil

1 medium brown onion (150g), chopped finely

2 cloves garlic, crushed

10 slices prosciutto (150g), chopped coarsely

1 trimmed celery stalk (100g), chopped finely

1 medium carrot (120g), chopped finely

1 medium green zucchini (120g), chopped finely

2 x 400g cans crushed tomatoes

1.5 litres (6 cups) chicken stock

1 medium potato (200g), chopped finely

1 cup (170g) ditalini

1 cup (80g) finely shredded savoy cabbage

1 cup (50g) finely shredded spinach

1 tablespoon finely shredded fresh basil

½ cup (40g) finely grated parmesan

1 Place beans in medium bowl, cover with water; stand overnight, drain.

2 Heat oil in large saucepan; cook onion and garlic, stirring, until onion softens. Add prosciutto, celery, carrot and zucchini; cook, stirring, 5 minutes. Stir in undrained tomatoes and stock; bring to a boil. Reduce heat; simmer, uncovered, 30 minutes.

3 Stir in beans and potato; simmer, uncovered, 15 minutes.

4 Add pasta; simmer, uncovered, about 10 minutes or until pasta is tender.

5 Just before serving, stir in cabbage, spinach and basil; serve soup sprinkled with grated cheese.

PER SERVING 7.0g total fat (2.7g saturated); 1191kj (285 cal); 34.7g carbohydrate; 17.5g protein; 6.4g fibre

---

Pumpkin soup

PREPARATION TIME 25 MINUTES **COOKING TIME** 30 MINUTES **SERVES** 4

Here's a variation on the pumpkin soup theme: fry two finely chopped bacon rashers, the chopped pumpkin and onion together, stirring until the bacon is crisp and the pumpkin is lightly browned. Follow the rest of the method at left, replacing the chicken stock with beef stock and the cream with marsala. Serve sprinkled with a few roasted pumpkin seeds.

2½ cups (625ml) water

1kg pumpkin, chopped coarsely

1 large brown onion (200g), chopped coarsely

2 medium tomatoes (300g), seeded, chopped coarsely

4cm piece fresh ginger (20g), grated

1 cup (250ml) chicken stock

½ cup (125ml) cream

1 Place the water, pumpkin, onion, tomato, ginger and stock in large saucepan; bring to a boil. Reduce heat; simmer, covered, about 20 minutes or until pumpkin is tender. Cool 10 minutes.

2 Blend or process soup, in batches, until smooth. Return soup to same pan. Stir in cream; stir over heat, without boiling, until soup is heated through.

PER SERVING 14.7g total fat (9.7g saturated); 986kj (236 cal); 18.0g carbohydrate; 6.6g protein; 3.6g fibre

Ever wondered about the different types of tofu? Chinese-style firm tofu is best used for cutting into cubes for stir-fries, soups and salads, as it will hold its shape. Japanese-style silken tofu, on the other hand, is much creamier, softer and better for making dips, desserts or any recipe that requires the tofu to be smooth.

Vietnamese beef, chicken and tofu soup *(pho bo)*

PREPARATION TIME 20 MINUTES **COOKING TIME** 1 HOUR 10 MINUTES **SERVES** 4

3 litres (12 cups) water
500g gravy beef
1 star anise
3cm piece fresh galangal (15g), halved
¼ cup (60ml) light soy sauce
2 tablespoons fish sauce
350g chicken breast fillets
1 ½ cups (120g) bean sprouts
1 cup loosely packed fresh coriander leaves
4 green onions, sliced thinly
2 fresh small red thai chillies, sliced thinly
⅓ cup (80ml) lime juice
300g firm tofu

1 Combine the water, beef, star anise, galangal and sauces in large saucepan; bring to a boil. Reduce heat; simmer, covered, 30 minutes. Uncover; simmer, 20 minutes. Add chicken; simmer, uncovered, 10 minutes.
2 Combine sprouts, coriander, onion, chilli and juice in medium bowl.
3 Remove beef and chicken from pan; reserve stock. Discard fat and sinew from beef; slice thinly. Slice chicken thinly. Return beef and chicken to pan; reheat soup.
4 Divide tofu among serving bowls; ladle hot soup over top, sprinkle with sprout mixture.

PER SERVING 16.3g total fat (4.9g saturated); 1659kj (397 cal); 3.6g carbohydrate; 56.8g protein; 3.1g fibre

For a crunchy and flavoursome garnish, combine ½ cup coarse stale breadcrumbs, 2 crushed garlic cloves, 1 tablespoon finely chopped rosemary, 2 tablespoons olive oil and ¼ cup coarsely chopped blanched almonds; bake in a hot oven for 5 minutes or until golden. Cool and sprinkle over the gazpacho. Vodka is optional but gives the soup an added zing.

Gazpacho

PREPARATION TIME 25 MINUTES (PLUS REFRIGERATION TIME) **SERVES** 4

3 cups (750ml) tomato juice
8 medium egg tomatoes (600g), chopped coarsely
1 medium red onion (170g), chopped coarsely
1 clove garlic, quartered
1 lebanese cucumber (130g), chopped coarsely
1 small red capsicum (150g), chopped coarsely
2 teaspoons Tabasco
4 green onions, chopped finely
½ lebanese cucumber (65g), seeded, chopped finely
½ small yellow capsicum (75g), chopped finely
2 teaspoons olive oil
1 tablespoon vodka
2 tablespoons finely chopped fresh coriander

1 Blend or process juice, tomato, onion, garlic, coarsely chopped cucumber and red capsicum, in batches, until pureed. Strain into large bowl, cover; refrigerate soup 3 hours.
2 Divide soup among serving bowls; top with combined remaining ingredients.

PER SERVING 2.6g total fat (0.3g saturated); 556kj (133 cal); 16.9g carbohydrate; 4.8g protein; 4.9g fibre

VIETNAMESE BEEF, CHICKEN AND TOFU SOUP (PHO BO)

Tom yum is the most popular soup in Thailand and renowned among lovers of Thai food the world over. Translated loosely as broth or stock (tom) and spicy/sour (yum), it has a complex, beautifully balanced blend of flavours.

Spicy sour prawn soup *(tom yum goong)*

PREPARATION TIME 20 MINUTES **COOKING TIME** 40 MINUTES **SERVES** 4

- 900g uncooked large king prawns
- 1 tablespoon peanut oil
- 1.5 litres (6 cups) water
- 2 tablespoons red curry paste
- 1 tablespoon tamarind concentrate
- 10cm stick (20g) finely chopped fresh lemon grass
- 1 teaspoon ground turmeric
- 1 fresh small red thai chilli, chopped coarsely
- 4cm piece fresh ginger (20g), grated
- 6 fresh kaffir lime leaves, shredded finely
- 1 teaspoon grated palm sugar
- 100g fresh shiitake mushrooms, halved
- 2 tablespoons fish sauce
- 2 tablespoons lime juice
- ¼ cup loosely packed fresh vietnamese mint leaves
- ¼ cup loosely packed fresh coriander leaves

1 Shell and devein prawns, leaving tails intact. Reserve heads and shells.

2 Heat oil in large saucepan; cook prawn heads and shells, stirring, about 5 minutes or until shells and heads are deep orange in colour.

3 Add 1 cup of the water and curry paste to pan; bring to a boil, stirring. Add remaining water; return to a boil. Reduce heat; simmer, uncovered, 20 minutes. Strain stock through muslin into large heatproof bowl; discard solids.

4 Return stock to same cleaned pan. Add tamarind, lemon grass, turmeric, chilli, ginger, lime leaves and sugar; bring to a boil. Boil, stirring, 2 minutes. Add mushrooms, reduce heat; simmer, stirring, 3 minutes. Add prawns; cook, stirring, until prawns are changed in colour. Remove from heat; stir in fish sauce and juice. Serve soup hot, topped with mint and coriander.

PER SERVING 9.0g total fat (1.3g saturated); 861kj (206 cal); 3.7g carbohydrate; 25.7g protein; 3.0g fibre

---

Ladle the soup into four flameproof serving bowls placed on an oven tray; top each with a slice of toasted baguette then sprinkle a tablespoon of grated gruyère or emmental cheese over the toast. Place the soup bowls, on the tray, under a preheated grill until the cheese melts and browns lightly.

French onion soup

PREPARATION TIME 30 MINUTES **COOKING TIME** 50 MINUTES **SERVES** 4

- 50g butter
- 4 large brown onions (800g), halved, sliced thinly
- ¾ cup (180ml) dry white wine
- 3 cups (750ml) water
- 1 litre (4 cups) beef stock
- 1 bay leaf
- 1 tablespoon plain flour
- 1 teaspoon fresh thyme leaves

1 Melt butter in large saucepan; cook onion, stirring occasionally, over medium heat, about 30 minutes or until caramelised.

2 Meanwhile, bring wine to a boil in medium saucepan; boil, uncovered, 1 minute. Stir in the water, stock and bay leaf; return to a boil. Remove from heat.

3 Stir flour into onion mixture; cook, stirring, until mixture bubbles and thickens. Gradually add hot stock mixture, stirring until mixture boils and thickens slightly. Reduce heat; simmer, uncovered, stirring occasionally, 20 minutes. Discard bay leaf; stir in thyme.
4 Divide soup among bowls; top with cheese croutes (see note, page 94), if desired.

PER SERVING 11.0g total fat (7.0g saturated); 903kj (216 cal); 14.6g carbohydrate; 6.3g protein; 2.7g fibre

---

Borscht

Originating in Russia, borscht is served hot in winter and cold in summer. It can be pureed or chunky, meatless or made with shredded beef and is nearly always served with sour cream.

PREPARATION TIME 1 HOUR 30 MINUTES (PLUS REFRIGERATION TIME)
COOKING TIME 5 HOURS 50 MINUTES **SERVES** 6

- 1kg beef bones (shin or shank, cut into pieces)
- 3 medium brown onions (450g), unpeeled, quartered
- 6 litres (24 cups) water
- 2 trimmed celery stalks (200g), chopped coarsely
- 2 medium carrots (240g), chopped coarsely
- 2 bay leaves
- 1 teaspoon black peppercorns
- 20g butter
- 1 large brown onion (200g), chopped finely
- 2 medium carrots (240g), chopped finely
- 3 trimmed celery stalks (300g), chopped finely
- 1 medium leek (350g), chopped finely
- 3 bacon rashers (210g), rind removed, chopped finely
- 5 medium beetroots (1.5kg), peeled, chopped finely
- 3 medium tomatoes (450g), peeled, chopped finely
- ¼ small savoy cabbage (300g), shredded finely

1 Preheat oven to hot (220°C/200°C fan-forced); roast bones and unpeeled onion on oven tray, uncovered, about 1 hour or until browned.
2 Combine bones and onion with the water, coarsely chopped celery and carrot, bay leaves and peppercorns in large saucepan or boiler; bring to a boil. Reduce heat; simmer, uncovered, 3½ hours. Strain stock through muslin-lined sieve or colander into large bowl; discard solids. Allow stock to cool, cover; refrigerate until cold.
3 Heat butter in large saucepan; cook finely chopped onion, carrot and celery, leek and bacon, stirring, until vegetables just soften. Discard fat from surface of stock. Add stock to pan with beetroot, tomato and cabbage; bring to a boil. Reduce heat; simmer, uncovered, about 1 hour.
4 Blend or process half the borscht, in batches, until smooth, then return to pan. Reheat till hot, then divide borscht among bowls. Serve with a dollop of dill cream (see page 97), if desired.

PER SERVING 28.3g total fat (16.7g saturated); 2065kj (494 cal); 35.0g carbohydrate; 18.6g protein; 15.1g fibre

Soup accompaniments

The following quick and easy ideas are the ideal way to jazz up your favourite home-made or bought soup.

PAPRIKA BUTTER
Melt 60g butter in a small frying pan; add 2 teaspoons hot paprika. Cook, stirring, 2 minutes; remove from the heat. Stir in 2 finely chopped green onions.

CHILLI PARMESAN CRISPS
Combine 1 cup finely grated parmesan and ½ finely chopped long red chilli; drop level tablespoons of mixture onto a baking-paper-lined oven tray. Bake in a hot oven about 3 minutes; stand until set.

GREMOLATA
Combine ⅓ cup finely chopped fresh flat-leaf parsley, 1 tablespoon finely grated lemon rind and 2 cloves finely chopped garlic in a small bowl. Keep covered in the fridge.

TORTILLA CRISPS
Slice corn tortillas into thin strips; shallow-fry in vegetable oil, in batches, until browned lightly. Drain on absorbent paper.

BACON TOASTS
Thinly slice a loaf of ciabatta; toast slices on one side under a preheated grill. Turn slices and spread with wholegrain mustard. Top with a mixture of coarsely chopped cooked crisp bacon and finely grated parmesan; grill until browned lightly.

CINNAMON CREAM
Lightly whip thickened cream until soft peaks form; mix in a little ground cinnamon to taste. Dollop on top of soup.

GRUYERE TOASTS

Cut a french bread stick into thick slices; toast slices on one side under a preheated grill. Turn slices and sprinkle with finely grated gruyère; grill until the cheese melts.

SPICED YOGURT

Dry-fry 1 teaspoon ground coriander, 1 teaspoon ground cumin and ½ teaspoon hot paprika until fragrant. Combine spices in a small bowl with 1 cup yogurt and ¼ cup finely chopped fresh mint.

PISTOU

Blend or process 2 cups fresh basil leaves, 1 quartered clove garlic, ¼ cup finely grated parmesan and ¼ cup olive oil until smooth. Keep covered in the fridge.

DILL CREAM

Combine ½ cup sour cream with 1 tablespoon finely chopped fresh dill in a small bowl. Dollop on top of soup; serve sprinkled with chopped dill.

ANCHOVY TOASTS

Combine 6 finely chopped anchovy fillets, 2 tablespoons finely chopped fresh garlic chives and 50g softened butter in a bowl. Toast bread slices on one side under a preheated grill. Spread untoasted side with anchovy butter; grill until browned lightly.

CUCUMBER AND ONION SALSA

Combine ¼ cup sour cream, 1 finely chopped, seeded Lebanese cucumber, 1 finely chopped small red onion and 1 finely chopped small red thai chilli in a small bowl.

1

2

3

4

Vichyssoise

PREPARATION TIME 20 MINUTES (PLUS REFRIGERATION TIME) **COOKING TIME** 50 MINUTES **SERVES** 6

Cold numbs taste buds so cold soups need to be highly flavoured. Pay close attention to seasoning and use a really good stock, preferably home-made, for a well-rounded flavour. Use only the white part of the leeks in this recipe to preserve the creamy whiteness of the soup.

50g butter

2 medium leeks (700g), trimmed, white part sliced thinly

750g coliban potatoes, chopped coarsely

2 cups (500ml) chicken stock

2 cups (500ml) water

300ml cream

2 tablespoons coarsely chopped fresh chives

1 Melt butter in large saucepan; cook leek, covered, about 20 minutes or until softened.
2 Add potato, stock and the water; bring to a boil. Reduce heat; simmer, covered, until potato is tender. Cool 10 minutes.
3 Blend or process soup, in batches, until smooth. Place soup in large bowl; stir in cream. Cover; refrigerate 3 hours or overnight. Divide among serving bowls; sprinkle with chives.

PER SERVING 29.2g total fat (19g saturated); 1584kj (379 cal); 21.3g carbohydrate; 6.4g protein; 4.6g fibre

---

Cuban black bean soup

PREPARATION TIME 30 MINUTES (PLUS STANDING TIME) **COOKING TIME** 2 HOURS 15 MINUTES **SERVES** 8

For a smoother, thicker soup mash half the black beans then return them to the soup.

2½ cups (500g) dried black beans

1kg ham bone

¼ cup (60ml) olive oil

2 medium brown onions (300g), chopped finely

1 medium red capsicum (200g), chopped finely

4 cloves garlic, crushed

1 tablespoon ground cumin

1 teaspoon dried chilli flakes

400g can chopped tomatoes

2.5 litres (10 cups) water

1 tablespoon dried oregano

2 teaspoons cracked black pepper

¼ cup (60ml) lime juice

2 medium tomatoes (300g), chopped finely

¼ cup coarsely chopped fresh coriander

1 Place beans in medium bowl, cover with water; stand overnight, drain. Rinse well; drain.
2 Preheat oven to hot (220°C/200°C fan-forced); place ham bone on oven tray; roast, uncovered, 30 minutes.
3 Meanwhile, heat oil in large saucepan; cook onion, capsicum and garlic until soft. Add cumin and chilli; cook, stirring, 1 minute. Add beans and ham bone with undrained tomatoes, the water, oregano and pepper; bring to a boil. Simmer, uncovered, 1½ hours.
4 Remove bone from soup; shred ham. Add to soup, stirring until heated through. Stir juice, tomato and coriander into soup just before serving.

PER SERVING 7.5g total fat (1.1g saturated); 502kj (120 cal); 6.8g carbohydrate; 4.6g protein; 3.3g fibre

Black beans, also known as turtle beans, are popular in Caribbean and Latin American dishes. They are available from health-food shops and gourmet food outlets. Don't use Chinese black beans, which are fermented soybeans.

1 VICHYSSOISE **2** CUBAN BLACK BEAN SOUP **3** HARIRA [P100]
4 ROASTED PARSNIP AND GARLIC SOUP [P101]

In North Africa many Muslims fasting for Ramadan break the day's fast by starting their meal with this hearty soup. While recipes vary from family to family, they will always include chickpeas and lamb.

Harira

PREPARATION TIME 25 MINUTES (PLUS STANDING TIME) **COOKING TIME** 2 HOURS 15 MINUTES **SERVES** 8

1 cup (200g) dried chickpeas
20g butter
2 medium brown onions (300g), chopped finely
2 trimmed celery stalks (200g), chopped finely
2 cloves garlic, crushed
4cm piece fresh ginger (20g), grated
1 teaspoon ground cinnamon
½ teaspoon cracked black pepper
pinch saffron threads
500g diced lamb
3 large tomatoes (660g), seeded, chopped coarsely
2 litres (8 cups) hot water
½ cup (100g) brown lentils
2 tablespoons plain flour
½ cup (100g) white long-grain rice
½ cup firmly packed fresh coriander leaves
2 tablespoons lemon juice

1 Place chickpeas in medium bowl, cover with water; stand overnight, drain. Rinse under cold water; drain.
2 Heat butter in large saucepan; cook onion, celery and garlic, stirring, until onion softens. Add ginger, cinnamon, pepper and saffron; cook, stirring, about 2 minutes or until fragrant. Add lamb; cook, stirring, about 5 minutes or until lamb is browned.
3 Add chickpeas and tomato; cook, stirring, about 5 minutes or until tomato softens.
4 Stir in the water; bring to a boil. Reduce heat; simmer, covered, 45 minutes. Add lentils; simmer, covered, 1 hour.
5 Blend flour with ½ cup of the slightly cooled cooking liquid in small bowl; stir into lamb mixture with rice. Cook, stirring, until mixture boils and thickens.
6 Stir coriander and juice into harira just before serving. Top with extra coriander leaves, if desired.

PER SERVING 9.5g total fat (4.1g saturated); 1279kj (306 cal); 29.2g carbohydrate; 22.7g protein; 6.7g fibre

Blue boilers (or field peas) are a special variety of pea grown specifically for being dried and used whole; when dried and halved, they're called split peas.

Pea and ham soup

PREPARATION TIME 15 MINUTES **COOKING TIME** 2 HOURS 10 MINUTES **SERVES** 6

2 cups (375g) dried peas (blue boilers)
1 medium brown onion (150g), chopped coarsely
2 trimmed celery stalks (200g), chopped coarsely
2 bay leaves
1.5kg ham bone
2.5 litres (10 cups) water
1 teaspoon cracked black pepper

1 Combine ingredients in large saucepan; bring to a boil. Reduce heat; simmer, covered, about 2 hours or until peas are tender.
2 Remove ham bone; when cool enough to handle, remove ham from bone, shred finely. Discard bone and fat; discard bay leaves.

3 Blend or process half of the pea mixture, in batches, until pureed. Return to pan with remaining unprocessed pea mixture and ham. Reheat soup, stirring, until hot.

PER SERVING 1.8g total fat (0.3g saturated); 928kj (222 cal); 31.1g carbohydrate; 17.5g protein; 7.1g fibre

---

Roasted parsnip and garlic soup

PREPARATION TIME 25 MINUTES **COOKING TIME** 1 HOUR 20 MINUTES **SERVES** 4

When peeling the parsnips, make sure you remove all of the bitter outer layer.

1 garlic bulb

2 tablespoons olive oil

1kg parsnips, chopped coarsely

1 tablespoon olive oil, extra

1 small brown onion (80g), chopped finely

1 medium potato (200g), chopped coarsely

1 litre (4 cups) chicken stock

300ml cream

¾ cup (180ml) milk

2 tablespoons finely chopped fresh garlic chives

1 Preheat oven to moderately hot (200°C/180°C fan-forced).
2 Place whole unpeeled garlic bulb in large shallow baking dish; roast, uncovered, about 10 minutes. Add combined oil and parsnip; roast, uncovered, 30 minutes or until garlic and parsnip are tender. When garlic is cool enough to handle, halve garlic bulb crossways; use fingers to squeeze garlic puree into small bowl. Reserve.
3 Heat extra oil in large saucepan; cook onion, stirring, until soft. Add parsnip with potato and stock; bring to a boil. Reduce heat; simmer, uncovered, stirring occasionally, about 20 minutes or until potato is softened.
4 Blend or process soup with reserved garlic puree, in batches, until smooth. Reheat soup in same pan, stir in cream and milk; bring to a boil. Ladle soup into serving bowls; sprinkle with chives. Serve soup with anchovy toasts (see page 97), if desired.

If you're not a fan of anchovies you could make parsnip chips as an accompaniment to this soup. Simply slice a peeled parsnip very thinly and deep-fry in vegetable oil.

PER SERVING 49.6g total fat (25.1g saturated); 2684kj (642 cal); 35.1g carbohydrate; 11.5g protein; 7.9g fibre

If you prefer, you can roast the garlic before using it for the aïoli and rouille. Toss the garlic cloves, with skins on, in a little olive oil and roast in a hot oven for about 20 minutes. Remove the skins to reveal a soft butter-like flesh with a delicious mellow flavour. If you roast a whole bulb the garlic paste will keep for a week in the fridge; 3 months in the freezer.

Bouillabaisse with aïoli and rouille

PREPARATION TIME 1 HOUR 15 MINUTES **COOKING TIME** 40 MINUTES **SERVES** 6

700g uncooked large king prawns

2 uncooked medium blue swimmer crabs (650g)

500g small black mussels

10 small tomatoes (900g)

1 tablespoon olive oil

1 clove garlic, crushed

1 large brown onion (200g), chopped coarsely

1 medium leek (350g), chopped coarsely

1 untrimmed baby fennel bulb (130g), chopped coarsely

1 fresh small red thai chilli, chopped coarsely

1 bay leaf

pinch saffron threads

10cm strip orange rind

1.5 litres (6 cups) water

1 cup (250ml) dry white wine

750g firm white fish fillets, chopped coarsely

½ cup coarsely chopped fresh flat-leaf parsley

1 long french bread stick

AIOLI

3 cloves garlic, quartered

2 egg yolks

2 tablespoons lemon juice

½ teaspoon dijon mustard

⅔ cup (160ml) olive oil

ROUILLE

1 medium red capsicum (200g)

1 fresh small red thai chilli, seeded, chopped finely

1 clove garlic, quartered

1 cup (70g) stale breadcrumbs

1 tablespoon lemon juice

¼ cup (60ml) olive oil

1 Shell and devein prawns, leaving tails intact. Reserve heads and shells; place prawn meat in medium bowl. Slide knife under top of crab shell at back, lever off; reserve with prawn shells. Discard gills; rinse crabs under cold water. Cut crab bodies into quarters; place in bowl with prawn meat. Scrub mussels; remove beards.

2 Chop four of the tomatoes coarsely; reserve with seafood shells.

3 Core then cut shallow cross in base of remaining tomatoes, place in large heatproof bowl; cover with boiling water. Stand 2 minutes; drain then peel, from cross end towards top. Quarter tomatoes; scoop out seeds, reserve with seafood shells. Chop tomato flesh finely; reserve.

4 Heat oil in large saucepan; cook reserved seafood shell mixture with the coarsely chopped tomato, garlic, onion, leek, fennel, chilli, bay leaf, saffron and rind, stirring, about 10 minutes or until shells change in colour and vegetables soften. Add the water and wine, cover; bring to a boil. Reduce heat; simmer, covered, 10 minutes. Remove crab shells.

5 Blend or process seafood mixture (including prawn shells), in batches, until smooth; using wooden spoon, push each batch through large sieve into large saucepan. Discard solids in sieve. Reserve ¼ cup strained seafood mixture for rouille (see below).

6 Make aïoli and rouille.

7 Add finely chopped tomatoes to strained seafood mixture; bring to a boil. Add fish and mussels, return to a boil; cook, covered, 5 minutes. Add reserved prawn meat and crab pieces; cook, covered, 5 minutes. Stir parsley into bouillabaisse; serve with sliced toasted bread, aïoli and rouille.

AIOLI Blend or process garlic, yolks, juice and mustard until smooth. With motor operating, gradually add oil in thin, steady stream; process until aïoli thickens.

ROUILLE Quarter capsicum; discard seeds and membrane. Roast under preheated grill or in very hot oven, skin-side up, until skin blackens. Cover capsicum pieces in plastic or paper for 5 minutes; peel away skin, then chop coarsely. Blend or process capsicum with chilli, garlic, breadcrumbs, juice and reserved ¼ cup strained seafood mixture liquid until smooth. With motor operating, gradually add oil in thin, steady stream; process until rouille thickens.

PER SERVING 44.0g total fat (7g saturated); 3361kj (804 cal); 38.8g carbohydrate; 53.2g protein; 6.5g fibre

---

Smoked cod chowder

PREPARATION TIME 25 MINUTES **COOKING TIME** 45 MINUTES **SERVES** 4

You can use smoked trout which is already cooked instead of the cod; add it to the recipe where it says "flake fish".

- 600g smoked cod fillets
- 1 litre (4 cups) milk
- 2 bay leaves
- 8 black peppercorns
- 2 bacon rashers (140g), rind removed, chopped finely
- 40g butter
- 1 medium leek (350g), sliced thinly
- 1 tablespoon plain flour
- 1 cup (250ml) dry white wine
- 4 medium potatoes (800g), diced into 2cm pieces
- 300ml cream
- 2 tablespoons coarsely chopped fresh flat-leaf parsley

For a lower-fat version, use evaporated milk instead of cream.

1 Place fish in large heavy-based frying pan. Pour half the milk over fish; heat almost to a boil. Drain fish; discard milk. Return fish to pan with remaining milk, bay leaves and peppercorns; heat almost to a boil. Drain over large bowl; reserve milk and fish, discard bay leaves and peppercorns.
2 Cook bacon in same cleaned heated pan, stirring, until browned and crisp; drain on absorbent paper.
3 Melt butter in same cleaned pan; cook leek, stirring, until softened. Add flour; cook, stirring, until mixture thickens and bubbles. Gradually add wine; stir until mixture boils and thickens. Add potato and reserved milk, reduce heat; simmer, uncovered, stirring occasionally, about 20 minutes or until potato is tender.
4 Meanwhile, discard skin and bones from fish. Flake fish into large pieces.
5 Add fish to chowder with cream; cook, stirring gently, until heated through. Remove from heat; stir in parsley. Serve bowls of chowder sprinkled with bacon and accompanied by warm sourdough rolls, if desired.

PER SERVING 57.0g total fat (35.4g saturated); 3829kj (916 cal); 39.8g carbohydrate; 50.3g protein; 4.3g fibre

Some of the best dishes to be found in South-East Asia are at "hawker stalls", also known as street markets. In Malaysia the spicy noodle soup known as laksa is the most popular hawker dish and can now be found in restaurants around the world.

Prawn laksa

PREPARATION TIME 45 MINUTES **COOKING TIME** 1 HOUR 20 MINUTES **SERVES** 6

2kg uncooked medium king prawns

2 bunches fresh coriander (approximately 100g)

4 trimmed celery stalks (400g), chopped coarsely

3 litres (12 cups) water

2 medium carrots (240g), chopped coarsely

2 large brown onions (400g), chopped coarsely

2 sticks lemon grass, chopped coarsely

2 fresh small red thai chillies, chopped coarsely

1 teaspoon ground turmeric

¼ cup coarsely chopped fresh vietnamese mint

2 cloves garlic, crushed

4cm piece fresh ginger (20g), grated

4cm piece fresh galangal (20g), grated

1 tablespoon fresh shrimp paste

1 tablespoon ground coriander

2 tablespoons peanut oil

1⅔ cups (410ml) coconut milk

100g fresh singapore egg noodles

200g fried tofu

1¼ cups (100g) bean sprouts

4 green onions, sliced thinly

1 Shell and devein prawns; reserve heads and shells. Cut roots from coriander; wash leaves and roots well, reserve both separately.

2 Combine prawns heads and shells, coriander roots, celery, carrot, the water and half the brown onion in large saucepan; bring to a boil. Reduce heat; simmer, uncovered, about 30 minutes. Strain through muslin-lined strainer into large bowl; reserve broth, discard solids.

3 Blend or process remaining brown onion with a loosely packed ¼ cup of the coriander leaves, lemon grass, chilli, turmeric, mint, garlic, ginger, galangal, shrimp paste, ground coriander and half of the oil until mixture forms a coarse paste.

4 Heat remaining oil in large saucepan; cook laksa paste, stirring, about 2 minutes or until fragrant. Stir in reserved broth and coconut milk; bring to a boil. Reduce heat; simmer, uncovered, 20 minutes. Stir in prawns; cook, stirring, about 10 minutes or until prawns are changed in colour.

5 Meanwhile, place noodles in large heatproof bowl, cover with boiling water; stand 3 minutes, drain. Cut tofu into 2cm cubes.

6 Just before serving, stir noodles, tofu, sprouts, green onion and 2 tablespoons finely chopped coriander leaves into laksa. Serve laksa topped with extra coriander leaves, sprouts and green onion, if desired.

PER SERVING 24.4g total fat (14.1g saturated); 2006kj (480 cal); 19.8g carbohydrate; 42.7g protein; 6.4g fibre

PRAWN LAKSA

One of the earliest green vegetables recorded, watercress can be traced back to the Romans.

Creamy watercress soup

PREPARATION TIME 30 MINUTES **COOKING TIME** 30 MINUTES **SERVES** 4

1 tablespoon olive oil

1 small brown onion (80g), chopped finely

1 small leek (200g), sliced thinly

3 medium potatoes (600g), chopped coarsely

1 litre (4 cups) chicken stock

350g watercress, trimmed

⅓ cup (80g) sour cream

Watercress has long been known as one of the "superfoods" of the world, containing more iron than spinach, more calcium than milk and three times as much vitamin E as lettuce.

1 Heat oil in large saucepan; cook onion and leek, stirring over low heat, until vegetables soften. Add potato and stock; bring to a boil. Reduce heat; simmer, covered, 20 minutes or until potato is almost tender.

2 Reserve four watercress sprigs; stir remaining watercress into pan. Simmer soup, uncovered, about 5 minutes or until potato is tender.

3 Blend or process soup, in batches, until smooth. Reheat soup in same pan then divide among serving bowls; top each with 1 tablespoon of the sour cream then a reserved watercress sprig.

PER SERVING 14.1g total fat (6.3g saturated); 1095kj (262 cal); 21.2g carbohydrate; 9.6g protein; 6.4g fibre

---

Merguez, traditionally made with lamb, garlic and chilli, can be replaced in this recipe with chorizo. You can reduce the cooking time of this recipe dramatically by adding rinsed and drained canned white beans along with the other ingredients in step 2; once the soup comes to a boil, simmer for about 10 minutes.

White bean, leek and garlic sausage soup

PREPARATION TIME 30 MINUTES (PLUS STANDING TIME) **COOKING TIME** 1 HOUR 15 MINUTES **SERVES** 6

1 cup (200g) dried small white beans

40g butter

2 bacon rashers (140g), rind removed, chopped finely

2 cloves garlic, crushed

1 medium leek (350g), sliced thinly

2 trimmed celery stalks (200g), chopped finely

2 medium carrots (240g), chopped finely

1.5 litres (6 cups) chicken stock

1 bay leaf

4 merguez sausages (320g)

1 Place beans in medium bowl, cover with water; soak overnight, drain. Rinse under cold water; drain.

2 Melt butter in large saucepan; cook bacon, garlic, leek, celery and carrot, stirring, until vegetables soften. Stir in stock, bay leaf and beans; bring to a boil. Reduce heat; simmer soup, covered, about 1 hour or until beans are tender.

3 Heat oiled medium frying pan; cook sausages until browned. Drain, chop coarsely.

4 Just before serving, ladle soup into serving bowls; top with sausage. Serve with a dollop of pistou (see page 97), if desired.

PER SERVING 33.6g total fat (13.6g saturated); 1697kj (406 cal); 7.9g carbohydrate; 17.0g protein; 5.2g fibre

Chicken and corn soup

PREPARATION TIME 15 MINUTES **COOKING TIME** 20 MINUTES **SERVES** 6

Ask most chefs which cut of chicken is the most succulent and flavoursome, chances are they will say chicken thighs. Unfortunately, thighs are one of the most under-rated and under-utilised parts of the chicken. To achieve the best flavour in this soup choose thighs over breasts.

1.5 litres (6 cups) chicken stock
310g can creamed corn
⅔ cup (130g) canned corn kernels, drained
½ teaspoon grated fresh ginger
1 teaspoon sesame oil
8 green onions, sliced thinly
¼ cup (35g) cornflour
¼ cup (60ml) water
2 egg whites
2 tablespoons water, extra
1 cup (170g) shredded cooked chicken
2 slices lean ham (80g), sliced thinly

1 Combine stock, creamed corn, corn kernels, ginger, oil and onion in large saucepan; bring to a boil.
2 Blend cornflour and the water in small jug; add to stock mixture. Cook, stirring, until mixture boils and thickens; reduce heat.
3 Combine egg whites and the extra water in small jug; add to soup in thin stream, stirring. Stir in chicken and ham; cook, uncovered, until heated through.

PER SERVING 6.0g total fat (1.7g saturated); 844kj (202 cal); 20.4g carbohydrate; 15.5g protein; 2.7g fibre

---

Swiss brown mushroom and barley soup

PREPARATION TIME 10 MINUTES **COOKING TIME** 55 MINUTES **SERVES** 4

Swiss brown mushrooms have a stronger, fuller flavour than white or field mushrooms. When larger, they are called portobello mushrooms.

300g swiss brown mushrooms, quartered
1 clove garlic, crushed
2 teaspoons soy sauce
2 teaspoons water
1 small brown onion (80g), chopped finely
1 litre (4 cups) chicken stock
1 litre (4 cups) water, extra
½ cup (100g) pearl barley
1 trimmed celery stalk (100g), chopped coarsely
2 small carrots (140g), chopped coarsely

1 Cook mushrooms, garlic, soy sauce and the water in heated large frying pan until mushrooms soften.
2 Cook onion in heated lightly oiled large saucepan, stirring, until softened. Add stock and the extra water; bring to a boil. Add barley, reduce heat; simmer, covered, 30 minutes.
3 Add mushroom mixture to saucepan with remaining ingredients; cook, uncovered, about 20 minutes or until barley and vegetables are tender.

PER SERVING 1.9g total fat (0.6g saturated); 627kj (150 cal); 21.5g carbohydrate; 8.5g protein; 6.4g fibre

STARTERS

Starters

You can use the recipes in this chapter as first courses for dinner parties, or as perfect ideas for the kind of meal you'd eat in a stylish cafe – light, interesting, not too filling, with fruit and cheese or a delicious little dessert to finish. Or, if you're planning a meal around a serious pudding, you might serve a soup first, then one of these dishes as a main course, so that the diners will still have appetites for the star turn.

CHOOSING A FIRST COURSE

If the main course will have a rich sauce, then a light, fresh first course is the right choice. If a plain roast or grill is to follow, a rich and luscious first course will be perfect. Also think about how your kitchen will cope, and ensure that the first course won't have to compete with one of the other courses for the oven or the grill, or for bench or fridge space.

OTHER IDEAS One of the world's best-loved ways to open a meal is with an array of mixed appetisers, either arranged on individual plates or presented on large platters and in bowls for diners to help themselves.This is an especially good idea if you haven't a lot of time, because you can mix home-made and good-quality bought items. See page 124 for a selection of the traditional mezze that are served throughout the Middle East and in Greece. The marvellous antipasto of Italy is another version, mixing bought items such as salami, sardines, olives and artichoke hearts with fresh items such as tomato wedges, radishes and capsicum strips, plus something warm and home-made. The French serve mixed hors d'oeuvre, which might include smoked or canned fish, sliced cold meats, cornichons (baby gherkins) and other bought delicacies such as pâté or quiche, plus simple home-made items such as asparagus with lemon and melted butter.

You don't have to stick to a theme of a particular country, simply mix things that you would like to eat together. As a general rule, serve at least one fresh salad vegetable and one warm home-made item plus a few bought items. Below is a list of possibilities.

FROM THE SUPERMARKET AND DELICATESSEN

- Frozen dim sims, spring rolls, mixed yum cha, pastizzi and other filled savoury pastries, and large or individual quiches
- Hummus, baba ganoush, tzatziki, smoked salmon and other dips
- Quality mayonnaise, aïoli and other dressings
- Chicken liver, smoked salmon and other pâtés
- Salami, smoked pork and beef, ham and other cold meats

- Cold-smoked salmon and ocean trout (thin slices, in packs or loose)
- Hot-smoked salmon and ocean trout (thick cuts)
- Canned or bottled anchovies, sardines, herring, tuna packed in olive oil
- Marinated and glazed chicken wings and kebabs
- Char-grilled capsicum and eggplant
- Semi-dried tomatoes
- Marinated mushrooms and artichoke hearts
- Plain and baked ricotta; plain and marinated fetta
- Soft cheeses: brie, camembert, goat cheese, blue cheese
- Eggs (hard-boil, halve lengthways, top with mayonnaise and chives)
- Olives, plain and marinated
- Pickled cucumbers, gherkins, cornichons
- Pickled onions
- Tabbouli and other prepared salads

FROM THE GREENGROCER

- Salad vegetables: baby leaves, cherry or other small tomatoes, cucumber, radish, celery, carrot, capsicum, watercress
- Vegetables to cook: asparagus, whole baby beans, baby potatoes and carrots (serve warm with melted butter and lemon for the asparagus and beans, chopped mint for the potatoes and carrots)

FROM THE FISHMONGER

- Prawns
- Oysters
- Whole smoked fresh-water trout (remove skin, lift fillets off bones, feel for pin-bones and pull out with tweezers)

FROM THE BUTCHER

- Lamb cutlets trimmed of all fat and skin and with bones cleaned (char-grill and top with a dob of spicy tomato salsa)

FROM YOUR LOCAL INDIAN, THAI OR CHINESE RESTAURANT

- Samosas, pakoras, Thai fish cakes, curry puffs, dim sims

FROM YOUR OWN FRIDGE OR FREEZER

- A planned left-over batch of your favourite soup, stowed away the last time you made it, to serve piping hot in demitasse cups holding just a few delicious mouthfuls.

PRESENTATION

The first course should usher in the meal with a flourish, so it is especially important to make it look tempting and interesting. Have a look at the photographs in this chapter for suggestions on how to present the food. For plates of mixed appetisers, look for colours and shapes that will look good next to each other. Arrange the different foods close beside each other, not spaced out round the edge of the plate. As a general rule, keep the garnish to just one telling effect: a single bouquet of parsley or watercress is better than small bits dotted about, or you might lay a stalk or two of dill, flat-leaf parsley or another herb, casually crossed, beside the food.

Sang choy bow

PREPARATION TIME 15 MINUTES **COOKING TIME** 15 MINUTES **SERVES** 4

These lettuce parcels are delicious but notorious for dripping. Place a finger bowl of warm water and lemon slices in the centre of the table, for guests to dip their fingertips in, and don't forget plenty of napkins.

1 tablespoon peanut oil
750g pork mince
2 cloves garlic, crushed
225g can water chestnuts, drained, chopped finely
1 teaspoon sambal oelek
1 tablespoon lime juice
1 medium red capsicum (200g), chopped finely
1 trimmed celery stalk (100g), chopped finely
2 tablespoons light soy sauce
2 tablespoons rice vinegar
100g packet fried noodles
8 large iceberg lettuce leaves
2 green onions, sliced thinly

1 Heat oil in wok; stir-fry pork and garlic about 5 minutes or until pork changes colour.
2 Add water chestnuts, sambal, juice, capsicum, celery, sauce and vinegar; stir-fry until vegetables are just tender. Remove from heat; stir in noodles.
3 Divide pork mixture among lettuce leaves; sprinkle each with onion.

PER SERVING 22.3g total fat (6.8g saturated); 1797kj (430 cal); 11.4g carbohydrate; 43g protein; 4.2g fibre

---

Risotto primavera on grilled flat mushrooms

PREPARATION TIME 20 MINUTES **COOKING TIME** 45 MINUTES **SERVES** 4

Primavera is Italian for spring. When used in a recipe it represents the freshest of seasonal vegetables.

1 litre (4 cups) chicken stock
1 cup (250ml) dry white wine
20g butter
1 tablespoon olive oil
1 medium brown onion (150g), chopped finely
1 clove garlic, crushed
1¼ cups (250g) arborio rice
100g snow peas, trimmed, halved
100g sugar snap peas, trimmed
250g asparagus, trimmed, sliced thickly
¼ cup finely chopped fresh chives
¼ cup (60ml) cream
¼ cup (20g) finely grated parmesan
4 flat mushrooms (320g)

1 Combine stock and wine in medium saucepan; bring to a boil, then simmer, covered.
2 Heat butter and oil in large saucepan; cook onion and garlic, stirring, until onion softens. Add rice; stir to coat. Stir in 1 cup hot stock; cook, stirring, over low heat until liquid is absorbed. Continue adding stock, in 1-cup batches, stirring, until liquid is absorbed after each addition. Total cooking time should be about 35 minutes or until rice is tender.
3 Stir in peas, asparagus, chives, cream and cheese; cook, uncovered, until just tender.
4 Meanwhile, cook mushrooms on heated oiled grill plate (or grill or barbecue) until browned and tender. Serve risotto on mushrooms.

There is no need to use a knife to remove the woody ends from the asparagus spears; simply snap them with your fingers. The asparagus will break at the point between the tender tips and the tougher ends.

PER SERVING 18.5g total fat (9.2g saturated); 2132kj (510 cal); 58.1g carbohydrate; 15.3g protein; 4.9g fibre

SANG CHOY BOW

Left-over red onion jam is a great addition to a beef sandwich, served with a cheeseboard or spread over a sheet of puff pastry, topped with soft goat or blue cheese and sprinkled with 1 tablespoon fresh thyme leaves. Bake in a hot oven for 20 minutes and cut into squares to serve.

Duck liver parfait with red onion jam

PREPARATION TIME 25 MINUTES **COOKING TIME** 40 MINUTES (PLUS REFRIGERATION TIME) **SERVES** 8

30g butter
6 shallots (150g), chopped finely
2 cloves garlic, crushed
½ teaspoon ground allspice
1 tablespoon finely chopped fresh thyme
1 teaspoon cracked black pepper
⅔ cup (160ml) brandy
400g duck livers, trimmed
¾ cup (180ml) cream
4 eggs
150g butter, melted, cooled
2 bay leaves, halved
2 sprigs thyme, halved
100g butter, extra

RED ONION JAM
50g butter
4 medium red onions (680g), sliced thinly
¼ cup (55g) white sugar
¾ cup (180ml) dry red wine
¼ cup (60ml) port
¼ cup (60ml) red wine vinegar

1 Preheat oven to slow (150°C/130°C fan-forced). Lightly oil 1.5-litre (6-cup) ovenproof terrine dish.
2 Melt butter in small frying pan; cook shallot and garlic, stirring, until shallot softens. Add allspice, thyme, pepper and brandy; bring to a boil. Reduce heat; simmer, uncovered, about 2 minutes or until liquid is reduced to about 1 tablespoon.
3 Blend or process shallot mixture with livers, cream, eggs and melted butter until mixture is smooth. Push parfait mixture through fine sieve into medium bowl; repeat process through same cleaned sieve.
4 Pour parfait mixture into terrine dish; place dish in baking dish. Pour enough boiling water into baking dish to come halfway up sides of terrine; cover terrine with foil. Cook, covered, about 40 minutes or until liver parfait is just set. Remove terrine from baking dish; cool parfait 10 minutes.
5 Meanwhile, make red onion jam.
6 Decorate parfait with bay leaves and thyme. Melt extra butter in small pan; cool 2 minutes then carefully pour butter fat over parfait, leaving milk solids in pan. Cover parfait in terrine; refrigerate 3 hours or overnight.
7 Turn parfait onto board. Using hot, wet knife, cut parfait into eight slices; serve with red onion jam and, if desired, toasted brioche.

RED ONION JAM Melt butter in large frying pan; cook onion and sugar, stirring occasionally, over medium heat, 20 minutes or until onion starts to caramelise. Add wine, port and vinegar; bring to a boil. Simmer, uncovered, 30 minutes or until jam thickens.

PER SERVING 50.1g total fat (30.7g saturated); 2650kj (634 cal); 15.3g carbohydrate; 16.0g protein; 1.4g fibre

DUCK LIVER PARFAIT WITH RED ONION JAM

Smoked salmon and prawns are among the most popular of all starters. This recipe also makes a brilliant main course to serve four.

Smoked salmon with avocado salsa and prawns

PREPARATION TIME 35 MINUTES **MAKES** 8

24 small slices smoked salmon (400g)

16 cooked medium king prawns (720g)

1 tablespoon salmon roe

8 fresh dill sprigs

AVOCADO SALSA

2 medium egg tomatoes (150g), seeded, chopped finely

2 small avocados (400g), chopped finely

½ small red onion (50g), chopped finely

1 tablespoon finely chopped fresh chives

2 teaspoons finely chopped fresh dill

1 teaspoon finely grated lemon rind

2 tablespoons lemon juice

LEMON CHIVE DRESSING

¼ cup (60ml) olive oil

2 tablespoons lemon juice

1 tablespoon finely chopped fresh chives

1 Make avocado salsa.

2 Line eight holes of a 12-hole (⅓-cup/80ml) muffin pan with plastic wrap, bringing the plastic 3cm above the edge of the holes. Place one salmon slice in base of each hole and fold over excess. Top each slice with 2 tablespoons of the salsa; lay another slice of salmon in each hole. Top with another 2 tablespoons of the salsa; lay another slice of salmon in each hole. Fold over plastic to seal; refrigerate until required.

3 Shell and devein prawns, leaving tails intact.

4 Make lemon chive dressing.

5 Turn out and unwrap salmon parcels. Divide parcels among serving plates; top with prawns, roe and dill, drizzle with dressing.

AVOCADO SALSA Combine ingredients in small bowl.

LIME CHIVE DRESSING Place ingredients in screw-top jar; shake well.

PER PARCEL 17.5g total fat (3.2g saturated); 1049kj (251 cal); 0.9g carbohydrate; 22.1g protein; 0.7g fibre

Minced lamb in vine leaves

PREPARATION TIME 15 MINUTES **COOKING TIME** 30 MINUTES **SERVES** 8

Grapevine leaves are preserved in brine and people often complain that they are too salty. To reduce the saltiness and improve the flavour of the leaves, blanch them by submerging them in boiling water then quickly placing them in cold water.

16 grapevine leaves in brine, rinsed, drained

250g packet frozen spinach, thawed, drained

500g lamb mince

1 small brown onion (80g), chopped finely

2 cloves garlic, crushed

2 tablespoons finely chopped fresh flat-leaf parsley

2 teaspoons lemon juice

2 tablespoons olive oil

1 cup (120g) seeded black olives, chopped finely

1 Preheat oven to moderately hot (200°C/180°C fan-forced). Lightly oil eight ½-cup (125ml) ovenproof dishes.

2 Line each dish with vine leaves, shiny-side down; allow edges to overhang dishes. Using hand, squeeze excess liquid from spinach. Combine spinach in large bowl with mince, onion, garlic, parsley, juice and oil in large bowl.

3 Divide olives among dishes; top with mince mixture, pressing firmly. Fold overhanging leaves over mince mixture; cover dishes with foil. Place dishes in large baking dish; pour enough boiling water to come halfway up sides of ovenproof dishes. Bake, uncovered, about 30 minutes or until cooked through. Remove dishes from water; cool 10 minutes.

4 Just before serving, drain dishes; turn onto serving plates.

☐ **PER SERVING** 10.3g total fat (3.2g saturated); 690kj (165 cal); 4.1g carbohydrate; 13.8g protein; 0.9g fibre

---

Stir-fried garlic prawns

PREPARATION TIME 15 MINUTES **COOKING TIME** 5 MINUTES **SERVES** 4

If you're planning a barbecue, you can marinate the prawns in the remaining ingredients overnight, then thread onto skewers to grill.

1 kg uncooked large king prawns

¼ cup (60ml) olive oil

6 cloves garlic, crushed

1 fresh small red thai chilli, chopped finely

2 tablespoons finely chopped fresh flat-leaf parsley

1 Shell and devein prawns, leaving tails intact.

2 Heat oil in wok; stir-fry garlic and chilli until fragrant. Add prawns; stir-fry until just changed in colour.

3 Serve prawns sprinkled with parsley.

☐ **PER SERVING** 14.5g total fat (2.1g saturated); 995kj (238 cal); 0.5g carbohydrate; 26.0g protein; 0.9g fibre

Fast starters

These fantastic fast starters also work well as a substantial snack or an elegant lunch.

PROSCIUTTO WITH WILD ROCKET
Arrange thin slices of prosciutto on serving plates; toss together wild rocket leaves, parmesan flakes, olive oil and lemon juice in a small bowl. Top prosciutto with rocket salad.

ASPARAGUS AND TOMATO SALAD
Combine steamed asparagus, halved teardrop tomatoes, baby spinach leaves, sliced avocado and torn basil leaves. Mix together 2 tablespoon olive oil, 1 tablespoon lemon juice, 2 teaspoons basil pesto and 1 clove crushed garlic. Drizzle over the salad.

GRILLED FETTA
Place 200g piece fetta on a baking-paper-lined oven tray; sprinkle with 2 tablespoons olive oil, 1 teaspoon dried chilli flakes and 1 tablespoon chopped fresh oregano. Cook under a preheated grill until browned lightly.

OYSTERS WITH MIRIN
Boil 2 tablespoons mirin, 1 tablespoon each light soy sauce and Chinese cooking wine and ½ teaspoon wasabi. Drizzle over oysters; top with chopped green onion and cucumber.

LEMON RICOTTA ZUCCHINI FLOWERS
Combine 200g ricotta with ¼ cup grated parmesan, ½ cup roasted pine nuts, 2 teaspoons grated lemon rind, 2 tablespoons lemon juice and ¼ cup chopped fresh chives. Discard the stamens; fill the flowers with the ricotta. Cook on a grill plate until browned.

PRAWNS WITH MANGO SALSA
Combine 1 chopped mango with 1 thinly sliced red onion, ½ cup fresh coriander leaves, 1 finely chopped long red chilli, 2 tablespoons lime juice and 2 tablespoons olive oil. Serve with grilled unshelled large prawns.

MOROCCAN LAMB CUTLETS

Combine 12 french-trimmed lamb cutlets with 1 tablespoon Moroccan seasoning, 1 clove crushed garlic and 2 tablespoons olive oil. Cook on a grill plate until cooked as desired; serve with baba ghanoush.

SMOKED CHICKEN AND PEAR SALAD

Toss together 50g torn radicchio leaves, 100g torn green mignonette lettuce leaves, 1 thinly sliced pear, 1 thinly sliced red onion and 200g thinly sliced smoked chicken. Drizzle with ¼ cup red wine vinegar and 2 tablespoons olive oil.

OLIVE AND TOMATO BRUSCHETTA

Combine 1 cup each chopped black and green olives and chopped semi-dried tomatoes with 1 tablespoon baby capers, ¼ cup shredded basil and 2 tablespoons red wine vinegar. Spoon mixture onto toasted ciabatta.

STEAMED MUSSELS WITH SAFFRON

Boil 1 teaspoon grated fresh ginger, 2 thinly sliced red thai chillies, ¾ cup dry white wine, ¼ teaspoon saffron threads and 1 tablespoon fish sauce. Add 2kg mussels. Cook, covered, until the mussels open; serve with coriander.

ROASTED VEGETABLE SALAD

Combine 4 sliced baby eggplants, 1 sliced yellow capsicum, 250g sliced pumpkin and 2 tablespoons olive oil in a baking dish; roast in a very hot oven until tender. Serve with 100g semi-dried tomatoes, 100g crumbled goat cheese and 1 tablespoon balsamic vinegar.

SALMON, RISONI AND PEA SALAD

Poach 500g salmon fillets; flake the fish into chunks. Combine with 3 cups cooked risoni, 1½ cups cooked baby peas, 100g baby spinach leaves, 2 tablespoons olive oil and ¼ cup lemon juice.

This famous Chinese dish is prized for the crunchy duck skin. Chinese restaurants serve two dishes using the peking duck: the pancakes are served with skin and little meat, while the remaining duck meat is often served in a noodle or stir-fry dish.

Peking duck pancakes

PREPARATION TIME 1 HOUR (PLUS REFRIGERATION TIME) **COOKING TIME** 30 MINUTES **MAKES** 30

1 cup (150g) plain flour
½ teaspoon salt
1 egg
2 cups (500ml) milk
200g garlic chives

1 chinese barbecued duck (1kg)
2 tablespoons hoisin sauce
2 tablespoons plum sauce
2 lebanese cucumbers (260g), seeded, cut into 4cm lengths

1 Combine flour and salt in medium bowl; gradually whisk in combined egg and milk until mixture is smooth. Strain mixture into large jug.
2 Finely chop enough chives to make ¼ cup coarsely chopped chives; stir chopped chives into batter. Cover; refrigerate 1 hour.
3 Meanwhile, remove skin and meat from duck; discard bones. Discard excess fat from under meat and skin; slice both as thinly as possible.
4 Pour ¼ cup of the batter into heated oiled 20cm frying pan; cook until pancake is browned lightly both sides. Repeat with remaining batter.
5 Using 8cm cutter, cut three rounds from each pancake. Spread each round with a little of the combined sauces; top with duck and cucumber.
6 Place remaining chives in small heatproof bowl; cover with boiling water. Stand until chives are wilted; drain. Fold in edges of rounds; roll to enclose filling. Tie a chive around each roll to secure; trim chive ends.

PER PANCAKE 4.7g total fat (1.6g saturated); 372kj (89 cal); 5.9g carbohydrate; 5.6g protein; 0.6g fibre

---

A chopped apple added to the caramelised onion mixture makes a delicious stuffing for a chicken breast. Wrap the breasts in proscuitto or bacon, place on a baking-paper-lined oven tray and bake in a moderately hot oven for about 25 minutes.

Caramelised onion and brie tart

PREPARATION TIME 30 MINUTES (PLUS REFRIGERATION AND COOLING TIME)
COOKING TIME 1 HOUR 20 MINUTES **SERVES** 6

30g butter
2 large brown onions (400g), sliced thinly
2 teaspoons brown sugar
150g brie, chopped coarsely
⅓ cup (80ml) cream
2 eggs
¼ teaspoon ground nutmeg

PASTRY
1¼ cups (185g) plain flour
125g cold butter, chopped
2 egg yolks
2 tablespoons iced water

1 Make pastry.
2 Melt butter in large frying pan; cook onion, stirring, 15 minutes or until soft. Add sugar; cook, stirring occasionally, about 15 minutes or until onion caramelises. Remove from heat; stir in cheese. Cool. Reduce oven temperature to moderate (180°C/160°C fan-forced).

3 Spoon onion mixture into pastry case; pour over combined cream, eggs and nutmeg. Bake, uncovered, about 30 minutes or until filling is almost set. Stand 10 minutes.
4 Serve tart with rocket leaves, if desired.

PASTRY Process flour and butter until crumbly. Add egg yolks and the water; process until ingredients just come together. Knead dough gently on floured surface until smooth, cover; refrigerate 30 minutes. Preheat oven to moderately hot (200°C/180°C fan-forced). Lightly oil 11cm x 35cm rectangular or 23cm-round flan tin. Roll pastry between sheets of baking paper until large enough to line tin. Lift pastry into tin; press into sides then trim edges. Place tin on oven tray; cover pastry with baking paper, fill with dried beans or rice. Bake, uncovered, 10 minutes. Remove paper and beans; bake 10 minutes or until browned lightly. Cool pastry case to room temperature.

PER SERVING 38.3g total fat (23.6g saturated); 2111kj (505 cal); 27.5g carbohydrate; 12.8g protein; 2.g fibre

---

Mixed satay sticks

PREPARATION TIME 20 MINUTES (PLUS REFRIGERATION TIME) **COOKING TIME** 15 MINUTES
MAKES 12 SKEWERS

Soak bamboo skewers in water for at least an hour before threading the meat on to help keep them from splintering or scorching. If a bamboo skewer does start to char, wrap a folded piece of foil around it to protect it.

- 250g chicken breast fillets
- 250g beef eye fillet
- 250g pork fillet
- 2 cloves garlic, crushed
- 2 teaspoons brown sugar
- ¼ teaspoon sambal oelek
- 1 teaspoon ground turmeric
- ¼ teaspoon curry powder
- ½ teaspoon ground cumin
- ½ teaspoon ground coriander
- 2 tablespoons peanut oil

SATAY SAUCE
- ½ cup (70g) roasted unsalted peanuts
- 2 tablespoons red curry paste
- ¾ cup (180ml) coconut milk
- ¼ cup (60ml) chicken stock
- 1 tablespoon kaffir lime juice
- 1 tablespoon brown sugar

1 Cut chicken, beef and pork into long 1.5cm-thick strips; thread strips onto skewers. Place skewers, in single layer, in shallow baking dish; brush with combined garlic, sugar, sambal, spices and oil. Cover; refrigerate 3 hours or overnight.
2 Make satay sauce.
3 Cook skewers on heated oiled grill plate (or grill or barbecue) until chicken is cooked through and beef and pork are cooked as desired. Serve skewers with satay sauce.

Skewers of meat and chicken can be brushed with combined garlic, spices and oil a day ahead, then covered and kept in the fridge until required. They can also be frozen for up to a month.

SATAY SAUCE Blend or process nuts until chopped finely; add paste, process until just combined. Bring coconut milk to a boil in small saucepan; add peanut mixture, whisking until smooth. Add stock, reduce heat; simmer, stirring, about 3 minutes or until sauce thickens slightly. Add juice and sugar; cook, stirring, until sugar dissolves.

PER SKEWER (INCLUDING SAUCE) 14.2g total fat (5.3g saturated); 844kj (202 cal); 3.1g carbohydrate; 15.3g protein; 1.2g fibre

Spinach soufflé with fresh tomato sauce

PREPARATION TIME 25 MINUTES **COOKING TIME** 25 MINUTES **SERVES** 6

¼ cup (25g) packaged breadcrumbs

30g butter

1 small brown onion (80g), chopped finely

250g packet frozen spinach

¼ teaspoon ground nutmeg

¼ cup (20g) finely grated parmesan

60g butter, extra

¼ cup (35g) plain flour

¾ cup (180ml) milk

3 eggs, separated

1 egg white, extra

FRESH TOMATO SAUCE

60g butter

1 clove garlic, crushed

500g ripe tomatoes, chopped coarsely

To add the egg whites, first stir in a large spoonful to lighten the base, then scoop the rest of the whites onto the surface and gently fold in. See also "Fold" on page 11.

1 Preheat oven to moderately hot (200°C/180°C fan-forced). Lightly oil six ¾-cup (180ml) soufflé dishes; sprinkle with breadcrumbs, shake away excess.

2 Make fresh tomato sauce.

3 Meanwhile, melt butter in medium saucepan; cook onion, stirring, until soft. Transfer to medium bowl. Cook spinach in same pan, stirring, over low heat, until spinach is thawed and dried out. Add spinach to onion with nutmeg and cheese; stir to combine.

4 Melt extra butter in same cleaned pan, add flour; cook, stirring, 1 minute. Gradually add milk; stir until mixture boils and thickens. Cool 10 minutes. Add egg yolks, one at a time, beating well after each addition. Stir in spinach mixture.

5 Beat all egg whites in small bowl until firm peaks form; gently fold egg whites into spinach mixture, in two batches.

6 Place soufflé dishes on oven tray; pour spinach mixture into dishes. Bake, uncovered, about 12 minutes or until puffed and browned lightly. Serve with fresh tomato sauce.

FRESH TOMATO SAUCE Melt butter in medium saucepan; cook garlic, stirring, until fragrant. Add tomato; bring to a boil. Reduce heat; simmer, covered, 15 minutes. Push mixture through sieve into medium bowl; discard solids. Cover to keep warm.

You can make the soufflé ahead through the end of step 4. Just before you intend to fold in the egg whites and bake the soufflé, warm the prepared egg yolk and spinach base by standing the bowl in warm water a few minutes.

☐ **PER SERVING** 25.8g total fat (15.8g saturated); 1313kj (314 cal); 11.2g carbohydrate; 9.1g protein; 2.2g fibre

SPINACH SOUFFLE WITH FRESH TOMATO SAUCE

Mezze platter

The Spanish have tapas, the French hors d'oeuvre, Italians antipasto, and Greece and Middle Eastern countries have mezze – all meaning a group of appetisers served as an entree.

PICKLED CAULIFLOWER

PREPARATION TIME 15 MINUTES **COOKING TIME** 5 MINUTES **MAKES** 4½ CUPS

Combine 3 cups water, 1½ cups white wine vinegar and ¼ cup salt in medium saucepan; bring to a boil. Boil, uncovered, 3 minutes. Pack florets of ½ small cauliflower, wedges of 1 medium turnip, wedges of 8 baby beetroots and 1 thinly sliced garlic clove into hot sterilised 1.5-litre (6-cup) glass jar with tight-fitting lid; pour in enough boiling vinegar mixture to leave 1cm space between vegetable pieces and top of jar. Seal while hot. Store in cool, dark place for at least 3 days; once opened, store in fridge.

PER ¼ CUP 0.1g total fat (0.0g saturated); 75kj (18 cal); 2.0g carbohydrate; 1.0g protein; 1.2g fibre

Many mezze dishes, especially the dips have become world-wide favourites, and are available in most supermarkets. While not quite as good as home-made, they are useful when time is short.

LAHMA BI AJEEN (MINI LAMB PIES)

PREPARATION TIME 30 MINUTES (PLUS STANDING TIME) **COOKING TIME** 10 MINUTES **MAKES** 20

Process 1 cup plain flour, 1 teaspoon dried yeast, ½ teaspoon sea salt flakes, 1 tablespoon olive oil and approximately ½ cup warm water until mixture forms a ball. Place ball of dough in oiled medium bowl; coat dough with oil spray. Cover; stand in warm place 1 hour or until dough doubles in size. Meanwhile, make spiced lamb topping. Preheat oven to moderately hot (200°C/180°C fan-forced). Lightly oil two oven trays. Knead dough on lightly floured surface 5 minutes; roll dough to 2mm thickness. Using 7cm cutter, cut 20 rounds from dough; place rounds on trays. Divide topping among rounds, spreading to edge to completely cover round. Bake, uncovered, 10 minutes or until cooked through.

SPICED LAMB TOPPING Combine 100g lamb mince, 1 finely chopped medium tomato, 1 teaspoon ground cumin, 1 teaspoon ground coriander and 2 teaspoons coarsely chopped roasted pine nuts in small bowl.

PER PIE 1.7g total fat (0.4g saturated); 188kj (45 cal); 5.2g carbohydrate; 2.0g protein; 0.4g fibre

SPINACH FILLO TRIANGLES

PREPARATION TIME 45 MINUTES **COOKING TIME** 15 MINUTES **MAKES** 16

Preheat oven to moderately hot (200°C/180°C fan-forced). Lightly oil oven tray. Boil, steam or microwave 250g finely shredded trimmed spinach until wilted; drain. When cool enough to handle, squeeze excess liquid from spinach. Combine spinach in small bowl with 2 teaspoons sumac, 2 finely chopped green onions and 1 tablespoon lemon juice. Cut four sheets fillo pastry into four strips each. Place one strip on board; cover remaining strips with baking paper, then with damp tea-towel. Spray strip with oil spray; place 1 rounded teaspoon of the spinach filling on one corner, 5mm from edge, flatten slightly. Fold opposite corner of strip diagonally across filling to form triangle; continue folding to end of strip, retaining triangular shape. Place fillo triangle on tray, seam-side down; repeat process with remaining strips and filling. Spray tops of fillo triangles lightly with oil; bake 10 minutes or until crisp and browned lightly.

PER TRIANGLE 0.2g total fat (0.0g saturated); 71kj (17 cal); 2.7g carbohydrate; 0.9g protein; 0.5g fibre

LABNE

This recipe must be prepared at least 2 days before you want to serve the mezze platter.

PREPARATION TIME 20 MINUTES (PLUS REFRIGERATION TIME) **MAKES** 24

Combine 3 cups greek-style yogurt and 3 teaspoons salt in medium bowl; pour into muslin-lined large sieve or colander set over large bowl. Gather corners of muslin together, twist, then tie with kitchen string. Place heavy can on muslin to weight yogurt mixture; refrigerate 24 to 36 hours until yogurt thickens (yogurt will lose about half its weight in water; discard water in bowl). Place thickened yogurt in small bowl; discard muslin. Roll level tablespoons of yogurt into balls; place balls on platter, drizzle with ¼ cup olive oil.

☐ **PER BALL** 3.6g total fat (1.1g saturated); 192kj (46 cal); 1.6g carbohydrate; 1.6g protein; 0.0g fibre

HUMMUS

PREPARATION TIME 10 MINUTES **COOKING TIME** 15 MINUTES **MAKES** 2 CUPS

Place 2 cups water and 2 x 300g cans rinsed, drained chickpeas in medium saucepan; bring to a boil. Boil, uncovered, about 10 minutes or until chickpeas are tender. Drain chickpeas over medium bowl; reserve 1 cup cooking liquid. Blend or process chickpeas and reserved cooking liquid with ¼ cup lemon juice, ¼ cup olive oil, ⅓ cup tahini and 3 crushed garlic cloves until just smooth. Serve hummus drizzled with extra oil, if desired.

☐ **PER ¼ CUP** 13.9g total fat (1.9g saturated); 752kj (180 cal); 7.2g carbohydrate; 5.2g protein; 3.8g fibre

BABA GHANOUSH

PREPARATION TIME 15 MINUTES (PLUS STANDING TIME) **COOKING TIME** 30 MINUTES **MAKES** 2 CUPS

Preheat grill. Pierce 2 large eggplants all over with fork or skewer; place on oiled oven tray under grill about 30 minutes or until skin blackens and eggplant is soft, turning occasionally. Stand 15 minutes. When cool enough to handle, peel eggplants; discard skin. Drain eggplant flesh in colander 10 minutes, then blend or process with 3 crushed garlic cloves, 2 tablespoons tahini, ¼ cup lemon juice, 2 tablespoons olive oil and ½ teaspoon sweet paprika until just smooth.

☐ **PER ¼ CUP** 8.0g total fat (1.0g saturated); 431kj (103 cal); 3.6g carbohydrate; 2.5g protein; 3.7g fibre

TABBOULEH

To prevent mint from blackening, chop it using a very sharp knife to avoid bruising the leaf, and do it just before assembling the tabbouleh.

PREPARATION TIME 30 MINUTES (PLUS REFRIGERATION TIME) **MAKES** 4½ CUPS

Place ¼ cup burghul in small shallow bowl. Halve 3 medium tomatoes; using small spoon, scoop pulp from tomato halves over burghul. Chop remaining tomato flesh finely; spread over burghul so surface is completely covered with tomato. Cover bowl; refrigerate 1 hour. Place burghul mixture in large bowl with 3 cups coarsely chopped fresh flat-leaf parsley, 2 finely chopped green onions, ¼ cup finely chopped fresh mint, ¼ cup lemon juice and ¼ cup olive oil; toss tabbouleh gently to combine.

☐ **PER ¼ CUP** 3.3g total fat (0.5g saturated); 184kj (44 cal); 2.2g carbohydrate; 0.8g protein; 1.3g fibre

Mussels should be alive when you buy them; don't store them in water or resealable plastic bags as that will kill them. Just keep them cool in the fridge. Before cooking, check the shells are tightly closed or close when tapped, indicating they are alive. Discard mussels that don't close or have broken shells. Once cooked all shells should be open; NEVER eat a mussel whose shell is still closed.

Mussels in fragrant thai broth

PREPARATION TIME 20 MINUTES **COOKING TIME** 15 MINUTES **SERVES** 4

½ cup (100g) jasmine rice
1kg small black mussels
1 tablespoon vegetable oil
2 tablespoons green curry paste
1½ cups (375ml) water
1½ cups (375ml) fish stock
2 teaspoons fish sauce
2 teaspoons brown sugar
1⅔ cups (400ml) coconut milk
¼ cup coarsely chopped fresh coriander
4 green onions, chopped finely
1 tablespoon lime juice

1 Cook rice in large saucepan of boiling water, uncovered, until just tender; drain. Cover to keep warm.
2 Meanwhile, scrub mussels; remove beards. Heat oil in large saucepan; cook paste, stirring, until fragrant. Add the water, stock, sauce and sugar; bring to a boil. Add coconut milk; return to a boil. Reduce heat; simmer, stirring, 1 minute. Add mussels; cook, covered, about 5 minutes or until mussels open (discard any that do not). Remove from heat; stir in coriander, onion and juice.
3 Divide rice among serving bowls; top with mussels and broth.

PER SERVING 30g total fat (19.5g saturated); 1839kj (440 cal); 29.7g carbohydrate; 11.7g protein; 3.5g fibre

---

This stylish salad also makes a lovely light lunch for a hot day, or an elegant dish for a buffet party.

Quail, fig and orange salad

PREPARATION TIME 15 MINUTES **COOKING TIME** 20 MINUTES **SERVES** 4

6 quails (1.2kg)
3 medium oranges (720g)
4 medium fresh figs (240g), quartered
100g mizuna
½ cup (60g) coarsely chopped roasted pecans

MAPLE AND ORANGE DRESSING
⅓ cup (80ml) orange juice
¼ cup (60ml) olive oil
2 tablespoons pure maple syrup
1 clove garlic, crushed

1 Make maple and orange dressing.
2 Rinse quails under cold water; pat dry with absorbent paper. Discard necks from quails. Using kitchen scissors, cut along each side of quails' backbone; discard backbones. Halve quails along breastbone; brush quail halves with half of the dressing. Cook quails on heated oiled grill plate (or grill or barbecue) until cooked through.
3 Meanwhile, segment oranges over large bowl. Add remaining ingredients and remaining dressing; toss gently to combine.
4 Divide salad among serving plates; top with quails.

MAPLE AND ORANGE DRESSING Place ingredients in screw-top jar; shake well.

PER SERVING 41.5g total fat (7.0g saturated); 2571kj (615 cal); 26.8g carbohydrate; 32.3g protein; 5.9g fibre

Duck ravioli in asian broth

PREPARATION TIME 30 MINUTES (PLUS STANDING TIME) **COOKING TIME** 2 HOURS **SERVES** 10

Many people are put off making ravioli as it can be a time-consuming process. Here we make life simpler by using wonton wrappers and a barbecued duck, purchased from Asian barbecue takeaway shops. Use fresh lasagne sheets in place of wonton wrappers, if you prefer.

- 1 chinese barbecued duck (1kg)
- 3 litres (12 cups) water
- 1 medium brown onion (150g), chopped coarsely
- 1 trimmed celery stalk (100g), chopped coarsely
- 1 medium carrot (120g), chopped coarsely
- 4 black peppercorns
- 5cm piece fresh ginger (25g), chopped coarsely
- 5 dried shiitake mushrooms
- ¼ cup (60ml) boiling water
- 2 green onions
- 40 round wonton wrappers
- 1 egg, beaten lightly
- 2 teaspoons soy sauce

1 Discard skin from duck; reserve meat and bones. Chop meat finely, cover; refrigerate.
2 Combine bones with the water, brown onion, celery, carrot, peppercorns and ginger in large saucepan; bring to a boil. Reduce heat; simmer, uncovered, 1½ hours. Strain through muslin-lined strainer into large bowl; discard solids. Return broth to same cleaned pan.
3 Meanwhile, combine mushrooms and the boiling water in small heatproof bowl; stand 20 minutes, drain. Discard mushroom stems; chop caps finely, reserve.
4 Chop 1 of the green onions finely; combine in medium bowl with meat and mushroom. Place 1 tablespoon of filling in centre of one wrapper; brush edges with egg. Top with another wrapper, press edges together. Repeat with remaining filling, wrappers and egg.
5 Add sauce to broth; bring to a boil. Add ravioli, simmer, uncovered, about 10 minutes or until ravioli are tender. Serve sprinkled with thinly sliced remaining green onion.

PER SERVING 12.0g total fat (3.6g saturated); 1074kj (257 cal); 19.9g carbohydrate; 17.0g protein; 0.8g fibre

---

Calamari stuffed with fetta and chilli

PREPARATION TIME 40 MINUTES **COOKING TIME** 10 MINUTES **SERVES** 8 AS PART OF A MENU

The calamari, a member of the squid family, is ideal for stuffing as its body, if cleaned carefully, makes a whole tube, without tearing. Calamari, as a rule, is more tender and less coarse than its near relatives, octopus and cuttlefish, and makes better eating.

- 8 (600g) whole calamari
- 400g firm fetta
- 1 teaspoon dried chilli flakes
- ⅓ cup finely chopped fresh oregano
- ⅓ cup (80ml) olive oil
- 2 teaspoons finely grated lemon rind
- 1 clove garlic, crushed

1 Clean calamari; separate tubes from tentacles (see page 157).
2 Mash fetta, chilli, half of the oregano and half of the oil together in small bowl. Fill calamari tubes with fetta mixture. Use toothpicks to secure opening. Place calamari and tentacles in a shallow dish.
3 Combine remaining ingredients; pour over calamari; cover and refrigerate for 3 hours, turning occasionally.
4 Cook calamari on oiled grill plate (or grill or barbecue) about 3 minutes each side.

PER SERVING 21.7g total fat (9.2g saturated); 1170kj (280 cal); 0.2g carbohydrate; 21.5g protein; 0.1g fibre

1

2

3

4

Radicchio with thai crab salad

PREPARATION TIME 20 MINUTES (PLUS REFRIGERATION TIME) **COOKING TIME** 5 MINUTES **SERVES** 6

Some people find the bitterness of radicchio a little overpowering. Try brushing each whole radicchio with oil and grill or barbecue until the outside leaves are charred and the inside is tender. This will give a sweeter smokey flavour. Slices of mango or paw paw make a nice addition to this salad.

1 tablespoon water

2 tablespoons lime juice

1 tablespoon white sugar

1 fresh small red thai chilli, chopped finely

250g fresh crab meat

½ lebanese cucumber (65g), seeded, chopped finely

½ small red capsicum (75g), chopped finely

1 green onion, sliced thinly

3 radicchio

1 Combine the water, juice, sugar and chilli in small saucepan, stir over heat, without boiling, until sugar dissolves; bring to a boil. Remove from heat, cool 10 minutes. Cover; refrigerate dressing until cold.

2 Combine crab, cucumber, capsicum, onion and dressing in medium bowl.

3 Trim ends from radicchio; separate leaves (you need 30 leaves). Place 1 heaped teaspoon of the crab salad on each leaf.

4 Serve cold.

PER LEAF 0.1g total fat (0.0g saturated); 46kj (11 cal); 1.0g carbohydrate; 1.3g protein; 0.4g fibre

---

Spinach and ricotta gnocchi with sage butter

PREPARATION TIME 25 MINUTES (PLUS REFRIGERATION TIME) **COOKING TIME** 10 MINUTES **SERVES** 4

Sage butter is a traditional Italian sauce for pasta or veal. The nutty butter flavour marries perfectly with the sage.

250g packet frozen spinach, thawed

500g firm fresh ricotta

1 cup (80g) finely grated parmesan

½ cup (75g) plain flour

2 eggs, beaten lightly

1 tablespoon olive oil

80g butter, chopped

16 fresh sage leaves

¼ cup (20g) flaked parmesan

1 Using hands, squeeze spinach to remove excess liquid; chop spinach finely.

2 Combine spinach, ricotta, grated parmesan, flour, eggs and oil in large bowl. Drop level tablespoons of the mixture onto tray, cover; refrigerate about 1 hour or until firm.

3 Shape spinach mixture into ovals. Drop gnocchi, in batches, into large saucepan of boiling water; cook, without stirring, until gnocchi floats to the surface. Using slotted spoon, remove gnocchi.

4 Meanwhile, melt butter in small frying pan; heat until butter is browned lightly. Add sage; remove from heat.

5 Divide gnocchi among plates; drizzle with sage butter. Serve topped with parmesan flakes and black pepper, if desired.

PER SERVING 46g total fat (26.4g saturated); 2466kj (590 cal); 15.4g carbohydrate; 29g protein; 1.6g fibre

---

1 RADICCHIO WITH THAI CRAB SALAD **2** SPINACH AND RICOTTA GNOCCHI WITH SAGE BUTTER
3 VEGETABLE TEMPURA WITH WASABI AIOLI (P 130) **4** SALT AND PEPPER BUTTERFLIED PRAWNS (P 130)

The secrets of making perfect tempura are: use the freshest vegetables you can find; make sure both the vegetables and the batter are really cold (this prevents the batter from soaking up too much oil); maintain a constant temperature by only frying a few pieces at a time; make the batter just before required; finally, don't overmix the batter – lumpy is good.

Vegetable tempura with wasabi aïoli

PREPARATION TIME 20 MINUTES **COOKING TIME** 15 MINUTES **SERVES** 6

2 medium carrots (240g)
2 medium red capsicums (400g)
1 large brown onion (200g)
2 egg whites
1 cup (150g) plain flour
½ cup (75g) cornflour
1 ¼ cups (310ml) iced water
vegetable oil, for deep-frying
800g pumpkin, sliced thinly
400g broccolini
½ cup (125ml) light soy sauce

WASABI AIOLI
2 egg yolks
1 tablespoon lemon juice
1 tablespoon wasabi paste
1 clove garlic, quartered
½ cup (125ml) vegetable oil
1 tablespoon hot water

1 Make wasabi aïoli.
2 Using vegetable peeler, cut carrots into long thin ribbons. Halve capsicums; discard seeds and membranes. Cut capsicum into 2cm-thick slices. Cut onion into thin wedges.
3 Whisk egg whites in small bowl until soft peaks form. Sift flours into large bowl. Stir in the water; fold in egg white.
4 Heat oil in wok. Dip vegetables, one piece at a time, in batter; deep-fry until browned lightly; drain. Serve tempura with soy sauce and wasabi aïoli.

WASABI AIOLI Blend or process egg yolks, juice, wasabi and garlic until smooth. With motor operating, gradually add oil in thin, steady stream; process until mixture thickens. Thin aïoli with the hot water, if desired.

PER SERVING 38.2g total fat (5.4g saturated); 2424kj (580 cal); 42.9g carbohydrate; 13.2g protein; 7.g fibre

---

For a delicious salad roughly break up the crisp wontons and toss together with 100g mixed salad leaves, 2 spring onions, sliced finely, half a cucumber chopped into cubes, ¼ cup coriander leaves and the stir-fried prawn mixture. Dress the salad with 2 teaspoons sesame oil, 1 tablespoon sweet chilli sauce and 2 tablespoons lime juice.

Salt and pepper butterflied prawns

PREPARATION TIME 25 MINUTES **COOKING TIME** 15 MINUTES **SERVES** 4

4 x 9cm-square wonton wrappers
1kg uncooked medium king prawns
vegetable oil, for shallow-frying
1 tablespoon peanut oil
2 cloves garlic, crushed
1 fresh small red thai chilli, sliced thinly
1 tablespoon lime juice
2 tablespoons sweet chilli sauce
3 green onions, sliced thinly
2 teaspoons roasted sesame seeds

SEASONING
½ teaspoon black peppercorns
¼ teaspoon coriander seeds
¾ teaspoon sea salt flakes
¼ teaspoon lemon pepper

1 Cut wrappers in half diagonally. Shell and devein prawns, leaving tails intact. Cut along back of prawns, taking care not to cut all the way through; flatten prawns slightly.

2 Heat vegetable oil in wok; shallow-fry wrappers, in batches, until browned lightly, drain on absorbent paper. Reheat oil; shallow-fry prawns, in batches, about 30 seconds or until prawns are almost tender and just changed in colour, drain on absorbent paper.

3 Meanwhile, make seasoning.

4 Heat peanut oil in same cleaned wok; stir-fry garlic and chilli until fragrant. Add prawns, juice, sauce and seasoning; stir-fry until heated through. Stir in onion.

5 Serve prawns on wontons wrappers; sprinkle with sesame seeds.

SEASONING Using mortar and pestle, lightly crush peppercorns and seeds; stir in salt and lemon pepper.

PER SERVING 19.8g total fat (2.8g saturated); 1321kj (316 cal); 7.0g carbohydrate; 27.1g protein; 1.0g fibre

---

Ocean trout sashimi rolls with lemon dipping sauce

For this recipe, buy fish labelled sashimi grade, an assurance that the fish has been handled correctly, for the purpose of eating raw. It will cost more than other fish as it is the highest quality fresh fish on the market. This is not a recipe where you can cut corners.

PREPARATION TIME 25 MINUTES (PLUS STANDING TIME) **COOKING TIME** 5 MINUTES **MAKES** 16

200g piece sashimi ocean trout

¼ medium red capsicum (50g)

½ lebanese cucumber (65g)

1 green onion

LEMON DIPPING SAUCE

½ cup (125ml) rice vinegar

¼ cup (55g) caster sugar

2 teaspoons light soy sauce

½ teaspoon finely grated lemon rind

1 Make lemon dipping sauce.

2 Using sharp knife, cut trout into paper-thin slices (you need 16 slices).

3 Discard seeds and membranes from capsicum; halve cucumber lengthways, scoop out seeds. Halve onion lengthways. Slice capsicum, cucumber and onion into 8cm pieces.

4 Lay trout slices on board in single layer; divide capsicum, cucumber and onion among trout slices, mounding at one of the narrow edges. Roll slices around filling; place rolls, seam-side down, on serving platter.

5 Serve immediately with lemon dipping sauce.

LEMON DIPPING SAUCE Heat vinegar, sugar and soy sauce in small saucepan, stirring, until sugar dissolves. Remove from heat, add rind; stand 10 minutes. Strain sauce into serving bowl; discard rind.

PER ROLL (INCLUDING SAUCE) 0.5g total fat (0.1g saturated); 125kj (30 cal); 3.7g carbohydrate; 2.5g protein; 0.1g fibre

SALADS

Salads

A salad can be anything – first course, main course, nourishing light meal, accompaniment, picnic-goer, buffet star; casual or elegant, warm or cold, vegetarian or not. The one thing a modern salad is not likely to be is the kind of all-purpose "mixed salad" our mothers made – a chilly jumble of everything they found in the fridge. We've learnt to take one or two good ingredients and bring out their charm by surrounding them with just the right supporting flavours and textures.

We are exceptionally fortunate to have an abundance, year-round, of beautiful fruits and vegetables and every other kind of fresh food from seafood to meats, poultry, eggs and fine cheeses. It only remains for us to choose carefully and use each ingredient to the best effect.

BUYING, STORING AND HANDLING SALAD VEGETABLES

LETTUCE AND OTHER LEAVES Leaf vegetables should be crisp and brightly coloured for their type, and have a sheen. Buy only as much soft-leaf lettuce or other soft leaves as you plan to use within a day or two. If buying iceberg or cos lettuce or cabbage, choose a size you will use in less than a week. Buy witlof and radicchio no more than 2 or 3 days ahead. Except for watercress, store leaf vegetables in paper bags enclosed in plastic bags, in the fridge. Trim watercress stems, gather them into a bouquet, slip a rubber band loosely round the stems and stand in 2 to 3cm of water in a bowl. Drop a plastic bag over the top and store in the fridge. Wash salad leaves up to 12 hours ahead of using, dry in a salad spinner or by shaking gently in a towel, and store as above until needed.

SPROUTS AND SHOOTS Buy no more than a day ahead, and store in a bowl of water in the fridge.

TOMATOES The ideal is to buy tomatoes that have been fully sun-ripened on the bush or vine but, in spite of many claims to this, the mechanics of marketing make true vine-ripened tomatoes a rarity. Truss tomatoes look convincing, but feel them and buy only if they give slightly. You can improve reasonably ripe tomatoes by enclosing them in a paper bag with a banana, at warmish room temperature, for a day or two. Oxheart tomatoes, a pointed pink variety available only in the warmer months, are probably the best bet when you can get them. They don't look thrilling, but their flesh is bright red, tender, juicy and flavoursome in the old-fashioned way.

Never put tomatoes in the fridge – chilling damages their cell structure. Store at room temperature, away from sunlight (which collapses them and reduces their vitamin content) and, preferably, in a single layer, not touching. Fully ripened tomatoes should be used within 2 or 3 days.

To peel tomatoes, cut a tiny cross in the skin at the base of each one, place them in a bowl, pour boiling water over them and stand for 20 seconds. Drain and run cold water over them, then pull off the skin with your fingers or a knife, starting at the base.

AVOCADOS Avocados to be eaten that day should yield all over when gently pressed. Avocados to be eaten in the next day or so should be just yielding at the neck end and firm elsewhere. In a greengrocer's shop, you are usually asked not to squeeze the produce but to ask the assistant to choose avocados of the required degree of ripeness. In a supermarket, you must test them yourself. Store at room temperature. If one is slow to ripen, you can help it along by enclosing it in a paper bag with a ripe apple or banana.

FIRM VEGETABLES Cucumbers, capsicum, celery, green onions, celeriac, zucchini and mushrooms should be perfectly firm with no soft or discoloured spots. Capsicums should be glossy, the other vegetables should have a sheen. Buy only as much of these vegetables as you will use within 4 or 5 days. Store cucumbers and capsicum unwrapped in a covered crisper, store the other vegetables in paper bags enclosed in plastic bags, in the fridge. Wash and cut up as close to serving time as possible (though don't wash mushrooms, simply wipe them with a damp cloth).

There are several ways to roast a capsicum and remove the skin: place it under a preheated grill on high heat, or in a hot oven; or hold it on a fork over a gas flame; or place pieces of capsicum, skin-side down, on a heat-spreading mat over a gas flame. Leave until the skin is blistered and charred all over, then place in a paper bag or place a bowl over the pieces and allow to steam for about 5 minutes. Peel the skin away with your fingers.

VEGETABLES TO BE COOKED Asparagus, artichokes, beans and snow, sugar or ordinary peas should be firm and crisp, with an almost moist-looking sheen. Corn should be brightly coloured and glossy. Buy these vegetables only a day or two ahead. Stand asparagus upright in 2 to 3cm of water in a jar or other container, drop a plastic bag over the top and store in the fridge. Store the other vegetables in paper bags enclosed in plastic bags in the fridge. Cook them only until they are on the firm side of tender, and as close as possible to serving. Once cooked, they can be dropped into ice water to arrest cooking, but the ideal is to cook, drain and add them to the salad while they are still just warm.

BEETROOT, CARROTS AND OTHER ROOT VEGETABLES Buy up to 4 or 5 days ahead and store in a covered crisper. They are often used raw and finely sliced or grated, but if you are cooking them, do it a day ahead at most and store, covered, in the fridge. Like nearly all vegetables, they are at their absolute best when freshly cooked and eaten just warm.

For another way to cook haloumi, coat 1cm-thick slices of the cheese in flour; dip into beaten egg then coat all over in a mixture of stale breadcrumbs, finely grated lemon rind and chopped fresh oregano. Fry in garlic or chilli oil until golden on both sides.

Haloumi, asparagus and rocket salad

PREPARATION TIME 20 MINUTES **COOKING TIME** 15 MINUTES **SERVES** 4

150g baby green beans, trimmed

1 tablespoon olive oil

500g asparagus, trimmed, halved crossways

500g haloumi cheese, sliced thinly

1 large avocado (320g), sliced thinly

½ cup (70g) roasted macadamia nuts, chopped coarsely

200g rocket

MACADAMIA DRESSING

1 teaspoon mild english mustard

¼ cup (60ml) macadamia oil

¼ cup (60ml) sherry vinegar

1 Make macadamia dressing.

2 Boil, steam or microwave beans until just tender; drain. Rinse under cold water; drain.

3 Meanwhile, heat half of the oil in large frying pan; cook asparagus, in batches, until just tender.

4 Heat remaining oil in same pan; cook cheese, in batches, until browned both sides. Drain on absorbent paper.

5 Place beans, asparagus and cheese in large bowl with dressing and remaining ingredients; toss gently to combine.

MACADAMIA DRESSING Place ingredients in screw-top jar; shake well.

PER SERVING 66.2g total fat (20.9g saturated); 3168kj (758 cal); 6.5g carbohydrate; 33.3g protein; 5g fibre

You have to love this recipe; it's got it all, well almost. It's sweet, spicy and salty, and if you like, add some fresh red chilli for heat. Try using fish, chicken or duck instead of the pork.

Asian pork and apple salad

PREPARATION TIME 20 MINUTES (PLUS REFRIGERATION TIME) **COOKING TIME** 20 MINUTES **SERVES** 4

⅓ cup (80ml) hoisin sauce

1 tablespoon fish sauce

1 tablespoon light soy sauce

2 tablespoons rice vinegar

¼ cup (90g) honey

2 cloves garlic, crushed

2cm piece fresh ginger (10g), grated

½ teaspoon five-spice powder

750g pork fillets, halved lengthways

1 tablespoon water

½ medium iceberg lettuce, chopped coarsely

50g bean sprouts

50g snow pea sprouts

1 small red onion (100g), sliced thinly

1 medium green apple (150g), unpeeled, sliced thinly

⅓ cup firmly packed fresh mint leaves

1 Combine sauces, vinegar, honey, garlic, ginger and five-spice in medium jug.

2 Pour ½ cup of the sauce mixture into medium bowl; add pork, turn to coat in marinade. Cover; refrigerate 3 hours or overnight.

3 Stir the water into remaining sauce mixture, cover; refrigerate.
4 Drain pork, reserve marinade. Cook pork on heated lightly oiled grill plate (or grill or barbecue) about 20 minutes or until cooked as desired, brushing occasionally with marinade (discard any remaining marinade). Cover; stand 10 minutes then slice thickly.
5 Meanwhile, place remaining ingredients in medium bowl; toss to combine. Divide salad among serving plates; top with pork then drizzle with reserved sauce.

PER SERVING 16.5g total fat (5.3g saturated); 1986kj (475 cal); 35.4g carbohydrate; 43.7g protein; 6g fibre

---

Tuscan white bean salad

PREPARATION TIME 20 MINUTES **SERVES** 4

If your rocket is looking a little tired, place it in a bowl of iced water for 15 minutes to revive it.

2 x 400g cans white beans, rinsed, drained

1 medium red onion (170g), chopped finely

⅔ cup (100g) drained semi-dried tomatoes

150g mozzarella, diced into 1cm pieces

½ cup (75g) seeded kalamata olives

150g rocket

OREGANO BALSAMIC VINAIGRETTE

1 clove garlic, crushed

1 tablespoon finely chopped fresh oregano

¼ cup (60ml) balsamic vinegar

¼ cup (60ml) olive oil

1 Make oregano balsamic vinaigrette.
2 Place beans, onion, tomato, cheese, olives and dressing in medium bowl; toss gently to combine.
3 Serve salad with rocket.

OREGANO BALSAMIC VINAIGRETTE Place ingredients in screw-top jar; shake well.

PER SERVING 23.8g total fat (7.5g saturated); 1576kj (377 cal); 19.3g carbohydrate; 17.3g protein; 7.8g fibre

---

Baby rocket and parmesan salad

PREPARATION TIME 20 MINUTES **SERVES** 8

Roast nuts by spreading them on an oven tray and roasting in a moderate oven, checking and stirring to ensure even browning. Alternatively, do them on the stovetop: place the nuts in a dry frying pan over low to medium heat and move them around frequently until they are just golden.

60g piece parmesan

200g baby rocket leaves

½ cup (75g) drained semi-dried tomatoes, halved lengthways

¼ cup (40g) roasted pine nuts

¼ cup (60ml) balsamic vinegar

¼ cup (60ml) olive oil

1 Using vegetable peeler, shave cheese into long pieces.
2 Place cheese in large bowl with rocket, tomato, nuts and combined vinegar and oil; toss gently to combine.

PER SERVING 13.4g total fat (2.8g saturated); 673kj (161 cal); 4.1g carbohydrate; 5.2g protein; 2.0g fibre

Gado gado translates roughly as "mixed mixed" which might explain why there are so many variations for this traditional Indonesian dish. This salad can use any selection of vegetables, raw, cooked or a mixture of both, and is always served with a delicious spicy peanut sauce.

Gado gado

PREPARATION TIME 1 HOUR **COOKING TIME** 35 MINUTES **SERVES** 4

2 medium potatoes (400g), sliced thickly

2 medium carrots (240g), sliced thickly

150g green beans, trimmed, chopped coarsely

½ small cabbage (600g)

vegetable oil, for deep-frying

300g firm tofu, diced into 2cm pieces

2 medium tomatoes (300g), cut into thick wedges

2 lebanese cucumbers (260g), sliced thickly

2 cups (160g) bean sprouts

4 hard-boiled eggs, quartered

PEANUT SAUCE

1 cup (140g) roasted unsalted peanuts

1 tablespoon peanut oil

1 small brown onion (80g), chopped finely

1 clove garlic, crushed

2 fresh small red thai chillies, chopped finely

4cm piece fresh galangal (20g), grated

1 tablespoon lime juice

1 tablespoon brown sugar

½ teaspoon shrimp paste

1 cup (250ml) coconut milk

1 tablespoon kecap manis

1 Boil, steam or microwave potato, carrot and beans, separately, until vegetables are just tender; drain.

2 Meanwhile, drop cabbage leaves into large saucepan of boiling water; remove leaves and quickly plunge into large bowl of cold water. Drain cabbage; slice thinly.

3 Make peanut sauce.

4 Heat oil in small saucepan; deep-fry tofu, in batches, until browned all over. Drain on absorbent paper.

5 Divide potato, carrot, beans, cabbage, tofu, tomato, cucumber, sprouts and egg among serving plates; serve with peanut sauce.

PEANUT SAUCE Blend or process nuts until chopped coarsely. Heat oil in small saucepan; cook onion, garlic and chilli, stirring, until onion is browned lightly. Add nuts and remaining ingredients; bring to a boil. Reduce heat; simmer, uncovered, about 5 minutes or until mixture thickens. Cool 10 minutes.

PER SERVING 49.1g total fat (17.5g saturated); 3148kj (753 cal); 35.6g carbohydrate; 34.3g protein; 18.7g fibre

GADO GADO

For a lower-fat alternative, spray pitta pieces with cooking-oil spray then bake, uncovered, in a hot oven until crisp; break into small pieces over the salad.

Fattoush

PREPARATION TIME 30 MINUTES **COOKING TIME** 5 MINUTES **SERVES** 4

6 pocket pitta (500g)

olive oil, for shallow-frying

3 medium tomatoes (450g), chopped coarsely

1 large green capsicum (350g), chopped coarsely

2 lebanese cucumbers (260g), seeded, sliced thinly

10 trimmed red radishes (150g), sliced thinly

4 spring onions (100g), sliced thinly

1 ½ cups firmly packed fresh flat-leaf parsley leaves

½ cup coarsely chopped fresh mint

LEMON GARLIC DRESSING

2 cloves garlic, crushed

¼ cup (60ml) olive oil

¼ cup (60ml) lemon juice

1 Make lemon garlic dressing.

2 Halve pitta horizontally; cut into 2.5cm pieces. Heat oil in wok or large frying pan; shallow-fry pitta, in batches, until browned lightly and crisp. Drain on absorbent paper.

3 Place about three-quarters of the pitta in large bowl with remaining ingredients and dressing; toss gently to combine.

4 Serve salad sprinkled with remaining pitta.

LEMON GARLIC DRESSING Place ingredients in screw-top jar; shake well.

PER SERVING 30.6g total fat (4.2g saturated); 2688kj (643 cal); 72g carbohydrate; 15.5g protein; 8.7g fibre

---

This is a recipe where the quality of ingredients really matters. Make sure you choose vine-ripened tomatoes that have a deep colour and strong aroma, as this salad will showcase their magnificent flavour.

Avocado caprese salad

PREPARATION TIME 10 MINUTES **SERVES** 4

4 large vine-ripened truss tomatoes (480g)

250g cherry bocconcini

1 large avocado (320g), halved

¼ cup loosely packed fresh basil leaves

2 tablespoons olive oil

1 tablespoon balsamic vinegar

1 Slice tomatoes, cheese and avocado thickly.

2 Place tomato, cheese and avocado on serving platter; top with basil leaves, drizzle with combined oil and vinegar. Sprinkle with cracked black pepper, if desired.

PER SERVING 31.4g total fat (10.3g saturated); 1455kj (348 cal); 2.5g carbohydrate; 13.1g protein; 2.4g fibre

Char-grilled thai beef salad

PREPARATION TIME 15 MINUTES (PLUS REFRIGERATION TIME) **COOKING TIME** 10 MINUTES **SERVES** 4

In Thailand the beef is always served rare. To avoid toughening it, never turn the beef more than once during cooking. Standing meat after cooking allows it to relax and the juices to settle so that it is more succulent.

- 500g beef rump steak
- ¼ cup (60ml) fish sauce
- ¼ cup (60ml) lime juice
- 3 lebanese cucumbers (390g), seeded, sliced thinly
- 4 fresh small red thai chillies, sliced thinly
- 8 green onions, sliced thinly
- 250g cherry tomatoes, quartered
- 1 cup loosely packed vietnamese mint leaves
- 1 cup loosely packed coriander leaves
- 1 tablespoon grated palm sugar
- 2 teaspoons dark soy sauce
- 1 clove garlic, crushed

1 Combine beef with 2 tablespoons of the fish sauce and 1 tablespoon of the juice in large bowl, cover; refrigerate 3 hours or overnight.
2 Drain beef; discard marinade. Cook beef on heated oiled grill plate (or grill or barbecue) until browned both sides and cooked as desired. Cover beef, stand 5 minutes; slice thinly.
3 Meanwhile, combine cucumber, chilli, onion, tomato and herbs in large bowl. Place remaining fish sauce and remaining juice with sugar, soy sauce and garlic in screw-top jar; shake well. Add beef and dressing to salad; toss gently to combine.

PER SERVING 7.8g total fat (3.2g saturated); 978kj (234 cal); 8.9g carbohydrate; 29.8g protein; 3.9g fibre

Old-fashioned chicken salad

PREPARATION TIME 40 MINUTES **COOKING TIME** 15 MINUTES **SERVES** 4

Cooling chicken in the poaching liquid keeps it moist and flavoursome.

- 1 litre (4 cups) boiling water
- 1 litre (4 cups) chicken stock
- 700g chicken breast fillets
- 1 long french bread stick, sliced thinly
- 2 tablespoons olive oil
- ½ cup (150g) mayonnaise
- ½ cup (120g) sour cream
- 2 tablespoons lemon juice
- 4 trimmed celery stalks (400g), sliced thinly
- 1 medium white onion (150g), chopped finely
- 3 dill pickles (150g), sliced thinly
- 2 tablespoons finely chopped fresh flat-leaf parsley
- 1 tablespoon finely chopped fresh tarragon
- 1 large butter lettuce

1 Bring the water and stock to a boil in large frying pan; poach chicken, covered, about 10 minutes or until cooked. Cool chicken in liquid 10 minutes; slice thinly. Discard liquid.
2 Meanwhile, preheat grill. Brush both sides of bread slices with oil; toast under grill until browned lightly both sides.
3 Whisk mayonnaise, sour cream and juice in small bowl. Place chicken in large bowl with celery, onion, pickle and herbs; toss gently to combine.
4 Place lettuce leaves on serving platter; top with salad and bread, then mayonnaise.

PER SERVING 40.3g total fat (12.4g saturated); 3377kj (808 cal); 55.4g carbohydrate; 52.4g protein; 7.7g fibre

Lettuces & other leaves

Buy them in small quantities, use them while they're spanking fresh and be famous for your leafy salads.

MIZUNA
A Japanese mustard green now widely grown and used in Australia, either alone or in mesclun (see below). Its jagged green leaves have a mild, aromatic flavour.

WATERCRESS
Sprigs of dark-green watercress look pretty and give a fresh, peppery tang to a salad or a sandwich. Lovely dressed with walnut or hazelnut oil and lemon juice, with a few nuts scattered over the top.

CORAL LETTUCE
A soft lettuce with either red or green, tightly crinkled leaves; one of the baby greens that makes up the mixture sold as mesclun. Dress lightly and use within a day or two of purchase.

COS LETTUCE
Robust and flavoursome, cos is just right for rich dressings and substantial companions such as egg or bacon. Its outer leaves are often coarse. Baby cos, a miniature variety, has less wastage.

LAMB'S LETTUCE (MACHE)
The tender, velvety leaves of lamb's lettuce are considered a luxury. It has a mild, refreshing, almost nutty flavour, best with a light dressing. Sold in punnets and available in the cooler months.

CURLY ENDIVE
Also known as frisée, curly endive belongs to the chicory family and has its characteristic bitterness played against grassy freshness. Particularly good with beetroot.

OAK-LEAF LETTUCE

The soft, floppy leaves of red or green oak-leaf lettuce are decoratively indented and curled. An ideal lettuce to grow because the leaves can be harvested one at a time.

MIGNONETTE LETTUCE

This is a small, soft-leafed lettuce, but crisper and glossier than coral or oak-leaf. It has a good grassy flavour with just a delicate suggestion of bitterness. Comes in red and green varieties.

WITLOF (BELGIAN ENDIVE, CHICORY)

Crisp, tightly furled witlof tastes mild and fresh with a touch of bitterness. It is grown in the dark to keep the leaves white and minimise bitterness. Comes in red-tipped and green-tipped varieties.

ROCKET

The assertive flavour of rocket has been described as roast beef with a peppery tang. Good with char-grilled vegetables, strong cheeses and balsamic vinegar. Does not store well; buy it the day you will use it.

RADICCHIO

A sturdy member of the chicory family whose refreshing bitter flavour is appreciated both raw and cooked. Comes in numerous varieties, often called after their places of origin, such as round-headed Verona or long-headed Treviso.

MESCLUN

An assortment of baby greens, which may include coral, mignonette, oak-leaf or butter lettuce, rocket, spinach, curly endive, mizuna and/or radicchio. Buy more than you need and discard any tired bits.

This makes a delicious light lunch. For a more substantial meal add slices of grilled chicken, crisp bacon and quartered hard-boiled eggs.

Caesar salad

PREPARATION TIME 25 MINUTES **COOKING TIME** 5 MINUTES **SERVES** 4

7 slices thick white bread
2 tablespoons light olive oil
100g parmesan
1 large cos lettuce, torn
5 anchovy fillets, drained, halved lengthways

CAESAR DRESSING
1 egg
1 clove garlic, crushed
2 tablespoons lemon juice
½ teaspoon dijon mustard
5 drained anchovy fillets
¾ cup (180ml) light olive oil

1 Discard crusts; cut bread into 1cm cubes. Heat oil in large frying pan; cook bread, stirring, until browned and crisp. Drain croutons on absorbent paper.
2 Meanwhile, make caesar dressing.
3 Using vegetable peeler, shave cheese into long pieces.
4 Place lettuce, half of the croutons, half of the cheese, half of the anchovies and half of the dressing in large bowl; toss gently to combine.
5 Serve salad sprinkled with remaining croutons, anchovies and cheese and drizzle with remaining dressing.

CAESAR DRESSING Blend or process egg, garlic, juice, mustard and anchovy fillets until smooth. With motor operating, add oil in thin, steady stream; process until dressing thickens.

PER SERVING 61.8g total fat (12.9g saturated); 3118kj (746 cal); 26g carbohydrate; 20.3g protein; 5.8g fibre

---

This classic German salad is good with ham and hot or cold corned beef. To make it into a one-dish meal, use continental frankfurters instead of bacon; add 2 teaspoons wholegrain mustard and 1 tablespoon finely chopped fresh dill to the dressing.

German hot potato salad

PREPARATION TIME 10 MINUTES **COOKING TIME** 15 MINUTES **SERVES** 4

4 eggs
4 bacon rashers (280g), rind removed, chopped coarsely
750g baby new potatoes
2 pickled gherkins, chopped finely
1 tablespoon finely chopped fresh flat-leaf parsley
⅔ cup (200ml) mayonnaise
⅓ cup (80g) sour cream
2 teaspoons lemon juice

1 Cover eggs with water in medium saucepan; cover pan, bring to a boil. Reduce heat; simmer, uncovered, 7 minutes. Drain. Cool eggs under cold water; shell and halve.
2 Meanwhile, cook bacon in medium heated frying pan until browned and crisp; drain on absorbent paper. Combine egg and bacon in large bowl.
3 Boil, steam or microwave potatoes until tender; drain. Halve potatoes, add to bowl.
4 Combine remaining ingredients in small saucepan; stir over low heat until warm. Pour over potato mixture; mix gently.

PER SERVING 37.6g total fat (12.0g saturated); 2546kj (609 cal); 40.2g carbohydrate; 25.6g protein; 4.2g fibre

Salade niçoise

PREPARATION TIME 1 HOUR **COOKING TIME** 5 MINUTES **SERVES** 4

There are many versions of this popular dish, but an authentic salade niçoise (originally from the provençal city of Nice) always includes ingredients that speak of this sun-kissed region of France: tomatoes, capers, olives and garlic. A typical recipe includes anchovies, tuna, egg and raw vegetables.

200g green beans, trimmed

1 medium red onion (170g), cut into thin wedges

4 medium egg tomatoes (300g), seeded, cut into thin wedges

3 trimmed celery stalks (300g), sliced thinly

3 hard-boiled eggs, quartered

12 anchovy fillets, drained, halved lengthways

425g can tuna in oil, drained, flaked

¾ cup (100g) niçoise olives

2 tablespoons drained baby capers, rinsed

2 tablespoons finely shredded fresh basil leaves

LEMON GARLIC DRESSING

½ cup (125ml) olive oil

¼ cup (60ml) lemon juice

1 clove garlic, crushed

1 teaspoon white sugar

1 Boil, steam or microwave beans until just tender, drain. Rinse under cold water; drain.

2 Meanwhile, make lemon garlic dressing.

3 Layer onion, tomato, celery, egg, beans, anchovy fillets and tuna on serving platter, sprinkle with olives, capers and basil; drizzle with dressing.

LEMON GARLIC DRESSING Place ingredients in screw-top jar; shake well.

PER SERVING 44.3g total fat (7.1g saturated); 2424kj (580 cal); 14g carbohydrate; 29.9g protein; 4.5g fibre

---

Greek salad

PREPARATION TIME 25 MINUTES **SERVES** 4

The authentic way of presenting this salad is to leave the fetta in a whole piece and sit it on the top of the salad.

4 medium egg tomatoes (300g), chopped coarsely

2 lebanese cucumbers (260g), chopped coarsely

2 medium green capsicums (400g), sliced thinly

1 medium red onion (170g), cut into thin wedges

1 cup (150g) seeded kalamata olives

150g greek sheep-milk fetta

1 teaspoon crushed dried rigani

½ cup (125ml) olive oil

1 Combine tomato, cucumber, capsicum, onion and olives in large bowl.

2 Break cheese into large pieces; top salad with cheese. Sprinkle with rigani; drizzle with olive oil.

PER SERVING 37.8g total fat (9.8g saturated); 1852kj (443 cal); 15.4g carbohydrate; 9.8g protein; 3.4g fibre

1

2

3

4

Chef's salad

PREPARATION TIME 20 MINUTES **COOKING TIME** 25 MINUTES **SERVES** 4

This universal favourite appears on hotel room-service menus all over the world.

350g chicken breast fillets

1 large cos lettuce, torn

3 medium egg tomatoes (225g), cut into thick wedges

200g thinly sliced leg ham

100g thinly sliced jarlsberg cheese

3 hard-boiled eggs, quartered

WHITE WINE VINAIGRETTE

½ cup (125ml) olive oil

¼ cup (60ml) white wine vinegar

2 teaspoons wholegrain mustard

1 teaspoon white sugar

1 Preheat oven to moderate (180°C/160°C fan-forced).
2 Cook chicken in heated oiled large frying pan until browned both sides.
3 Place chicken in shallow baking dish; bake, uncovered, about 15 minutes or until cooked through. Cover chicken, stand 5 minutes; slice thinly.
4 Meanwhile, make white wine vinaigrette.
5 Divide lettuce among serving bowls; layer with chicken, tomato, ham, cheese and egg, then drizzle with vinaigrette.

WHITE WINE VINAIGRETTE Place ingredients in screw-top jar; shake well.

PER SERVING 44.3g total fat (11g saturated); 2537kj (607 cal); 5.7g carbohydrate; 44.5g protein; 4.6g fibre

For a creamier dressing, place the ingredients in a blender and process until thick and opaque.

Panzanella

PREPARATION TIME 25 MINUTES **SERVES** 4

Panzanella is a traditional Italian bread salad. As a variation, cut the soft white centre of the bread into small cubes, drizzle with 2 tablespoons olive oil; toss until well coated. Place the bread cubes on an oven tray, sprinkle on 2 tablespoons finely grated parmesan and toast in a moderate oven for about 10 minutes.

½ long loaf stale ciabatta

6 medium tomatoes (900g), seeded, chopped coarsely

2 trimmed celery stalks (200g), chopped coarsely

1 lebanese cucumber (130g), peeled, seeded, chopped coarsely

1 medium red onion (170g), chopped coarsely

RED WINE VINAIGRETTE

¼ cup (60ml) red wine vinegar

½ cup (125ml) olive oil

1 clove garlic, crushed

¼ cup finely shredded fresh basil leaves

1 Discard soft centre from bread; cut crust into 2cm cubes.
2 Make red wine vinaigrette.
3 Place bread in large bowl with tomato, celery, cucumber, onion and dressing; toss gently to combine.

RED WINE VINAIGRETTE Place ingredients in screw-top jar; shake well.

PER SERVING 30.8g total fat (4.3g saturated); 1906kj (456 cal); 35.3g carbohydrate; 7.0g protein; 4.9g fibre

1 CHEF'S SALAD **2** PANZANELLA **3** CRUNCHY FRIED NOODLE COLESLAW [P 148] **4** WITLOF AND NASHI SALAD [P 148]

To make this salad a light meal toss through shredded barbecued chicken with the other ingredients. For extra heat, add 1 tablespoon Thai sweet chilli sauce to the dressing.

Crunchy fried noodle coleslaw

PREPARATION TIME 35 MINUTES **SERVES** 8

10 trimmed red radishes (150g)

1 large red capsicum (350g), sliced thinly

1 small chinese cabbage (700g), shredded finely

6 green onions, chopped finely

1 cup (80g) bean sprouts

½ cup (70g) roasted slivered almonds

2 x 100g packets fried noodles

SWEET AND SOUR DRESSING

⅔ cup (160ml) peanut oil

2 tablespoons white wine vinegar

2 tablespoons brown sugar

2 tablespoons light soy sauce

2 teaspoons sesame oil

1 clove garlic, crushed

1 Slice radishes into matchstick-sized pieces.

2 Make sweet and sour dressing.

3 Place radish in large bowl with vegetables, sprouts, almonds, noodles and dressing; toss gently to combine.

SWEET AND SOUR DRESSING Place ingredients in screw-top jar; shake well.

PER SERVING 26.5g total fat (4.7g saturated); 1230kj (311 cal); 11.8g carbohydrate; 5.0g protein; 3.7g fibre

---

If you prefer, you could use other soft cheeses, such as cream cheese, ricotta, goat cheese or fetta, instead of the blue cheese.

Witlof and nashi salad

PREPARATION TIME 35 MINUTES **COOKING TIME** 15 MINUTES **SERVES** 4

3 pieces lavash

150g blue cheese

½ cup (125ml) buttermilk

2 tablespoons milk

20g butter

2 teaspoons brown sugar

2 medium apples (300g), cored, cut into thick wedges

500g witlof, leaves separated

2 small green oak-leaf lettuces, torn

2 medium nashi (400g), cut into thin wedges

1 cup (120g) roasted pecans

1 Preheat oven to moderate (180°C/160°C fan-forced).

2 Cut lavash into 3cm-wide strips. Place on oven tray; toast, uncovered, about 8 minutes or until crisp.

3 Meanwhile, blend or process cheese, buttermilk and milk until smooth. Place buttermilk dressing in small bowl; cover surface with plastic wrap to prevent skin forming.

4 Heat butter and sugar in medium frying pan; cook apple, turning occasionally, until coated all over with caramel mixture.

5 Divide lavash among serving plates, top with witlof, lettuce, apple, nashi and nuts; drizzle with dressing.

PER SERVING 40.6g total fat (12.6g saturated); 2608kj (624 cal); 40.1g carbohydrate; 19.5g protein; 12.9g fibre

Grilled vegetable salad

PREPARATION TIME 15 MINUTES **COOKING TIME** 20 MINUTES **SERVES** 6

So that the flavours of the grilled vegetables and the dressing can infuse and soften, make this salad the day before you serve it.

- 2 medium green capsicums (400g)
- 2 medium red capsicums (400g)
- 2 medium yellow capsicums (400g)
- 1 large red onion (300g), cut into thick wedges
- 2 medium green zucchini (240g), sliced thinly lengthways
- 2 medium yellow zucchini (240g), sliced thinly lengthways
- 6 baby eggplants (360g), sliced thinly lengthways

BALSAMIC DRESSING

- 2 tablespoons lemon juice
- 1 clove garlic, crushed
- ¼ cup (60ml) olive oil
- 2 tablespoons balsamic vinegar
- 1 tablespoon finely chopped fresh oregano

1 Quarter capsicums; discard seeds and membranes. Cut into thick strips.

2 Cook vegetables, in batches, on heated oiled grill plate (or grill or barbecue) until browned all over and tender.

3 Meanwhile, make balsamic dressing.

4 Place vegetables and dressing in large bowl; toss gently to combine.

BALSAMIC DRESSING Place ingredients in screw-top jar; shake well.

Left-over salad is great served on an antipasto platter, as a topping for pizza or in a pasta sauce.

PER SERVING 9.8g total fat (1.3g saturated); 669kj (160 cal); 10.5g carbohydrate; 4.9g protein; 5.0g fibre

---

Potato salad

PREPARATION TIME 25 MINUTES (PLUS COOLING TIME) **COOKING TIME** 20 MINUTES **SERVES** 8

This is the perfect salad for a picnic or barbecue. If you wish, you can make it ahead, omitting the tarragon, eggs and chives, and store in the fridge overnight. Add these ingredients shortly before serving and mix in lightly.

- 7 large pontiac potatoes (2kg), diced into 2cm pieces
- 2 tablespoons cider vinegar
- 1 large brown onion (200g), chopped finely
- 6 green onions, chopped finely
- 2 tablespoons finely chopped fresh tarragon
- 5 hard-boiled eggs, chopped coarsely
- ¾ cup (225g) mayonnaise
- ¾ cup (180g) sour cream
- 1 tablespoon wholegrain mustard
- 1 clove garlic, crushed
- 2 tablespoons finely chopped fresh chives

1 Boil, steam or microwave potato until just tender; drain. Place potato, in single layer, on tray; sprinkle with vinegar. Cool 15 minutes.

2 Place potato in large bowl with onions, tarragon, egg and combined remaining ingredients; toss gently to combine.

PER SERVING 21.5g total fat (8.0g saturated); 1630kj (390 cal); 36.0g carbohydrate; 10.6g protein; 4.2g fibre

Larb chicken

PREPARATION TIME 25 MINUTES **COOKING TIME** 20 MINUTES **SERVES** 4

Originating in northern Thailand, this salad is traditionally served cold; it is just the thing for those hot days when all you want is a light meal with refreshing flavours. If preferred, you can substitute pork or beef mince for the chicken mince. If you want to serve the salad cold, allow the meat to cool before combining it with the remaining ingredients.

2 tablespoons uncooked white long-grain rice

1 tablespoon peanut oil

5cm stick (10g) finely chopped fresh lemon grass

2 fresh small red thai chillies, chopped finely

2 cloves garlic, crushed

4cm piece fresh galangal (20g), chopped finely

750g chicken mince

1 lebanese cucumber (130g), seeded, sliced thinly

1 small red onion (100g), sliced thinly

1¼ cups (100g) bean sprouts

½ cup loosely packed fresh thai basil leaves

1 cup loosely packed fresh coriander leaves

4 large iceberg lettuce leaves

LARB DRESSING

⅓ cup (80ml) lime juice

2 tablespoons fish sauce

2 tablespoons kecap manis

2 tablespoons peanut oil

2 teaspoons grated palm sugar

½ teaspoon sambal oelek

1 Make larb dressing.

2 Heat dry wok; stir-fry rice until browned lightly. Blend or process (or crush using mortar and pestle) rice until it resembles fine breadcrumbs.

3 Heat oil in same wok; stir-fry lemon grass, chilli, garlic and galangal until fragrant. Remove from wok. Stir-fry chicken in same wok, in batches, until cooked through.

4 Return chicken and lemon grass mixture to wok with about a third of the dressing; stir-fry 5 minutes or until mixture thickens slightly.

5 Place chicken mixture in large bowl with cucumber, onion, sprouts, herbs and remaining dressing; toss gently to combine. Place lettuce leaves on serving plates; divide larb among leaves, sprinkle with ground rice.

LARB DRESSING Place ingredients in screw-top jar; shake well.

PER SERVING 21.9g total fat (4.7g saturated); 1781kj (426 cal); 12.3g carbohydrate; 43.0g protein; 3.2g fibre

LARB CHICKEN

This salad makes the perfect accompaniment to grilled or barbecued meat, especially lamb.

Three-bean salad

PREPARATION TIME 35 MINUTES **SERVES** 6

300g can white beans, rinsed, drained

300g can red kidney beans, rinsed, drained

500g packet frozen broad beans, thawed, peeled

1 medium tomato (150g), peeled, seeded, chopped coarsely

1 small red onion (100g), chopped coarsely

¼ cup coarsely chopped fresh flat-leaf parsley

LEMON AND GARLIC DRESSING

¼ cup (60ml) olive oil

¼ cup (60ml) lemon juice

1 clove garlic, crushed

½ teaspoon white sugar

1 Make lemon and garlic dressing.

2 Place ingredients and dressing in large bowl; toss gently to combine.

LEMON AND GARLIC DRESSING Place ingredients in screw-top jar; shake well.

PER SERVING 9.9g total fat (1.4g saturated); 757kj (181 cal); 9.3g carbohydrate; 9.3g protein; 8.7g fibre

---

There is a good range of flavoured canned tuna on the market these days. For something a little different try using lemon pepper, smoked or chilli-flavoured tuna. This recipe also works well with canned salmon.

Tuna pasta salad

PREPARATION TIME 20 MINUTES **COOKING TIME** 10 MINUTES **SERVES** 4

500g spiral pasta

2 x 425g cans tuna in oil

440g can corn kernels, drained

1 small red onion (100g), sliced thinly

1 medium red capsicum (200g), sliced thinly

2 trimmed celery stalks (200g), sliced thinly

¼ cup chopped fresh flat-leaf parsley

¼ cup (75g) mayonnaise

1 tablespoon yogurt

1 clove garlic, crushed

2 teaspoons finely grated lemon rind

2 tablespoons lemon juice

2 tablespoons wholegrain mustard

1 Cook pasta in large saucepan of boiling water until pasta is just tender; drain.

2 Meanwhile, drain tuna; reserve 2 tablespoons of the oil.

3 Place pasta and tuna in large bowl with corn, onion, capsicum, celery and parsley.

4 Combine remaining ingredients and reserved tuna oil in small bowl. Add to pasta mixture; toss gently to combine.

PER SERVING 30.4g total fat (4.6g saturated); 4021kj (962 cal); 109.0g carbohydrate; 57.2g protein; 8.9g fibre

Gremolata lamb pasta salad

PREPARATION TIME 20 MINUTES **COOKING TIME** 20 MINUTES **SERVES** 4

For a delicious crumb coating for chicken or fish, combine 2 tablespoons olive oil and 1 cup fresh breadcrumbs with the gremolata ingredients

250g farfalle

600g asparagus, trimmed, halved

200g green beans, trimmed, halved crossways

1 tablespoon vegetable oil

800g lamb backstraps

2 teaspoons dijon mustard

3 shallots (75g), sliced thinly

⅓ cup (50g) roasted pine nuts

⅓ cup loosely packed fresh flat-leaf parsley leaves

LEMON DIJON DRESSING

2 tablespoons lemon juice

2 tablespoons olive oil

2 teaspoons dijon mustard

GREMOLATA

2 cloves garlic, chopped finely

1 tablespoon finely grated lemon rind

½ cup finely chopped fresh flat-leaf parsley

1 Make lemon dijon dressing and gremolata.
2 Cook pasta until just tender; drain. Rinse under cold water; drain.
3 Meanwhile, boil, steam or microwave asparagus and beans, separately, until tender.
4 Heat oil in large frying pan; cook lamb, uncovered, until cooked as desired. Spread lamb with mustard; then gremolata. Cover; stand 5 minutes. Slice lamb thickly.
5 Combine pasta, vegetables and lamb in large bowl with shallots, pine nuts, parsley and dressing; toss gently to combine.

LEMON DIJON DRESSING Combine ingredients in screw-top jar; shake well.
GREMOLATA Combine ingredients in small bowl.

PER SERVING 41.2g total fat (10.5g saturated); 3319kj (794 cal); 47.4g carbohydrate; 55g protein; 7.1g fibre

---

Simple pasta salad

PREPARATION TIME 30 MINUTES **COOKING TIME** 15 MINUTES **SERVES** 6

The secret of a great pasta salad is to cook the pasta to just "al dente", which means that it should still be slightly chewy; the pasta will then be able to absorb some of the dressing and still remain slightly firm to the bite.

375g shell pasta

6 bacon rashers

1½ cups (450ml) mayonnaise

⅓ cup (95g) wholegrain mustard

¾ cup (180ml) buttermilk

3 trimmed celery stalks (300g), sliced thinly

1 large red capsicum (350g), chopped finely

1 bunch (15g) fresh chives, chopped finely

2 tablespoons finely chopped fresh flat-leaf parsley

1 Cook pasta in large saucepan of boiling water, uncovered, until just tender. Cool.
2 Meanwhile, remove rind from bacon then cut bacon into small pieces. Cook bacon, stirring, in heated medium frying pan until brown and crisp; drain on absorbent paper.
3 Whisk mayonnaise, mustard and buttermilk in large bowl.
4 Add pasta, bacon, remaining ingredients and dressing to bowl; toss gently to combine.

PER SERVE 29.2g total fat (5.0g saturated); 2466kj (590 cal); 61.7g carbohydrate; 18.0g protein; 4.5g fibre

SEAFOOD

Seafood

Fish is the gourmet's delight, immensely versatile and the basis of some exquisite dishes. It is also the hurried cook's friend, being easy to prepare and quick to cook, and is highly nutritious but low in fat. Even that small amount of fat gives us omega-3 fatty acids which help to prevent heart disease.

BUYING AND STORING FISH AND SHELLFISH

- Fresh fish and shellfish smell fishy but fresh. Whole fish feel springy, have full, bright eyes, red gills and shiny, slippery skin. Fillets and cutlets have a sheen and feel springy.
- Cooked shellfish should smell pleasant; the shells should be clean and undamaged.
- Buy crabs, lobsters and shellfish alive or cooked, but never uncooked (green or raw) unless they've been frozen correctly. Once killed, they deteriorate rapidly.
- Refrigerate fresh seafood, loosely covered with foil, as soon as you get home. Don't refrigerate live shellfish; store in a clean, damp hessian bag in a cool place.
- Commercially frozen seafood is better than home-frozen because the process is faster.

CLEANING, FILLETING AND SKINNING FRESH FISH

SCALING Working on plenty of newspaper, grasp the tail and scrape firmly from the tail to the head with a rigid knife or serrated fish-scaler. Repeat on the other side.

CLEANING Slit open along the belly from the vent (near the tail) to the head, pull out the guts and scrape away any dark blood from the backbone. Rinse well.

FILLETING Remove the head, hold the tail and, starting from the tail, using a thin, flexible knife, cut along the backbone towards the head to remove the meat in one piece. Repeat on the other side. For flat fish, cut down the centre and remove the fillets on each side.

SKINNING Place the fillet on a board, skin-side down and tail end towards you. Dip the fingers of one hand in salt and hold the tail end firmly, while with the other hand you ease a thin knife between the flesh and skin, pushing rather than cutting the flesh off the skin.

COOKING FISH AND SHELLFISH

The simple imperatives for this do not change. Give all seafood your undivided attention while it is on the heat. Take fish (or shellfish) off the heat the moment it turns opaque and white (or lighter pink, for prawns and pink fish such as salmon). To check whole fish, push a toothpick into the thickest part; when it slides in easily, the fish is done. Take whole prawns off the heat as soon as their shells change colour. For larger whole shellfish, see recipes. Have everything else needed for the meal ready and serve all seafood immediately.

PREPARING SHELLFISH

A fishmonger usually does this, but if you are preparing it yourself, proceed as follows.

CLAMS, COCKLES AND PIPIS Place in a bucket of cold, salted water for 1 hour to purge. Open by steaming or, if only the meat is wanted, open uncooked as for mussels.

CRABS Kill crabs as humanely as possible; we recommend freezing for at least 2 hours before cooking. When cooked, to obtain the meat, protect your hands with gloves; twist off the claws and legs, prise off the undershell, discard the spongy gills from the body and cut the undershell in two. Pick out the body meat, breaking the shell as needed. Reserve the creamy "mustard" from the top shell. Crack the claws and legs and pull out the meat.

LOBSTERS, BALMAIN BUGS, SCAMPI, YABBIES, MARRON Freeze live lobsters, bugs and scampi for at least 2 hours before cooking, as for crabs. Kill yabbies and marron by freezing for 2 hours. When cooked, to obtain the meat, cut in half lengthways, discard the intestine and head sac and reserve any roe and brown "mustard" or tomalley. Loosen the tail flesh from the shell, then return to the cleaned shell for serving, if you wish.

MUSSELS Never buy mussels that are open; choose tightly closed ones and keep them refrigerated until you're ready to cook them. Scrub mussels all over with a stiff brush, remove the beards by pulling sharply downwards, then rinse again. Open by steaming or, if only the meat is wanted, place in warm, salted water; as the mussels open, insert the point of a short knife between the shells and slide toward the hinge to sever the muscle.

OCTOPUS Cut off the head/body section below the eyes to remove the tentacles in one piece. Push the beak up through the centre of the tentacles, cut off and discard. If using the body, cut out the eyes with kitchen shears or a very sharp knife then turn the body inside out and discard all organs and the ink sac, unless it is to be used in the recipe. Rinse well. To tenderise, pound with a heavy mallet, rub with salt and rub off the skin under running water. Baby octopus should not need tenderising but if in doubt, freeze overnight then thaw, which partially breaks down the structure of the flesh and makes it more tender.

OYSTERS To open, protect your hands with metal-mesh or other tough gloves and, using an oyster knife, insert the tip between the shells near the hinge, where there is a small gap, and lever the shells apart. Cut through the muscle joining the oyster to the upper shell.

PRAWNS For cooked prawns, remove the head, shell, legs and tail (unless the recipe specifies otherwise) and remove the intestinal vein by slitting down the back and pulling it out. For uncooked prawns to be cooked in the shell, make a small slit in the centre back, insert a toothpick under the vein and draw it out.

SCALLOPS To open live scallops, put them on ice. When they start to open, hold each one, dark-side up and hinge facing away, insert the point of a strong knife from the right-hand side between shells and slide along to cut the hinge. Discard the top shell and peel the dark mantle and gut off the pale meat by scraping from hinge to front, pinching the mantle firmly to the knife. Slide the knife under the meat to separate it from the shell and trim off any remaining dark threads or wispy brown beard.

SQUID, CALAMARI, CUTTLEFISH All cephalopods, or molluscs without shells, with the calamari being a tender, imminently edible, variety of squid. Pull the head and tentacles from the body; the guts will come out with them. Cut off the tentacles in one piece, press the centre and discard the beak that pops out, along with the head and guts. Remove the transparent quill from inside the body, and pull off the fins. Dip your fingers in salt and rub off the skin from the body, fins and tentacles. Rinse well.

Seared tuna with kipfler smash and salsa verde

PREPARATION TIME 25 MINUTES **COOKING TIME** 20 MINUTES **SERVES** 4

If your kipfler potatoes are young and quite small, scrubbing (as opposed to peeling) them will be sufficient.

1kg kipfler potatoes, peeled, halved
30g butter
1 tablespoon olive oil
4 x 175g tuna steaks
80g baby rocket leaves

SALSA VERDE
½ cup firmly packed fresh parsley
¼ cup loosely packed fresh mint
⅔ cup (160ml) olive oil
¼ cup (50g) drained capers, rinsed
2 teaspoons dijon mustard
2 tablespoons lemon juice
8 anchovy fillets, drained
1 clove garlic, quartered

1 Boil, steam or microwave potato until tender; drain. Using potato masher, crush potato roughly in large bowl with butter and oil. Cover to keep warm.
2 Meanwhile, make salsa verde. Cook fish, in batches, on heated oiled grill plate (or grill or barbecue) until browned both sides and cooked as desired.
3 Divide rocket and potato among serving plates; top with fish, drizzle with salsa verde.

Salsa verde, with mayonnaise replacing the olive oil and half the lemon juice, makes a splendid dressing for potato salad.

SALSA VERDE Blend or process ingredients until just combined.

PER SERVING 57.9g total fat (14g saturated); 3674kj (879 cal); 34.9g carbohydrate; 52.6g protein; 6.3g fibre

Sardines in chermoulla with tomato salsa

PREPARATION TIME 25 MINUTES (PLUS REFRIGERATION TIME) **COOKING TIME** 10 MINUTES **SERVES** 6

Popular in Morocco, chermoulla (also tchermila, chermoula, charmoula or sharmula) combines fragrant seasonings with oil. Dried chermoulla spice mixes are now readily available.

½ cup firmly packed fresh flat-leaf parsley leaves
½ cup firmly packed fresh coriander leaves
4 cloves garlic, crushed
1 teaspoon finely grated lemon rind
1 teaspoon ground cumin
1 teaspoon sweet paprika
1cm piece fresh ginger (5g), grated
⅓ cup (80ml) peanut oil
1 medium red onion (170g), chopped finely
24 fresh sardines (1kg), boned
4 medium tomatoes (600g), seeded, chopped finely

1 Blend or process herbs, garlic, rind, cumin, paprika, ginger, ¼ cup of the oil and half of the onion until smooth. Reserve 2 tablespoons of the chermoulla.
2 Combine sardines with chermoulla in large bowl, cover; refrigerate 1 hour. Combine tomato, remaining onion and oil and reserved chermoulla in small bowl to make a salsa.
3 Cook sardines on heated oiled grill plate (or grill or barbecue); serve with tomato salsa.

PER SERVING 15.8g total fat (9.2g saturated); 1597kj (382 cal); 39.8g carbohydrate; 18g protein; 4.2g fibre

SEARED TUNA WITH KIPFLER SMASH AND SALSA VERDE

If you are watching your weight, make a delicious, healthy salsa instead of the dressing. Combine the corn, onion, chilli and coriander with 1 chopped mango and 2 chopped vine-ripened tomatoes, and season with lime juice.

Grilled mahi mahi with roasted corn and chilli salad

PREPARATION TIME 30 MINUTES **COOKING TIME** 25 MINUTES **SERVES** 4

8 trimmed corn cobs (2kg)

1 egg yolk

1 clove garlic, crushed

2 tablespoons lime juice

1 teaspoon dijon mustard

¾ cup (180ml) olive oil

1 medium red onion (170g), chopped finely

2 fresh small red thai chillies, chopped finely

⅓ cup coarsely chopped fresh coriander

4 x 200g mahi mahi steaks

1 Cook corn on heated oiled grill plate (or grill or barbecue) until browned lightly and tender.

2 Meanwhile, blend or process egg yolk, garlic, juice and mustard until smooth. With motor operating, gradually add oil in thin, steady stream; process until mayonnaise thickens slightly.

3 Using sharp knife, remove kernels from cobs. Place kernels in large bowl with onion, chilli, coriander and half of the mayonnaise; toss gently to combine.

4 Cook fish on same heated grill plate until browned both sides and cooked as desired. Divide corn salad among serving plates; top with fish, drizzle with remaining mayonnaise.

PER SERVING 51.3g total fat (8g saturated); 4071kj (974 cal); 62.5g carbohydrate; 57.8g protein; 17.4g fibre

---

Balmain bug heads and shells don't make good stock – they often have a strong iodine taste. Use scampi if balmain bugs are unavailable.

Balmain bugs and citrus salad

PREPARATION TIME 20 MINUTES **COOKING TIME** 15 MINUTES **SERVES** 4

2kg uncooked balmain bugs

1 tablespoon olive oil

2 teaspoons finely grated orange rind

2 tablespoons orange juice

1 tablespoon wholegrain mustard

CITRUS SALAD

1 medium grapefruit (425g)

1 large orange (300g)

1 lemon (140g)

150g curly endive, chopped coarsely

1 large fennel bulb (550g), trimmed, sliced thinly

1 tablespoon wholegrain mustard

1 tablespoon olive oil

1 Make citrus salad.

2 Place balmain bugs upside down on board; cut tail from body, discard body. Halve tail lengthways; discard back vein. Cook bugs on heated grill plate until cooked through.

3 Place bugs in large bowl with combined oil, rind, juice and mustard; toss to coat in mixture. Serve with citrus salad.

CITRUS SALAD Cut unpeeled grapefruit, orange and lemon into thick wedges; cook on heated oiled grill plate (or grill or barbecue) until browned. Place fruit in large bowl with endive, fennel and combined mustard and oil; toss gently to combine.

PER SERVING 11.0g total fat (1.6g saturated); 1254kj (300 cal); 11.8g carbohydrate; 35.8g protein; 5.1g fibre

---

Salt-baked whole ocean trout in saffron cream sauce

PREPARATION TIME 30 MINUTES **COOKING TIME** 1 HOUR 10 MINUTES **SERVES** 6

Cooking salt is coarser than table salt but not as large-grained as sea salt; it is sold packaged in bags in most supermarkets. You need a large (approximately 28cm x 38cm) baking dish in order to accommodate the fish used in this recipe.

- 3kg coarse cooking salt
- 4 egg whites
- 2.4kg whole ocean trout
- 1.5kg baby new potatoes
- 3 whole unpeeled bulbs garlic, halved horizontally
- ¼ cup (60ml) olive oil
- 15 sprigs fresh thyme
- 350g watercress, trimmed

SAFFRON CREAM SAUCE

- ¾ cup (180ml) dry white wine
- ¼ cup (60ml) white wine vinegar
- 1 tablespoon lemon juice
- pinch saffron threads
- ½ cup (125ml) cream
- 170g butter, chilled, chopped finely

1 Preheat oven to moderately hot (200°C/180°C fan-forced).
2 Mix salt with egg whites in medium bowl (mixture will have the consistency of wet sand). Spread about half of the salt mixture evenly over the base of a large baking dish; place fish on salt mixture then cover completely (except for tail) with remaining salt mixture. Bake 1 hour.
3 Meanwhile, combine potatoes, garlic, oil and thyme in large shallow baking dish; place in oven on shelf below fish. Bake, uncovered, 50 minutes or until potatoes are tender.
4 Make saffron cream sauce.
5 Remove fish from oven; break salt crust with heavy knife, taking care not to cut into fish. Discard salt crust; transfer fish to large serving plate. Carefully remove skin from fish; flake meat into large pieces.
6 Divide watercress, potatoes and garlic among serving plates; top with fish, drizzle sauce over fish.

SAFFRON CREAM SAUCE Combine wine, vinegar, juice and saffron in medium saucepan; bring to a boil. Boil, uncovered, until mixture is reduced to about a third. Add cream; return to a boil. Whisk in butter, one piece at a time, until mixture thickens slightly. Pour into medium jug; cover to keep warm.

PER SERVING 49.9g total fat (24.5g saturated); 3453kj (826 cal); 34.4g carbohydrate; 52.0g protein; 7.5g fibre

Make a Vietnamese-style main-course salad by tossing the grilled prawns, raw fruits and herb sauce (to which you've added a finely chopped red chilli and a teaspoon of fish sauce) with softened and chilled rice vermicelli.

Grilled prawns with tropical fruits

PREPARATION TIME 15 MINUTES **COOKING TIME** 15 MINUTES **SERVES** 4

24 uncooked large king prawns (1.6kg)

¼ medium pineapple (300g), chopped coarsely

1 slightly firm large mango (600g), chopped coarsely

1 slightly firm large banana (230g), chopped coarsely

¼ cup loosely packed fresh mint leaves

2 tablespoons lime juice

HERB SAUCE

½ cup loosely packed fresh mint leaves

½ cup loosely packed fresh flat-leaf parsley leaves

1 clove garlic, quartered

2 tablespoons lime juice

1 tablespoon olive oil

1 Make herb sauce.
2 Cook prawns on heated oiled grill plate (or grill or barbecue) until cooked through.
3 Meanwhile, cook fruit on same heated grill plate until browned lightly.
4 Combine prawns and fruit in large bowl with mint and juice. Divide prawn mixture among serving bowls; drizzle with sauce.

HERB SAUCE Blend or process ingredients until combined.

PER SERVING 6.2g total fat (0.9g saturated); 1434kj (343 cal); 25.0g carbohydrate; 43.8g protein; 4.5g fibre

---

Never fill a saucepan or wok more than half-full with oil for deep-frying as it may boil up suddenly when the food is added. The oil is hot enough when a piece of potato or bread dropped in the oil sizzles briskly and browns in about a minute.

Fish in beer batter with chips

PREPARATION TIME 30 MINUTES (PLUS REFRIGERATION TIME) **COOKING TIME** 30 MINUTES **SERVES** 4

1½ cups (225g) self-raising flour

1 egg

1½ cups (375ml) beer

5 large potatoes (1.5kg)

vegetable oil, for deep-frying

8 flathead fillets (880g)

TARTARE SAUCE

¾ cup (180g) crème fraîche

2 teaspoons finely grated lemon rind

2 teaspoons lemon juice

2 tablespoons finely chopped sweet gherkins

2 tablespoons drained capers, rinsed, chopped finely

1 tablespoon finely chopped fresh chives

1 fresh small red thai chilli, chopped finely

1 Whisk flour, egg and beer in medium bowl until smooth, cover; refrigerate 1 hour.
2 Meanwhile, preheat oven to moderate (180°C/160°C fan-forced). Cut peeled potatoes into 1cm slices; cut slices into 1cm-thick chips. Pat potato chips dry with absorbent paper.
3 Heat oil in wok or large saucepan; deep-fry chips, in batches, until browned and cooked through. Place chips on absorbent paper on oven tray; place, uncovered, in oven.

4 Reheat oil. Dip fish in beer batter; drain away excess batter. Deep-fry fish, in batches, until browned and crisp.

5 Meanwhile, make tartare sauce.

6 Divide fish and chips among serving plates; serve with tartare sauce.

TARTARE SAUCE Combine ingredients in small bowl.

▭ **PER SERVING** 41.5g total fat (15.9g saturated); 4025kj (963 cal); 82.9g carbohydrate; 60.4g protein; 7.3g fibre

The best varieties of potato to use for chips are bintje, nicola or russet burbank.

Thai fish burgers with sour and sweet green salad

PREPARATION TIME 20 MINUTES **COOKING TIME** 15 MINUTES **SERVES** 4

Gently shape and pat the burgers to an even thickness so they will cook evenly. To stop them sticking, spray or brush them lightly with oil; make sure you have a good spatula for turning them.

500g blue-eye fillets, chopped coarsely

1 tablespoon fish sauce

1 tablespoon kecap manis

1 clove garlic, quartered

1 fresh small red thai chilli, quartered

50g green beans, trimmed, chopped coarsely

¼ cup (20g) shredded coconut

¼ cup finely chopped fresh coriander

½ loaf turkish bread (215g)

⅓ cup (80ml) sweet chilli sauce

SOUR AND SWEET GREEN SALAD

2 cups (120g) finely shredded iceberg lettuce

40g snow pea sprouts, chopped coarsely

1 telegraph cucumber (400g), seeded, sliced thinly

2 tablespoons lime juice

1 tablespoon fish sauce

1 tablespoon brown sugar

1 Blend or process fish, fish sauce, kecap manis, garlic and chilli until smooth. Using hand, combine fish mixture in large bowl with beans, coconut and coriander; shape mixture into four burgers.

2 Cook burgers on heated oiled grill plate (or grill or barbecue) about 15 minutes or until cooked through.

3 Meanwhile, make sour and sweet green salad.

4 Cut bread in half; split halves horizontally. Toast, cut-side up. Divide bread among serving plates; top with salad, burgers and chilli sauce.

SOUR AND SWEET GREEN SALAD Place ingredients in medium bowl; toss gently.

▭ **PER SERVING** 8.6g total fat (4.1g saturated); 1559kj (373 cal); 36.6g carbohydrate; 33.9g protein; 5.7g fibre

Bought teriyaki sauce may be used, but it's stronger than home-made. Dilute it with mirin, sake or water.

Salmon teriyaki

PREPARATION TIME 10 MINUTES (PLUS SOAKING TIME) **COOKING TIME** 10 MINUTES **SERVES** 4

4 salmon fillets (700g), skinned

½ cup (120g) finely grated white radish

TERIYAKI MARINADE

⅔ cup (160ml) japanese soy sauce

⅔ cup (160ml) mirin

2 tablespoons sake

1 tablespoon caster sugar

1 Make teriyaki marinade. Add salmon, stand 10 minutes. Drain; reserve marinade.
2 Meanwhile, soak radish in small bowl of iced water for 15 minutes; drain well.
3 Cook salmon on heated oiled grill plate (or grill or barbecue), brushing occasionally with marinade, until cooked as desired. Bring reserved marinade to a boil in small saucepan; simmer, uncovered, 5 minutes. Serve salmon with radish, drizzle with sauce.

TERIYAKI MARINADE Combine ingredients in medium bowl; stir until sugar dissolves.

PER SERVING 12.5g total fat (2.8g saturated); 1350kj (323 cal); 7.8g carbohydrate; 36.6g protein; 0.5g fibre

---

To add a distinctly Spanish flavour to this dish add ¼ teaspoon smoked paprika to the onion and garlic.

Octopus braised in red wine

PREPARATION TIME 15 MINUTES **COOKING TIME** 1 HOUR 45 MINUTES **SERVES** 6

⅓ cup (80ml) olive oil

600g baby onions, halved

4 cloves garlic, crushed

1.5kg cleaned baby octopus

1½ cups (375ml) dry red wine

⅓ cup (95g) tomato paste

⅓ cup (80ml) red wine vinegar

3 large tomatoes (660g), peeled, seeded, chopped coarsely

2 bay leaves

1 fresh long red chilli, chopped finely

10 anchovy fillets, drained, chopped coarsely

⅓ cup finely chopped fresh oregano

1 cup coarsely chopped fresh flat-leaf parsley

1 Heat oil in large saucepan; cook onion and garlic, stirring, until onion softens. Add octopus; cook, stirring, until just changed in colour.
2 Add wine; cook, stirring, about 5 minutes or until liquid is reduced by about a third. Add paste, vinegar, tomato, bay leaves, chilli and anchovies; bring to a boil. Reduce heat; simmer, covered, 1 hour. Uncover; simmer about 30 minutes or until sauce thickens and octopus is tender. Remove from heat; stir in oregano and parsley.

PER SERVING 17.2g total fat (2.8g saturated); 2111kj (505 cal); 7.9g carbohydrate; 67.5g protein; 2.8g fibre

1 SALMON TERIYAKI **2** OCTOPUS BRAISED IN RED WINE **3** BARBECUED SEAFOOD AND GREEN MANGO SALAD [P 166] **4** DEEP-FRIED PERCH WITH CHILLI LIME DRESSING [P 166]

1

2

3

4

The lemon grass dressing can be made a day ahead and shaken up again just before using. Any left-over dressing is good on cold fish or chicken.

Barbecued seafood and green mango salad

PREPARATION TIME 40 MINUTES (PLUS REFRIGERATION TIME) **COOKING TIME** 15 MINUTES **SERVES** 4

250g squid hoods

500g uncooked medium king prawns

500g cleaned baby octopus, halved lengthways

1 large green mango (600g)

200g mizuna

250g cherry tomatoes, halved

100g snow pea sprouts

1 cup loosely packed fresh vietnamese mint leaves

LEMON GRASS DRESSING

2 fresh small red thai chillies, chopped finely

2 tablespoons fish sauce

1 tablespoon grated palm sugar

⅓ cup (80ml) peanut oil

15cm stick (30g) finely chopped fresh lemon grass

¼ cup (60ml) lime juice

1 Make lemon grass dressing.

2 Cut squid down centre to open out; score the inside in diagonal pattern then cut into 5cm squares. Shell and devein prawns, leaving tails intact. Combine squid and prawns in large bowl with octopus and half of the dressing, cover; refrigerate 2 hours.

3 Meanwhile, slice mango thinly; cut slices into matchstick-sized pieces.

4 Cook seafood, in batches, on heated oiled grill plate (or grill or barbecue) until browned and cooked as desired.

5 Place seafood and mango in large bowl with remaining dressing and remaining ingredients; toss gently to combine.

LEMON GRASS DRESSING Place ingredients in screw-top jar; shake well.

PER SERVING 22.6g total fat (4.2g saturated); 2387kj (571 cal); 27.5g carbohydrate; 61g protein; 5.6g fibre

---

To make this into a more substantial salad, combine some shredded Chinese cabbage, 2 tablespoons roasted cashews, ½ cup bean sprouts and about 100g fried noodles with the cucumber and carrots.

Deep-fried perch with chilli lime dressing

PREPARATION TIME 15 MINUTES **COOKING TIME** 20 MINUTES **SERVES** 4

3 lebanese cucumbers (390g)

3 medium carrots (360g)

4 x 400g whole ocean perch, cleaned

vegetable oil, for deep-frying

½ cup (75g) plain flour

2 teaspoons salt

2 teaspoons ground white pepper

CHILLI LIME DRESSING

⅓ cup (80ml) sweet chilli sauce

2 teaspoons fish sauce

¼ cup (60ml) lime juice

1 teaspoon sesame oil

2 tablespoons coarsely chopped fresh thai basil

2 tablespoons coarsely chopped fresh vietnamese mint

2 tablespoons water

1 Using vegetable peeler, slice cucumbers and carrots lengthways into thin strips; combine in medium bowl.

2 Discard fish heads; score each fish three times both sides.

3 Heat oil in wok or large saucepan. Combine flour, salt and pepper in medium shallow bowl; coat fish in flour mixture. Deep-fry fish, in two batches, until browned lightly and cooked through; drain on absorbent paper.
4 Meanwhile, make chilli lime dressing.
5 Divide carrot mixture among serving plates; top with fish, drizzle with dressing.

CHILLI LIME DRESSING Place ingredients in screw-top jar; shake well.

PER SERVING 26.6g total fat (3.5g saturated); 2638kj (631 cal); 24.1g carbohydrate; 70.9g protein; 5.3g fibre

Lobster with flavoured butter and lemon grass mash

PREPARATION TIME 20 MINUTES (PLUS REFRIGERATION AND FREEZING TIME)
COOKING TIME 30 MINUTES **SERVES** 4

- 2 medium live lobsters (1.5kg)
- 100g butter, softened
- 2 tablespoons coarsely chopped fresh vietnamese mint
- 2 tablespoons coarsely chopped fresh thai basil
- 1 tablespoon coarsely chopped garlic chives
- 1 clove garlic, crushed
- 2 stalks lemon grass
- 4 large potatoes (1.2kg), chopped coarsely
- 10cm piece fresh ginger (50g), sliced thickly
- 2½ cups (625ml) milk

1 Place lobsters in freezer for 2 hours; this is the most humane way of killing them. Place lobster, upside down, on chopping board; cut through body and tail. Turn lobster around and cut through head; pull lobster halves apart. Discard white gills, the light-green liver and grey thread running down centre back of tail. Refrigerate, covered, until required.
2 Combine butter, herbs and garlic in small bowl, cover; refrigerate until required.
3 Cut each lemon grass stalk into three pieces. Combine lemon grass, potato, ginger and milk in medium saucepan; bring to a boil. Reduce heat; simmer, covered, stirring occasionally, about 25 minutes or until potato is tender. Strain potato mixture over medium bowl; reserve ¼ cup spiced milk. Discard ginger and lemon grass; return potato to pan. Mash over low heat until smooth; stir in reserved spiced milk.
4 Meanwhile, cook lobster on heated oiled grill plate (or grill or barbecue) until browned and just changed in colour.
5 Serve lobster, topped with flavoured butter, on lemon grass mash.

PER SERVING 29.7g total fat (18.1g saturated); 3139kj (751 cal); 40.0g carbohydrate; 78.3g protein; 4.5g fibre

For a hearty thick soup use fish stock in place of half the milk and cook the potatoes until soft; process in batches until smooth, then stir in the chopped herbs and top with pieces of cooked lobster.

Herbs

Fresh herbs are a culinary gift – their beauty, their fragrance and, of course, the difference they make to your cooking.

CHERVIL
Fennel-flavoured chervil is elegant in a salad and with fish, poultry and vegetables. One of the classic French fines herbes (along with parsley, chives and tarragon).

DILL
Feathery, dark green, anise-flavoured dill looks decorative and tastes brilliant with fresh, smoked and cured fish, shellfish, cucumber, beetroot, potatoes and rice, and in a vinaigrette or mayonnaise.

VIETNAMESE MINT
Not really a mint, but a smooth-leafed herb with a flavour rather like peppery coriander. Used all over South-East Asia in laksas, salads, stir-fries and curries; also, shredded, as a garnish.

CORIANDER
Coriander is essential to South-East Asian, Latin American and Middle Eastern cooking. Every part of the plant has its distinctive lemon/anise/sage flavour, and all parts are used – leaves, stems and roots.

OREGANO
The big savoury taste and scent of oregano speak of Mediterranean cooking, from Greek moussaka and zucchini or eggplant dishes to Italian pizza and pasta sauces. Unlike most herbs, it has the best taste and greatest pungency when dried.

GARLIC CHIVES
Their flat, dark-green leaves are a great Asian ingredient, used in soups, stir-fries, egg dishes and noodle dishes. Also good for snipping over salads and into mayonnaise and cream cheese.

THAI BASIL

Quite different from common or sweet basil, Thai basil has pungent aniseed-flavoured leaves. An essential ingredient in many Thai curries, soups and other dishes; also a customary garnish.

TARRAGON

French tarragon, with its subtle aniseed flavour, is the desirable one; Russian and Mexican tarragon are more coarse-tasting. Tarragon complements chicken, eggs and veal, and is sublime in sauce béarnaise.

BASIL

The soul of pesto and the herb that makes tomatoes sing. A summer annual, but you can enjoy its clove-and-anise perfume in winter by processing with a little olive oil and freezing.

SAGE

The pungent, balsamic taste and scent of sage are classic in stuffings for duck and pork and with veal and prosciutto for saltimbocca. Deep-fried sage leaves are a delicious garnish for veal, liver, brains and pumpkin ravioli.

MARJORAM

Closely related to and similar in flavour to oregano, but milder and sweeter. Delicious in herb mixtures for omelettes, stuffings, herb scones and herb and cream-cheese sandwiches. As with oregano, many chefs prefer dried marjoram to fresh.

PARSLEY

The trusty workhorse of herbs, as right for a fresh garnish as it is in potato salad, scrambled eggs or a sauce for corned beef. Flat-leaf (also called continental) parsley has a stronger taste than curly parsley.

For a professional touch, wrap lemon halves in muslin, which prevents squirting and catches any pips.

Hot seafood platter

PREPARATION TIME 40 MINUTES (PLUS REFRIGERATION TIME) **COOKING TIME** 25 MINUTES **SERVES** 4

- 500g dhufish cutlets, skinned
- 500g calamari rings
- 1 cup (150g) plain flour
- ¼ cup (60ml) milk
- 4 eggs, beaten lightly
- 2 cups (140g) stale breadcrumbs
- ⅓ cup finely chopped fresh flat-leaf parsley
- ½ cup (40g) finely grated parmesan
- 1 tablespoon finely grated lemon rind
- 1 medium tomato (150g), halved
- 1 tablespoon vodka
- ¼ teaspoon Tabasco
- 2 teaspoons worcestershire sauce
- 1 teaspoon lemon juice
- vegetable oil, for shallow-frying
- 12 oysters, on the half shell
- 1 trimmed celery stalk (100g), chopped finely
- 3 slices pancetta (45g), chopped finely
- 8 uncooked large king prawns (560g)
- 2 lemons, cut into wedges

1 Halve fish lengthways, discard bones; cut each half into three pieces. Coat fish and calamari in flour, then in combined milk and egg, and finally in combined breadcrumbs, parsley, cheese and rind. Cover; refrigerate 15 minutes.
2 Meanwhile, using largest holes on a four-sided grater, grate tomato halves, from cut-side, into small bowl; discard skin. Stir in vodka, sauces and juice.
3 Heat oil in large deep frying pan; shallow-fry fish and calamari, in batches, until browned and cooked through. Drain on absorbent paper.
4 Meanwhile, preheat grill. Place oysters on oven tray. Divide tomato mixture among oysters; top with celery and pancetta. Place under grill 5 minutes or until pancetta is crisp.
5 Cook prawns on heated oiled grill plate (or grill or barbecue) until browned lightly and cooked through. Arrange seafood and lemon wedges on large serving platter.

PER SERVING 39.8g total fat (9.5g saturated); 3917kj (937 cal); 52.8g carbohydrate; 87g protein; 4g fibre

---

Tenderising squid in coconut milk with 1 tablespoon fish sauce will also impart a wonderful flavour.

Salt and pepper squid

PREPARATION 15 MINUTES **COOKING TIME** 5 MINUTES **SERVES** 4

- 500g squid hoods
- ¾ cup (110g) plain flour
- 1 tablespoon coarse cooking salt
- 1 tablespoon cracked black pepper
- vegetable oil, for deep-frying
- 150g mesclun

CHILLI DRESSING

- ½ cup (125ml) sweet chilli sauce
- 1 teaspoon fish sauce
- ¼ cup (60ml) lime juice
- 1 clove garlic, crushed

1 Cut squid down centre to open out; score the inside in diagonal pattern then cut into 2cm strips.

2 Combine flour, salt and pepper in large bowl; add squid. Coat in flour mixture; shake off excess.
3 Heat oil in wok or large saucepan; deep-fry squid, in batches, until tender and browned lightly. Drain on absorbent paper.
4 Meanwhile, make chilli dressing.
5 Serve squid, on mesclun, drizzled with chilli dressing.

CHILLI DRESSING Place ingredients in screw-top jar; shake well.

PER SERVING 9.8g total fat (1.6g saturated); 1267kj (303 cal); 26.7g carbohydrate; 24.9g protein; 3.4g fibre

For a quick way to coat squid, place the flour, salt and pepper in a strong plastic bag with the squid; grip the bag tightly closed, then gently shake. Remove the squid from the bag; shake off any excess flour.

Macadamia prawn cakes

PREPARATION TIME 30 MINUTES **COOKING TIME** 30 MINUTES **SERVES** 4

Roasted cashews or peanuts can be used instead of macadamias. For a touch of heat, add a tablespoon of sweet chilli sauce to the prawn mixture.

¾ cup (180ml) orange juice
¼ cup (60ml) lemon juice
2cm piece fresh ginger (10g), chopped coarsely
1 teaspoon black peppercorns
2 tablespoons white vinegar
½ cup (125ml) dry white wine
½ cup (70g) roasted macadamias
750g cooked shelled small king prawns
1 egg, beaten lightly
1 tablespoon finely grated orange rind
4 green onions, chopped finely
1 ½ cups (105g) stale breadcrumbs
1 loaf turkish bread (430g)
2 tablespoons vegetable oil
4 egg yolks
250g butter, melted
80g watercress, trimmed

1 Combine juices, ginger, peppercorns, vinegar and wine in small saucepan; bring to a boil. Reduce heat; simmer, uncovered, about 5 minutes or until citrus mixture reduces to ½ cup. Remove from heat; strain into small jug.
2 Meanwhile, blend or process nuts until chopped finely; place in large bowl. Blend or process 500g of the prawns until mixture forms a paste; place in bowl with nuts. Add remaining prawns, egg, rind, onion and 1 cup of the breadcrumbs to nut mixture; mix well. Shape mixture into eight cakes. Press remaining breadcrumbs onto both sides of cakes; place on tray.
3 Cut bread into four pieces; split each piece in half horizontally. Toast, cut-side up; cover to keep warm.
4 Heat oil in large frying pan; cook cakes, in batches, until browned both sides and cooked through. Cover to keep warm.
5 Meanwhile, blend or process egg yolks with citrus mixture until combined. With motor operating, add butter in thin, steady stream; process until sauce thickens.
6 Place two pieces of toast on each serving plate; top with watercress then two cakes and drizzle with sauce.

PER SERVING 86.0g total fat (40.0g saturated); 5208kj (1246 cal); 71.6g carbohydrate; 40.1g protein; 6.2g fibre

A well-known secret among oyster farmers is to cook whole unopened oysters in their shells, on hot coals. They acquire a subtle smoked flavour, cooking in their own juices, and their lids pop open when they are ready to eat.

Dressing up oysters

JAPANESE OYSTERS WITH SHIITAKE MUSHROOMS

Combine 1 tablespoon sake, 2 tablespoons mirin, 1 tablespoon rice vinegar and 1 tablespoon tamari in small jug. Heat 1 tablespoon sesame oil in small frying pan; cook 100g thinly sliced fresh shiitake mushrooms, stirring, until tender. Add half of the sake mixture; cook, stirring, until liquid is absorbed. Divide mushroom mixture evenly among 12 oysters on the half shell; spoon remaining sake mixture over oysters. Serve oysters topped with thinly sliced green onions.

PER OYSTER 1.8g total fat (0.3g saturated); 117kj (28 cal); 0.5g carbohydrate; 1.5g protein; 0.2g fibre

OYSTERS WITH SALSA VERDE

Blend or process ⅓ cup coarsely chopped fresh flat-leaf parsley, 2 tablespoons coarsely chopped fresh mint, 2 teaspoons drained capers, 1 drained anchovy fillet, 1 quartered garlic clove, ½ teaspoon finely grated lemon rind, 1 teaspoon lemon juice and ½ teaspoon dijon mustard until chopped finely. With motor operating, add ⅓ cup olive oil in thin, steady stream; process until almost smooth. Divide salsa verde among 12 oysters on the half shell; sprinkle with a little finely grated lemon rind.

PER OYSTER 6.3g total fat (1.0g saturated); 263kj (63 cal); 0.2g carbohydrate; 1.4g protein; 0.2g fibre

GARLIC AND FENNEL CREAM OYSTERS

Melt 20g butter in small frying pan; cook 1 small thinly sliced fennel bulb and 1 clove crushed garlic, stirring, 5 minutes or until fennel is tender. Add 2 tablespoons dry white wine; cook, stirring, until wine evaporates. Stir in ⅓ cup cream; cook, stirring, until mixture thickens. Stir in 1 tablespoon finely chopped drained capers and 2 teaspoons finely chopped fresh flat-leaf parsley. Divide fennel mixture among 12 oysters on the half shell.

PER OYSTER 4.5g total fat (2.9g saturated); 209kj (50 cal); 0.6g carbohydrate; 1.4g protein; 0.2g fibre

OYSTERS WITH TOMATO, BACON AND BASIL

Heat 1 tablespoon olive oil in small frying pan; cook ½ small finely chopped red onion and 1 clove crushed garlic, stirring, until onion softens. Add 2 finely chopped rindless bacon rashers; cook, stirring, until browned lightly. Add 2 medium finely chopped seeded tomatoes; cook, stirring, until tomato just softens. Stir in 1 tablespoon finely shredded fresh basil. Preheat grill. Place 12 oysters on the half shell on oven tray; divide tomato mixture among oysters, top each with 1 teaspoon finely grated parmesan. Place under grill until cheese melts and is browned lightly.

PER OYSTER 3.1g total fat (1.0g saturated); 184kj (44 cal); 0.7g carbohydrate; 3.3g protein; 0.2g fibre

MEXICAN-STYLE FRIED OYSTERS

Preheat oven to moderate (180°C/160°C fan-forced). Make salsa by combining 1 small finely chopped tomato, ½ finely chopped yellow capsicum, ½ medium finely chopped red onion, 1 tablespoon finely chopped fresh coriander, 1 tablespoon olive oil, 1 tablespoon lime juice and 1 fresh small finely chopped red thai chilli in small bowl. Remove 12 oysters from shells. Heat shells on oven tray 5 minutes. Combine ½ cup polenta, ⅓ cup milk,

1 beaten egg and pinch cayenne pepper in small bowl. Heat enough vegetable oil to deep-fry in medium saucepan, dip oysters in polenta batter; deep-fry until browned lightly. Drain on absorbent paper. Return oysters to shells; top with salsa.

PER OYSTER 2.6g total fat (0.6g saturated); 238kj (57 cal); 5.4g carbohydrate; 2.8g protein; 0.5g fibre

CHEESE AND CHIVE SOUFFLED OYSTERS
Preheat oven to hot (220°C/200°C fan-forced). Melt 20g butter in small saucepan; add 2 teaspoons plain flour and cook, stirring, until mixture thickens and bubbles. Gradually add ¼ cup milk; cook, stirring, until mixture boils and thickens. Remove from heat; stir in 1 egg yolk, 2 tablespoons finely grated parmesan and 1 tablespoon finely chopped fresh chives. Beat 1 egg white in small bowl with electric mixer until soft peaks form; fold into yolk mixture. Place 12 oysters on the half shell on oven tray. Top oysters with soufflé mixture; sprinkle with combined 1 tablespoon stale breadcrumbs and ¼ teaspoon sweet paprika. Bake, uncovered, 5 minutes or until puffed. Serve immediately.

PER OYSTER 2.7g total fat (1.5g saturated); 163kj (39 cal); 1.2g carbohydrate; 2.6g protein; 0.1g fibre

---

Malaysian swordfish curry

PREPARATION TIME 25 MINUTES **COOKING TIME** 35 MINUTES **SERVES** 4

If you can't find shallots, substitute a medium brown onion and a small clove of crushed garlic.

- 6 fresh small red thai chillies, chopped coarsely
- 2 cloves garlic, quartered
- 10 shallots (250g), chopped coarsely
- 2 x 15cm sticks (60g) fresh lemon grass, coarsely chopped
- 5cm piece galangal (25g), quartered
- 1 teaspoon curry powder
- 1 teaspoon ground coriander
- ¼ teaspoon ground turmeric
- 2 tablespoons vegetable oil
- 1 tablespoon fish sauce
- 1⅔ cups (400ml) coconut milk
- 1⅔ cups (400ml) coconut cream
- 2 cups (400g) jasmine rice
- 4 x 220g swordfish steaks, skinned
- ¼ cup (10g) roasted flaked coconut
- 4 fresh kaffir lime leaves, shredded finely

1 Blend or process chilli, garlic, shallot, lemon grass, galangal, curry powder, coriander, turmeric and half of the oil until mixture forms a paste.
2 Heat remaining oil in large frying pan; cook paste, stirring, over medium heat about 3 minutes or until fragrant. Add sauce, coconut milk and cream; bring to a boil. Reduce heat; simmer, uncovered, about 15 minutes or until mixture thickens slightly.
3 Meanwhile, cook rice in large saucepan of boiling water, uncovered, until tender; drain.
4 Cook swordfish on heated oiled grill plate (or grill or barbecue), in batches, until browned both sides and cooked as desired.
5 Divide fish among serving bowls; top with sauce, sprinkle with coconut and lime leaves. Serve rice in separate bowl.

PER SERVING 57.8g total fat (40.6g saturated); 4661kj (1115 cal); 89g carbohydrate; 57g protein; 5.7g fibre

As easy as raita is to make, if you are in a hurry you can cheat and buy tzatziki, which is the Greek eqivalent of the Indian raita.

Curried blue-eye with lentils and raita

PREPARATION TIME 30 MINUTES **COOKING TIME** 45 MINUTES **SERVES** 4

1 cup (200g) brown lentils

1 cup (200g) green split peas

1 tablespoon vegetable oil

2 medium brown onions (300g), chopped finely

2 cloves garlic, crushed

4 dried curry leaves

2 bay leaves

2 cinnamon sticks

6 cardamom pods

6 cloves

½ teaspoon curry powder

¼ teaspoon ground coriander

1½ cups (375ml) chicken stock

4 x 200g blue-eye fillets, skinned

2 tablespoons mild curry paste

½ cup finely chopped fresh flat-leaf parsley

RAITA

2 lebanese cucumbers (260g), seeded

1 cup (280g) greek-style yogurt

1 tablespoon finely shredded fresh mint leaves

1 Cook lentils and split peas in separate medium saucepans of boiling water, uncovered, until just tender; drain.

2 Meanwhile, make raita.

3 Heat oil in large frying pan; cook onion and garlic, stirring, until onion softens. Add leaves, cinnamon, cardamom, cloves, curry powder and coriander; cook, stirring, until fragrant. Add stock; cook, stirring, 2 minutes. Remove from heat.

4 Spread fish with curry paste; cook on heated oiled grill plate (or grill or barbecue) until browned both sides and cooked as desired.

5 Meanwhile, place lentils, split peas and parsley in frying pan with spicy onion mixture; stir over heat until heated through. Serve fish on lentil mixture; top with raita.

RAITA Grate cucumber coarsely; drain in fine sieve 10 minutes. Combine drained cucumber in small bowl with yogurt and mint.

PER SERVING 17.5g total fat (4.3g saturated); 2859kj (684 cal); 52.3g carbohydrate; 70.9g protein; 15.3g fibre

CURRIED BLUE-EYE WITH LENTILS AND RAITA

Sashimi-grade salmon can be used in place of the tuna, and for extra heat in the dressing, add ¼ teaspoon wasabi or 1 finely chopped fresh small red thai chilli.

Tuna tartare

PREPARATION TIME 45 MINUTES **COOKING TIME** 5 MINUTES **SERVES** 4

200g green beans, trimmed, halved

600g piece sashimi tuna, diced into 1cm pieces

3 cups (240g) finely shredded chinese cabbage

4 green onions, sliced thinly

½ cup firmly packed fresh coriander leaves

2 cups (160g) bean sprouts

GINGER DRESSING

7cm piece fresh ginger (35g)

⅓ cup (80ml) lime juice

¼ cup (60ml) olive oil

1 tablespoon light soy sauce

2 teaspoons finely chopped coriander root

2 cloves garlic, crushed

2 teaspoons sesame oil

2 teaspoons caster sugar

1 Boil, steam or microwave beans until just tender; drain. Rinse under cold water; drain.

2 Make ginger dressing.

3 Place tuna in medium bowl with a third of the dressing; toss gently to combine.

4 Combine beans in large bowl with remaining ingredients and remaining dressing.

5 Divide undrained tuna among serving plates, shaping into mound; serve with salad.

GINGER DRESSING Cut ginger into thin strips; combine ginger with remaining ingredients.

PER SERVING 17.1g total fat (2.6g saturated); 899kj (215 cal); 5.8g carbohydrate; 7.7g protein; 4.5g fibre

---

Another delicious curing mixture for salmon is a combination of sugar, salt and pepper with ¼ cup vodka, 1 tablepoon lemon juice and 2 tablespoons each of finely grated lemon and orange rind. Follow the method given here.

Gravlax

PREPARATION TIME 20 MINUTES (PLUS REFRIGERATION TIME) **SERVES** 4

375g salmon fillet

⅓ cup (75g) caster sugar

¼ cup (70g) coarse cooking salt

2 tablespoons cracked black pepper

⅓ cup coarsely chopped fresh dill

⅓ cup coarsely chopped fresh chives

VINAIGRETTE

¼ cup (60ml) olive oil

1 tablespoon white wine vinegar

1 teaspoon lime juice

1 teaspoon cracked black pepper

1 tablespoon chopped fresh dill

1 Remove skin, bones and any fat from fish.

2 Combine sugar, salt, pepper, dill and chives in small bowl. Sprinkle half of the sugar mixture on tray lined with plastic wrap. Place fish on top of sugar mixture and sprinkle remaining sugar mixture over fish. Cover tightly with plastic wrap; refrigerate overnight.

3 Make vinaigrette.

4 Wash fish; pat dry. Slice fish thinly; serve fish topped with vinaigrette.

VINAIGRETTE Place ingredients in screw-top jar; shake well.

PER SERVING 20.3g total fat (3.4g saturated); 1384kj (331 cal); 18.9g carbohydrate; 18.4g protein; 0.1g fibre

Tuna, kingfish and salmon carpaccio

PREPARATION TIME 50 MINUTES (PLUS FREEZING AND REFRIGERATION TIME) **SERVES** 6

Carpaccio should be sliced paper-thin, and freezing the fish beforehand to firm it really helps to achieve this. Make sure you buy the freshest fish you can, from a reputable supplier.

- 350g piece sashimi tuna
- 350g piece sashimi kingfish
- 350g piece sashimi salmon
- ⅓ cup (80ml) lime juice
- ⅔ cup (160ml) lemon juice
- 4cm piece fresh ginger (20g), grated
- ¼ cup (60ml) light soy sauce
- 1 baby fennel (130g)
- ⅓ cup (80ml) olive oil
- 1 tablespoon drained baby capers, rinsed
- ½ small red onion (50g), sliced thinly
- 1 teaspoon finely chopped fresh dill

1 Tightly wrap fish, separately, in plastic wrap; freeze about 1 hour or until slightly firm.
2 Unwrap fish then slice as thinly as possible. Arrange slices on separate platters; drizzle tuna with lime juice, drizzle kingfish and salmon with lemon juice. Cover platters; refrigerate 1 hour.
3 Meanwhile, combine ginger and soy sauce in small jug; stand while fish is under refrigeration. Finely chop enough fennel leaves to make 1 level tablespoon; discard remaining leaves. Chop fennel bulb finely.
4 Drain excess juice from platters. To serve, divide fish among serving plates: drizzle tuna with strained sauce mixture; sprinkle kingfish with fennel, leaves and half of the oil; sprinkle salmon with capers, onion, dill and remaining oil. Serve carpaccio with crusty bread, if desired.

PER SERVING 21.1g total fat (4.5g saturated); 1488kj (356 cal); 2.4g carbohydrate; 39.2g protein; 0.6g fibre

---

Steamed scallops with asian flavours

PREPARATION TIME 15 MINUTES **COOKING TIME** 15 MINUTES **SERVES** 4

Scallops lend themselves to quick grilling, poaching, frying or steaming. If overcooked they shrivel and become tough. They are cooked as soon as the flesh becomes opaque.

- 1½ cups (300g) jasmine rice
- 3cm piece fresh ginger (15g)
- 20 scallops (800g), in half shell
- 10cm stick (20g) fresh lemon grass, thinly sliced
- 4 green onions, sliced thinly
- 1 tablespoon sesame oil
- ¼ cup (60ml) kecap manis
- ¼ cup (60ml) light soy sauce

1 Cook rice in large saucepan of boiling water, uncovered, until just tender; drain.
2 Meanwhile, slice ginger thinly; cut slices into thin strips. Place scallops, in batches, in single layer in large bamboo steamer fitted over large saucepan of boiling water; top with ginger, lemon grass and onion. Steam, covered, 5 minutes or until cooked as desired.
3 Divide scallops among serving plates; top with combined remaining ingredients. Serve with rice.

PER SERVING 5.5g total fat (0.9g saturated); 1513kj (362 cal); 61.2g carbohydrate; 15.6g protein; 0.9g fibre

Mussels or "moules" served with french fries or "frites" are the national dish of Belgium. You can substitute wine for beer or add ½ cup cream once the mussels are cooked.

Steamed belgian mussels

PREPARATION TIME 30 MINUTES **COOKING TIME** 10 MINUTES **SERVES** 4

1.3kg large black mussels
2 teaspoons olive oil
2 cloves garlic, crushed
3 shallots (75g), sliced thinly
2 trimmed celery stalks (200g), sliced thinly
2 large egg tomatoes (180g), chopped finely
½ cup (125ml) dry white wine
200g curly endive
½ cup loosely packed fresh flat-leaf parsley leaves
¼ cup coarsely chopped fresh chives
¼ cup (60ml) lemon juice

1 Scrub mussels; remove beards.
2 Heat oil in wok; stir-fry garlic, shallot and celery until shallot softens. Add tomato; stir-fry 30 seconds. Add wine; bring to a boil. Reduce heat; simmer, uncovered, until liquid reduces by half. Add mussels; simmer, covered, about 5 minutes or until mussels open (discard any that do not).
3 Add remaining ingredients to wok; toss gently to combine. Serve mussels with broth in large serving bowls.

PER SERVING 4.0g total fat (0.7g saturated); 548kj (131 cal); 6.8g carbohydrate; 10.4g protein; 2.9g fibre

Notoriously difficult to eat, but irresistibly delicious. Have finger bowls filled with warm water and lemon slices – and plenty of large napkins – with this dish. And don't wear a white shirt or eat this on a first date.

Singapore chilli crab

PREPARATION TIME 45 MINUTES (PLUS STANDING TIME) **COOKING TIME** 35 MINUTES **SERVES** 4

2 live mud crabs (1.5kg)
2 tablespoons peanut oil
1 fresh long red chilli, chopped finely
2 cloves garlic, crushed
2cm piece fresh ginger (10g), grated
⅓ cup (80ml) chinese cooking wine
400g can crushed tomatoes
1 cup (250ml) water
1 tablespoon brown sugar
2 lebanese cucumbers (260g), halved lengthways, sliced thinly
10cm piece fresh ginger (50g), sliced thinly
3 green onions, sliced thinly
¼ cup loosely packed fresh coriander leaves
2 fresh long red chillies, sliced thinly

1 Place crabs in in freezer for 2 hours. Remove back shell from crabs; discard grey gills. Rinse crab; using cleaver or heavy knife, chop each body into six pieces.
2 Heat oil in wok; stir-fry chopped chilli, garlic and grated ginger until fragrant. Add wine; cook until liquid has reduced by half. Add undrained tomatoes, the water and sugar; bring to a boil. Remove and reserve half of the sauce in small bowl.
3 Add half of the crab to wok, reduce heat; simmer, covered, about 15 minutes or until crab has changed in colour. Stir in half of the cucumber. Transfer to large serving bowl; cover to keep warm. Repeat with reserved sauce, remaining crab and cucumber.

4 Cut sliced ginger into thin strips. Combine with onion, coriander and sliced chilli; sprinkle over crab. Serve with steamed jasmine rice, if desired.

☐ **PER SERVING** 10.5g total fat (1.8g saturated); 1066kj (255 cal); 11.2g carbohydrate; 23.7g protein; 2.6g fibre

---

Hot and sour fish steamed in banana leaves

PREPARATION TIME 25 MINUTES (PLUS MARINATING TIME) **COOKING TIME** 20 MINUTES **SERVES** 4

The advantage of steaming in a bamboo steamer compared with a metal one is that the steam disperses instead of condensing and dripping onto the food. If you have to use a metal steamer, cover the fish with baking paper to protect it.

4 medium whole bream (1kg)

1 large banana leaf

3 fresh small red thai chillies, sliced thinly

2 fresh kaffir lime leaves, shredded finely

2 green onions, sliced thinly

¼ cup loosely packed fresh coriander leaves

¼ cup loosely packed fresh thai basil leaves

2 sticks fresh lemon grass

kitchen string

LIME AND SWEET CHILLI DRESSING

¼ cup (60ml) sweet chilli sauce

2 tablespoons fish sauce

2 tablespoons lime juice

2 tablespoons peanut oil

1 clove garlic, crushed

1cm piece fresh ginger (5g), grated

1 Make lime and sweet chilli dressing.

2 Score fish both sides through thickest part of flesh; place on large tray, drizzle with half of the lime and sweet chilli dressing. Cover; refrigerate 1 hour.

3 Meanwhile, trim banana leaf into four 30cm squares. Using tongs, dip one square at a time into large saucepan of boiling water; remove immediately. Rinse under cold water; pat dry with absorbent paper.

4 Place leaves on work surface. Combine chilli, lime leaves, onion, coriander and basil in medium bowl. Halve lemon grass sticks lengthways, then halve crossways; you will have eight pieces.

5 Place two pieces cut lemon grass on each leaf; place one fish on each. Top fish with equal amounts of the herb mixture then fold opposite corners of the leaf to enclose centre part of fish; secure each parcel with kitchen string.

6 Place parcels, in single layer, in large bamboo steamer fitted over large saucepan of boiling water; steam, covered, in two batches, about 15 minutes or until fish is cooked through. Serve fish still in parcel, sprinkled with remaining dressing.

LIME AND SWEET CHILLI DRESSING Place ingredients in screw-top jar; shake well.

☐ **PER SERVING** 16.4g total fat (4.1g saturated); 1150kj (275 cal); 4.1g carbohydrate; 27.3g protein; 1.4g fibre

Cioppino

PREPARATION TIME 30 MINUTES **COOKING TIME** 40 MINUTES **SERVES** 4

New England is famous for chowder, and California for cioppino. Developed in San Francisco by southern European immigrants, it is an adaptation of Italian and Portuguese seafood stews. Try serving this tasty dish with linguine, or add potatoes or risoni for a meal in a bowl.

2 teaspoons olive oil

1 medium brown onion (150g), chopped coarsely

1 baby fennel bulb (130g), trimmed, chopped coarsely

3 cloves garlic, crushed

6 medium tomatoes (900g), chopped coarsely

425g can crushed tomatoes

½ cup (125ml) dry white wine

1½ cups (375ml) fish stock

2 cooked blue swimmer crabs (650g)

500g uncooked large king prawns

450g swordfish steaks

400g clams, rinsed

150g scallops

¼ cup coarsely chopped fresh basil

½ cup coarsely chopped fresh flat-leaf parsley

1 Heat oil in large saucepan; cook onion, fennel and garlic, stirring, until onion softens. Add fresh tomato; cook, stirring, about 5 minutes or until pulpy. Stir in undrained tomatoes, wine and stock; bring to a boil. Reduce heat; simmer, covered, 20 minutes.

2 Meanwhile, remove back shell from crabs; discard grey gills. Rinse crab; chop each crab into four pieces. Shell and devein prawns, leaving tails intact. Chop fish into 2cm pieces.

3 Add clams to pan; simmer, covered, about 5 minutes or until clams open (discard any that do not). Add remaining seafood; cook, stirring occasionally, about 5 minutes or until seafood has changed in colour and is cooked as desired. Remove from heat; stir in herbs.

PER SERVING 6.5g total fat (1.4g saturated); 1492kj (357 cal); 12.1g carbohydrate; 54.0g protein; 5.8g fibre

---

Lime and ginger ceviche

PREPARATION TIME 20 MINUTES (PLUS REFRIGERATION TIME) **SERVES** 4

Ceviche is the national dish of Peru, and uses citrus juice to partially "cook" raw seafood. When selecting fish choose a sashimi-grade firm-fleshed white fish. In Peru many believe that ceviche is the best cure for a hangover.

24 scallops (600g), roe removed

400g piece sashimi kingfish, sliced thinly

¼ cup finely grated lime rind

1½ teaspoons sea salt

1 teaspoon cracked black pepper

4 green onions, sliced thinly

8cm piece fresh ginger (40g), grated

4 fresh kaffir lime leaves, shredded finely

1 cup (250ml) lime juice

1 Split scallops in half through centre. Place in large shallow dish with remaining ingredients; toss to coat seafood in marinade. Spread evenly in dish to ensure seafood is submerged in marinade. Cover; refrigerate, stirring occasionally, about 1½ hours or until seafood softens and is almost opaque.

2 Divide ceviche among serving plates; serve with crusty bread and lime wedges, if desired.

PER SERVING 2.9g total fat (0.9g saturated); 631kj (151 cal); 2.3g carbohydrate; 28.0g protein; 1.0g fibre

CIOPPINO

How do you know if the oil is hot enough? Dip in a wooden chopstick or the handle of a wooden spoon; the oil is hot enough when bubbles form all around the object.

Honey prawns

PREPARATION TIME 30 MINUTES **COOKING TIME** 15 MINUTES **SERVES** 4

1.5kg uncooked large king prawns
1 cup (150g) self-raising flour
1 ¼ cups (310ml) water
1 egg
⅓ cup (50g) cornflour
vegetable oil, for deep-frying
2 teaspoons peanut oil
¼ cup (90g) honey
100g snow pea sprouts
2 tablespoons roasted sesame seeds

1 Shell and devein prawns, leaving tails intact. Sift self-raising flour into medium bowl; gradually whisk in the water and egg until batter is smooth. Coat prawns in cornflour; shake off excess. Dip into batter, one at a time; shake off excess.
2 Heat vegetable oil in wok or large frying pan; deep-fry prawns, in batches, until browned lightly. Drain on absorbent paper.
3 Heat peanut oil in same cleaned wok; heat honey, uncovered, until bubbling. Add prawns; coat with honey. Serve prawns on snow pea sprouts and sprinkle with seeds.

PER SERVING 16.8g total fat (2.6g saturated); 2487kj (595 cal); 62g carbohydrate; 46.5g protein; 2.8g fibre

---

An interesting addition to this recipe is to add ½ teaspoon sichuan pepper to the salt and pepper mixture or use chilli powder instead of the black pepper.

Salt and pepper salmon cutlets with white radish and snow pea salad

PREPARATION TIME 25 MINUTES **COOKING TIME** 10 MINUTES **SERVES** 4

2 teaspoons sea salt
1 teaspoon cracked black pepper
4 x 265g salmon cutlets
1 tablespoon peanut oil
½ small white radish (200g)
150g snow pea sprouts
200g snow peas, trimmed, sliced thinly
1 fresh long red chilli, sliced thinly
½ cup loosely packed fresh thai basil leaves
½ cup loosely packed fresh vietnamese mint leaves
2 small pink grapefruit (460g)

CHILLI AND LIME VINAIGRETTE
2 tablespoons sweet chilli sauce
2 tablespoons lime juice
1 tablespoon rice vinegar
5cm stick (10g) finely chopped fresh lemon grass
1 clove garlic, crushed
2 teaspoons brown sugar

1 Make chilli and lime vinaigrette.
2 Combine salt and pepper in large bowl, add fish; turn to coat in mixture. Heat oil in large frying pan; cook fish, in batches, until browned both sides and cooked as desired.
3 Meanwhile, slice radish thinly lengthways; cut slices into matchsticks. Combine radish in large bowl with sprouts, snow peas, chilli and herbs.

4 Segment grapefruit over salad. Add half of the vinaigrette to salad; toss gently to combine. Divide salad among serving plates; top with fish, drizzle with remaining vinaigrette.

CHILLI AND LIME VINAIGRETTE Place ingredients in screw-top jar; shake well.

PER SERVING 20.6g total fat (4.4g saturated); 1956kj (468 cal); 20.2g carbohydrate; 47.6g protein; 5.2g fibre

---

Whiting parcels with porcini and sun-dried tomatoes on soft polenta

A modern take on the traditional method of cooking "en papillote" (in sealed packets), this recipe uses aluminium foil rather than baking paper to enclose the ingredients. Cooking this way reduces the need for any added oil and allows the flavours to mingle and intensify.

PREPARATION TIME 20 MINUTES (PLUS STANDING TIME) **COOKING TIME** 20 MINUTES **SERVES** 4

30g dried porcini mushrooms
30g butter, melted
1 clove garlic, crushed
½ cup (75g) drained sun-dried tomatoes, chopped coarsely
2 tablespoons finely shredded fresh sage
8 x 120g whiting fillets, with skin
2 tablespoons lemon juice

SOFT POLENTA
2 cups (500ml) chicken stock
2 cups (500ml) milk
1 cup (250ml) water
1 cup (170g) polenta
⅓ cup (25g) coarsely grated parmesan

1 Place mushrooms in small heatproof bowl, cover with boiling water; stand 20 minutes. Drain; chop coarsely. Combine mushrooms in medium bowl with butter, garlic, tomato and sage.
2 Preheat oven to hot (220°C/200°C fan-forced).
3 Centre four of the fillets, skin-side down, on four 60cm-pieces of lightly oiled foil; top each fillet with equal amounts of the mushroom mixture. Top with remaining fillets, skin-side up; drizzle with juice. Gather corners of foil together above fillets; twist to enclose securely. Place parcels on oven tray. Cook 15 minutes or until fish is cooked as desired.
4 Meanwhile, make soft polenta.
5 Discard foil from parcels just before serving fish on polenta.

SOFT POLENTA Combine stock, milk and the water in medium saucepan; bring to a boil. Gradually add polenta to liquid, stirring constantly. Reduce heat; simmer, stirring, about 10 minutes or until polenta thickens. Stir in cheese.

PER SERVING 15.8g total fat (9.2g saturated); 1597kj (382 cal); 39.8g carbohydrate; 18.2g protein; 4.2g fibre

To add extra flavour to this recipe add 1 finely chopped fresh small red thai chilli to the fish crust and ¼ cup seeded black olives and 2 tablespoons drained, rinsed baby capers to the potatoes when adding the capsicum.

Barramundi with kipflers and roasted capsicum

PREPARATION TIME 25 MINUTES **COOKING TIME** 40 MINUTES **SERVES** 4

½ cup (125ml) vegetable stock
1 tablespoon lemon juice
700g kipfler potatoes, halved lengthways
1 tablespoon finely grated lemon rind
⅓ cup coarsely chopped fresh oregano
1.2kg whole barramundi, cleaned
1 large red capsicum (350g), sliced thinly
1 large yellow capsicum (350g), sliced thinly
2 cloves garlic, crushed

1 Preheat oven to moderate (180°C/160°C fan-forced).
2 Combine stock, juice and potato in large baking dish; roast, uncovered, 10 minutes.
3 Meanwhile, combine rind and oregano in small bowl. Score fish both sides; press rind mixture into cuts and inside cavity. Place fish in lightly oiled large baking dish. Roast, uncovered, about 30 minutes.
4 Meanwhile, add capsicums and garlic to potato mixture; stir to combine. Roast, uncovered, about 30 minutes or until potato is tender.
5 Serve fish with vegetables, drizzled with any pan juices; sprinkle fish with oregano leaves, if desired.

PER SERVING 2.5g total fat (0.7g saturated); 1296kj (310 cal); 28.1g carbohydrate; 40.5g protein; 5.3g fibre

---

This recipe is also delicious with hot-smoked salmon, smoked tofu or smoked chicken instead of trout. For extra crunch add ¼ chinese cabbage, shredded, 2 shredded carrots and 1 tablespoon roasted sesame seeds.

Hot-smoked trout and vermicelli salad

PREPARATION TIME 25 MINUTES **COOKING TIME** 5 MINUTES **SERVES** 4

200g rice vermicelli
400g hot-smoked trout fillets
2 trimmed celery stalks (200g), sliced thinly
2 lebanese cucumbers (260g), seeded, sliced thinly
½ cup (70g) roasted shelled pistachios
¼ cup coarsely chopped fresh mint
¼ cup coarsely chopped fresh thai basil
⅓ cup (80ml) lime juice
1 teaspoon chilli oil
1 tablespoon sesame oil
2 tablespoons fish sauce
1 clove garlic, crushed

1 Place vermicelli in large heatproof bowl; cover with boiling water. Stand until just tender; drain. Rinse noodles under cold water; drain.
2 Meanwhile, discard skin and bones from fish. Flake fish into large pieces in large bowl; add vermicelli, celery, cucumber, nuts and herbs.
3 Place remaining ingredients in screw-top jar; shake well. Drizzle dressing over salad; toss gently to combine.

PER SERVING 15.4g total fat (2.4g saturated); 1396kj (334 cal); 15.8g carbohydrate; 31.2g protein; 3.7g fibre

Citrus-ginger steamed bream

PREPARATION TIME 20 MINUTES **COOKING TIME** 15 MINUTES **SERVES** 4

- 1 medium lemon (140g)
- 2 medium oranges (480g)
- 2 cloves garlic, crushed
- 2cm piece fresh ginger (10g), grated
- 4 x 250g whole bream, cleaned
- 2 cups (400g) jasmine rice
- ⅓ cup loosely packed fresh basil leaves, torn

1 Using vegetable peeler, peel rind carefully from lemon and one orange; cut rind into thin strips. Squeeze juice of both oranges and lemon into large shallow dish. Stir in rind, garlic and ginger. Score fish both sides; add to dish, turn to coat in marinade.

2 Fold 80cm-long piece of foil in half crossways; place one fish on foil, spoon a quarter of the marinade onto fish. Fold foil over fish to tightly enclose. Repeat process with remaining fish and marinade.

3 Place fish parcels in large steamer fitted over large saucepan of boiling water; steam, covered, about 15 minutes or until cooked as desired.

4 Meanwhile, cook rice in large saucepan of boiling water, uncovered, until just tender; drain. Divide rice among serving plates; top with fish, drizzle with cooking juices, sprinkle with basil.

PER SERVING 3.6g total fat (1.0g saturated); 2215kj (530 cal); 86.4g carbohydrate; 34.8g protein; 3.4g fibre

For a delicate aromatic rice that marries perfectly with the citrus flavours of the fish, add a cinnamon stick, a few cardomom pods and a star anise to the water when adding the rice. Be sure to remove the spices from the rice before serving.

Pipis stir-fried in coconut milk

PREPARATION TIME 15 MINUTES (PLUS STANDING TIME) **COOKING TIME** 10 MINUTES **SERVES** 4

- 1 tablespoon peanut oil
- 1 medium brown onion (150g), chopped coarsely
- 2 cm piece fresh ginger (10g), grated
- 2 cloves garlic, crushed
- 1 tablespoon finely chopped fresh lemon grass
- 2 teaspoons ground cumin
- 2 teaspoons ground coriander
- 1 teaspoon ground turmeric
- 1kg pipis, prepared
- 2 tablespoons lime juice
- 2 teaspoons fish sauce
- 400ml coconut milk
- 2 teaspoons brown sugar
- 500g choy sum, chopped coarsely
- 2 tablespoons fresh coriander leaves

1 Heat the oil in wok or large pan, add onion, ginger, garlic, lemon grass and ground spices; stir-fry until fragrant.

2 Add rinsed and drained pipis, juice, sauce, milk and sugar; stir-fry until pipis open, discard any that do not.

3 Add choy sum; stir-fry until leaves are just wilted. Serve sprinkled with fresh coriander.

PER SERVE 26.5g total fat (19.3g saturated); 1384kj (331 cal); 11.6g carbohydrate; 10.2g protein; 4.4g fibre

To avoid wastage, peel a whole piece of ginger, use what you need and store the rest in the freezer for next time. Frozen ginger is a dream to grate and there are no stringy bits.

See page 157 for information on how to prepare pipis.

POULTRY & GAME BIRDS

Poultry & Game Birds

You have only to look at the recipes in this chapter to realise just how many good, interesting and very different ways there are to cook with chicken. Suitable for finger food, pizza toppings, salads, curries, burgers, stir-fries and casseroles, this versatile bird is amazing.

Then there are those other choice birds: duck, quail and turkey. Though wild duck and quail are sometimes hunted, the ones you will buy are farmed so you can be confident they will be tender. Duck, quail and turkey are now readily available, yet they still seem special enough to mark a meal as an occasion. Other birds, such as geese, pheasant and pigeon, usually need to be ordered in for you.

CHOOSING POULTRY AND GAME BIRDS

CHICKEN Try to choose fresh, free-range, organic chicken, either whole or cut into pieces. Second-best is fresh, but not free-range, chicken. If cooking a frozen chicken, give it time to thaw out in the fridge first. It will lose some of its juices as it thaws, but will lose less this way. Thaw, uncovered, on several thicknesses of absorbent paper on a plate in the fridge.
DUCK, QUAIL AND TURKEY Choose these using the same criteria discussed for chicken.

STORING AND HANDLING POULTRY AND GAME BIRDS

Remove chicken and other birds from their wrappings and refrigerate on a clean plate, loosely covered with foil or a damp disposable cloth, as soon as you get them home. Use fresh birds or portions within 3 days, thawed frozen birds or portions within 2 days. Never cook a partially frozen bird: it may appear to be cooked through, but unless the internal temperature reached 75°C or higher during cooking, dangerous micro-organisms such as salmonella may have survived. Be scrupulous about hygiene. Wash your hands before and after handling raw poultry and game birds. Rinse cutting boards promptly, scrub with coarse cooking salt and rinse again. Also thoroughly clean any knife you have used.

POULTRY AND GAME BIRD CUTS

Chickens are sold whole or cut into portions, as follows:

- **Breast** Whole or halved, with skin and bone intact
- **Breast fillet** Skinless, boneless half-breast; double fillet means full breast
- **Thigh cutlet (chicken chop)** Skin-on thigh with one bone
- **Thigh fillet** Skinless, boneless thigh
- **Drumstick** Skin-on, bone-in leg

- **Wing** Skin-on, bone-in wing
- **Drumette** Wing trimmed to resemble a miniature drumstick
- **Maryland** Skin-on, joined thigh and drumstick, bone-in
- **Chicken livers** are readily available.

SPATCHCOCK are small chickens, usually weighing between 300g and 600g. Note that "spatchcock" in overseas cookbooks means a chicken or game bird split down the back and flattened out for grilling. What we call spatchcock is called poussin or baby chicken.

DUCKS are sold whole, and you can also buy boneless breast fillets (half-breasts), either skin-on or skinless, and marylands (thigh and leg attached, skin and bone intact). Duck livers are available but may have to be ordered ahead.

TURKEYS are sold whole, and you can also buy turkey breast fillet (skinless, boneless breast meat) and turkey buffe, a whole, skin-on breast on the bone.

QUAIL are sold whole or butterflied, with the body boned but the wings, thighs and legs intact. You can also buy boneless, skin-on breast fillets.

HOW MUCH TO BUY

The amounts given here are a general guide only.

CHICKEN 375g per person for roast or fried chicken; 500g per person of chicken on the bone for grilling or barbecuing; 250g to 500g per person of chicken on the bone for casseroling; 150 to 200g per person of boneless chicken (skin-on or skinless).

ONE SPATCHCOCK serves 1.

DUCK has a larger carcass and thinner meat covering than chicken. A 1.4kg duck will serve 2 or 3, a 1.6kg one 2 or 4, a 2kg one 4, and a 2.5kg one 5 or 6.

ONE DUCK MARYLAND serves 1.

ONE SKIN-ON OR SKINLESS DUCK BREAST FILLET serves 1.

TURKEY a 3 to 4kg turkey serves 8 to 10, a 4 to 6kg turkey serves 10 to 14, a 6 to 8kg turkey serves 14 to 16. Allow 375g of turkey buffe per person; 150 to 200g of turkey breast fillet per person.

QUAIL 2 or 3 quail, either whole or boned, per person; 125 to 150g quail fillets per person.

JUDGING WHEN POULTRY AND GAME BIRDS ARE DONE

CHICKEN should be cooked through but not overdone. Check small pieces by pressing with your finger or the back of tongs; they should feel springy. Check a whole chicken by inserting a fine skewer into the thickest part of the thigh near the body; the juices should run clear with no tinge of pink.

A WHOLE DUCK or a maryland should be cooked through but not overdone; check it as for chicken, above.

DUCK BREAST FILLETS may be rare or cooked through, according to taste. Rare meat feels soft and spongy, medium-rare soft but springy; meat cooked through but not overdone feels firm but still springy

A WHOLE TURKEY or turkey buffe should be cooked through but not overdone. Check by inserting a fine skewer into the thickest part of the breast; the skewer should go in easily and the juice that runs out should be clear, with no tinge of pink.

TURKEY BREAST FILLET portions may be rare or cooked through, according to taste. Check as for duck breast fillets, above.

For a tasty rice salad cook 1 ½ cups basmati rice. Combine with 1 chopped cucumber, 2 chopped vine-ripened tomatoes, 1 finely chopped red onion, 70g baby spinach, 50g snow pea sprouts and 2 tablespoons chopped mint. Top with the chicken pieces and dress with raita.

Chicken tandoori pockets with raita

PREPARATION TIME 10 MINUTES **COOKING TIME** 10 MINUTES **MAKES** 8

1 tablespoon lime juice

⅓ cup (100g) tandoori paste

¼ cup (70g) yogurt

400g chicken tenderloins

8 large flour tortillas

60g snow pea sprouts

RAITA

1 cup (280g) yogurt

1 lebanese cucumber (130g), seeded, chopped finely

1 tablespoon finely chopped fresh mint

1 Combine juice, paste and yogurt in medium bowl, add chicken; turn to coat in mixture.

2 Cook chicken, in batches, on heated oiled grill plate (or grill or barbecue) until cooked through. Stand 5 minutes; slice thickly.

3 Meanwhile, heat tortillas according to manufacturer's instructions.

4 Make raita.

5 Place equal amounts of each of the chicken, sprouts and raita on a quarter section of each tortilla; fold tortilla in half and then in half again to enclose filling and form triangle-shaped pockets.

RAITA Combine ingredients in small bowl.

PER POCKET 10.8g total fat (2.5g saturated); 1225kj (293 cal); 29.2g carbohydrate; 17.8g protein; 3.2g fibre

---

To avoid oil bubbling over when the chicken is added make sure the wok is only one-third filled with oil. To prevent splattering, bring the chicken up to room temperature before deep-frying.

Crisp-skinned soy chicken with spiced salt

PREPARATION TIME 20 MINUTES (PLUS STANDING AND REFRIGERATION TIME)
COOKING TIME 30 MINUTES **SERVES** 4

4 litres (16 cups) water

1 cup (250ml) light soy sauce

5cm piece fresh ginger (25g), sliced thickly

2 cloves garlic, crushed

2 teaspoons five-spice powder

1.5kg chicken

vegetable oil, for deep-frying

SOY MARINADE

1 tablespoon honey

1 tablespoon light soy sauce

1 tablespoon dry sherry

½ teaspoon five-spice powder

½ teaspoon sesame oil

SPICED SALT

¼ cup (30g) sea salt flakes

½ teaspoon cracked black pepper

1 teaspoon five-spice powder

1 Combine the water, sauce, ginger, garlic and five-spice in large saucepan; bring to a boil. Boil, uncovered, 2 minutes. Add chicken; return to a boil. Reduce heat; simmer, uncovered, 10 minutes, turning once during cooking. Remove from heat, cover; stand 30 minutes. Remove chicken from stock; pat dry with absorbent paper. Discard stock.

2 Make soy marinade and spiced salt.

3 Cut chicken in half through breastbone and along sides of backbone; remove legs and wings. Place pieces on tray; brush skin with soy marinade. Cover; refrigerate 2 hours.

4 Heat oil in wok or large deep frying pan; deep-fry chicken, in batches, until browned all over; drain on absorbent paper.
5 Cut chicken into serving-sized pieces; serve with spiced salt.

SOY MARINADE Combine ingredients in small bowl.

SPICED SALT Heat small frying pan; cook salt and pepper, stirring, 2 minutes. Add five-spice; cook, stirring, about 1 minute or until fragrant.

☐ **PER SERVING** 21.4g total fat (4.1g saturated); 1768kj (423 cal); 8.2g carbohydrate; 48.1g protein; 0.4g fibre

Chicken enchiladas with corn salsa

PREPARATION TIME 30 MINUTES **COOKING TIME** 35 MINUTES **SERVES** 4

Corn salsa is also delicious with grilled chicken or lamb. For another version, roast the capsicum for a sweeter, slightly smokey flavour; place the corn kernels in a hot frying pan and toss until lightly roasted, which will give a nutty flavour. You could also add some diced tomato, onion and chilli.

1 large red onion (300g), chopped finely

2 tablespoons vegetable oil

2 cloves garlic, crushed

1 tablespoon tomato paste

¼ cup (45g) drained bottled jalapeño chillies, chopped coarsely

400g can crushed tomatoes

1 cup (250ml) chicken stock

500g chicken breast fillets, sliced thinly

10 corn tortillas

2 cups (240g) coarsely grated cheddar

½ cup (120g) sour cream

CORN SALSA

1 small red capsicum (150g), chopped finely

310g can corn kernels, drained

1 tablespoon lime juice

1 cup coarsely chopped fresh coriander

1 Reserve a quarter of the onion for the corn salsa. Preheat oven to moderate (180°C/160°C fan-forced). Oil 3-litre (12-cup) shallow ovenproof dish.
2 Heat oil in large frying pan; cook remaining onion with garlic, stirring, until onion softens. Add paste, chilli, undrained tomatoes, stock and chicken; bring to a boil. Reduce heat; simmer, uncovered, until chicken is cooked through. Remove chicken from pan; cover to keep warm.
3 Heat tortillas according to manufacturer's instructions. Dip tortillas, one at a time, in tomato mixture; place on board. Divide chicken and half the cheese among tortillas; roll tortillas to enclose filling. Place enchiladas, seam-side down, in dish; enchiladas should fit snugly, without overcrowding.
4 Pour remaining tomato mixture over enchiladas; top with sour cream and remaining cheese. Bake, uncovered, about 15 minutes or until heated through.
5 Make corn salsa; serve with enchiladas.

CORN SALSA Combine reserved onion in small bowl with remaining ingredients.

☐ **PER SERVING** 50.4g total fat (23.9g saturated); 3917kj (937 cal); 63g carbohydrate; 53g protein; 10.9g fibre

Chicken liver salad with polenta croutons

PREPARATION TIME 30 MINUTES (PLUS STANDING TIME)
COOKING TIME 45 MINUTES (PLUS REFRIGERATION TIME) **SERVES** 6

Soaking the livers in milk is an important part of this recipe; the enzymes in the milk help neutralise the bitter flavour that can occur in liver.

2 cups (500ml) water
2 cups (500ml) chicken stock
1 cup (170g) polenta
20g butter
2 tablespoons finely grated parmesan
cooking-oil spray
1kg chicken livers, trimmed
1 cup (250ml) milk
½ cup (75g) plain flour
1 teaspoon salt
1 teaspoon cracked black pepper
¼ cup (60ml) olive oil
150g baby spinach leaves
1 small red onion (100g), sliced thinly
60g firm blue cheese

SHALLOT DRESSING
3 shallots (75g), chopped finely
2 tablespoons red wine vinegar
2 tablespoons olive oil

1 Lightly oil 19cm x 29cm slice pan.
2 Place the water and stock in large saucepan; bring to a boil. Gradually add polenta, stirring constantly. Reduce heat; cook, stirring, about 10 minutes or until polenta thickens. Stir in butter and parmesan then spread into pan; cool 10 minutes. Cover; refrigerate about 3 hours or until firm. Cut polenta into 2cm-square croutons.
3 Meanwhile, make shallot dressing.
4 Preheat oven to moderate (180°C/160°C fan-forced). Oil two oven trays.
5 Place polenta croutons, in single layer, on trays. Spray croutons with oil; bake, uncovered, about 30 minutes or until browned lightly.
6 Meanwhile, soak livers in milk in medium bowl 30 minutes. Separate livers into halves by cutting lobes apart. Coat liver in combined flour, salt and pepper; shake off excess.
7 Heat oil in large frying pan; cook liver, over high heat, about 5 minutes or until browned and cooked as desired (do not overcook). Drain on absorbent paper.
8 Place spinach, onion, croutons, liver and dressing in large bowl; toss gently to combine. Serve salad sprinkled with blue cheese.

SHALLOT DRESSING Place ingredients in screw-top jar; shake well.

PER SERVING 31.4g total fat (10.0g saturated); 2391kj (572 cal); 32.1g carbohydrate; 39.6g protein; 2.2g fibre

CHICKEN LIVER SALAD WITH POLENTA CROUTONS

This dish was originally created for the 1953 coronation of Queen Elizabeth II. It makes a mouth-watering filling for a sandwich or wrap, with finely sliced cucumber and shredded iceberg lettuce.

Coronation chicken

PREPARATION TIME 15 MINUTES **COOKING TIME** 20 MINUTES **SERVES** 4

1½ cups (300g) basmati rice
700g chicken breast fillets
1 cup (300g) mayonnaise
½ cup (120g) sour cream
1 teaspoon curry powder
2 cups loosely packed fresh basil leaves
5 ripe nectarines (850g), cut into thick wedges
2 cups (300g) roasted unsalted cashews

1 Cook rice in large saucepan of boiling water, uncovered, until tender; drain. Rinse under cold water; drain.
2 Meanwhile, poach chicken, covered, in large frying pan of boiling water about 10 minutes or until cooked through. Cool chicken in liquid 10 minutes; slice thinly.
3 Combine mayonnaise, cream and curry powder in large bowl. Add chicken, basil, nectarine and three-quarters of the nuts; toss gently to combine.
4 Divide rice among serving plates; top with chicken mixture and remaining nuts.

PER SERVING 80.8g total fat (19.2g saturated); 5773kj (1381 cal); 101.7g carbohydrate; 57.5g protein; 10.5g fibre

Half a quail makes a good first course for a winter dinner party. Be sure to provide sharp, pointed knives, as cutting the meat off quail can be fiddly.

Roast bacon-wrapped quail with muscat sauce

PREPARATION TIME 15 MINUTES **COOKING TIME** 30 MINUTES **SERVES** 4

4 quails (640g)
1 lemon
20g butter
4 bacon rashers (280g), rind removed
⅓ cup (80ml) muscat
250g green beans, trimmed
½ cup (125ml) chicken stock
150g fresh muscatel grapes, halved

1 Preheat oven to moderately hot (200°C/180°C fan-forced).
2 Discard necks from quails. Wash quails under cold water; pat dry with absorbent paper.
3 Halve lemon; cut one lemon half into four wedges. Place one lemon wedge and a quarter of the butter inside each quail. Tuck legs along body, wrapping tightly with bacon rasher to hold legs in place.
4 Place quails in medium flameproof casserole dish; drizzle with 1 tablespoon of the muscat and juice of remaining lemon half. Roast, uncovered, about 25 minutes or until quails are browned and cooked through. Remove quails from dish; cover to keep warm.
5 Meanwhile, boil, steam or microwave beans until tender; drain. Keep warm.
6 Return dish with pan juices to heat, add remaining muscat and stock; stir until sauce boils and reduces to about ½ cup. Add grapes; stir until heated though. Serve quail on beans topped with muscat sauce.

PER SERVING 22.6g total fat (8.5g saturated); 1680kj (402 cal); 12.2g carbohydrate; 30.8g protein; 3g fibre

Chicken and mixed mushroom stir-fry

PREPARATION TIME 15 MINUTES **COOKING TIME** 15 MINUTES **SERVES** 4

The chicken and vegetables are cooked separately to prevent the vegetables from overcooking – the chicken takes a little longer. It also allows the chicken and vegetables to retain their individual flavours.

- 600g hokkien noodles
- 1 tablespoon peanut oil
- 750g chicken tenderloins, halved
- 200g button mushrooms, halved
- 200g flat mushrooms, sliced thickly
- 200g swiss brown mushrooms, halved
- 3 green onions, chopped finely
- 2 tablespoons mild chilli sauce
- ½ cup (125ml) oyster sauce

1 Place noodles in large heatproof bowl; cover with boiling water, separate with fork, drain.
2 Heat half of the oil in wok; stir-fry chicken, in batches, until just cooked through.
3 Heat remaining oil in wok; stir-fry mushrooms, in batches, until browned. Return chicken and mushrooms to wok with noodles, onion and sauces; stir-fry until heated through.

☐ **PER SERVING** 15.2g total fat (3.5g saturated); 3131kj (749 cal); 88.3g carbohydrate; 59.6g protein; 7.2g fibre

Chicken chow mein

PREPARATION TIME 15 MINUTES **COOKING TIME** 15 MINUTES **SERVES** 4

Tips for buying woks:
- *carbon steel woks are the best and often the cheapest*
- *flat-bottom woks are best for electric stoves.*

- 1 tablespoon peanut oil
- 500g chicken thigh fillets, sliced thinly
- 2 medium brown onions (300g), sliced thinly
- 2 cloves garlic, crushed
- 4cm piece fresh ginger (20g), grated
- 2 trimmed celery stalks (200g), sliced thinly
- 1 medium red capsicum (200g), sliced thinly
- 2 teaspoons cornflour
- ½ cup (125ml) chicken stock
- ¼ cup (60ml) light soy sauce
- 5 green onions, sliced thickly
- 1 cup (80g) bean sprouts
- 2 cups (160g) finely shredded chinese cabbage
- 2 x 100g packets fried noodles

1 Heat half of the oil in wok; stir-fry chicken, in batches, until just cooked through.
2 Heat remaining oil in same wok; stir-fry brown onion, garlic and ginger until fragrant. Add celery and capsicum; stir-fry until vegetables are just tender.
3 Blend cornflour with stock and sauce in small jug. Return chicken to wok with cornflour mixture; stir-fry until sauce boils and thickens. Add green onion, sprouts and cabbage; stir-fry until heated through. Serve on fried noodles.

☐ **PER SERVING** 14.6g total fat (4.2g saturated); 1463kj (350 cal); 19.7g carbohydrate; 32.1g protein; 5.4g fibre

1

2

3

4

Chicken tagine with olives and preserved lemon

PREPARATION TIME 15 MINUTES **COOKING TIME** 45 MINUTES **SERVES** 4

- 1 tablespoon olive oil
- 1 tablespoon butter
- 8 chicken thigh cutlets (1.6kg)
- 1 large red onion (300g), chopped finely
- ½ teaspoon saffron threads, roasted, crushed
- 1 teaspoon ground cinnamon
- 1 teaspoon ground ginger
- 1½ cups (375ml) chicken stock
- 1 cup (120g) seeded large green olives
- 2 tablespoons finely chopped preserved lemon peel

1 Heat oil and butter in large heavy-based saucepan; cook skinned chicken until browned.

2 Place onion and spices in same pan; cook until onion softens. Return chicken to pan with stock; bring to a boil then simmer, covered, 30 minutes or until chicken is cooked.

3 Remove chicken from pan; cover to keep warm. Skim and discard fat from top of sauce; bring to a boil. Reduce heat; cook, stirring, until sauce reduces by half.

4 Return chicken to pan with olives and lemon; stir over medium heat until heated through.

PER SERVING 21.2g total fat (6.9g saturated); 2019kj (483 cal); 11.0g carbohydrate; 60.6g protein; 2.5g fibre

For a traditional accompaniment bring 1½ cups chicken stock to the boil; remove from the heat. Stir in 1½ cups couscous; rest for about 5 minutes, fluffing with a fork occasionally. Stir in ½ cup chopped fresh coriander and 2 tablespoons lemon juice.

Poached chicken with ruby grapefruit salad

PREPARATION TIME 40 MINUTES **COOKING TIME** 10 MINUTES **SERVES** 4

- 2½ cups (625ml) water
- 2½ cups (625ml) chicken stock
- 700g chicken breast fillets
- 4 ruby grapefruits (2kg)
- 1 small red onion (100g), cut into thin wedges
- 4 green onions, sliced thinly
- 2 fresh small red thai chillies, sliced thinly
- 1 cup coarsely chopped fresh coriander
- ¼ cup (35g) roasted unsalted peanuts
- 100g baby spinach leaves
- 2 cloves garlic, crushed
- 1 tablespoon grated palm sugar
- 1 tablespoon lime juice
- 1 tablespoon light soy sauce

1 Combine the water and stock in large frying pan; bring to a boil. Add chicken; return to a boil. Reduce heat; simmer, covered, about 10 minutes or until cooked through. Cool chicken in poaching liquid 10 minutes. Remove chicken from pan; discard poaching liquid. Slice chicken thinly.

2 Segment peeled grapefruit over large bowl to catch juice; add grapefruit segments to bowl with chicken, onions, chilli, coriander, nuts and spinach.

3 Place remaining ingredients in small jug; whisk until sugar dissolves. Pour dressing over salad; toss gently to combine.

PER SERVING 13.0g total fat (3.0g saturated); 1668kj (399 cal); 23g carbohydrate; 44.9g protein; 4.9g fibre

Brown sugar can be used in place of palm sugar.

1 CHICKEN TAGINE WITH OLIVES AND PRESERVED LEMON **2** POACHED CHICKEN WITH RUBY GRAPEFRUIT SALAD **3** DUCK BREASTS WITH FIG SAUCE AND SPINACH RISONI [P 198] **4** BUTTER CHICKEN [P 198]

For a more piquant sauce, you can use ½ cup halved, drained morello cherries plus the juice of half an orange, instead of the figs. If you would like a thicker sauce, blend 2 teaspoons cornflour with 2 teaspoons water and add to the pan with the port and stock.

Duck breasts with fig sauce and spinach risoni

PREPARATION TIME 20 MINUTES **COOKING TIME** 25 MINUTES **SERVES** 4

4 duck breast fillets (600g)
4 sprigs fresh rosemary
4 bay leaves
1 cup (220g) risoni
20g butter
200g baby spinach leaves
1 small brown onion (80g), chopped finely
6 dried figs (90g), quartered
1 cup (250ml) port
1 cup (250ml) chicken stock
20g butter, extra

1 Use fingers to make pocket between meat and fat of each duck breast; press one sprig rosemary and one bay leaf into each pocket. Prick duck skins with fork several times; cook duck, skin-side down, in heated large lightly oiled frying pan about 8 minutes or until browned and crisp. Turn duck; cook about 5 minutes or until cooked as desired. Remove from pan; cover to keep warm. Drain fat from pan.
2 Cook pasta in large saucepan of boiling water, uncovered, until just tender; drain. Place pasta in large bowl with butter and spinach; toss gently to combine. Cover to keep warm.
3 Meanwhile, cook onion in same frying pan, stirring, until soft. Add fig, port and stock; bring to a boil. Reduce heat; simmer, stirring, 5 minutes. Add extra butter; whisk until sauce thickens slightly. Slice duck thinly; serve with risoni and fig sauce.

☐ **PER SERVING** 17.5g total fat (8g saturated); 2374kj (568 cal); 49.3g carbohydrate; 35.5g protein; 3.9g fibre

---

For a great pie filling add 2 large cooked potatoes, chopped, and 100g baby spinach leaves to the butter chicken. Spoon the filling into a deep pie dish and top with a sheet of ready-rolled puff pastry. Brush with beaten egg, snip two air holes in the top and bake in a hot oven for 25 minutes or until the pastry is golden.

Butter chicken

PREPARATION TIME 20 MINUTES (PLUS REFRIGERATION TIME) **COOKING TIME** 50 MINUTES **SERVES** 8

1.5kg chicken thigh fillets, halved
4 cloves garlic, crushed
2 teaspoons garam masala
2 teaspoons ground coriander
2 teaspoons ground cumin
½ teaspoon chilli powder
2 teaspoons sweet paprika
½ cup (140g) yogurt
80g butter, chopped
2 tablespoons white vinegar
2 tablespoons tomato paste
410g can tomato puree
¾ cup (180ml) chicken stock
5 cardamom pods, bruised
1 cinnamon stick
300ml cream
⅓ cup coarsely chopped fresh coriander

1 Combine chicken, garlic, spices and yogurt in large bowl, cover; refrigerate 3 hours.
2 Melt butter in large saucepan; cook chicken mixture, stirring, until chicken browns lightly. Add vinegar, paste, puree, stock, cardamom and cinnamon; bring to a boil. Reduce heat; simmer, uncovered, stirring occasionally, about 30 minutes or until chicken is cooked through. Add cream; stir until heated through. Stir in coriander.

☐ **PER SERVING** 33g total fat (18.8g saturated); 2036kj (487 cal); 5.5g carbohydrate; 41.7g protein; 1.6g fibre

Chicken, caramelised onion and fig pizza

PREPARATION TIME 30 MINUTES (PLUS STANDING TIME) **COOKING TIME** 55 MINUTES **SERVES** 4

Dusting polenta onto pizza trays prevents the bases from sticking and gives extra crunch to the crust. If you don't have a pizza wheel, cut the pizza with kitchen scissors – you'll find it far easier and cleaner than using a knife.

200g chicken breast fillet

2 teaspoons olive oil

2 cloves garlic, crushed

425g can crushed tomatoes

1 tablespoon polenta

100g firm goat cheese

4 large fresh figs (320g), quartered

50g baby rocket leaves

PIZZA DOUGH

2 teaspoons dried yeast

½ teaspoon salt

2½ cups (375g) plain flour

1 cup (250ml) warm water

2 teaspoons olive oil

CARAMELISED ONION

1 tablespoon olive oil

3 large brown onions (600g), sliced thinly

2 tablespoons brown sugar

2 tablespoons balsamic vinegar

1 Make pizza dough and caramelised onion.

2 Preheat oven to moderately hot (200°C/180°C fan-forced).

3 Cook chicken in heated lightly oiled small frying pan until cooked through. Cool 10 minutes; slice thinly.

4 Meanwhile, heat oil in small saucepan; cook garlic, stirring, until fragrant. Add undrained tomatoes; bring to a boil. Reduce heat; simmer, uncovered, about 15 minutes or until mixture thickens.

5 Sprinkle polenta onto two 30cm-pizza trays. Halve pizza dough; roll each half on lightly floured surface to form 30cm-round pizza base. Place one base on each tray; divide tomato sauce and caramelised onion between bases.

6 Cook pizzas, uncovered, 10 minutes. Divide chicken, cheese and fig between pizzas; cook, uncovered, about 5 minutes or until bases are crisp. Sprinkle each with baby rocket leaves before serving.

PIZZA DOUGH Combine yeast, salt and flour in large bowl; gradually stir in the water and oil. Turn dough onto lightly floured surface; knead until smooth. Place dough in lightly oiled large bowl; cover tightly with plastic wrap then a tea-towel. Stand in warm place 45 minutes or until dough has doubled in size. Knead dough on floured surface until smooth.

CARAMELISED ONION Heat oil in large frying pan; cook onion, stirring, until softened. Add sugar and vinegar; cook, stirring occasionally, about 15 minutes or until onion caramelises.

PER SERVING 17.1g total fat (4.7g saturated); 2809kj (672 cal); 94.5g carbohydrate; 29g protein; 9.7g fibre

Broad beans are enclosed in flat, green pods, which are usually discarded. Each bean has a chewy skin which is often removed after cooking, as in this recipe, to reveal the bright green, tender inner bean. In dishes where the beans will be pureed, for example soups and dips, the skins are usually left on.

Mixed pea, broad bean and turkey salad with lemon mustard dressing

PREPARATION TIME 1 HOUR 15 MINUTES **COOKING TIME** 1 HOUR **SERVES** 6

1.2kg single turkey breast
1 tablespoon olive oil
1 tablespoon sea salt
½ teaspoon cracked black pepper
2 teaspoons finely grated lemon rind
1½ cups (330g) risoni
750g fresh broad beans
1¾ cups (280g) shelled fresh peas
300g sugar snap peas, trimmed
200g snow peas, trimmed
¼ cup coarsely chopped fresh mint
200g snow pea tendrils
50g baby rocket leaves

LEMON MUSTARD DRESSING
2 tablespoons lemon juice
2 teaspoons wholegrain mustard
2 tablespoons white wine vinegar
1 teaspoon caster sugar
⅓ cup (80ml) olive oil

1 Preheat oven to moderately hot (200°C/180°C fan-forced). Oil oven tray.
2 Tie turkey breast at 6cm intervals with kitchen string. Place on tray; rub with combined oil, salt, pepper and rind. Cover with foil; bake 40 minutes. Remove foil; bake 10 minutes or until cooked through.
3 Meanwhile, make lemon mustard dressing.
4 Cook risoni in large saucepan of boiling water, uncovered, until just tender; drain. Rinse under cold water; drain.
5 Shell broad beans; discard pods. Boil, steam or microwave beans until just tender; drain. Rinse under cold water; drain. Peel away grey-coloured outer shells.
6 Meanwhile, boil, steam or microwave all peas together, until just tender; drain. Rinse under cold water; drain.
7 Place risoni, beans and pea mixture in large bowl with mint, tendrils, rocket and dressing; toss gently to combine. Slice turkey thinly; serve turkey on salad.

LEMON MUSTARD DRESSING Place ingredients in screw-top jar; shake well.

PER SERVING 25.7g total fat (4.6g saturated); 3135kj (750 cal); 57.6g carbohydrate; 63.5g protein; 16.0g fibre

MIXED PEA, BROAD BEAN AND TURKEY SALAD WITH LEMON MUSTARD DRESSING

Fast barbecued chicken ideas

You will need one large barbecued chicken weighing about 900g for these recipes.

CHICKEN WRAPS

Top flour tortillas with chopped tomato, sliced avocado, chopped red onion, shredded cooked chicken, coriander leaves and chunky salsa. Roll the tortilla to enclose the filling.

CHICKEN CHILLI PIZZA

Spread small pizza bases with a mixture of tomato paste and barbecue sauce. Top with thinly sliced mushroom, chopped red chilli, shredded cooked chicken and grated pizza cheese. Cook in a hot oven about 20 minutes.

PESTO AND CHICKEN GNOCCHI

Simmer 300ml cream and ¼ cup basil pesto in a large frying pan 5 minutes. Add 2 cups coarsely chopped cooked chicken and 500g cooked gnocchi. Sprinkle with baby basil leaves.

TERIYAKI RICE PAPER ROLLS

Combine shredded cooked chicken, grated carrot, sliced red capsicum, snow pea sprouts, teriyaki sauce and sweet chilli sauce in a bowl. Soften the rice paper in warm water; top with filling and roll to enclose.

CHICKEN NACHOS

Combine 425g can drained Mexican-style beans, 3 cups shredded cooked chicken and a 390g jar nachos sauce in a frying pan; stir until warm. Place corn chips on a heatproof plate, top with chicken and pizza cheese; grill until the cheese melts. Serve with sour cream.

PECAN CHICKEN OPEN SANDWICH

Mix together finely chopped cooked chicken, sliced green onion, chopped roasted pecans, finely chopped celery and whole-egg mayonnaise. Spoon the mixture onto halved or quaretered french bread sticks.

CHICKEN CAESAR SALAD

Toss together 1 sliced cos lettuce, 3 rashers chopped crisp bacon, 3 cups shredded cooked chicken, 4 quartered hard-boiled eggs, ½ cup shaved parmesan and ½ cup Caesar dressing.

CHICKEN PASTA SALAD

Combine 4 cups cooked penne with 150g crumbled fetta, 150g chopped char-grilled capsicum, 3 cups chopped cooked chicken, ⅓ cup roasted chopped walnuts, 1 cup basil leaves and ½ cup Italian dressing.

CHICKEN AND AVOCADO SANDWICH

Spread slices of wholegrain bread with softened cream cheese; top with coarsley shredded cooked chicken, thickly sliced avocado and mixed salad leaves.

CHICKEN FRIED RICE

Stir-fry 5 cups cooked long-grain white rice with 1 cup frozen peas, 1 cup corn kernels, 3 cups shredded cooked chicken, 6 sliced green onions, 1 finely chopped red capsicum and ⅓ cup light soy sauce; toss until heated through.

ITALIAN-STYLE TOASTED SANDWICH

Cut a piece of pide in half horizontally; spread base with basil pesto. Top with char-grilled vegetables, coarsely chopped cooked chicken and mozzarella. Top with the remaining bread; cook in preheated sandwich press until browned lightly.

CHICKEN AND ZUCCHINI SOUP

Cook 1 chopped brown onion in a large saucepan until soft; add 3 cups chopped cooked chicken, 2 coarsely grated zucchini, 310g can creamed corn, 4 cups chicken stock and ½ cup cream. Stir until heated through.

To save time you can buy pancakes in several sizes at Asian grocery stores. The small pancakes make great canapé bases (see page 120).

Peking duck

PREPARATION TIME 30 MINUTES (PLUS REFRIGERATION TIME) **COOKING TIME** 1 HOUR **SERVES** 4

2kg duck
1/3 cup (80ml) water
1 tablespoon treacle
1 teaspoon rice vinegar
1 tablespoon dry sherry
1 teaspoon five-spice powder
4cm piece fresh ginger (20g), sliced thickly
2 star anise
1 lebanese cucumber (130g)
5 green onions

PANCAKES
2 cups (300g) plain flour
1 1/2 cups (375ml) boiling water
2 teaspoons peanut oil

PEANUT AND HOISIN SAUCE
1 tablespoon peanut butter
2 tablespoons hoisin sauce
1 tablespoon peanut oil
1 teaspoon rice vinegar

Honey can be used instead of treacle in this recipe.

1 Wash duck under cold water; pat dry inside and out with absorbent paper. Tie string around neck of duck. Lower duck into large saucepan of boiling water for 30 seconds; remove from pan. Drain well; pat dry with absorbent paper. Tie string to refrigerator shelf and suspend duck, uncovered, over drip tray overnight.
2 Preheat oven to very hot (240°C/220°C fan-forced).
3 Tuck wings under duck. Place duck, breast-side up, on wire rack in large baking dish; brush entire duck with combined water, treacle, vinegar, sherry and five-spice. Place ginger and star anise inside cavity of duck. Roast, uncovered, 10 minutes; turn duck. Brush with marinade; roast, uncovered, 10 minutes. Turn duck breast-side up; brush with marinade.
4 Reduce oven temperature to moderately hot (200°C/180°C fan-forced); roast, uncovered, about 30 minutes or until duck is cooked as desired. Brush occasionally with remaining marinade.
5 Increase oven temperature to very hot (240°C/220°C fan-forced); roast, uncovered, about 10 minutes or until skin is crisp and browned.
6 Meanwhile, make pancakes and peanut and hoisin sauce.
7 Place duck on chopping board; remove skin. Slice skin and duck meat thickly. Using teaspoon, remove seeds from cucumber. Cut cucumber and onions into 5cm strips. Serve warm pancakes with duck meat, crisp skin, cucumber, onion and sauce.

PANCAKES Sift flour into large bowl; add the water. Stir quickly using wooden spoon until ingredients cling together. Knead dough on floured surface about 10 minutes or until smooth. Divide dough into 20 pieces; roll pieces into balls, flatten slightly. Brush tops of dough with oil. Place one piece of dough on top of another, oiled surfaces together, and roll out into a 18cm pancake. Repeat with remaining balls. Cook pancakes, one at a time, in small lightly oiled frying pan, over medium heat, about 30 seconds or until browned lightly. Turn pancake; brown other side. Pull pancakes apart with fingers to make two thin pancakes. Wrap pancakes in foil after each is cooked to prevent drying out.

PEANUT AND HOISIN SAUCE Combine ingredients in small bowl.

PER SERVING 27.2g total fat (6.6g saturated); 3206kj (767 cal); 64.5g carbohydrate; 61.2g protein; 5.5g fibre

Roasted chicken with 40 cloves of garlic

This provençal favourite will surprise you with how mild and creamy the garlic becomes after its long roasting. It's a good idea to roast extra bulbs whose cloves can be peeled, made into a paste and frozen for later use.

PREPARATION TIME 20 MINUTES **COOKING TIME** 1 HOUR 20 MINUTES (PLUS STANDING TIME) **SERVES** 4

3 bulbs garlic
60g butter, softened
1.5kg chicken
2 teaspoons salt
2 teaspoons cracked black pepper
1 cup (250ml) water

ROASTED POTATOES
1kg baby new potatoes
cooking-oil spray

1 Preheat oven to moderately hot (200°C/180°C fan forced).
2 Separate cloves from garlic bulb, leaving skins intact. Rub butter over outside of chicken and inside cavity; press combined salt and pepper onto skin and inside cavity. Place half of the garlic inside cavity; tie legs together with kitchen string.
3 Place remaining garlic cloves, in single layer, in medium baking dish; place chicken on top. Pour the water carefully into dish; roast chicken, uncovered, brushing occasionally with pan juices, about 1 hour 20 minutes or until cooked through.
4 Meanwhile, make roasted potatoes.
5 Stand chicken, covered, 15 minutes before serving with roasted garlic and potatoes.

ROASTED POTATOES Boil, steam or microwave potatoes 5 minutes; drain. Pat dry with absorbent paper; cool 10 minutes. Place potatoes, in single layer, in large oiled baking dish; spray with oil. Roast, uncovered, for the last 30 minutes of chicken cooking time or until potatoes are tender.

☐ **PER SERVING** 22.9g total fat (10.9g saturated); 2420kj (579 cal); 36g carbohydrate; 52.2g protein; 10g fibre

---

Classic buffalo wings

Rather than wasting the chicken wing tips use them for making stock.

PREPARATION TIME 15 MINUTES (PLUS REFRIGERATION TIME) **COOKING TIME** 15 MINUTES **SERVES** 4

½ cup (150g) mayonnaise
½ cup (120g) sour cream
¼ cup (60ml) buttermilk
2 teaspoons lemon juice
¼ teaspoon hot paprika
1 small brown onion (80g), chopped coarsely
100g danish blue cheese
16 small chicken wings (1.3kg)
vegetable oil, for deep-frying
⅓ cup (80ml) hot chilli sauce
80g butter, melted
4 trimmed celery stalks (400g), cut into sticks

1 Blend mayonnaise, cream, milk, juice, paprika, onion and half of the crumbled cheese until smooth; stir in remaining crumbled cheese. Cover; refrigerate 2 hours.
2 Cut wings into three pieces; discard tips. Heat oil in large saucepan; deep-fry chicken until cooked through, drain. Combine chicken in large bowl with sauce and butter. Serve chicken with mayonnaise mixture and celery.

☐ **PER SERVING** 66.6g total fat (28.9g saturated); 3503kj (838 cal); 15.1g carbohydrate; 44.8g protein; 2.8g fibre

The crumb mixture lends itself to the addition of extra flavours, such as grated parmesan, grated lemon rind, chopped thyme, chopped rosemary, chilli or mustard powder.

Chicken schnitzel burgers

PREPARATION TIME 10 MINUTES **COOKING TIME** 20 MINUTES **SERVES** 4

- 4 single chicken breast fillets (800g)
- ¼ cup (35g) plain flour
- 2 eggs, beaten lightly
- 1 tablespoon milk
- ½ cup (80g) corn flake crumbs
- ½ cup (50g) packaged breadcrumbs
- 2 medium tomatoes (300g), seeded, chopped finely
- 1 medium avocado (250g), chopped finely
- 2 teaspoons lemon juice
- 1 loaf turkish bread (430g)
- ½ cup (150g) mayonnaise
- 1 small white onion (80g), chopped finely
- 2 tablespoons french dressing
- 1 tablespoon sweet fruit chutney
- 40g baby rocket leaves

1 Preheat oven to hot (220°C/200°C fan-forced).

2 Using meat mallet, gently pound chicken between sheets of plastic wrap until 1cm thick.

3 Combine flour, egg and milk in medium bowl; combine corn flakes and breadcrumbs in another medium bowl. Coat chicken, one piece at a time, first in flour mixture then in breadcrumb mixture.

4 Place chicken, in single layer, on oiled oven tray; bake, uncovered, about 20 minutes or until chicken is browned lightly all over and cooked through.

5 Meanwhile, combine tomato, avocado and juice in small bowl. Quarter turkish bread, split pieces horizontally; toast, cut-side up. Whisk mayonnaise, onion, dressing and chutney in separate small bowl until combined.

6 To serve, sandwich rocket, chicken, tomato mixture and mayonnaise mixture between two pieces of toasted bread.

PER SERVING 40.0g total fat (7.9g saturated); 4147kj (992 cal); 93.5g carbohydrate; 60.8g protein; 6.4g fibre

---

In Japan the sauce is often used as a marinade for the chicken, or brushed over it as a glaze during cooking, which enhances its flavour.

Yakitori with sesame dipping sauce

PREPARATION TIME 20 MINUTES **COOKING TIME** 10 MINUTES **MAKES** 32

- 1kg chicken breast fillets
- ¼ cup (60ml) light soy sauce
- 2 tablespoons mirin
- 3 teaspoons caster sugar
- ½ teaspoon sesame oil
- 1 teaspoon sesame seeds

1 Cut chicken into 32 long thin slices; thread each slice on a skewer. Cook, in batches, on heated oiled grill plate (or grill or barbecue) until yakitori is browned and cooked through.

2 Meanwhile, combine remaining ingredients in small bowl.

3 Serve yakitori with sauce.

PER YAKITORI (INCLUDING SAUCE) 1.4g total fat (0.4g saturated); 176kj (42 cal); 0.5g carbohydrate; 6.6g protein; 0.0g fibre

Braised spatchcock with peas and lettuce

PREPARATION TIME 30 MINUTES **COOKING TIME** 1 HOUR **SERVES** 6

Any leftovers make a delicious hearty soup. Remove the spatchcock meat from the bone. Mix some of the mashed potato into the braising mixture (depending on how thick you want it) and stir until well combined. Add the meat and heat through. You may have to add extra stock, depending on how much sauce is left.

3 x 500g spatchcocks
1 medium leek (350g)
2 bay leaves
1 sprig fresh thyme
1 sprig fresh rosemary
4 fresh flat-leaf parsley stalks
50g butter
2 cloves garlic, crushed
1 large brown onion (200g), chopped finely
8 bacon rashers (560g), rind removed, chopped coarsely
¼ cup (35g) plain flour
1½ cups (375ml) dry white wine
3 cups (750ml) chicken stock
1.5kg potatoes, chopped coarsely
¾ cup (180ml) milk, warmed
50g butter, softened
500g frozen peas
1 large butter lettuce, shredded finely
½ cup coarsely chopped fresh mint

1 Cut along both sides of spatchcocks' backbones; discard backbones. Cut in half between breasts. Rinse spatchcock halves under cold water; pat dry with absorbent paper.

2 Cut leek in half crossways; chop white bottom half finely, reserve. Using kitchen string, tie green top half of the leek, bay leaves, thyme, rosemary and parsley stalks into a bundle.

3 Heat butter in large saucepan; cook spatchcock, in batches, until browned lightly both sides.

4 Cook reserved chopped leek, garlic, onion and bacon in same pan, stirring, about 10 minutes or until onion softens. Add flour; cook, stirring, 2 minutes. Gradually add wine and stock; bring to a boil, stirring constantly until mixture boils and thickens. Return spatchcock to pan with herb bundle, reduce heat; simmer, covered, 30 minutes.

5 Meanwhile, boil, steam or microwave potato until tender; drain. Mash potato with milk and butter in large bowl until smooth. Cover to keep warm.

6 Discard herb bundle. Add peas, lettuce and mint to pan; simmer, uncovered, about 5 minutes or until peas are just tender.

7 Divide mashed potato among serving plates; top with spatchcock mixture.

PER SERVING 34.7g total fat (16.3g saturated); 3465kj (829 cal); 48.8g carbohydrate; 63.6g protein; 14.1g fibre

Chicken green curry

PREPARATION TIME 45 MINUTES **COOKING TIME** 25 MINUTES **SERVES** 4

3¼ cups (800ml) coconut milk
2 fresh kaffir lime leaves, torn
1kg chicken thigh fillets
2 tablespoons peanut oil
2 tablespoons fish sauce
2 tablespoons lime juice
1 tablespoon grated palm sugar
150g pea eggplants, quartered
1 large zucchini (150g), cut into 5cm pieces
⅓ cup loosely packed fresh thai basil leaves
¼ cup coarsely chopped fresh coriander
1 tablespoon fresh coriander leaves
1 long green chilli, sliced thinly
2 green onions, sliced thinly

GREEN CURRY PASTE
2 teaspoons ground coriander
2 teaspoons ground cumin
10 long green chillies, chopped coarsely
10 small green chillies, chopped coarsely
1 large clove garlic, quartered
4 green onions, chopped coarsely
1 stick fresh lemon grass, sliced thinly
2 fresh kaffir lime leaves, sliced thinly
1 teaspoon finely chopped fresh galangal
¼ cup coarsely chopped fresh coriander root and stem mixture
1 teaspoon shrimp paste
1 tablespoon peanut oil

Instead of serving plain rice with this curry, place 1 cup rinsed basmati or Thai jasmine rice in a medium saucepan; cover with 2 cups water, ¼ cup coconut cream, 2 kaffir lime leaves and a stick of lemon grass. Bring to a boil; stir, cover and reduce to a simmer. Cook for about 10 minutes. Remove from the heat; rest for 5 minutes.

1 Make green curry paste. Measure ¼ cup of the paste for this recipe, then freeze the remainder, covered, for future use.
2 Place ¼ cup of the curry paste in large saucepan; stir over heat until fragrant. Add coconut milk and lime leaves; bring to a boil. Reduce heat; simmer, stirring, 5 minutes.
3 Meanwhile, quarter chicken pieces. Heat oil in large frying pan; cook chicken, in batches, until just browned. Drain on absorbent paper.
4 Add chicken to curry mixture with sauce, juice, sugar and eggplants; simmer, covered, about 5 minutes or until eggplants are tender and chicken is cooked through. Add zucchini, thai basil and chopped coriander; cook, stirring, until zucchini is just tender.
5 Place curry in serving bowl; sprinkle with coriander leaves, sliced chilli and onion.

GREEN CURRY PASTE Dry-fry ground coriander and cumin in small heated frying pan over medium heat until fragrant. Blend or process roasted spices with remaining ingredients, except for the oil, until mixture forms a paste, pausing to scrape down sides of machine occasionally during blending. Add oil to paste mixture; continue to blend in machine or using mortar and pestle until smooth.

☐ **PER SERVING** 66.0g total fat (41.8g saturated); 3708kj (887 cal); 13.5g carbohydrate; 58.2g protein; 6.0g fibre

CHICKEN GREEN CURRY

This is a great salad to take to a picnic, as the chicken legs are good warm or cold and the salad will carry well. Take the dressing separately and add it just before you're ready to eat.

Spicy chicken legs with mango salad

PREPARATION TIME 40 MINUTES **COOKING TIME** 30 MINUTES **SERVES** 4

½ cup (125ml) chicken stock
2 teaspoons honey
2 tablespoons rice vinegar
1 teaspoon five-spice powder
6 cloves garlic, crushed
¼ cup (60ml) light soy sauce
½ cup (125ml) water
2 teaspoons sesame oil
8 chicken drumsticks (1.2kg)

MANGO SALAD
1 green mango (350g)
4 green onions, sliced thinly
1 cup loosely packed fresh coriander leaves
150g snow peas, trimmed, halved
2 lebanese cucumbers (260g), seeded, sliced thinly
1 ½ cups (120g) bean sprouts
¼ cup (60ml) lime juice
¼ cup (60ml) rice vinegar
2 teaspoons peanut oil

1 Combine stock, honey, vinegar, five-spice, garlic, soy sauce and the water in medium jug.
2 Heat oil in large deep frying pan; cook chicken, in batches, until browned all over. Return chicken to pan with stock mixture; bring to a boil. Reduce heat; simmer, covered, about 20 minutes or until chicken is cooked through.
4 Meanwhile, make mango salad.
5 Divide chicken and salad among serving plates; drizzle remaining pan juices over chicken.

MANGO SALAD Cut mango into strips; combine with remaining ingredients in large bowl.

PER SERVING 13.2g total fat (3.1g saturated); 1555kj (372 cal); 15.7g carbohydrate; 44.7g protein; 5g fibre

---

For a great accompaniment roast 1kg potatoes and serve as they are, or toss with ½ cup mayonnaise, 1 crushed garlic clove (or 2 roasted garlic cloves) and ½ teaspoon smoked paprika.

Portuguese-style grilled spatchcock

PREPARATION TIME 15 MINUTES **COOKING TIME** 40 MINUTES **SERVES** 4

4 x 500g spatchcocks
1 tablespoon cracked black pepper
1 tablespoon ground cumin
1 tablespoon lemon juice
1 tablespoon olive oil
½ teaspoon chilli powder
½ teaspoon hot paprika
¼ teaspoon cayenne pepper
1 clove garlic, crushed

1 Cut along both sides of spatchcocks' backbones; discard backbones. Insert metal skewer through thigh and opposite wing. Repeat with other thigh and wing.
2 Combine remaining ingredients in small bowl. Rub paste all over spatchcock. Cook, covered, on heated oiled grill plate (or grill or barbecue) 20 minutes. Turn spatchcock; cook about 20 minutes or until browned all over and tender.

PER SERVING 16.3g total fat (4.0g saturated); 1593kj (381 cal); 0.2g carbohydrate; 58.0g protein; 0.1g fibre

SPICY CHICKEN LEGS WITH MANGO SALAD

Anchovies are a "secret" ingredient in many savoury dishes, merging into the flavours of the other ingredients to add depth and richness. Soaking them first in milk removes their fishy taste and some of their saltiness.

Chicken cacciatore

PREPARATION TIME 30 MINUTES (PLUS STANDING TIME) **COOKING TIME** 1 HOUR 20 MINUTES **SERVES** 4

2 tablespoons olive oil

1.5kg chicken pieces

1 medium brown onion (150g), chopped finely

1 clove garlic, crushed

½ cup (125ml) dry white wine

1 tablespoon white vinegar

½ cup (125ml) chicken stock

410g can crushed tomatoes

1 tablespoon tomato paste

1 teaspoon finely chopped fresh basil

1 teaspoon white sugar

3 anchovy fillets, drained, chopped finely

¼ cup (60ml) milk

⅓ cup (55g) seeded kalamata olives, halved

1 tablespoon finely chopped fresh flat-leaf parsley

1 Preheat oven to moderate (180°C/160°C fan-forced).
2 Heat oil in large frying pan; cook chicken, in batches, until browned all over. Place chicken in ovenproof dish.
3 Cook onion and garlic in same pan, stirring, until onion softens. Add wine and vinegar; bring to a boil. Boil, uncovered, until liquid reduces by half. Add stock, undrained tomatoes, paste, basil and sugar; cook, uncovered, 5 minutes. Pour tomato mixture over chicken pieces. Cover; bake about 1 hour or until chicken is cooked through.
4 Soak anchovies in milk 5 minutes; drain. Place chicken on serving dish; cover. Pour pan juices into medium saucepan; bring to a boil. Boil, uncovered, 1 minute. Add anchovy, olives and parsley; stir until heated through. Pour sauce over chicken.

PER SERVING 20.4g total fat (4.7g saturated); 1945kj (465 cal); 11g carbohydrate; 52.9g protein; 2.3g fibre

---

Luscious as duck confit is, no-one could call it low-fat. If you prefer a lower-fat way of cooking the duck, salt it (preferably overnight) then cook it in an aromatic chicken stock flavoured with thyme, orange rind, cinnamon, juniper berries and peppercorns. When tender, drain and pat dry with absorbent paper. Heat 2 tablespoons olive oil in a heavy-based frying pan and pan-fry the duck until the skin is golden and crisp.

Duck confit with pan-fried kipflers and pear and watercress salad

PREPARATION TIME 1 HOUR (PLUS REFRIGERATION TIME) **COOKING TIME** 3 HOURS **SERVES** 6

2 x 2kg ducks

1 tablespoon coarse cooking salt

2 cloves garlic, sliced thinly

1 dried bay leaf, crumbled

2 sprigs fresh thyme

2 teaspoons black peppercorns

2 cups (500ml) olive oil, approximately

750g kipfler potatoes

PEAR AND WATERCRESS SALAD

350g watercress, trimmed

1 large pear (330g), sliced thinly

1 tablespoon wholegrain mustard

1 tablespoon white wine vinegar

1 teaspoon white sugar

¼ cup (60ml) olive oil

1 Using sharp knife, cut marylands and breasts off ducks. Remove as much fat as possible from carcasses; reserve. Discard wings and carcasses. Combine duck pieces, salt, garlic, bay leaf, thyme and peppercorns in medium bowl, cover; refrigerate until required.

2 Meanwhile, place reserved fat in large saucepan; cook, uncovered, over low heat, 1 hour or until fat has melted. Strain mixture through fine sieve into large bowl; discard solids.
3 Preheat oven to slow (150°C/130°C fan-forced).
4 Rinse duck pieces under cold water; pat dry with absorbent paper. Place in large baking dish. Reserve 2 tablespoons of the fat for potatoes; pour remaining fat over duck. Top up with olive oil, making sure duck is submerged. Bake, uncovered, 2 hours.
5 Boil, steam or microwave potato until tender; drain. Heat reserved fat in large frying pan; cook potato, in batches, until browned. Cover to keep warm.
6 Meanwhile, make pear and watercress salad.
7 Place duck in same large frying pan; cook, skin-side down, until skin is crisp.
8 Serve duck with potato and salad.

PEAR AND WATERCRESS SALAD Place watercress, pear and combined remaining ingredients in large bowl; toss gently to combine.

☐ **PER SERVING** 106.3g total fat (18.1g saturated); 5589kj (1337 cal); 22.4g carbohydrate; 72.7g protein; 6.1g fibre

---

Asian chicken burger with pickled cucumber and wasabi mayonnaise

PREPARATION TIME 15 MINUTES (PLUS REFRIGERATION TIME) **COOKING TIME** 15 MINUTES **SERVES** 4

For chilli burgers, add 1 tablespoon finely chopped pickled ginger and 1 finely chopped red chilli to the burger mixture. After shaping the burgers, dip them into a mixture of plain and black sesame seeds, before cooking.

500g chicken mince
1 tablespoon dark soy sauce
1 egg
1 cup (70g) stale breadcrumbs
1 teaspoon sesame oil
2 green onions, chopped finely
4 hamburger buns
50g mizuna

PICKLED CUCUMBER
1 lebanese cucumber (130g)
¼ cup (70g) drained pickled pink ginger
½ cup (125ml) rice vinegar
1 teaspoon salt
1 tablespoon caster sugar

WASABI MAYONNAISE
¼ cup (75g) mayonnaise
2 teaspoons wasabi paste

1 Make pickled cucumber and wasabi mayonnaise.
2 Meanwhile, using hand, combine mince, soy sauce, egg, breadcrumbs, oil and onion in large bowl; shape mixture into four burgers. Cook burgers on heated oiled grill plate (or grill or barbecue) about 15 minutes or until cooked through.
3 Meanwhile, split buns in half horizontally; toast, cut-side up. Spread wasabi mayonnaise on bun bases; sandwich mizuna, burgers and drained pickled cucumber between bun halves.

PICKLED CUCUMBER Using sharp knife, mandoline or v-slicer, slice cucumber thinly. Combine cucumber in small bowl with remaining ingredients. Cover; refrigerate 30 minutes.

WASABI MAYONNAISE Combine ingredients in small bowl.

☐ **PER SERVING** 16.4g total fat (3.2g saturated); 2165kj (518 cal); 53.1g carbohydrate; 37.0g protein; 4.0g fibre

Chicken drumettes in crisp spicy batter

PREPARATION TIME 25 MINUTES **COOKING TIME** 30 MINUTES **MAKES** 16

Besan flour is made from chickpeas. It adds crispness and a nutty flavour to the spices used in the batter. As the drumettes are cooked, place them on an oven tray lined with crumpled absorbent paper and keep them warm in a slow oven until they are all done.

16 chicken drumettes (1.1kg)
2 tablespoons besan flour
¼ cup (35g) self-raising flour
½ teaspoon chilli powder
½ teaspoon garam masala
¼ teaspoon ground cumin
¼ teaspoon ground coriander
½ cup (125ml) water
vegetable oil, for deep-frying

DIPPING SAUCE
½ cup (125ml) char siu sauce
¼ cup (60ml) water
1 fresh small red thai chilli, chopped finely

1 Trim around bone of drumettes with sharp knife; cut, scrape and push meat down to large end. Pull skin and meat down over ends of bones; they will resemble baby drumsticks.
2 Sift dry ingredients into medium bowl; gradually stir in the water.
3 Make dipping sauce.
4 Dip drumettes into batter; shake off excess. Heat oil in wok or large saucepan; deep-fry drumettes, in batches, until browned lightly and cooked through. Serve with sauce.

DIPPING SAUCE Combine ingredients in small saucepan; bring to a boil.

PER DRUMETTE (INCLUDING SAUCE) 4.2g total fat (0.8g saturated); 397kj (95 cal); 4.9g carbohydrate; 8.7g protein; 1.1g fibre

---

Cajun chicken with pineapple salsa

PREPARATION TIME 15 MINUTES **COOKING TIME** 15 MINUTES **SERVES** 4

Make this salsa just before serving and add the bacon last. It must be eaten the same day as the enzymes in the fresh pineapple will gradually cause the bacon to go mushy.

1 tablespoon sweet paprika
1 teaspoon cayenne pepper
2 teaspoons garlic powder
2 teaspoons dried oregano
1 tablespoon olive oil
8 chicken thigh fillets (880g)

PINEAPPLE SALSA
4 bacon rashers (280g), rind removed
1 small pineapple (900g), chopped finely
1 fresh small red thai chilli, chopped finely
¼ cup coarsely chopped fresh flat-leaf parsley
1 medium red capsicum (200g), chopped coarsely
¼ cup (60ml) lime juice
1 teaspoon olive oil

1 Combine spices, oregano and oil in large bowl; add chicken, turn to coat in mixture.
2 Make pineapple salsa.
3 Meanwhile, cook chicken on heated oiled flat plate, uncovered, until cooked through.
4 Serve chicken with salsa and lemon wedges, if desired.

PINEAPPLE SALSA Cook bacon on heated oiled flat plate until crisp; drain then chop coarsely. Place bacon in medium bowl with remaining ingredients; toss gently to combine.

☐ **PER SERVING** 24.5g total fat (6.9g saturated); 2169kj (519 cal); 11.7g carbohydrate; 61.2g protein; 3.4g fibre

---

Steamed chicken in banana leaf

PREPARATION TIME 25 MINUTES **COOKING TIME** 15 MINUTES **SERVES** 4

If banana leaves are unavailable, foil or baking paper can be used to enclose the chicken. Any firm white-fleshed fish (such as bream or snapper) can also be cooked using this method.

4 single chicken breast fillets (800g)

5 cloves garlic, crushed

4cm piece fresh ginger (20g), grated

15cm stick (30g) finely chopped fresh lemon grass

2 fresh small red thai chillies, chopped finely

½ cup coarsely chopped fresh coriander

⅓ cup (80ml) lime juice

1 tablespoon peanut oil

1 large banana leaf

300g snow peas, trimmed

¼ cup (40g) roasted pine nuts

THAI DRESSING

2 tablespoons lime juice

2 tablespoons brown sugar

1 tablespoon rice wine

1 tablespoon fish sauce

½ teaspoon sesame oil

1cm piece fresh ginger (5g), grated

1 clove garlic, crushed

2 teaspoons sweet chilli sauce

1 Using sharp knife, make three shallow cuts on smooth side of each fillet.
2 Combine garlic, ginger, lemon grass, chilli, coriander, juice and peanut oil in large bowl. Press spice mixture all over chicken, pressing into cuts. Cover; refrigerate while preparing banana leaf.
3 Cut banana leaf into four 30cm squares. Using tongs, dip one square at a time into large saucepan of boiling water; remove immediately. Rinse under cold water; pat dry with absorbent paper. Leaves should be soft and pliable.
4 Centre each undrained fillet on a banana leaf square. Fold leaf over fillet to enclose; secure each parcel with kitchen string. Place parcels in bamboo steamer over wok or large saucepan of boiling water; steam, covered, about 15 minutes or until chicken is cooked.
5 Meanwhile, boil, steam or microwave snow peas until just tender; drain. Rinse under cold water; drain.
6 Make thai dressing.
7 Place snow peas in medium bowl with pine nuts and dressing; toss gently to combine. Serve snow peas with chicken and steamed jasmine rice, if desired.

THAI DRESSING Place ingredients in screw-top jar; shake well.

☐ **PER SERVING** 21.0g total fat (3.8g saturated); 1818kj (435 cal); 12.5g carbohydrate; 46.2g protein; 3.8g fibre

BEEF & VEAL

Beef & Veal

Beef stands for great family meals and generous hospitality. It is highly nutritious, supplying first-class protein, B vitamins, zinc and iron. As well, up-to-date research shows that, contrary to some earlier opinions, lean beef is not a threat to our cholesterol levels.

CHOOSING CUTS OF MEAT

In all table animals, the most tender and expensive cuts come from the parts that have had the least exercise – those that lie along the back. Cheapter cuts from parts that have had more exercise have developed more connective tissue, the main cause of toughness. This does *not* mean that it is always desirable to use the most tender and expensive cut you can afford. Braises and stews get their deep flavour and richness from cuts with plenty of connective tissue, which breaks down when it is cooked slowly with liquid.

STORING AND HANDLING FRESH MEAT

Refrigerate fresh meat as soon as you get it home, storing it in one layer in a container covered loosely with foil. The more it has been cut and handled, the less time it will keep.

RECOMMENDED REFRIGERATION TIMES

Mince and sausages	2 days
Diced or cubed meat	3 days
Steaks, chops or cutlets	4 days
Roasting joints, bone-in	3 to 5 days
Roasting joints, boned and rolled	2 to 3 days
Corned meat	1 week

BE SCRUPULOUS ABOUT HYGIENE Wash your hands before and after handling raw meat After cutting it up, rinse the cutting board promptly, scrub it with coarse cooking salt and rinse again. Defrost frozen meat in the fridge, not at room temperature.

KINDS OF BEEF

Beef may be grass-fed (fed entirely on pasture) or grain-fed (fed on grain-dominated feed for 3 months before slaughter). All beef is aged (ie, stored, packaged in cryovac, in coolroom conditions) for about 2 weeks before sale so natural enzyme action can enhance tenderness.

BEEF CUTS

- **Roasting** cuts are fillet, sirloin, rump, scotch fillet and rib either on the bone ("standing") or boned and rolled. Cheaper cuts marked "roasting" are often tough.
- **Grilling, char-grilling, barbecuing or pan-frying** steaks are fillet, rump, T-bone, New York cut, porterhouse and rib (entrecote). Oyster blade is good for pan-frying if cut thin. Cheaper cuts marked "grilling" or "barbecuing" may disappoint.
- **Pot-roasting** (braising in one piece) cuts are round, topside, silverside and bolar blade.
- Beef for cutting up and **casseroling** can be chuck, blade, skirt, brisket, gravy beef or any of the pot-roasting cuts above.
- **Corned beef** may be silverside (lean) or rolled brisket (fatty).
- **Ox kidney** is good for steak and kidney.

HOW MUCH TO BUY

The amount for each serving varies with individual appetites and the type of dish. As a guide, allow 125 to 150g per person of boneless beef and 150 to 200g of beef with some bone, such as T-bone steak or bone-in roast.

JUDGING WHEN BEEF IS DONE TO YOUR TASTE

STEAK Press the surface with a finger or the back of tongs. Rare steak feels soft and spongy, medium-rare soft but springy, medium-done firm but still springy, and well-done quite firm. Rest the steaks, wrapped or covered with foil, for 5 minutes before serving.

ROAST BEEF Use a meat thermometer, or insert a fine skewer into the centre and check the juice that runs out. Red juice means rare, pink means medium, clear means well done. To enhance juiciness, rest a cooked roast, wrapped in foil, for 15 minutes before serving.

KINDS OF VEAL

Veal from calves that have fed on grass is pink or pinky-red. Veal from calves fed on milk only is very pale, delicate in flavour, supremely tender and more expensive.

VEAL CUTS

- **Roasting** cuts are loin on the bone or boned and rolled, rib, rump, topside (cushion), silverside, round (nut) and boned and rolled rib.
- Cuts for **pan-frying, grilling or char-grilling** are chops, cutlets and leg or fillet steaks. Schnitzel (scaloppine) is for pan-frying but does not suit grilling.
- Cuts for **pot-roasting** (braising in one piece) are shoulder on the bone or boned and rolled, stuffed and rolled breast (brisket) or any of the roasting cuts above.
- Veal for cutting up and **casseroling** can be boneless shoulder, neck, breast, shin (shank), or any of the pot-roasting cuts above.
- Veal **sweetbreads** (thymus glands), **kidneys** and calf's **liver** are prized for their delicacy.

COOKING VEAL

Moist cooking methods and low to moderate heat are the general rule. The exceptions are roasts (protected by very frequent basting), schnitzel, which is briefly cooked on high heat, and pan-fried chops, steaks and cutlets, which are browned quickly on high heat, then cooked on low heat.

When browning meat make sure the meat is dry and that the oil is hot (the surface should shimmer). It is important to brown the beef in batches to prevent overcrowding in the pan, which causes the meat to stew, rather than brown. Well-browned meat is very important for the flavour of a stew.

Beef and horseradish stew with kumara potato mash

PREPARATION TIME 40 MINUTES **COOKING TIME** 3 HOURS 30 MINUTES **SERVES** 6

2 tablespoons olive oil

1.5kg chuck steak, diced into 5cm pieces

3 medium brown onions (450g), sliced into thick wedges

3 cloves garlic, crushed

8cm piece fresh ginger (40g), grated

2 teaspoons curry powder

¼ cup (35g) plain flour

3 cups (750ml) beef stock

1 tablespoon worcestershire sauce

2 tablespoons horseradish cream

¼ cup coarsely chopped fresh flat-leaf parsley

KUMARA POTATO MASH

1kg kumara, chopped coarsely

500g potatoes, chopped coarsely

¾ cup (180ml) cream

50g butter

1 Preheat oven to very slow (120°C/100°C fan-forced).

2 Heat oil in large flameproof casserole dish; cook beef, in batches, until browned. Cook onion, garlic and ginger in same dish, stirring, about 5 minutes or until onion softens. Add curry powder and flour; cook, stirring, 5 minutes.

3 Return beef to dish with stock and sauce; stir over heat until mixture boils and thickens. Cover dish tightly; bake for 3 hours, stirring occasionally.

4 Meanwhile, make kumara potato mash.

5 Stir horseradish cream and parsley into beef mixture off the heat just before serving; serve with kumara potato mash.

KUMARA POTATO MASH Boil, steam or microwave kumara and potato, separately, until tender; drain. Mash kumara and potato in large bowl with warmed cream and butter until smooth; cover to keep warm.

☐ **PER SERVING** 42.1g total fat (20.8g saturated); 3336kj (798 cal); 40.8g carbohydrate; 61.5g protein; 5.5g fibre

Beef, bean and chorizo stew

PREPARATION TIME 20 MINUTES **COOKING TIME** 2 HOURS 30 MINUTES **SERVES** 6

If you're unable to find chorizo, use herb and garlic sausages. To replace the distinct smokey flavour of the chorizo, change the hot paprika to hot smoked paprika or add ½ teaspoon chopped chipotle chilli.

¼ cup (60ml) olive oil

1.5kg chuck steak, diced

2 medium brown onions (300g), sliced thickly

4 cloves garlic, crushed

1 tablespoon hot paprika

2 chorizo sausages (340g), sliced thinly

¼ cup (70g) tomato paste

2 x 400g cans crushed tomatoes

2 tablespoons finely chopped fresh thyme

1 cup (250ml) dry red wine

2 x 300g cans white beans, rinsed, drained

1 Heat 2 tablespoons of the oil in large saucepan; cook beef, in batches, until browned.

2 Heat remaining oil in same pan; cook onion, garlic, paprika and sausages, stirring, until onion softens. Return beef to pan with paste, undrained tomatoes, thyme and wine; bring to a boil. Reduce heat; simmer, covered, about 1½ hours or until beef is tender.

3 Uncover; simmer, stirring occasionally, about 30 minutes or until thickened slightly. Add beans; stir until heated through.

PER SERVING 41.4g total fat (13.8g saturated); 3022kj (723 cal); 11g carbohydrate; 67.8g protein; 4.6g fibre

---

Traditional beef pot roast

PREPARATION TIME 15 MINUTES **COOKING TIME** 3 HOURS **SERVES** 8

Keep the heat fairly high while browning the beef and turn several times to ensure that it is a good, rich brown all over. Don't hurry the process – much of the flavour of the pot roast comes from the caramelised surface of the meat.

1 tablespoon olive oil

125g butter

2kg corner topside roast

4 medium carrots (480g), cut into 3cm lengths

2 large potatoes (600g), chopped coarsely

1 large brown onion (200g), sliced thickly

3 medium parsnips (750g), cut into 3cm lengths

¼ cup (35g) plain flour

1 litre (4 cups) beef stock

½ cup (125ml) dry red wine

¼ cup (70g) tomato paste

¼ cup (60ml) worcestershire sauce

1 Heat oil and 20g of the butter in large saucepan; cook beef until browned all over. Remove from pan.

2 Melt another 20g of the butter in same pan; cook carrot, potato, onion and parsnip, stirring, until vegetables just soften and brown lightly. Remove from pan.

3 Heat remaining butter in same pan, add flour; cook, stirring, until browned lightly. Remove from heat. Gradually stir in stock and wine; stir over heat until sauce boils and thickens. Stir in paste and sauce.

4 Return beef and any juices to pan; bring to a boil. Reduce heat; simmer, covered, about 2 hours or until beef is tender, turning occasionally. Return vegetables to pan; simmer, uncovered, about 20 minutes or until sauce thickens slightly.

PER SERVING 30.5g total fat (15.1g saturated); 2700kj (646 cal); 27.9g carbohydrate; 59.4g protein; 5.7g fibre

Long, slow cooking is the key to massaman curry. The meat needs to be so tender that it practically falls apart. For something a little different try using lamb shanks instead of the beef.

Beef massaman curry

PREPARATION TIME 20 MINUTES **COOKING TIME** 2 HOURS **SERVES** 4

1kg skirt steak, diced into 3cm pieces

1½ cups (375ml) beef stock

3¼ cups (810ml) coconut milk

5 cardamom pods, bruised

¼ teaspoon ground clove

2 star anise

1 tablespoon grated palm sugar

2 tablespoons fish sauce

1 tablespoon tamarind concentrate

2 teaspoons tamarind concentrate, extra

½ cup (125ml) beef stock, extra

8 baby brown onions (200g), halved

1 medium kumara (400g), chopped coarsely

¼ cup (35g) coarsely chopped unsalted roasted peanuts

2 green onions, sliced thinly

MASSAMAN CURRY PASTE

20 dried long red chillies

1 teaspoon ground coriander

2 teaspoons ground cumin

2 teaspoons ground cinnamon

½ teaspoon ground cardamom

½ teaspoon ground clove

5 large cloves garlic, quartered

1 large brown onion (200g), chopped coarsely

2 sticks fresh lemon grass, sliced thinly

3 fresh kaffir lime leaves, sliced thinly

4cm piece fresh ginger (20g), chopped coarsely

2 teaspoons shrimp paste

1 tablespoon peanut oil

1 Place beef, stock, 1½ cups of the coconut milk, cardamom, clove, star anise, sugar, sauce and tamarind in large saucepan; bring to a boil. Reduce heat; simmer, uncovered, about 1½ hours or until beef is almost tender. Strain beef over large bowl; reserve 1 cup of the beef sauce, discard cardamom and star anise.

2 Meanwhile, make massaman curry paste.

3 Place 2 tablespoons of the curry paste in same cleaned pan; cook, stirring, until fragrant. Add remaining coconut milk, extra tamarind and extra stock; bring to a boil. Boil, stirring, 1 minute or until mixture is smooth. Add beef, brown onion, kumara and reserved beef sauce; cook, uncovered, about 30 minutes or until vegetables are tender.

4 Place curry in serving bowl; sprinkle with nuts and green onion.

MASSAMAN CURRY PASTE Preheat oven to moderate (180°C/160°C fan-forced). Place chillies in small heatproof jug, cover with boiling water; stand 15 minutes, drain. Meanwhile, dry-fry ground coriander, cumin, cinnamon, cardamom and clove in small heated frying pan, stirring, over medium heat, until fragrant. Place chillies and roasted spices in small shallow baking dish with remaining ingredients. Roast, uncovered, for 15 minutes. Blend or process curry paste mixture until smooth.

☐ **PER SERVING** 57.4g total fat (40.9g saturated); 3883kj (929 cal); 31.4g carbohydrate; 68.5g protein; 8.2g fibre

Pat the steaks dry before cooking. Keep the heat high and cook one side until beads of moisture appear on the top surface. Turn once only. Cook the second side, lowering the heat to medium after 2 minutes, until the steaks are cooked to your liking.

T-bones with blue-cheese butter and pear salad

PREPARATION TIME 15 MINUTES **COOKING TIME** 10 MINUTES **SERVES** 4

4 t-bone steaks (1.2kg)
2 tablespoons olive oil
50g soft blue cheese
50g butter, softened
2 green onions, chopped finely
1 tablespoon wholegrain mustard
1 teaspoon honey
¼ cup (60ml) olive oil, extra
1 tablespoon red wine vinegar
100g mesclun
1 large pear (330g), sliced thinly
½ cup (60g) roasted pecans

1 Brush beef with oil; cook on heated grill plate (or grill or barbecue) until browned both sides and cooked as desired.

2 Meanwhile, combine cheese, butter and onion in small bowl. Place mustard, honey, extra oil and vinegar in screw-top jar; shake well.

3 Gently toss mesclun, pear, nuts and mustard dressing in medium bowl.

4 Spread blue-cheese butter on hot beef; serve with salad.

PER SERVING 59.4g total fat (18.0g saturated); 3168kj (758 cal); 10g carbohydrate; 45.6g protein; 3.7g fibre

---

Dusting meat with flour before browning adds extra flavour, as the flour acquires a nutty taste. The flour also helps to thicken the sauce. Browning the pieces of oxtail carefully and thoroughly is probably the most important part of making this recipe.

Braised oxtails with orange gremolata

PREPARATION TIME 20 MINUTES **COOKING TIME** 3 HOURS 15 MINUTES **SERVES** 4

1.5kg oxtails, cut into 5cm pieces
2 tablespoons plain flour
2 tablespoons olive oil
1 medium brown onion (150g), chopped coarsely
2 cloves garlic, crushed
½ cup (125ml) sweet sherry
400g can crushed tomatoes
1 cup (250ml) beef stock
1 cup (250ml) water
4 sprigs fresh thyme
2 bay leaves
10cm strip orange rind
4 medium tomatoes (600g), chopped coarsely

ORANGE GREMOLATA

¼ cup finely chopped fresh flat-leaf parsley
1 tablespoon finely grated orange rind
1 clove garlic, crushed

1 Preheat oven to moderately slow (170°C/150°C fan-forced).

2 Coat oxtail in flour; shake off excess. Heat half of the oil in large flameproof casserole dish; cook oxtail pieces, in batches, until browned all over.

3 Heat remaining oil in same dish; cook onion and garlic, stirring, until onion softens. Return oxtails to dish with sherry, undrained crushed tomatoes, stock, the water, herbs and rind, cover; bake about 3 hours or until oxtail is tender. Stir in chopped tomato.

4 Make orange gremolata by combining ingredients in small bowl.
5 Serve oxtail sprinkled with gremolata on mashed potato, if desired.

PER SERVING 110.3g total fat (40.0g saturated); 5706kj (1365 cal); 16.9g carbohydrate; 69.8g protein; 4.4g fibre

---

Osso buco

Osso buco is traditionally served with risotto milanese, also known as saffron risotto (see recipe on page 390). It is also good with plain rice or ribbon noodles.

PREPARATION TIME 30 MINUTES **COOKING TIME** 2 HOURS 30 MINUTES **SERVES** 4

1 tablespoon olive oil
8 pieces veal osso buco (2kg)
1 medium brown onion (150g), chopped coarsely
2 cloves garlic, crushed
1 trimmed celery stalk (100g), chopped coarsely
1 large carrot (180g), chopped coarsely
2 tablespoons tomato paste
½ cup (125ml) dry white wine
1 cup (250ml) beef stock
1 cup (250ml) water
400g can crushed tomatoes
1 teaspoon fresh rosemary leaves
1 medium eggplant (300g), chopped coarsely
1 medium green capsicum (200g), chopped coarsely
1 medium yellow capsicum (200g), chopped coarsely

GREMOLATA
2 teaspoons finely grated lemon rind
¼ cup finely chopped fresh flat-leaf parsley
1 tablespoon finely chopped fresh rosemary
1 clove garlic, chopped finely

1 Heat half of the oil in large saucepan; cook veal, in batches, until browned all over.
2 Heat remaining oil in same pan; cook onion, garlic, celery and carrot, stirring, until vegetables soften. Stir in paste, wine, stock, the water, undrained tomatoes and rosemary; bring to a boil.
3 Return veal to pan, fitting pieces upright and tightly together in single layer; return to a boil. Reduce heat; simmer, covered, 1½ hours. Add eggplant; cook, uncovered, about 15 minutes, stirring occasionally. Add capsicums; cook, uncovered, 15 minutes or until vegetables are tender.
4 Meanwhile, make gremolata by combining ingredients in small bowl.
5 Remove veal and vegetables from pan; cover to keep warm. Bring sauce to a boil; boil, uncovered, about 10 minutes or until sauce thickens slightly.
6 Divide veal and vegetables among serving plates; top with sauce, then gremolata.

PER SERVING 10.3g total fat (2.1g saturated); 2111kj (505 cal); 13.9g carbohydrate; 79.8g protein; 6.8g fibre

Chile con carne

PREPARATION TIME 25 MINUTES (PLUS STANDING TIME)
COOKING TIME 3 HOURS 40 MINUTES (PLUS COOLING TIME) **SERVES** 8 **MAKES** 12 MUFFINS

If you can find fresh jalapeño chillies, use two, seeded and finely chopped, in both the chile con carne and the muffins. Jalapeños also add a delicious depth of flavour to home-made baked beans, salsas, marinades and stews.

1 cup (200g) dried kidney beans
1.5kg chuck steak
2 litres (8 cups) water
1 tablespoon olive oil
2 medium brown onions (300g), chopped coarsely
2 cloves garlic, crushed
2 teaspoons ground cumin
2 teaspoons ground coriander
½ teaspoon cayenne pepper
2 teaspoons sweet paprika
2 x 400g cans crushed tomatoes
1 tablespoon tomato paste
4 green onions, chopped coarsely
2 tablespoons coarsely chopped fresh coriander
⅓ cup (65g) drained bottled jalapeño chillies, chopped finely

JALAPEÑO CORN MUFFINS
½ cup (125g) plain flour
½ cup (125g) self-raising flour
2 cups (340g) polenta
2 teaspoons salt
1 cup (250ml) milk
2 cups (500ml) buttermilk
2 tablespoons olive oil
2 eggs, beaten lightly
1⅓ cups (160g) finely grated cheddar
⅓ cup (65g) drained bottled jalapeño chillies, chopped finely

1 Place beans in medium bowl, cover with water, stand overnight; drain.
2 Combine beef with the water in large saucepan; bring to a boil. Reduce heat; simmer, covered, 1½ hours. Cool 15 minutes.
3 Drain beef in large muslin-lined strainer placed over large bowl; reserve 3½ cups (875ml) of the cooking liquid. Using two forks, shred beef coarsely.
4 Heat oil in same cleaned pan; cook brown onion and garlic, stirring, until onion softens. Add spices; cook, stirring, until fragrant. Add beans, undrained tomatoes, paste and 2 cups of the reserved cooking liquid; bring to a boil. Simmer, covered, 1 hour.
5 Add beef and remaining cooking liquid to pan; simmer, covered, about 30 minutes or until beans are tender.
6 Meanwhile, make jalapeño corn muffins.
7 Stir green onion, coriander and chilli into chile con carne. Serve with muffins.

JALAPEÑO CORN MUFFINS Preheat oven to moderate (180°C/160°C fan-forced). Sift flours into large bowl; add remaining ingredients, mix until combined. Spoon muffin mixture into greased 12-hole (½-cup/125ml) muffin pan. Bake, uncovered, 35 minutes.

PER SERVING CHILE CON CARNE 11.5g total fat (3.9g saturated); 1501kj (359 cal); 14.8g carbohydrate; 45.1g protein; 7.7g fibre

PER MUFFIN 10.8g total fat (4.8g saturated); 1137kj (272 cal); 32.1g carbohydrate; 10.7g protein; 1.4g fibre

CHILE CON CARNE

Try adding 1 tablespoon horseradish cream or 1 teaspoon English dry mustard or dried thyme to the Yorkshire pudding mixture. You can also add ale or beef stock instead of the water. For light fluffy Yorkshire puddings it is essential that the batter is well rested and cold, and that the oven and dripping are both very hot.

Roast beef with yorkshire puddings

PREPARATION TIME 35 MINUTES (PLUS REFRIGERATION AND STANDING TIME)

COOKING TIME 2 HOURS **SERVES** 8

2 cups (500ml) dry red wine
2 bay leaves
6 black peppercorns
¼ cup (70g) wholegrain mustard
4 cloves garlic, sliced thinly
4 sprigs fresh thyme
1 medium brown onion (150g), chopped coarsely
2kg corner piece topside roast
2 medium carrots (240g), chopped coarsely
1 large leek (500g), chopped coarsely
2 trimmed celery stalks (200g), chopped coarsely
2 tablespoons olive oil
2 tablespoons plain flour
1½ cups (375ml) beef stock

YORKSHIRE PUDDINGS

1 cup (150g) plain flour
½ teaspoon salt
2 eggs
½ cup (125ml) milk
½ cup (125ml) water

1 Combine wine, bay leaves, peppercorns, mustard, garlic, thyme and onion in large bowl, add beef; turn to coat beef in marinade. Cover; refrigerate 3 hours or overnight.

2 Preheat oven to moderate (180°C/160°C fan-forced). Strain beef over medium bowl; reserve 1 cup of the marinade. Combine carrot, leek and celery in large flameproof baking dish, top with beef; brush beef with oil. Roast, uncovered, about 1½ hours or until beef is browned and cooked as desired. Make batter for yorkshire puddings after beef has been roasting for 1 hour.

3 Remove beef from pan, wrap in foil; stand 20 minutes. Using slotted spoon, discard vegetables. Pour juices from dish into large jug; skim 1½ tablespoons of the fat from juice, reserve for yorkshire puddings. Skim and discard remaining fat from juice. Reserve 2 tablespoons of juice for gravy; discard remaining juice. Finish puddings.

4 Meanwhile, heat reserved pan juices for gravy in same baking dish, add flour; cook, stirring, until mixture bubbles and thickens. Gradually add reserved marinade and stock; cook, stirring, until mixture boils and thickens, strain gravy into large jug.

5 Serve beef with yorkshire puddings and gravy, and roasted vegetables, if desired.

YORKSHIRE PUDDINGS Increase oven temperature to hot (220°C/200°C fan-forced). Sift flour and salt into bowl, make well in centre; add combined egg, milk and the water. Using wooden spoon, gradually stir in flour until batter is smooth. Cover; refrigerate 30 minutes. Divide reserved fat among 16 holes of mini (1½-tablespoon/30ml) muffin pans; heat in oven 2 minutes. Pour batter into pan holes; bake 10 minutes or until puffed and golden.

PER SERVING 22.1g total fat (7.8g saturated); 2404kj (575 cal); 21.4g carbohydrate; 60g protein; 3.9g fibre

Beef spareribs

PREPARATION TIME 10 MINUTES (PLUS REFRIGERATION TIME) **COOKING TIME** 20 MINUTES **SERVES** 4

Ribs lend themselves to slow cooking, so if you don't feel like firing up the barbecue, bake them in a slow oven for 2 hours. Turn them after an hour, basting them with the marinade.

2 cups (500ml) tomato sauce

½ cup (125ml) worcestershire sauce

¾ cup (180ml) vegetable oil

½ cup (125ml) water

¼ cup (60ml) white wine vinegar

⅓ cup (75g) firmly packed brown sugar

1 medium brown onion (150g), chopped finely

1.5kg spare ribs

1 Combine sauces, oil, the water, vinegar, sugar and onion in large shallow dish, add ribs; turn to coat in marinade. Cover; refrigerate 3 hours or overnight.

2 Drain ribs; reserve marinade.

3 Place reserved marinade in small saucepan; bring to a boil. Reduce heat; simmer, uncovered, until thickened slightly.

4 Cook ribs on heated oiled grill plate (or grill or barbecue), uncovered, until browned and cooked through. Pour sauce over ribs; serve with salad, if desired.

PER SERVING 58.4g total fat (12.2g saturated); 4230kj (1012 cal); 58.5g carbohydrate; 62.3g protein; 3.2g fibre

---

Sausages with caramelised onions, kipflers and mushrooms

PREPARATION TIME 10 MINUTES **COOKING TIME** 25 MINUTES **SERVES** 4

For a tasty picnic frittata chop the cooked sausages, potatoes and mushrooms into bite-sized pieces. Combine with the caramelised onion, 2 teaspoons fresh thyme and 6 eggs in a 22cm oiled frying pan. Cook over low heat until the base of the frittata is browned. Place the pan under a hot grill; cook until the top is browned and the frittata is set.

750g kipfler potatoes

olive-oil cooking spray

¼ cup coarsely chopped fresh chives

200g swiss brown mushrooms, sliced thickly

8 thick beef sausages (1.2kg)

2 large red onions (600g), sliced thinly

1 tablespoon balsamic vinegar

1 tablespoon brown sugar

1 Boil, steam or microwave potatoes until just tender; drain. Place on heated oiled grill plate (or grill or barbecue); spray with oil. Cook potatoes, uncovered, until browned. Remove from heat; sprinkle with chives.

2 Meanwhile, cook mushrooms and sausages on same grill plate, uncovered, until mushrooms are browned and sausages are cooked through.

3 Cook onion, stirring, on oiled flat plate or large frying pan until soft. Sprinkle with vinegar and sugar; cook, stirring, until onion is caramelised.

4 Divide potatoes, sausages and mushrooms among plates; top with caramelised onion.

PER SERVING 60.4g total fat (28.6g saturated); 3632kj (869 cal); 40.9g carbohydrate; 35.6g protein; 13.1g fibre

The best oils for deep-frying have a high smoking point, which means they can be heated to a high temperature without burning. Oils heated beyond their smoking point will taste bitter. The most suitable oils for deep-frying are peanut, rice bran and grapeseed oils.

Twice-fried sichuan beef

PREPARATION TIME 20 MINUTES **COOKING TIME** 25 MINUTES **SERVES** 4

- 2 tablespoons dry sherry
- ⅓ cup (80ml) dark soy sauce
- 3 teaspoons brown sugar
- 600g eye fillet, sliced thinly
- ½ cup (75g) cornflour
- 1½ cups (300g) jasmine rice
- vegetable oil, for deep-frying
- 2 teaspoons sesame oil
- 1 clove garlic, crushed
- 1 fresh small red thai chilli, chopped finely
- 1 medium brown onion (150g), sliced thickly
- 1 medium carrot (120g), halved, sliced thinly
- 1 small red capsicum (150g), sliced thinly
- 500g gai lan, chopped coarsely
- 1 tablespoon cracked sichuan peppercorns
- 2 tablespoons oyster sauce
- ½ cup (125ml) beef stock

This is quite a salty recipe, so you might prefer to use a salt-reduced soy sauce.

1 Combine sherry, half the soy sauce and half the sugar in medium bowl, add beef; turn to coat in mixture. Stand 10 minutes; drain. Toss beef in cornflour; shake off excess.
2 Cook rice in large saucepan of boiling water, uncovered, until just tender; drain. Cover.
3 Heat vegetable oil in wok or large saucepan; deep-fry beef, in batches, until crisp. Drain.
4 Heat sesame oil in same cleaned wok; stir-fry garlic, chilli and onion until onion just softens. Add carrot and capsicum; stir-fry until just tender. Add gai lan; stir-fry until just wilted. Return beef to wok with peppercorns, oyster sauce, remaining soy sauce, stock and remaining sugar; stir-fry until heated through. Serve with rice.

PER SERVING 20.3g total fat (5.3g saturated); 3072kj (735 cal); 88.2g carbohydrate; 42.9g protein; 7g fibre

---

For a slightly smoky flavour char-grill the eggplant slices instead of pan-frying.

Veal and eggplant parmigiana

PREPARATION TIME 10 MINUTES **COOKING TIME** 20 MINUTES **SERVES** 4

- ½ medium eggplant (150g)
- ¼ cup (60ml) olive oil
- 4 veal scaloppine (400g)
- 500g bottled tomato pasta sauce
- 1 tablespoon fresh sage leaves
- 200g bocconcini, sliced thinly

1 Cut eggplant into four 1cm slices. Heat 2 tablespoons of the oil in large frying pan; cook eggplant, uncovered, until browned both sides and tender. Drain on absorbent paper.
2 Heat remaining oil in same pan; cook veal, uncovered, until browned both sides.
3 Remove pan from heat. Top veal with eggplant, 1 tablespoon of the pasta sauce, sage and bocconcini. Spoon remaining sauce around veal.
4 Preheat grill. Return pan to heat; simmer, covered, about 5 minutes or until veal is heated through. Place pan under grill until cheese melts and browns lightly.

PER SERVING 23.7g total fat (7.5g saturated); 1680kj (402 cal); 12.7g carbohydrate; 33.1g protein; 3g fibre

1 TWICE-FRIED SICHUAN BEEF **2** VEAL AND EGGPLANT PARMIGIANA **3** NEW YORK STEAKS WITH LEMON-THYME BUTTER (P 232) **4** VEAL RACK WITH ROSEMARY AND ROCKET PESTO (P 232)

1

2

3

4

New York steaks are also known as boneless sirloin, striploin and porterhouse steaks – a tender and flavoursome cut.

New york steaks with lemon-thyme butter

PREPARATION TIME 15 MINUTES (PLUS REFRIGERATION TIME) **COOKING TIME** 45 MINUTES **SERVES** 4

4 large potatoes (1.2kg), cut into wedges

2 medium red onions (340g), cut into wedges

1 lemon, cut into wedges

2 teaspoons fresh thyme leaves

¼ cup (60ml) olive oil

4 new york-cut steaks (880g)

LEMON-THYME BUTTER

60g butter, softened

2 teaspoons finely grated lemon rind

1 teaspoon finely chopped fresh thyme

1 clove garlic, crushed

1 Preheat oven to hot (220°C/200°C fan-forced). Make lemon-thyme butter.

2 Combine potato, onion, lemon, thyme and oil in large deep baking dish. Roast, uncovered, stirring occasionally, 45 minutes or until potato wedges are browned and crisp.

3 Meanwhile, cook steaks, in batches, on heated oiled grill plate (or grill or barbecue) until browned both sides and cooked as desired.

4 Serve steaks with potato wedges and topped with lemon-thyme butter.

LEMON-THYME BUTTER Combine ingredients in small bowl. Cover; refrigerate until firm.

PER SERVING 46.4g total fat (19.1g saturated); 3453kj (826 cal); 44.5g carbohydrate; 54.4g protein; 7.8g fibre

---

The rich juices of the crusty meat and cheesy potatoes are all the sauce that the asparagus needs. You might like to put a fresh green salad on the table too, to eat with the last of those glorious juices.

Veal rack with rosemary and rocket pesto

PREPARATION TIME 15 MINUTES **COOKING TIME** 1 HOUR 5 MINUTES (PLUS STANDING TIME) **SERVES** 4

1kg baby new potatoes

1 clove garlic, quartered

50g baby rocket leaves

¼ cup (60ml) olive oil

¼ cup coarsely chopped fresh rosemary

1kg veal rack (8 cutlets)

½ cup (40g) finely grated parmesan

1 tablespoon plain flour

¾ cup (180ml) beef stock

¼ cup (60ml) dry white wine

1 tablespoon redcurrant jelly

500g asparagus, trimmed

1 Preheat oven to moderately hot (200°C/180°C fan-forced). Lightly oil shallow medium baking dish.

2 Place potatoes in dish; roast, uncovered, about 50 minutes or until tender.

3 Meanwhile, blend or process garlic, rocket, oil and 2 tablespoons of the rosemary until mixture forms a paste. Stir remaining rosemary into pesto.

4 Place veal rack on wire rack over large shallow flameproof baking dish; coat veal with pesto. Roast, uncovered, about 40 minutes or until veal is browned and cooked as desired. Remove veal from dish; cover to keep warm.

5 When potatoes are tender, sprinkle with cheese; roast, uncovered, about 5 minutes or until cheese melts.

6 Place baking dish holding veal juices over heat, add flour; cook, stirring, until mixture thickens and bubbles. Gradually add stock, wine and jelly, stirring, until sauce boils and thickens slightly.

7 Meanwhile, boil, steam or microwave asparagus until just tender; drain.

8 Serve veal, sliced into cutlets, with potatoes, asparagus and sauce.

PER SERVING 22.1g total fat (5.4g saturated); 2533kj (606 cal); 37.5g carbohydrate; 58.3g protein; 6.7g fibre

---

Steak sandwich revisited

PREPARATION TIME 20 MINUTES **COOKING TIME** 1 HOUR 20 MINUTES **SERVES** 4

Chilli tomato jam partners barbecued meats perfectly, especially a simple sausage sandwich. With sour cream stirred in, it becomes a quick and easy dip or you could spoon it over corn chips with cheese and guacamole for a speedy nachos.

4 scotch fillet steaks (800g)

8 thick slices ciabatta (280g)

2 tablespoons olive oil

60g rocket

CHILLI TOMATO JAM

1 tablespoon olive oil

2 cloves garlic, crushed

4 medium tomatoes (600g), chopped coarsely

1 tablespoon worcestershire sauce

½ cup (125ml) sweet chilli sauce

⅓ cup (75g) firmly packed brown sugar

1 tablespoon coarsely chopped fresh coriander

CARAMELISED LEEK

30g butter

1 medium leek (350g), sliced thinly

2 tablespoons brown sugar

2 tablespoons dry white wine

1 Make chilli tomato jam and caramelised leek.

2 Cook steaks on heated oiled grill plate (or grill or barbecue) until browned both sides and cooked as desired.

3 Meanwhile, brush both sides of bread slices with oil; toast both sides.

4 Sandwich rocket, steaks, chilli tomato jam and caramelised leek between bread slices.

CHILLI TOMATO JAM Heat oil in medium saucepan; cook garlic, stirring, until browned lightly. Add tomato, sauces and sugar; bring to a boil. Reduce heat; simmer, uncovered, about 45 minutes or until mixture thickens. Stand 10 minutes; stir in coriander.

CARAMELISED LEEK Melt butter in medium frying pan; cook leek, stirring, until softened. Add sugar and wine; cook, stirring occasionally, 20 minutes or until leek caramelises.

PER SERVING 35.0g total fat (11.4g saturated); 3419kj (818 cal); 68.5g carbohydrate; 51.6g protein; 7.4g fibre

Fast barbecue ideas

Some great ideas for starters, mains, accompaniments and even a few desserts.

CHILLI GARLIC OCTOPUS
Combine 500g baby octopus in a small bowl with 1 tablespoon lemon juice, ¼ cup sweet chilli sauce and 2 cloves crushed garlic. Cook on a grill plate until cooked through.

SKEWERED LEMON PRAWNS
Shell 24 large uncooked king prawns, leaving the tails intact. Thread onto skewers; place in a large dish with ⅓ cup olive oil, 1 tablespoon finely grated lemon rind and 1 teaspoon sea salt. Refrigerate 1 hour; cook on a grill plate.

TIKKA DRUMETTES
Combine ¼ cup tikka paste and 2 tablespoons yogurt in a small bowl. Add 1kg chicken drumettes; toss to coat in the mixture. Cook, covered, on a grill plate. Serve with extra yogurt.

POTATO AND ONION HASH
Slice 1 large brown onion. Grate 1kg potatoes; stir in 1 teaspoon salt. Squeeze the moisture from the potato. Combine the onion and potato, then cook on a heated oiled flat plate until browned and tender.

THAI RED CURRY BEEF SKEWERS
Thread 500g diced beef and cherry tomatoes onto skewers with one lime wedge. Combine 2 tablespoons red curry paste, 1 tablespoon brown sugar and 1 tablespoon lime juice; brush over the skewers and grill until cooked.

ROSEMARY AND LAMB KEBABS
Remove the leaves from eight 15cm rosemary stalks. Chop 2 tablespoons of leaves, mix with 2 tablespoons olive oil and 1 clove crushed garlic. Thread 800g diced lamb onto the skewers; brush with garlic oil. Grill.

PESTO CHICKEN

Brush four chicken breast fillets with a mixture of 1 teaspoon finely grated lemon rind, ¼ cup basil pesto and 1 tablespoon balsamic vinegar. Cook on a grill plate until cooked through.

GRILLED ASPARAGUS WITH CHILLI BUTTER

Combine 50g soft butter with ½ teaspoon dried chilli flakes. Push skewers crossways through some asparagus spears; brush with olive oil. Cook on a grill plate until tender. Serve with the chilli butter.

SALMON LEMON GRASS SKEWERS

Cut three lemon grass sticks in half lengthways then widthways. Cut 600g salmon fillets into 12 squares; cut a slit through the centre of each. Thread onto each skewer; cook on a grill.

CHOCOLATE BANANAS

Cut a 12cm slit in four unpeeled bananas; place on pieces of foil. Chop 150g dark eating chocolate; divide among the slits in the bananas. Drizzle with 2 tablespoons rum, then wrap in foil. Cook on a grill plate 30 minutes.

SUGARED LIME AND MANGO CHEEKS

Slice the cheeks from two mangoes; score in a criss-cross pattern. Drizzle with combined 1 tablespoon finely grated lime rind and 1 tablespoon lime juice then sprinkle each with a teaspoon of brown sugar. Cook on a grill, flesh-side down, until browned lightly.

PINEAPPLE WITH PASSIONFRUIT

Peel and core half a small pineapple; cut lengthways into 10 wedges. Brown the wedges on a grill plate. Combine 2 tablespoons Malibu and ⅓ cup passionfruit pulp; drizzle over the pineapple to serve.

This is one curry that is best eaten as soon as it is made, as the tender beef fillet becomes tough and dry if left to stand.

Beef rendang

PREPARATION TIME 15 MINUTES **COOKING TIME** 15 MINUTES **SERVES** 4

- 2 cloves garlic, quartered
- 4cm piece fresh ginger (20g), chopped coarsely
- 5cm stick (10g) finely chopped fresh lemon grass
- 2 medium brown onions (300g)
- 1 tablespoon peanut oil
- 1kg beef fillet, sliced thinly
- 1 cinnamon stick
- 2 whole cloves
- 1 tablespoon ground coriander
- 1 tablespoon ground cumin
- ½ cup (40g) desiccated coconut
- 1 tablespoon tamarind concentrate
- ¼ cup (60ml) coconut cream

1 Blend or process garlic, ginger, lemon grass and one quartered onion until mixture is almost smooth. Finely chop remaining onion.

2 Heat oil in wok; stir-fry beef and chopped onion, in batches, until beef is browned all over.

3 Place lemon grass mixture in wok with spices and coconut; stir-fry until fragrant. Return beef mixture to wok with tamarind and coconut cream; stir-fry until rendang is almost dry.

PER SERVING 29.0g total fat (15.6g saturated); 2128kj (509 cal); 5.7g carbohydrate; 55.1g protein; 3g fibre

---

You can vary the flavour by adding 2 tablespoons roasted walnuts and 1 teaspoon chopped sage to the gorgonzola cream. Replace the marinated artichokes with thinly sliced kumara that has been cooked on a grill plate.

Hamburger with a twist

PREPARATION TIME 15 MINUTES **COOKING TIME** 10 MINUTES **SERVES** 4

- 80g gorgonzola cheese, crumbled
- ¼ cup (60g) sour cream
- 400g beef mince
- 120g sausage mince
- 1 small brown onion (80g), chopped finely
- 1 tablespoon barbecue sauce
- 2 teaspoons worcestershire sauce
- ½ cup (75g) drained sun-dried tomatoes, chopped finely
- 4 hamburger buns
- 50g baby rocket leaves
- 170g marinated artichoke hearts, drained, quartered

1 Blend or process half of the cheese with sour cream until mixture is smooth. Stir in remaining cheese.

2 Using hands, combine minces, onion, sauces and tomato in medium bowl; shape mixture into four patties.

3 Cook patties in large lightly oiled heated frying pan until cooked through.

4 Meanwhile, halve buns; toast, cut-side up.

5 Sandwich rocket, patties, gorgonzola cream and artichoke in toasted buns.

PER SERVING 28.3g total fat (14.1g saturated); 2508kj (600 cal); 44.2g carbohydrate; 38.6g protein; 7.1g fibre

Fajitas with salsa cruda and avocado mash

PREPARATION TIME 25 MINUTES (PLUS REFRIGERATION TIME) **COOKING TIME** 15 MINUTES **SERVES** 4

2 tablespoons vegetable oil

⅓ cup (80ml) lime juice

¼ cup coarsely chopped fresh oregano

2 cloves garlic, crushed

¼ cup coarsely chopped fresh coriander

2 teaspoons ground cumin

800g skirt steak

1 medium red capsicum (200g), sliced thickly

1 medium green capsicum (200g), sliced thickly

1 medium yellow capsicum (200g), sliced thickly

1 large red onion (300g), sliced thickly

20 small flour tortillas

SALSA CRUDA

2 cloves garlic, crushed

3 medium tomatoes (450g), seeded, chopped finely

1 small white onion (80g), chopped finely

2 trimmed red radishes (30g), chopped finely

1 lebanese cucumber (130g), chopped finely

2 tablespoons coarsely chopped fresh coriander

1 fresh long red chilli, chopped finely

2 tablespoons lime juice

AVOCADO MASH

2 small avocados (400g)

2 tablespoons lime juice

1 Combine oil, juice, oregano, garlic, coriander and cumin in large bowl, add beef; turn to coat in marinade. Cover; refrigerate overnight.

2 Cook beef, capsicums and onion on heated oiled grill plate (or grill or barbecue) until beef is cooked as desired and vegetables are just tender. Cover to keep warm.

3 Meanwhile, make salsa cruda and avocado mash.

4 Make four foil parcels of five tortillas each; heat parcels both sides on same grill plate until tortillas are warm and just softened.

5 Cut beef into 1cm slices; combine with cooked vegetables in large bowl. Serve with salsa cruda, avocado mash and tortillas.

SALSA CRUDA Combine ingredients in small bowl.

AVOCADO MASH Mash ingredients in small bowl.

PER SERVING 44.5g total fat (8.8g saturated); 4875kj (1166 cal); 116.5g carbohydrate; 68.3g protein; 11.6g fibre

Skirt steak is a long, flat piece of beef cut from the diaphragm muscle. It's sometimes referred to as butchers steak and is often not on display, as it's a less popular cut. It is very flavoursome due to the high marbling of fat, which makes it a juicy steak when cooked correctly. Because it's a tougher cut, skirt steak is best marinated and should be sliced across the grain for serving.

Cold meatloaf makes a delicious sandwich filling on sourdough bread. Serve with melted cheese, mixed salad leaves and a chunky beetroot relish.

Barbecue-glazed meatloaf

PREPARATION TIME 20 MINUTES **COOKING TIME** 50 MINUTES **SERVES** 4

1 small red capsicum (150g)

400g beef mince

150g sausage mince

1 medium brown onion (150g), chopped finely

2 cloves garlic, crushed

¼ cup (25g) packaged breadcrumbs

1 egg, beaten lightly

½ cup (80g) coarsely chopped seeded green olives

¼ cup coarsely chopped fresh basil

1 tablespoon coarsely chopped fresh oregano

8 bacon rashers (560g), rind removed, sliced thickly lengthways

BARBECUE GLAZE

¼ cup (60ml) water

1 tablespoon tomato paste

1 tablespoon red wine vinegar

2 tablespoons brown sugar

1 Quarter capsicum; discard seeds and membrane. Roast under grill or in very hot oven, skin-side up, until skin blisters and blackens. Cover capsicum pieces with plastic or paper for 5 minutes. Peel away skin; slice capsicum thinly.

2 Preheat oven to moderate (180°C/160°C fan-forced). Line 8cm x 25cm bar cake pan with plastic wrap. Lightly oil 25cm x 30cm swiss roll pan.

3 Using hand, combine minces, onion, garlic, breadcrumbs, egg, olives and herbs in large bowl. Press half of the meatloaf mixture into bar pan. Lay capsicum strips over top, leaving 1cm border; press remaining meatloaf mixture over capsicum.

4 Turn bar pan onto swiss roll pan; remove plastic wrap from meatloaf. Cover top and sides of meatloaf with bacon, overlapping slices. Bake, uncovered, 15 minutes.

5 Meanwhile, make barbecue glaze.

6 Pour off any excess fat from meatloaf, brush with glaze; bake, uncovered, 25 minutes or until meatloaf is cooked through. Stand 10 minutes before serving.

BARBECUE GLAZE Combine ingredients in small saucepan; bring to a boil. Reduce heat; simmer, uncovered, 5 minutes.

PER SERVING 35.3g total fat (13.7g saturated); 2633kj (630 cal); 20.6g carbohydrate; 56.6g protein; 2.6g fibre

BARBECUE-GLAZED MEATLOAF

Beef burritos

PREPARATION TIME 20 MINUTES **COOKING TIME** 35 MINUTES **SERVES** 4

For a vegetarian alternative replace the beef mince with refried beans, either plain or chilli flavoured. And for vegetarians and meat eaters alike, this is delicious served with a dollop of guacamole.

4 x 25cm-round flour tortillas

1 cup (120g) coarsely grated cheddar

1 teaspoon hot paprika

¾ cup (180g) sour cream

1 tablespoon coarsely chopped fresh coriander

BEAN AND BEEF FILLING

1 tablespoon olive oil

1 medium brown onion (150g), chopped finely

1 clove garlic, crushed

500g beef mince

400g can crushed tomatoes

35g packet taco seasoning mix

½ cup (125ml) water

300g can kidney beans, rinsed, drained

1 Preheat oven to moderately hot (200°C/180°C fan-forced).

2 Make bean and beef filling.

3 Divide warm filling among tortillas, roll; secure with toothpicks.

4 Place filled tortillas on oiled oven tray; sprinkle with cheese and paprika. Bake, uncovered, about 10 minutes or until heated through.

5 Remove toothpicks; top with sour cream and coriander.

BEAN AND BEEF FILLING Heat oil in medium frying pan; cook onion and garlic, stirring, until onion softens. Add beef; cook, stirring, until browned. Stir in remaining ingredients; bring to a boil. Reduce heat; simmer, uncovered, 15 minutes or until mixture thickens.

PER SERVING 44.0g total fat (22.6g saturated); 3135kj (750 cal); 41g carbohydrate; 44.3g protein; 7.4g fibre

Beef carpaccio with fennel salad

PREPARATION TIME 10 MINUTES (PLUS FREEZING TIME) **SERVES** 4

Variations: add ¼ cup seeded halved green olives and 2 teaspoons finely chopped preserved lemon peel to the fennel salad, or scatter shavings of parmesan and crisp fried capers over the carpaccio. Serve with ciabatta bread.

400g piece eye fillet

2 medium fennel bulbs (600g), trimmed

2 trimmed celery stalks (200g)

2 tablespoons finely chopped fresh flat-leaf parsley

2 tablespoons lemon juice

1 clove garlic, crushed

½ teaspoon dijon mustard

⅓ cup (80ml) olive oil

1 Wrap fillet tightly in plastic wrap; freeze about 1 hour. Slice fillet as thinly as possible.

2 Slice fennel and celery thinly. Toss in medium bowl with remaining ingredients.

3 Arrange carpaccio slices, in single layer, on serving plates; top with fennel salad. Serve with sliced italian bread.

PER SERVING 24.4g total fat (5.1g saturated); 1367kj (327 cal); 3.6g carbohydrate; 22.4g protein; 3.4g fibre

BEEF BURRITOS

A French classic, this was a favourite dinner-party dish 20 or 30 years ago. Thanks to the resurgence in popularity of rich and rustic comfort food, it has now reappeared on restaurant menus and in the repertoire of many home cooks.

Beef bourguignon

PREPARATION TIME 30 MINUTES **COOKING TIME** 2 HOURS 30 MINUTES **SERVES** 6

- 350g shallots
- 2 tablespoons olive oil
- 2kg gravy beef, trimmed, diced into 2.5cm pieces
- 30g butter
- 4 bacon rashers (280g), rind removed, chopped coarsely
- 400g mushrooms, halved
- 2 cloves garlic, crushed
- ¼ cup (35g) plain flour
- 1¼ cups (310ml) beef stock
- 2½ cups (625ml) dry red wine
- 2 bay leaves
- 2 sprigs fresh thyme
- ½ cup coarsely chopped fresh flat-leaf parsley

1 Peel shallots, leaving root end intact so shallots remain whole during cooking.
2 Heat oil in large flameproof casserole dish; cook beef, in batches, until browned.
3 Heat butter in same dish; cook shallots, bacon, mushrooms and garlic, stirring, until shallots are browned lightly.
4 Sprinkle flour over shallot mixture; cook, stirring, until flour mixture bubbles and thickens. Gradually add stock and wine; stir over heat until mixture boils and thickens. Return beef and any juices to dish with bay leaves and thyme; bring to a boil. Reduce heat; simmer, covered, about 2 hours or until beef is tender, stirring every 30 minutes.
5 Discard bay leaf; stir in parsley just before serving.

PER SERVING 31.9g total fat (12.2g saturated); 2976kj (712 cal); 6.6g carbohydrate; 81.1g protein; 2.8g fibre

---

Persillade is a mixture of chopped garlic and parsley traditionally used either as a garnish or to flavour a sauce, as we have done here.

The secret of tender calves liver is to slice it into thin scallops, then quickly sear it. Overcooking will toughen its delicate texture.

Seared calves liver with persillade and parsnip mash

PREPARATION TIME 15 MINUTES **COOKING TIME** 30 MINUTES **SERVES** 4

- 1kg parsnips, chopped coarsely
- 1 large potato (300g), chopped coarsely
- 3 cloves garlic
- ½ cup (125ml) cream
- 100g butter
- 250g asparagus, trimmed
- 400g piece calves liver, sliced thinly
- 1 shallot (25g), chopped finely
- ½ cup (125ml) chicken stock
- 1 tablespoon lemon juice
- ⅓ cup finely chopped fresh flat-leaf parsley

1 Boil, steam or microwave parsnip and potato, separately, until tender; drain. Crush 2 cloves of the garlic; mash in large bowl with parsnip, potato, cream and half of the butter. Cover to keep warm.
2 Boil, steam or microwave asparagus until just tender; drain. Cover to keep warm.
3 Pat liver dry with absorbent paper. Melt about 1 tablespoon of the remaining butter in large frying pan; cook liver quickly, in batches, over high heat until browned both sides and cooked as desired (do not overcook). Cover to keep warm.

4 Heat remaining butter in same pan. Finely chop remaining clove of garlic; cook garlic and shallot, stirring, until shallot softens. Add stock and juice; bring to a boil, stirring. Remove from heat; stir in parsley.

5 Serve sliced liver with parsnip mash and asparagus; top liver with persillade.

▭ **PER SERVING** 43.3g total fat (25.3g saturated); 2688kj (643 cal); 33.0g carbohydrate; 27.5g protein; 7.3g fibre

---

Braised beef cheeks in red wine

Beef cheeks are an inexpensive cut, worth the long, slow cooking and absolutely delicious. A nice addition to this stew would be cannellini or butter beans.

PREPARATION TIME 20 MINUTES **COOKING TIME** 3 HOURS 10 MINUTES **SERVES** 4

- 2 tablespoons olive oil
- 1.6kg beef cheeks, trimmed
- 1 medium brown onion (150g), chopped coarsely
- 1 medium carrot (120g), chopped coarsely
- 3 cups (750ml) dry red wine
- ¼ cup (60ml) red wine vinegar
- 2 x 400g cans whole tomatoes
- ¼ cup (55g) firmly packed brown sugar
- 2 sprigs fresh rosemary
- 6 black peppercorns
- 2 tablespoons fresh oregano leaves
- 1 large fennel bulb (550g), trimmed, cut into thin wedges
- 400g spring onions, trimmed, halved
- 200g swiss brown mushrooms

CHEESY POLENTA

- 2⅓ cups (580ml) water
- 2⅓ cups (580ml) milk
- 1 cup (170g) polenta
- ½ cup (40g) finely grated parmesan
- 30g butter

1 Preheat oven to moderately slow (170°C/150°C fan-forced).

2 Heat half of the oil in large flameproof dish; cook beef, in batches, until browned.

3 Heat remaining oil in same dish; cook brown onion and carrot, stirring, until onion softens. Return beef to dish with wine, vinegar, undrained tomatoes, sugar, rosemary, peppercorns, oregano and fennel; bring to a boil. Cover; cook 2 hours.

4 Stir in spring onion and mushrooms; cook, uncovered, about 45 minutes or until beef is tender.

5 Meanwhile, make cheesy polenta. Serve beef with polenta.

CHEESY POLENTA Combine the water and milk in large saucepan; bring to a boil. Gradually add polenta to liquid, stirring constantly. Reduce heat; simmer, stirring, about 10 minutes or until polenta thickens. Add cheese and butter; stir until cheese melts.

▭ **PER SERVING** 57.5g total fat (24.9g saturated); 5087kj (1217 cal); 65.6g carbohydrate; 101.7g protein; 10.1g fibre

A standing rib roast is also known as a bone-in rib roast. After draining the marinade from the beef, you can dry it and rub with sea salt and dry mustard for a delicious crust.

Standing rib roast with lemon and garlic

PREPARATION TIME 15 MINUTES (PLUS REFRIGERATION AND STANDING TIME)
COOKING TIME 1 HOUR 40 MINUTES **SERVES** 6

2kg standing rib roast
¾ cup (180ml) lemon juice
⅓ cup (80ml) olive oil
6 cloves garlic, chopped coarsely
2 tablespoons coarsely chopped fresh rosemary
4 lemons
1 bulb garlic (70g)
4 sprigs fresh rosemary
1 cup (250ml) beef stock
1 cup (250ml) water
1 tablespoon cornflour
1 tablespoon water, extra

1 Place beef in large bowl; pour combined juice, oil, chopped garlic and chopped rosemary over beef. Cover; refrigerate 3 hours or overnight, turning the roast occasionally.
2 Preheat oven to moderate (180°C/160°C fan-forced). Oil large flameproof baking dish.
3 Drain beef; discard marinade. Cut each lemon into six wedges. Break garlic bulb into separate cloves; do not peel cloves. Combine lemon, garlic and rosemary sprigs in dish. Place beef on lemon mixture; roast, uncovered, 1½ hours or until beef is cooked as desired. Remove beef from dish, cover; stand 20 minutes. Remove lemons and garlic from dish, drain on absorbent paper; cover to keep warm.
4 Meanwhile, pour pan juices into medium jug; skim fat from pan juices. Return juices to dish with stock and the water; cook, stirring, until mixture boils. Stir in blended cornflour and extra water; cook, stirring, until sauce boils and thickens. Strain.
5 Serve beef with lemon, garlic and sauce.

PER SERVING 30.4g total fat (9.5g saturated); 2303kj (551 cal); 4.6g carbohydrate; 63.4g protein; 3.1g fibre

---

Finely sliced mushrooms are often added to this dish in Italy. Try adding 150g mushrooms after browning the veal. A perfect accompaniment would be spinach flavoured with sautéed onion and garlic.

Veal marsala

PREP TIME 15 MINUTES **COOK TIME** 15 MINUTES **SERVES** 4

8 veal leg schnitzels (800g)
¼ cup (35g) plain flour
2 tablespoons vegetable oil
20g butter
⅓ cup (80ml) marsala
¾ cup (180ml) cream
½ teaspoon cracked black pepper
2 tablespoons finely chopped fresh chives

1 Toss veal in flour; shake off excess. Heat oil and butter in large frying pan; cook veal, in batches, until cooked as desired. Cover to keep warm.
2 Drain fat from pan, place remaining ingredients in pan; bring to a boil. Reduce heat; simmer, stirring, until sauce thickens slightly. Return veal and any juices to pan. Turn veal to coat in sauce.

PER SERVING 35.9g total fat (17.5g saturated); 2383kj (570 cal); 10.1g carbohydrate; 46.5g protein; 0.4g fibre

Steak diane

PREPARATION TIME 10 MINUTES **COOKING TIME** 15 MINUTES **SERVES** 4

No one really knows the origin of Steak Diane; chefs in Australia, Brazil and the US have all claimed to be its creators. The dish was extremely popular in restaurants in the 1950s and 1960s, often being cooked at the table. Steak Diane now features regularly on pub and bistro menus.

1 tablespoon olive oil
8 thin slices beef fillet (800g)
20g butter
3 cloves garlic, crushed
3 green onions, sliced thinly
1 tablespoon brandy
2 tablespoons worcestershire sauce
300ml cream

1 Heat oil in large frying pan; cook beef, in batches, until cooked as desired.
2 Melt butter in same pan; cook garlic and onion until onion softens. Add brandy and sauce; bring to a boil. Stir in cream, simmer, uncovered, 3 minutes. Serve beef with sauce.

☐ **PER SERVING** 53g total fat (29.8g saturated); 2842kj (680 cal); 4.9g carbohydrate; 44.3g protein; 0.6g fibre

---

Beef and buk choy with black bean sauce

PREPARATION TIME 25 MINUTES (PLUS REFRIGERATION TIME) **COOKING TIME** 25 MINUTES **SERVES** 4

Beef in black bean sauce is one of the most popular Chinese stir-fries, and it can be made with broccoli, gai lan or choy sum instead of the asparagus and buk choy we use here. A little freshly chopped chilli stir-fried with the onion and garlic will add a spark to the finished dish.

800g beef rump steak, sliced thinly
1 tablespoon sesame oil
1 tablespoon fish sauce
¼ cup (35g) cornflour
1 egg, beaten lightly
¼ cup (60ml) peanut oil
2 medium brown onions (300g), sliced thinly
3 cloves garlic, crushed
5cm stick (10g) finely chopped fresh lemon grass
4cm piece fresh ginger (20g), grated
300g baby buk choy, halved
250g asparagus, trimmed, halved

BLACK BEAN SAUCE
2 teaspoons cornflour
½ cup (125ml) water
¼ cup (60ml) black bean sauce
1 tablespoon fish sauce
1 tablespoon brown sugar

1 Combine beef, sesame oil and sauce in large bowl, cover; refrigerate 30 minutes.
2 Meanwhile, make black bean sauce. Stir cornflour and egg into beef mixture.
3 Heat half of the peanut oil in cleaned wok; stir-fry beef, in batches, until browned.
4 Heat remaining peanut oil in same wok; stir-fry onion, garlic, lemon grass and ginger until onion just softens. Add buk choy and asparagus, stir-fry until buk choy is just wilted. Place vegetables on serving plate; top with beef mixture, drizzle with black bean sauce.

BLACK BEAN SAUCE Blend cornflour and water with remaining ingredients in wok; stir over heat until mixture boils and thickens. Remove from wok; cover to keep warm.

☐ **PER SERVING** 33.9g total fat (9.7g saturated); 2533kj (606 cal); 22.4g carbohydrate; 51.2g protein; 3.8g fibre

Cold cabbage mash is a great base for making up-market bubble and squeak. Add 150g flaked smoked trout, 1 egg, 2 tablespoons chopped dill, 1 tablespoon chopped parsley and ¼ cup grated cheddar. Shape into patties, then dust with flour. Heat 2 tablespoons olive oil in a large frying pan and cook the patties until golden on both sides. Serve with lemon wedges.

Rissoles with cabbage mash

PREPARATION TIME 25 MINUTES **COOKING TIME** 20 MINUTES **SERVES** 4

- 2 bacon rashers (140g), rind removed, chopped finely
- 1 small brown onion (80g), chopped finely
- 1 clove garlic, crushed
- 1 fresh small red thai chilli, chopped finely
- 1 tablespoon worcestershire sauce
- 1 cup (70g) stale breadcrumbs
- 1 egg
- ¼ cup coarsely chopped fresh flat-leaf parsley
- 500g beef mince
- 2 tablespoons barbecue sauce
- 1 tablespoon vegetable oil
- 1 tablespoon dijon mustard
- 2 cups (500ml) beef stock
- 1 tablespoon cornflour
- 2 tablespoons water

CABBAGE MASH

- 1kg potatoes, quartered
- ¼ cup (60ml) cream
- 30g butter, chopped
- 200g finely shredded savoy cabbage
- 1 small white onion (80g), chopped finely

1 Cook potato for cabbage mash. Cover to keep warm.

2 Cook bacon, onion, garlic and chilli in medium frying pan, stirring, until onion softens. Remove from heat.

3 Using hand, combine worcestershire sauce, breadcrumbs, egg, parsley, mince and half of the barbecue sauce with bacon mixture in large bowl; shape mixture into eight rissoles.

4 Heat oil in same pan; cook rissoles, in batches, until browned both sides and cooked through. Cover to keep warm.

5 Place mustard, stock and remaining barbecue sauce in same pan; bring to a boil. Stir in blended cornflour and water; cook, stirring, until gravy boils and thickens slightly.

6 Finish cabbage mash. Serve rissoles, topped with gravy, with cabbage mash.

CABBAGE MASH Boil, steam or microwave potato until tender; drain. Mash potato with cream and butter until smooth; stir in cabbage and onion.

PER SERVING 31.9g total fat (14.4g saturated); 2876kj (688 cal); 51.1g carbohydrate; 45.8g protein; 6.7g fibre

Buy the freshest beef available; it is always a good idea to check with your butcher to find out whether the meat you are purchasing can be eaten raw. It is very important to keep the beef as cold as possible when preparing this recipe. Use a sharp knife to chop the beef so that it neither tears nor becomes overly minced.

Steak tartare

PREPARATION TIME 40 MINUTES **SERVES** 4

600g piece eye fillet, trimmed

2 cloves garlic, crushed

1 tablespoon dijon mustard

½ teaspoon Tabasco

1 teaspoon worcestershire sauce

4 quail eggs

1 small red onion (100g), chopped finely

1 tablespoon drained capers, rinsed, chopped finely

4 anchovy fillets, drained, chopped finely

¼ cup finely chopped fresh flat-leaf parsley

1 Chop beef finely; combine beef in large chilled bowl with garlic, mustard and sauces. Divide tartare mixture evenly among serving plates, making a small well in the centre of each mound.

2 Crack one egg carefully into each well. Divide onion, capers, anchovy and parsley among serving plates; serve immediately.

PER SERVING 10.6g total fat (4.2g saturated); 1028kj (246 cal); 2.3g carbohydrate; 34.8g protein; 0.8g fibre

Spaetzle is traditionally served throughout Germany, Switzerland, Austria and the French region of Alsace. Best described as tiny noodle-like dumplings, they are made by pushing a batter through the holes of a colander or strainer into a pan of boiling water or stock. The cooked spaetzle are generally tossed with melted butter, herbs or gravy then served as a side dish, or added to soups or stews in place of pasta or potatoes.

Wiener schnitzel with lemon spaetzle

PREPARATION TIME 20 MINUTES (PLUS REFRIGERATION TIME) **COOKING TIME** 20 MINUTES **SERVES** 4

½ cup (75g) plain flour

3 eggs, beaten lightly

2 tablespoons milk

2 cups (140g) stale breadcrumbs

¾ cup (75g) packaged breadcrumbs

½ cup (40g) finely grated parmesan

8 veal schnitzels (800g)

vegetable oil, for shallow-frying

LEMON SPAETZLE

2 cups (300g) plain flour

4 eggs, beaten lightly

½ cup (125ml) water

2 teaspoons finely grated lemon rind

40g butter, chopped

1 Whisk flour, egg and milk in medium shallow bowl; combine breadcrumbs and cheese in another medium shallow bowl. Coat schnitzels, one at a time, in flour mixture then in breadcrumb mixture. Place, in single layer, on tray. Cover; refrigerate 15 minutes.

2 Make lemon spaetzle.

3 Heat oil in large frying pan; cook schnitzels, in batches, until browned both sides and cooked through.

4 Serve schnitzel with lemon spaetzle.

LEMON SPAETZLE Place flour in large bowl, make well in centre. Gradually add eggs and the water, stirring, until batter is smooth. Stir in rind. Pour half of the batter into metal colander set over large saucepan of boiling water; using wooden spoon, push batter through holes of colander, remove colander. When water returns to a boil, boil, uncovered, about 2 minutes or until spaetzle float to the surface. Use slotted spoon to remove spaetzle; drain, place in large bowl. Add half of the butter; toss spaetzle gently until butter melts. Keep warm; repeat with remaining batter and butter.

PER SERVING 26.6g total fat (5.8g saturated); 4046kj (968 cal); 103.6g carbohydrate; 74.0g protein; 5.8g fibre

---

Veal sweetbreads with duxelles and herb salad

Duxelles, a classic French mixture generally used in sauces, pâtés and terrines, stuffings and soup bases, is made of finely chopped mushrooms and various herbs sautéed in butter with shallots or green onions. Here, we serve it as an accompaniment to the mild creaminess of the sweetbreads.

PREPARATION TIME 45 MINUTES (PLUS REFRIGERATION TIME)
COOKING TIME 20 MINUTES (PLUS COOLING TIME) **SERVES** 4

500g veal sweetbreads
¼ cup (35g) plain flour
1 teaspoon salt
½ teaspoon cracked black pepper
¼ cup (60ml) olive oil
1 cup loosely packed fresh flat-leaf parsley leaves
1 cup loosely packed fresh basil leaves
1 cup loosely packed fresh chervil leaves
¾ cup coarsely chopped fresh chives
2 tablespoons olive oil, extra
2 tablespoons red wine vinegar

DUXELLES
40g butter
400g swiss brown mushrooms, chopped finely
8 shallots (200g), chopped finely
¼ cup (60ml) port
⅓ cup (80ml) beef stock
2 tablespoons finely chopped fresh flat-leaf parsley

1 Place sweetbreads in medium bowl, cover with cold water; refrigerate 4 hours, changing water once an hour, until sweetbreads whiten and water is clear. Cook sweetbreads, uncovered, in medium saucepan of boiling water about 5 minutes. Drain; cool 10 minutes. Remove outer membranes then slice sweetbreads thickly.
2 Meanwhile, make duxelles.
3 Coat sweetbreads in combined flour, salt and pepper; shake away excess. Heat oil in large frying pan; cook sweetbreads, in batches, about 5 minutes or until browned lightly and cooked as desired.
4 Meanwhile, combine herbs in large bowl with extra oil and vinegar; toss gently.
5 Serve sweetbreads with duxelles and herb salad.

DUXELLES Heat butter in large frying pan; cook mushrooms and shallot, stirring, until shallot softens. Add port and stock; bring to a boil. Reduce heat; simmer, uncovered, about 15 minutes or until liquid is evaporated. Remove from heat; stir in parsley.

PER SERVING 38.5g total fat (10.9g saturated); 2253kj (539 cal); 14.2g carbohydrate; 29.1g protein; 4.6g fibre

PORK

Pork

Because pigs don't need pasture but can live in a sty in the yard and be fed on scraps, they have always been the meat that peasants could raise. This has meant that, over many generations, hearty and rustic pork dishes have evolved. In both East and West, but especially in Europe where winters were long and bitter, pigs also provided the salted, smoked and potted meats, branching out over the years into hams, sausages and other delicious smallgoods that sustained the family when fresh meat was scarce.

We are the lucky inheritors of all these traditions and you will find dishes from all of them in this chapter. You will also find dishes with a very modern attitude to pork, made from lean cuts designed for quick, easy, low-fat cooking which are readily available at most butchers.

CHOOSING PORK

Pork may be pale pink or reddish pink and should be fine-grained with firm white fat and thin, smooth skin. It is naturally tender but cuts from parts with more connective tissue will require slow, moist cooking to ensure tenderness. Pork from female pigs is generally considered the choicest.

STORING AND HANDLING PORK

For advice about storing and handling all fresh meats including pork, please read "Storing and handling fresh meat" on page 218.

PORK CUTS

- **Roasting** cuts are the loin, bone-in or boned and sometimes rolled, which serves 8 to 10 and is often cut into two smaller roasts; the leg, also very large and often divided into the fillet end and the shank end, the latter often being boned and rolled; fillet; rump; individual leg muscles seamed out for small, boneless roasts; and shoulder, either on the bone or boned and rolled. Cheaper cuts marked "roasting" are often tough.
- **Grilling, char-grilling and pan-frying** cuts are fillet, traditional loin chops and cutlets with some fat, and fatless chops, medallions and steaks. The more traditional cuts are also suitable for **barbecuing**, but the very lean cuts are not. Pork schnitzel is pan-fried but does not suit grilling. Cheaper cuts marked "grilling" or "barbecuing" may disappoint.
- Cuts for **pot-roasting** (braising in one piece) are topside, silverside, boned and rolled shoulder and boned and rolled foreloin (neck).

- Pork for cutting up and **casseroling** are all the pot-roasting cuts, above, and meat from belly or forequarter (usually sold already cubed). Pork belly, in particular, has enjoyed great popularity as of late, consumed in dishes from confit to pizza. Pork hock (lower shank), fresh, cured (salted) or smoked, may be simmered whole in slow-cooked dishes, removed and the meat taken off the bone, cut up and returned to the pot.
- **Spareribs** may be Chinese-style spareribs, a meaty and fatty cut from the belly, which are usually available. American-style spareribs from the rib area, with more bone and less meat, may have to be especially ordered.

HOW MUCH TO BUY

As a general guide, allow 125 to 200g per serving of boneless pork, 150 to 250g of pork with some bone, such as chops, cutlets or Chinese-style spareribs; 375 to 500g of bony cuts such as bone-in shoulder or American-style spareribs.

COOKING PORK

- It used to be considered that pork must be thoroughly cooked to destroy any parasites, but modern pig-raising methods produce clean and healthy animals with no such problems.
- Small cuts, especially the modern, lean cuts, are more juicy and tender if not too well done, and should be cooked, over medium heat, only until medium done, when the meat feels springy if you press the surface with a finger or the back of the tongs. Before cooking lean cuts, brush them with oil to guard against dryness.
- Rest grilled or pan-fried pork, wrapped in foil, for 5 to 10 minutes, depending on size, before serving to contain the juices and help prevent the meat from drying out.
- Most people enjoy roast pork best if it is cooked through but not overcooked. Allow 30 minutes per 500g if the roast is over 3kg, 40 minutes per kg if the roast is under 3kg, and use a meat thermometer or check by inserting a fine skewer into the centre towards the end of the cooking time. If the skewer goes in easily and the juices that run out are clear, the meat is done.
- Rest a cooked roast, wrapped or covered tightly in foil, for 15 minutes before carving. This allows the juices to settle into the meat and makes it more succulent.
- The rind on a roast provides one of pork's greatest joys: crisp and bubbly crackling. Have the rind scored by the butcher, or do it yourself by cutting through the rind into the underlying fat at 1cm intervals. Rub with oil and coarse cooking salt. Cook the roast in a preheated oven at the highest heat for 20 minutes or until the skin bubbles, then reduce the heat to moderate and continue cooking. Don't baste, cover or turn roasts that have crackling. The initial 20 minutes is included in the total cooking time as calculated above.
- You can also buy rindless pork roasts. Cook these for 10 minutes in a moderately hot oven, then reduce the heat to moderate for the remainder of the cooking time. Calculate the cooking time as for a rind-on roast (above). Baste a rindless roast every 15 minutes.

You can use canned beans to reduce the preparation time for this recipe – you will need three 300g cans. Drain and rinse the beans before using.

Cassoulet

PREPARATION TIME 40 MINUTES (PLUS STANDING TIME) **COOKING TIME** 2 HOURS 10 MINUTES **SERVES** 6

- 1½ cups (300g) dried white beans
- 300g boned pork belly, rind removed, sliced thinly
- 150g piece streaky bacon, rind removed, diced into 1cm pieces
- 800g piece boned lamb shoulder, diced into 3cm pieces
- 1 large brown onion (200g), chopped finely
- 1 small leek (200g), sliced thinly
- 2 cloves garlic, crushed
- 3 sprigs fresh thyme
- 400g can crushed tomatoes
- 2 bay leaves
- 1 cup (250ml) water
- 1 cup (250ml) chicken stock
- 2 cups (140g) stale breadcrumbs
- ⅓ cup coarsely chopped fresh flat-leaf parsley

1 Place beans in medium bowl, cover with water; soak overnight, drain. Rinse under cold water; drain. Place beans in medium saucepan of boiling water; bring to a boil. Reduce heat; simmer, covered, about 15 minutes or until beans are just tender. Drain.
2 Preheat oven to moderately slow (170°C/150°C fan-forced).
3 Cook pork in large flameproof casserole dish over heat, pressing down with back of spoon on pork until browned all over; remove from dish. Cook bacon in same pan, stirring, until crisp; remove from dish. Cook lamb, in batches, in same pan, until browned; remove.
4 Cook onion, leek and garlic in same dish, stirring, until onion softens. Add thyme, undrained tomatoes, leaves, the water, stock, beans and meat; bring to a boil. Cover; bake 45 minutes. Remove from oven; sprinkle with combined breadcrumbs and parsley. Return to oven; bake, uncovered, about 45 minutes or until liquid is nearly absorbed and beans are tender.

PER SERVING 26.0g total fat (10.1g saturated); 2153kj (515 cal); 21.5g carbohydrate; 46.8g protein; 4g fibre

---

Don't be tempted to put more filling in each leaf than the recipe directs. The rice will absorb moisture and swell as it cooks, so too much filling would burst the roll.

Pork cabbage rolls

PREPARATION TIME 1 HOUR **COOKING TIME** 1 HOUR 40 MINUTES **SERVES** 6

- 18 large cabbage leaves
- ½ cup (100g) uncooked white long-grain rice
- 250g pork mince
- 1 medium brown onion (150g), chopped finely
- ¼ cup finely chopped fresh dill
- 1 clove garlic, crushed
- 1 tablespoon tomato paste
- 2 teaspoons ground cumin
- 1 teaspoon ground coriander
- 1 teaspoon ground allspice
- 4 cloves garlic, quartered
- 2 medium tomatoes (300g), chopped coarsely
- 2 x 400g cans crushed tomatoes
- ¼ cup (60ml) lemon juice

1 Discard thick stems from 15 cabbage leaves; reserve remaining leaves. Boil, steam or microwave trimmed leaves until just pliable; drain. Rinse under cold water; drain. Pat dry with absorbent paper.

2 Using hand, combine rice, pork, onion, dill, crushed garlic, paste and spices in medium bowl.
3 Place one trimmed leaf, vein-side up, on board; cut leaf in half lengthways. Place 1 rounded teaspoon of the pork mixture at stem end of each half; roll each half firmly to enclose filling. Repeat with remaining trimmed leaves.
4 Place reserved leaves in base of large saucepan. Place only enough rolls, seam-side down, in single layer, to completely cover leaves in base of saucepan. Top with quartered garlic, chopped fresh tomato then remaining rolls.
5 Pour undrained tomatoes and juice over cabbage rolls; bring to a boil. Reduce heat; simmer, covered, 1 hour. Uncover; simmer about 30 minutes or until cabbage rolls are cooked through.
6 Serve with greek-style yogurt flavoured with a little finely chopped preserved lemon, if desired.

PER SERVING 4.0g total fat (1.2g saturated); 903kj (216 cal); 24.7g carbohydrate; 15.3g protein; 9.4g fibre

---

Pork rissoles on potato rösti with leek puree

PREPARATION TIME 30 MINUTES (PLUS REFRIGERATION TIME) **COOKING TIME** 45 MINUTES **SERVES** 6

For a different flavour, make the rösti with half ordinary potato and half sweet potato, and add 2 teaspoons fresh thyme leaves.

- 1kg lean pork mince
- 2 cloves garlic, crushed
- 1 medium brown onion (150g), chopped finely
- ½ cup coarsely chopped fresh mint
- 1 egg white
- 1 cup (70g) stale breadcrumbs
- 5 medium potatoes (1kg)
- ¼ cup (35g) plain flour
- 1 egg white, extra
- 2 large leeks (1kg), chopped coarsely
- 2 tablespoons milk

1 Preheat oven to hot (220°C/200°C fan-forced).
2 Using hand, combine pork, garlic, onion, mint, egg white and breadcrumbs in large bowl; shape pork mixture into 18 patties. Place on oiled tray, cover; refrigerate 30 minutes.
3 Meanwhile, peel and coarsely grate potatoes; using hand, squeeze out excess moisture. Combine potato, flour and extra egg white in large bowl; shape potato mixture into 12 patties. Place potato rösti, in single layer, on lightly oiled oven trays; bake, uncovered, turning once, about 30 minutes or until rösti are browned both sides.
4 Heat large oiled heavy-based saucepan; cook leek, stirring, until soft. Blend or process leek with milk until mixture forms a thick puree.
5 Meanwhile, heat large oiled frying pan; cook rissoles, in batches, until browned both sides and cooked through.
6 Stack three patties and two rösti on each serving plate; top with leek puree.

PER SERVING 14.4g total fat (4.6g saturated); 1944kj (465 cal); 35.3g carbohydrate; 44.7g protein; 6.6g fibre

Packed with flavour, this curry demonstrates how hot, sour, sweet, salty and bitter flavours can be balanced beautifully, which is the secret of Thai cuisine. This recipe makes 1 cup of curry paste which will keep, tightly covered, in the fridge for a week, or in the freezer for 3 months.

Panang pork curry with pickled snake beans

PREPARATION TIME 30 MINUTES (PLUS COOLING AND REFRIGERATION TIMES)
COOKING TIME 1 HOUR 30 MINUTES **SERVES** 6

- 3⅓ cups (830ml) water
- 2¾ cups (680ml) coconut milk
- 1.5kg pork shoulder, trimmed, diced into 2cm pieces
- 1⅔ cups (410ml) coconut cream
- ¼ cup (65g) grated palm sugar
- ¼ cup (60ml) fish sauce
- 6 fresh kaffir lime leaves, sliced thinly
- 190g can sliced bamboo shoots, rinsed, drained
- ⅓ cup coarsely chopped fresh thai basil
- ¼ cup coarsely chopped fresh coriander
- 2 fresh long red chillies, sliced thinly

PICKLED SNAKE BEANS

- 350g snake beans, trimmed
- 1 cup (250ml) water
- 1 cup (250ml) white vinegar
- 1 tablespoon malt vinegar
- 1 cup (220g) white sugar
- 2 tablespoons coarse cooking salt

PANANG PASTE

- 6 fresh long red chillies, chopped coarsely
- 2 teaspoons coarsely chopped coriander root
- 2 tablespoons finely chopped fresh galangal
- 10cm stick (20g) fresh lemon grass, chopped finely
- 2 thai purple shallots (50g), chopped coarsely
- 3 cloves garlic, quartered
- ¼ cup (60ml) water
- ½ cup (75g) roasted unsalted peanuts

1 Make pickled snake beans and panang paste.
2 Combine the water and half of the coconut milk in medium saucepan; bring to a boil. Add pork; return to a boil. Reduce heat; simmer, uncovered, about 1 hour or until tender. Remove from heat; cool pork in liquid 30 minutes.
3 Heat coconut cream in large saucepan about 10 minutes or until fat separates from cream. Add ⅓ cup panang paste; cook, stirring, 10 minutes. Stir in sugar, fish sauce, 1 cup pork cooking liquid (discard any remaining liquid), remaining coconut milk, lime leaves, bamboo shoots and drained pork; simmer, uncovered, until heated through.
4 Stir thai basil and coriander through curry off the heat, sprinkle with chilli; serve with pickled snake beans and, if desired, steamed jasmine rice.

PICKLED SNAKE BEANS Cut beans into 5cm lengths; place in medium heatproof bowl. Stir the water, vinegars, sugar and salt in small saucepan until sugar dissolves; bring to a boil. Remove from heat; cool pickling liquid 10 minutes, then pour over beans. Refrigerate beans, covered, 3 hours or overnight before serving.

PANANG PASTE Blend or process chilli, coriander root, galangal, lemon grass, shallot, garlic and the water until mixture forms a paste; add nuts, pulse until just combined.

PER SERVING 63.8g total fat (40.6g saturated); 4460kj (1067 cal); 57.6g carbohydrate; 62.9g protein; 7.1g fibre

American-style spareribs

PREPARATION TIME 25 MINUTES (PLUS REFRIGERATION TIME)
COOKING TIME 2 HOURS 10 MINUTES **SERVES** 8

3.5kg slabs of american-style pork spareribs

BARBECUE SAUCE

2¼ cups (560ml) tomato sauce

1½ cups (375ml) apple cider vinegar

⅓ cup (80ml) olive oil

½ cup (125ml) worcestershire sauce

¾ cup (165g) firmly packed brown sugar

⅓ cup (95g) american-style mustard

1½ teaspoons cracked black pepper

3 fresh small red thai chillies, chopped finely

3 cloves garlic, crushed

¼ cup (60ml) lemon juice

For sticky Asian-style ribs, combine ¼ cup each of hoisin sauce, sweet chilli sauce, tomato sauce, dark soy sauce and dry sherry, 2 crushed cloves garlic and 1 tablespoon grated fresh ginger, and use instead of the barbecue sauce.

1 Make barbecue sauce.
2 Place slabs of ribs in large deep baking dish; brush both sides of each slab with sauce. Pour remaining sauce over slabs, cover; refrigerate overnight, turning slabs occasionally in the sauce.
3 Preheat oven to moderately slow (170°C/150°C fan-forced). Drain slabs, reserving sauce. Divide slabs of ribs between two wire racks over two large shallow baking dishes. Roast, covered, about 1½ hours, brushing with sauce every 20 minutes. Turn slabs midway through cooking time.
4 Increase oven temperature to hot (220°C/200°C fan-forced). Uncover slabs; roast, brushing frequently with sauce, until slabs are browned and cooked through, turning after 15 minutes.
5 Place remaining barbecue sauce in small saucepan; bring to a boil. Reduce heat; simmer, stirring, 5 minutes or until sauce thickens slightly. Using scissors, cut slabs in portions of two or three ribs; serve ribs with hot barbecue sauce.

BARBECUE SAUCE Combine ingredients in medium saucepan; bring to a boil. Remove from heat; cool 15 minutes.

☐ **PER SERVING** 25.5g total fat (6.6g saturated); 2416kj (578 cal); 42.1g carbohydrate; 43.8g protein; 2.2g fibre

American-style spareribs can also be cooked by the indirect method on a covered barbecue. Baste the ribs with barbecue sauce every 15 minutes or so; this keeps them moist and succulent. Encourage your guests to use their fingers when eating spareribs by serving them with stacks of paper napkins.

Italian blt

PREPARATION TIME 15 MINUTES **COOKING TIME** 15 MINUTES **SERVES** 4

For a vegetarian alternative replace the pancetta with slices of grilled eggplant or sweet potato.

4 medium egg tomatoes (300g), quartered

1 tablespoon balsamic vinegar

1 tablespoon finely chopped fresh basil

¼ cup (60ml) olive oil

8 slices pancetta (120g)

1 loaf ciabatta (440g)

1 clove garlic, crushed

100g bocconcini, sliced thickly

25g baby rocket leaves

1 Place tomato in medium bowl with vinegar, basil and 1 tablespoon of the oil; toss tomato to coat in mixture.

2 Cook tomato and pancetta on heated oiled grill plate (or grill or barbecue) until tomato is browned and pancetta crisp.

3 Cut bread into quarters, split quarters in half horizontally; brush cut sides with combined garlic and remaining oil. Toast bread, cut-side down, on same grill plate.

4 Sandwich tomato, pancetta, bocconcini and rocket between bread pieces.

PER SERVING 24.5g total fat (6.4g saturated); 2149kj (514 cal); 51g carbohydrate; 20.2g protein; 4.2g fibre

---

Pork fillet with mash and wilted cabbage

PREPARATION TIME 15 MINUTES **COOKING TIME** 35 MINUTES **SERVES** 4

To smarten up the cabbage for a dinner party add 1 sliced onion, 1 crushed clove garlic and 3 chopped rashers of bacon to the butter; cooking until the onion is soft. Add the cabbage with 1 tablespoon fennel seeds, stirring, until barely wilted.

1.2kg potatoes, quartered

½ cup (125ml) cream

100g butter, chopped

1 tablespoon olive oil

750g pork fillets, sliced thickly

1 cup (250ml) chicken stock

¾ cup (180ml) port

¼ cup (80g) cranberry sauce

½ small cabbage (500g), trimmed, sliced thickly

1 Boil, steam or microwave potato until tender; drain. Mash potato in large bowl with cream and half of the butter.

2 Meanwhile, heat oil in large frying pan; cook pork, in batches, until browned both sides. Cover to keep warm.

3 Place stock and port in same pan; bring to a boil. Reduce heat; simmer, uncovered, until mixture reduces by half. Stir in cranberry sauce. Return pork to pan; cook, uncovered, until pork is cooked through.

4 Heat remaining butter in separate large frying pan; cook cabbage, stirring, until wilted.

5 Serve pork and sauce with cabbage and mash.

PER SERVING 54.2g total fat (28.3g saturated); 3929kj (940 cal); 49.6g carbohydrate; 49.2g protein; 8.1g fibre

ITALIAN BLT

Unusual ingredients

Some of the wonderful things that have appeared in recent years, and stayed to add interest to our cooking.

CHIPOTLE
The name given to jalapeño chillies which have been dried and smoked. Like fresh jalapeños, chipotles are rated medium-hot. Used to flavour stews, salsas, soups and sauces.

GALANGAL
The juicy rhizome of a plant related to ginger, looking like boldly orange- and brown-striped ginger and reminiscent of ginger in flavour but with additional citrus and camphor notes. From Asian stores and many greengrocers.

CHORIZO
Spanish sausage made of coarsely ground pork, seasoned with garlic and chilli. Now made in Australia and available from delicatessens and many butchers. Used in stews and rice dishes.

LEMON MYRTLE
The intensely lemon/lime-scented leaf of a small Australian tree. Add to rice as it cooks or to the milk for custard, use for summer drinks, chop and rub into fish, poultry, lamb or veal before cooking.

PURPLE SHALLOT
Also called Thai, Asian or pink shallot, an intensely flavoured variety used throughout South-East Asia. They are used fresh in salads or deep-fried and used as an accompaniment or condiment prized both for flavour and for crunchy texture.

POMEGRANATE
These leathery dark-skinned fruit the size of oranges are filled with many seeds, each wrapped in edible pulp that gives a sweet-sour flavour.

PEA EGGPLANT
Pea-size green or purple and white Thai eggplant, rather bitter in flavour and prized for its crispness. Used as an interesting textural note in curries and relishes.

HORSERADISH
The highly pungent root of a perennial herb, which is grated and mixed with vinegar and sugar or with cream, lemon juice and sugar for a fiery relish or sauce for roast or corned beef, pork, ham or tongue.

KECAP MANIS
Dark, thick Indonesian/Malaysian soy sauce whose saltiness is balanced by the sweetness of palm sugar. Used in marinades, dressings and dips, as a condiment and seasoning for stir-fries.

WASABI
Japanese horseradish, from a plant related to European horseradish but even more fiery. Sold either as a pale-green powder or as a paste in tubes.

TURMERIC
Turmeric is the rhizome of a tropical plant, sold fresh in Asian food stores and some greengrocers, though more widely available in its dried form as a bright yellow powder. It gives food a golden colour and contributes a warm, earthy flavour.

TAMARIND
The astringent, sweet-sour, fibrous pulp of the seed pods from an African tree. Available from Asian food stores in dried blocks (reconstitute in hot water) or as a pulp or concentrate.

Sweet and sour sauce is often described as the "yin yang" of Chinese cooking. The Chinese consider the two flavours essential to a well-balanced meal.

Sweet and sour pork

PREPARATION TIME 15 MINUTES **COOKING TIME** 15 MINUTES **SERVES** 4

750g pork fillets
¼ cup (35g) cornflour
440g can pineapple pieces in natural juice
vegetable oil, for deep-frying
1 tablespoon peanut oil
1 medium brown onion (150g), sliced thickly
1 medium red capsicum (200g), chopped coarsely
1 medium green capsicum (200g), chopped coarsely
1 trimmed celery stalk (100g), chopped coarsely
2 tablespoons tomato sauce
2 tablespoons plum sauce
2 tablespoons light soy sauce
¼ cup (60ml) white vinegar
1 tablespoon cornflour, extra
¼ cup (60ml) chicken stock

1 Slice pork into 1cm slices. Coat pork in cornflour; shake off excess.
2 Drain pineapple over small bowl; reserve juice and pineapple separately.
3 Heat vegetable oil in medium frying pan; deep-fry pork, in batches, until browned all over. Drain on absorbent paper.
4 Heat peanut oil in wok; stir-fry onion until just soft. Add capsicums and celery; stir-fry until vegetables are just tender. Stir in combined sauces, vinegar, and extra cornflour blended with stock and reserved juice; cook, stirring, until mixture boils and thickens.
5 Add pork and pineapple; stir-fry until heated through.

☐ **PER SERVING** 25.0g total fat (6.6g saturated); 2270kj (543 cal); 34.6g carbohydrate; 43.2g protein; 3.4g fibre

---

This is often the hottest dish on a restaurant menu. To counteract the heat or "chilli burn", drink milk or a lassi (yogurt drink).

Pork vindaloo

PREPARATION TIME 15 MINUTES (PLUS REFRIGERATION TIME)
COOKING TIME 1 HOUR 15 MINUTES (PLUS COOLING TIME) **SERVES** 6

2 teaspoons cumin seeds
2 teaspoons garam masala
4cm piece fresh ginger (20g), grated
6 cloves garlic, crushed
8 fresh small red thai chillies, chopped finely
1 tablespoon white vinegar
1 tablespoon tamarind concentrate
1kg diced pork
2 tablespoons ghee
2 large brown onions (400g), chopped coarsely
2 cinnamon sticks
6 cloves
2 teaspoons plain flour
1 litre (4 cups) beef stock
8 curry leaves
2 tablespoons grated palm sugar

1 Dry-fry cumin and garam masala in large heated saucepan, stirring, until fragrant; cool 5 minutes.

2 Combine cumin mixture with ginger, garlic, chilli, vinegar, tamarind and pork in large bowl; cover, refrigerate 1 hour.

3 Heat ghee in same pan; cook onion, cinnamon and cloves, stirring, until onion browns lightly. Add pork mixture; cook, stirring, about 5 minutes or until pork is browned lightly. Stir in flour.

4 Gradually add stock, stir in leaves; simmer, covered, 30 minutes. Uncover; simmer about 30 minutes or until pork is tender and sauce thickens. Stir in palm sugar.

PER SERVING 19.6g total fat (8.5g saturated); 1563kj (374 cal); 10.0g carbohydrate; 38.7g protein; 1.6g fibre

---

Pork cutlet with stuffed apple and peppercorn cider sauce

PREPARATION TIME 20 MINUTES **COOKING TIME** 1 HOUR **SERVES** 4

The apple skins are pierced to prevent the skins from splitting while baking, which would cause the apples to collapse.

40g butter

1 small brown onion (80g), chopped finely

1 clove garlic, crushed

1 bacon rasher (70g), rind removed, chopped finely

¼ cup (15g) stale breadcrumbs

2 seeded prunes (20g), chopped finely

2 tablespoons finely chopped fresh chives

2 large apples (400g)

10g butter, melted

4 pork cutlets (940g)

½ cup (125ml) sparkling apple cider

2 teaspoons drained green peppercorns, crushed

300ml cream

1 Preheat oven to moderate (180°C/160°C fan-forced).

2 Melt butter in large frying pan; cook onion, garlic and bacon, stirring, until onion softens. Stir in breadcrumbs, prunes and half of the chives.

3 Core apples; pierce apples in several places with fork. Press breadcrumb mixture into apple centres; place in large deep flameproof baking dish. Brush melted butter all over apples. Bake, uncovered, 30 minutes.

4 Meanwhile, lightly oil same cleaned pan; cook pork, uncovered, about 2 minutes each side or until browned. Place pork in same dish with apples; cover with foil. Bake with apples about 15 minutes or until pork is cooked as desired.

5 Remove pork and apples from dish; cover to keep warm. Stir cider and peppercorns into juices in dish; cook, stirring, 1 minute. Add cream; bring to a boil. Reduce heat; simmer, uncovered, until sauce thickens slightly. Stir in remaining chives.

6 Halve apples; serve with pork, drizzle with sauce and serve with mash, if desired.

PER SERVING 61.7g total fat (34.7g saturated); 3219kj (770 cal); 18.2g carbohydrate; 34.1g protein; 2.5g fibre

For a different flavour, marinate the pork steaks overnight in ¼ cup olive oil, the rind and juice of a lemon, and 2 teaspoons fresh thyme leaves.

Butterflied pork steaks with pear and apple salsa

PREPARATION TIME 15 MINUTES **COOKING TIME** 10 MINUTES **SERVES** 4

1 tablespoon water

2 tablespoons lemon juice

2 teaspoons caster sugar

1 medium green apple (150g), diced into 1cm pieces

1 medium red apple (150g), diced into 1cm pieces

1 small pear (180g), diced into 1cm pieces

1 long green chilli, chopped finely

1 tablespoon finely chopped fresh mint

8 x 100g butterflied pork steaks, trimmed

1 Stir the water, juice and sugar in medium bowl until sugar dissolves. Add apples, pear, chilli and mint; toss gently to combine.

2 Cook pork on heated oiled grill plate (or grill or barbecue) until browned both sides and cooked as desired. Serve pork with salsa.

PER SERVING 14.5g total fat (4.8g saturated); 1555kj (372 cal); 12.8g carbohydrate; 46.2g protein; 1.9g fibre

---

Wetting your hands before shaping the burgers will help prevent the meat from sticking to them.

Pork burgers with caramelised pears

PREPARATION TIME 15 MINUTES **COOKING TIME** 15 MINUTES **SERVES** 4

500g pork mince

2 cloves garlic, crushed

3 green onions, chopped finely

1 fresh small red thai chilli, chopped finely

1 egg

2 tablespoons barbecue sauce

½ cup (35g) stale breadcrumbs

4 small pears (720g), sliced thinly

1 medium red onion (170g), sliced thinly

¼ cup (60ml) balsamic vinegar

1 tablespoon brown sugar

1 long french bread stick (300g)

2 tablespoons dijonnaise

50g mizuna

1 Using hand, combine pork, garlic, green onion, chilli, egg, sauce and breadcrumbs in medium bowl; shape mixture into four burgers. Cook burgers on heated oiled grill plate (or grill or barbecue) until cooked through.

2 Meanwhile, cook pear and red onion on same heated grill plate until onion softens. Sprinkle combined vinegar and sugar over pear and red onion; cook, turning, about 10 minutes or until mixture caramelises.

3 Cut bread into quarters; split quarters in half horizontally. Spread dijonnaise on cut sides; sandwich mizuna, burgers and caramelised pear and red onion between bread pieces.

PER SERVING 14.0g total fat (4.2g saturated); 2119kj (507 cal); 54.8g carbohydrate; 37.3g protein; 5.0g fibre

1 BUTTERFLIED PORK STEAKS WITH PEAR AND APPLE SALSA **2** PORK BURGERS WITH CARAMELISED PEARS **3** PORK CHOPS WITH CRANBERRY SAUCE AND KUMARA CRAISIN SALAD [P 266] **4** ASIAN-SPICED ROASTED PORK BELLY [P 266]

1

2

3

4

The richness of pork works perfectly with fresh and aromatic flavours, as in the coating mixture and salad for this recipe. Loin chops have a fatty edge – trim it if you wish, but don't remove it as it makes the meat flavoursome and luscious.

Pork chops with cranberry sauce and kumara craisin salad

PREPARATION TIME 15 MINUTES **COOKING TIME** 30 MINUTES **SERVES** 4

1 tablespoon ground ginger

1 tablespoon ground coriander

1 teaspoon sweet paprika

½ cup (160g) cranberry sauce

2 tablespoons orange juice

2 tablespoons lemon juice

1 tablespoon dijon mustard

4 pork loin chops (1.2kg)

KUMARA CRAISIN SALAD

3 large kumara (1.5kg), diced into 2cm pieces

2 tablespoons olive oil

½ cup (80g) roasted pine nuts

⅓ cup (45g) craisins

1 cup coarsely chopped fresh coriander

¼ cup (60ml) white wine vinegar

2 teaspoons olive oil, extra

1 Combine ginger, coriander, paprika, sauce, juices and mustard in large bowl, add pork; toss pork to coat in mixture.

2 Make kumara craisin salad.

3 Cook pork on heated grill plate until cooked as desired. Serve pork with salad.

KUMARA CRAISIN SALAD Boil, steam or microwave kumara until just tender; drain. Combine kumara with oil in large bowl; cook kumara on heated oiled grill plate (or grill or barbecue) until browned lightly. Return kumara to same bowl with remaining ingredients; toss gently to combine.

PER SERVING 46.9g total fat (9.6g saturated); 3637kj (870 cal); 63.4g carbohydrate; 45g protein; 7.9g fibre

Pork belly is prized for its rich taste and succulence. It is a fatty cut, but much of the fat is melted away during the simmering in plain water that is the first step of this classic recipe.

Asian-spiced roasted pork belly

PREPARATION TIME 10 MINUTES (PLUS REFRIGERATION TIME) **COOKING TIME** 1 HOUR 25 MINUTES **SERVES** 6

1kg pork belly, skin on, boned

½ cup (125ml) chinese cooking wine

¼ cup (60ml) dark soy sauce

1 tablespoon tamarind concentrate

2 tablespoons honey

½ teaspoon sesame oil

4cm piece fresh ginger (20g), chopped finely

3 cloves garlic, crushed

2 teaspoons five-spice powder

1 star anise

1 dried long red chilli

1 teaspoon sichuan pepper

3 cups (750ml) water

900g baby buk choy, halved lengthways

1 Place pork in large saucepan of boiling water; return to a boil. Reduce heat; simmer, uncovered, about 40 minutes or until pork is cooked through, drain.

2 Meanwhile, combine wine, soy sauce, tamarind, honey, oil, ginger, garlic, five-spice, star anise, chilli, pepper and the water in large bowl. Add pork; turn to coat pork in marinade. Cover; refrigerate 3 hours or overnight.

3 Preheat oven to hot (220°C/200°C fan-forced).

4 Place pork, skin-side up, on wire rack in large shallow baking dish; reserve marinade. Pour enough water into baking dish to come halfway up side of dish. Roast pork, uncovered, about 30 minutes or until browned.

5 Meanwhile, strain marinade into small saucepan; bring to a boil. Boil, uncovered, about 20 minutes or until sauce reduces to about 1 cup.

6 Boil, steam or microwave buk choy until just tender; drain.

7 Serve pork with sauce and buk choy and, if desired, steamed jasmine rice.

PER SERVING 34.2g total fat (11.5g saturated); 2094kj (501 cal); 12.5g carbohydrate; 29.5g protein; 2.3g fibre

---

Caramelised barbecued pork neck

PREPARATION TIME 15 MINUTES **COOKING TIME** 1 HOUR 30 MINUTES (PLUS STANDING TIME) **SERVES** 8

Pork neck is the traditional cut for this dish. It is slightly fatty, making it ideal for slow cooking, as it doesn't dry out. Don't try substituting a lean cut like fillet or you'll be bitterly disappointed with the tough results.

1.2kg piece pork neck

1 clove garlic, sliced thinly

4cm piece fresh ginger (20g), sliced thinly

2 star anise, quartered

2 tablespoons sea salt

HOT AND SWEET GLAZE

1 ¼ cups (310ml) water

1 ¾ cups (470g) grated palm sugar

3 fresh long red chillies, sliced thinly

2 fresh small red thai chillies, sliced thinly

1 star anise

⅓ cup (80ml) dark soy sauce

½ cup (125ml) lime juice

1 Make hot and sweet glaze.

2 Using sharp knife, make eight small cuts in pork. Press garlic, ginger and star anise pieces into cuts; rub pork with salt. Brush ¼ cup of the glaze over pork.

3 Place pork on heated barbecue; cook, covered, over low heat 30 minutes. Turn pork; cook, covered, further 30 minutes. Uncover; cook pork 10 minutes, brushing with remaining glaze constantly. Increase heat to high; cook 5 minutes, turning and brushing with glaze constantly. Remove pork from heat; stand 15 minutes before slicing.

HOT AND SWEET GLAZE Combine the water and sugar in medium saucepan; bring to a boil. Reduce heat; simmer, uncovered, about 10 minutes or until glaze thickens slightly. Remove from heat; stir in chillies, star anise, soy sauce and juice.

PER SERVING 12.1g total fat (4.1g saturated); 1977kj (473 cal); 57.5g carbohydrate; 32.6g protein; 0.2g fibre

Potted pork also can be spread on bread, toast or melba toast (see page 89) and served as an appetiser with drinks.

Traditionally, this type of recipe was packed in pork fat, then covered with more fat to preserve the meat.

Potted pork with witlof and cornichons

PREPARATION TIME 30 MINUTES **COOKING TIME** 2 HOURS 30 MINUTES **SERVES** 8

¼ cup (60ml) water

1kg boned pork belly, rind removed, diced into 5cm pieces

3 bay leaves

2 cloves garlic, chopped coarsely

¼ cup (60ml) dry white wine

2 teaspoons salt

1 teaspoon cracked black pepper

1 small red onion (100g), chopped finely

1 tablespoon finely chopped fresh flat-leaf parsley

⅔ cup (120g) drained cornichons

6 witlof (750g), trimmed, leaves separated

1 Preheat oven to slow (150°C/130°C fan-forced).

2 Combine the water, pork, leaves, garlic, wine, salt and pepper in large shallow baking dish. Cook, covered, about 2½ hours or until pork is very tender.

3 Discard bay leaves; using two forks, shred pork finely in dish with pan juices. Stir in onion and parsley. Serve pork with cornichons and witlof.

☐ **PER SERVING** 10.1g total fat (3.4g saturated); 936kj (224 cal); 3.1g carbohydrate; 27.8g protein; 2.0g fibre

---

Rest the pork, wrapped in foil, in a warm place for at least 15 minutes before serving. This allows the juices to settle and makes the meat more succulent.

Roast rack of pork with lemon and garlic

PREPARATION TIME 20 MINUTES **COOKING TIME** 2 HOURS **SERVES** 10

2 tablespoons finely grated lemon rind

3 cloves garlic, crushed

1 teaspoon cracked black pepper

1 tablespoon olive oil

2.6kg rack of pork

6 bay leaves

1 tablespoon olive oil, extra

2 teaspoons coarse cooking salt

½ cup (125ml) dry white wine

2½ cups (625ml) chicken stock

2 teaspoons cornflour

1 tablespoon water

1 Preheat oven to very hot (240°C/220°C fan-forced).

2 Combine rind, garlic, pepper and oil in small bowl. Rub underside of pork with lemon mixture. Place leaves on wire rack in large, shallow flameproof baking dish; top with pork.

3 Rub pork rind with extra oil; sprinkle with salt. Roast, uncovered, about 30 minutes or until the rind blisters. Reduce oven temperature to moderate (180°C/160°C fan-forced); roast, uncovered, about 1 hour 15 minutes or until just cooked through.

4 Remove pork from dish; cover to keep warm. Drain excess fat from baking dish.

5 Place baking dish on top of stove; add wine. Cook, stirring, until wine is reduced by half. Add stock; bring to a boil. Stir in blended cornflour and the water; cook, stirring, until mixture boils and thickens. Strain.

6 Serve pork with sauce.

☐ **PER SERVING** 22.1g total fat (6.9g saturated); 1409kj (337 cal); 1.1g carbohydrate; 31.8g protein; 0.2g fibre

Steamed pork buns

PREPARATION TIME 45 MINUTES (PLUS STANDING TIME) **COOKING TIME** 50 MINUTES **MAKES** 18

If you can't find a warm place for the dough to rise, open your preheated oven and sit the bowl at the top end of the open door.

cooking-oil spray
1 ½ teaspoons dried yeast
¼ cup (55g) caster sugar
1 ¼ cups (310ml) warm water
3 cups (450g) plain flour
1 teaspoon baking powder

FILLING
2 dried shiitake mushrooms
2 teaspoons peanut oil
1 clove garlic, crushed
300g chinese barbecued pork, chopped finely
2 tablespoons low-salt soy sauce
1 tablespoon hoisin sauce
1 tablespoon oyster sauce
2 teaspoons cornflour
½ cup (125ml) water

1 Mark 18 x 5cm squares on baking paper; spray paper with oil and cut out squares.
2 Combine yeast, 1 tablespoon of the sugar and ¼ cup of the water in small bowl, cover; stand in warm place about 15 minutes or until the mixture is frothy.
3 Sift flour and baking powder into large bowl; stir in the remaining sugar. Stir in yeast mixture and remaining water; mix to a soft dough. Knead dough on floured surface about 5 minutes or until dough is smooth and elastic. Place dough in large oiled bowl, cover; stand in warm place about 1 ½ hours or until dough has doubled in size.
4 Meanwhile, make filling.
5 Turn dough onto floured surface; knead for 3 minutes. Divide dough into 18 pieces.
6 Roll one piece of dough into 10cm round on floured surface. Using ¼-cup measuring cup, ease dough into cup. Place level tablespoon of the filling into centre; press filling down. Dip your fingers in water, gather dough together with fingers, twist at the top. Place a piece of the oiled paper over the join; turn bun out onto paper. Repeat with remaining dough and filling.
7 Place buns, paper-side down, on baking paper-lined trays. Cover, stand in warm place about 20 minutes or until the buns have increased in size.
8 Make a cross in the top of the buns with small, sharp knife. Steam buns on paper square in batches in large bamboo steamer, covered, over large saucepan of boiling water about 15 minutes or until buns are puffed and cooked through.

FILLING Cover mushrooms with boiling water in small bowl; stand 20 minutes. Drain mushrooms; discard stems, chop caps finely. Heat oil in medium frying pan; cook garlic and mushrooms, stirring, until fragrant. Add pork, sauces and blended cornflour and water; cook, stirring, until mixture boils and thickens. Cool 15 minutes.

PER BUN 3.6g total fat (1.2g saturated); 644kj (154 cal); 22.8g carbohydrate; 6.6g protein; 1.7g fibre

For added crunch, add roasted black and white sesame seeds and crispy fried noodles. Chinese barbecued duck makes a delicious substitute for the pork.

Mixed cabbage coleslaw with chinese barbecued pork

PREPARATION TIME 30 MINUTES **SERVES** 4

3 cups (240g) finely shredded savoy cabbage

3 cups (240g) finely shredded red cabbage

3 cups (240g) finely shredded chinese cabbage

2 medium carrots (240g), grated coarsely

⅓ cup coarsely chopped fresh coriander

1 fresh long red chilli, sliced thinly

500g chinese barbecued pork, sliced thinly

SWEET SOY DRESSING

1 tablespoon sesame oil

1 tablespoon fish sauce

2 tablespoons light soy sauce

1 tablespoon brown sugar

1 Make sweet soy dressing.

2 Place ingredients and dressing in large bowl; toss gently to combine.

SWEET SOY DRESSING Place ingredients in screw-top jar; shake well.

PER SERVING 4.9g total fat (0.6g saturated); 485kj (116 cal); 10.3g carbohydrate; 4.4g protein; 6.8g fibre

---

This sturdy, big-flavoured salad topped with a warm poached egg is a beloved classic of French country cooking. When the egg is cut, the yolk runs out to mingle richly with the speck and other ingredients. A marvellous one-dish meal, needing only good bread on the side.

Spinach, speck and poached egg salad

PREPARATION TIME 15 MINUTES **COOKING TIME** 15 MINUTES **SERVES** 4

300g speck, sliced thinly

200g baby spinach leaves

¼ cup coarsely chopped fresh basil

50g pecorino cheese, shaved

4 eggs

GARLIC VINAIGRETTE

2 cloves garlic, crushed

1 teaspoon dijon mustard

⅓ cup (80ml) olive oil

¼ cup (60ml) balsamic vinegar

1 Cook speck in large frying pan, stirring occasionally, until crisp. Drain on absorbent paper; cool 10 minutes.

2 Meanwhile, make garlic vinaigrette.

3 Place speck in medium bowl with spinach, basil and cheese; toss gently to combine.

4 Poach eggs until just cooked (see page 327).

5 Divide salad among serving plates; top each with an egg then drizzle with vinaigrette.

GARLIC VINAIGRETTE Place ingredients in screw-top jar; shake well.

PER SERVING 37.6g total fat (10.5g saturated); 1898kj (454 cal); 1g carbohydrate; 28.5g protein; 1.7g fibre

MIXED CABBAGE COLESLAW WITH CHINESE BARBECUED PORK

LAMB

Lamb

If Australia has a national dish, it is roast lamb. We love the old standbys, from shepherd's pie to the trusty crumbed cutlet, but we also embrace flavours and cooking methods from all over the world. Today, we may roast the lamb slowly and anoint it with lemon as Greek cooks do, turn a stew into a fragrant Middle Eastern tagine or cook cutlets with tandoori spices as Indian cooks do. They're all here, old and new favourites alike.

In recent years, the lamb industry has been promoting lean cuts, making for quick and easy low-fat cooking. These trimmed cuts are available in most butchers' shops along with the traditional cuts. Both kinds have their place and you will find them well represented in this chapter.

CHOOSING CUTS

For advice about choosing cuts of all fresh meats including lamb, please read "Choosing cuts of meat" on page 218.

STORING AND HANDLING LAMB

For advice about storing and handling all fresh meats including lamb, please read "Storing and handling fresh meat" on page 218.

KINDS OF LAMB

Ordinary lamb comes from animals younger than 12 months, having no permanent teeth. Spring lamb comes from animals 3 to 10 months old and has a sweet and delicate flavour. There is a limited amount of milk-fed lamb on the market, coming from animals of about 8 weeks or less that have fed only on milk. Their meat is soft, delicate and meltingly tender.

LAMB CUTS

- **Roasting** cuts are the leg, loin, shoulder or forequarter roast (the last two usually boned and rolled), rack (ribs), rump, and boned and rolled breast, a fatty cut. Trimmed roasts are usually individual leg muscles seamed out to make small, fatless roasts.
- **Grilling, char-grilling and barbecuing** cuts are chump and loin chops, preferably cut double-thick if they are to be barbecued; trimmed lamb steaks; butterflied leg (boned, cut almost in half lengthways and opened out flat). Cutlets can be char-grilled quickly but, unless cut double-thick, are too thin for grilling or barbecuing. Cheaper cuts may be marked "grilling" or "barbecuing" but they often disappoint.

- Cuts for **pan-frying** are cutlets (plain or crumbed); fillet; leg steaks; trimmed steaks.
- Cuts for **pot-roasting** (braising in one piece) are rolled shoulder or forequarter roast and trimmed roasts.
- Lamb for **casseroling** can be neck chops or other forequarter chops; cubed meat from the forequarter or breast; shank.
- Lamb **kidneys, liver (lamb's fry) and brains** are popular for breakfast or brunch.

HOW MUCH TO BUY

As a general guide, allow 125 to 200g per serving of boneless lamb; 150 to 250g of lamb with some bone, such as chops or cutlets.

JUDGING WHEN LAMB IS DONE TO YOUR TASTE

CHOPS, CUTLETS AND STEAKS Press the surface with a finger or the back of tongs. Rare meat feels soft and spongy, medium-rare is soft but springy, medium-done firm but still springy, and well-done is quite firm.

ROAST LAMB Use a meat thermometer, or insert a fine skewer into the centre and check the juice that runs out. Red juice means rare, pink means medium, clear means well done.

COOKING LAMB

- Today, most people enjoy grilled, pan-fried or roast lamb best when it is browned outside but still pink and juicy inside. When it is medium-done (see above), it will be fairly firm and blush-pink, with clear or slightly pinkish juice; when medium-rare (see above), the interior will be soft and reddish pink and the juices "bloody".
- It can be tricky to get a small piece of meat like a lamb chop or steak appetisingly brown and crusty on the outside yet still pink inside. The first step is to ensure that the meat has been brought to room temperature and that the grill or pan is very hot when the meat goes on. Cook until the first side is well browned, then turn and cook just until the meat feels right for how you want it cooked on the inside (see above). Immediately it feels right, take it off whether the second side is properly browned or not. Serve with the well-browned side upward and the diner will neither know nor care how brown the underside is. This works with both plain and crumbed meat.
- Rest all grilled or pan-fried meat, wrapped in foil, in a warm place for 5 to 10 minutes, depending on size, before serving. This allows the juices to settle into the meat and makes it more succulent.
- Put roasts in a preheated hot oven and cook for 20 minutes, then reduce the heat to moderate for the remainder of the cooking time. Baste with pan juices about every 20 minutes. Trimmed roasts, being lean, need to be brushed with oil before cooking and basted every 10 minutes. Allow 10 to 15 minutes per 500g, depending on whether you want fairly rare or firm but pink lamb; 20 minutes per 500g will give well-done lamb that is just pink in the middle. Start checking towards the end of the cooking time (see above).
- Rest a cooked roast, wrapped or tightly covered in foil, in a warm place for about 15 to 20 minutes, depending on size, before carving to allow it to recover from the high roasting temperature and become more tender.

When it comes to the science of marinating remember the following:

- *acid = tender*
- *sweet = flavour and sticky caramelisation of meat*
- *oil = flavour and succulence*
- *herbs and spices = flavour.*

Barbecued lamb chops with three marinades

PREPARATION TIME 20 MINUTES (PLUS REFRIGERATION TIME) **COOKING TIME** 15 MINUTES **SERVES** 4

1 Make marinade of your choice. Add four lamb loin chops to marinade; turn to coat in marinade. Cover; refrigerate 3 hours or overnight. Drain.
2 Cook lamb on heated oiled grill plate (or grill or barbecue) until cooked as desired.

HERB AND BALSAMIC Combine 2 teaspoons finely chopped fresh thyme, 2 crushed garlic cloves, ⅓ cup balsamic vinegar, 2 teaspoons brown sugar and 2 tablespoons olive oil in large bowl.

PER SERVING 17.3g total fat (5.1g saturated); 1158kj (277 cal); 1.7g carbohydrate; 28.6g protein; 0.3g fibre

CHILLI AND KAFFIR LIME Combine 1 crushed garlic clove, 2 finely shredded kaffir lime leaves, 2 tablespoons fish sauce, 1 fresh small finely chopped red thai chilli and 2 tablespoons peanut oil in large bowl.

PER SERVING 17.3g total fat (5.5g saturated); 1154kj (276 cal); 0.6g carbohydrate; 29.4g protein; 0.3g fibre

HONEY AND SOY Combine 2 tablespoons honey, ⅓ cup light soy sauce and 1 teaspoon sesame oil in large bowl.

PER SERVING 9.3 total fat (4.0g saturated); 1058kj (253 cal); 12.3g carbohydrate; 29.6g protein; 0.0g fibre

---

Use full fat or Greek-style yogurt in this recipe, and add it a little at a time, stirring constantly, to prevent curdling. Like most curries, this one tastes all the better for being made a day ahead and reheated when wanted.

Rogan josh

PREPARATION TIME 10 MINUTES **COOKING TIME** 2 HOURS 10 MINUTES **SERVES** 6

2 teaspoons ground cardamom
1 teaspoon ground fennel
2 teaspoons ground cumin
2 teaspoons ground coriander
1.4kg trimmed diced lamb shoulder
¼ cup (60ml) vegetable oil
2 medium brown onions (300g), chopped finely
4cm piece fresh ginger (20g), grated
4 fresh small red thai chillies, sliced thinly
4 cloves garlic, crushed
400g can crushed tomatoes
¼ teaspoon saffron threads
2 bay leaves
2 cinnamon sticks
¼ cup (40g) poppy seeds
1 cup (280g) greek-style yogurt
2 teaspoons brown sugar

1 Combine ground spices in medium bowl, add lamb; toss to cover lamb in spice mix.
2 Heat half of the oil in large saucepan; cook lamb, in batches, until browned all over.
3 Heat remaining oil in same pan; cook onion, ginger, chilli and garlic, stirring, until onion softens. Return lamb to pan with undrained tomatoes, saffron, leaves, cinnamon and poppy seeds. Add yogurt, 1 tablespoon at a time, stirring well between each addition; bring to a boil. Reduce heat to very low; simmer, covered, about 1¾ hours or until lamb is very tender. Stir in sugar; cook, uncovered, about 10 minutes or until thickened.

PER SERVING 34.6g total fat (11.9g saturated); 2358kj (564 cal); 8.7g carbohydrate; 53.6g protein; 3g fibre

Chilli lamb cutlets with grilled corn and garlic

PREPARATION TIME 15 MINUTES (PLUS REFRIGERATION TIME) **COOKING TIME** 15 MINUTES **SERVES** 4

Garlic bulbs consist of many cloves of garlic. The bulbs are also known as heads or knobs of garlic.

1 tablespoon crushed chilli

2 tablespoons olive oil

12 lamb cutlets (900g)

4 fresh corn cobs (1.6kg), husks on

4 bulbs garlic

CHILLI BUTTER

1 teaspoon crushed chilli

80g butter, softened

1 Combine chilli, oil and lamb in large bowl. Cover; refrigerate overnight.

2 Pull husk down corn cob, leaving it attached at base; remove silk. Bring husk back over cob. Tie each cob with kitchen string to hold husk in place; soak overnight in cold water.

3 Make chilli butter. Divide half among garlic bulbs; wrap each bulb in foil.

4 Drain corn. Cook corn and garlic parcels on heated oiled grill plate (or grill or barbecue) about 15 minutes or until corn and garlic are tender.

5 Meanwhile, cook lamb on same heated grill plate until cooked as desired. Spread corn with remaining chilli butter; serve with lamb and garlic.

CHILLI BUTTER Combine ingredients in small bowl.

PER SERVING 41g total fat (17.8g saturated); 3340kj (799 cal); 56.6g carbohydrate; 40.4g protein; 21g fibre

---

Lamb kofta with hummus

PREPARATION TIME 1 HOUR (PLUS STANDING TIME) **COOKING TIME** 15 MINUTES **SERVES** 6

Bite-sized lamb koftas served on cocktail sticks or individually wrapped in a strip of Lebanese bread, with hummus or minted yogurt, make a popular appetiser. To make, roll tablespoons of the lamb mixture into balls; brown in a frying pan with 1 tablespoon olive oil. Transfer to an oven tray; bake, uncovered, in a moderate oven for about 15 minutes.

½ cup (80g) burghul

1kg lamb mince

1 small brown onion (80g), chopped finely

1 teaspoon ground allspice

1 clove garlic, crushed

1 cup (75g) stale breadcrumbs

1 egg

200g yogurt

¼ cup finely chopped fresh mint

HUMMUS

2 x 300g cans chickpeas, rinsed, drained

1 teaspoon salt

1 clove garlic, quartered

⅓ cup (90g) tahini

¼ cup (60ml) lemon juice

⅓ cup (80ml) water

1 Cover burghul with cold water in small bowl; stand 20 minutes or until burghul softens. Drain burghul, squeezing with hands to remove as much water as possible.

2 Meanwhile, make hummus by blending or processing ingredients until smooth.

3 Combine burghul with lamb, onion, allspice, garlic, breadcrumbs and egg in large bowl. Divide mixture into 12 balls; mould balls around 12 skewers to form sausage shape.

4 Cook kofta on heated oiled grill plate (or grill or barbecue) until cooked through.

5 Serve kofta with hummus, combined yogurt and mint, and tabbouleh, if desired.

PER SERVING 27.9g total fat (9.1g saturated); 2395kj (573 cal); 28g carbohydrate; 48.2g protein; 8.3g fibre

See page 278 for our recipe for tabbouleh.

Other uses for sumac: pour olive oil over 1 tablespoon sumac in a small bowl and serve with bread for dipping. Sprinkle over pitta bread strips brushed with olive oil and bake in a moderately hot oven for 5 minutes or until crisp, for tasty pitta crisps to serve with dips. Sumac also makes a delicious seasoning for salads, especially partnered with oranges.

Lamb and tabbouleh wrap

PREPARATION TIME 35 MINUTES (PLUS STANDING TIME) **COOKING TIME** 10 MINUTES **MAKES** 8 WRAPS

1 cup (250ml) water
½ cup (80g) burghul
300g can chickpeas, drained, rinsed
⅓ cup (95g) low-fat yogurt
1 teaspoon finely grated lemon rind
2 tablespoons lemon juice
2 medium tomatoes (300g), seeded, chopped finely
3 green onions, sliced thinly
1 lebanese cucumber (130g), seeded, chopped finely
1 cup coarsely chopped fresh flat-leaf parsley
½ cup coarsely chopped fresh mint
250g lean lamb strips
2 tablespoons sumac
8 slices lavash bread

1 Combine the water and burghul in small bowl; stand 30 minutes. Drain. Squeeze burghul with hands to remove excess water.
2 Blend or process chickpeas, yogurt, rind and half of the juice until hummus is smooth.
3 Combine burghul in large bowl with tomato, onion, cucumber, herbs and remaining juice.
4 Toss lamb in sumac; cook on heated oiled grill plate until cooked as desired. Spread hummus over half of each slice of bread, top with lamb and tabbouleh; roll to enclose filling.

☐ **PER WRAP** 5.5g total fat (1.8g saturated); 1292kj (309 cal); 45.1g carbohydrate; 16.4g protein; 5.6g fibre

If you have a barbecue with a lid, try browning the lamb on the barbecue and finishing it off in a baking dish (on the barbecue) with the lid down.

Asian mini lamb roasts

PREPARATION TIME 15 MINUTES **COOKING TIME** 30 MINUTES **SERVES** 4

2 lamb mini roasts (700g)
2 tablespoons kecap manis
1 tablespoon sesame seeds
2 cloves garlic, crushed
2 teaspoons sesame oil
1cm piece fresh ginger (5g), grated
1 small red capsicum (150g), sliced thinly
600g gai lan, chopped coarsely
⅓ cup (80ml) oyster sauce
2 tablespoons water
1 tablespoon lime juice

1 Preheat oven to moderately hot (200°C/180°C fan-forced).
2 Cook lamb in heated oiled wok until browned. Place lamb on oiled wire rack in baking dish; brush with combined kecap manis, seeds and half of the garlic. Roast, uncovered, about 25 minutes or until cooked as desired. Cover; stand 5 minutes, slice thickly.
3 Meanwhile, heat oil in same wok; stir-fry ginger and remaining garlic until fragrant. Add remaining ingredients; stir-fry until gai lan is just wilted. Serve lamb on gai lan mixture.

☐ **PER SERVING** 19.9g total fat (7.6g saturated); 1655kj (396 cal); 8.6g carbohydrate; 42.7g protein; 6.5g fibre

1 LAMB AND TABBOULEH WRAP **2** ASIAN MINI LAMB ROASTS
3 TANDOORI LAMB CUTLETS WITH CHUTNEY [P 280] **4** SLOW-ROASTED GREEK LAMB [P 280]

1

2
3

4

A tandoor is a clay oven used in the north of India to cook this popular style of food, which is a "dry" curry, rather than one in a sauce.

Tandoori lamb cutlets with chutney

PREPARATION TIME 20 MINUTES (PLUS 30 MINUTES REFRIGERATION)
COOKING TIME 10 MINUTES **SERVES** 4

200g yogurt

1 medium brown onion (150g), chopped coarsely

2 tablespoons lemon juice

1 tablespoon vegetable oil

2cm piece fresh ginger (10g), grated

3 cloves garlic, crushed

2 teaspoons chilli powder

1 teaspoon garam masala

1 teaspoon ground cumin

½ teaspoon red food colouring

12 lamb cutlets (960g)

CHUTNEY

1 tablespoon vegetable oil

1 small red onion (100g), chopped finely

2 large tomatoes (440g), chopped finely

1 tablespoon lime juice

1 tablespoon sweet chilli sauce

2 tablespoons finely chopped fresh coriander

RAITA

1 lebanese cucumber (130g), seeded, chopped finely

2 tablespoons finely chopped fresh mint

200g yogurt

1 Blend or process yogurt, onion, juice, oil, ginger, garlic, spices and colouring until smooth. Combine paste with lamb in large bowl.

2 Meanwhile, make chutney and raita.

3 Heat oil in large frying pan; cook lamb, in batches, until cooked as desired.

4 Serve lamb with separate bowls of chutney and raita.

CHUTNEY Combine ingredients in small bowl.

RAITA Combine ingredients in small bowl.

PER SERVING 39.2g total fat (9.9g saturated); 2266kj (542 cal); 12g carbohydrate; 33.1g protein; 6.2g fibre

---

To maximise the amount of juice extracted from lemons and limes, make sure they are at room temperature, then roll each one, pressing down firmly, on the kitchen bench. This helps release juice from the pulp; any excess juice can be frozen in an ice-cube container.

Slow-roasted greek lamb

PREPARATION TIME 30 MINUTES **COOKING TIME** 3 HOURS 45 MINUTES **SERVES** 4

2kg leg of lamb

3 cloves garlic, quartered

12 sprigs fresh oregano

½ cup (125ml) dry white wine

1 cup (250ml) chicken stock

⅓ cup (80ml) lemon juice

1kg baby new potatoes, quartered lengthways

2 medium lemons (280g), quartered

⅔ cup (80g) seeded black olives

1 tablespoon olive oil

2 tablespoons plain flour

1 cup (250ml) water

1 Preheat oven to hot (220°C/200°C fan-forced). Using sharp knife, pierce 12 cuts into lamb; press garlic and oregano into cuts.

2 Place lamb in large flameproof baking dish; pour wine, stock and juice over lamb. Cover tightly; roast lamb 30 minutes. Reduce oven temperature to moderate (180°C/160°C fan-forced); roast lamb, covered tightly, brushing occasionally with pan juices, about 3 hours or until lamb is very tender.
3 Meanwhile, combine potato, lemon, olives and oil in separate large baking dish. Roast, uncovered, for last hour of lamb cooking time.
4 Transfer lamb to serving dish; cover to keep warm. Transfer lamb juices to medium jug.
5 Heat 1 tablespoon of the reserved lamb juices in same flameproof baking dish, add flour; cook, stirring, until mixture is well browned. Gradually stir in remaining lamb juices and the water; cook, stirring, until gravy boils and thickens.
6 Slice lamb; serve with potato mixture and gravy.

PER SERVING 25.5g total fat (9.7g saturated); 3340kj (799 cal); 43.3g carbohydrate; 89.8g protein; 7g fibre

---

Shepherd's pie

PREPARATION TIME 20 MINUTES **COOKING TIME** 45 MINUTES **SERVES** 4

30g butter
1 medium brown onion (150g), chopped finely
1 medium carrot (120g), chopped finely
½ teaspoon dried mixed herbs
4 cups (750g) chopped cooked lamb
¼ cup (70g) tomato paste
¼ cup (60ml) tomato sauce
2 tablespoons worcestershire sauce
2 cups (500ml) beef stock
2 tablespoons plain flour
⅓ cup (80ml) water

POTATO TOPPING
5 medium potatoes (1kg), chopped
60g butter, chopped
¼ cup (60ml) milk

1 Preheat oven to moderately hot (200°C/180°C fan-forced). Oil shallow 2.5-litre (10-cup) ovenproof dish.
2 Make potato topping.
3 Heat butter in large saucepan; cook onion and carrot, stirring, until tender. Add mixed herbs and lamb; cook, stirring, 2 minutes. Stir in paste, sauces and stock, then blended flour and water; stir over heat until mixture boils and thickens. Pour into dish.
4 Place heaped tablespoons of the potato topping on lamb mixture. Bake, uncovered, about 20 minutes or until browned lightly and heated through.

POTATO TOPPING Boil, steam or microwave potato until tender; drain. Mash with butter and milk until smooth.

PER SERVING 36.2g total fat (20.2g saturated); 2934kj (702 cal); 43g carbohydrate; 48.4g protein; 5.7g fibre

The debate over the difference between shepherd's pie and cottage pie has been going on for years. Some say shepherd's pie must use cooked left-over lamb (such as last night's roast) and cottage pie must use uncooked beef mince and vegetables.

Lamb and quince tagine with pistachio couscous

PREPARATION TIME 20 MINUTES **COOKING TIME** 1 HOUR 30 MINUTES **SERVES** 4

As a flavour variation, add ¼ cup quince paste to the pan with the spices and 1 tablespoon chopped preserved lemon peel with the tomatoes. You can also add a can of drained, rinsed chickpeas with the tomatoes.

40g butter

600g diced lamb

1 medium red onion (170g), chopped coarsely

2 cloves garlic, crushed

1 cinnamon stick

2 teaspoons ground coriander

1 teaspoon ground cumin

1 teaspoon ground ginger

1 teaspoon dried chilli flakes

1½ cups (375ml) water

425g can crushed tomatoes

2 medium quinces (700g), peeled, quartered

1 large green zucchini (150g), chopped coarsely

2 tablespoons coarsely chopped fresh coriander

PISTACHIO COUSCOUS

1½ cups (300g) couscous

1 cup (250ml) boiling water

20g butter

½ cup finely chopped fresh coriander

¼ cup (35g) roasted shelled pistachios, chopped coarsely

1 Melt butter in large saucepan; cook lamb, in batches, until browned.

2 Add onion to same pan; cook, stirring, until softened. Add garlic, cinnamon, ground coriander, cumin, ginger and chilli; cook, stirring, until mixture is fragrant.

3 Return lamb to pan. Stir in the water, undrained tomatoes and quince; bring to a boil. Reduce heat; simmer, covered, 30 minutes. Uncover; simmer, stirring occasionally, about 1 hour or until lamb and quince are tender.

4 Add zucchini; cook, stirring, about 10 minutes or until zucchini is just tender.

5 Meanwhile, make pistachio couscous.

6 Serve tagine with couscous, sprinkled with coriander.

PISTACHIO COUSCOUS Combine couscous with the water and butter in large heatproof bowl, cover; stand 5 minutes or until water is absorbed, fluffing with fork occasionally. Stir in coriander and nuts.

PER SERVING 31.0g total fat (14.7g saturated); 3361kj (804 cal); 78.5g carbohydrate; 45.5g protein; 13.7g fibre

LAMB AND QUINCE TAGINE WITH PISTACHIO COUSCOUS

Don't discard the wispy green fennel fronds in the middle of the fennel bulb; chop them finely and scatter them over the cooked fennel.

Lamb cutlets with olive salsa, polenta and fennel

PREPARATION TIME 10 MINUTES **COOKING TIME** 10 MINUTES **SERVES** 4

12 french-trimmed lamb cutlets (600g)

1 ½ cups (375ml) water

2 cups (500ml) chicken stock

1 cup (170g) polenta

⅓ cup (25g) finely grated parmesan

½ cup (125ml) cream

2 tablespoons olive oil

600g baby fennel, trimmed, sliced thinly

¾ cup (90g) seeded black olives, chopped coarsely

2 tablespoons lemon juice

1 clove garlic, crushed

1 tablespoon coarsely chopped fresh flat-leaf parsley

1 Cook lamb on heated oiled grill plate (or grill or barbecue) until browned both sides and cooked as desired.

2 Meanwhile, combine the water and stock in medium saucepan; bring to a boil. Gradually add polenta to liquid, stirring constantly. Reduce heat; simmer, stirring, about 10 minutes or until polenta thickens. Stir in cheese and cream.

3 Heat half of the oil in medium frying pan; cook fennel, stirring, until tender.

4 Combine remaining oil with olives, juice, garlic and parsley in small bowl. Serve cutlets with polenta, fennel and olive salsa.

PER SERVING 33.3g total fat (15.3g saturated); 2366kj (566 cal); 39g carbohydrate; 25.8g protein; 4g fibre

---

As an accompaniment, serve mashed potato with a little coconut milk stirred through, or rice cooked with a couple of kaffir lime leaves, a cinnamon stick, a few cardamom pods and a star anise.

Lamb shanks in five-spice, tamarind and ginger

PREPARATION TIME 20 MINUTES **COOKING TIME** 2 HOURS 10 MINUTES **SERVES** 4

2 teaspoons five-spice powder

1 teaspoon dried chilli flakes

1 cinnamon stick

2 star anise

¼ cup (60ml) dark soy sauce

½ cup (125ml) chinese cooking wine

2 tablespoons tamarind concentrate

2 tablespoons brown sugar

8cm piece fresh ginger (40g), grated

2 cloves garlic, chopped coarsely

1 ¼ cups (310ml) water

8 french-trimmed lamb shanks (2kg)

500g choy sum, chopped into 10cm lengths

150g sugar snap peas, trimmed

1 Preheat oven to moderate (180°C/160°C fan-forced).

2 Dry-fry spices in small frying pan, stirring, until fragrant. Combine with soy, wine, tamarind, sugar, ginger, garlic and the water in medium jug.

3 Place shanks, in single layer, in large shallow baking dish; drizzle with spice mixture. Roast, covered, turning shanks occasionally, about 2 hours or until meat is almost falling off the bone. Remove shanks from dish; cover to keep warm. Skim away excess fat; strain sauce into small saucepan.

4 Bring sauce to a boil. Boil, uncovered, 2 minutes.
5 Meanwhile, boil, steam or microwave choy sum and peas, separately, until tender; drain.
6 Divide vegetables among serving plates; serve with shanks, drizzled with sauce.

PER SERVING 15.7g total fat (7.0g saturated); 1948kj (466 cal); 11.8g carbohydrate; 61.1g protein; 3.0g fibre

---

Braised lamb shanks with white bean puree

PREPARATION TIME 40 MINUTES **COOKING TIME** 2 HOURS 30 MINUTES **SERVES** 4

White bean puree is wonderful spread on bruschetta, then topped with roasted red capsicum, semi-dried tomatoes or parma ham and simply drizzled with plain or flavoured olive oil.

1 tablespoon olive oil
8 french-trimmed lamb shanks (2kg)
1 large red onion (300g), chopped coarsely
2 cloves garlic, crushed
1 cup (250ml) chicken stock
2 cups (500ml) water
400g can diced tomatoes
1 tablespoon fresh rosemary leaves
4 anchovy fillets, drained, chopped coarsely
2 large red capsicums (700g)
2 large green capsicums (700g)

WHITE BEAN PUREE
20g butter
1 small brown onion (80g), chopped finely
1 clove garlic, crushed
¼ cup (60ml) dry white wine
¾ cup (180ml) chicken stock
2 x 400g cans white beans, rinsed, drained
2 tablespoons cream

1 Heat oil in large deep saucepan; cook lamb, in batches, until browned all over.
2 Cook onion and garlic in same pan, stirring, until onion softens. Add stock, the water, undrained tomatoes, rosemary and anchovy; bring to a boil. Return lamb to pan, reduce heat; simmer, covered, 1 hour, stirring occasionally. Uncover; simmer about 45 minutes or until lamb is tender.
3 Meanwhile, quarter capsicums; discard seeds and membranes. Roast under hot grill or in very hot oven, skin-side up, until skin blisters and blackens. Cover capsicum pieces with plastic wrap or paper for 5 minutes; peel away skin, slice thickly.
4 Meanwhile, make white bean puree.
5 Add capsicum to lamb; cook, uncovered, 5 minutes.
6 Serve lamb on white bean puree.

WHITE BEAN PUREE Melt butter in medium frying pan; cook onion and garlic, stirring, until onion softens. Add wine; cook, stirring, until liquid is reduced by half. Add stock and beans; bring to a boil. Reduce heat; simmer, uncovered, about 10 minutes or until liquid is almost evaporated. Blend or process bean mixture and cream until smooth.

PER SERVING 29.7g total fat (13.5g saturated); 2738kj (655 cal); 21.4g carbohydrate; 69.0g protein; 8.4g fibre

A roast joint should be rested before serving to allow the meat to relax. The heat of the oven causes the meat fibres to tighten, so as meat rests the fibres will relax, allowing the meat juices to redistribute themselves throughout the joint. Try to carve the joint across the grain so that each slice has short fibres which feel tender to eat.

Traditional roast dinner

PREPARATION TIME 30 MINUTES **COOKING TIME** 1 HOUR 10 MINUTES **SERVES** 6

2kg leg of lamb

3 sprigs fresh rosemary, chopped coarsely

½ teaspoon sweet paprika

1kg potatoes, chopped coarsely

500g pumpkin, chopped coarsely

3 small brown onions (240g), halved

2 tablespoons olive oil

2 tablespoons plain flour

1 cup (250ml) chicken stock

¼ cup (60ml) dry red wine

CAULIFLOWER MORNAY

1 small cauliflower (1kg), cut into florets

50g butter

¼ cup (35g) plain flour

2 cups (500ml) hot milk

¾ cup (90g) coarsely grated cheddar

1 Preheat oven to moderately hot (200°C/180°C fan-forced).

2 Place lamb in large lightly oiled baking dish; using sharp knife, score skin at 2cm intervals, sprinkle with rosemary and paprika. Roast lamb, uncovered, 15 minutes.

3 Reduce oven temperature to moderate (180°C/160°C fan-forced); roast lamb, uncovered, about 45 minutes or until cooked as desired.

4 Meanwhile, place potato, pumpkin and onion, in single layer, in large shallow baking dish; drizzle with oil. Roast, uncovered, for last 45 minutes of lamb cooking time.

5 Make cauliflower mornay.

6 Remove lamb and vegetables from oven; cover to keep warm. Strain pan juices from lamb into medium jug. Return ¼ cup of the pan juices to flameproof dish over medium heat, add flour; cook, stirring, 5 minutes or until mixture is browned. Gradually add stock and wine; cook, stirring, until gravy boils and thickens.

7 Strain gravy; serve with sliced lamb, roasted vegetables and cauliflower mornay.

CAULIFLOWER MORNAY Boil, steam or microwave cauliflower until tender; drain. Melt butter in medium saucepan, add flour; cook, stirring, until mixture thickens and bubbles. Gradually add milk; cook, stirring, until mixture boils and thickens. Stir in half of the cheese. Preheat grill. Place cauliflower in 1.5-litre (6-cup) shallow flameproof dish; pour mornay sauce over cauliflower, sprinkle with remaining cheese. Place under grill about 10 minutes or until browned lightly.

PER SERVING 35.6g total fat (17.0g saturated); 3244kj (776 cal); 40.5g carbohydrate; 71.9g protein; 7.0g fibre

Fast lamb cutlets

Everybody loves lamb cutlets; they're perfect at picnics, fabulous as finger food and make a mean main meal.

LEMON AND GARLIC MARINADE
Marinate lamb cutlets in a mixture of olive oil, grated lemon rind, lemon juice and crushed garlic for up to 3 hours. Grill the drained cutlets until cooked as desired.

CHILLI AND PAPRIKA RUB
Combine crushed garlic, dried chilli flakes, sweet paprika, ground cumin and olive oil in a small bowl. Rub into cutlets; cover and refrigerate 3 hours. Pan-fry the cutlets until cooked as desired.

HARISSA BUTTER
Combine 3 teaspoons harissa with 2 tablespoons finely chopped fresh flat-leaf parsley and 80g softened butter. Serve the cooked cutlets with a dollop of harissa butter.

MUSTARD BALSAMIC MARINADE
Marinate lamb cutlets in a mixture of garlic, wholegrain mustard, balsamic vinegar and olive oil for up to 3 hours. Grill the drained cutlets until cooked as desired.

TAMARIND AND DATE CHUTNEY
Combine ½ cup tamarind concentrate, 1 teaspoon ground cumin, 1 cup coarsely chopped seeded dates, ½ cup brown sugar and ½ cup water in a medium saucepan. Simmer, uncovered, 5 minutes. Serve with grilled cutlets.

ZA'ATAR CRUSTED CUTLETS
Combine1 tablespoon sesame seeds, 1 tablespoon sumac, 2 teaspoons dried thyme and 1 teaspoon chopped fresh marjoram. Rub onto cutlets; pan-fry until cooked as desired.

PESTO BUTTER

Combine 2 tablespoons basil pesto with 1 teaspoon finely grated lemon rind and 80g softened butter. Serve the cooked cutlets with a dollop of pesto butter and fresh basil.

CARDAMOM-CRUMBED CUTLETS

Toss cutlets in flour; dip in combined egg and milk and then in a mixture of breadcrumbs, lemon rind, finely chopped fresh flat-leaf parsley and ground cardamom. Shallow-fry the cutlets in oil until browned lightly.

CHAR SUI AND HONEY MARINADE

Marinate lamb cutlets in a mixture of char sui sauce, peanut oil, honey and finely grated fresh ginger for up to 3 hours. Grill the drained cutlets until cooked as desired.

CHILLI LEMON GRASS MARINADE

Marinate lamb cutlets in a mixture of finely chopped lemon grass, crushed garlic, chopped red chilli, fish sauce and peanut oil for up to 3 hours. Drain; grill the cutlets until cooked as desired.

TANDOORI LAMB CUTLETS

Mix ½ cup tandoori paste with ¾ cup yogurt; coat cutlets in the mixture. Grill the cutlets until cooked as desired. Serve with extra yogurt and sprinkle with chopped cucumber.

MUSTARD AND ROSEMARY CREAM

Mix together crème fraîche, dijon mustard and finely chopped fresh rosemary leaves. Serve as a dipping sauce with grilled cutlets.

This is a classic peasant dish from Ireland that traditionally uses mutton and the cheapest local ingredients available, which are root vegetables and barley.

Irish stew with herb dumplings

PREPARATION TIME 30 MINUTES **COOKING TIME** 1 HOUR 45 MINUTES **SERVES** 6

1kg diced lamb
2 tablespoons plain flour
1 teaspoon cracked black pepper
2 large brown onions (400g), sliced thickly
2 large potatoes (600g), sliced thickly
1 large carrot (180g), sliced thickly
½ cup (100g) pearl barley
2 teaspoons finely chopped fresh thyme
1½ cups (375ml) vegetable stock
1 litre (4 cups) hot water

HERB DUMPLINGS

1 cup (150g) self-raising flour
50g cold butter, chopped
1 tablespoon finely chopped fresh flat-leaf parsley
1 tablespoon finely chopped fresh thyme
1 egg, beaten lightly
¼ cup (60ml) milk, approximately

1 Coat lamb with combined flour and pepper in large bowl; shake off excess.

2 Layer half of the onion, potato, carrot and lamb in large heavy-based saucepan; repeat layering with the remaining vegetables and lamb. Sprinkle with barley and thyme, pour on combined stock and the water; bring to a boil. Skim surface of stew, reduce heat; simmer, covered, 1½ hours.

3 Make herb dumplings. Uncover stew; drop heaped tablespoons of dumpling mixture, 2cm apart, on top. Cover; simmer about 15 minutes or until dumplings are cooked through.

HERB DUMPLINGS Sift flour into medium bowl; rub in butter. Stir in herbs, egg and enough milk to mix to a soft, sticky dough.

PER SERVING 23.9g total fat (11.9g saturated); 2483kj (594 cal); 47g carbohydrate; 44.4g protein; 5.9g fibre

---

Beurre blanc or "white butter" is not only wonderful with lamb, but with any meat, poultry, fish or vegetable. To stop this sauce from curdling, use well-chilled butter and loads of elbow grease when whisking it in. Don't reheat – it is meant to be served just warm.

Lamb backstraps with vegetable crisps and beurre blanc

PREPARATION TIME 20 MINUTES **COOKING TIME** 35 MINUTES **SERVES** 4

½ small kumara (125g)
1 small parsnip (120g)
1 large beetroot (200g), trimmed
1 tablespoon olive oil
4 x 200g lamb backstraps
vegetable oil, for deep-frying

BEURRE BLANC

¼ cup (60ml) dry white wine
1 tablespoon lemon juice
¼ cup (60ml) cream
125g cold butter, chopped

1 Using vegetable peeler, slice kumara and parsnip into ribbons. Slice beetroot thinly.

2 Heat olive oil in large frying pan; cook lamb, in batches, until cooked as desired.

3 Make beurre blanc.

4 Heat vegetable oil in wok or large saucepan; deep-fry vegetables, in batches, about 2 minutes per batch or until crisp. Drain on absorbent paper.
5 Cut each piece of lamb into three pieces. Divide half of the sauce among serving plates; top with lamb, remaining sauce and vegetable crisps.

BEURRE BLANC Combine wine and juice in medium saucepan; bring to a boil. Boil, without stirring, until reduced by two-thirds. Add cream; return to a boil. Whisk in cold butter, piece by piece, whisking between additions. Pour into medium jug; cover to keep warm.

▭ **PER SERVING** 65.4g total fat (31.2g saturated); 3407kj (815 cal); 10.7g carbohydrate; 44g protein; 2.4g fibre

---

Moussaka

PREPARATION TIME 40 MINUTES (PLUS STANDING TIME) **COOKING TIME** 1 HOUR 30 MINUTES **SERVES** 6

If you can cook the eggplant on a grill pan or barbecue do so – it will take on an amazing smokey flavour, which will add a delicious element to the moussaka.

- 2 large eggplants (1kg), sliced thinly
- 1 tablespoon coarse cooking salt
- ¼ cup (60ml) olive oil
- 1 large brown onion (200g), chopped finely
- 2 cloves garlic, crushed
- 1kg lamb mince
- 425g can crushed tomatoes
- ½ cup (125ml) dry white wine
- 1 teaspoon ground cinnamon
- ¼ cup (20g) finely grated parmesan

WHITE SAUCE

- 80g butter
- ⅓ cup (50g) plain flour
- 2 cups (500ml) hot milk

1 Place eggplant in colander, sprinkle all over with salt; stand 30 minutes. Rinse under cold water; drain. Pat dry with absorbent paper. Heat oil in large frying pan; cook eggplant, in batches, until browned both sides; drain on absorbent paper.
2 Cook onion and garlic in same pan, stirring, until onion softens. Add lamb; cook, stirring, until lamb changes colour. Stir in undrained tomatoes, wine and cinnamon; bring to a boil. Reduce heat; simmer, uncovered, about 30 minutes or until liquid has evaporated.
3 Meanwhile, preheat oven to moderate (180°C/160°C fan-forced). Oil shallow 2-litre (8-cup) rectangular baking dish.
4 Make white sauce.
5 Place a third of the eggplant, overlapping slices slightly, in dish; spread half of the meat sauce over eggplant. Repeat layering, finishing with layer of eggplant. Spread white sauce over top; sprinkle with cheese. Cook, uncovered, about 40 minutes or until top browns lightly. Cover moussaka; stand 10 minutes before serving.

WHITE SAUCE Melt butter in medium saucepan, add flour; cook, stirring, until mixture thickens and bubbles. Gradually add milk; cook, stirring, until mixture boils and thickens.

▭ **PER SERVING** 36.6g total fat (16.5g saturated); 2420kj (579 cal); 18.0g carbohydrate; 41.8g protein; 5.3g fibre

Raan with lemon pilau

PREPARATION TIME 25 MINUTES (PLUS REFRIGERATION TIME)
COOKING TIME 2 HOURS 35 MINUTES **SERVES** 6

If you're ever invited home for a lamb roast in northern India, this traditional recipe is probably what you'll be served. Break with tradition and try it at home for your next Sunday roast.

2 teaspoons coriander seeds
1 teaspoon cumin seeds
5 cardamom pods, bruised
1 teaspoon chilli powder
1 teaspoon ground turmeric
1 cinnamon stick
2 cloves
2 star anise
1 medium brown onion (150g), chopped coarsely
4 cloves garlic, peeled
2cm piece fresh ginger (10g), grated
¼ cup (40g) blanched almonds
½ cup (140g) yogurt
2 tablespoons lemon juice
2kg leg of lamb, trimmed

LEMON PILAU
1 tablespoon vegetable oil
5 cardamom pods, bruised
4 cloves
1 cinnamon stick
¼ teaspoon saffron threads
2 cups (400g) white long-grain rice
3 cups (750ml) boiling water
⅓ cup (80ml) lemon juice
1 tablespoon white sugar
20g butter
2 teaspoons finely grated lemon rind
2 tablespoons slivered roasted almonds

1 Dry-fry seeds, cardamom, chilli, turmeric, cinnamon, cloves and star anise in small frying pan, stirring, until fragrant. Blend or process spices with onion, garlic, ginger, nuts, yogurt and juice until mixture forms a paste.
2 Pierce lamb all over with sharp knife; place on wire rack in large shallow baking dish. Spread paste over lamb, pressing firmly into cuts. Cover; refrigerate overnight.
3 Preheat oven to moderately hot (200°C/180°C fan-forced).
4 Remove lamb from refrigerator; pour enough water into baking dish to completely cover base. Cover dish with foil; roast lamb 30 minutes. Reduce oven temperature to slow (150°C/130°C fan-forced); roast lamb, covered with foil, 1½ hours. Uncover; roast about 30 minutes or until lamb is cooked as desired.
5 Meanwhile, make lemon pilau.
6 Cover lamb; stand 10 minutes before slicing. Serve with pilau and, if desired, yogurt with coarsely chopped fresh coriander stirred through it.

LEMON PILAU Heat oil in large saucepan; cook spices, stirring, until fragrant. Add rice; stir until rice is coated in spice mixture. Add the water, juice and sugar; bring to a boil. Reduce heat; simmer rice, partially covered, about 10 minutes or until steam holes appear on surface. Reduce heat to as low as possible, cover rice tightly; steam 10 minutes (do not remove lid). Remove from heat; stand 10 minutes without removing lid. Fluff with fork, then stir in butter, rind and nuts.

PER SERVING 25.2g total fat (9g saturated); 3010kj (720 cal); 59.2g carbohydrate; 62.4g protein; 2.1g fibre

RAAN WITH LEMON PILAU

This popular Chinese restaurant dish has its origins in the campfire-braised meats, packed with masses of garlic, eaten by mongol herders in the vast expanses of the Euro-asian steppes.

Mongolian garlic lamb

PREPARATION TIME 10 MINUTES **COOKING TIME** 15 MINUTES **SERVES** 4

750g lamb fillets, sliced thinly
3 cloves garlic, crushed
1 tablespoon cornflour
¼ cup (60ml) dark soy sauce
⅓ cup (80ml) sweet sherry
2 tablespoons vegetable oil
1 tablespoon brown sugar
1 teaspoon sesame oil
8 green onions, sliced thinly

1 Combine lamb, garlic, cornflour, half of the sauce and half of the sherry in large bowl.
2 Heat vegetable oil in wok; stir-fry lamb mixture, in batches, until browned all over.
3 Return lamb mixture to wok. Add remaining sauce, remaining sherry, sugar and sesame oil; stir-fry until sauce boils and thickens slightly. Remove from heat; stir in onion.

PER SERVING 27.0g total fat (8.8g saturated); 1927kj (461 cal); 9.3g carbohydrate; 40.5g protein; 0.8g fibre

Give this pizza another layer of flavour by garnishing with crumbled fetta, extra roasted pine nuts and extra mint leaves just before serving.

Turkish herbed lamb pizza

PREPARATION TIME 45 MINUTES (PLUS STANDING TIME) **COOKING TIME** 35 MINUTES **SERVES** 4

¾ teaspoon dried yeast
1 teaspoon white sugar
¾ cup (180ml) warm water
2 cups (300g) plain flour
1 teaspoon salt
cooking-oil spray
600g lamb mince
1 tablespoon olive oil
1 small brown onion (80g), chopped finely
1 clove garlic, crushed
½ teaspoon ground cinnamon
1½ teaspoons ground allspice
¼ cup (40g) pine nuts, chopped coarsely
¼ cup (70g) tomato paste
2 medium tomatoes (300g), seeded, chopped finely
1 cup (250ml) chicken stock
2 tablespoons lemon juice
¼ cup finely chopped fresh flat-leaf parsley
¼ cup finely chopped fresh mint
½ cup (140g) greek-style yogurt
2 tablespoons cold water

1 Whisk yeast, sugar and the warm water in small bowl, cover; stand in warm place about 15 minutes or until mixture is frothy.
2 Combine flour and salt in large bowl; stir in yeast mixture, mix to a soft dough. Knead on floured surface about 10 minutes or until smooth and elastic. Place in large oiled bowl, turning dough once to coat in oil. Cover dough; stand in warm place about 1 hour or until dough has doubled in size.
3 Halve dough; knead each portion until smooth then roll out to oval shape measuring approximately 12cm x 35cm. Place each oval on a lightly oiled oven tray; spray lightly with oil. Cover; stand in warm place 30 minutes.
4 Preheat oven to very hot (240°C/220°C fan-forced).

5 Heat large oiled frying pan, add mince; cook, stirring, until cooked through. Place in medium bowl.

6 Heat oil in same pan; cook onion and garlic, stirring, until onion softens. Add spices and nuts; cook, stirring, about 5 minutes or until nuts are just roasted. Return mince to pan with paste, tomato, stock and juice; cook, stirring, about 5 minutes or until liquid is almost evaporated. Remove pan from heat; stir in herbs.

7 Spoon mince mixture over pizza bases; cook, uncovered, about 15 minutes or until bases are cooked through and tops are browned lightly. Serve drizzled with combined yogurt and the cold water.

PER SERVING 26.5g total fat (7.7g saturated); 2805kj (671 cal); 63.0g carbohydrate; 44.2g protein; 5.3g fibre

---

Herb-crusted lamb racks with kipfler potatoes and leek

As a variation on the crust, add 3 teaspoons wholegrain mustard and 1 tablespoon olive oil instead of the pesto.

PREPARATION TIME 25 MINUTES **COOKING TIME** 55 MINUTES (PLUS STANDING TIME) **SERVES** 4

- 4 x 3-cutlet racks of lamb (750g)
- ¼ cup (15g) stale white breadcrumbs
- 1 tablespoon finely chopped fresh rosemary
- 1 tablespoon finely chopped fresh flat-leaf parsley
- 2 teaspoons finely chopped fresh thyme
- 3 cloves garlic, crushed
- 3 teaspoons bottled coriander pesto
- 1kg kipfler potatoes, halved lengthways
- cooking-oil spray
- 1 teaspoon sea salt
- 2 medium leeks (700g), trimmed
- 10g butter
- ¼ cup (60ml) chicken stock
- ¼ cup (60ml) dry white wine

1 Preheat oven to moderately hot (200°C/180°C fan-forced).

2 Remove any excess fat from lamb. Combine breadcrumbs, herbs, garlic and pesto in small bowl. Press breadcrumb mixture onto lamb racks, cover; refrigerate until required.

3 Place potato in large shallow baking dish; spray with oil, sprinkle with salt. Roast, uncovered, 20 minutes.

4 Place lamb on top of the potato; roast, uncovered, about 10 minutes. Reduce oven temperature to slow (150°C/130°C fan-forced); cook 20 minutes or until potato is tender and lamb is cooked as desired.

5 Meanwhile, cut leeks into 10cm lengths; slice thinly lengthways. Melt butter in large frying pan; cook leek, stirring, until leek softens. Stir in stock and wine; bring to a boil. Reduce heat; simmer, uncovered, until liquid reduces by half.

6 Stand lamb 5 minutes before cutting racks into cutlets; serve with potato and leek.

PER SERVING 13.6g total fat (6g saturated); 1806kj (432 cal); 39.8g carbohydrate; 30.4g protein; 8.8g fibre

For a change, add 2 teaspoons finely grated lemon rind to the breadcrumb mixture.

Parmesan-breaded lamb cutlets

PREPARATION TIME 15 MINUTES **COOKING TIME** 15 MINUTES **SERVES** 4

12 lamb cutlets (900g)
⅓ cup (50g) plain flour
2 eggs
2 tablespoons milk
1 clove garlic, crushed
½ cup (35g) stale breadcrumbs
½ cup (50g) packaged breadcrumbs
½ cup (40g) finely grated parmesan
1 tablespoon finely chopped fresh oregano
2 tablespoons olive oil

1 Coat lamb in flour; shake off excess. Combine eggs, milk and garlic in medium shallow bowl; combine breadcrumbs, cheese and oregano in another medium shallow bowl. Dip cutlets, one at a time, into egg mixture, then in breadcrumb mixture.
2 Heat oil in large frying pan; cook cutlets, in batches, until cooked as desired.

PER SERVING 26.7g total fat (9.6g saturated); 2031kj (486 cal); 23.6g carbohydrate; 37g protein; 1.5g fibre

---

Celeriac remoulade has long been one of the temptations of the hors d'oeuvre trolley in top French restaurants. It provides just the right, piquant balance to the rich crumbed brains.

Crumbed brains with celeriac remoulade

PREPARATION TIME 30 MINUTES (PLUS REFRIGERATION TIME)
COOKING TIME 20 MINUTES (PLUS COOLING TIME) **SERVES** 4

6 sets lamb brains (600g)
1 litre (4 cups) water
1 tablespoon lemon juice
1 teaspoon salt
1 cup (70g) stale breadcrumbs
2 green onions, chopped finely
1 tablespoon finely chopped fresh flat-leaf parsley
2 tablespoons finely chopped fresh tarragon
¼ cup (35g) plain flour
1 egg
2 tablespoons milk
vegetable oil, for deep-frying

CELERIAC REMOULADE
½ cup (150g) mayonnaise
200g celeriac, grated coarsely
2 anchovy fillets, drained, chopped finely
2 tablespoons drained capers, rinsed, chopped finely
1 tablespoon finely chopped fresh flat-leaf parsley
1 tablespoon lemon juice

1 Remove brain stem by pulling away gently with fingers; divide each set of brains into two lobes. Place in large bowl, cover with cold water; refrigerate, covered, 2 hours. Drain.
2 Combine brains in medium saucepan with the water, juice and salt; bring to a boil. Reduce heat; simmer, uncovered, 5 minutes. Drain; cool 10 minutes.
3 Meanwhile, make celeriac remoulade by combining ingredients in medium bowl.
4 Combine breadcrumbs, onion and herbs in large bowl. Coat brains in flour; shake away excess. Dip brains in combined egg and milk then coat in breadcrumb mixture.

5 Heat oil in wok or large saucepan; deep-fry brains, in batches, until browned lightly.

6 Serve brains with celeriac remoulade and assorted salad greens, if desired.

PER SERVING 34.9g total fat (6.6g saturated); 2232kj (534 cal); 28.6g carbohydrate; 25.4g protein; 3.4g fibre

Za'atar lamb with warm chickpea salad

Za'atar, a mixture of roasted sesame seeds, dried marjoram, thyme and sumac, can be found already blended in Middle Eastern food stores. Alternatively, you can make your own blend, as we have here.

PREPARATION TIME 45 MINUTES (PLUS STANDING AND REFRIGERATION TIME)

COOKING TIME 40 MINUTES **SERVES** 4

1 cup (200g) dried chickpeas
1 bay leaf
4 x 200g lamb backstraps
20g butter
1 tablespoon olive oil
12 baby onions (300g), halved
1 large carrot (180g), chopped finely
2 trimmed celery stalks (200g), chopped finely
2 small fennel bulbs (400g), trimmed, sliced thinly
1 cup firmly packed fresh flat-leaf parsley leaves

ZA'ATAR

2 tablespoons olive oil
1 tablespoon sumac
1 tablespoon roasted sesame seeds
1 teaspoon dried thyme leaves
1 teaspoon dried oregano leaves
1 teaspoon dried marjoram
1 teaspoon sweet paprika

SUMAC DRESSING

1 tablespoon sumac
1 teaspoon dijon mustard
¼ cup (60ml) olive oil
¼ cup (60ml) lemon juice

1 Place chickpeas in large bowl of cold water; stand overnight. Drain.

2 Cook chickpeas and bay leaf in medium saucepan of boiling water, uncovered, until just tender; drain. Rinse under cold water; drain.

3 Meanwhile, combine za'atar ingredients in large bowl; mix well. Add lamb; turn to coat in za'atar mixture. Cover; refrigerate 30 minutes.

4 Make sumac dressing by placing ingredients in screw-top jar. Shake well.

5 Heat butter and oil in large frying pan; cook onion, stirring, until browned lightly and softened. Add carrot, celery and fennel; cook, stirring, until vegetables are just tender.

6 Meanwhile, cook lamb, in batches, on heated oiled grill plate (or grill or barbecue) until browned and cooked as desired. Cover lamb, stand 5 minutes; slice lamb thickly.

7 Combine chickpeas, parsley and half of the dressing with vegetables; cook, stirring, to warm through. Divide chickpea salad among plates; top with lamb and remaining dressing.

PER SERVING 52.1g total fat (14.9g saturated); 3102kj (742 cal); 16.7g carbohydrate; 48.8g protein; 8.3g fibre

Skordalia is a pungent Greek sauce or dip made with bread (or sometimes potato), garlic, lemon juice and olive oil. It can be served with almost any kind of dish – from grilled meats and poultry to fish and raw vegetables.

Greek lamb salad

PREPARATION TIME 40 MINUTES (PLUS REFRIGERATION TIME) **COOKING TIME** 10 MINUTES **SERVES** 4

2 tablespoons olive oil

2 teaspoons finely grated lemon rind

1 teaspoon finely chopped fresh marjoram

1 clove garlic, crushed

600g lamb fillets, trimmed

1 large green capsicum (350g), sliced thinly

1 telegraph cucumber (400g), diced into 2cm pieces

400g grape tomatoes, halved

2 trimmed celery stalks (200g), sliced thinly

4 green onions, sliced thinly

2 baby cos lettuces, chopped coarsely

1 cup (150g) seeded kalamata olives

200g goat fetta, crumbled

SKORDALIA

2 slices stale white bread

2 cloves garlic, crushed

2 tablespoons olive oil

2 teaspoons white wine vinegar

1 tablespoon lemon juice

⅓ cup (80ml) water

MARJORAM DRESSING

2 tablespoons olive oil

2 tablespoons white wine vinegar

1 tablespoon finely chopped fresh marjoram

pinch cayenne pepper

1 Place oil, rind, marjoram and garlic in large bowl, add lamb; turn to coat in marinade. Cover; refrigerate 1 hour.

2 Meanwhile, make skordalia and marjoram dressing.

3 Heat large oiled frying pan; cook lamb, in batches, until browned and cooked as desired. Cover; stand 5 minutes. Slice lamb thickly.

4 Place lamb in large bowl with remaining ingredients and dressing; toss gently to combine. Divide salad among serving plates; drizzle with skordalia.

SKORDALIA Discard crusts from bread, soak in small bowl of cold water; drain. Squeeze out excess water; blend or process bread and remaining ingredients until smooth.

MARJORAM DRESSING Place ingredients in screw-top jar; shake well.

PER SERVING 53.7g total fat (17.7g saturated); 3244kj (776 cal); 25.1g carbohydrate; 45.9g protein; 7.0g fibre

GREEK LAMB SALAD

VEGETABLES

Vegetables

It may seem that nothing could excel the appeal of a plain, fresh vegetable carefully cooked and presented in all its simple perfection – but then, what about a luscious vegetable lasagne, a fragrant vegetable curry, crunchy Asian greens played against a rich sauce, mushrooms, with their buttery juices soaking into soft polenta, or the joy of hot chips rustling onto the plate?

BUYING VEGETABLES

Buy greens and vegetable flowers and fruits such as globe artichokes, broccoli, cauliflower, eggplant, capsicum and zucchini in quantities you will use within a few days, and root vegetables in quantities you will use within a week or so. Peas and sweetcorn should be eaten the day you buy them because they gradually lose sweetness and tenderness.

Fresh vegetables look brisk and upstanding; most have a sheen. Greens should be taut and bright, the cabbage family firm and tightly packed, tomatoes gleaming and richly coloured, eggplant and capsicum smooth and glossy, root vegetables well shaped, clean and unmarked (though potatoes are even better if they are still dirty, as the high-pressure hoses used to clean them can damage their skins). Select potatoes by variety. High-starch, floury varieties which bake well can collapse if boiled, while lower-starch, waxy ones which boil well will not bake satisfactorily. Spunta, russet burbank, kipfler and king Edward are good for baking; desiree, pontiac and bintje boil and mash well; while nicola and pink fir apple are excellent all-rounders and sebago are acceptable ones.

STORING AND HANDLING VEGETABLES

Please also read "Buying, storing and handling salad vegetables" on page 134.

- Don't wash vegetables until you are about to prepare them (except for some salad ingredients, see page 134).
- Store leaf vegetables, peas, beans, corn, globe artichokes, okra, broccoli, cauliflower, cut pumpkin and beetroot in paper bags or loosely wrapped in greaseproof paper, enclosed in plastic bags, in the fridge.
- Store eggplant, capsicum and carrots unwrapped in a covered crisper.
- Store onions and potatoes in a cool, dark place on racks or in baskets off the floor.

JUDGING WHEN VEGETABLES ARE DONE

- Spinach and cabbage are done as soon as they wilt and lose volume.
- Check small vegetables or pieces by taking one out and biting.
- Check larger vegetables or pieces by inserting a fine skewer; when it meets no resistance, they are done.

BASIC WAYS OF COOKING VEGETABLES

BOILING Vegetables that grow underground "in the cold and dark" should be boiled "in the cold and dark", that is, placed in cold salted water to cover and cooked with the lid on (the exceptions are tiny ones, which go into boiling water). Drain, return to the saucepan and shake briefly over low heat to dry.

Vegetables that grow above-ground "in the heat and light" should be boiled "in the heat and light", that is, placed in boiling water and cooked without a lid.

STEAMING Place the vegetables in a metal steamer which fits over a saucepan containing boiling water, or a bamboo steamer, or stand a collapsible metal steamer in boiling water in a saucepan (the water should not touch the steamer or the vegetables). Cover with a tight-fitting lid. Steaming takes almost as long as boiling, depending on how tightly the lid fits.

BRAISING Blanch for a few minutes in boiling water, drain, then add to a little melted butter in a shallow pan or dish. Add enough stock to come halfway up the vegetables, season, then cover and cook slowly on the stovetop or in the oven until the vegetables are very tender and the liquid has reduced to make a sauce.

CHAR-GRILLING, BARBECUING Brush vegetables with melted butter or oil, place on a well-heated ridged grill pan or barbecue bars, press down with tongs and grill, turning as needed, until barely tender and well marked with char stripes.

ROASTING, BAKING For vegetables to accompany a roast, par-boil for 5 minutes, dry as for boiled root vegetables and score the surfaces with a fork. Place around the roast for half an hour before the meat will be done, spoon the pan juices over and cook, turning once. For a crunchier roast potato, roast them on a well-oiled oven tray by themselves. For olive-oil-roasted vegetables, cut into smallish pieces, coat with a little oil in a shallow baking dish, season and roast in a moderately hot oven, turning once or twice, until crisp and tender. For potatoes baked in their skins, wash, dry and brush with oil for soft skin or rub the oiled potato with coarse salt for crisp skin. Bake on the oven bars in a moderately hot oven until done (45 minutes to 1 hour depending on size).

STIR-FRYING Cut vegetables into uniform pieces, slices or shreds. Heat a wok over high heat and add enough vegetable oil to coat the food generously; add sliced or chopped ginger and/or garlic if you wish, removing with a slotted spoon as soon as they are lightly coloured. Add vegetables in the order of the time they take to par-cook (they should still be crunchy): longest-cooking first, shortest-cooking last. Before the last vegetables go in, return the ginger and garlic to the wok if you wish and add seasonings such as soy or other sauces or sesame oil. Add the last vegetables, toss once or twice more and turn into a heated serving dish.

PAN-FRYING Heat a little oil or butter, or a mixture of both, over medium heat until the oil gives off a haze or the butter stops sizzling. Fry the vegetables until browned and tender, turning once; remove with a slotted spoon or tongs and drain on crumpled absorbent paper.

DEEP-FRYING Barely half-fill a deep fryer or large saucepan with vegetable oil. For hot chips (french fries) cut peeled potatoes into sticks, wash and dry. Heat the oil to 170°C – it is ready when a square of day-old bread browns in 60 seconds. Add the chips in a frying basket (in batches if necessary – don't crowd them) and cook until soft but not coloured. Remove and allow to cool a little or completely (this can be done several hours ahead). Heat the oil to 190°C (when bread browns in 30 seconds), return the chips to the fryer and cook until crisp and golden. Drain on absorbent paper and salt lightly.

For vegetable fritters, heat the oil to 190°C, add batter-coated vegetable pieces, a few at a time, and cook until golden. Drain and salt as for chips.

For an impresive starter or light lunch cut one sheet of ready-rolled puff pastry into four equal squares. Place the pastry squares on an oven tray, bake in a moderately hot oven for 20 minutes or until golden. Serve the pastry squares topped with a dressed salad and a slice or two of pan-fried haloumi.

Pan-fried haloumi with green salad

PREPARATION TIME 15 MINUTES **COOKING TIME** 5 MINUTES **SERVES** 4

150g curly endive

50g baby spinach leaves

½ cup loosely packed fresh flat-leaf parsley leaves

⅔ cup (100g) drained semi-dried tomatoes, chopped coarsely

250g haloumi cheese

LEMON DIJON DRESSING

¼ cup (60ml) lemon juice

1 clove garlic, crushed

1 tablespoon water

1 teaspoon white sugar

1 teaspoon dijon mustard

¼ teaspoon ground cumin

pinch cayenne pepper

1 Combine endive, spinach, parsley and tomato in medium bowl.

2 Cut haloumi into eight slices. Heat lightly oiled medium frying pan; cook cheese, in batches, until browned both sides.

3 Meanwhile, make lemon dijon dressing.

4 Add dressing to salad; toss gently to combine. Serve salad topped with cheese.

LEMON DIJON DRESSING Place ingredients in screw-top jar; shake well.

☐ **PER SERVING** 12.2g total fat (7g saturated); 1003kj (240 cal); 12.4g carbohydrate; 17.7g protein; 5.1g fibre

Traditionally in India curries are served with accompaniments such as basmati rice, naan or roti, pappadums and mango chutney.

Chickpea, pumpkin and eggplant curry

PREPARATION TIME 15 MINUTES **COOKING TIME** 40 MINUTES **SERVES** 4

1 tablespoon vegetable oil

1 medium brown onion (150g), chopped coarsely

2 cloves garlic, crushed

4 baby eggplants (240g), chopped coarsely

¼ cup (75g) medium curry paste

600g pumpkin, chopped coarsely

½ small cauliflower (500g), cut into florets

1½ cups (375ml) vegetable stock

425g can crushed tomatoes

400g can chickpeas, rinsed, drained

1 cup (280g) yogurt

½ cup finely shredded fresh mint

1 Heat oil in large saucepan; cook onion, garlic and eggplant, stirring, until just tender. Add curry paste; cook, stirring, until fragrant.

2 Add pumpkin, cauliflower, stock and undrained tomatoes; bring to a boil. Reduce heat; simmer, covered, 20 minutes. Add chickpeas; simmer, covered, about 10 minutes or until vegetables are tender.

3 Meanwhile, combine yogurt and mint in small bowl. Serve curry with yogurt mixture.

☐ **PER SERVING** 15.9g total fat (3.5g saturated); 1526kj (365 cal); 32.2g carbohydrate; 17g protein; 12.6g fibre

1 PAN-FRIED HALOUMI WITH GREEN SALAD **2** CHICKPEA, PUMPKIN AND EGGPLANT CURRY **3** STIR-FRIED ASIAN GREENS IN BLACK BEAN SAUCE [P 306] **4** STEAMED SPINACH DUMPLINGS WITH FRESH TOMATO AND HERB SAUCE [P 306]

1

2

3

4

To make this into a one-dish meal, cut 150g firm tofu into bite-sized cubes. If you prefer the edges of the tofu to be crispy, cook the tofu cubes in a frying pan with ¼ cup vegetable oil until golden.

Stir-fried asian greens in black bean sauce

PREPARATION TIME 10 MINUTES **COOKING TIME** 15 MINUTES **SERVES** 4

2 cups (400g) jasmine rice

1 tablespoon sesame oil

150g sugar snap peas, trimmed

400g gai lan, chopped coarsely

200g snake beans, trimmed, cut into 5cm lengths

2 cloves garlic, sliced thinly

1 fresh small red thai chilli, chopped finely

2 medium zucchini (240g), sliced thickly

2 tablespoons black bean sauce

1 tablespoon kecap manis

⅓ cup (50g) roasted unsalted cashews, chopped coarsely

1 Cook rice in large saucepan of boiling water, uncovered, until just tender; drain.

2 Meanwhile, heat oil in wok; stir-fry peas, gai lan stems, beans, garlic, chilli and zucchini until stems are just tender.

3 Add sauces, gai lan leaves and nuts; stir-fry until leaves are just wilted. Serve with rice.

PER SERVING 12.3g total fat (2g saturated); 2249kj (538 cal); 88.4g carbohydrate; 14.2g protein; 6.6g fibre

---

Egg white plays a vital function in binding these dumplings together.

Steamed spinach dumplings with fresh tomato and herb sauce

PREPARATION TIME 30 MINUTES (PLUS STANDING TIME) **COOKING TIME** 20 MINUTES **SERVES** 4

2 x 250g packets frozen spinach, thawed

200g ricotta cheese

1 clove garlic, crushed

1 egg white

1 tablespoon plain flour

¼ cup (20g) finely grated parmesan

1½ cups (110g) stale breadcrumbs

¼ teaspoon ground nutmeg

1 tablespoon finely chopped fresh chives

2 tablespoons finely grated parmesan, extra

FRESH TOMATO AND HERB SAUCE

½ cup (125ml) dry white wine

4 medium tomatoes (600g), chopped finely

2 tablespoons finely chopped fresh flat-leaf parsley

1 teaspoon white sugar

1 Squeeze excess liquid from spinach. Combine spinach in large bowl with ricotta, garlic, egg white, flour, parmesan, breadcrumbs, nutmeg and chives; roll level tablespoons of the mixture into balls. Place balls, in single layer, about 2cm apart in baking-paper-lined bamboo steamer fitted over large saucepan of boiling water. Steam, covered, 10 minutes or until dumplings are heated through.

2 Meanwhile, make fresh tomato and herb sauce.
3 Serve dumplings with sauce and extra parmesan.

FRESH TOMATO AND HERB SAUCE Bring wine to a boil in medium saucepan. Reduce heat; simmer, uncovered, until reduced by half. Add tomato; return to a boil. Boil, uncovered, about 10 minutes or until thickened slightly. Stir in parsley and sugar.

PER SERVING 9.8g total fat (5.5g saturated); 1200kj (287 cal); 25.3g carbohydrate; 16.6g protein; 5.1g fibre

---

Yellow curry

PREPARATION TIME 20 MINUTES **COOKING TIME** 30 MINUTES **SERVES** 4

- 1⅔ cups (410ml) light coconut milk
- 1 cup (250ml) salt-reduced vegetable stock
- 1 large kumara (500g), chopped coarsely
- 200g green beans, trimmed
- 150g firm tofu, diced into 2cm pieces
- 2 tablespoons lime juice
- ¼ cup coarsely chopped fresh coriander
- 2 cups (400g) jasmine rice

YELLOW CURRY PASTE

- 1 teaspoon ground coriander
- 1 teaspoon ground cumin
- 1 teaspoon ground cinnamon
- 4cm piece fresh ginger (20g), chopped coarsely
- 2 cloves garlic, quartered
- 5 fresh long red chillies, chopped coarsely
- 5cm stick (10g) coarsely chopped fresh lemon grass
- 3 green onions, chopped coarsely
- 1 teaspoon salt
- 2 teaspoons curry powder
- 1 medium brown onion (150g), chopped coarsely

For a quick satay sauce for skewered vegetables, chicken or meat, place 1 tablespoon each of this yellow curry paste and vegetable oil in a small saucepan; cook for about 2 minutes. Add 1 cup coconut milk, ½ cup crunchy peanut butter, 1 tablespoon each of soy sauce and brown sugar; bring to a boil, stirring. Reduce the heat and simmer, uncovered, for 5 minutes.

1 Make yellow curry paste.
2 Cook half of the curry paste in large saucepan, stirring, until fragrant. Add coconut milk and stock; bring to a boil. Reduce heat; simmer, stirring, 5 minutes. Add kumara; simmer, covered, about 10 minutes or until kumara is tender. Add beans, tofu and juice; cook, stirring, until beans are tender. Stir in coriander.
3 Meanwhile, cook rice in large saucepan of boiling water, uncovered, until just tender; drain rice.
4 Serve curry with rice topped with fresh coriander leaves, if desired.

The remaining half of the curry paste can be refrigerated, tightly covered, for up to a week, or frozen for 3 months.

YELLOW CURRY PASTE Dry-fry coriander, cumin and cinnamon in small frying pan, stirring, until fragrant. Blend or process spices with remaining ingredients until mixture forms a paste.

PER SERVING 24.9g total fat (19.2g saturated); 3035kj (726 cal); 103.1g carbohydrate; 17.9g protein; 7.9g fibre

In Morocco it's popular to cook savoury meals utilising fruit and nuts of the region. Try adding ¼ cup roasted whole almonds, 2 tablespoons coarsely chopped fresh coriander and 6 coarsely chopped fresh seeded dates to the couscous.

Vegetable tagine

PREPARATION TIME 25 MINUTES **COOKING TIME** 40 MINUTES **SERVES** 6

- 1 tablespoon coriander seeds
- 1 tablespoon cumin seeds
- 1 tablespoon caraway seeds
- 1 tablespoon vegetable oil
- 3 cloves garlic, crushed
- 2 large brown onions (400g), chopped finely
- 2 teaspoons sweet paprika
- 2 teaspoons ground ginger
- 1 tablespoon tomato paste
- 2 cups (500ml) water
- 2 x 400g cans diced tomatoes
- 600g pumpkin, chopped coarsely
- 8 yellow patty-pan squash (240g), quartered
- 200g baby green beans, trimmed, halved
- 300g can chickpeas, rinsed, drained

LEMON COUSCOUS

- 2 cups (400g) couscous
- 2 cups (500ml) boiling water
- 2 teaspoons coarsely grated lemon rind
- 2 teaspoons lemon juice
- 2 tablespoons coarsely chopped fresh flat-leaf parsley

1 Using mortar and pestle, crush coriander, cumin and caraway seeds to a fine powder. Sift into small bowl; discard husks.

2 Heat oil in large saucepan; cook garlic and onion, stirring, until onion softens. Add crushed seeds, paprika and ginger; cook, stirring, until fragrant.

3 Add paste, the water, undrained tomatoes and pumpkin; bring to a boil. Reduce heat; simmer, uncovered, 20 minutes. Stir in squash, beans and chickpeas; simmer, covered, about 10 minutes or until squash is tender.

4 Meanwhile, make lemon couscous.

5 Serve tagine with couscous.

LEMON COUSCOUS Combine couscous with the water in large heatproof bowl, cover; stand about 5 minutes or until water is absorbed, fluffing with fork occasionally. Stir in remaining ingredients.

PER SERVING 5.0g total fat (0.8g saturated); 1735kj (415 cal); 71.3g carbohydrate; 16.4g protein; 7.9g fibre

Potato and vegetable mashes

EACH OF THESE MASHES IS ENOUGH TO SERVE 4 PEOPLE AS A SIDE DISH.

There are many methods for making the perfect mashed potato, evolving from the "classic French style" or the "Anglo-american style". The difference is that the French use waxy potatoes (less starch) to make a smooth puree consistency and Anglo-americans use floury potatoes (higher starch) to make a thick, light, fluffy consistency. For this recipe we used lasoda potatoes, an all-purpose potato, which is a hybrid of the two varieties.

CAPSICUM MASH

Quarter 2 medium red capsicums; discard seeds and membranes. Roast under grill or in very hot oven, skin-side up, until skin blisters and blackens. Cover capsicum pieces with plastic or paper 5 minutes; peel away skin, then chop capsicum coarsely. Blend or process capsicum until smooth. Meanwhile, boil, steam or microwave 1kg peeled, coarsely chopped lasoda potato until tender; drain. Mash potato in large bowl; stir in ½ cup hot cream and 20g softened butter. Add capsicum to mash; stir until combined.

PER SERVING 18.0g total fat (11.6g saturated); 1329kj (318 cal); 30.5g carbohydrate; 6.8g protein; 4.2g fibre

FENNEL MASH

Slice 1 large trimmed fennel bulb thinly. Melt 60g butter in large frying pan; cook fennel, covered, over low heat, 10 minutes or until very soft. Blend or process fennel until smooth. Meanwhile, boil, steam or microwave 1kg peeled, coarsely chopped lasoda potato until tender; drain. Mash potato in large bowl; stir in ½ cup hot cream and fennel mixture.

PER SERVING 26.1g total fat (17.0g saturated); 1618kj (387 cal); 30.0g carbohydrate; 6.2g protein; 5.4g fibre

SPINACH MASH

Boil, steam or microwave 1kg peeled, coarsely chopped lasoda potato until tender; drain. Meanwhile, boil, steam or microwave 220g spinach until wilted; drain. Squeeze out excess liquid. Blend or process spinach with 40g softened butter until almost smooth. Mash potato in large bowl; stir in ½ cup hot cream and spinach mixture.

PER SERVING 22.1g total fat (17.0g saturated); 1434kj (343 cal); 27.5g carbohydrate; 6.8g protein; 4.7g fibre

PEA MASH

Boil, steam or microwave 1kg peeled, coarsely chopped lasoda potato and 1½ cups frozen peas, separately, until tender; drain. Mash potato in large bowl; stir in ¾ cup hot milk and 50g softened butter. Using fork, mash peas in small bowl; stir into mash.

When mashing potatoes never try to make them extra smooth by whizzing them in a food processor; the result will be something like glue.

PER SERVING 12.5g total fat (8.0g saturated); 1229kj (294 cal); 32.0g carbohydrate; 9.9g protein; 6.7g fibre

CELERIAC MASH

Boil, steam or microwave 800g peeled, coarsely chopped lasoda potato and 1kg peeled, coarsely chopped celeriac, separately, until tender; drain. Mash potato and celeriac in large bowl; stir in ½ cup hot cream and 60g softened butter.

PER SERVING 26.4g total fat (17g saturated); 1739kj (416 cal); 31.9g carbohydrate; 7.7g protein; 11.4g fibre

PUMPKIN MASH

Boil, steam or microwave 500g peeled, coarsely chopped lasoda potato and 500g peeled, coarsely chopped pumpkin together until tender; drain. Mash potato and pumpkin in large bowl; stir in 30g softened butter.

PER SERVING 6.7g total fat (4.4g saturated); 681kj (163 cal); 19.7g carbohydrate; 4.6g protein; 2.8g fibre

These aromatic vegetables make a wonderful first course (or main course with couscous) for a vegetarian meal, and also a delicious accompaniment to corned beef or pork chops.

Braised root vegetables with gremolata

PREPARATION TIME 15 MINUTES **COOKING TIME** 50 MINUTES **SERVES** 4

1 tablespoon olive oil

2 cloves garlic, crushed

2 large parsnips (700g), chopped coarsely

2 large carrots (360g), chopped coarsely

2 medium turnips (450g), chopped coarsely

1 cup (250ml) vegetable stock

3 medium beetroots (500g), cut into thin wedges

¼ cup (60ml) lemon juice

GREMOLATA

1 cup finely chopped fresh flat-leaf parsley

1 tablespoon finely grated lemon rind

1 clove garlic, crushed

1 Preheat oven to moderately hot (200°C/180°C fan-forced).

2 Heat half of the oil in large frying pan; cook garlic, parsnip, carrot and turnip, stirring, until vegetables browned lightly. Add stock; bring to a boil. Reduce heat; simmer, covered, about 40 minutes or until vegetables are tender.

3 Meanwhile, combine remaining oil and beetroot in medium shallow baking dish; roast, uncovered, about 40 minutes or until beetroot is tender.

4 Make gremolata.

5 Stir juice and beetroot into braised vegetables. Divide vegetables among serving plates; top with gremolata. Serve with couscous, if desired.

GREMOLATA Combine ingredients in small bowl.

☐ **PER SERVING** 5.4g total fat (0.8g saturated); 970kj (232 cal); 31.7g carbohydrate; 7.7g protein; 12.9g fibre

---

Try rubbing the potato skin with olive oil and sea salt, before wrapping it in foil, for a delicious crisp edge. Another way to serve these potatoes is to scoop out the fluffy cooked potato on the inside, mix it with your topping of choice and then spoon it back into the potato skins. You can also use russet burbank or spunta potatoes to make this recipe.

Baked potatoes

PREPARATION TIME 5 MINUTES **COOKING TIME** 1 HOUR **MAKES** 8

8 king edward potatoes (1.4kg), unpeeled

1 Preheat oven to moderate (180°C/160°C fan-forced).

2 Pierce skin of each potato with fork; wrap each potato in foil, place on oven tray. Bake about 1 hour or until tender. Top with one of the variations below.

☐ **PER POTATO** 0.2g total fat (0.0g saturated); 493kj (118 cal); 22.9g carbohydrate; 4.2g protein; 3.7g fibre

CREAM CHEESE AND PESTO TOPPING

PREPARATION TIME 5 MINUTES **MAKES** 8

Combine ⅔ cup spreadable cream cheese, ½ teaspoon cracked black pepper and ⅓ cup pesto in small bowl; cover and refrigerate until required.

☐ **PER POTATO** 10.6g total fat (5.0g saturated); 936kj (224 cal); 23.6g carbohydrate; 6.8g protein; 3.7g fibre

LIME AND CHILLI YOGURT TOPPING

PREPARATION TIME 5 MINUTES **MAKES** 8

Combine ⅔ cup yogurt, 2 tablespoons coarsely chopped fresh coriander, 1 finely chopped fresh small red thai chilli and 1 teaspoon finely grated lime rind in small bowl; cover and refrigerate until required.

PER POTATO 1.0g total fat (0.5g saturated); 564kj (135 cal); 24.1g carbohydrate; 5.3g protein; 3.6g fibre

MUSTARD AND WALNUT BUTTER TOPPING

PREPARATION TIME 5 MINUTES **MAKES** 8

Mash 60g softened butter, 1 teaspoon wholegrain mustard and 2 tablespoons finely chopped roasted walnuts in small bowl until mixture forms a paste; cover and refrigerate until required.

PER POTATO 7.9g total fat (4.1g saturated); 790kj (189 cal); 23.1g carbohydrate; 4.6g protein; 3.7g fibre

---

Barbecued vegetarian pizzas

PREPARATION TIME 20 MINUTES **COOKING TIME** 55 MINUTES **SERVES** 4

- 4 small beetroot (400g), sliced thickly
- 2 medium red onions (340g), sliced thinly
- 1 tablespoon olive oil
- 2 tablespoons red wine vinegar
- 1 teaspoon brown sugar
- 2 cloves garlic, sliced thinly
- 6 sprigs fresh thyme
- 100g fetta, crumbled
- ⅔ cup (170g) bottled tomato pasta sauce
- 4 pocket pittas
- ¼ cup finely shredded fresh basil

HERB SALAD

- 1 cup loosely packed fresh flat-leaf parsley leaves
- ½ cup loosely packed fresh basil leaves
- ½ cup loosely packed fresh chervil sprigs
- ½ cup coarsely chopped fresh chives
- 50g baby rocket leaves
- 1 teaspoon olive oil
- 2 teaspoons red wine vinegar

1 Preheat oven to moderately hot (200°C/180°C fan-forced). Oil large baking dish.

2 Combine beetroot, onion, oil, vinegar, sugar, garlic and thyme in dish. Roast, uncovered, 50 minutes or until beetroot is tender, stirring halfway through cooking time. Stir in cheese.

3 Spread pasta sauce equally over each pitta; top each with beetroot mixture.

4 Cover barbecue flat plate with double thickness of lightly oiled foil; place pizzas on foil. Cook, covered, over medium heat, 5 minutes or until heated through and bases are crisp.

5 Meanwhile, make herb salad.

6 Top pizzas with basil; serve with herb salad.

HERB SALAD Combine ingredients in large bowl.

PER SERVING 13.1g total fat (4.8g saturated); 1384kj (331 cal); 37.3g carbohydrate; 12.4g protein; 7.2g fibre

You may like to add some seeded kalamata olives (which are divine when roasted) to the baking dish. If beetroot isn't your thing use kumara or pumpkin instead. To serve, sprinkle some roasted pine nuts over the pizza and serve with tzatziki.

Asian greens

Cook these wonderful greens quickly and simply with a range of complementary flavours, as Asian cooks do.

TAT SOI
A mild-flavoured cabbage also known as rosette, flat or spoon cabbage because of its spoon-shaped leaves and the way it grows. Eaten raw in salads.

BUK CHOY (BOK CHOY)
Usually sold in bundles of three or four plants, buk choy has crisp white stems and tender, mildly cabbage-flavoured leaves with an acid tang. Often used in stir-fries or cooked alone and dressed with Chinese sauces.

CHOY SUM
Also called flowering buk choy or buk choy sum, this has small yellow flowers which are eaten with the leaves and stems. It has a mild mustard sort of flavour; can be steamed or stir-fried.

LEMON GRASS
A very fibrous plant, so only the inner stem is used. Cut the stalks short and peel away the tough outer layers until you come to the more tender white part at the base.

OYSTER MUSHROOMS
These are delicate in flavour and texture, so should not be used with strong-flavoured ingredients that would overwhelm them. Use raw or cook briefly – they become unpleasantly slippery if cooked for too long.

GREEN PAPAYA
This is simply underripe papaya. It varies in length and shape, and is mostly used, raw or cooked, in Thai recipes.

CHINESE CABBAGE (WOMBOK)
This crunchy cabbage is delicious raw, stir-fried, steamed or braised for Asian dishes, but you might also want to try serving it instead of European cabbage as part of a Western-style meal.

KAFFIR LIME LEAVES
Quite different in scent and flavour from ordinary lime leaves, these give a heady citrus freshness to soups, curries, fish and poultry dishes. They are rather tough, so shred finely or, if used whole, remove them before serving.

SHIITAKE MUSHROOMS
The earthy fragrance and flavour of shiitake are quite different from those of any other mushroom. Available fresh or dried; soak dried caps in warm water and discard the tough stems.

GAI LAN (CHINESE BROCCOLI)
This is prized for its crunchy texture and flavour resembling that of European broccoli. The white flowers, stems and leaves are eaten. Often cooked with oyster sauce; can be steamed, boiled or stir-fried.

KANG KONG (WATER SPINACH)
A delicate green vegetable with long, hollow stems and thin leaves. Use the leaves and top half of the stems, cut into 5cm lengths. Stir-fry, dip in batter and deep-fry, or serve steamed with kecap manis or a savoury paste.

BETEL LEAVES
Sold in bunches, often under their Vietnamese name, lã lôp; these leaves are used as a wrapping for rice, minced meat etc. The betel used for chewing is related but a different plant.

Eggplant, fetta and capsicum stack with mesclun salad

This is the kind of food – light and stylish – that we enjoy in cafes and bistros. It's best served warm.

PREPARATION TIME 15 MINUTES **COOKING TIME** 15 MINUTES **SERVES** 4

2 medium red capsicums (400g)
¼ cup (60ml) olive oil
2 tablespoons lemon juice
1 clove garlic, crushed
1 large eggplant (500g)
1 cup (150g) drained sun-dried tomatoes, chopped coarsely
¼ cup (40g) seeded kalamata olives, chopped coarsely
½ cup loosely packed fresh basil, torn
100g mesclun
2 tablespoons red wine vinegar
200g fetta, cut into 8 slices
1 tablespoon small fresh basil leaves, extra

1 Quarter capsicums; discard seeds and membranes. Roast on heated oiled grill plate (or grill or barbecue), skin-side down, until skin blisters and blackens. Cover with plastic or paper for 5 minutes; peel away skin.
2 Meanwhile, combine 2 tablespoons of the oil in small bowl with juice and garlic. Cut eggplant lengthways into eight slices; brush eggplant with a little of the garlic mixture. Cook on same grill plate, brushing occasionally with remaining garlic mixture, until just tender.
3 Combine tomato, olives and basil in small bowl. Place mesclun in medium bowl with vinegar and remaining oil; toss gently to combine.
4 Place one slice of the eggplant on each serving plate; top each with two slices of the cheese, two pieces of the capsicum and one remaining eggplant slice. Top with tomato mixture, sprinkle with extra basil leaves; serve with salad.

PER SERVING 27.8g total fat (9.8g saturated); 1777kj (425 cal); 23g carbohydrate; 16.4g protein; 10.3g fibre

Mustard and honey-glazed roasted kumara

Kumara works really well as an accompaniment to a roast or barbecued meats. Slice into 5mm rounds, place in little stacks on baking paper-lined shallow baking dishes and spray with olive oil. These will roast in about 30 minutes.

PREPARATION TIME 10 MINUTES **COOKING TIME** 1 HOUR **SERVES** 8

⅔ cup (230g) honey
⅓ cup (95g) wholegrain mustard
2 tablespoons coarsely chopped fresh rosemary
2.5kg kumara, unpeeled, cut into thick wedges

1 Preheat oven to hot (220°C/200°C fan-forced).
2 Combine honey, mustard and rosemary in large bowl, add kumara; toss to coat in mixture. Divide kumara mixture between two large shallow baking dishes. Roast, uncovered, about 1 hour or until kumara is tender and slightly caramelised.

PER SERVING 0.6g total fat (0.0g saturated); 12.2kj (290 cal); 61.8g carbohydrate; 5.8g protein; 5.3g fibre

EGGPLANT, FETTA AND CAPSICUM STACK WITH MESCLUN SALAD

Quinoa, pronounced keen-wa, is a gluten-free grain. It has a delicate, slightly nutty taste and chewy texture, partnering rich or spicy foods perfectly. Quinoa makes a nice change from rice for a pilaf and couscous for a salad. Cooking it in stock boosts its flavour.

Barbecued fennel, orange and red onion with quinoa

PREPARATION TIME 20 MINUTES **COOKING TIME** 30 MINUTES **SERVES** 4

5 small fennel bulbs (1kg), trimmed, quartered lengthways

1 large red onion (300g), cut into thick wedges

¼ cup (60ml) olive oil

2 cups (500ml) water

1 cup (100g) quinoa

½ cup (125ml) white wine vinegar

¼ cup coarsely chopped fresh dill

1 medium orange (240g), segmented

1 cup firmly packed fresh flat-leaf parsley leaves

1 Cook fennel and onion on heated oiled grill plate (or grill or barbecue) until vegetables are just tender, brushing with 1 tablespoon of the oil occasionally.

2 Meanwhile, bring the water to a boil in small saucepan. Add quinoa, reduce heat; simmer, covered, about 10 minutes or until water is absorbed, drain.

3 Place fennel, onion and quinoa in large bowl with remaining ingredients and remaining oil; toss gently to combine.

PER SERVING 14.4g total fat (2g saturated); 1170kj (280 cal); 26.9g carbohydrate; 5.8g protein; 10.6g fibre

---

This is traditional lasagne redesigned for vegetarians, but the flavours are so rich that meat-eaters will love it too. Use scissors to trim the sheets of lasagne to fit into your baking dish: you may only require three sheets in total.

Roasted vegetable lasagne

PREPARATION TIME 40 MINUTES (PLUS STANDING TIME) **COOKING TIME** 1 HOUR **SERVES** 6

3 medium red capsicums (600g)

2 medium eggplants (600g), sliced thinly

2 tablespoons coarse cooking salt

2 medium zucchini (240g), sliced thinly

600g kumara, sliced thinly

cooking-oil spray

700g bottled tomato pasta sauce

4 fresh lasagne sheets

150g ricotta, crumbled

1 tablespoon finely grated parmesan

WHITE SAUCE

40g butter

¼ cup (35g) plain flour

1½ cups (375ml) hot milk

2 tablespoons coarsely grated parmesan

1 Quarter capsicums; discard seeds and membranes. Roast under grill or in very hot oven, skin-side up, until skin blisters and blackens. Cover capsicum pieces with plastic or paper for 5 minutes; peel away skin.

2 Preheat oven to moderately hot (200°C/180°C fan-forced). Oil deep rectangular 2.5-litre (10-cup) ovenproof dish.

3 Place eggplant in colander, sprinkle with salt; stand 20 minutes. Rinse eggplant under cold water; pat dry with absorbent paper.

4 Place eggplant, zucchini and kumara, in single layer, on oven trays; spray with oil. Roast, uncovered, about 15 minutes or until tender.
5 Meanwhile, make white sauce.
6 Spread 1 cup pasta sauce over base of ovenproof dish; top with half of the eggplant and half of the capsicum. Layer with lasagne, trimmed if necessary to fit dish; top with ½ cup of the pasta sauce, ricotta, kumara and zucchini. Layer with more lasagne; top with remaining pasta sauce, remaining eggplant and remaining capsicum. Layer remaining lasagne over vegetables; top with white sauce, sprinkle with parmesan. Bake, uncovered, 45 minutes or until browned lightly. Stand 5 minutes before serving.

WHITE SAUCE Melt butter in small saucepan, add flour; cook, stirring, until mixture thickens and bubbles. Gradually stir in milk; cook, stirring, until mixture boils and thickens. Remove from heat; stir in cheese.

PER SERVING 13.5g total fat (7.7g saturated); 1634kj (391 cal); 48.1g carbohydrate; 14.6g protein; 8.4g fibre

---

Mixed mushroom ragout with soft polenta

A winner for brunch, lunch or dinner. Never wash mushrooms as they soak up water like a sponge and become heavy and watery. Simply wipe them with a damp cloth.

PREPARATION TIME 20 MINUTES **COOKING TIME** 50 MINUTES **SERVES** 8

- 2 tablespoons butter
- 2 large brown onions (400g), chopped coarsely
- 3 cloves garlic, crushed
- ¼ cup (35g) plain flour
- 400g button mushrooms
- 400g swiss brown mushrooms, quartered
- 400g flat mushrooms, sliced thickly
- 2 tablespoons tomato paste
- ⅔ cup (160ml) dry red wine
- 1.25 litres (5 cups) water
- 1 litre (4 cups) vegetable stock
- 2 teaspoons finely chopped fresh thyme
- 2 cups (340g) polenta
- 1 cup (250ml) milk
- ¼ cup (20g) finely grated parmesan

1 Melt butter in large saucepan; cook onion and garlic, stirring, until onion softens. Add flour; cook, stirring, until mixture bubbles. Add mushrooms; cook, stirring, until mushrooms are just tender.
2 Add paste and wine to mushroom mixture; bring to a boil. Reduce heat; simmer, uncovered, until liquid reduces by half. Add 2 cups of the water and half of the stock; return to a boil. Reduce heat; simmer, uncovered, 30 minutes. Stir in thyme.
3 Meanwhile, combine the remaining water and remaining stock in another large saucepan; bring to a boil. Gradually add polenta to liquid, stirring constantly. Reduce heat; simmer, stirring, about 10 minutes or until polenta thickens. Add milk and cheese; stir until cheese melts.
4 Serve mushroom ragout on polenta.

PER SERVING 7.9g total fat (4.3g saturated); 1287kj (308 cal); 35.4g carbohydrate; 13.7g protein; 6.1g fibre

For a vegetarian version of shepherd's pie, top the bean and vegetable mixture with herby mashed potato. Cook 800g potatoes until tender, drain well, then mash the potato with 60g butter and ¼ cup milk until smooth. Stir in 1 tablespoon chopped fresh parsley, 1 teaspoon chopped fresh thyme and ¼ cup finely grated cheddar.

Vegetable cassoulet

PREPARATION TIME 20 MINUTES (PLUS STANDING TIME) **COOKING TIME** 1 HOUR 25 MINUTES **SERVES** 4

½ cup (100g) dried borlotti beans

½ cup (100g) dried great northern beans

2 teaspoons olive oil

4 shallots (100g), halved

3 cloves garlic, sliced thinly

2 medium carrots (240g), chopped coarsely

200g mushrooms, halved

1 cup (250ml) dry white wine

2 medium zucchini (240g), chopped coarsely

1½ cups (375ml) vegetable stock

700g bottled tomato pasta sauce

1 teaspoon finely chopped fresh thyme

BREAD TOPPING

1 tablespoon olive oil

1 small brown onion (80g), chopped finely

2 teaspoons finely grated lemon rind

1 clove garlic, crushed

2 teaspoons finely chopped fresh thyme

½ ciabatta (220g), diced into 2cm pieces

2 tablespoons coarsely chopped fresh flat-leaf parsley

1 Place beans in medium bowl, cover with water; stand overnight, drain. Rinse under cold water; drain. Place beans in medium saucepan of boiling water; return to a boil. Reduce heat; simmer, uncovered, about 15 minutes or until beans are just tender; drain.

2 Preheat oven to moderate (180°C/160°C fan-forced).

3 Heat oil in large flameproof casserole dish; cook shallots, garlic, carrot and mushroom, stirring, until vegetables are just tender. Add wine; bring to a boil. Boil, uncovered, until liquid is reduced by half. Add beans, zucchini, stock, sauce and thyme; return to a boil. Bake, covered, 50 minutes.

4 Meanwhile, make bread topping.

5 Sprinkle cassoulet with bread topping; bake, uncovered, about 10 minutes or until bread topping is browned.

BREAD TOPPING Heat oil in large frying pan; cook onion, stirring, until soft. Add rind, garlic, thyme and bread; cook, stirring, about 10 minutes or until bread browns lightly. Stir in parsley.

PER SERVING 10.7g total fat (1.7g saturated); 1969kj (471 cal); 61.1g carbohydrate; 16.4g protein; 11.4g fibre

It is sometimes thought that Thai eggplant and pea eggplant are the same thing; they're not. Thai eggplant are golf-ball sized and pea eggplant are the size of large green peas. You will find both varieties of eggplants in specialist Asian supermarkets.

Tofu and thai eggplant massaman curry

PREPARATION TIME 30 MINUTES **COOKING TIME** 25 MINUTES **SERVES** 4

2 teaspoons peanut oil

1 cup (250ml) coconut milk

4 baby eggplants (240g), sliced thickly

350g thai eggplants, quartered

3 medium potatoes (600g), chopped coarsely

200g firm tofu, sliced thickly

1 tablespoon grated palm sugar

1 tablespoon lime juice

¼ cup loosely packed fresh coriander leaves

MASSAMAN CURRY PASTE

2 teaspoons ground coriander

½ teaspoon ground cumin

½ teaspoon ground cinnamon

¼ teaspoon ground nutmeg

¼ teaspoon ground cardamom

2 fresh long red chillies, chopped coarsely

3 shallots (75g), chopped coarsely

3 cloves garlic, crushed

2cm piece fresh galangal (10g), grated

10cm stick (20g) fresh lemon grass, chopped finely

4 coriander roots, chopped finely

1 tablespoon roasted peanuts

1 Make massaman curry paste.

2 Heat oil in large saucepan; cook curry paste, stirring, until fragrant. Add coconut milk, eggplant and potato; bring to a boil. Reduce heat; simmer, covered, about 15 minutes or until potato is tender.

3 Add tofu, sugar and juice; stir until tofu is heated through.

4 Divide curry among serving plates; top with coriander. Serve with steamed jasmine rice, if desired.

MASSAMAN CURRY PASTE Dry-fry spices in small frying pan, stirring, until fragrant. Blend or process spices and remaining ingredients until mixture forms a smooth paste.

PER SERVING 20.6g total fat (12.5g saturated); 1517kj (363 cal); 27.6g carbohydrate; 13g protein; 8.4g fibre

---

Serve as a starter with 200g baby rocket leaves, 100g crumbled soft goat cheese and ¼ cup chopped roasted walnuts.

Baby beetroot with caper vinaigrette

PREPARATION TIME 10 MINUTES **COOKING TIME** 20 MINUTES **SERVES** 8

1kg baby beetroot

1 tablespoon drained baby capers, rinsed

2 tablespoons white wine vinegar

2 tablespoons olive oil

1 teaspoon dijon mustard

1 Remove stems from beetroot; cook beetroot in large saucepan of boiling water, uncovered, about 20 minutes or until tender. Drain; cool 10 minutes. Peel beetroot.

2 Place beetroot in large bowl with remaining ingredients; toss gently to combine.

PER SERVING 4.7g total fat (0.6g saturated); 397kj (95 cal); 9.4g carbohydrate; 2.1g protein; 3.5g fibre

Ricotta and herb calzones

PREPARATION TIME 30 MINUTES (PLUS STANDING TIME)
COOKING TIME 25 MINUTES (PLUS COOLING TIME) **MAKES** 4

Pizzas and calzone are a speciality of Naples. A calzone is simply a pizza "turnover", enclosing the filling. To achieve a crispier bottom crust, slide the calzone directly onto the oven rack for the last 5 minutes of baking time.

- 2 cups (300g) plain flour
- 1 ¼ teaspoons dried yeast
- ½ teaspoon salt
- 2 teaspoons olive oil
- ¾ cup (180ml) warm water
- 8 sun-dried tomatoes (20g)
- 1 clove garlic, crushed
- ¼ teaspoon dried chilli flakes
- 1 medium green capsicum (200g), sliced thinly
- 1 cup (240g) ricotta cheese
- ⅓ cup (35g) coarsely grated mozzarella cheese
- ⅓ cup (25g) finely grated parmesan
- 1 tablespoon coarsely chopped fresh oregano
- 1 tablespoon coarsely chopped fresh flat-leaf parsley
- 1 egg white, beaten lightly

1 Place flour, yeast and salt in large bowl; gradually stir in oil and the water, mix to a soft dough. Knead dough on floured surface about 5 minutes or until smooth and elastic. Place dough in large oiled bowl, turning dough once to coat in oil. Cover; stand in warm place about 1 hour or until dough doubles in size.

2 Meanwhile, place tomatoes in small heatproof bowl, cover with boiling water; stand 20 minutes, drain. Chop tomatoes coarsely.

3 Cook garlic, chilli and capsicum in medium heated lightly oiled frying pan 5 minutes or until capsicum has softened. Remove from heat; stir in tomato. Cool to room temperature. Combine capsicum mixture in medium bowl with cheeses and herbs.

4 Preheat oven to very hot (240°C/220°C fan-forced). Lightly oil two oven trays.

5 Turn dough onto lightly floured surface; knead until smooth. Divide dough into quarters; using rolling pin, flatten dough and roll each quarter out to a 18cm round. Place a quarter of the cheese mixture in centre of dough; brush one edge of dough with a little of the egg white; fold over to enclose filling, press edge to seal. Repeat with remaining dough, cheese mixture and egg white.

6 Place calzones onto trays; brush with remaining egg white. Carefully cut two slits in top of dough; bake, uncovered, about 15 minutes or until browned lightly.

PER SERVING 14.3g total fat (7.3g saturated); 1914kj (458 cal); 57.7g carbohydrate; 21.7g protein; 4.6g fibre

If you've never cooked globe artichokes before, here are a few tips.

- *Remove the pointed ends of the leaves with scissors before cooking.*
- *The choke is the centre of the artichoke, which is inedible. Use a spoon to gently scoop out the pale fibres.*
- *Add some lemon slices to the cooking water to prevent the artichoke discolouring.*

Artichoke and broad bean salad

PREPARATION TIME 20 MINUTES (PLUS REFRIGERATION TIME) **COOKING TIME** 20 MINUTES **SERVES** 4

4 medium globe artichokes (800g)

500g packet frozen broad beans

¼ cup (60ml) lemon juice

½ cup (125ml) olive oil

1 teaspoon white sugar

1 clove garlic, crushed

⅓ cup coarsely chopped fresh mint

1⅓ cups (200g) seeded kalamata olives

1 Boil, steam or microwave artichokes until just tender; drain. Quarter artichokes; remove and discard choke.

2 Boil, steam or microwave beans until just tender; drain. Peel away grey-coloured outer shells.

3 Place juice, oil, sugar, garlic and mint in screw-top jar; shake well.

4 Place warm artichokes, beans, olives and dressing in large bowl; toss gently to combine. Cover; refrigerate 3 hours or overnight.

PER SERVING 30.0g total fat (4.2g saturated); 1697kj (406 cal); 17.2g carbohydrate; 13g protein; 9.9g fibre

---

If you like smoked tofu, you can use it instead of plain firm tofu, giving this dish an added dimension.

To save your hands from being beetroot-coloured for days, wear disposable gloves when handling them.

Pan-fried tofu with beetroot hummus

PREPARATION TIME 15 MINUTES **COOKING TIME** 30 MINUTES **SERVES** 4

1 medium beetroot (175g)

4 small red onions (400g), quartered

420g can chickpeas, rinsed, drained

2 cloves garlic, quartered

¼ cup (60ml) lemon juice

3 teaspoons tahini

300g firm tofu, diced into 3cm pieces

2 tablespoons sumac

100g baby spinach leaves

100g rocket

1 Peel beetroot; cut into thin wedges.

2 Heat medium lightly oiled frying pan; cook onion, stirring occasionally, until just tender. Transfer to large bowl.

3 Cook beetroot in same pan, covered, about 15 minutes or until tender.

4 Meanwhile, cook chickpeas in small saucepan of boiling water, uncovered, 10 minutes or until chickpeas are just tender; drain, reserving ¼ cup of the cooking liquid.

5 Blend or process beetroot, chickpeas, reserved cooking liquid, garlic, juice and tahini until smooth.

6 Combine tofu and sumac in medium bowl; cook tofu, in batches, in same cleaned lightly oiled frying pan until browned all over.

7 Add spinach and rocket to onion in large bowl; toss gently to combine. Serve onion mixture topped with tofu and beetroot hummus.

PER SERVING 9.3g total fat (1.3g saturated); 1058kj (253 cal); 20.4g carbohydrate; 17.6g protein; 8.9g fibre

Middle-eastern roasted pumpkin, carrot and parsnip

PREPARATION TIME 20 MINUTES **COOKING TIME** 25 MINUTES **SERVES** 8

Alternatively you could toss the uncooked vegetables in the spice paste and roast them for about 40 minutes. Delicious served with ½ cup Greek-style yogurt mixed with about 2 tablespoons coriander pesto.

900g pumpkin, unpeeled, sliced thinly

1 tablespoon olive oil

4 large carrots (720g), halved, sliced thickly

2 large parsnips (700g), chopped coarsely

⅓ cup firmly packed fresh flat-leaf parsley leaves

¼ cup (40g) roasted pine nuts

SPICE PASTE

2 cloves garlic, quartered

1 teaspoon cumin seeds

1 teaspoon coriander seeds

½ teaspoon ground cinnamon

1 teaspoon sea salt

1 tablespoon olive oil

20g butter

¼ cup (55g) firmly packed brown sugar

1½ cups (375ml) apple juice

1 Preheat oven to moderately hot (200°C/180°C fan-forced).

2 Combine pumpkin and oil in large baking dish. Roast, uncovered, about 25 minutes or until just tender.

3 Meanwhile, boil, steam or microwave carrot and parsnip, separately, until just tender.

4 Make spice paste.

5 Place vegetables, parsley and nuts in large bowl with spice paste; toss to combine.

SPICE PASTE Using mortar and pestle or small electric spice blender, crush garlic, cumin, coriander, cinnamon, salt and oil until mixture forms a thick paste. Melt butter in large frying pan; cook paste, stirring, until fragrant. Add sugar and juice; bring to a boil. Cook, stirring, about 10 minutes or until spice paste thickens slightly.

☐ **PER SERVING** 10.7g total fat (2.5g saturated); 1012kj (242 cal); 29.0g carbohydrate; 4.6g protein; 5.6g fibre

---

Broccolini polonaise

PREPARATION TIME 10 MINUTES **COOKING TIME** 10 MINUTES **SERVES** 8

Polonaise topping originates from Poland and is a popular partner for all of the brassica family (cauliflower, cabbage, kale, spinach, broccoli and sprouts).

60g butter

1 cup (70g) stale breadcrumbs

4 hard-boiled eggs, chopped finely

¼ cup finely chopped fresh flat-leaf parsley

750g broccolini

60g butter, melted

1 Melt butter in large frying pan; cook breadcrumbs, stirring, until browned and crisp. Combine breadcrumbs in small bowl with egg and parsley.

2 Boil, steam or microwave broccolini until just tender; drain.

3 Top broccolini with polonaise mixture then drizzle with the melted butter.

☐ **PER SERVING** 15.5g total fat (9.0g saturated); 874kj (209 cal); 6.5g carbohydrate; 9.1g protein; 4.3g fibre

EGGS

Eggs

What would we do without the marvellous egg? What a lot we'd miss, from motherly custard to aristocratic hollandaise and béarnaise; from meringues to soufflés; from soups and sauces made rich and silky with egg to pastries made shiny and golden by egg. Saddest of all, we'd never know the solace, when we're tired or out of sorts, of the undemanding pleasures of boiled eggs with buttered toast.

EGG SIZES AND VARIETIES

HEN EGGS come in small (about 50g), medium (about 55g) and large (about 60g) sizes. Use large eggs for cakes etc unless the recipe says otherwise.

DUCK EGGS average about 90g and are richer-tasting than hen eggs. They are used mainly for baking; duck-egg whites do not whisk up well.

QUAIL EGGS taste like hen eggs and are prized for their miniature charm.

BUYING AND STORING EGGS

Shell colour does not indicate yolk colour or nutritional value; this depends on the hen's diet. Free-range eggs come from happier hens, and do taste much better. Store eggs in the fridge in their cartons to protect from odours which might penetrate their porous shells. To check freshness, place in a bowl of water; fresh eggs sink, stale ones float big-end up.

TO SEPARATE EGGS

Have ready two non-plastic bowls and a cup, all dry and grease-free. Crack an egg on the cup and tip the contents onto your hand. Hold over the cup and allow the white to run through your fingers into the cup, then drop the yolk into a bowl. Check the white is free of shell and yolk, then tip it into the other bowl. Remove any bits of shell with a broken piece of shell; any yolk will stop the white from beating up properly, so it must be discarded.

TO WHISK EGG WHITES

Ideally, use a copper bowl, as copper reacts with whites to form a very stable foam, though glass, stainless steel or china bowls are also fine. Mostly we use a stand-alone electric mixer for beating egg whites, though a whisk (balloon is best), hand-held electric beater or rotary beater will also do the job. All utensils must be dry and grease-free. Whisk plain whites to a soft snow which forms drooping peaks on the whisk. For meringue, start adding sugar gradually at the soft-foam stage and continue whisking until the mixture forms soft upright peaks.

BASIC WAYS TO COOK EGGS

Before you start, bring the eggs to room temperature. Have accompaniments such as bacon or toast ready and keeping warm on heated plates. Cooking times here are for large (60g) eggs.

BOILED There are two method for perfect boiled eggs: place in salted boiling water and boil gently for 3 minutes for soft yolks and firm whites. For hard-boiled eggs, boil for 7 minutes, drain and put immediately into cold water, then tap each egg all over to crack the shell and stand a few minutes before peeling. Alternatively, put the eggs snugly in a saucepan, barely cover them with cold water, cover and bring to a boil. As soon as the water boils, remove the lid and boil gently for 2½ minutes, or 7 minutes for hard-boiled.

FRIED Over medium heat, melt enough butter, bacon fat or oil in a frying pan to cover the bottom. Break each egg into a cup. When the butter begins to give off a haze, slide the eggs into the pan – the butter should sizzle gently; if not, adjust the heat. Spoon butter over the yolks to set the "veil" of white. When the whites are set but the yolks still wobble, use a spatula to lift the eggs out and serve at once.

POACHED Half-fill a lidded frying pan with water, add a dash of white vinegar and bring to the boil. Break each egg into a cup. When the water boils, add the eggs; allow the water to return to the boil then immediately move the pan off the heat, put the lid on and stand for 3 to 4 minutes or until a light film of egg white has set over the yolks. Use a spatula to lift out each egg, place it for a moment (still on the spatula) on absorbent paper to blot up any water and serve immediately. The chefs' method of gently lowering eggs, one at a time, into a deep, fairly large saucepan of simmering water works like a charm, but it takes practice to perfect. Poach no more than three or four eggs at a time using this method.

SCRAMBLED EGGS Whisk two to three eggs per person with salt, pepper and a tablespoon of milk or cream per egg. Have ready any additional ingredients such as herbs or smoked fish. Over low heat, melt enough butter in a frying pan to cover the bottom generously. When the butter foams slightly, add the eggs and stir with a wooden spoon, reaching right to the edges. When the eggs are a little softer than you want them, add the herbs etc, stir once more, remove from heat and serve immediately.

BAKED EGGS Grease small porcelain dishes such as soufflé dishes, break an egg into each, season and cover with a teaspoon of warm cream or melted butter. Bake in a preheated moderate oven for about 10 minutes or until the whites are set and the yolks are still soft. Serve in the dishes.

OMELETTES Make each person's omelette individually. Beat two or three eggs lightly with a fork and stir in salt and pepper, 2 teaspoons water and any flavouring such as herbs or grated cheese. Have any filling ready and warmed. In a small frying pan over fairly high heat, melt enough butter to cover the bottom. When the butter foams, pour the eggs into the pan. Using a palette knife or small spatula, continuously pull the egg from the sides to the centre, allowing the uncooked mixture to run underneath, until the omelette is set underneath but still slightly runny on top. Spoon any filling across the centre and, using the spatula to help, fold a third of the omelette over the centre; fold the other side over and tilt the pan over the warmed plate so that the omelette rolls out. Run a dab of butter on the point of a knife along the top and serve immediately.

1

2

3

4

Chorizo and kumara frittata

PREPARATION TIME 15 MINUTES **COOKING TIME** 30 MINUTES **SERVES** 4

This recipe also makes impressive canapés. Cut the frittata into bite-sized squares and top with crumbled goat cheese, chopped olives and a basil leaf.

500g kumara, sliced thinly
¼ cup coarsely chopped fresh basil
8 eggs
½ cup (125ml) milk
1 tablespoon olive oil
1 large brown onion (200g), sliced thinly
2 chorizo sausages (340g), sliced thinly
120g mesclun
¼ cup (60ml) french dressing

1 Preheat oven to hot (220°C/200°C fan-forced). Oil deep 23cm-square cake pan.
2 Boil, steam or microwave kumara until just tender; drain.
3 Meanwhile, whisk basil, eggs and milk in large bowl. Heat oil in medium frying pan; cook onion and chorizo, stirring, until onion softens and chorizo is browned. Drain on absorbent paper.
4 Add kumara and chorizo mixture to egg mixture; pour into pan. Bake, uncovered, 20 minutes or until frittata is just set. Serve with combined mesclun and dressing.

☐ **PER SERVING** 15.5g total fat (9.0g saturated); 874kj (209 cal); 6.5g carbohydrate; 9.1g protein; 4.3g fibre

---

Eggs ranchero-style

PREPARATION TIME 10 MINUTES **COOKING TIME** 30 MINUTES **SERVES** 4

To serve as a tortilla pizza, brush the tortillas with oil, place on oven trays and bake in a moderate oven for about 5 minutes. Spoon the tomato mixture over each tortilla, making a shallow well in the centre of each; crack an egg into each well. Bake for about 8 minutes. Serve topped with fresh coriander leaves.

1 small red onion (100g), chopped finely
4 medium tomatoes (600g), chopped coarsely
2 tablespoons water
1 tablespoon balsamic vinegar
1 medium red capsicum (200g), chopped finely
4 eggs
4 corn tortillas

1 Cook onion in lightly oiled large frying pan, stirring, until softened. Add tomato, the water and vinegar; bring to a boil. Reduce heat; simmer, uncovered, about 15 minutes, stirring occasionally. Add capsicum; cook, uncovered, 5 minutes.
2 Using large shallow mixing spoon, press four shallow depressions into tomato mixture. Working quickly, break eggs, one at a time, into cup, sliding each egg into one of the hollows in tomato mixture. Cover; cook over low heat, 5 minutes or until eggs are just set.
3 Divide warmed tortillas among plates. Use spatula to carefully lift egg and tomato mixture onto each tortilla.

☐ **PER SERVING** 6g total fat (1.7g saturated fat); 619kJ (148 cal); 13.1g carbohydrate; 10.1g protein; 3.4g fibre

1 CHORIZO AND KUMARA FRITTATA **2** EGGS RANCHERO-STYLE **3** BAKED EGGS WITH PANCETTA [P 330] **4** SAFFRON SCRAMBLED EGGS ON CORN CAKES [P 330]

This is the perfect brunch dish for entertaining, as you don't have to stand over it while it cooks. The capsicum mixture can be prepared ahead.

Baked eggs with pancetta

PREPARATION TIME 15 MINUTES **COOKING TIME** 20 MINUTES **SERVES** 4

2 teaspoons olive oil

1 small red capsicum (150g), chopped finely

6 slices pancetta (90g), chopped finely

100g mushrooms, chopped finely

4 green onions, chopped finely

⅔ cup (50g) finely grated parmesan

8 eggs

2 teaspoons coarsely chopped fresh flat-leaf parsley

1 Preheat oven to moderately hot (200°C/180°C fan-forced). Oil four ¾-cup (180ml) ovenproof dishes.

2 Heat oil in medium frying pan; cook capsicum and pancetta, stirring, until capsicum is just tender. Add mushroom and onion; cook, stirring, until onion just softens. Remove from heat; stir in half of the cheese.

3 Divide capsicum mixture among dishes; break two eggs into each dish. Bake, uncovered, 5 minutes. Sprinkle remaining cheese over eggs; bake, 5 minutes or until eggs are just set. Sprinkle with parsley just before serving.

PER SERVING 20.1g total fat (7.3g saturated); 1195kj (286 cal); 2.2g carbohydrate; 24.0g protein; 1.2g fibre

---

For a more substantial meal serve the corn cakes and scrambled egg with thick slices of pan-fried chorizo sausage.

Saffron scrambled eggs on corn cakes

PREPARATION TIME 20 MINUTES **COOKING TIME** 15 MINUTES **SERVES** 4

1 trimmed corn cob (250g)

¾ cup (110g) plain flour

1 teaspoon sweet paprika

1 tablespoon finely chopped fresh coriander

¼ cup (60ml) milk

3 egg whites

3 eggs

2 egg whites, extra

pinch saffron threads

You can use the remaining egg yolks in home-made sauces or dressings.

1 Cut corn kernels from cob. Combine corn, flour, paprika and coriander in medium bowl; stir in milk.

2 Beat egg whites in small bowl with electric mixer until soft peaks form; fold egg whites into corn mixture. Cook ¼-cup measures of corn mixture in heated oiled large frying pan until browned both sides and cooked through.

3 Using fork, lightly beat eggs, extra egg whites and saffron in medium bowl. Cook egg mixture in medium lightly oiled frying pan, stirring gently, until just set.

4 Serve scrambled eggs with corn cakes.

PER SERVING 5.4g total fat (1.7g saturated); 957kj (229 cal); 28.3g carbohydrate; 14.9g protein; 3.2g fibre

Crab fried rice in omelette

PREPARATION TIME 15 MINUTES **COOKING TIME** 25 MINUTES **SERVES** 4

¼ cup (60ml) peanut oil

4 green onions, chopped finely

2 fresh small red thai chillies, chopped finely

1 tablespoon red curry paste

2 cups cooked jasmine rice

250g cooked crab meat

2 tablespoons lime juice

2 tablespoons fish sauce

8 eggs

2 tablespoons water

1 lime, cut into wedges

1 Heat 1 tablespoon of the oil in wok; stir-fry onion and chilli until onion softens. Add paste; stir-fry until mixture is fragrant. Add rice; stir-fry until heated through. Remove from heat; place in large bowl. Add crab meat, juice and fish sauce; toss to combine.

2 Whisk eggs with the water in medium bowl. Heat 2 teaspoons of the remaining oil in same cleaned wok; pour a quarter of the egg mixture into wok. Cook, tilting wok, over low heat until almost set. Spoon a quarter of the fried rice into centre of the omelette; using spatula, fold four sides of omelette over to enclose filling.

3 Press omelette firmly with spatula; turn carefully to brown other side. Remove omelette from wok; cover to keep warm. Repeat process with remaining oil, egg mixture and fried rice. Place omelettes on serving plates; serve with lime.

☐ **PER SERVING** 26.9g total fat (6g saturated); 2934kj (702 cal); 83.8g carbohydrate; 29.5g protein; 2.1g fibre

The reason water is added to the eggs is because water turns to steam, which gives the omelette a light texture.

If you would prefer the filling to be more evenly distributed throughout the omelette, add the rice mixture to the whisked eggs, before adding them to the pan.

Corned beef hash with poached eggs

PREPARATION TIME 10 MINUTES **COOKING TIME** 10 MINUTES **SERVES** 2

1 medium brown onion (150g), chopped finely

3 medium potatoes (600g), grated coarsely

500g cooked corned beef, shredded finely

2 tablespoons finely chopped fresh flat-leaf parsley

2 tablespoons plain flour

2 eggs

1 tablespoon vegetable oil

4 eggs, extra

1 Combine onion, potato, beef, parsley, flour and eggs in large bowl; shape hash mixture into four patties. Heat oil in large heavy-based frying pan; cook patties, uncovered, until browned both sides and potato is tender.

2 Half-fill a large shallow frying pan with water; bring to a boil. Place four oiled egg rings in water. One at a time, break extra eggs into cup and slide into egg rings, return water to a boil. Cover pan, turn off heat; stand about 4 minutes or until a light film of egg white sets over yolks. One at a time, remove eggs, using slotted spoon, and place on absorbent-paper-lined saucer to blot poaching liquid. Carefully remove egg rings.

3 Serve hash patties topped with poached eggs; top with shredded basil, if desired.

☐ **PER SERVING** 41.7g total fat (13.3g saturated); 3557kj (851 cal); 44g carbohydrate; 72.3g protein; 5.5g fibre

For many people, this classic way of using left-over corned beef is even more of a treat than the meat at its first appearance. Have the plates hot as it takes a couple of minutes to spoon out the hash and top with the eggs, and this dish should be hot when served.

To make quick curried egg sandwiches mash 4 hard-boiled eggs with ¼ cup mayonnaise, 1 teaspoon curry powder, 1 tablespoon chopped coriander, and salt and pepper. Spread onto slices of bread and top with thinly sliced cucumber.

Curried eggs

PREPARATION TIME 10 MINUTES **COOKING TIME** 20 MINUTES **SERVES** 4

¼ cup (60ml) peanut oil
8 hard-boiled eggs
1 teaspoon black mustard seeds
1 clove garlic, crushed
1 cm piece fresh ginger (5g), grated
1 small brown onion (80g), sliced thinly
1 teaspoon ground cumin
2 tablespoons curry powder
½ teaspoon ground cardamom
425g can crushed tomatoes
1 teaspoon white sugar
½ cup (125ml) water

1 Heat oil in medium saucepan; cook eggs, stirring occasionally, until eggs are well browned all over. Drain on absorbent paper.
2 Reserve 1 tablespoon of the oil from saucepan; discard remaining oil. Reheat reserved oil in same pan; cook seeds, covered, about 30 seconds or until seeds begin to crack. Stir in garlic, ginger and onion; cook, stirring, until onion softens. Stir in cumin, curry powder, cardamom, undrained tomatoes, sugar and the water; bring to a boil. Add eggs, reduce heat; simmer, covered, 5 minutes or until thickened slightly. Serve with rice, if desired.

PER SERVING 24.4g total fat (5.7g saturated); 1262kj (302 cal); 5.9g carbohydrate; 14.5g protein; 1.7g fibre

---

A favourite for dieters around the world, egg-white omelettes have been made famous by many a celebrity. If you're not counting calories and are wondering how to use the egg yolks, make a custard, mayonnaise, lemon butter or hollandaise.

Egg-white omelette

PREPARATION TIME 25 MINUTES **COOKING TIME** 20 MINUTES **SERVES** 4

12 egg whites
4 green onions, chopped finely
¼ cup finely chopped fresh chives
¼ cup finely chopped fresh chervil
½ cup finely chopped fresh flat-leaf parsley
½ cup (60g) coarsely grated cheddar
½ cup (50g) coarsely grated mozzarella cheese

1 Preheat grill.
2 Beat a quarter of the egg white in small bowl with electric mixer until soft peaks form; fold in a quarter of the combined onion and herbs.
3 Pour mixture into 20cm heated lightly oiled frying pan; cook, uncovered, over low heat until omelette is just browned lightly on the bottom.
4 Sprinkle a quarter of the combined cheeses on half of the omelette. Place pan under grill until cheese begins to melt and omelette sets; fold omelette over to completely cover cheese. Carefully slide onto serving plate; cover to keep warm.
5 Repeat process with remaining egg white, onion and herb mixture, and cheese to make four omelettes.

PER SERVING 7.9g total fat (5.0g saturated); 623kj (149 cal); 1.0g carbohydrate; 18.2g protein; 0.7g fibre

Eggs benedict

PREPARATION TIME 20 MINUTES **COOKING TIME** 30 MINUTES (PLUS COOLING TIME) **SERVES** 8

8 eggs
8 english muffins
200g shaved ham

HOLLANDAISE SAUCE
¼ cup (60ml) white wine vinegar
3 black peppercorns
1 bay leaf
2 egg yolks
125g butter, melted
1 teaspoon lemon juice

1 Make hollandaise sauce.
2 Half-fill a large shallow frying pan with water; bring to a boil. One at a time, break four eggs into cup and slide into pan. When eggs are in pan, allow water to return to a boil. Cover pan, turn off heat; stand about 4 minutes or until a light film of egg white sets over yolks. One at a time, remove eggs, using slotted spoon, and place on absorbent-paper-lined saucer to blot poaching liquid. Repeat with remaining eggs.
3 Meanwhile, split muffins in half; toast until just crisp. Place two muffin halves on each serving plate; layer ham on one muffin half. Top with an egg and hollandaise sauce.

HOLLANDAISE SAUCE Bring vinegar, peppercorns and bay leaf to a boil in small saucepan. Reduce heat; simmer, uncovered, until reduced by half. Strain into small jug; cool. Blend or process egg yolks until smooth. With motor operating, gradually add 1 teaspoon of the melted butter (it must be bubbling hot) to yolks; blend or process until mixture starts to thicken. Then, with motor operating, add 2 teaspoons of the vinegar mixture at a time, alternating with 2 teaspoons of the remaining melted butter, processing until sauce thickens and all butter and vinegar mixture have been incorporated; stir in juice.

☐ **PER SERVING** 21.3g total fat (11g saturated); 1517kj (363 cal); 23.7g carbohydrate; 18.5g protein; 1.9g fibre

Hollandaise is renowned for being impossible to re-heat because it curdles. To help stabilise the sauce, whisk the egg whites to soft peaks and fold them into the thickened sauce. This will make the sauce much lighter, and allow you to gently re-warm it in a bowl set over simmering water. Fold gently while warming and take off the heat when the sauce is warm.

Florentine eggs with bacon and pecorino

PREPARATION TIME 5 MINUTES **COOKING TIME** 10 MINUTES **SERVES** 4

600g spinach, chopped coarsely
4 bacon rashers (280g), rind removed
4 eggs
⅓ cup (40g) shaved pecorino cheese

1 Boil, steam or microwave spinach until just wilted; drain. Cover to keep warm.
2 Meanwhile, cook bacon in large heated frying pan until crisp. Drain.
3 Half-fill a large shallow frying pan with water; bring to a boil. Break eggs into cup, one at a time, then slide into pan. When all eggs are in pan, allow water to return to a boil. Cover pan, turn off heat; stand about 4 minutes or until a light film of egg white sets over yolks. Remove eggs, one at a time, using slotted spoon, and place on absorbent-paper-lined saucer to blot up poaching liquid.
4 Divide spinach among serving plates; top each with bacon, egg and cheese.

☐ **PER SERVING** 20.7g total fat (8.0g saturated); 1396kj (334 cal); 1.7g carbohydrate; 33.4g protein; 4.1g fibre

Very fresh eggs are best for poaching. They can be cooked ahead and stored in a large bowl of cold water. When ready to serve, immerse them in barely simmering water for 1 to 2 minutes.

Cheeses

Cheese means a world of flavours. Here are some of our favourites to relish as great ingredients or splendid snacks.

HALOUMI
A rubbery, salty Greek cheese, now also made in Australia. Always sliced and fried in olive oil or brushed with oil and grilled, which makes the texture firm but tender.

FETTA
A salty, crumbly Greek/Turkish/Bulgarian cheese, now also made here. Its milky, fresh acidity is short-lived, so it is often preserved in olive oil. Originally a sheep milk cheese, it is now often made from cow milk.

GOAT
Goat cheeses range from strong-tasting, firm, mature styles, often rolled in ash or herbs, to moist, delicate, white curd cheese, always with the earthy flavour of goat milk.

RACLETTE
A soft, sweet Swiss cheese noted for its readiness to melt smoothly, and also the name of the Swiss speciality of cheese melted over the fire and eaten with potatoes, salted cucumbers and pickled onions.

PARMESAN
The king of Italian hard cheeses, now also made here. The best is Parmigiano-reggiano from the strictly defined Emilia-Romagna cheese-making region in northern Italy. Much used for grating, but also a splendid table cheese.

RICOTTA
Soft white cheese made from whey, to which fresh milk and acid are added. Sweet and moist, it is often used for desserts and in baking. Use within a day or two of purchase.

FONTINA

A smooth, firm cheese with a brown or red rind, originally from the Italian Alps. It is usually matured in caves or tunnels, adding a slightly earthy overtone to its nutty flavour.

PROVOLONE

A firm, smooth-textured Italian cheese, now also made in Australia, which is mild and rather like mozzarella when young (provolone dolce), maturing to a sharp, strong and often salty flavour (provolone piccante).

BOCCONCINI

Small balls of fresh mozzarella, this Italian cheese was originally made from buffalo milk but now also from cow milk. Soft and white, they keep for 2 days in brine in the fridge.

ASIAGO

Mature asiago is a firm, salty and tangy Italian cheese which, when aged, can be grated like parmesan. There is also young asiago, a lightly pressed cheese ripened for a few weeks, which is delicate and sweet.

BRIE

Originally French, brie is now made by a number of fine Australian cheesemakers. Savoury/earthy/mushroomy in flavour, it has a bloomy white rind and a creamy centre which becomes runnier as it ripens.

MASCARPONE

Midway between heavy cream and fresh cheese in texture and flavour, mascarpone is made by adding a culture to cream. Its slight tang and reckless richness (75% fat content) are perfect with fresh fruits.

Many cooks believe that the key to perfectly risen soufflés is "bottom heat". Preheat an oven tray, place the filled ramekins onto this, and return to the oven immediately.

Goat cheese soufflé with creamed spinach sauce

PREPARATION TIME 15 MINUTES (PLUS COOLING TIME) **COOKING TIME** 25 MINUTES **SERVES** 6

¼ cup (25g) packaged breadcrumbs

30g butter

2 tablespoons plain flour

1 cup (250ml) hot milk

4 eggs, separated

¼ teaspoon cayenne pepper

150g firm goat cheese, crumbled

CREAMED SPINACH SAUCE

180g baby spinach leaves

⅔ cup (160ml) cream, warmed

1 Preheat oven to moderately hot (200°C/180°C fan-forced). Lightly oil six 1-cup (250ml) soufflé dishes, sprinkle with breadcrumbs; place on oven tray.
2 Melt butter in small saucepan, add flour; cook, stirring, until mixture thickens and bubbles. Gradually add milk; cook, stirring, until mixture boils and thickens. Transfer to large bowl; stir in egg yolks, pepper and cheese; cool 5 minutes.
3 Beat egg whites in small bowl with electric mixer until soft peaks form; gently fold whites into cheese mixture, in two batches.
4 Divide mixture among dishes. Bake, uncovered, about 15 minutes or until soufflés are puffed and browned lightly.
5 Meanwhile, make creamed spinach sauce.
6 Serve soufflés with sauce.

CREAMED SPINACH SAUCE Boil, steam or microwave spinach until just wilted; drain. Using hand, squeeze out excess liquid. Blend or process spinach until almost smooth. With motor operating, gradually add cream; process until smooth.

PER SERVING 24.9g total fat (15.1g saturated); 1271kj (304 cal); 8.8g carbohydrate; 11.3g protein; 1.1g fibre

---

Extremely fresh eggs do not peel easily. If you only have really fresh eggs available, add some salt to the water; this will make the peeling process a lot easier.

Creamy stuffed eggs

PREPARATION TIME 20 MINUTES (PLUS STANDING TIME) **COOKING TIME** 15 MINUTES **MAKES** 24

12 eggs

1 tablespoon mayonnaise

1 tablespoon sour cream

1 teaspoon french mustard

1 Place eggs in large saucepan, cover with cold water, stir constantly but gently over high heat until water comes to boil. Boil, uncovered, 10 minutes; drain.
2 Crack shells of eggs under cold running water; stand in cold water 5 minutes.
3 Remove shells; cut eggs in half lengthways. Mash egg yolks in medium bowl; stir in mayonnaise, sour cream and mustard. Pipe mixture into egg whites; serve as appetisers.

PER EGG 3.2g total fat (1.1g saturated); 180kj (43 cal); 0.3g carbohydrate; 3.4g protein; 0.0g fibre

GOAT CHEESE SOUFFLE WITH CREAMED SPINACH SAUCE

In the US this omelette is often served with lashings of hickory or barbecue sauce.

Denver omelette

PREPARATION TIME 10 MINUTES **COOKING TIME** 15 MINUTES **SERVES** 4

10 eggs

⅓ cup (80g) sour cream

1 fresh small red thai chilli, chopped finely

2 teaspoons vegetable oil

3 green onions, sliced thinly

1 medium green capsicum (200g), chopped finely

100g leg ham, chopped finely

2 small tomatoes (180g), seeded, chopped finely

½ cup (60g) coarsely grated cheddar

1 Whisk eggs, sour cream and chilli in large bowl.

2 Heat oil in large frying pan; cook onion and capsicum, stirring, until onion softens. Combine onion mixture in medium bowl with ham, tomato and cheese.

3 Pour ½ cup of the egg mixture into same lightly oiled frying pan; cook, tilting pan, over low heat until almost set. Sprinkle about ⅓ cup of the filling over half of the omelette; using spatula, fold omelette over to completely cover filling.

4 Pour ¼ cup of the egg mixture into empty half of pan; cook over low heat until almost set. Sprinkle about ⅓ cup of the filling over folded omelette, fold omelette over top of first omelette to cover filling. Repeat twice more, using ¼ cup of the egg mixture each time, to form one large layered omelette. Carefully slide omelette onto plate; cover to keep warm.

5 Repeat steps 3 and 4 to make second omelette, using remaining egg mixture and filling. Cut each denver omelette in half.

PER SERVING 29.4g total fat (13g saturated); 1588kj (380 cal); 2.6g carbohydrate; 26.5g protein; 0.8g fibre

---

You can use goat cheese instead of the blue cheese, and try adding 1 teaspoon chopped thyme.

Twice-cooked cheese soufflés

PREPARATION TIME 15 MINUTES

COOKING TIME 45 MINUTES (PLUS STANDING AND REFRIGERATION TIME) **SERVES** 6

60g butter

⅓ cup (50g) plain flour

¾ cup (180ml) hot milk

70g firm blue cheese, crumbled

1 tablespoon finely grated parmesan

6 eggs, separated

⅔ cup (160ml) thickened cream

1 Preheat oven to moderate (180°C/160°C fan-forced). Lightly oil six (¾-cup/180ml) soufflé dishes.

2 Melt butter in small saucepan, add flour; cook, stirring, 1 minute. Gradually stir in milk; cook, stirring, until sauce boils and thickens. Remove from heat; stir in cheeses and egg yolks. Transfer mixture to large bowl.

3 Beat egg whites in medium bowl with electric mixer until soft peaks form. Fold egg whites into cheese mixture, in two batches.

4 Divide mixture among dishes. Place dishes in medium baking dish with enough boiling water to come halfway up sides of dishes. Bake, uncovered, about 25 minutes or until puffed and golden. Remove dishes from water; stand 10 minutes. Invert soufflés into oiled individual gratin dishes or an ovenproof dish. Cover; refrigerate up to 6 hours.

5 Preheat oven to moderate (180°C/160°C fan-forced. Spoon cream over soufflés; bake, uncovered, about 15 minutes or until browned.

☐ **PER SERVING** 28.8g total fat (17.0g saturated); 1413kj (338 cal); 8.5g carbohydrate; 12g protein; 0.3g fibre

---

Braised leek and witlof salad with poached eggs and roasted kipflers

PREPARATION TIME 20 MINUTES **COOKING TIME** 50 MINUTES **SERVES** 4

To test eggs for freshness place them in a bowl of water. Fresh eggs should stay at the bottom of the bowl as they only contain a small amount of air. Older eggs will stand up or float as the ageing egg absorbs air, enlarging the air cell, which makes the egg lighter.

1kg kipfler potatoes, halved lengthways

2 teaspoons sea salt

½ teaspoon cracked black pepper

2 cloves garlic, crushed

cooking-oil spray

1 tablespoon olive oil

20 baby leeks (1.6kg), trimmed to 15cm in length

6 white witlof (750g), halved lengthways

⅔ cup (160ml) dry white wine

1 cup (250ml) vegetable stock

1 teaspoon white sugar

8 eggs

CREAMY CHERVIL DRESSING

2 tablespoons lemon juice

1 tablespoon wholegrain mustard

⅔ cup (160ml) cream

¼ cup loosely packed fresh chervil leaves

1 Preheat oven to moderately hot (200°C/180°C fan-forced).

2 Make creamy chervil dressing.

3 Toss potato with salt, pepper and garlic in large baking dish; coat lightly with spray. Roast, uncovered, about 50 minutes or until tender and crisp.

4 Meanwhile, heat oil in large flameproof baking dish; cook leeks and witlof, cut-side down, in single layer, 1 minute. Add wine, stock and sugar; bring to a boil. Reduce heat; simmer, uncovered, 2 minutes. Cover tightly; bake in oven for last 20 minutes of potato cooking time.

5 With 10 minutes left of potato cooking time, half-fill a large shallow frying pan with water; bring to a boil. One at a time, break eggs into cup and slide into pan. When all eggs are in pan, allow water to return to a boil. Cover pan, turn off heat; stand about 4 minutes or until a light film of egg white sets over yolks. One at a time, remove eggs, using slotted spoon, and place on absorbent-paper-lined saucer to blot poaching liquid.

6 Divide potato and witlof among serving plates; top with leeks and two eggs each, drizzle with dressing.

CREAMY CHERVIL DRESSING Place ingredients in screw-top jar; shake well.

☐ **PER SERVING** 34.6g total fat (15.5g saturated); 2767kj (662 cal); 46.5g carbohydrate; 27.7g protein; 15.6g fibre

For a chunkier dhal with a little bite, replace half the red lentils with yellow split peas.

Dhal with egg and eggplant

PREPARATION TIME 10 MINUTES **COOKING TIME** 1 HOUR **SERVES** 4

2 cups (400g) red lentils

2 teaspoons vegetable oil

1 medium brown onion (150g), chopped finely

1 clove garlic, crushed

2 teaspoons ground cumin

½ teaspoon cumin seeds

1 tablespoon tomato paste

1 litre (4 cups) water

2 cups (500ml) vegetable stock

1 large tomato (220g), chopped coarsely

3 baby eggplants (180g), chopped coarsely

4 hard-boiled eggs

1 Rinse lentils in large colander under cold water until water runs clear; drain.

2 Heat oil in large heavy-based saucepan; cook onion, garlic, ground cumin, seeds and paste, stirring, 5 minutes. Add lentils with the water and stock; bring to a boil. Simmer, uncovered, about 40 minutes or until dhal thickens slightly, stirring occasionally.

3 Add tomato and eggplant; simmer, uncovered, 20 minutes or until dhal is thickened and eggplant is tender, stirring occasionally. Add eggs; stir gently until heated through.

PER SERVING 10.3g total fat (2.5g saturated); 1835kj (439 cal); 43.8g carbohydrate; 34.0g protein; 16.2g fibre

---

You can make the cream mixture (known as a panada) well ahead of time. Mix in the cheese and egg yolks, cover and refrigerate. Bring back to room temperature before folding in the egg whites.

Red capsicum and cheese soufflés

PREPARATION TIME 15 MINUTES **COOKING TIME** 45 MINUTES (PLUS COOLING TIME) **SERVES** 4

1 medium red capsicum (200g)

60g butter

1 medium leek (350g), sliced thinly

2 tablespoons plain flour

1 cup (250ml) hot milk

½ cup (125ml) cream

1 tablespoon wholegrain mustard

⅓ cup (25g) finely grated parmesan

4 eggs, separated

1 Preheat oven to moderately hot (200°C/180°C fan-forced). Lightly oil four 1-cup (250ml) ovenproof dishes on oven tray.

2 Quarter capsicum; discard seeds and membrane. Roast under grill or in very hot oven, skin-side up, until skin blisters and blackens. Cover capsicum with plastic or paper for 5 minutes; peel away skin, then finely chop capsicum.

3 Heat butter in large frying pan; cook leek, stirring, until soft. Stir in flour, stir over heat until mixture bubbles. Remove pan from heat; gradually stir in milk, cream, mustard and capsicum. Stir over heat until mixture boils and thickens; cool 5 minutes.

4 Stir cheese and egg yolks into cream mixture. Beat egg whites in small bowl until soft peaks form; gently fold egg whites into cream mixture, in two batches. Spoon mixture into dishes. Bake, uncovered, 20 minutes or until soufflés are puffed and browned lightly.

PER SERVING 36.0g total fat (21.6g saturated); 1797kj (430 cal); 12g carbohydrate; 14.3g protein; 2.4g fibre

Smoked salmon caper and dill frittata

PREPARATION TIME 5 MINUTES **COOKING TIME** 30 MINUTES **SERVES** 4

To make a larger frittata, add 200g cooked, sliced new potatoes and 100g soft goat cheese.

6 eggs

½ cup (125ml) cream

1 teaspoon finely grated lemon rind

1 small red onion (100g), sliced thinly

½ cup coarsely chopped fresh dill

2 tablespoons drained baby capers, rinsed

200g sliced smoked salmon

1 Preheat oven to moderate (180°C/160°C fan-forced). Oil deep 19cm-square cake pan; line base and sides with baking paper.

2 Whisk eggs, cream and rind in medium bowl.

3 Combine onion, dill and capers in small bowl. Spread a third of the onion mixture in pan; top with half of the salmon then pour half of the egg mixture over salmon. Place half of the remaining onion mixture and remaining salmon in pan. Sprinkle remaining onion mixture over salmon then pour in remaining egg mixture.

4 Bake, uncovered, 30 minutes or until frittata is set; stand 5 minutes before cutting.

☐ **PER SERVING** 21.7g total fat (10.4g saturated); 1229kj (294 cal); 2.8g carbohydrate; 22.5g protein; 0.5g fibre

---

Creamy egg and lettuce finger sandwiches

PREPARATION TIME 30 MINUTES **MAKES** 48

The classic combination of egg and smoked salmon makes delectable sandwiches. Add 100g finely chopped smoked salmon and 1 tablespoon chopped dill to the egg mixture and use snow pea sprouts instead of lettuce.

18 hard-boiled eggs, chopped finely

½ cup (150g) whole-egg mayonnaise

2 tablespoons cream

¼ cup finely chopped fresh chives

48 slices wholemeal bread

1 small iceberg lettuce, trimmed, shredded finely

80g butter, softened

1 Combine egg, mayonnaise, cream and chives in large bowl. Divide half of the egg mixture among 16 slices of the bread; top with half of the lettuce.

2 Butter 16 slices of the remaining bread both sides; place each slice on top of lettuce. Divide remaining egg mixture among sandwiches; top with remaining lettuce and remaining bread slices.

3 Remove crusts; cut sandwiches into thirds.

4 Serve at room temperature.

☐ **PER FINGER SANDWICH** 5.5g total fat (2.0g saturated); 502kj (120 cal); 11.3g carbohydrate; 5.3g protein; 1.9g fibre

PASTA & NOODLES

Pasta & Noodles

Italians eat pasta as a first course but we tend to eat it as a main course or a one-dish meal. Italian cooks also use much less sauce on pasta than we do; they consider the pasta itself as the dish and the sauce as more of a dressing. Try it and you may find you too relish the flavour of good pasta.

The ever-growing variety of Asian noodles on display in supermarkets tells the story of our increasing interest in their possibilities. We are serving fragrant noodle mixtures in broth, stir-frying them with meats or seafood and vegetables, and tossing them with Asian sauces for fast lunches or any-time snacks.

KINDS OF PASTA

DRIED PASTA is the mass-produced kind in packets and boxes on the supermarket shelves. Mass-produced does not necessarily mean lesser quality – some of the biggest pasta factories produce top-quality pasta.

FRESH PASTA is soft and pliable; it cooks more quickly than dried but cannot be stored for as long. Fresh pasta is not superior to dried pasta, simply different. When properly cooked, both kinds have the same taste and consistency.

EGG PASTA is available fresh or dried, and is made with egg and softer wheat flour than the hard-wheat flour used for plain pasta. Egg pasta can be homemade.

WHOLEMEAL PASTA is made with part wholemeal and part white flour.

FLAVOURED PASTA is flavoured and coloured with spinach, tomato, basil, chilli and so on.

PASTA SHAPES

- **Long strands, round in section:** spaghetti, spaghettoni (thicker) spaghettini (thinner), capellini (very thin), angel hair (fine and delicate, usually shaped into a nest).
- **Tubular:** macaroni (short and thick), elbow macaroni (with a bend in the middle), rigatoni (short and wide, with ridged surface), bucatini (long and thin).
- **Flat ribbons:** fettuccine, plain or verde (green, spinach-flavoured), tagliatelle (wider), tagliolini (narrower), linguine (narrower still).
- **Large sheets:** lasagne, flat or with ripple edges, plain or verde (green, spinach-flavoured). Instant lasagne needs no pre-boiling before being layered with sauce and cheese and baked.
- **Pasta for soup:** tiny shapes such as stelline (stars) and orzo or risoni (rice-grain shapes).
- **Stuffed pasta:** ravioli (square or round), agnolotti (turnovers), tortellini (turnovers twisted into a ring).

- **Small pasta shapes with holes or crevices to hold chunky sauces:** penne (quills or pens), conchiglie (shells, in several sizes), fusilli (corkscrews), orecchiette (little ears), farfalle (butterflies or bow-ties).

CHOOSING AND STORING PASTA

Both Italy and Australia produce quality dried pasta made from durum (hard) wheat flour. Look for labelling such as "made from durum wheat" or "pasta di semola di Grano Duro". Dried pasta will keep indefinitely, in a cool, dry place, in its unopened packaging or in an airtight jar or box after opening. Fresh pasta will keep for 3 to 4 days in the fridge; it tends to stick together if kept longer. It can be frozen but may glue together as it thaws.

COOKING PASTA

With the exception of instant lasagne, pasta is always boiled even if it is then to be baked. Use a large saucepan. Bring the water to a rolling boil, add salt, then the pasta gradually so the water does not go off the boil. Add long pasta by holding the strands and feeding them in gradually as they soften. Keep the water boiling fast to keep the pasta moving. Test by biting a piece of pasta. It is done when it is *al dente* – cooked through but still firm to the bite (2 to 3 minutes for fresh pasta, 5 to12 minutes, depending on freshness and thickness, for dried). Drain into a colander in the sink, moving onto a bowl for the last few moments in case you need a little cooking water to thin the sauce. Do not rinse. Turn into a heated serving bowl, add sauce, toss and serve at once. Serve cheese separately if using.

CHINESE NOODLES

EGG NOODLES, fresh or dried, made from wheat flour, egg and water, are all-purpose, long noodles in thin threads or wider flat ribbons. They are cooked in the same way as pasta.
WHEAT NOODLES may be fresh or dried and are cooked in the same way as pasta.
HOKKIEN NOODLES are fresh, long, fat wheat noodles for stir-frying or noodles in broth. They need no cooking, but may be softened by covering with boiling water.
RICE NOODLES may be fresh or dried and come in ribbons, sticks or sheets. They do not need boiling, but are usually softened in hot water and used in soups or stir-fried. Dried rice vermicelli may also be cut into short lengths and deep-fried, which crisps it up.
BEAN THREAD (CELLOPHANE) NOODLES are fine, dried, transparent noodles made from ground mung beans. They are used in the same way as rice noodles and are softened in hot water or deep-fried in the same way as rice vermicelli.

JAPANESE NOODLES

SOBA are buckwheat noodles, cooked in the same way as pasta. They can be eaten plain or topped with seafood or meat and vegetables.
UDON are wheat noodles, cooked in the same way as pasta and typically served in broth.
RAMEN are wheat noodles, and cooked in the same way as pasta.
SOMEN are fine, delicate, white wheat noodles, cooked in the same way as pasta.

STORING NOODLES

Store fresh and dried Asian noodles in the same way as fresh and dried pasta.

In Italian alla Marinara means "sailor-style". It is a tomato-based sauce with garlic and oregano that was given to the sailors of Naples when they returned from sea. It did not originally include seafood, though today it usually does. It is also used on pizzas and in risottos.

Spaghetti marinara

PREPARATION TIME 20 MINUTES **COOKING TIME** 20 MINUTES **SERVES** 4

- 500g cooked medium king prawns
- 375g spaghetti
- ½ cup (125ml) water
- ½ cup (125ml) dry white wine
- 250g scallops, halved
- 2 tablespoons olive oil
- 5 large tomatoes (1.1kg), chopped coarsely
- 2 cloves garlic, crushed
- 1 tablespoon tomato paste
- 8 oysters
- 45g can anchovy fillets, drained, chopped finely
- 1 tablespoon finely chopped fresh parsley
- 1 tablespoon finely chopped fresh mint

1 Shell and devein prawns.

2 Cook pasta in large saucepan of boiling water, uncovered, until tender; drain.

3 Meanwhile, combine the water and wine in large saucepan; cook scallops, uncovered, 1 minute, drain.

4 Heat oil in large frying pan; cook tomato, garlic and paste, stirring, 2 minutes. Stir in seafood; cook, uncovered, 1 minute. Stir in herbs.

5 Serve marinara over pasta.

PER SERVING 12.1g total fat (2.0g saturated); 2437kj (583 cal); 70.5g carbohydrate; 38.1g protein; 7.g fibre

---

This dish is considered one of Singapore's classic fried noodle dishes. It is cooked at hawker stalls and uses wide fresh rice noodles, cooked in oil or lard.

Char kway teow

PREPARATION TIME 25 MINUTES **COOKING TIME** 10 MINUTES **SERVES** 6

- 1kg fresh rice noodles
- 500g uncooked small king prawns
- 2 tablespoons peanut oil
- 340g chicken breast fillets, chopped coarsely
- 3 fresh small red thai chillies, chopped finely
- 2 cloves garlic, crushed
- 2cm piece fresh ginger (10g), grated
- 5 green onions, sliced thinly
- 2 cups (160g) bean sprouts
- ⅓ cup (80ml) light soy sauce
- ¼ teaspoon sesame oil
- 1 teaspoon brown sugar

1 Cover noodles with boiling water in large heatproof bowl; separate with fork, drain.

2 Shell and devein prawns, leaving tails intact; halve prawns crossways.

3 Heat half of the peanut oil in wok; stir-fry chicken, chilli, garlic and ginger until chicken is cooked through. Remove from wok.

4 Heat remaining peanut oil in wok; stir-fry prawns until just changed in colour. Remove from wok. Stir-fry onion and sprouts in wok until onion softens. Add noodles and combined remaining ingredients; stir-fry 1 minute.

5 Return chicken mixture and prawns to wok; stir-fry until heated through.

PER SERVING 9.6g total fat (1.9g saturated); 1442kj (345 cal); 37.6g carbohydrate; 25.4g protein; 2.1g fibre

Lasagne bolognese

PREPARATION TIME 1 HOUR 15 MINUTES **COOKING TIME** 2 HOURS 45 MINUTES (PLUS STANDING TIME)
SERVES 8

In Bologna, a lasagne sauce is traditionally made with chicken liver and milk in the sauce. Made this way, lasagne is worthy of a dinner party. Fresh or dried lasagne sheets can be substituted for the home-made pasta; follow directions on the packet for cooking times.

2 teaspoons olive oil
6 slices pancetta (90g), chopped finely
1 large white onion (200g), chopped finely
1 medium carrot (120g), chopped finely
2 trimmed celery stalks (200g), chopped finely
1kg beef mince
150g chicken livers, trimmed, chopped finely
2 cups (500ml) milk
60g butter
2 cups (500ml) beef stock
1 cup (250ml) dry red wine
410g can tomato puree
2 tablespoons tomato paste
¼ cup finely chopped fresh flat-leaf parsley
2 cups (160g) finely grated parmesan

PASTA

1 cup (150g) plain flour
¼ cup (45g) semolina flour
2 eggs
1 tablespoon olive oil
semolina flour, for dusting, extra

WHITE SAUCE

125g butter
¾ cup (110g) plain flour
1.25 litres (5 cups) hot milk

1 Heat oil in large heavy-based saucepan; cook pancetta until crisp. Add onion, carrot and celery; cook, stirring, until vegetables soften. Add beef and liver; cook until beef just changes colour. Stir in milk and butter; cook until liquid reduces to about half. Add stock, wine, puree and paste; simmer, uncovered, 1½ hours. Remove from heat; stir in parsley.
2 Meanwhile, make pasta and white sauce. Oil deep 26cm x 35cm baking dish.
3 Preheat oven to moderately hot (200°C/180°C fan-forced).
4 Spread about ½ cup of the white sauce over base of dish. Layer two pasta sheets, a quarter of the meat sauce, ¼ cup of the cheese and about 1 cup of white sauce in dish. Repeat layering, ending with white sauce (four layers in total). Top with remaining cheese. Bake, uncovered, 40 minutes or until browned lightly. Stand 15 minutes before serving.

PASTA Process flours, eggs and oil until combined. Knead on floured surface 5 minutes. Divide dough into quarters; roll each piece through pasta machine (see side note). Cook pasta in large saucepan of boiling salted water, in batches, about 1 minute or until pasta rises to the surface. Transfer to bowl of iced water; drain, pat dry with absorbent paper.

WHITE SAUCE Melt butter in medium saucepan, add flour; cook, stirring, until mixture thickens and bubbles. Gradually stir in milk; cook, stirring, until mixture boils and thickens.

To roll dough through a pasta machine, fold the long sides of dough into the centre, then roll through the machine on its thickest setting. Repeat rolling several times, adjusting the setting so the pasta sheets become thinner with each roll; dust the pasta with extra semolina flour when necessary. Roll to the second thinnest setting (1mm thick), making sure the pasta is at least 10cm wide. Cut the pasta into 35cm lengths.

PER SERVING 49.1g total fat (27.2g saturated); 3603kj (862 cal); 43.5g carbohydrate; 55.2g protein; 3.5g fibre

Pad thai *(thai fried rice stick noodles)*

PREPARATION TIME 20 MINUTES (PLUS STANDING TIME) **COOKING TIME** 10 MINUTES **SERVES** 4

Tamarind is an important ingredient in Thai cooking, used mainly as a souring agent in marinades, pastes and dressings. The paste in this recipe can be made using a mortar and pestle if you prefer.

40g tamarind pulp
½ cup (125ml) boiling water
2 tablespoons grated palm sugar
⅓ cup (80ml) sweet chilli sauce
⅓ cup (80ml) fish sauce
375g rice stick noodles
12 uncooked medium king prawns (500g)
2 cloves garlic, crushed
2 tablespoons finely chopped preserved turnip
4cm piece fresh ginger (20g), grated
2 tablespoons dried shrimp
1 fresh small red thai chilli, chopped coarsely
1 tablespoon peanut oil
250g pork mince
3 eggs, beaten lightly
2 cups (160g) bean sprouts
4 green onions, sliced thinly
⅓ cup coarsely chopped fresh coriander
¼ cup (35g) coarsely chopped roasted unsalted peanuts
1 lime, quartered

1 Soak tamarind pulp in the boiling water for 30 minutes. Push through fine strainer over small bowl. Discard any tamarind solids left in strainer; reserve pulp liquid. Stir sugar and sauces into bowl with tamarind; reserve.
2 Cover noodles with boiling water in large heatproof bowl; stand until just soft, drain.
3 Shell and devein prawns, leaving tails intact.
4 Blend or process garlic, turnip, ginger, shrimp and chilli until mixture forms a paste.
5 Heat oil in wok; stir-fry paste until fragrant. Add pork, stir-fry until just cooked through. Add prawns, stir-fry 1 minute. Add egg, stir-fry until egg just sets. Add noodles, tamarind mixture, bean sprouts and half of the onion; stir-fry until combined. Remove from heat; toss in remaining green onion, coriander and nuts. Serve with lime wedges.

PER SERVING 19.2g total fat (4.5g saturated); 2006kj (480 cal); 34.3g carbohydrate; 39.8g protein; 5g fibre

---

Fettuccine carbonara

PREPARATION TIME 10 MINUTES **COOKING TIME** 10 MINUTES **SERVES** 4

Italian recipes vary from region to region, reflecting the ingredients available there. While "charcoal burners' fettuccine" is made without cream in the south, it includes cream, as our recipe does, in the north of the country.

375g fettuccine
4 bacon rashers (280g), rind removed, chopped coarsely
3 egg yolks, beaten lightly
1 cup (250ml) cream
½ cup (40g) finely grated parmesan
2 tablespoons coarsely chopped fresh chives

1 Cook pasta in large saucepan of boiling water, uncovered, until just tender; drain.
2 Meanwhile, cook bacon in heated small frying pan, stirring, until crisp; drain.
3 Combine bacon, pasta, egg yolks, cream and cheese. Serve sprinkled with chives.

PER SERVING 44.8g total fat (24.8g saturated); 3336kj (798 cal); 66g carbohydrate; 31.4g protein; 3.1g fibre

PAD THAI (THAI FRIED RICE STICK NOODLES)

In Italian primavera means "spring". This sauce was created to celebrate the abundance of spring vegetables available in Italy. Spiral pasta (fusilli) is used because its crevices will hold the chunky sauce.

Pasta primavera

PREPARATION TIME 15 MINUTES **COOKING TIME** 15 MINUTES **SERVES** 4

- 375g small spirals
- 1 medium carrot (120g)
- 1 tablespoon olive oil
- 1 medium brown onion (150g), chopped finely
- 3 cloves garlic, crushed
- 300g yellow patty-pan squash, quartered
- 1 medium red capsicum (200g), sliced thinly
- 200g sugar snap peas, trimmed
- 300ml cream
- 1 tablespoon wholegrain mustard
- 2 tablespoons coarsely chopped fresh flat-leaf parsley

1 Cook pasta in large saucepan of boiling water, uncovered, until just tender; drain.
2 Meanwhile, using vegetable peeler, cut carrot lengthways into ribbons. Heat oil in large saucepan; cook onion and garlic, stirring, until onion softens. Add squash; cook, stirring, until just tender. Add carrot, capsicum and peas; cook, stirring, until capsicum is tender.
3 Add pasta to vegetable mixture with combined remaining ingredients; stir over low heat until just heated through.

PER SERVING 38.5g total fat (22.3g saturated); 3081kj (737 cal); 76.4g carbohydrate; 17.1g protein; 8.3g fibre

---

Selecting the right potatoes is the key to light, tender gnocchi. The potatoes need to be floury (russet burbank, lasoda, king Edward) with low water content and high starch.

Gnocchi with burnt butter and tomato

PREPARATION TIME 40 MINUTES (PLUS REFRIGERATION TIME) **COOKING TIME** 25 MINUTES **SERVES** 4

- 3 large potatoes (900g), chopped coarsely
- 1 clove garlic, crushed
- 2 tablespoons milk
- 2 egg yolks
- ⅓ cup (25g) finely grated parmesan
- 1 cup (150g) plain flour, approximately
- 100g butter, chopped
- ⅓ cup loosely packed baby basil leaves
- 3 medium egg tomatoes (225g), chopped coarsely

1 Boil or steam potato until tender; drain. Cool 10 minutes. Mash with a masher, ricer or mouli until smooth; stir in garlic and milk. Stir in egg yolks, cheese and enough of the sifted flour to form a firm dough.
2 On lightly floured surface, roll a quarter of the dough into 2cm thick log. Cut log into 1.5cm pieces; roll pieces into balls. Roll each ball along the inside tines of a floured fork, pressing lightly on top of ball with index finger to form classic gnocchi shape – grooves on one side and a dimple on the other. Place gnocchi, in single layer, on lightly floured tray. Repeat with remaining dough. Cover; refrigerate 1 hour.
3 Cook gnocchi, in batches, in large saucepan of boiling water about 3 minutes or until they float to the surface. Remove with a slotted spoon; drain well.

4 Meanwhile, heat butter in medium frying pan until golden brown; cook basil leaves until crisp. Remove basil from pan with a slotted spoon; drain on absorbent paper. Add tomato; cook, stirring, until tomato softens.

5 Place drained gnocchi and tomato mixture in large bowl; toss gently to combine. Divide among serving dishes; sprinkle with basil. Serve with extra grated parmesan, if desired.

PER SERVING 26.5g total fat (16g saturated); 2140kj (512 cal); 52.4g carbohydrate; 13.5g protein; 5.2g fibre

---

Udon casseroles

If you fancy a little heat in this recipe add 1 finely sliced long red chilli and 2 teaspoons grated ginger at stage 4. Serve pickled ginger as a garnish.

PREPARATION TIME 15 MINUTES (PLUS STANDING TIME) **COOKING TIME** 20 MINUTES **SERVES** 4

- 400g dried thick udon noodles
- 200g chicken breast fillet, chopped coarsely
- 2 teaspoons japanese soy sauce
- 2 teaspoons sake
- 250g spinach, trimmed
- 1 teaspoon instant dashi powder
- 2½ cups (625ml) water
- 2 tablespoons japanese soy sauce, extra
- 1 tablespoon mirin
- 1 medium carrot (120g), sliced thinly
- 4 fresh shiitake mushrooms, sliced thinly
- 2 green onions, chopped coarsely
- 4 eggs
- ¼ teaspoon seven-spice mix (shichimi togarashi)

1 Cook noodles in large saucepan of boiling water, uncovered, until just tender; drain. Rinse under cold water, drain.

2 Combine chicken, soy sauce and sake in small bowl; stand, covered, 10 minutes.

3 Boil, steam or microwave spinach until just wilted; drain. Rinse under cold water; drain. Slice spinach thickly; squeeze out excess water.

4 Combine dashi, the water, extra soy sauce and mirin in medium saucepan; bring to a boil. Cover. keep hot over low heat.

5 Place ½ cup of the broth and carrot in small saucepan; cook, uncovered, 2 minutes. Add chicken; cook, uncovered, 2 minutes. Add mushrooms; cook, uncovered, until chicken is cooked through.

6 Divide noodles among four 2½-cup (625ml) flameproof pots, arrange carrot, chicken, mushrooms, spinach and onion among pots. Cover with hot broth.

7 Using back of a spoon, make a small hollow in noodles; break eggs, one at a time, into small bowl, slide an egg into each hollow. Cover pots; stand, covered, until egg just sets. Just before serving, sprinkle each pot with a tiny pinch of seven-spice mix.

PER SERVING 8.7g total fat (2.4g saturated); 2132kj (510 cal); 71.0g carbohydrate; 31.1g protein; 6.1g fibre

Noodles

The Asian custom of eating noodles with vegetables, a little meat and flavoursome condiments is delicious and healthy.

HOKKIEN
Fat, yellow, fresh wheat noodles which need no pre-cooking, only a dip in hot water to rinse off their oil coating and separate the strands. Used in broths and stir-fries.

FRIED
Commercially prepared deep-fried egg noodles, also called crispy noodles. The frying gives them crunch and savour and, it should be noted, makes them a high-fat food. Often used for sang choy bow.

BEAN THREAD
Also called cellophane or glass noodles, these are made from mung bean flour and are either softened in hot water (needing no further cooking) or fried, making them crisp and puffed.

SOBA
Japanese noodles made from buckwheat flour and wheat flour. Can be eaten chilled with a dipping sauce as a snack, or in soups or served with seafood or meat and vegetables.

SHANGHAI
Fresh flat noodles similar to hokkien but paler in colour, and generally sold unoiled; dip in hot water to separate the strands. Also available dried, as a thin white noodle which is boiled like other dried noodles.

RAMEN
Japanese wheat noodles, sold in dried, fresh, steamed and instant forms. A popular fast food in the many ramen bars in Japan, they are also a diet staple for students.

FRESH RICE
Also known as pho and ho fun, these noodles are white and chewy. They need no pre-cooking, only a short soak in hot water to soften them. They come in various sizes, including sheets.

RICE STICK
Thin ones are used in soups, wide ones in stir-fries. They need no pre-cooking, only a short soak in hot water to soften them. They can also be fried, which makes them crisp and puffed.

RICE VERMICELLI
Like rice sticks, these need only a short soak in hot water to soften them. They can also be fried to make them crisp and puffed. Can be substituted for bean-thread noodles.

SOMEN
These very thin wheat noodles from Japan are labelled somen if they are eggless, tamago somen if they were made with egg. Can be eaten chilled or served in warm broth. Don't overcook them as they quickly become gluggy.

UDON
Broad, white Japanese wheat noodles. Particularly popular in southern Japan, udon are best known as soup noodles, but are also good in stir-fries and hotpots. Available fresh and dried, in round, square or ribbon shapes.

FRESH EGG
Made from wheat flour and eggs, these noodles are sold fresh or dried. They range in width from fine to quite wide. Golden in colour, they only need softening and separating in hot water.

Use fresh egg noodles that are actually made from wheat flour and egg: many so-called egg noodles are just wheat noodles tinted with yellow food colouring. Buy the thinnest fresh noodles you can find for this recipe.

Singapore noodles

PREPARATION TIME 15 MINUTES **COOKING TIME** 10 MINUTES **SERVES** 12

200g thin fresh egg noodles

2 tablespoons peanut oil

250g beef rump steak, sliced thinly

1 small brown onion (80g), sliced thinly

2 fresh long red chillies, chopped finely

1 medium red capsicum (200g), sliced thinly

1 tablespoon mild curry paste

4 green onions, sliced thinly

2½ cups (200g) bean sprouts

100g snow peas, trimmed, sliced thinly

200g chinese barbecued pork, chopped coarsely

2 tablespoons oyster sauce

⅓ cup (80ml) light soy sauce

2 tablespoons sesame oil

1 Cover noodles with hot water in medium heatproof bowl; separate with fork, drain.

2 Meanwhile, heat half of the peanut oil in wok; stir-fry beef, in batches, until browned. Remove from wok.

3 Heat remaining peanut oil in wok; stir-fry brown onion, chilli and capsicum until onion softens. Add curry paste; stir-fry until fragrant.

4 Add green onions, sprouts, snow peas and pork; stir-fry 1 minute. Return beef to wok with sauces, sesame oil and noodles; stir-fry until heated through.

5 Divide singapore noodles among bowls or takeaway boxes.

PER SERVING 10.9g total fat (2.8g saturated); 819kj (196 cal); 12.1g carbohydrate; 11.5g protein; 2.0g fibre

This dish makes a terrific salad. Allow the risoni to cool before tossing with the tomatoes, spinach leaves, 1 cup cooked peas, 100g blanched sugar snap peas, 150g flaked smoked trout, finely grated rind of ½ lemon, juice of 1 lemon and a drizzle of olive oil.

Risoni with spinach and semi-dried tomatoes

PREPARATION TIME 5 MINUTES **COOKING TIME** 25 MINUTES **SERVES** 4

30g butter

2 medium brown onions (300g), chopped finely

3 cloves garlic, crushed

500g risoni

1 litre (4 cups) chicken stock

½ cup (125ml) dry white wine

1 cup (150g) drained semi-dried tomatoes, halved

100g baby spinach leaves

⅓ cup (25g) finely grated parmesan

1 Melt butter in large saucepan; cook onion and garlic, stirring, until onion softens.

2 Stir in risoni, then stock and wine; bring to a boil. Reduce heat; simmer, stirring, until liquid is absorbed and risoni is just tender. Stir in tomato, spinach and cheese.

PER SERVING 12.5g total fat (6.4g saturated); 2842kj (680 cal); 104.8g carbohydrate; 25.3g protein; 11.7g fibre

1 SINGAPORE NOODLES **2** RISONI WITH SPINACH AND SEMI-DRIED TOMATOES **3** SAGANAKI PRAWN RAVIOLI [P 356] **4** ORECCHIETTE WITH HAM, ARTICHOKES AND SUN-DRIED TOMATOES [P 356]

1

2

3

4

These large, luxurious ravioli with their light tomato sauce make a lovely opener to a dinner party or, served with a fresh green salad, a stylish little lunch.

Saganaki prawn ravioli

PREPARATION TIME 50 MINUTES **COOKING TIME** 20 MINUTES **SERVES** 4

¼ cup (60ml) olive oil

5 large tomatoes (1.1kg), seeded, chopped coarsely

4 cloves garlic, crushed

¼ cup finely chopped fresh lemon thyme

700g uncooked medium prawns

⅓ cup (80g) sour cream

1 teaspoon finely grated lemon rind

200g fetta, crumbled

40 wonton wrappers

1 Heat 2 tablespoons of the oil in large saucepan; cook tomato, garlic and 2 tablespoons of the thyme, stirring, 2 minutes. Cover; cook over low heat 5 minutes.
2 Meanwhile, shell and devein prawns; chop prawn meat coarsely. Combine prawn meat in medium bowl with sour cream, rind, 150g of the cheese and remaining thyme.
3 Centre a level tablespoon of the prawn mixture on one wrapper; brush around edges with a little water. Top with another wrapper, press edges together to seal. Repeat with remaining prawn mixture and wrappers; you will have 20 ravioli.
4 Cook ravioli, in two batches, in large saucepan of boiling water, uncovered, until ravioli float to the surface and are cooked through; drain.
5 Divide ravioli among serving plates, top with hot tomato mixture, sprinkle with remaining cheese then drizzle with remaining oil. Top with extra lemon thyme, if desired.

☐ **PER SERVING** 35.2g total fat (15.2g saturated); 2491kj (596 cal); 34.3g carbohydrate; 34.2g protein; 3.5g fibre

---

Orecchiette, meaning "little ears", is the typical pasta of Puglia. For a traditional sauce place 2 tablespoons olive oil, 1 chopped onion, 2 crushed cloves garlic, 1 finely chopped red chilli and 4 anchovy fillets in a medium saucepan and cook for 5 minutes. Add 500g finely chopped steamed broccoli, ⅓ cup grated parmesan and 1 tablespoon grated lemon rind. Toss gently with the cooked pasta.

Orecchiette with ham, artichokes and sun-dried tomatoes

PREPARATION TIME 10 MINUTES **COOKING TIME** 15 MINUTES **SERVES** 4

375g orecchiette

500g leg ham, chopped coarsely

340g jar marinated artichoke hearts, drained, quartered

½ cup (75g) drained sun-dried tomatoes, halved

1 cup (80g) flaked parmesan

1 cup loosely packed fresh flat-leaf parsley leaves

2 tablespoons lemon juice

1 tablespoon wholegrain mustard

1 tablespoon honey

1 clove garlic, crushed

½ cup (125ml) olive oil

1 Cook pasta in large saucepan of boiling water, uncovered, until just tender; drain.
2 Place pasta in large bowl with ham, artichoke, tomato, cheese, parsley and combined remaining ingredients; toss gently to combine.

☐ **PER SERVING** 18.9g total fat (6.9g saturated); 2872kj (687 cal); 77.9g carbohydrate; 45.7g protein; 8.9g fibre

Spaghetti bolognese

PREPARATION TIME 15 MINUTES **COOKING TIME** 2 HOURS 15 MINUTES **SERVES** 4

Pasta-lovers the world over have made spaghetti bolognese their own. This recipe is slightly simplified from the original, but is still rich and fragrant enough to be worthy of the name. One secret of a good bolognese is long, slow cooking to concentrate the flavour.

2 tablespoons olive oil

1 large brown onion (200g), chopped finely

2 cloves garlic, crushed

750g beef mince

2 x 410g cans crushed tomatoes

⅓ cup (95g) tomato paste

1 litre (4 cups) water

1 tablespoon finely shredded fresh basil

1 tablespoon finely chopped fresh oregano

2 teaspoons finely chopped fresh thyme

375g spaghetti

⅓ cup (25g) finely grated parmesan

1 Heat oil in medium frying pan; add onion and garlic, cook until soft. Add mince; cook, stirring, until browned.

2 Push tomatoes with their liquid through sieve in medium bowl, add to pan with paste and the water; bring to a boil. Reduce heat; simmer, uncovered, about 2 hours or until nearly all liquid is evaporated. Stir in herbs.

3 Cook pasta in large saucepan of boiling water, uncovered, until tender; drain.

4 Divide pasta among serving bowls; top with sauce. Sprinkle with cheese.

PER SERVING 23.8g total fat (7.5g saturated); 3168kj (758 cal); 75.6g carbohydrate; 55.8g protein; 7.5g fibre

---

Tagliatelle puttanesca

PREPARATION TIME 10 MINUTES **COOKING TIME** 20 MINUTES **SERVES** 4

This powerful piquant pasta sauce has a historical link to the "ladies of the night" in southern Italy. For a tasty pizza sauce, reduce the sauce for 10 minutes or until it has thickened.

2 teaspoons vegetable oil

1 large brown onion (200g), sliced thickly

3 cloves garlic, crushed

3 fresh small red thai chillies, chopped finely

600ml bottled tomato pasta sauce

¼ cup (50g) drained capers, rinsed

1 cup (150g) seeded kalamata olives

8 anchovy fillets, drained, halved

½ cup coarsely chopped fresh flat-leaf parsley

375g tagliatelle

1 Heat oil in large frying pan; cook onion, garlic and chilli, stirring, until onion softens. Add sauce, capers, olives and anchovies; bring to a boil. Reduce heat; simmer, uncovered, about 5 minutes or until sauce thickens slightly. Stir in parsley.

2 Meanwhile, cook pasta in large saucepan of boiling water, uncovered, until just tender; drain. Serve pasta with sauce.

PER SERVING 5.5g total fat (0.8g saturated); 2140kj (512 cal); 94.0g carbohydrate; 16.1g protein; 8.5g fibre

Pastitsio

PREPARATION TIME 30 MINUTES (PLUS STANDING TIME)
COOKING TIME 1 HOUR 45 MINUTES (PLUS COOLING TIME) **SERVES** 6

Pastitsio is a popular party dish in Italy. If you put it in the oven shortly before people arrive, it will look after itself while drinks and appetisers are served – just check it once or twice in case it needs turning to brown evenly.

250g macaroni

2 eggs, beaten lightly

¾ cup (60g) finely grated parmesan

2 tablespoons stale breadcrumbs

MEAT SAUCE

2 tablespoons olive oil

2 medium brown onions (300g), chopped finely

750g beef mince

400g can crushed tomatoes

⅓ cup (95g) tomato paste

½ cup (125ml) beef stock

¼ cup (60ml) dry white wine

½ teaspoon ground cinnamon

1 egg

TOPPING

90g butter

½ cup (75g) plain flour

3½ cups (875ml) hot milk

1 cup (80g) finely grated parmesan

2 egg yolks

1 Preheat oven to moderate (180°C/160°C fan-forced). Oil shallow 2.5-litre (10-cup) ovenproof dish.

2 Make meat sauce and topping.

3 Cook pasta in large saucepan of boiling water, uncovered, until just tender; drain.

4 Combine hot pasta, egg and cheese in large bowl. Press pasta over base of dish. Top pasta evenly with meat sauce; pour on topping, smooth surface then sprinkle with breadcrumbs. Bake, uncovered, 1 hour or until browned lightly. Stand 10 minutes before serving with green salad, if desired.

MEAT SAUCE Heat oil in large saucepan; cook onion and mince, stirring, until mince is browned. Stir in undrained tomatoes, paste, stock, wine and cinnamon; bring to a boil. Reduce heat; simmer, uncovered, until sauce thickens. Cool 20 minutes; stir in egg.

TOPPING Melt butter in medium saucepan, add flour; cook, stirring, until mixture thickens and bubbles. Gradually stir in milk; cook, stirring, until sauce boils and thickens. Stir in cheese, cool 10 minutes. Stir in egg yolks.

☐ **PER SERVING** 44.5g total fat (22.2g saturated); 3515kj (841 cal); 53.5g carbohydrate; 53.3g protein; 4.1g fibre

PASTITSIO

The Japanese celebrate New Year's Eve by eating soba noodles as the clock strikes midnight. This is known as "Toshi-koshi soba", which literally means "Across the Years Noodles". The noodles symbolise longevity.

Chilled soba

PREPARATION TIME 5 MINUTES **COOKING TIME** 15 MINUTES (PLUS CHILLING TIME) **SERVES** 4

250g dried soba noodles
½ teaspoon instant dashi powder
¾ cup (180ml) water
2 tablespoons japanese soy sauce
2 tablespoons mirin
½ teaspoon white sugar
2 green onions, chopped finely
1 teaspoon wasabi paste
½ toasted seaweed sheet (yaki-nori), sliced thinly

1 Cook noodles in large saucepan of boiling water, uncovered, until just tender; drain. Rinse under cold water; drain.

2 Heat dashi, the water, soy sauce, mirin and sugar in small saucepan, stirring, until sugar dissolves; cool dipping sauce.

3 Divide dipping sauce, onion and wasabi among individual side dishes.

4 Just before serving, place noodles in a strainer and immerse in iced water to chill; drain. Divide among serving baskets or dishes; top with seaweed strips.

5 Add onion and wasabi to dipping sauce, to taste; dip noodles in sauce before eating.

PER SERVING 0.7g total fat (0.1g saturated); 957kj (229 cal); 44.1g carbohydrate; 7.7g protein; 2.2g fibre

---

This delicate and decorative pasta dish is a speciality of Venice.

Spaghetti alla vongole

PREPARATION TIME 30 MINUTES (PLUS SOAKING TIME) **COOKING TIME** 40 MINUTES **SERVES** 6

1.5kg clams
1 tablespoon coarse cooking salt
¼ cup (60ml) olive oil
1 medium brown onion (150g), chopped finely
2 cloves garlic, crushed
2 anchovy fillets, drained, chopped finely
1 fresh small red thai chilli, chopped finely
2 teaspoons coarsely chopped fresh thyme
20 medium egg tomatoes (1.5kg), peeled, seeded, chopped finely
2 tablespoons coarsely chopped fresh flat-leaf parsley
500g spaghetti

1 Rinse clams under cold water; drain. Place in large bowl; sprinkle with salt; cover with cold water and soak for 2 hours (this purges them of any grit). Discard water, rinse clams thoroughly; drain.

2 Heat 2 tablespoons of the oil in large saucepan; cook clams, covered with tight-fitting lid, about 8 minutes or until all clams have opened.

3 Strain clam cooking liquid through fine cloth or tea-towel. Return liquid to clean pan; cook, uncovered, until liquid is reduced to 1 cup. Reserve clam stock.

4 Heat remaining oil in same cleaned saucepan; cook onion, garlic, anchovy, chilli and thyme, stirring, until onion softens. Add tomato and reserved clam stock; cook, uncovered, 10 minutes or until sauce thickens. Add clams; stir until heated through. Stir in parsley before serving.

5 Meanwhile, cook pasta in another large saucepan of boiling water, uncovered, until just tender; drain.
6 Add pasta to clam sauce; toss gently to combine.

PER SERVING 10.4g total fat (1.5g saturated); 1789kj (428 cal); 60.8g carbohydrate; 19.8g protein; 4.5g fibre

---

Chicken and prosciutto cannelloni

This is a great dish for entertaining. Ahead of time, prepare and assemble up to the point of putting the chicken and pasta rolls into the dishes. One hour before you want to serve it, preheat the oven and add the remaining tomato sauce and cheese. Put the dishes in the oven and check once or twice during cooking.

PREPARATION TIME 30 MINUTES **COOKING TIME** 1 HOUR 10 MINUTES (PLUS COOLING TIME) **SERVES** 8

- 50g butter
- ¼ cup (35g) plain flour
- ⅔ cup (160ml) milk
- 1½ cups (375ml) chicken stock
- ½ cup (40g) finely grated parmesan
- 400g fontina cheese, grated coarsely
- 1 tablespoon olive oil
- 2 medium brown onions (300g), chopped finely
- 3 cloves garlic, crushed
- 1kg chicken mince
- 2 tablespoons finely chopped fresh sage
- 810g can crushed tomatoes
- ½ cup (125ml) dry white wine
- ¼ cup (70g) tomato paste
- 3 teaspoons white sugar
- 12 fresh lasagne sheets
- 24 slices prosciutto (360g)

1 Preheat oven to moderate (180°C/160°C fan-forced). Lightly oil two 3-litre (12-cup) ovenproof dishes.
2 Heat butter in medium saucepan, add flour; cook, stirring, until mixture thickens and bubbles. Remove from heat. Gradually stir in milk and stock; cook, stirring, until sauce boils and thickens. Remove from heat; stir in parmesan and a quarter of the fontina.
3 Heat oil in large saucepan; cook onion and garlic, stirring, until onion softens. Add chicken; cook, stirring, until browned. Stir in sage. Combine chicken and cheese sauce in large bowl; cool 10 minutes.
4 Combine undrained tomatoes, wine, paste and sugar in same large pan; cook, stirring, 10 minutes. Cool 10 minutes; blend or process, in batches, until smooth.
5 Cut pasta sheets and prosciutto slices in half crossways. Place two pieces of prosciutto on each piece of pasta. Top each with ¼ cup chicken mixture; roll to enclose filling. Repeat with remaining pasta, prosciutto and chicken mixture.
6 Pour a quarter of the tomato sauce into base of each dish; divide pasta rolls, seam-side down, between dishes. Pour remaining tomato sauce over rolls; sprinkle each dish with remaining fontina. Bake, covered, 30 minutes. Uncover, bake about 15 minutes or until cheese melts and browns. Serve with a green salad, if desired.

PER SERVING 31.8g total fat (16.4g saturated); 2638kj (631 cal); 27.3g carbohydrate; 55.0g protein; 3.1g fibre

You can put frozen gnocchi straight into boiling water; as with fresh gnocchi they will rise to the surface when cooked – it will just take a little longer.

Gnocchi al quattro formaggi

PREPARATION TIME 10 MINUTES **COOKING TIME** 10 MINUTES **SERVES** 4

¼ cup (60ml) dry white wine
1 cup (250g) mascarpone cheese
¼ cup (60ml) milk
1 cup (120g) coarsely grated fontina cheese
½ cup (40g) coarsely grated parmesan
625g gnocchi
75g gorgonzola cheese, crumbled

1 Bring wine to a boil in large saucepan; boil, uncovered, until wine reduces by half. Reduce heat, add mascarpone; stir until smooth. Add milk, fontina and parmesan; cook, stirring, until cheeses melt and sauce is smooth.
2 Meanwhile, cook gnocchi in large saucepan of boiling water, uncovered, until gnocchi rise to the surface; drain.
3 Add gnocchi and gorgonzola to sauce; toss gently to combine.

PER SERVING 55g total fat (35.7g saturated); 3315kj (793 cal); 47.4g carbohydrate; 23.5g protein; 3.6g fibre

---

The food of Thailand's northern region, around the city of Chiang Mai, is richer and less chilli-hot than the food of the south. Here, chilli is used as a garnish to let individual diners decide how much fire they want.

Chiang mai noodles

PREPARATION TIME 20 MINUTES **COOKING TIME** 20 MINUTES **SERVES** 4

vegetable oil, for deep-frying
500g fresh thin egg noodles
1 large brown onion (200g), sliced thinly
2 green onions, sliced thinly
¼ cup loosely packed fresh coriander leaves
¼ cup (75g) red curry paste
2 cloves garlic, crushed
¼ teaspoon ground turmeric
2 cups (500ml) water
400ml can coconut milk
500g chicken breast fillets, sliced thinly
¼ cup (60ml) fish sauce
1 tablespoon light soy sauce
2 tablespoons grated palm sugar
2 teaspoons lime juice
2 tablespoons coarsely chopped fresh coriander
1 fresh long red thai chilli, sliced thinly

1 Heat oil in wok; deep-fry about 100g of the noodles, in batches, until crisp. Drain.
2 Using same heated oil, deep-fry brown onion, in batches, until browned lightly and crisp. Drain on absorbent paper. Combine fried noodles, fried onion, green onion and coriander leaves in small bowl. Cool oil; remove from wok and reserve for another use.
3 Place remaining noodles in large heatproof bowl; cover with boiling water, separate with fork, drain.
4 Cook paste, garlic and turmeric in same cleaned wok, add the water and coconut milk. Bring to a boil; simmer, stirring, 2 minutes. Add chicken; cook 5 minutes or until cooked. Add sauces, sugar and juice; cook, stirring, until sugar dissolves. Stir in chopped coriander.
5 Divide noodles among serving bowls; spoon chicken curry mixture into each bowl, then top with fried noodle mixture. Sprinkle with chilli.

PER SERVING 34.7g total fat (20.7g saturated); 3436kj (822 cal); 80g carbohydrate; 43g protein; 7.6g fibre

Spaghetti napoletana

This recipe, from the southern Italian region around Naples, is typical of Italy's traditional and wonderful "foods of the poor", which have become favourite quick meals all over the world.

PREPARATION TIME 5 MINUTES **COOKING TIME** 25 MINUTES **SERVES** 4

- 2 teaspoons olive oil
- 1 small brown onion (80g), chopped finely
- 3 cloves garlic, crushed
- 3 x 415g cans crushed tomatoes
- ⅓ cup coarsely chopped fresh basil
- ½ cup coarsely chopped fresh flat-leaf parsley
- 375g spaghetti

1 Heat oil in medium saucepan; cook onion and garlic, stirring, until onion softens. Add undrained tomatoes; bring to a boil. Reduce heat; simmer, uncovered, about 20 minutes or until reduced by about a third. Stir in herbs.

2 Meanwhile, cook pasta in large saucepan of boiling water, uncovered, until just tender; drain. Serve pasta topped with napoletana sauce.

PER SERVING 3.8g total fat (0.5g saturated); 1630kj (390 cal); 71.8g carbohydrate; 12.8g protein; 6.7g fibre

---

Hokkien mee noodles

Garnish these noodles with crisp fried shallots or garlic, which can be found in Asian supermarkets.

PREPARATION 15 MINUTES **COOKING TIME** 5 MINUTES **SERVES** 4

- 600g hokkien noodles
- 2 tablespoons vegetable oil
- 2 cloves garlic, crushed
- 2cm piece fresh ginger (10g), grated
- 3 fresh kaffir lime leaves, chopped finely
- 1 large red capsicum (350g), sliced thinly
- 6 green onions, chopped coarsely
- 500g baby buk choy, chopped coarsely
- 1 cup (80g) bean sprouts
- 1 teaspoon cornflour
- ⅓ cup (80ml) kecap manis
- 2 tablespoons sweet chilli sauce
- 1 teaspoon sesame oil
- 1 tablespoon water

1 Cover noodles with boiling water in large heatproof bowl; separate with fork, drain.

2 Meanwhile, heat vegetable oil in wok; stir-fry garlic, ginger, lime leaves, capsicum and buk choy about 2 minutes or until vegetables are almost tender.

3 Add onion, sprouts and noodles; stir-fry to combine. Blend cornflour with sauces, sesame oil and the water, add to wok; stir-fry until mixture boils and thickens slightly.

PER SERVING 12.8g total fat (1.7g saturated); 2312kj (553 cal); 86.1g carbohydrate; 18.8g protein; 7.0g fibre

For a meat version, combine ¼ cup pesto, 2 tablespoons roasted pine nuts and 500g Italian sausages (skin removed); add to the spinach mixture, with the cottage cheese reduced to 200g. Spoon the mixture into the shells.

Ricotta and spinach stuffed pasta shells

PREPARATION TIME 20 MINUTES **COOKING TIME** 1 HOUR 5 MINUTES **SERVES** 4

32 large pasta shells (280g)
500g spinach, trimmed
250g ricotta cheese
500g cottage cheese
600g bottled tomato pasta sauce
1 cup (250ml) vegetable stock
1 tablespoon finely grated parmesan

1 Preheat oven to moderate (180°C/160°C fan-forced). Oil shallow 2-litre (8-cup) ovenproof dish

2 Cook pasta in large saucepan of boiling water, uncovered, 3 minutes; drain. Cool 10 minutes.

3 Meanwhile, boil, steam or microwave spinach until just wilted; drain. Chop spinach finely; squeeze out excess liquid.

4 Combine spinach in large bowl with ricotta and cottage cheese; spoon spinach mixture into pasta shells.

5 Combine sauce and stock in dish; place pasta shells on top, sprinkle with parmesan. Bake, covered, about 1 hour or until pasta is tender.

PER SERVING 9.9g total fat (5.3g saturated); 2295kj (549 cal); 66.7g carbohydrate; 43g protein; 8.4g fibre

---

For a good chicken pie, add 500g chopped, cooked new potatoes instead of the fettuccine to the creamy chicken sauce with 200g cooked green peas. Spoon the chicken mixture into a deep pie dish, top with puff pastry; brush with beaten egg. Bake in a moderately hot oven for 20 minutes or until the pastry is puffed and brown.

Fettuccine boscaiola with chicken

PREPARATION TIME 10 MINUTES **COOKING TIME** 10 MINUTES **SERVES** 4

500g fettuccine
1 tablespoon olive oil
1 medium brown onion (150g), chopped finely
2 bacon rashers (140g), rind removed, chopped finely
200g mushrooms, sliced thinly
¼ cup (60ml) dry white wine
⅔ cup (160ml) cream
1 cup (250ml) milk
1 cup (170g) thinly sliced cooked chicken
¼ cup (20g) finely grated parmesan
2 tablespoons coarsely chopped fresh flat-leaf parsley

1 Cook pasta in large saucepan of boiling water, uncovered, until just tender; drain, reserving ½ cup of the cooking liquid.

2 Meanwhile, heat oil in large saucepan; cook onion, stirring, until soft. Add bacon and mushrooms; cook, stirring, 1 minute. Add wine, cream and milk; bring to a boil. Reduce heat; simmer, stirring, 5 minutes. Add chicken; stir until combined.

3 Add pasta, cheese, parsley and reserved cooking liquid to chicken mixture; stir until heated through.

PER SERVING 33.9g total fat (17.2g saturated); 3486kj (834 cal); 91.7g carbohydrate; 36.7g protein; 6.0g fibre

RICOTTA AND SPINACH STUFFED PASTA SHELLS

This sauce is also delicious served with pumpkin gnocchi or steaks, or to make a quick starter, put ½ canned pear in a ramekin, top with the sauce and some breadcrumbs and grill until golden.

Cheese and spinach tortellini with gorgonzola sauce

PREPARATION TIME 5 MINUTES **COOKING TIME** 15 MINUTES **SERVES** 4

30g butter
2 tablespoons plain flour
1 cup (250ml) hot milk
¾ cup (180ml) cream
100g gorgonzola cheese, chopped coarsely
750g cheese and spinach tortellini
¼ cup loosely packed fresh flat-leaf parsley leaves

1 Melt butter in medium saucepan, add flour; cook, stirring, until mixture thickens and bubbles. Gradually add milk and cream; cook, stirring, until mixture boils and thickens. Remove from heat; stir in cheese.
2 Meanwhile, cook pasta in large saucepan of boiling water, uncovered, until just tender; drain. Combine pasta and sauce in large bowl; serve pasta topped with parsley.

PER SERVING 49.3g total fat (31.8g saturated); 2876kj (688 cal); 36.5g carbohydrate; 23.6g protein; 3.6g fibre

---

This classic fried noodle dish has become a Thai "fast food", eaten by people all over the country for lunch and as a snack.

Sweet soy fried noodles

PREPARATION TIME 15 MINUTES **COOKING TIME** 15 MINUTES **SERVES** 4

1kg fresh wide rice noodles
2 teaspoons sesame oil
2 cloves garlic, crushed
2 fresh small red thai chillies, sliced thinly
600g chicken thigh fillets, chopped coarsely
250g baby buk choy, quartered lengthways
4 green onions, sliced thinly
2 tablespoons kecap manis
1 tablespoon oyster sauce
1 tablespoon fish sauce
1 tablespoon grated palm sugar
¼ cup coarsely chopped fresh coriander
1 tablespoon fried onion

1 Cover noodles with hot water in large heatproof bowl; separate with fork, drain.
2 Heat oil in wok; stir-fry garlic and chilli until fragrant. Add chicken; stir-fry until browned lightly. Add buk choy and green onion; stir-fry until chicken is cooked through.
3 Add noodles with kecap manis, sauces and sugar; stir-fry until heated through. Remove from heat; add coriander, tossing to combine. Serve noodles sprinkled with fried onion.

PER SERVING 9.9g total fat (2.2g saturated); 2052kj (491 cal); 59.8g carbohydrate; 38.2g protein; 2.8g fibre

Creamy farfalle with fried zucchini

PREPARATION TIME 10 MINUTES **COOKING TIME** 20 MINUTES **SERVES** 4

375g farfalle

2 tablespoons olive oil

3 cloves garlic, crushed

6 small zucchini (540g), grated coarsely

2 teaspoons finely grated lemon rind

1 tablespoon finely chopped fresh flat-leaf parsley

3 green onions, sliced thinly

½ cup (40g) finely grated parmesan

300ml cream

1 Cook pasta in large saucepan of boiling water, uncovered, until just tender; drain.

2 Meanwhile, heat oil in large frying pan; cook garlic, stirring, until fragrant. Add zucchini; cook, stirring, 2 minutes.

3 Combine rind, parsley, onion and cheese in small bowl.

4 Add cream and hot pasta to zucchini mixture; stir gently over low heat until heated through. Serve pasta topped with cheese mixture.

PER SERVING 46.3g total fat (25.0g saturated); 3227kj (772 cal); 68.8g carbohydrate; 17.7g protein; 5.9g fibre

For a seafood version, add 1 finely chopped fresh small red chilli with the garlic. Roast, grill or poach 400g salmon or ocean trout fillet and flake into the pasta.

Baked three-cheese pasta

PREPARATION TIME 10 MINUTES **COOKING TIME** 30 MINUTES **SERVES** 4

375g macaroni

300ml cream

⅓ cup (80ml) vegetable stock

1 ¼ cups (125g) grated fontina cheese

⅓ cup (75g) crumbled gorgonzola cheese

1 ¼ cups (100g) coarsely grated parmesan

1 teaspoon dijon mustard

2 tablespoons chopped flat-leaf parsley

1 tablespoon chopped fresh chives

1 Preheat oven to moderate (180°C/160°C fan-forced).

2 Cook pasta, uncovered, in large saucepan of boiling water until just tender; drain.

3 Meanwhile, heat cream and stock in medium saucepan until hot. Remove from heat, add fontina, gorgonzola and half of the parmesan; stir until melted. Add mustard and herbs. Combine cream mixture with drained pasta.

4 Pour pasta mixture into 2.5-litre (10-cup) ovenproof dish; top with remaining parmesan. Bake, uncovered, 20 minutes or until browned.

PER SERVING 56.1g total fat (36.1g saturated); 3804kj (910 cal); 66.4g carbohydrate; 33.9g protein; 3.3g fibre

This sauce makes a memorable cauliflower cheese or pumpkin and potato gratin with a topping of 1 ½ cups stale breadcrumbs mixed with ½ cup roasted, finely chopped walnuts, 1 teaspoon fresh thyme and 30g melted butter.

RICE

Rice

Rice can be anything you want it to be: first course, main course, dessert, accompaniment; finger food, party dish or lunch for a toddler; exotic as you like – Chinese, Japanese, Thai, Italian, Spanish, Middle Eastern, Indian, Latin American – or motherly British rice pudding.

KINDS OF RICE

All rice is long-grained, medium-grained or short-grained. Within these three types there are many variations: brown, white, red, black, fragrant, soft-cooking, firm-cooking, creamy-cooking, sticky, quick-cooking and more.

TYPES OF GRAIN

LONG-GRAINED rice cooks to give the separate, fluffy grains required for rice as an accompaniment, and for pilafs, salads, stuffings and most savoury dishes.

MEDIUM-GRAINED rice is slightly more clingy than long-grain when cooked. It is ideal for rice croquettes and moulds, and also for eating with chopsticks. Special varieties are used for risotto (see arborio rice, page 380).

SHORT-GRAINED rice cooks to soft, moist grains that cling together, perfect for puddings and a good food for babies before they get teeth.

Note: Some rices are border-line medium/short types and may be labelled by either description. If you need short but can't find it, use medium. If you need medium but can't find it, use long for croquettes and moulds, short for puddings.

BUYING AND STORING RICE

You can now buy Australian rices in many of the special styles, such as arborio, basmati, jasmine and sushi, that were once available only as imports. The originals are still readily available too. Virtually all plain rices on the Australian market are produced here. We are fortunate as our rices are admired overseas for their flavour and high standard of purity.

White rice will keep in an airtight container in a cool, dry place for up to 2 years. The oil in the bran coating of brown rice and the bran nutrients of par-boiled rice shorten their storage time; they will keep in the same conditions as white rice for 6 months.

RICE COOKING METHODS

The aim is to cook the rice grains until tender but separate rather than stuck together in lumps. There are three main methods of achieving this.

BOILED RICE This method makes it very easy to keep the grains separate, but you do throw away some of the rice flavour with the cooking water. Bring a large saucepan of lightly salted water to a rolling boil (check proportions and cooking times in the chart below). Slowly sprinkle in the rice through your fingers, stir once then cook, uncovered, keeping the water at a brisk boil. Start testing after 10 minutes. The rice should be tender but firm in the centre, not mushy. Drain and run hot water through to separate the grains.

ABSORPTION METHODS These methods retain all the flavour of the rice. Rinse the rice in a sieve in several changes of cold water, rubbing it with your fingers to help dislodge surface starch. Bring to the boil twice as much water, by volume, as the amount of rice you want to cook, salt lightly, cover and bring to a brisk boil over high heat. Uncover and slowly sprinkle in the rice, keeping the heat high so the water does not go off the boil. Stir once, then cover again with a really tight-fitting lid and turn the heat very low, using a heat-spreading mat if necessary. Cook for 10 minutes; don't lift the lid. Remove from the heat, stand with the lid on for at least another 10 minutes, then fluff up with a fork.

Here is a slightly different method. Experiment with both, using the same saucepan, to see which you like best. Rinse the rice as above, place in a wide saucepan, add a pinch of salt and cold water to cover, and shake the pan gently from side to side to level the surface. Place the tip of your forefinger on the surface of the rice and add more cold water until it comes up to your first finger joint (this applies no matter what quantity you are cooking). Bring to the boil and cook until the water evaporates, leaving steam holes in the rice, then cover with a tight-fitting lid and turn the heat very low, using a heat-spreading mat if necessary. Cook for 10 minutes or until the rice is tender but firm in the centre. Don't lift the lid until the last minute or two of cooking, then quickly remove a few grains of rice to test and replace the lid immediately. When cooked, remove from the heat, stand with the lid on for 10 minutes, then fluff up with a fork.

COOKING TIMES FOR RICE

Note: we used an 830 watt microwave oven

WHITE RICE Method	Quantity of rice	Quantity of water	Cooking time
Absorption	1½ cups (300g)	3 cups/750ml	10 minutes
Microwave	1½ cups (300g)	3 cups/750ml	10 minutes
Baked	1½ cups (300g)	2½ cups/625ml	25 minutes
Boiled	1½ cups (300g)	8 cups/2 litres	12 minutes

BROWN RICE Method	Quantity of rice	Quantity of water	Cooking time
Absorption	1½ cups (300g)	3½ cups/875ml	30 minutes
Microwave	1½ cups (300g)	3½ cups/875ml	25 minutes
Baked	1½ cups (300g)	3½ cups/875ml	1 hour
Boiled	1½ cups (300g)	8 cups/2 litres	25 minutes

WILD RICE Method	Quantity of rice	Quantity of water	Cooking time
Absorption	½ cup (100g)	1½ cups/375ml	40 minutes
Microwave	½ cup (100g)	2 cups/500ml	25 minutes
Baked	½ cup (100g)	½ cup/125ml	30 minutes
Boiled	½ cup (100g)	4 cups/1 litre	20 minutes

For a lamb pilaf, marinate 450g lamb backstrap, cut into bite-sized pieces, in the spices for 30 minutes. Brown the lamb in batches; set aside. Add the garlic then the rice and follow the recipe. Stir in the lamb with the nuts, adding 2 tablespoons chopped mint. This may sound strange, but a delicious addition is some chopped fresh paw paw.

Tunisian spicy nut pilaf

PREPARATION TIME 10 MINUTES **COOKING TIME** 20 MINUTES (PLUS STANDING TIME) **SERVES** 4

2 tablespoons ghee
1 clove garlic, crushed
2 teaspoons ground cinnamon
pinch saffron threads
1 tablespoon ground cumin
1 tablespoon ground coriander
2 cups (400g) basmati rice
2 cups (500ml) vegetable stock
2 cups (500ml) water
2 large brown onions (400g), sliced thinly
2 medium carrots (240g), sliced thickly
¼ cup (35g) roasted shelled pistachios
¼ cup (40g) roasted pine nuts

1 Melt half of the ghee in large saucepan; cook garlic and spices, stirring, until fragrant. Stir in rice; cook, stirring, 1 minute.
2 Stir in stock and the water; bring to a boil. Reduce heat; simmer, covered, 15 minutes or until rice is just tender. Remove from heat; stand, covered, 10 minutes.
3 Meanwhile, melt remaining ghee in medium frying pan; cook onion, stirring, until browned lightly. Remove from pan.
4 Cook carrot in same pan, stirring, until just tender.
5 Stir onion, carrot and nuts into pilaf.

☐ **PER SERVING** 21.3g total fat (7.0g saturated); 2571kj (615 cal); 90.0g carbohydrate; 12.9g protein; 5.0g fibre

---

We used a 930-watt microwave oven for this recipe. Increase the cooking time if the wattage of your oven is lower, or reduce the cooking time if it is higher.

Microwave mushroom risotto

PREPARATION TIME 10 MINUTES **COOKING TIME** 30 MINUTES **SERVES** 4

40g butter
1 medium brown onion (150g), chopped coarsely
2 cloves garlic, crushed
2 cups (400g) arborio rice
250g button mushrooms, quartered
250g swiss brown mushrooms, halved
½ cup (125ml) dry white wine
2 cups (500ml) chicken stock
1¾ cups (430ml) boiling water
2 green onions, sliced thinly
¼ cup (20g) finely grated parmesan
1 tablespoon olive oil

1 Place the butter, brown onion and garlic in large microwave-safe bowl; cook on high (100%) about 2 minutes or until onion softens. Add rice and mushrooms, stir well. Cook, covered, on high for 3 minutes.
2 Add the wine; cook, uncovered, on high for 2 minutes. Add stock and the water, stir well. Cook, covered, on high about 20 minutes or until rice is just tender, stirring every 5 minutes.
3 Stir in green onion, cheese and oil.

☐ **PER SERVING** 15.7g total fat (7.4g saturated); 2320kj (555 cal); 83.7g carbohydrate; 13.4g protein; 3.5g fibre

Chicken jambalaya

PREPARATION TIME 15 MINUTES **COOKING TIME** 30 MINUTES **SERVES** 4

There are many recipes for jambalaya, a creole dish from New Orleans. You can use prawns, crab, chicken or ham instead of the sausages.

1 tablespoon olive oil

1 medium brown onion (150g), chopped coarsely

1 medium red capsicum (200g), chopped coarsely

1 clove garlic, crushed

2 trimmed celery stalks (200g), sliced thinly

2 fresh small red thai chillies, sliced thinly

1½ cups (300g) basmati and wild rice blend

½ cup (125ml) dry white wine

2½ cups (625ml) chicken stock

425g can crushed tomatoes

1 tablespoon tomato paste

700g chicken and herb sausages

⅓ cup coarsely chopped fresh coriander

1 Heat oil in large saucepan; cook onion, capsicum, garlic, celery and chilli, stirring, until vegetables soften. Stir in rice, wine, stock, undrained tomatoes and paste; bring to a boil. Reduce heat; simmer, covered, about 20 minutes or until liquid is absorbed.

2 Meanwhile, cook sausages in large frying pan, uncovered, until browned and cooked through. Drain on absorbent paper; slice thickly.

3 Stir sausage and coriander into jambalaya just before serving.

PER SERVING 45.5g total fat (14.3g saturated); 3566kj (853 cal); 73g carbohydrate; 29.7g protein; 8.6g fibre

---

Oven-baked risotto with italian sausages

PREPARATION TIME 15 MINUTES **COOKING TIME** 40 MINUTES **SERVES** 6

Risotto is one rice dish where it's important not to wash the rice, as it would remove the starch that helps make risotto creamy.

1 litre (4 cups) chicken stock

6 spicy italian-style sausages (500g)

1 tablespoon olive oil

40g butter

2 large brown onions (400g), chopped coarsely

1 clove garlic, crushed

2 cups (400g) arborio rice

¾ cup (180ml) dry white wine

1 cup (150g) drained semi-dried tomatoes

¼ cup loosely packed fresh basil leaves

¼ cup (20g) finely grated parmesan

1 Preheat oven to moderate (180°C/160°C fan-forced).

2 Bring stock to a boil in medium saucepan. Reduce heat; simmer, covered.

3 Meanwhile, heat large flameproof casserole dish on stovetop; cook sausages, uncovered, until browned all over and cooked through. Remove from dish; slice thickly.

4 Heat oil and butter in same dish; cook onion and garlic, stirring, until soft. Add rice; stir to coat in butter mixture. Add wine; bring to a boil. Reduce heat; simmer, uncovered, 1 minute. Add stock, sausages and tomato, cover; bake about 25 minutes or until liquid is absorbed and rice is tender, stirring halfway through cooking.

5 Stir in basil and cheese.

PER SERVING 36.8g total fat (14.4g saturated); 3114kj (745 cal); 69.0g carbohydrate; 27.6g protein; 5.5g fibre

Dolmades

PREPARATION TIME 30 MINUTES **COOKING TIME** 1 HOUR 20 MINUTES (PLUS COOLING TIME) **MAKES** 24

300g packet grapevine leaves in brine

1 tablespoon lemon juice

¾ cup (180ml) water

1 tablespoon olive oil

FILLING

¼ cup (60ml) olive oil

1 medium brown onion (150g), chopped finely

2 tablespoons pine nuts

½ cup (100g) white medium-grain rice

2 tablespoons dried currants

½ cup (125ml) water

2 tablespoons finely chopped fresh flat-leaf parsley

1 Make filling.

2 Rinse vine leaves under cold water; drain well. Place vine leaves, vein-side up, on bench, place rounded teaspoons of the filling on each leaf; roll up firmly, folding in sides.

3 Place any torn or small leaves on bottom of heavy-based medium saucepan; place dolmades, in single layer, in pan. Add juice, water and oil. Place a heatproof plate on top of dolmades; bring to a boil. Simmer, covered, 1 hour or until dolmades are cooked.

FILLING Heat oil in medium saucepan; cook onion, stirring, until soft. Add nuts; cook, stirring, until browned lightly. Add rice and currants; stir to coat rice in onion mixture. Add the water; bring to a boil. Reduce heat; simmer, covered, about 10 minutes or until liquid is absorbed. Remove pan from heat; cool 15 minutes. Stir in parsley.

PER ROLL 3.9g total fat (0.5g saturated); 242kj (58 cal); 4.4g carbohydrate; 1.0g protein; 0.8g fibre

The dolmades are cooked, seam-side down, to prevent them from opening during cooking. If the plate is a light one, weight it with a can of food lying on its side.

If you have access to a grapevine in springtime, by all means use the fresh leaves when making dolmades. Harvest only the most tender and same-size leaves; submerge them, one at a time, in boiling water to make pliable, then pat dry with absorbent paper before filling them as instructed in step 2.

Yellow coconut rice

PREPARATION TIME 5 MINUTES (PLUS STANDING TIME) **COOKING TIME** 15 MINUTES **SERVES** 4

1¾ cups (350g) white long-grain rice

1¼ cups (310ml) water

1⅔ cups (410ml) coconut cream

1 teaspoon white sugar

½ teaspoon ground turmeric

pinch saffron threads

1 Soak rice in large bowl of cold water for 30 minutes. Pour rice into strainer; rinse under cold water until water runs clear. Drain.

2 Place rice and remaining ingredients in large heavy-based saucepan, cover; bring to a boil, stirring occasionally. Reduce heat; simmer, covered, about 15 minutes or until rice is tender. Remove from heat; stand, covered, 5 minutes.

PER SERVING 21.7g total fat (18.7g saturated); 2207kj (528 cal); 74g carbohydrate; 7.8g protein; 2.5g fibre

In Tanzania they make an aromatic yellow rice by replacing the saffron with ¼ teaspoon each of ground cinnamon, ground clove and ground cardamon.

DOLMADES

As the name suggests california rolls were adaptated from traditional Japanese sushi rolls by American chefs, using cooked fish such as crab and tuna. For many people in the West, california rolls were their first introduction to this style of food, before Japanese-style sushi became so popular.

California handrolls

PREPARATION TIME 45 MINUTES **MAKES** 40

- 10 sheets toasted seaweed (yaki-nori)
- ⅓ cup (100g) mayonnaise
- 1 teaspoon wasabi paste
- ¼ portion sushi rice (page 382)
- 60g cooked crab, shredded coarsely
- 1 lebanese cucumber (130g), seeded, sliced thinly
- 1 small avocado (200g), sliced thinly
- 1 small red capsicum (150g), sliced thinly

1 Cut each sheet of seaweed into four squares. Combine mayonnaise and wasabi in small bowl.

2 Place a quarter sheet of seaweed, shiny-side down, diagonally across palm of left hand. Dip fingers of right hand in bowl of vinegared water; shake off excess. Mould rounded teaspoons of rice into oblong shape; place across centre of seaweed. Wet fingers; gently rake rice evenly over seaweed, making a slight groove down the middle of the rice for filling. Using finger, swipe a dab of wasabi mayonnaise along the groove, top with a little crab, cucumber, avocado and capsicum.

3 Fold one side of seaweed over; fold other side of seaweed over the first to form a cone. Tip of cone can be folded back to hold cone shape securely.

PER HANDROLL 0.8g total fat (0.1g saturated); 100kj (24 cal); 3.8g carbohydrate; 0.3g protein; 0.1g fibre

---

To make great fried rice you must stir-fry over as high a heat as possible in the briefest amount of time, so it is important that all ingredients are prepared and ready for use before you begin to heat your wok. Cook the rice the day before you make the recipe; you'll need 1⅓ cups uncooked rice to make this quantity of cooked rice.

Chicken and thai basil fried rice

PREPARATION TIME 15 MINUTES **COOKING TIME** 10 MINUTES **SERVES** 4

- ¼ cup (60ml) peanut oil
- 1 medium brown onion (150g), chopped finely
- 3 cloves garlic, crushed
- 2 long green chillies, chopped finely
- 1 tablespoon brown sugar
- 500g chicken breast fillets, chopped coarsely
- 2 medium red capsicums (400g), sliced thinly
- 200g green beans, trimmed, chopped coarsely
- 4 cups cooked jasmine rice
- 2 tablespoons fish sauce
- 2 tablespoons light soy sauce
- ½ cup loosely packed fresh thai basil leaves

1 Heat oil in wok; stir-fry onion, garlic and chilli until onion softens. Add sugar; stir-fry until dissolved. Add chicken; stir-fry until browned lightly. Add capsicum and beans; stir-fry until vegetables are just tender and chicken is cooked through.

2 Add rice and sauces; stir-fry to combine. Remove from heat, stir in basil leaves.

PER SERVING 20.3g total fat (4.2g saturated); 4473kj (1070 cal); 172.8g carbohydrate; 44.0g protein; 5.1g fibre

1 CALIFORNIA HANDROLLS **2** CHICKEN AND THAI BASIL FRIED RICE **3** COMBINATION FRIED RICE [P 378] **4** ROASTED EYE FILLET WITH RED WINE RISOTTO [P 378]

1

2

3

4

One of the secrets of perfect fried rice is that the rice needs to be cold. Frozen rice is particularly good for frying: after it has partially thawed, break the rice apart and spread it on sheets of absorbent paper before you start cooking. You will need 1 ⅓ cups uncooked rice to make the required quantity of cooked rice.

Combination fried rice

PREPARATION TIME 10 MINUTES (PLUS REFRIGERATION TIME)
COOKING TIME 10 MINUTES (PLUS COOLING TIME) **SERVES** 4

- 2 teaspoons peanut oil
- 3 eggs, beaten lightly
- 1 tablespoon peanut oil, extra
- 2 cloves garlic, crushed
- 2cm piece fresh ginger (10g), grated
- 6 green onions, sliced thinly
- 4 cups cooked white long-grain rice
- 200g cooked shelled small king prawns
- 200g chinese barbecued pork, sliced thinly
- 3 chinese sausages (100g), sliced thinly
- ¾ cup (90g) frozen peas, thawed
- 1 cup (80g) bean sprouts
- 2 tablespoons light soy sauce

1 Heat half of the oil in wok, add half of the egg; swirl wok so egg forms an omelette over base. Cook omelette until set; remove, cool 5 minutes. Repeat with remaining oil and remaining egg. Roll omelettes; slice thinly.

2 Heat extra oil in same wok; stir-fry garlic, ginger and onion until fragrant. Add rice, omelette, prawns, pork, sausage, peas, sprouts and sauce; stir-fry until heated through.

PER SERVING 5.7g total fat (1.8g saturated); 594kj (142 cal); 13.6g carbohydrate; 8.4g protein; 1.3g fibre

---

Never add cold stock to hot rice as the rice will not absorb it and won't cook properly. Keep the stock simmering slowly while adding it to the rice, to help maintain a constant cooking temperature.

Roasted eye fillet with red wine risotto

PREPARATION TIME 15 MINUTES **COOKING TIME** 40 MINUTES (PLUS STANDING TIME) **SERVES** 4

- 500g piece beef eye fillet
- 1 tablespoon olive oil
- 1 teaspoon cracked black pepper
- ¼ cup (60ml) dry red wine
- ½ cup (125ml) beef stock

RED WINE RISOTTO

- 3 cups (750ml) vegetable stock
- 40g butter
- 1 medium brown onion (150g), chopped finely
- 1 cup (200g) arborio rice
- 1 cup (250ml) dry red wine
- ¼ cup (20g) finely grated parmesan
- 3 green onions, sliced thinly

1 Preheat oven to moderately hot (200°C/180°C fan-forced).

2 Trim excess fat from beef; tie beef with kitchen string at 3cm intervals. Place beef in lightly oiled shallow flameproof baking dish; brush all over with oil, sprinkle with pepper. Roast, uncovered, about 20 minutes or until cooked as desired.

3 Meanwhile, make red wine risotto.

4 Remove beef from dish, cover; stand 10 minutes. Place baking dish over low heat, add wine; simmer, stirring, about 2 minutes or until mixture reduces by half. Add stock; bring to a boil, stirring. Strain sauce into small jug. Serve sliced beef with red wine risotto, drizzled with sauce.

RED WINE RISOTTO Bring stock to a boil in medium saucepan, then simmer, covered. Heat half of the butter in large saucepan; cook brown onion, stirring, until softened. Add rice; stir to coat rice in butter mixture. Add wine; bring to a boil. Reduce heat; simmer, stirring, 2 minutes. Stir in ½ cup of the simmering stock; cook, stirring, over low heat, until liquid is absorbed. Continue adding stock mixture, in ½-cup batches, stirring until absorbed after each addition. Total cooking time will be about 35 minutes or until rice is just tender. Add cheese, remaining butter and green onion; stir until butter melts.

PER SERVING 22.9g total fat (10.7g saturated); 2404kj (575 cal); 43.5g carbohydrate; 35.1g protein; 1.1g fibre

---

Paella

PREPARATION TIME 20 MINUTES (PLUS STANDING TIME) **COOKING TIME** 40 MINUTES **SERVES** 4

The traditional pan for this recipe is shallow and wide. If you don't have a paella pan or a large enough frying pan, use two smaller frying pans as the mixture should be only about 4cm deep. This recipe is best made as close to serving as possible.

- 500g clams
- 1 tablespoon coarse cooking salt
- 300g uncooked medium king prawns
- 500g small black mussels
- pinch saffron threads
- ¼ cup (60ml) water
- 2 tablespoons olive oil
- 2 chicken thigh fillets (220g), chopped coarsely
- 200g chorizo sausage, sliced thinly
- 1 large red onion (300g), chopped finely
- 1 medium red capsicum (200g), chopped finely
- 2 cloves garlic, crushed
- 2 teaspoons sweet paprika
- 1½ cups (300g) short-grain rice
- 3½ cups (875ml) chicken stock
- 1 cup (120g) frozen peas
- 2 medium tomatoes (300g), peeled, seeded, chopped finely

1 Rinse clams under cold water; place in large bowl. Sprinkle with salt, cover with cold water; stand for 2 hours. This purges them of any grit. Discard water then rinse clams thoroughly; drain.
2 Shell and devein prawns, leaving tails intact. Scrub mussels; remove beards. Combine saffron and the water in small bowl; stand for 30 minutes.
3 Heat oil in 40cm-wide shallow pan; cook chicken, uncovered, until browned; remove chicken. Cook chorizo in same pan, stirring, until browned; drain on absorbent paper. Cook onion, capsicum, garlic and paprika in same pan, stirring, until onion softens. Add rice; stir to coat in onion mixture. Return chicken and chorizo to pan; stir to combine.
4 Stir in stock and saffron mixture; bring to a boil. Reduce heat; simmer, uncovered, about 12 minutes or until rice is almost tender. Sprinkle peas and tomato over rice; simmer, uncovered, 3 minutes.
5 Place clams, mussels and prawns on rice mixture. Cover pan with foil; simmer about 5 minutes or until clams and mussels have opened and prawns are cooked. Discard any unopened shells.

The Spanish grow two varieties of short-grain rice especially for paella: calasparra and bomba. Seek these out if you wish but feel confident that using locally grown arborio rice will make a very satisfactory paella.

PER SERVING 19.7g total fat (6.8g saturated); 2780kj (665 cal); 71.8g carbohydrate; 47.3g protein; 4.6g fibre

Rice

This staple is one of the good carbohydrates that we should eat often: each grain is a package of health and energy.

ARBORIO
The best-known of the Italian risotto rices (the others are Carnaroli and Vialone), which give risotto its creaminess and tender, but not mushy, consistency.

JASMINE
A fragrant, long-grain Thai rice, now also grown in Australia, jasmine rice is the perfect accompaniment for South-East Asian food. It should be cooked by the absorption method to preserve its delicate perfume and taste.

BASMATI
A fragrant long-grain rice imported from Pakistan and also now grown in Australia. It should be cooked by the absorption method so that its warm aroma and taste are preserved.

GLUTINOUS
Also known as sticky rice, with short, fat, distinctively flavoured grains that cling together when cooked, so it is easily formed into small balls to dip into savoury dishes to soak up the sauce.

NISHIKI
A medium-grain rice which, like Koshihikari (above) cooks to the tender, soft and lightly clinging texture that is right for sushi. A Japanese variety now grown in California and available here from Asian food stores.

WILD RICE BLEND
A packaged mixture of white long-grain and dark brown wild rice. The latter has a distinctively crunchy, resilient texture that contrasts nicely with the softer white rice.

WILD
Not a member of the rice family at all but the seed of a flowering aquatic grass native to the cold climates of North America. The dark-brown, almost black, long grain has a nutty flavour.

BLACK
Also known as purple rice, black rice is un-milled, leaving the dark husk in place which colours the grain when cooked. It has a nutty flavour and crunchy texture. There are hundreds of varieties of black rice across Asia.

KOSHIHIKARI
Rice with small, round grains which cook to tender softness with just enough cling to be eaten with chop-sticks. Perfect for sushi and rice desserts. Sold as "sushi rice".

LONG-GRAIN
The right rice for most savoury uses. When cooked, it gives the separate, fluffy grains needed for rice as a plain accompaniment, for rice salads and stuffings and for Indian, Middle Eastern, Italian and Spanish dishes.

CALROSE
A medium-grain variety developed by Australian growers, Sunrice, as an all-purpose rice that can substitute for either short- and long-grain. White Calrose is medium-soft and slightly clingy; brown Calrose is firm, slightly chewy and separated.

BROWN
Brown rice has had the outer hull removed but retains the nutritious, nutty-tasting bran coating that covers the white inner grain. It takes longer to cook than white rice, has a chewier texture and the grains stay separate.

Adding too much stock towards the end of cooking can result in overcooked risotto. Start checking the rice at about 15 minutes and continue cooking until "al dente", which means that the rice is still firm to the bite

Prawn and asparagus risotto

PREPARATION TIME 30 MINUTES **COOKING TIME** 50 MINUTES **SERVES** 6

1.5kg uncooked medium king prawns

500g asparagus, trimmed

1.5 litres (6 cups) chicken stock

1½ cups (375ml) dry white wine

30g butter

2 cloves garlic, crushed

1 large brown onion (200g), chopped finely

3 cups (600g) arborio rice

2 medium tomatoes (300g), seeded, chopped finely

⅓ cup coarsely chopped fresh flat-leaf parsley

1 Shell and devein prawns, leaving tails intact. Cut asparagus diagonally into 3cm lengths.
2 Combine stock and wine in large saucepan; bring to a boil, then simmer, covered.
3 Melt butter in large saucepan; cook garlic and onion, stirring, until onion softens. Add rice; stir to coat in butter mixture. Stir in 1 cup of the hot stock mixture; cook, stirring, over low heat until liquid is absorbed. Continue adding stock mixture, in 1-cup batches, stirring, until liquid is absorbed after each addition. Total cooking time should be about 35 minutes or until rice is just tender.
4 Add prawns, asparagus, tomato and parsley; cook, stirring, until prawns are just changed in colour and asparagus is tender.

PER SERVING 6.5g total fat (3.4g saturated); 2487kj (595 cal); 84.1g carbohydrate; 37.4g protein; 2.7g fibre

The success of sushi largely depends on perfectly cooked sumeshi – cooled vinegared rice. Use short-grain rice such as Australian-grown koshihikari or the nishiki variety from California. These varieties have the ideal texture and consistency to just stick together without being gluggy. If you use medium-grain rice, you may need to add a little more water.

Sushi rice

PREPARATION TIME 10 MINUTES (PLUS DRAINING TIME)
COOKING TIME 12 MINUTES (PLUS STANDING TIME) **MAKES** 9 CUPS

3 cups (600g) white short-grain rice

3 cups (750ml) water

SUSHI VINEGAR

½ cup (125ml) rice vinegar

¼ cup (55g) caster sugar

½ teaspoon salt

1 Place rice in large bowl, fill with cold water, stir with hand; drain. Repeat process until water is almost clear. Drain rice in strainer or colander at least 30 minutes.
2 Meanwhile, make sushi vinegar.
3 To cook rice in rice cooker: place drained rice and the water in rice cooker, cover; switch onto "cook". When cooker automatically switches to "keep warm" position, allow rice to stand, covered, 10 minutes.
4 To cook rice in saucepan: place drained rice and the water in medium saucepan, cover tightly; bring to a boil. Reduce heat; simmer, covered, about 10 minutes or until water is absorbed. Remove from heat; allow rice to stand, covered, 10 minutes.
5 Spread rice in large, non-metallic flat-bottomed bowl or wooden tub. Using rice paddle, large flat wooden spoon or plastic spatula, repeatedly slice through the rice at a sharp angle to break up lumps and separate grains, gradually pouring in the sushi vinegar at the same time. Not all of the vinegar may be required; the rice shouldn't be too wet or mushy.

6 Continue to slice (don't stir because it crushes the rice grains) with one hand, lifting and turning the rice from the outside into the centre (this action is similar to folding beaten egg whites into a cake or soufflé mixture).

7 Meanwhile, using the other hand, fan the rice until it is almost cool; this will take about 5 minutes (an electric fan, on the low setting, can be used instead of a hand-held fan if you prefer). Do not over-cool rice or it will harden. Performing these two actions together will give you glossy, slightly sticky but still separate sushi rice. Keep the rice covered with a damp cloth to stop it drying out while making sushi.

SUSHI VINEGAR Stir ingredients in small bowl until sugar dissolves. To make this mixture slightly less astringent, heat it gently just before using.

When preparing the sushi rice you can add either a little mirin or sake to the sushi vinegar mixture if you like, or you can use ½ cup ready-made sushi vinegar (see page 382).

PER CUP 0.3g total fat (0.1g saturated); 1091kj (261 cal); 58.8g carbohydrate; 4.4g protein; 0.5g fibre

---

Tuna and cucumber mini maki

PREPARATION TIME 30 MINUTES **MAKES** 48

- 4 sheets toasted seaweed (yaki-nori)
- ¼ portion sushi rice (page 382)
- 2 teaspoons wasabi paste
- 120g piece sashimi tuna, cut into 5mm strips
- 1 lebanese cucumber (130g), seeded, cut into thin strips
- ¼ cup (60ml) japanese soy sauce

1 Fold one sheet of seaweed in half parallel with lines marked on rough side of sheet; cut along fold. Place a half sheet, shiny-side down, lengthways across bamboo mat about 2cm from edge closest to you.

2 Dip fingers in bowl of vinegared water; shake off excess. Mould ¼ cup of the rice into oblong shape; place across centre half of seaweed.

3 Wet fingers again; gently rake rice evenly over seaweed, leaving 2cm strip at far end of seaweed uncovered.

4 Using finger, swipe a dab of wasabi across centre of rice, flattening it out evenly. Place tuna strips, end to end, in a row over wasabi across centre of rice; repeat with cucumber.

5 Starting with edge closest to you, pick up mat with thumb and index finger of both hands; use remaining fingers to hold filling in place as you roll mat. Roll forward, pressing gently but tightly, wrapping seaweed around rice and filling. When roll is complete, the strip of uncovered seaweed will stick to the roll to form a join.

6 Unroll mat; place sushi roll, join-down, on board. Wipe very sharp knife with damp cloth; cut roll into six pieces of mini maki.

7 Working quickly, repeat process with remaining seaweed, rice, wasabi, tuna and cucumber. Serve mini maki with soy sauce and more wasabi, if desired.

PER MINI MAKI 0.2g total fat (0.1g saturated); 71kj (17 cal); 2.8g carbohydrate; 0.9g protein; 0.1g fibre

For a different filling combine two 170g cans drained crab meat, 500g ricotta, ¼ cup finely grated parmesan, finely grated rind of 1 lemon, 150g baby spinach, 2 tablespoons torn basil leaves and 1 egg white; mix well. Fill the flowers, following the remainder of the recipe.

Risotto-filled zucchini flowers

PREPARATION TIME 50 MINUTES **COOKING TIME** 50 MINUTES **MAKES** 48

- 1 cup (250ml) dry white wine
- 2 cups (500ml) vegetable stock
- ½ cup (125ml) water
- 1 tablespoon olive oil
- 1 small brown onion (80g), chopped finely
- 1 clove garlic, crushed
- 1 cup (200g) arborio rice
- 150g mushrooms, sliced thinly
- 2 trimmed silverbeet leaves (160g), chopped finely
- ¼ cup (20g) finely grated parmesan
- 48 tiny zucchini with flowers attached
- cooking-oil spray

1 Combine wine, stock and the water in large saucepan; bring to a boil. Reduce heat; simmer, covered.
2 Heat oil in large saucepan; cook onion and garlic, stirring, until onion softens. Add rice; stir to coat in onion mixture. Stir in 1 cup of the simmering stock mixture; cook, stirring, over low heat until liquid is absorbed. Continue adding stock mixture, in 1-cup batches, stirring, until liquid is absorbed after each addition. Total cooking time should be about 35 minutes or until rice is tender.
3 Stir in mushroom and silverbeet; cook until mushroom is just tender. Stir in cheese.
4 Remove and discard stamens from centre of flowers; fill flowers with risotto, twist petal tops to enclose filling.
5 Cook zucchini with flowers, in batches, on heated oiled grill plate (or grill or barbecue) until zucchini are just tender and risotto is heated through.

PER FLOWER 0.8g total fat (0.2g saturated); 125kj (30 cal); 3.8g carbohydrate; 1.0g protein; 0.6g fibre

---

Taking the name from Baltistan, a mountainous region in northern Pakistan, balti curries often use beef and are fairly similar to the curries of northern India – rich and aromatic rather than extremely spicy.

Balti biryani

PREPARATION TIME 20 MINUTES (PLUS REFRIGERATION AND STANDING TIME)
COOKING TIME 1 HOUR 30 MINUTES **SERVES** 4

- 750g beef skirt steak, diced into 2cm pieces
- ¾ cup (225g) balti curry paste
- 2 cups (400g) basmati rice
- 8 cloves garlic, unpeeled
- 1 tablespoon ghee
- 4 cardamom pods, bruised
- 4 cloves
- 1 cinnamon stick
- 3 green onions, sliced thinly
- 2 cups (500ml) beef stock
- ¾ cup (100g) roasted slivered almonds
- ¼ cup loosely packed fresh coriander leaves
- 2 fresh small red thai chillies, sliced thinly

1 Preheat oven to moderate (180°C/160°C fan-forced).
2 Combine beef and curry paste in medium bowl, cover; refrigerate 1 hour.
3 Meanwhile, place rice in medium bowl, cover with water; stand 30 minutes. Drain rice in strainer; rinse under cold water, drain.

4 Place garlic in small baking dish; roast, uncovered, about 20 minutes or until soft.
5 Melt ghee in large saucepan; cook cardamom, cloves, cinnamon and onion, stirring, until fragrant. Add beef mixture, reduce heat; simmer, covered, stirring occasionally, about 45 minutes or until beef is tender.
6 Add rice with stock to pan; simmer, covered, stirring occasionally, about 15 minutes or until rice is just tender.
7 Peel garlic; chop finely. Add garlic, almonds and coriander to biryani, cover; stand 5 minutes. Sprinkle biryani with chilli; serve with raita and naan, if desired.

PER SERVING 41.8g total fat (8.1g saturated); 4088kj (978 cal); 86.2g carbohydrate; 59g protein; 10g fibre

---

Cheesy rice croquettes

PREPARATION TIME 30 MINUTES (PLUS REFRIGERATION TIME) **COOKING TIME** 20 MINUTES **SERVES** 6

Don't have the oil too hot as the croquettes will colour too quickly, before the cheese is melted inside. Check by dropping a spoonful of the rice mixture into the oil; if it sizzles steadily and browns in 2 minutes, the oil is the right temperature. After deep-frying, the croquettes can be kept warm in a slow oven.

- 2 tablespoons olive oil
- 1 small brown onion (80g), chopped finely
- 1 clove garlic, crushed
- 300g pork and veal mince
- 400g can crushed tomatoes
- ½ cup (100g) white medium-grain rice
- 2 small chicken stock cubes
- 1½ cups (375ml) water
- 2 tablespoons tomato paste
- 1 tablespoon finely chopped fresh basil
- 3 cups (210g) stale breadcrumbs
- 100g piece mozzarella cheese
- ½ cup (75g) plain flour
- 2 eggs
- 2 tablespoons milk
- 1¼ cups (125g) packaged breadcrumbs
- vegetable oil, for deep-frying.

1 Heat olive oil in large saucepan; cook onion and garlic, stirring, until onion softens. Add mince; cook, stirring, until browned. Stir in undrained tomatoes, rice, crumbled stock cubes, the water, paste and basil; bring to a boil. Reduce heat; simmer, uncovered, about 12 minutes or until rice is tender and mixture is thick. Cool 10 minutes; stir in stale breadcrumbs. Refrigerate until cold.
2 Cut cheese into 1cm x 5cm pieces. Roll 2 tablespoons of the mince mixture into log, press one piece of the cheese in centre; re-mould mince mixture to enclose cheese. Repeat using remaining mince mixture and cheese.
3 Toss croquettes in flour, shake away excess. Dip into combined eggs and milk; coat in packaged breadcrumbs.
4 Heat vegetable oil in wok or large saucepan; deep-fry croquette, in batches, until browned and heated through. Drain on absorbent paper.

PER SERVING 25.1g total fat (6.7g saturated); 2516kj (602 cal); 63.2g carbohydrate; 28.4g protein; 4.3g fibre

Arancini, which means "little oranges" in Italian due to their golden colour, make an excellent finger food or light lunch with salad. The risotto mixture can be made a day ahead. Arancini can be fried several hours beforehand and reheated gently in a slow oven.

Arancini

PREPARATION TIME 20 MINUTES (PLUS COOLING TIME) **COOKING TIME** 45 MINUTES **MAKES** 18

2½ cups (625ml) salt-reduced chicken stock

1 tablespoon olive oil

1 small brown onion (80g), chopped finely

1 clove garlic, crushed

½ cup (100g) arborio rice

½ cup (125ml) dry white wine

½ cup (60g) frozen peas

40g ham, chopped finely

½ cup (40g) finely grated parmesan

100g piece mozzarella cheese

1 egg, beaten lightly

½ cup (75g) plain flour

1 egg, beaten lightly, extra

1 tablespoon milk

1 cup (100g) packaged breadcrumbs

vegetable oil, for deep-frying

1 Bring the stock to a boil in medium saucepan. Reduce heat; simmer, covered.

2 Heat olive oil in medium saucepan; cook onion and garlic, stirring, until onion softens. Add rice; stir to coat in onion mixture. Add wine; cook, stirring, until wine has evaporated.

3 Add about ⅓ cup of the simmering stock; cook, stirring, over low heat until stock is absorbed. Continue adding stock, in ⅓-cup batches, stirring, until stock is absorbed after each addition. Total cooking time should be about 35 minutes or until rice is just tender.

4 Stir in peas and ham. Remove from heat; stir in parmesan. Transfer risotto to medium bowl; cool 15 minutes.

5 Chop mozzarella into 18 cubes.

6 Stir egg into the risotto. Roll 2 rounded tablespoons of the risotto into balls; press a piece of mozzarella into the centre of each ball. Re-mould rice to cover cheese. Toss balls in flour; shake away excess. Dip into combined extra egg and milk, then coat in breadcrumbs.

7 Heat vegetable oil in wok or large saucepan; deep-fry arancini, in batches, until browned and heated through.

8 Drain on absorbent paper. Serve hot with lemon wedges, if desired

PER ARANCINI 8.5g total fat (2.3g saturated); 640kj (153 cal); 11.8g carbohydrate; 5.7g protein; 0.7g fibre

Risotto cakes with basil sauce and pancetta

PREPARATION TIME 20 MINUTES **COOKING TIME** 45 MINUTES **SERVES** 4

½ cup (125ml) dry white wine

1 medium brown onion (150g), chopped finely

1 clove garlic, crushed

1 cup (200g) arborio rice

3 cups (750ml) chicken stock

2 tablespoons finely chopped fresh flat-leaf parsley

2 tablespoons finely chopped fresh chives

2 tablespoons finely grated parmesan

1 egg white, beaten lightly

4 slices pancetta (60g)

4 oak-leaf lettuce leaves

BASIL SAUCE

1 teaspoon cornflour

1 teaspoon water

¾ cup (180ml) evaporated milk

2 tablespoons finely chopped fresh basil

Risotto cakes came about as a way of using up left-over risotto. It is far easier to shape the cakes when the mixture is cold. It is worth lining oven trays with baking paper to stop the cakes sticking.

1 Preheat oven to hot (220°C/200°C fan-forced).

2 Heat 2 tablespoons of the wine in large saucepan; cook onion and garlic, stirring, about 2 minutes or until onion softens.

3 Add rice and remaining wine; cook, stirring, about 3 minutes or until wine reduces by half. Stir in stock; bring to a boil. Reduce heat; simmer, covered, 15 minutes, stirring halfway through cooking. Remove from heat; stir in parsley, chives and cheese. Cool 15 minutes; stir in egg white. Using hands, shape risotto mixture into four patties.

4 Place pancetta on oven tray. Bake, uncovered, about 5 minutes or until crisp; drain on absorbent paper. Break pancetta into pieces.

5 Reduce oven temperature to moderate (180°C/160°C fan-forced).

6 Cook risotto cakes in large heated lightly oiled frying pan until browned both sides. Place cakes on oven tray; bake, uncovered, 10 minutes or until heated through.

7 Meanwhile, make basil sauce.

8 Serve risotto cakes on lettuce leaves. Drizzle with basil sauce; top with pancetta.

BASIL SAUCE Blend cornflour with the water in small saucepan; stir in milk. Stir over heat until mixture boils and thickens slightly; stir in basil.

PER SERVING 5.3g total fat (2.6g saturated); 5802kj (1388 cal); 49.1g carbohydrate; 15.3g protein; 1.9g fibre

RISOTTO CAKES WITH BASIL SAUCE AND PANCETTA

For a crunchy Asian-style salad, add 1 cubed Lebanese cucumber, ⅓ cup roasted unsalted cashews and 1 chopped red capsicum. Dress with the chilli lime dressing on page 427.

Prawn, snow pea and wild rice salad

PREPARATION TIME 20 MINUTES **COOKING TIME** 20 MINUTES **SERVES** 4

24 uncooked medium king prawns (1kg)

1½ cups (300g) basmati and wild rice blend

150g snow peas, trimmed, halved lengthways

1 small red onion (100g), sliced thinly

½ cup coarsely chopped fresh flat-leaf parsley

150g snow pea tendrils

RASPBERRY VINEGAR DRESSING

⅓ cup (80ml) raspberry vinegar

2 tablespoons olive oil

1 tablespoon dijon mustard

2 cloves garlic, crushed

2 tablespoons lemon juice

2 teaspoons white sugar

1 Shell and devein prawns, leaving tails intact.
2 Make raspberry vinegar dressing.
3 Cook rice in large saucepan of boiling water, uncovered, until tender; drain.
4 Meanwhile, boil, steam or microwave snow peas until just tender; drain.
5 Cook prawns on heated oiled grill plate (or grill or barbecue) until changed in colour.
6 Place rice, peas, prawns, onion, parsley and tendrils in large bowl with dressing and toss gently to combine.

RASPBERRY VINEGAR DRESSING Place ingredients in screw-top jar; shake well.

PER SERVING 10.5g total fat (1.5g saturated); 1430kj (342 cal); 26.3g carbohydrate; 32.8g protein; 4.4g fibre

---

One of the classic dishes of Italy, risotto milanese is traditionally served with osso buco (see page 225). It would also go superbly with barbecued meats and a green salad.

Risotto milanese

PREPARATION TIME 15 MINUTES **COOKING TIME** 40 MINUTES **SERVES** 2

3½ cups (875ml) chicken stock

½ cup (125ml) dry white wine

¼ teaspoon saffron threads

50g butter

1 large brown onion (200g), chopped finely

1¾ cups (350g) arborio rice

2 tablespoons finely grated parmesan

1 Bring stock, wine and saffron to a boil in medium saucepan, then simmer, covered.
2 Heat half of the butter in large saucepan; cook onion, stirring, until soft. Add rice; stir to coat in butter mixture. Stir in 1 cup of the simmering stock mixture; cook, stirring, over low heat until liquid is absorbed. Continue adding stock mixture in, 1-cup batches, stirring, until liquid is absorbed after each addition. Total cooking time should be about 35 minutes or until rice is tender.
3 Stir in cheese and remaining butter.

PER SERVING 25.5g total fat (16.0g saturated); 3971kj (950 cal); 147.1g carbohydrate; 20.7g protein; 2.7g fibre

Italian brown rice salad

PREPARATION TIME 15 MINUTES **COOKING TIME** 1 HOUR **SERVES** 4

Many people dismiss brown rice as being too "healthy" and complain that it takes too long to cook. Cooked correctly, brown rice is lovely and chewy with a delicious nutty flavour that can add so much to a dish.

- 3 cups (750ml) vegetable stock
- 2 teaspoons olive oil
- 1 small brown onion (80g), chopped finely
- 1 ½ cups (300g) brown medium-grain rice
- 1 teaspoon finely grated lime rind
- 1 clove garlic, crushed
- ⅓ cup (45g) roasted slivered almonds
- 100g sun-dried tomatoes, chopped coarsely
- ½ cup (60g) seeded black olives, chopped coarsely
- ½ cup coarsely chopped fresh basil
- ¼ cup coarsely chopped fresh flat-leaf parsley

LIME AND MUSTARD DRESSING

- 2 tablespoons lime juice
- 2 tablespoons white wine vinegar
- 2 cloves garlic, crushed
- 2 teaspoons dijon mustard

1 Place stock in medium saucepan; bring to a boil. Reduce heat; simmer, covered.

2 Heat oil in large saucepan; cook onion, stirring, until soft. Add rice, rind and garlic; stir to coat rice in onion mixture. Add stock; bring to a boil. Reduce heat; simmer, covered, about 50 minutes or until rice is tender and liquid is absorbed.

3 Make lime and mustard dressing.

4 Place rice in large bowl with remaining ingredients and dressing; toss to combine.

5 Serve salad topped with fresh flat-leaf parsley, if desired.

LIME AND MUSTARD DRESSING Place ingredients in screw-top jar; shake well.

PER SERVING 12.3 g total fat (1.9g saturated fat); 1923kj (460 cal); 72.4g carbohydrate; 13.5g protein; 8g fibre

PULSES & GRAINS

Pulses & Grains

If dried beans, peas and lentils (collectively known as pulses) and grain foods, including bread, are eaten together, they supply all the forms of protein needed in the diet. Today, chefs and home cooks alike prize these "foods of the poor" because they offer such nutritious, yet deeply enjoyable, eating.

PULSES

BEANS

- **Adzuki beans:** small, reddish-brown, thin-skinned, sweet flavour.
- **Black beans (turtle beans):** small, black, very savoury flavour.
- **Black-eyed beans (black-eyed peas):** small, cream with a black spot, mild flavour.
- **Borlotti beans:** pinky-brown marbled with dark red; savoury flavour, fluffy texture.
- **Broad beans (fava beans):** large, green/pale brown, tough-skinned, strong flavour.
- **Butter (lima) beans:** large or small, mild flavour, smooth texture.
- **Chickpeas:** really a bean; round and creamy-beige, robust nutty flavour, crisp texture.
- **Flageolet beans:** green variety, delicate flavour.
- **Ful medames (Egyptian brown beans):** small, thinner-skinned, nutty flavour.
- **Haricot (cannellini, navy, soisson) beans:** different varieties of mild-flavoured white beans, interchangeable with each other in recipes.
- **Kidney beans:** red, full flavour, mealy texture.
- **Mung beans:** black or green, sweetish flavour; the bean usually used for sprouts.
- **Pinto beans:** brown-speckled beige, similar in flavour and texture to kidney beans.
- **Soybeans:** a source of complete protein; has a mild yet distinctive flavour.

PEAS

- **Blue boilers:** whole peas, grey-green colour, used for mushy peas, pea and ham soup.
- **Split peas:** skinless, yellow or green, sweet, definite pea flavour.

LENTILS

- **Brown (green, Continental) lentils:** pale brown to greenish, various sizes, but are interchangeable; skin-on, keep their shape when cooked, warm, slightly spicy flavour.
- **Puy lentils:** small, dark blue-green, exceptionally fine in flavour and texture; originally from the Le Puy district in France, they are very expensive.
- **Red (Egyptian) lentils:** skinned and split, tiny, orange-red, spicy flavour, cook to a puree.

BUYING AND STORING PULSES

The best dried pulses are those from a recent harvest; in storage, they gradually harden and take longer to cook. Buy from a shop with a high turnover. Store in airtight containers in a cool, dry place for no more than a year. Many dried beans are available pre-cooked in cans; they are softer than home-cooked beans. Drain and rinse them before using.

COOKING PULSES

Dried beans and peas are best soaked before cooking, but lentils do not need soaking.

- **Overnight soaking:** Cover with cold water in a large bowl to allow for swelling, and stand in a cool place for 6 to 8 hours – no longer or they may ferment. Drain. If you wish, you can soak double or triple the amount of beans required for a particular recipe then freeze the well-drained remainder, in individual cup measures, for later use.
- **Quick soaking:** Cover generously with cold water in a large saucepan, bring to the boil, then cover and cook for 2 minutes. Remove from the heat and stand for 1 hour. Drain.
- To cook pulses, cover with cold water and bring to the boil. Do not add salt, sugar or other flavouring as this will toughen them; add these just before the end of cooking.
- Indigestible sugars in dried beans can cause intestinal gas when eaten. These sugars leach into the water during cooking, so you can reduce their presence by discarding the first lot of water when it boils and starting again. Once boiling, put the lid on, turn the heat to low and simmer until tender. Lentils may take 20 minutes or less to cook; beans and peas 1 to 2 hours or longer. When tender, drain and use according to the recipe. Cooked pulses can be stored, covered, in the fridge for 2 to 3 days.

GRAINS

- **Barley:** Pearl barley is the type usually used for cooking. The barley grains have had the husk removed and been steamed and polished. It has a robust, nutty flavour.
- **Buckwheat:** Not a true grain, but the fruit of a plant related to rhubarb and sorrel. It is, however, used as a grain, being cooked into a porridge or ground into a flour which is used for pancakes and noodles. Buckwheat is naturally white, but the hulled kernels are often roasted to make *kasha*, which is ground to various degrees of fineness.
- **Burghul:** Made from cracked wheat which is hulled, par-boiled or steamed so that it becomes lighter-textured and milder-flavoured, then dehydrated. It needs no further cooking but, before use, should be soaked in cold water to soften and swell the grains. It is then drained, squeezed as dry as possible and spread on a tea-towel or absorbent paper to dry further.
- **Couscous:** Fine semolina (the first, grainy millings of the floury part of wheat grains, called the endosperm). Traditionally, couscous is first moistened to allow the grains to swell, then steamed over the pot in which the meat and vegetables for the meal are simmering. Pre-cooked "instant" couscous is also available.
- **Polenta:** Cornmeal ground to various degrees of fineness. It is prepared by boiling with water to make a porridge. It can be eaten like this (soft or wet polenta) or spread in a shallow pan, chilled to firm it, then brushed with oil and grilled, pan-fried or barbecued. Pre-cooked "instant" polenta is also available.

If you are unable to buy ghee, also known as "clarified butter", make your own. Heat some butter in a small pan until a white foamy layer appears on the surface; skim and discard. Pour off the butter leaving the sediment (milk solids) at the bottom of the pan; discard. Ghee will keep for several months in the fridge.

Mixed dhal

PREPARATION TIME 15 MINUTES **COOKING TIME** 1 HOUR 15 MINUTES **SERVES** 8

3 tablespoons ghee

2 medium brown onions (300g), chopped finely

2 cloves garlic, crushed

4cm piece fresh ginger (20g), grated

2 tablespoons black mustard seeds

2 tablespoons ground cumin

1 tablespoon ground coriander

2 teaspoons ground turmeric

¾ cup (150g) brown lentils

¾ cup (150g) red lentils

¾ cup (150g) yellow split peas

¾ cup (150g) green split peas

2 x 400g cans crushed tomatoes

1 litre (4 cups) vegetable stock

⅔ cup (160ml) coconut cream

½ cup coarsely chopped fresh coriander

1 Heat ghee in large heavy-based saucepan; cook onion, garlic and ginger, stirring, until onion softens. Add seeds and spices; cook, stirring, until fragrant.

2 Add lentils and peas to pan; stir to combine. Add undrained tomatoes and stock; bring to a boil. Reduce heat; simmer, covered, about 1 hour or until lentils are tender and mixture thickens, stirring occasionally.

3 Add coconut cream and coriander; stir over low heat until dhal is heated through.

PER SERVING 13.9g total fat (9.0g saturated); 1618kj (387 cal); 38.7g carbohydrate; 21g protein; 11.2g fibre

---

In the US, chickpeas are commonly known as garbanzos. Other names for chickpeas are channa, ceci bean, hummus and bengal gram.

Felafel

PREPARATION TIME 30 MINUTES (PLUS REFRIGERATION TIME) **COOKING TIME** 15 MINUTES **SERVES** 4

¾ cup (110g) frozen broad beans, thawed, peeled

420g can chickpeas, rinsed, drained

⅓ cup coarsely chopped fresh flat-leaf parsley

1 small red onion (100g), chopped coarsely

⅓ cup (50g) plain flour

2 teaspoons ground coriander

1 teaspoon ground cumin

1 teaspoon bicarbonate of soda

1 Blend or process beans, chickpeas, parsley, onion, flour, coriander, cumin and soda until almost smooth.

2 Shape rounded tablespoons of the mixture into ball-shaped patties; place on tray. Cover; refrigerate 30 minutes.

3 Cook felafel on heated oiled flat plate (or grill pan) until browned both sides.

PER SERVING 1.9g total fat (0.3g saturated); 660kj (158 cal); 23.3g carbohydrate; 8.2g protein; 7g fibre

Hummus bi tahini

PREPARATION TIME 10 MINUTES (PLUS STANDING TIME) **COOKING TIME** 55 MINUTES **MAKES** 2 CUPS

A food processor is better than a blender to make a really smooth hummus.

¾ cup (150g) dried chickpeas

1 teaspoon salt

1 clove garlic, quartered

⅓ cup (90g) tahini

¼ cup (60ml) lemon juice

pinch cayenne pepper

1 tablespoon finely chopped fresh flat-leaf parsley

2 teaspoons olive oil

1 Place chickpeas in medium bowl, cover with cold water; stand overnight, drain.

2 Place in medium saucepan, cover with fresh water; bring to a boil. Reduce heat; simmer, covered, about 50 minutes or until chickpeas are tender. Drain chickpeas over large bowl. Reserve ⅓ cup chickpea liquid; discard remaining liquid.

3 Blend or process chickpeas with salt, garlic, tahini, juice and reserved liquid until almost smooth.

4 Serve hummus sprinkled with pepper and parsley and drizzled with oil.

You can replace the dried chickpeas with a 420g can of rinsed and drained chickpeas.

PER TABLESPOON 2.8g total fat (0.4g saturated); 150kj (36 cal); 1.1g carbohydrate; 1.3g protein; 0.9g fibre

---

Quartet of beans in chilli lime sauce

REPARATION TIME 10 MINUTES **COOKING TIME** 20 MINUTES **SERVES** 4

A quick way to remove garlic skins from individual cloves is to place the flat side of a chef's knife onto a whole clove of garlic, gently tapping the heel of your hand against the flat side of the knife. You can then slip the garlic skin away from the slightly crushed clove.

300g rice stick noodles

250g frozen broad beans, thawed

150g green beans, trimmed, halved

150g snake beans, trimmed, chopped coarsely

150g butter beans, trimmed

vegetable oil, for deep-frying

¼ cup (40g) drained capers, rinsed

1 tablespoon olive oil

6 cloves garlic, crushed

1 small red onion (100g), cut into thick wedges

3 fresh small red thai chillies, chopped coarsely

2 tablespoons finely grated lime rind

1 cup (250ml) vegetable stock

1 Place noodles in medium heatproof bowl, cover with boiling water; stand until just tender, drain. Rinse under cold water; drain.

2 Meanwhile, boil, steam or microwave beans, separately, until just tender; drain. Peel away grey-coloured outer shells from broad beans.

3 Heat vegetable oil in small frying pan; deep-fry capers until crisp. Drain.

4 Heat olive oil in wok or large frying pan; stir-fry garlic, onion, chilli and rind until onion softens. Add stock, beans and noodles; stir-fry until sauce thickens. Sprinkle with capers.

PER SERVING 5.9g total fat (0.9g saturated); 844kj (202 cal); 22.9g carbohydrate; 10.1g protein; 8.5g fibre

Soybean patties with lemon and herb yogurt

PREPARATION TIME 20 MINUTES **COOKING TIME** 25 MINUTES **SERVES** 4

Make fresh breadcrumbs using a food processor or blender. Place the breadcrumbs in sealable plastic bags and keep them in the freezer. For dried breadcrumbs simply place them on an oven tray in a slow oven for 15 minutes.

1 tablespoon olive oil

1 medium red onion (170g), chopped finely

1 medium red capsicum (200g), chopped finely

2 cloves garlic, crushed

3 cups (210g) stale breadcrumbs

2 x 300g cans soybeans, rinsed, drained

2 eggs

½ cup finely chopped fresh flat-leaf parsley

2 teaspoons finely grated lemon rind

¾ cup (60g) finely grated parmesan

⅓ cup (50g) roasted pine nuts

LEMON AND HERB YOGURT

200g yogurt

1 clove garlic, crushed

1 tablespoon lemon juice

2 tablespoons finely chopped fresh flat-leaf parsley

2 tablespoons finely chopped fresh chives

1 Preheat oven to hot (220°C/200°C fan-forced). Lightly oil oven tray.

2 Heat oil in medium saucepan; cook onion, capsicum and garlic until onion softens.

3 Process onion mixture, breadcrumbs, beans, eggs, parsley, rind and half of the cheese until just combined; stir in nuts.

4 Shape ⅓-cup measures of the mixture into patties. Place patties on tray; sprinkle with remaining cheese. Bake, uncovered, about 20 minutes or until browned lightly, turning halfway during cooking.

5 Meanwhile, make lemon and herb yogurt.

6 Serve patties with lemon and herb yogurt and steamed asparagus and rocket leaves, if desired.

LEMON AND HERB YOGURT Combine ingredients in small bowl.

PER SERVING 30.2g total fat (7.4g saturated); 2475kj (592 cal); 44.9g carbohydrate; 30.6g protein; 9.7g fibre

SOYBEAN PATTIES WITH LEMON AND HERB YOGURT

Megadarra, a pilaf-style dish, is often referred to as the poor man's food of the Middle East. However, it is both nutritious and delicious, and served with a salad like tabbouleh or fattoush, makes a totally satisfying meal.

Megadarra

PREPARATION TIME 10 MINUTES **COOKING TIME** 35 MINUTES **SERVES** 4

2 cups (400g) brown lentils

1.5 litres (6 cups) boiling water

¾ cup (150g) white long-grain rice

1.25 litres (5 cups) boiling water, extra

1 ½ teaspoons ground allspice

1 teaspoon ground coriander

2 teaspoons salt

CARAMELISED ONION

¼ cup (60ml) olive oil

4 large onions (800g), sliced thinly

2 teaspoons white sugar

½ cup (125ml) water

1 Place lentils and the water in large saucepan; bring to a boil. Reduce heat; simmer, uncovered, about 15 minutes or until lentils are just tender. Drain.

2 Meanwhile, make caramelised onion. Cover to keep warm.

3 Combine rice, the extra water and spices in medium saucepan. Add half of the caramelised onion; bring to a boil. Reduce heat; simmer, uncovered, 12 minutes. Add lentils and salt; simmer, uncovered, about 3 minutes or until liquid is just absorbed. Spoon megadarra into serving bowls; top with remaining caramelised onion.

CARAMELISED ONION Heat oil in large frying pan; cook onion and sugar, stirring, 5 minutes. Add half of the water; bring to a boil. Reduce heat; simmer, uncovered, about 5 minutes. Add remaining water; simmer, stirring, about 5 minutes or until onion caramelises.

PER SERVING 16g total fat (2.3g saturated); 2587kj (619 cal); 80.4g carbohydrate; 29.5g protein; 16.6g fibre

---

Burghul is also known as bulgar. Left-over salad makes a delicious stuffing for chicken, lamb or turkey: add a beaten egg and ½ cup stale breadcrumbs to help bind it together.

Burghul salad with chickpeas

PREPARATION TIME 20 MINUTES (PLUS STANDING TIME) **COOKING TIME** 10 MINUTES **SERVES** 4

1 large red capsicum (350g)

1 cup (160g) burghul

1 cup (250ml) boiling water

420g can chickpeas, rinsed, drained

1 trimmed celery stalk (100g), chopped finely

50g baby spinach leaves

SUMAC AND HERB DRESSING

1 tablespoon sesame seeds

2 tablespoons sumac

1 tablespoon fresh thyme leaves

1 tablespoon coarsely chopped fresh oregano

½ cup (125ml) lime juice

1 tablespoon olive oil

1 clove garlic, crushed

1 Quarter capsicum; discard seeds and membranes. Roast under grill or in very hot oven, skin-side up, until skin blisters and blackens. Cover capsicum pieces with plastic or paper for 5 minutes; peel away skin, then slice capsicum thinly.

2 Meanwhile, place burghul in medium bowl, cover with the boiling water; stand about 10 minutes or until tender.

3 Make sumac and herb dressing.

4 Place burghul and capsicum in large bowl with chickpeas, celery, spinach and dressing; toss gently to combine.

SUMAC AND HERB DRESSING Place ingredients in screw-top jar; shake well.

☐ **PER SERVING** 8.5g total fat (1.2g saturated); 1225kj (293 cal); 37.0g carbohydrate; 11.1g protein; 11.7g fibre

---

New york steaks with grilled cheesy polenta triangles

For mustard lovers, add 1 tablespoon wholegrain mustard and 1 teaspoon chopped thyme with the butter and cheese.

PREPARATION TIME 10 MINUTES (PLUS REFRIGERATION TIME) **COOKING TIME** 25 MINUTES **SERVES** 4

1 litre (4 cups) water

1 cup (170g) polenta

20g butter

100g provolone cheese, chopped finely

2 tablespoons red wine vinegar

⅓ cup (80ml) dry red wine

1 clove garlic, crushed

4 beef new york-cut steaks (880g)

ROCKET SALAD

¼ cup (60ml) olive oil

2 tablespoons red wine vinegar

1 tablespoon wholegrain mustard

1 teaspoon white sugar

100g baby rocket leaves

1 Oil 19cm x 29cm slice pan.

2 Place the water in large saucepan; bring to a boil. Gradually add polenta to liquid, stirring constantly. Reduce heat; cook, stirring, about 10 minutes or until polenta thickens. Stir in butter and cheese then spread polenta into pan; cool 10 minutes. Cover; then refrigerate overnight.

3 Combine vinegar, wine and garlic in large bowl, add beef; turn to coat beef in marinade. Cover; refrigerate overnight.

4 Turn polenta onto board; trim edges. Cut polenta into six squares; cut each square in half diagonally to form two triangles. Cook polenta triangles on heated oiled grill plate (or grill or barbecue) until heated through. Cover to keep warm.

5 Drain steaks and cook on same heated oiled grill plate until cooked as desired. Cover steaks; stand 5 minutes.

6 Make rocket salad.

7 Serve steaks with salad and polenta triangles; drizzle steaks with dressing reserved from the salad.

ROCKET SALAD Place oil, vinegar, mustard and sugar in screw-top jar; shake well. Place rocket and half of the dressing in large bowl; toss to combine. Reserve remaining dressing.

☐ **PER SERVING** 46g total fat (18.3g saturated); 3214kj (769 cal); 31.2g carbohydrate; 57.1g protein; 1.8g fibre

Pulses & grains

Yes, they're cheap and good for you, but the best reason for serving them is the world of splendid eating they offer.

ADZUKI BEANS
Small russet beans with a cream stripe. Thin-skinned and sweetish, they are used in Japan in a paste for desserts and cakes, and are also good in stews and for sprouting.

BLACK BEANS
Also called turtle beans. Their big, savoury flavour makes them the stars of Caribbean and Latin-American cooking, famously for black-bean soup. Not the same as Chinese black beans, which are salted, fermented soybeans.

BLACK-EYED BEANS
Also called black-eyed peas or cow peas. Mild-flavoured and thin-skinned, so they cook faster than most other beans. Often served in the American south with pork and cornbread.

HARICOT BEANS
The haricot bean family includes navy beans for Boston baked beans and soissons for French cassoulet as well as cannellini. All are mild-flavoured white beans which can be interchanged with each other.

BURGHUL
Best-known in the refreshing Middle Eastern salad, tabbouleh, burghul is hulled, steamed or par-boiled and dried cracked wheat ground to various degrees of fineness. Before use, it is soaked briefly in water to soften and swell the grains, then squeezed dry.

PUY LENTILS
From the Le Puy district in southern France, these tiny dark gray-green lentils are delicious and very expensive. Local versions are available, sold under the name of French green or Bondi lentils.

BROAD BEANS
Also called fava beans. Large and mealy-textured, found fresh and dried. Used with chickpeas for felafel. Ful medames (Egyptian brown beans) are a small, nutty-flavoured variety.

SPLIT PEAS
Yellow or green varieties, both with a sweet, strong pea flavour. Best known for pea and ham soup and for traditional pease pudding (mashed with butter, mint, parsley and eggs, then steamed) to serve with corned beef.

CHICKPEAS
Also called garbanzos, channa or hummus, prized for their full, nutty flavour and crisp texture. Essential for the Italian soup *pasta e ceci*, and for the Middle Eastern *hummus bi tahini*.

POLENTA
Also known as cornmeal, made from dried corn ground to various degrees of fineness. It is boiled with water to a porridge (soft polenta), which may be chilled, cut into shapes, oiled and grilled for grilled polenta.

COUSCOUS
The staple cereal of North Africa, made from fine semolina. It is steamed over the pot in which the meat and vegetables are cooking, or, for sweet couscous, over water, then mixed with sugar, nuts and fruits.

CANNELLINI BEANS
Small, white Italian members of the haricot bean family. Used in minestrone and other soups and in Tuscan dishes such as beans baked with pancetta and garlic or chilled beans with tuna.

Mexican broad bean burgers

PREPARATION TIME 30 MINUTES (PLUS REFRIGERATION TIME)
COOKING TIME 1 HOUR 20 MINUTES **SERVES** 6

Mexican cuisine uses beans in adventurous ways. This recipe is an example of how interesting and satisfying vegetarian food can be.

½ cup (100g) pearl barley

1kg frozen broad beans

1 medium white onion (150g), grated

1¾ cups (120g) stale breadcrumbs

2 eggs

1 tablespoon milk

100g cheese-flavoured corn chips, crushed finely

1 tablespoon olive oil

2 medium red onions (340g), sliced thinly

6 hamburger buns

1 cup (240g) refried beans

1 medium avocado (250g), sliced thinly

½ cup (120g) sour cream

½ cup (125ml) mild chilli sauce

SALSA

1 medium tomato (150g), chopped finely

1 small red onion (100g), chopped finely

1 tablespoon coarsely chopped fresh coriander

1 tablespoon lime juice

1 teaspoon caster sugar

1 Cook barley in large saucepan of boiling water, uncovered, about 40 minutes or until tender; drain.

2 Pour boiling water over beans in medium heatproof bowl. Stand 2 minutes; drain. Peel away grey-coloured outer shells from beans; blend or process beans until smooth.

3 Combine barley, bean puree, white onion, 1 cup of the breadcrumbs and one of the eggs in large bowl. Shape mixture into six patties; dip in combined milk and remaining egg. Press on combined corn chips and remaining breadcrumbs. Place patties on lightly oiled oven tray. Cover; refrigerate 1 hour.

4 Preheat oven to moderately hot (200°C/180°C fan-forced).

5 Remove patties from refrigerator and bake, uncovered, 25 minutes or until firm.

6 Meanwhile, make salsa.

7 Heat oil in small frying pan; cook red onion, stirring, until soft.

8 Split buns in half; toast buns, cut-side up, until browned lightly. Sandwich patties, heated beans, avocado, salsa, red onion, sour cream and sauce between buns.

SALSA Combine ingredients in small bowl.

PER SERVING 29.6g total fat (10.4g saturated); 3298kj (789 cal); 88.4g carbohydrate; 30.9g protein; 22.4g fibre

MEXICAN BROAD BEAN BURGERS

To give this couscous a lovely citrus flavour to complement fish, replace the water with 2 cups hot chicken stock and 1 cup hot orange juice. Stir in the rind of an orange with the almonds, currants and coriander.

Almond coriander couscous

PREPARATION TIME 10 MINUTES (PLUS STANDING TIME) **COOKING TIME** 10 MINUTES **SERVES** 6

3 cups (600g) couscous
3 cups (750ml) boiling water
¼ cup (60ml) olive oil
1 clove garlic, crushed
2 green onions, sliced thinly
¾ cup (110g) roasted slivered almonds
⅓ cup (55g) dried currants
½ cup coarsely chopped fresh coriander

1 Combine couscous with the water in large heatproof bowl, cover; stand 5 minutes or until water is absorbed, fluffing with fork occasionally.
2 Heat oil in large frying pan; cook garlic and onion, stirring, until onion softens. Add couscous; stir until heated through. Stir in remaining ingredients.

☐ **PER SERVING** 19.9g total fat (2g saturated); 2470kj (591 cal); 83.7g carbohydrate; 16.9g protein; 3.3g fibre

---

This is a good salad for a barbecue as it keeps well and is not fussy about the temperature at which it is served.

Burghul and wild rice salad

PREPARATION TIME 40 MINUTES (PLUS STANDING TIME) **COOKING TIME** 55 MINUTES **SERVES** 4

2 cups (320g) burghul
⅔ cup (130g) wild rice
2 medium red capsicums (400g)
200g yellow patty-pan squash, quartered
4 green onions, chopped finely
⅔ cup (70g) walnuts
2 tablespoons finely chopped fresh flat-leaf parsley

DRESSING
⅔ cup (160ml) olive oil
2 tablespoons lemon juice
1 clove garlic, crushed

1 Place burghul in medium heatproof bowl; cover with boiling water. Stand 15 minutes; drain. Rinse under cold water; drain on absorbent paper.
2 Cook rice in large saucepan of boiling water, uncovered, about 35 minutes or until rice is tender; drain. Rinse under cold water; drain.
3 Quarter capsicums; discard seeds and membranes. Roast under grill or in very hot oven, skin-side up, until skin blisters and blackens. Cover capsicum pieces with plastic or paper for 5 minutes; peel away skin, then slice capsicum thickly.
4 Boil, steam or microwave squash until tender; drain. Rinse under cold water; drain.
5 Meanwhile, make dressing.
6 Combine burghul, rice, capsicum, squash, onion, nuts, parsley and dressing in large bowl.

DRESSING Place ingredients in screw-top jar; shake well.

☐ **PER SERVING** 50.3g total fat (6g saturated); 3277kj (784 cal); 60.2g carbohydrate; 15.2g protein; 17.2g fibre

1 ALMOND CORIANDER COUSCOUS **2** BURGHUL AND WILD RICE SALAD **3** BLACK-EYED BEANS, OKRA AND KUMARA GUMBO [P 408] **4** MUSHROOMS WITH BUCKWHEAT KERNELS [P 408]

1

2

3

4

One of the classic dishes of Louisiana, famous for creole and cajun cooking, gumbo takes its name from an African word for okra, without which this hearty vegetable stew would not be the same.

Black-eyed beans, okra and kumara gumbo

PREPARATION TIME 15 MINUTES (PLUS STANDING TIME) **COOKING TIME** 1 HOUR 15 MINUTES **SERVES** 6

- 1 cup (200g) black-eyed beans
- 2 teaspoons olive oil
- 1 large brown onion (200g), chopped coarsely
- 3 cloves garlic, crushed
- 1 teaspoon dried thyme
- 2 teaspoons dried oregano
- 3 teaspoons ground fennel
- 1 teaspoon cayenne pepper
- 500g okra
- 600g kumara, chopped coarsely
- 2 x 425g cans crushed tomatoes
- ¾ cup (180ml) water
- 1½ cups (300g) white long-grain rice
- 425g can baby corn, rinsed, drained

1 Place beans in medium bowl, cover with water; stand overnight, drain.
2 Rinse beans under cold water; drain. Place beans in medium saucepan of boiling water; return to a boil. Simmer, uncovered, about 30 minutes or until beans are just tender.
3 Heat oil in large saucepan; cook onion and garlic, stirring, until onion softens. Add dried herbs and spices; cook, stirring, until fragrant.
4 Add drained beans, okra, kumara, undrained tomatoes and the water; bring to a boil. Reduce heat; simmer, uncovered, about 30 minutes or until vegetables are tender.
5 Cook rice in medium saucepan of boiling water, uncovered, until just tender; drain.
6 Stir corn into gumbo; cook, uncovered, until corn is hot. Serve gumbo with rice.

PER SERVING 3.1g total fat (0.4g saturated); 1760kj (421 cal); 72.6g carbohydrate; 8.7g protein; 9.4g fibre

---

This recipe is inspired by the Russian passion for kasha, cooked grains such as buckwheat, millet or oats. Buckwheat kernels or groats are available from health-food stores.

Mushrooms with buckwheat kernels

PREPARATION TIME 10 MINUTES **COOKING TIME** 30 MINUTES **SERVES** 4

- 60g butter
- 1 large brown onion (200g), chopped finely
- 1½ cups (260g) buckwheat kernels
- 2½ cups (625ml) vegetable stock
- 2 tablespoons olive oil
- 250g button mushrooms, sliced thinly
- 250g flat mushrooms, sliced thinly
- 150g oyster mushrooms, sliced thinly
- 2 cloves garlic, crushed
- ⅓ cup coarsely chopped fresh chives

1 Heat half of the butter in medium saucepan; cook onion, stirring, until onion softens. Add buckwheat and stock; bring to a boil. Reduce heat; simmer, covered, 10 minutes. Uncover; simmer, about 5 minutes or until liquid is absorbed and grains are tender.
2 Meanwhile, heat remaining butter and oil in large frying pan; cook mushrooms and garlic, stirring, about 10 minutes or until mushrooms are tender and juices evaporate. Combine buckwheat mixture with mushroom mixture in large bowl; stir in chives.

PER SERVING 24.3g total fat (10.1g saturated); 2111kj (505 cal); 51.7g carbohydrate; 16.0g protein; 7.7g fibre

Leek and saffron barley

PREPARATION TIME 10 MINUTES **COOKING TIME** 35 MINUTES **SERVES** 4

Barley cooked this way is good with grilled or roasted lamb or chicken. To turn it into a hearty soup, add a can of chopped tomatoes, some grated lemon rind and enough chicken or vegetable stock to give a soup consistency.

1 tablespoon olive oil

2 medium leeks (700g), sliced thinly

3 cloves garlic, crushed

1 cup (200g) pearl barley

3 cups (750ml) vegetable stock

pinch saffron threads

⅓ cup finely chopped fresh flat-leaf parsley

1 Heat oil in large saucepan; cook leek and garlic, stirring, until leek softens.

2 Add barley, stock and saffron; bring to a boil. Reduce heat; simmer, covered, about 30 minutes or until barley softens, stirring occasionally. Stir in parsley.

▭ **PER SERVING** 7.0g total fat (1.2g saturated); 1095kj (262 cal); 36.3g carbohydrate; 8.7g protein; 9.4g fibre

---

Soft polenta

PREPARATION TIME 10 MINUTES **COOKING TIME** 30 MINUTES **SERVES** 4

Soft polenta is Italy's answer to mashed potato and is a treasured comfort food. Like mashed potato, it lends itself to the addition of flavoursome ingredients such as pesto, bacon, mushrooms, cheese, olives, semi-dried tomatoes and roasted vegetables.

1 litre (4 cups) milk

1 large brown onion (200g), quartered

4 bay leaves

4 cloves garlic, quartered

8 black peppercorns

1 cup (170g) polenta

40g butter, chopped

1 cup (80g) finely grated parmesan

1 Combine milk, onion, bay leaves, garlic and peppercorns in large saucepan; bring to a boil. Strain milk mixture over large bowl; discard solids. Return milk to same pan; return to a boil.

2 Gradually add polenta to milk, stirring constantly. Reduce heat; simmer, stirring, about 10 minutes or until polenta thickens. Stir in butter and cheese.

▭ **PER SERVING** 25.4g total fat (16.1g saturated); 2065kj (494 cal); 44.5g carbohydrate; 20.5g protein; 2.4g fibre

SAUCES, DRESSINGS & SALSAS

Sauces, Dressings & Salsas

Some of the sauces in this chapter have been familiar treasures for generations; many are fairly new to this country, though they come from long traditions elsewhere. All are ready to transform basics into food that sings. The classic sauces are one of the glories of cooking, and they will always be used. While snappy salsas, quick pasta sauces and easy Asian inspirations may be more in line with today's lighter eating and emphasis on fast and simple cooking, the bliss of fillet steak with béarnaise, asparagus or hot salmon with hollandaise, or cold salmon with homemade mayonnaise should also be at least an occasional part of everyone's life.

WHITE AND BROWN SAUCES

The sauces we classify as white range from the simple sauce we splash over cauliflower to pale golden velouté, made with stock instead of milk (and lovely on chicken, fish or veal), plus all their variations such as onion sauce for corned beef, cheese or mornay sauce in which to bake fish or eggs, mushroom sauce for chicken or steak, and many more.

The point to watch with white sauces is that they are not too thick. A sauce to be spooned over food should run freely off the spoon; a sauce in which food is to be cooked should be dense enough to coat the food, but not thick enough to hold its shape alone.

When you dine in a good restaurant and your main course comes with a deep-flavoured and silky, complex and savoury, sauce that plays harmony with the meat on your plate, you are probably eating either a classic espagnole, based on a roux made with meat stock and pan drippings, or its grander form, demi-glace. These and their variations can transform roast beef, steak or roast chicken into a major culinary event. As with white sauce, brown sauce should have body but be thin enough to run freely off the spoon.

BEARNAISE AND HOLLANDAISE

These superb egg and butter sauces can be made by hand or in a blender or food processor. When making by hand, the points to note are that you whisk the egg yolk mixture until it thickens enough to cling to the whisk when it is raised, and that you incorporate the butter completely before adding more. It is also important to keep the heat low and steady; many cooks prefer to make these sauces in a ceramic bowl over a saucepan, rather than in a metal or glass double boiler, because ceramic takes up heat more gradually then metal. If the sauces are too thick, or separate, whisk in a tablespoon or two of hot water until the mixture is smooth and creamy

GRAVY

Gravy may be at the other end of the scale, but it is a distant cousin of classic brown sauces such as demi-glace. Its savour comes from the meat or bird that has been roasted in the pan in which it is made; many cooks add a quartered onion to the pan while roasting, for the specific purpose of making the coagulated pan juices, and therefore the gravy, more flavoursome.

You can make a thin gravy (in French, jus) by pouring off all the fat and deglazing the pan with stock plus a little wine if you wish. Scrape and stir the coagulated juices into the liquid as it heats. Start with twice as much liquid as you want to end up with; when it has reduced by half, strain the liquid into a saucepan, season lightly, bring back to simmering point and add bits of butter, swirling or whisking them in to give the gravy a bit of body.

DRESSINGS

The two great basics, French dressing (vinaigrette) and mayonnaise, provide the basis for most salad dressings.

French dressing can be as simple as vinegar, oil, salt and pepper and perhaps a dollop of mustard, or it can take many variations and additions, changing its name along the way to Italian (with garlic, capsicum, onion and herbs), Roquefort (with crumbled Roquefort whisked in), salsa verde (with garlic, herbs and anchovy) and so on.

Mayonnaise can be sublimely simple or turn into aïoli with the addition of garlic, tartare sauce with gherkins, capers and herbs, remoulade with mustard, gherkins, herbs and anchovy and so on. Mayonnaise can be made by hand or in a blender or food processor.

Whatever the additions, the quality of the basic ingredients shows through. Use good oil – extra virgin olive oil or a fine cold-pressed nut oil. Buy in small quantities: oils are best when they are freshest. You may want to soften the taste of an assertive olive oil or nut oil with a little mild oil such as peanut, canola, grapeseed or a light olive oil.

Use a wine vinegar – red, white, or perhaps a sherry vinegar (meaning sherry was the base wine from which it was made). Good wine vinegar has been aged, and this should be indicated on the label. Balsamic vinegar, which comes at various prices depending on its age, is deep-flavoured and sharp-sweet. It can be mixed with a lighter wine vinegar.

SALSAS

While we may have just embraced the concept of salsas as spicy accompaniments to traditional main courses fairly recently, they have been tantalising mainstays in the Latin American kitchen forever, and they have equally flavoursome counterparts in cuisines throughout the world – from Mediterranean pesto, salsa verde and skordalia to South Asia's raita, sambal and satay sauce, to name but a few. While these may assume vastly different forms and be made out of myriad ingredients, the common denominator is that they are, collectively, condiments that raise the tempo of the food they're served with, enliven its flavour and give it heart.

A salsa fresca or cruda from Mexico can be as simple as a bowl of seeded, chopped tomatoes tossed with a bit of chilli, fresh coriander and lime juice, but it works marvellous magic on a plate of enchiladas; cooked thickened salsas, whether red or green, strained or chunky, give lift to barbecued meats and fish and add zest when slathered over tortillas that are eventually wrapped around beans, rice and salad to make burritos.

Béchamel is one of the "mother" or base sauces of classic French cooking and probably the one sauce that most people learn to cook before leaving home, often with the addition of cheese.

Béchamel sauce

PREPARATION TIME 5 MINUTES **COOKING TIME** 10 MINUTES (PLUS COOLING TIME) **MAKES** ¾ CUP

1 cup (250ml) milk
1 bay leaf
½ small brown onion (40g), sliced thickly
1 sprig fresh flat-leaf parsley
1 sprig fresh thyme
4 black peppercorns
20g butter
1 tablespoon plain flour

1 Combine milk, bay leaf, onion, parsley, thyme and peppercorns in medium saucepan; bring to a boil. Strain; cool 5 minutes.

2 Melt butter in same cleaned pan, add flour; cook, stirring, until mixture thickens and bubbles. Gradually stir in milk; cook, stirring, until sauce boils and thickens.

☐ **PER TABLESPOON** 2.9g total fat (1.9g saturated); 171kj (41 cal); 2.5g carbohydrate; 1.2g protein; 0.1g fibre

---

Velouté, meaning velvety, is another base sauce of French cuisine. Serve it on vegetables, chicken and veal or – with the addition of a little lemon juice or a reduction of shallot and white wine – on seafood.

Velouté sauce

PREPARATION TIME 5 MINUTES **COOKING TIME** 30 MINUTES **MAKES** 1¼ CUPS

50g butter
¼ cup (35g) plain flour
2 cups (500ml) hot chicken stock
1 bay leaf
1 sprig fresh thyme
1 sprig fresh flat-leaf parsley
5 black peppercorns

1 Melt butter in medium saucepan, add flour; cook, stirring, until mixture thickens and bubbles. Gradually stir in stock with bay leaf, thyme, parsley and peppercorns; cook, stirring, until mixture boils and thickens.

2 Reduce heat; simmer, uncovered, about 20 minutes, stirring occasionally, until thickened to desired consistency. Strain sauce through fine sieve.

☐ **PER TABLESPOON** 2.9g total fat (1.9g saturated); 150kj (36 cal); 1.9g carbohydrate; 0.6g protein; 0.1g fibre

---

For a quick fish pie, make this sauce and stir in a can of drained salmon, some baby spinach leaves and frozen peas, two chopped hard-boiled eggs, some finely chopped parsley and grated lemon rind. Spoon into a small shallow baking dish and top with mashed potato; bake in a moderate oven until golden.

Basic cheese sauce

PREPARATION TIME 5 MINUTES **COOKING TIME** 10 MINUTES (PLUS COOLING TIME) **MAKES** 1¼ CUPS

50g butter
¼ cup (35g) plain flour
1½ cups (375ml) hot milk
⅓ cup (40g) finely grated cheddar

1 Melt butter in medium saucepan, add flour; cook, stirring, until mixture thickens and bubbles. Gradually stir in milk; cook, stirring, until sauce boils and thickens. Cover surface of sauce with plastic wrap, stand 5 minutes; stir in cheese.

☐ **PER TABLESPOON** 4.6g total fat (3.0g saturated); 251kj (60 cal); 2.9g carbohydrate; 1.8g protein; 0.1g fibre

Hollandaise

PREPARATION TIME 5 MINUTES (PLUS COOLING TIME) **COOKING TIME** 15 MINUTES **MAKES** 1⅓ CUPS

- 1 tablespoon water
- ¼ cup (60ml) white wine vinegar
- 2 teaspoons lemon juice
- 1 bay leaf
- 2 green onions, chopped finely
- 1 teaspoon black peppercorns
- 3 egg yolks
- 185g butter, melted

1 Bring the water, vinegar, juice, bay leaf, onion and peppercorns to a boil in small saucepan. Reduce heat; simmer, uncovered, until liquid is reduced to 2 tablespoons. Strain and reserve liquid; cool 10 minutes.

2 Combine egg yolks and vinegar mixture in medium heatproof bowl over medium saucepan of simmering water; do not allow water to touch base of bowl. Whisk mixture constantly until thickened. Remove from heat; gradually add hot butter in thin, steady stream; whisk constantly until mixture is thick and creamy. If mixture is too thick, stir in 1 to 2 tablespoons of hot water to give desired consistency.

☐ **PER TABLESPOON** 11.2g total fat (7.0g saturated); 431kj (103 cal); 0.2g carbohydrate; 0.7g protein; 0g fibre

For a quick hollandaise, blend or process the egg yolks and hot vinegar until combined. With the motor operating, add the melted butter in a thin, steady stream until the hollandaise reaches the desired consistency. For tips on making hollandaise ahead and re-heating, turn to page 333.

Béarnaise

PREPARATION TIME 5 MINUTES **COOKING TIME** 15 MINUTES (PLUS COOLING TIME) **MAKES** 1¼ CUPS

- ½ cup (125ml) white wine vinegar
- 3 shallots (75g) chopped finely
- 8 black peppercorns
- 1 bay leaf
- 1 teaspoon fresh tarragon leaves
- 4 egg yolks
- 250g butter, melted, cooled

1 Bring vinegar, shallots, peppercorns, bay leaf and tarragon to a boil in small saucepan. Reduce heat; simmer, uncovered, until liquid is reduced to 2 tablespoons. Strain and reserve liquid; cool 10 minutes.

2 Place egg yolks in medium heatproof bowl over medium saucepan of simmering water; do not allow water to touch base of bowl. Whisk in reserved liquid. Place pan over low heat so water is barely simmering. Gradually add butter in thin, steady stream; whisk constantly until mixture thickens. If mixture is too thick, stir in 1 to 2 tablespoons of hot water to give desired consistency.

☐ **PER TABLESPOON** 15.2g total fat (9.5g saturated); 581kj (139 cal); 0.2g carbohydrate; 1.0g protein; 0g fibre

Serve this luscious sauce with roast beef or fillet steak. Try it, too, over a barbecued steak and roasted potatoes.

Serve with fish, shellfish, veal or globe artichokes. A citrus beurre blanc can be a wonderful twist: replace the white wine vinegar with lemon, lime or grapefruit juice.

Beurre blanc

PREPARATION TIME 5 MINUTES **COOKING TIME** 15 MINUTES **MAKES** 1¼ CUPS

2 green onions, chopped finely
2 tablespoons fish stock
2 tablespoons white wine vinegar
¼ cup (60ml) dry white wine
250g cold butter, chopped

1 Bring onion, stock, vinegar and wine to a boil in small saucepan. Reduce heat; simmer, uncovered until reduced to 2 tablespoons. Strain and reserve liquid.
2 Return liquid to pan. Whisk in two cubes of the butter; whisk until smooth. Whisk in remaining butter over low heat, one cube at a time, until sauce thickens to the consistency of pouring cream.

PER TABLESPOON 13.7g total fat (9.0g saturated); 523kj (125 cal); 0.2g carbohydrate; 0.2g protein; 0.0g fibre

---

A basic vehicle for your favourite flavours, try any of the following: drained and rinsed baby capers, black olives, mushrooms, chilli, anchovies, roasted vegetables, tuna, meatballs, spicy sausage, bacon and cheese, to name but a few.

Basic tomato sauce

PREPARATION TIME 10 MINUTES **COOKING TIME** 20 MINUTES **MAKES** 3 CUPS

2 tablespoons olive oil
1 medium brown onion (150g), chopped finely
3 cloves garlic, crushed
¼ cup (60ml) dry red wine
2 x 410g cans crushed tomatoes
2 tablespoons tomato paste
1 teaspoon white sugar
1 tablespoon finely chopped fresh thyme
1 tablespoon finely chopped fresh basil

1 Heat oil in medium saucepan; cook onion and garlic, stirring, until onion softens. Add wine; bring to a boil. Reduce heat; simmer, uncovered, until reduced by half.
2 Stir in undrained tomatoes, paste, sugar and thyme; simmer, uncovered, 10 minutes or until sauce thickens. Stir in basil.

PER TABLESPOON 1.1g total fat (0.1g saturated); 71kj (17 cal); 1.2g carbohydrate; 0.3g protein; 0.4g fibre

---

The important rule of thumb for cooking with any wine is that if it's not good enough to drink then it's not good enough to cook with. If it tastes like vinegar then no amount of cooking is going to make it taste better in your food!

Basic red wine sauce

PREPARATION TIME 5 MINUTES **COOKING TIME** 15 MINUTES **MAKES** 1 CUP

30g butter
3 shallots (75g), chopped finely
1 clove garlic, crushed
1 tablespoon plain flour
2 teaspoons finely chopped fresh thyme
⅓ cup (80ml) dry red wine
1 cup (250ml) beef stock

1 Melt butter in medium saucepan; cook shallots and garlic, stirring, until shallots soften. Add flour; cook, stirring, until browned lightly. Gradually stir in thyme, wine and stock; cook, stirring, until sauce boils and thickens. Strain.

PER TABLESPOON 2.1g total fat (1.4g saturated); 121kj (29 cal); 1.0g carbohydrate; 0.5g protein; 0.1g fibre

Gravy

PREPARATION TIME 5 MINUTES **COOKING TIME** 10 MINUTES **MAKES** 2 CUPS

2 tablespoons pan drippings
2 tablespoons plain flour
¾ cup (180ml) dry red wine
1 ¼ cups (310ml) beef stock
1 teaspoon worcestershire sauce

1 Heat reserved pan drippings in same baking dish that the meat was roasted in, add flour; cook, stirring, until mixture thickens, bubbles and browns. Gradually stir in wine, stock and sauce; cook, stirring, until gravy boils and thickens. Strain before serving.

PER TABLESPOON 1.5g total fat (0.4g saturated); 96kj (23 cal); 0.8g carbohydrate; 0.3g protein; 0g fibre

After the roast is removed from the oven and resting, make gravy with two tablespoons of the pan drippings. Remember that the colour of the gravy comes from the browning of the flour. Be patient: keep stirring the mixture until it browns. The darker this mixture is, the darker your gravy will be.

Mint sauce

PREPARATION TIME 5 MINUTES **COOKING TIME** 5 MINUTES (PLUS STANDING TIME) **MAKES** 1 CUP

2 cups firmly packed fresh mint leaves
¼ cup (60ml) water
¾ cup (180ml) white wine vinegar
2 tablespoons caster sugar

1 Chop half of the mint coarsely; place in small heatproof bowl.
2 Combine the water, vinegar and sugar in small saucepan; stir over heat, without boiling, until sugar dissolves. Pour liquid over chopped mint in bowl, cover; stand 3 hours.
3 Strain liquid into bowl; discard mint. Chop remaining mint coarsely; stir into liquid. Blend or process until chopped finely.

PER TABLESPOON 0.3g total fat (0.1g saturated fat); 234kJ (56 cal); 10.1g carbohydrate; 0.9g protein; 1.9g fibre

---

Cumberland sauce

PREPARATION TIME 5 MINUTES **COOKING TIME** 30 MINUTES (PLUS COOLING TIME) **MAKES** 1 CUP

1 shallot (25g), sliced thinly
½ cup (125ml) red wine vinegar
½ cup (125ml) port
½ teaspoon finely grated lemon rind
½ teaspoon finely grated orange rind
¼ cup (60g) red currant jelly
1 cup (250ml) beef stock

1 Place shallot and vinegar in small saucepan; bring to a boil then reduce heat. Simmer, uncovered, until mixture reduces by half.
2 Add remaining ingredients; bring to a boil then reduce heat. Simmer, uncovered, about 20 minutes or until mixture is reduced by half. Strain into small jug; cool.

PER TABLESPOON 0.1g total fat (0g saturated fat); 159kJ (38 cal); 6.1g carbohydrate; 0.7g protein; 0g fibre

This sauce can be frozen for 3 months. Serve with chicken, pork or beef skewers, crisp fried tofu, burgers, or mixed into a stir-fry; use as a marinade or make into a dressing for a salad.

Satay sauce

PREPARATION TIME 20 MINUTES **COOKING TIME** 20 MINUTES **MAKES** 3½ CUPS

- 1 cup (140g) roasted unsalted peanuts
- 1 medium brown onion (150g), chopped coarsely
- 3 cloves garlic, quartered
- 5cm piece fresh ginger (25g), chopped coarsely
- 5cm stick (10g) fresh lemon grass, coarsely chopped
- 1 fresh small red thai chilli, chopped coarsely
- 1 tablespoon finely grated lime rind
- ¼ cup coarsely chopped coriander root and stem mixture
- 2 teaspoons sesame oil
- 2 teaspoons vegetable oil
- 1 teaspoon cumin seeds
- ½ teaspoon ground turmeric
- 1⅔ cups (410ml) coconut milk
- 1 tablespoon fish sauce
- 3 teaspoons tamarind concentrate
- 1 tablespoon brown sugar

1 Blend or process nuts until chopped finely. Transfer to small bowl.

2 Blend or process onion, garlic, ginger, lemon grass, chilli, rind and coriander until chopped finely.

3 Heat oils in medium saucepan; cook onion mixture, stirring, over low heat, about 10 minutes or until fragrant. Add cumin and turmeric; cook, stirring, 1 minute. Stir in nuts, coconut milk, sauce, tamarind and sugar; bring to a boil. Reduce heat; simmer, uncovered, 5 minutes.

☐ **PER TABLESPOON** 4.0g total fat (2.1g saturated); 192kj (46 cal); 1.2g carbohydrate; 1.3g protein; 0.6g fibre

Serve with chicken breasts or pork fillets, or try adding 2 shredded chicken breasts to the sauce and mixing in some spinach fettuccine with shavings of parmesan.

Creamy tarragon and mushroom sauce

PREPARATION TIME 10 MINUTES **COOKING TIME** 15 MINUTES **MAKES** 2 CUPS

- 30g butter
- 250g mushrooms, sliced thinly
- ¼ cup (60ml) dry white wine
- 1 tablespoon brandy
- 300ml cream
- 1 tablespoon coarsely chopped fresh chives
- 1 tablespoon finely chopped fresh tarragon

1 Heat butter in medium saucepan; cook mushrooms, stirring, until tender. Add wine and brandy; bring to a boil. Reduce heat; simmer, uncovered, 5 minutes.

2 Stir in cream, bring to a boil then reduce heat and simmer, uncovered, about 5 minutes or until sauce thickens slightly. Stir in herbs.

☐ **PER TABLESPOON** 6.5g total fat (4.2g saturated); 272kj (65 cal); 0.4g carbohydrate; 0.6g protein; 0.3g fibre

Nuts & seeds

Freshness is vital so buy nuts and seeds from a high-turnover shop. If you must store them, keep them in the freezer.

PECANS
Like walnuts but sweeter and milder. Best known in the pecan pie of the American south. Good in salads, with soft cheeses, celery or apple, in cakes, cookies and breads

ALMONDS
The most useful nut for cooks, from trout or barramundi with almonds in brown butter to pilafs, chicken salad, Chinese and Indian cooking, almond bread and Christmas cake. Buy unblanched and blanch when needed.

BRAZIL NUTS
If buying in the shell, avoid any that rattle or feel light for their size. Use them as an interesting change from other nuts in biscuits and sweets – they are delicious in butterscotch.

WALNUTS
Magnificent fresh, but highly susceptible to becoming stale and rancid, walnuts are best bought in the shell, or vacuum-packed if shelled. Serve simply with cheese or in salads, cakes and desserts.

PISTACHIOS
Sold in their half-open shell and loose, salted as a snack or unsalted to use in cooking. Their flavour is mild and slightly resinous. Decoratively bright green, they are used to stud pâtés and terrines and in biscuits, cakes and confectionery.

PINE NUTS
Usually roasted or fried to bring out their warm savour, pine nuts are an essential ingredient of pesto, and are used to decorate Middle Eastern meat and rice dishes and in Mediterranean cooking.

HAZELNUTS

Wonderful with watercress, orange and rich meats such as duck, and in meringues, biscuits, cakes and anything to do with chocolate. Roasting brings out their rich taste.

MACADAMIAS

Expensive but worth it for their crisp texture and warm, buttery flavour. Wonderful roasted as a snack, and lovely in browned butter over beans or freshwater fish, and in biscuits, brownies and other chocolate confections.

CASHEWS

Roasted, salted and raw, they are second only to peanuts as a snack. Their full, sweetish flavour plays well against spices and in stir-fries; often used in Chinese and Indian cooking.

PEPITAS

Dried pumpkin seed kernels, mostly eaten salted as a snack, and also used in breakfast cereals, salads and rice dishes. Be sure to buy kernels, not seeds, as the outer husk is difficult to remove once the seed is dried.

SUNFLOWER SEEDS

For eating or cooking, you want the kernels of the dried seeds, not the whole seeds. Highly nutritious, they are eaten salted as a snack, and also used in breakfast cereals, salads and rice dishes.

SESAME SEEDS

Most familiar on breads, but also delicious fried in butter or oil and tossed with cooked carrot sticks or chunks of roasted pumpkin or sweet potato, or scattered on sweet teabreads or biscuits before baking.

In France this classic sauce is served with fish or mixed with shredded raw celeriac as an hors d'oeuvre. For a tasty salad, mix with finely shredded celeriac and crab meat, or with finely shredded cabbage and flaked smoked fish.

Remoulade

PREPARATION TIME 10 MINUTES **MAKES** 1 ½ CUPS

1 egg
1 egg yolk
1 cup (250ml) vegetable oil
2 teaspoons lemon juice
2 teaspoons dijon mustard
1 teaspoon wholegrain mustard
1 tablespoon finely chopped gherkins
2 teaspoons finely chopped fresh tarragon
2 drained anchovy fillets, chopped finely

1 Blend or process egg and egg yolk until smooth. With motor operating, gradually add oil in thin, steady, process until mixture thickens.
2 Transfer mixture to small bowl; stir in remaining ingredients.

▭ **PER TABLESPOON** 13.4g total fat (1.8g saturated); 510kj (122 cal); 0.2g carbohydrate; 0.7g protein; 0g fibre

---

Combine half this quantity of aïoli with 1 cup stewed apple for a delicious apple sauce to serve with roast pork.

Aïoli

PREPARATION TIME 15 MINUTES **MAKES** 1 CUP

4 cloves garlic, quartered
1 teaspoon sea salt
2 teaspoons lemon juice
1 cup (300g) mayonnaise

1 Using mortar and pestle, crush garlic and salt to a smooth paste.
2 Combine garlic and remaining ingredients in small bowl.

▭ **PER TABLESPOON** 6.2g total fat (0.7g saturated); 301kj (72 cal); 3.8g carbohydrate; 0.2g protein; 0.3g fibre

---

In India this is considered a salad and is served with hot and spicy food to help reduce the "burn" of the chilli. It often includes chopped tomato and onion.

Raita

PREPARATION TIME 10 MINUTES **MAKES** 1 CUP

200g yogurt
½ lebanese cucumber (65g), seeded, chopped finely
1 teaspoon cumin seeds, roasted
1 clove garlic, crushed
1 tablespoon lemon juice

1 Combine ingredients in small bowl.

▭ **PER TABLESPOON** 0.6g total fat (0.4g saturated); 54kj (13 cal); 1.0g carbohydrate; 0.8g protein; 1.0g fibre

Skordalia

PREPARATION TIME 15 MINUTES **COOKING TIME** 15 MINUTES **MAKES** 2 CUPS

Skordalia is a tangy Greek sauce or dip made with pureed potatoes and breadcrumbs or ground nuts (or, as in this case, both). It can be served with almost any kind of dish – from grilled meats and poultry to fish and raw vegetables

- 400g potatoes, chopped coarsely
- 2 slices white bread
- ½ cup (60g) almond meal
- 3 cloves garlic, crushed
- 2 tablespoons apple cider vinegar
- ⅓ cup (80ml) water
- ¼ cup (60ml) olive oil

1 Boil, steam or microwave potato until tender; drain. Mash potato in medium bowl.
2 Meanwhile, trim and discard crusts from bread. Soak bread in small bowl of cold water; drain. Squeeze out excess water.
3 Blend or process bread with almond meal, garlic, vinegar and the water until mixture is smooth. With motor operating, gradually add oil in a thin steady stream; process until mixture thickens slightly. Fold bread mixture into potato.

PER TABLESPOON 3.7g total fat (0.4g saturated); 209kj (50 cal); 2.9g carbohydrate; 1.0g protein; 0.6g fibre

---

Honey chilli sauce

PREPARATION TIME 10 MINUTES **COOKING TIME** 5 MINUTES **MAKES** ABOUT 1⅓ CUPS

Drizzle this sauce over cooked scallops or prawns with ribbons of carrot and shredded snow peas.

- ¼ cup (90g) honey
- 2 teaspoons sweet chilli sauce
- 2 teaspoons soy sauce
- 1cm piece fresh ginger (5g), grated
- ⅔ cup (160ml) fish stock
- 3 teaspoons cornflour
- ⅓ cup (60ml) dry white wine
- 1 green onion sliced thinly

1 Combine honey, sauces, ginger, stock and blended cornflour and wine in small saucepan; stir over heat until mixture boils and thickens. Stir in onion.

PER TABLESPOON 0.0g total fat (0.0g saturated); 113kj (27 cal); 5.7g carbohydrate; 0.2g protein; 0.1g fibre

---

Butterscotch sauce

PREPARATION TIME 5 MINUTES **COOKING TIME** 5 MINUTES **MAKES** 2¼ CUPS

For a lavish touch, add ¼ cup raisins and 1 tablespoon rum or brandy. Serve over ice-cream, baked apples, barbecued pineapple slices or bananas, pancakes or waffles.

- 1 cup (220g) firmly packed brown sugar
- 1 cup (250ml) cream
- 150g butter, chopped

1 Combine ingredients in small saucepan; stir over heat until sugar dissolves and butter melts. Reduce heat; simmer, uncovered, 3 minutes.

PER TABLESPOON 8.6g total fat (5.6g saturated); 460kj (110 cal); 8.2g carbohydrate; 0.2g protein; 0g fibre

Low heat and constant whisking are the key elements to a successful crème anglaise. Try flavouring the custard with liqueurs, finely grated citrus rind, chocolate, spices or coffee.

Crème anglaise

PREPARATION TIME 5 MINUTES (PLUS STANDING AND REFRIGERATION TIME)
COOKING TIME 10 MINUTES **MAKES** 1½ CUPS

1 vanilla bean
1½ cups (375ml) milk
1 tablespoon caster sugar
4 egg yolks
¼ cup (55g) caster sugar, extra

1 Split vanilla bean in half lengthways. Combine vanilla bean, milk and sugar in small saucepan; bring to a boil. Remove from heat; stand, covered, 20 minutes.
2 Combine egg yolks and extra sugar in medium bowl; whisk until smooth. Slowly pour milk mixture onto egg mixture, whisking constantly. Return mixture to pan, stir constantly over low heat, without boiling, until mixture thickens slightly and coats the back of a wooden spoon. Strain mixture; cover surface, refrigerate until cold.

☐ **PER TABLESPOON** 2.1g total fat (0.9g saturated); 188kj (45 cal); 5.1g carbohydrate; 1.4g protein; 0g fibre

---

To melt chocolate, place in a bowl over hot water to soften, then stir. Serve chocolate sauce with poached pears, banana splits, brownies, berries or ice-cream. Use any cold left-over sauce to make a very decadent iced chocolate.

Chocolate sauce

PREPARATION TIME 5 MINUTES **COOKING TIME** 5 MINUTES **MAKES** 2 CUPS

125g dark eating chocolate, melted
¼ cup (40g) icing sugar
300ml thickened cream
2 tablespoons coffee liqueur
1 teaspoon vanilla extract

1 Place chocolate in medium bowl; stir in sifted sugar, cream, liqueur and extract. Stir until smooth

☐ **PER TABLESPOON** 6.2g total fat (4.5g saturated); 351kj (84 cal); 5.9g carbohydrate; 0.5g protein; 0.2g fibre

---

Fold ½ cup coulis, the pulp of 2 passionfruit, ½ cup lightly crushed biscotti, 250g yogurt and 250g vanilla custard together until just combined. Serve in four glass tumblers.

Raspberry coulis

PREPARATION TIME 5 MINUTES **COOKING TIME** 10 MINUTES **MAKES** ¾ CUP

150g frozen raspberries, thawed
2 tablespoons caster sugar
4 cloves
½ cup (125ml) dry red wine

1 Combine raspberries and sugar in small saucepan; cook, without boiling, until sugar dissolves. Add cloves and wine; bring to a boil. Reduce heat; simmer, uncovered, about 5 minutes or until coulis thickens. Strain coulis into small jug.

☐ **PER TABLESPOON** 0.1g total fat (0.0g saturated); 138kj (33 cal); 5.0g carbohydrate; 0.2g protein; 0.9g fibre

Basic mayonnaise

PREPARATION TIME 10 MINUTES **MAKES** 1 CUP

If mayonnaise curdles, whisk an egg yolk in another bowl and slowly add to the curdled mayonnaise, whisking constantly until smooth. Alternatively, slowly drizzle in about 1 tablespoon boiling water, whisking until the mayonnaise emulsifies again.

2 egg yolks
1 teaspoon dijon mustard
½ cup (125ml) olive oil
½ cup (125ml) light olive oil
1 tablespoon lemon juice

1 Blend or process egg yolks and mustard until smooth.
2 With motor operating, gradually add combined oils in thin, steady stream; process until mixture thickens. Stir in juice.

PER TABLESPOON 19.9g total fat (3.0g saturated); 744kj (178 cal); 0.1g carbohydrate; 0.5g protein; 0g fibre

Tartare sauce

PREPARATION TIME 10 MINUTES **MAKES** 1¼ CUPS

Piquant tartare sauce is the classic one to slather on fried fish or hot or cold shellfish. Note that, unlike many commercial versions, the real thing does not contain sugar.

1 quantity basic mayonnaise (see above)
1 tablespoon drained capers, rinsed, chopped finely
1 tablespoon finely chopped gherkin
3 teaspoons finely chopped red onion
1 tablespoon finely chopped fresh flat-leaf parsley

1 Combine ingredients in small bowl.

PER TABLESPOON 15g total fat (2.4g saturated); 602kj (144 cal); 0.3g carbohydrate; 0.5g protein; 0.1g fibre

Thousand island dressing

PREPARATION TIME 5 MINUTES **MAKES** 1½ CUPS

This American dressing is great on sandwiches, in coleslaw and with seafood or chicken.

1 quantity basic mayonnaise (see above)
¼ cup (60ml) tomato sauce
½ small white onion, grated finely
8 pimiento-stuffed green olives, chopped finely
1 small red capsicum (150g), chopped finely

1 Combine ingredients in small bowl.

PER TABLESPOON 13.4g total fat (2.0g saturated); 527kj (126 cal); 1.0g carbohydrate; 0.5g protein; 0.3g fibre

1

2

3

4

Chilli lime dressing

PREPARATION TIME 10 MINUTES **MAKES** ½ CUP

This dressing makes an excellent marinade for seafood.

- 2 tablespoons lime juice
- 2 tablespoons brown sugar
- 1 tablespoon chinese cooking wine
- 1 tablespoon fish sauce
- ½ teaspoon sesame oil
- 1cm piece fresh ginger (5g), grated
- 1 clove garlic, crushed
- 2 teaspoons sweet chilli sauce

1 Place ingredients in screw-top jar; shake well.

PER TABLESPOON 0.5g total fat (0.1g saturated); 121kj (29 cal); 5.0g carbohydrate; 0.4g protein; 0.2g fibre

---

French dressing

PREPARATION TIME 5 MINUTES **MAKES** ⅔ CUP

Vary this great basic dressing by adding garlic, different vinegars (red wine, balsamic, sherry or apple cider), fresh or dried herbs, citrus juices instead of the vinegar, or honey or fruit concentrates instead of the sugar.

- ½ cup (125ml) olive oil
- 1 tablespoon white wine vinegar
- 2 teaspoons dijon mustard
- ½ teaspoon caster sugar

1 Place ingredients in screw-top jar; shake well.

PER TABLESPOON 14.2g total fat (2.0g saturated); 531kj (127 cal); 0.3g carbohydrate; 0g protein; 0g fibre

---

Italian dressing

PREPARATION TIME 10 MINUTES **MAKES** 1½ CUPS

If using to dress a pasta salad, make sure you only cook the pasta just to the "al dente" stage, then toss it with the dressing, so that the hot pasta absorbs the flavours.

- ½ cup (125ml) white wine vinegar
- 1 tablespoon lemon juice
- 1 teaspoon white sugar
- ½ cup (125ml) light olive oil
- ½ small white onion (40g), chopped finely
- 1 clove garlic, crushed
- ½ small red capsicum (75g), chopped finely
- ¼ cup finely chopped fresh flat-leaf parsley

1 Place ingredients in screw-top jar; shake well.

PER TABLESPOON 6.3g total fat (0.9g saturated); 247kj (59 cal); 0.5g carbohydrate; 0.1g protein; 0.1g fibre

1 CHILLI LIME DRESSING 2 FRENCH DRESSING 3 ITALIAN DRESSING 4 RANCH DRESSING (P 428)

As well as a dressing for a salad, this is a good sauce for spicy potato wedges, spicy chicken wings or crudités.

Ranch dressing

PREPARATION TIME 10 MINUTES **MAKES** 1 CUP

⅓ cup (95g) yogurt
⅓ cup (100g) mayonnaise
2 tablespoons buttermilk
1 clove garlic, crushed
1 small brown onion (80g), grated finely
1 tablespoon finely chopped fresh chives

1 Combine ingredients in small bowl.

☐ **PER TABLESPOON** 3.0g total fat (0.5g saturated); 167kj (40 cal); 2.5g carbohydrate; 0.7g protein; 0.2g fibre

---

For appetisers, chop all the ingredients finely, then spoon a little of this salsa onto bite-sized pieces of grilled tuna steak or individual corn chips.

Mango and avocado salsa

PREPARATION TIME 15 MINUTES **MAKES** 2½ CUPS

1 medium mango (430g), chopped coarsely
1 large avocado (320g), chopped coarsely
1 small red onion (100g), chopped finely
1 small red capsicum (150g), chopped finely
1 fresh small red thai chilli, chopped finely
2 tablespoons lime juice

1 Combine ingredients in medium bowl.

☐ **PER TABLESPOON** 1.7g total fat (0.4g saturated); 100kj (24 cal); 1.7g carbohydrate; 0.4g protein; 0.4g fibre

---

This Italian "green sauce" is sublime with grilled or poached fish. Spread onto bread as a sauce for a tuna sandwich, stir into mayonnaise for a great potato salad or spoon onto fishcakes.

Salsa verde

PREPARATION TIME 15 MINUTES **MAKES** ½ CUP

⅓ cup coarsely chopped fresh flat-leaf parsley
2 tablespoons coarsely chopped fresh mint
2 teaspoons drained capers, rinsed
1 anchovy fillet, drained
1 clove garlic, quartered
½ teaspoon finely grated lemon rind
1 teaspoon lemon juice
½ teaspoon dijon mustard
⅓ cup (80ml) olive oil

1 Blend or process parsley, mint, capers, anchovy, garlic, rind, juice and mustard until chopped finely. With motor operating, gradually add oil in thin, steady stream; process until mixture is almost smooth.

☐ **PER TABLESPOON** 12.2g total fat (1.7g saturated); 464kj (111 cal); 0.3g carbohydrate; 0.3g protein; 0.4g fibre

MANGO AND AVOCADO SALSA

Grilled corn and zucchini salsa

PREPARATION TIME 20 MINUTES **COOKING TIME** 10 MINUTES **MAKES** 7 CUPS

This salsa is delicious with grilled fish or chicken, pork, beef or lamb. Eat it just as it is, or as a salad, wrapped in lettuce or mixed through shredded Chinese cabbage.

- 2 corn cobs (800g), trimmed
- 100g baby zucchini, halved lengthways
- 2 large avocados (640g), chopped coarsely
- 200g grape tomatoes, halved
- 1 medium red onion (170g), sliced thickly
- ¼ cup coarsely chopped fresh coriander
- 1 tablespoon sweet chilli sauce
- ⅓ cup (80ml) lime juice
- 2 fresh small red thai chillies, sliced thinly

1 Cook corn and zucchini on heated oiled grill plate (or grill or barbecue) until tender and browned lightly. Using sharp knife, remove kernels from cobs.

2 Combine corn and zucchini in large bowl with avocado, tomato, onion and coriander. Add remaining ingredients; toss gently to combine.

PER TABLESPOON 1.3g total fat (0.3g saturated); 84kj (20 cal); 1.4g carbohydrate; 0.5g protein; 0.5g fibre

---

Caper and roasted capsicum salsa

PREPARATION TIME 15 MINUTES **COOKING TIME** 10 MINUTES **MAKES** 2 CUPS

For a light summer meal that is great for entertaining, grill or barbecue swordfish or tuna steaks. Serve the steaks on tuscan white bean salad (see page 137), replacing the mozzarella cheese with fetta, and top with caper and roasted capsicum salsa.

- 1 medium red capsicum (200g)
- 1 medium green capsicum (200g)
- 1 medium yellow capsicum (200g)
- 3 medium tomatoes (450g), peeled, seeded, sliced thinly
- 1 small red onion (100g), sliced thinly
- ¼ cup (50g) drained baby capers, rinsed
- ¼ cup finely shredded fresh basil
- 2 tablespoons balsamic vinegar
- ½ cup (125ml) olive oil
- 3 teaspoons black olive tapenade
- 2 cloves garlic, crushed

1 Quarter capsicums; discard seeds and membranes. Roast under grill or in very hot oven, skin-side up, until skin blisters and blackens. Cover capsicum pieces with plastic or paper for 5 minutes; peel away skin, then slice capsicum thinly.

2 Place capsicum in medium bowl with tomato, onion, capers, basil and combined vinegar, oil, tapenade and garlic; toss gently to combine.

PER TABLESPOON 4.8g total fat (0.7g saturated); 209kj (50 cal); 1.2g carbohydrate; 0.5g protein; 0.4g fibre

GRILLED CORN AND ZUCCHINI SALSA

CHRISTMAS & OTHER FESTIVITIES

Christmas & Other Festivities

One of the deepest pleasures of special festive times is the appearance of the traditional treats that have become an essential part of the whole joyous occasion. They may be treats that belong entirely to a particular festival, such as Christmas pudding, or they may be things that can appear at other times but always mean an important occasion, such as a baked ham. They may be simply family tradition, such as the special cake that is always baked for a birthday. All are treasured for what they mean beyond the pleasure of eating them: continuity, togetherness, the assurance that some things never change.

Or do they? Many of us can remember when Christmas always meant a hot roasted bird and a hot pudding, even in the heat of an Australian summer. The idea of having a cold Christmas lunch – cold seafood and a chilled or frozen pudding – started as a daringly original one, but caught on quickly until, today, it is a parallel tradition to the old ones. It's called having the best of both worlds.

MENU PLANNING

If your festive menu is part of never-to-be-changed tradition, we wouldn't dream of arguing. But bear in mind that you can buy, rather than make, quite a few time-consuming items. Specialty food stores and many chicken shops offer roasted turkeys plus instructions for reheating them. Delicatessens and the food section of department stores have a splendid array of top-quality sauces, and supermarkets now carry quality dressings, dips and pâtés.

Think about what can be done ahead of time, from preparing vegetables to baking the ham in the early morning of the festive day – it will be just deliciously warm and well set, making it easy to carve, by the time it is needed. Of course, the great do-ahead job is the pudding, which can and should be made weeks ahead if it is steamed and up to a year ahead if it is boiled. See page 442 for more information on how to store puddings.

PLANNING THE DAY

If your Christmas, New Year or other festive day adds up to a party big enough to need real planning, please read "Planning" on page 66. You may also want to read about serving party drinks on page 48. Even for a small party, planning makes the difference between feeling fraught and enjoying it all, both in the run-up to the day and on the day itself. Make a timetable of what has to be done and when you will do it. And don't forget that, especially for a family party, the tradition of each cook bringing a part of the meal is a delightful and sensible one.

CARVING

The first requisite for all carving is a razor-sharp knife. Ideally, it should be long, narrow and slightly flexible. It is easier to carve on a board than on a platter, as the meat won't slip. The board should have a channel to catch the juices.

All meat consists of muscles in which bundles of fibres run in one direction, and you should carve across the fibres (across the grain), not along them. This makes all the difference to the texture of the meat, as short lengths of fibre feel tender to eat while long ones feel chewy and tough.

A ham frill looks festive and provides a clean handle to hold while carving. Take a piece of white A4 office paper or the same shape in foil or decorative paper. Fold in half lengthways, repeat; flatten out the second fold and use scissors to cut down at 5mm intervals from the first fold to the line of the second fold, from one end of the paper to the other. Turn inside out, overlap the ends and secure with a paper clip. When needed, wrap round ham shank and glue or secure with sticky tape. If you don't have a ham stand, sit the ham on a pudding basin, right-side up so that the ham sits solidly while you're carving.

TURKEY

Cut off the wing then the hindquarter on the same side, cutting through the thigh bone.

Turn the bird on its side; place the cut-off wing and hindquarter under the bird to help keep it steady

Holding the bird firmly with a fork, carve across the breast at the top, running along the bird's torso.

Carve the leg and wing then turn the bird over and carve the other side in the same manner.

HAM

Cut a circle through the rind at the bone end; run your fingers around the edge, pull the rind back from the cut.

To begin carving, cut a small wedge from the top of the ham close to the remaining rind on the bone end.

Make long sweeps with the knife to get large thin slices. As you carve, the slices will increase in size.

As you continue slicing, the ham can be adjusted on the stand so it can be carved from the side.

Turkey breast tends to brown faster than the rest of the bird, so keep the greased foil used in the first part of the cooking and if the breast is browning too much, cover it with foil.

Traditional turkey with forcemeat stuffing

PREPARATION TIME 40 MINUTES **COOKING TIME** 3 HOURS 10 MINUTES (PLUS STANDING TIME) **SERVES** 10

4.5kg turkey

1 cup (250ml) water

80g butter, melted

¼ cup (35g) plain flour

3 cups (750ml) chicken stock

½ cup (125ml) dry white wine

FORCEMEAT STUFFING

40g butter

3 medium brown onions (450g), chopped finely

2 bacon rashers (140g), rind removed, chopped coarsely

1 cup (70g) stale breadcrumbs

2 tablespoons finely chopped fresh tarragon

½ cup coarsely chopped fresh flat-leaf parsley

½ cup (70g) coarsely chopped roasted pistachios

250g pork mince

250g chicken mince

To test if turkey is cooked, insert a skewer into the thickest part of the breast. If the juice runs clear, the turkey is cooked. Alternatively, insert a meat thermometer into the thickest part of the thigh, without touching any bone; the temperature should reach 90°C.

1 Make forcemeat stuffing.

2 Preheat oven to moderate (180°C/160°C fan-forced).

3 Discard neck from turkey. Rinse turkey under cold water; pat dry inside and out with absorbent paper. Fill neck cavity loosely with stuffing; secure skin over opening with poultry pins. Fill large cavity loosely with stuffing; tie legs together with kitchen string.

4 Place turkey on oiled wire rack in large shallow flameproof baking dish; pour the water into dish. Brush turkey all over with half of the butter; cover dish tightly with two layers of greased foil. Roast 2 hours. Uncover turkey; brush with remaining butter. Roast, uncovered, about 45 minutes or until browned all over and cooked through. Remove turkey from dish, cover turkey; stand 20 minutes.

5 Pour juice from dish into large jug; skim 1 tablespoon of the fat from juice, return to same dish. Skim and discard remaining fat from juice. Add flour to dish; cook, stirring, until mixture bubbles and is well browned. Gradually stir in stock, wine and remaining juice; bring to a boil, stirring, until gravy boils and thickens. Strain gravy into serving jug; serve turkey with gravy.

FORCEMEAT STUFFING Melt butter in medium frying pan; cook onion and bacon, stirring, until onion softens. Using hand, combine onion mixture in large bowl with remaining ingredients.

PER SERVING 47.4g total fat (17.2g saturated); 3097kj (741 cal); 11.3g carbohydrate; 65.2g protein; 1.8g fibre

1 TRADITIONAL TURKEY WITH FORCEMEAT STUFFING **2** PORK LOIN WITH SPINACH AND PANCETTA STUFFING [P 438] **3** ASIAN-SPICED BARBECUED TURKEY [P 438] **4** TRADITIONAL GLAZED HAM [P 439]

1

2

3

4

When you order the pork loin, ask your butcher to leave a flap measuring about 20cm in length to help make rolling the stuffed loin easier.

Pork loin with spinach and pancetta stuffing

PREPARATION TIME 30 MINUTES **COOKING TIME** 1 HOUR 30 MINUTES **SERVES** 10

4 slices white bread (180g)
2 tablespoons olive oil
2 cloves garlic, crushed
1 medium brown onion (150g), chopped coarsely
6 slices pancetta (90g), chopped coarsely
100g baby spinach leaves
¼ cup (35g) roasted macadamias, chopped coarsely
½ cup (125ml) chicken stock
2kg boned pork loin

PLUM AND RED WINE SAUCE
1½ cups (480g) plum jam
2 tablespoons dry red wine
⅔ cup (160ml) chicken stock

1 Preheat oven to moderately hot (200°C/180°C fan-forced).
2 Discard bread crusts; cut bread into 1cm cubes. Heat half of the oil in large frying pan; cook bread, stirring, until browned and crisp. Drain croutons on absorbent paper.
3 Heat remaining oil in same pan; cook garlic, onion and pancetta until onion browns lightly. Stir in spinach; remove from heat. Stir in croutons, nuts and stock.
4 Place pork on board, fat-side down; slice through thickest part of pork horizontally, without cutting through other side. Open out pork to form one large piece; press stuffing against loin along width of pork. Roll to enclose stuffing, secure with kitchen string.
5 Place rolled pork on rack in large shallow baking dish. Roast, uncovered, 1¼ hours or until cooked through. Cover; stand 10 minutes. Make plum and red wine sauce.
6 Serve sliced pork with sauce.

PLUM AND RED WINE SAUCE Combine ingredients in small saucepan; bring to a boil. Reduce heat; simmer, uncovered, about 10 minutes or until sauce thickens slightly.

PER SERVING 25.7g total fat (7.1g saturated); 2458kj (588 cal); 40.3g carbohydrate; 47g protein; 1.8g fibre

---

The indirect method is used in a covered barbecue. With gas, the food is placed in the barbecue; the burners directly under the food are turned off while the side burners remain on. With a charcoal barbecue, metal bars hold two stacks of coals against the barbecue's sides leaving the centre rack empty.

Asian-spiced barbecued turkey

PREPARATION TIME 25 MINUTES **COOKING TIME** 1 HOUR 50 MINUTES **SERVES** 8

4kg turkey
2 tablespoons sichuan peppercorns
2 star anise
1 tablespoon coriander seeds
1 tablespoon cumin seeds
2 teaspoons salt
2 teaspoons dried chilli flakes
1 teaspoon ground ginger
1 teaspoon five-spice powder
⅓ cup (80ml) vegetable oil

1 Discard neck from turkey. Rinse turkey under cold water; pat dry inside and out with absorbent paper. Using kitchen scissors, cut along each side of turkey's backbone; discard backbone. Turn turkey skin-side up; press down on breastbone to flatten turkey.

2 Using mortar and pestle, crush peppercorns, star anise, seeds and salt until mixture is crushed coarsely. Dry-fry peppercorn mixture with chilli, ginger and five-spice in small frying pan until fragrant. Remove from heat; stir in oil. Rub all over turkey.

3 Place turkey on heated barbecue; cook, covered, using indirect heat method, over low heat about 1¾ hours or until cooked through.

PER SERVING 40.7g total fat (10.7g saturated); 2404kj (575 cal); 0g carbohydrate; 53.0g protein; 0g fibre

---

Traditional glazed ham

For maximum impact and minimum fuss, nothing compares with a glazed and decorated ham in the centre of your Christmas table. Ham can be served warm or cold, so it is easy to prepare it the day before it is required, or skin and decorate the ham the day before, then bake it early the next morning.

PREPARATION TIME 30 MINUTES **COOKING TIME** 1 HOUR 5 MINUTES **SERVES** 20

8kg cooked leg of ham

thinly sliced glacé ginger and whole cloves, to decorate

½ cup (175g) honey

1 Preheat oven to moderate (180°C/160°C fan-forced).

2 Cut through rind about 10cm from shank end in decorative pattern; run thumb around edge of rind just under skin to remove rind. Carefully pull rind away from fat up to decorative pattern. (Reserved rind can be used to cover surface of ham to keep it moist during storage).

3 Gently cut diamond pattern into ham fat (not the flesh); decorate with ginger and cloves. Place ham on wire rack in large baking dish; cover shank with foil. Brush surface of ham with honey; bake, uncovered, 20 minutes.

4 Meanwhile, make desired glaze.

5 Brush ham with glaze. Bake, uncovered, about 45 minutes or until browned all over, brushing frequently with glaze during cooking.

LIME GLAZE Stir 1 cup lime marmalade, 2 tablespoons lime juice, ¼ cup firmly packed brown sugar and ¼ cup sweet sherry in small saucepan, over low heat, until marmalade melts.

PER SERVING (INCLUDING HAM) 16.9g total fat (6.2g saturated); 1743kj (417 cal); 10.7g carbohydrate; 54.3g protein; 0.0g fibre

CRANBERRY-CURRANT GLAZE Stir 340g jar redcurrant jelly and 290g jar cranberry sauce in medium saucepan, over low heat, without boiling, until jelly melts. Remove from heat; stir in 2 tablespoons lemon juice and ⅓ cup brandy. Strain.

PER SERVING (INCLUDING HAM) 13.0g total fat (4.8g saturated); 1367kj (327 cal); 8.6g carbohydrate; 42.0g protein; 0.0g fibre

PINEAPPLE-ORANGE GLAZE Stir ¼ cup pineapple juice, 2 tablespoons orange marmalade, ¼ cup firmly packed brown sugar and 1 tablespoon brandy in small saucepan, over low heat, until mixture boils. Reduce heat; simmer, uncovered 10 minutes.

PER SERVING (INCLUDING HAM) 3.0g total fat (4.9g saturated); 1258kj (301 cal); 3.6g carbohydrate; 41.7g protein; 0.0g fibre

Cold seafood platter with dipping sauces

PREPARATION TIME 1 HOUR **SERVES** 4

1 cooked large lobster (1.2kg)

2 cooked blue swimmer crabs (650g)

4 cooked balmain bugs (800g)

16 cooked large king prawns (1.1kg)

12 oysters, on the half shell

3 lemons, cut into wedges

SAMBAL MAYONNAISE

½ cup (150g) mayonnaise

1 tablespoon water

2 tablespoons tomato sauce

1 teaspoon worcestershire sauce

1 teaspoon sambal oelek

MUSTARD AND DILL

½ cup (150g) mayonnaise

1 tablespoon water

1 tablespoon drained baby capers, rinsed

1 teaspoon wholegrain mustard

1 tablespoon coarsely chopped fresh dill

CHILLI AND LIME

¼ cup (60ml) sweet chilli sauce

2 tablespoons lime juice

1 tablespoon water

1 teaspoon fish sauce

2 teaspoons finely chopped fresh vietnamese mint

Cold seafood platters have become a popular choice for Christmas in many households. Safe storage and handling are imperative and the following pointers should be noted.

- *Purchase seafood no more than a day ahead from a reputable supplier at the end of your shopping trip; take it home in an iced cool box and refrigerate immediately.*
- *Defrost any frozen seafood in the fridge.*
- *Prepare the platter just before serving.*

1 Place lobster upside-down. Cut through chest and tail; turn lobster around and cut through head. Pull halves apart; using small spoon, remove brain matter and liver. Rinse lobster carefully under cold water. Pat dry with absorbent paper.

2 Place one crab upside-down; lift tail flap then, with a peeling motion, lift off back shell. Remove and discard whitish gills, liver and brain matter; rinse crab well. Cut crab body in half; repeat with remaining crab. Rinse well under cold water.

3 Place bugs upside-down on chopping board; cut in half lengthways. Remove any green matter, liver and back vein from tails.

4 Shell and devein prawns, leaving heads and tails intact.

5 Make any or all of the dipping sauces.

6 Arrange seafood on large serving platter with lemon. Serve with dipping sauces.

If you can't find balmain bugs, use scampi instead.

DIPPING SAUCES Combine ingredients for each in small bowls.

☐ **PER SERVING (INCLUDING SAUCES)** 29.9g total fat (3.5g saturated); 3612kj (864 cal); 23.7g carbohydrate; 122.6g protein; 3.1g fibre

COLD SEAFOOD PLATTER WITH DIPPING SAUCE

To store the pudding, cool to room temperature then wrap in plastic wrap; refrigerate in the cleaned steamer, or seal tightly in an airtight container. Store the pudding in the fridge for up to 2 months or frozen for up to 12 months.

Steamed Christmas pudding

PREPARATION TIME 25 MINUTES **COOKING TIME** 4 HOURS 15 MINUTES (PLUS COOLING TIME) **SERVES** 10

3 cups (480g) chopped mixed dried fruit

¾ cup (120g) finely chopped seeded dried dates

¾ cup (120g) finely chopped raisins

¾ cup (180ml) water

1 cup (220g) firmly packed brown sugar

100g butter, chopped

1 teaspoon bicarbonate of soda

2 eggs, beaten lightly

¾ cup (110g) plain flour

¾ cup (110g) self-raising flour

1 teaspoon mixed spice

½ teaspoon ground cinnamon

2 tablespoons dark rum

To reheat the pudding, cover with plastic wrap; microwave on medium (55%) for 15 minutes or until hot. To reheat individual serves, place on a microwave-proof dish, cover with plastic wrap and microwave on high (100%) for 30 seconds. Or, you can reheat the pudding by steaming (step 4) for 1 ½ hours.

1 Combine fruit, the water, sugar and butter in medium saucepan. Stir over medium heat until butter melts and sugar dissolves; bring to a boil. Reduce heat; simmer, uncovered, 6 minutes. Stir in soda. Transfer mixture to large bowl; cool to room temperature.

2 Stir in eggs, sifted dry ingredients and rum.

3 Grease 2-litre (8-cup) pudding steamer; spoon mixture into steamer. Top with pleated baking paper and foil (to allow pudding to expand as it cooks); secure with kitchen string or tight-fitting lid.

4 Place pudding in large boiler with enough boiling water to come halfway up side of steamer. Cover with tight-fitting lid, boil for 4 hours, replenishing water as necessary to maintain level. Stand 10 minutes before turning onto plate; serve with cream, ice-cream, hard sauce (below) or vanilla custard (page 444).

PER SERVING 10.1g total fat (5.9g saturated); 1969kj (471 cal); 84.4g carbohydrate; 5.2g protein; 5.2g fibre

---

For a delicious twist to this festive favourite, replace the cream with 2 tablespoons orange juice and about 1 tablespoon finely grated orange rind.

Hard sauce

PREPARATION 15 MINUTES **SERVES** 12

250g soft butter

2 cups (320g) icing sugar, sifted

¼ cup (60ml) cream

⅓ cup (80ml) brandy

1 Beat butter and sugar in small bowl with electric mixer until mixture is as white as possible. Beat in cream, then brandy. Serve with steamed or boiled Christmas pudding.

PER SERVING 19.2g total fat (12.7g saturated); 1229kj (294 cal); 26.9g carbohydrate; 0.2g protein; 0g fibre

This custard makes a great festive trifle layered with tropical fruits, orange cake and passionfruit jelly. Top with whipped cream and fresh passionfruit pulp.

Vanilla custard

PREPARATION 10 MINUTES **COOKING** 25 MINUTES (PLUS STANDING TIME) **SERVES** 12

2 cups (500ml) milk
300ml thickened cream
1 vanilla bean, halved lengthways
6 egg yolks
⅓ cup (75g) caster sugar
2 teaspoons cornflour

1 Combine milk, cream and vanilla bean in medium saucepan; heat until just below boiling point. Stand 15 minutes; discard vanilla bean.
2 Beat egg yolks and sugar in small bowl with electric mixer until thick and creamy; beat in cornflour. Gradually whisk egg mixture into warm milk mixture.
3 Return milk mixture to pan; stir over low heat, without boiling, until custard thickens.
4 Strain into medium jug. Serve with steamed or boiled Christmas pudding.

PER SERVING 13.7g total fat (8.0g saturated); 727kj (174 cal); 9.4g carbohydrate; 3.5g protein; 0.0g fibre

---

This traditional German Christmas treat is often made with a layer of marzipan through the centre of the bread. Marzipan is the generic name for almond paste and can be purchased at some delicatessens and cake shops. To make your own combine 1 ¼ cups icing sugar, ½ cup almond meal, 1 tablespoon brandy, 1 egg yolk with enough lemon juice to make a firm paste.

Stollen

PREPARATION TIME 15 MINUTES **COOKING TIME** 3 HOURS (PLUS COOLING TIME) **SERVES** 18

1 ¼ cups (310ml) milk
1 teaspoon salt
½ cup (110g) caster sugar
2 teaspoons dried yeast
4 cups (600g) plain flour
160g butter, melted
2 eggs, beaten lightly
1 tablespoon finely grated lemon rind
¼ cup (40g) finely chopped raisins
¼ cup (50g) glacé cherries, quartered
¼ cup (40g) mixed peel
2 rings (55g) glacé pineapple, chopped finely
½ cup (80g) blanched almonds, chopped coarsely
½ teaspoon ground cinnamon
2 teaspoons caster sugar, extra
1 egg, extra

1 Stir milk, salt and sugar in small saucepan over heat until sugar dissolves and milk warms. Transfer to medium bowl. Whisk in yeast and 1 cup of the flour, cover; stand in warm place about 10 minutes or until mixture is frothy. Sift remaining flour into large bowl. Stir in butter, eggs, rind, fruit, yeast mixture and nuts; mix to a soft dough.
2 Turn dough onto floured surface; knead 5 minutes or until smooth. Halve dough; press each half into 18cm x 25cm oval. Sprinkle with cinnamon and extra sugar; fold dough almost in half. Place stollens on greased oven trays, cover with greased plastic wrap; stand in warm place 40 minutes or until risen slightly.
3 Preheat oven to moderately hot (200°C/180°C fan-forced).
4 Brush stollen with extra egg. Bake, uncovered, 10 minutes. Reduce oven temperature to moderate (180°C/160°C fan-forced); bake, uncovered, about 5 minutes or until cooked through.

PER SERVING 11.7g total fat (5.7g saturated); 1212kj (290 cal); 38.5g carbohydrate; 6.5g protein; 2.0g fibre

Christmas cookies

PREPARATION TIME 1 HOUR (PLUS REFRIGERATION TIME) **COOKING TIME** 1 HOUR (PLUS STANDING TIME)
MAKES 36 COOKIES

Make the cookies no more than a week before Christmas. They keep well in an airtight container, but they do slowly lose their fresh flavour if stored for too long. If you want to hang the cookies, make a small hole in the dough when you place the cookies on the trays in step 4. After the cookies are baked, and while they're still hot, use a skewer to make sure the hole is big enough for string or ribbon.

250g butter, softened
2 teaspoons finely grated lemon rind
½ teaspoon almond essence
¾ cup (165g) caster sugar
1 egg
1 tablespoon water
2¼ cups (335g) plain flour

ROYAL ICING
1½ cups (240g) pure icing sugar, approximately
1 egg white
½ teaspoon lemon juice

1 Preheat oven to moderate (180°C/160°C fan-forced). Line two oven trays with baking paper.
2 Beat butter, rind, essence, sugar, egg and the water in small bowl with electric mixer until smooth (do not overbeat). Transfer to large bowl; stir in sifted flour in two batches. Knead dough on floured surface until smooth, cover with plastic wrap; refrigerate about 30 minutes.
3 Roll dough between sheets of baking paper until 4mm thick. Cut shapes from dough using medium-sized cookie cutters.
4 Place cookies on oven trays; bake, uncovered, 10 minutes. Cool on oven trays.
5 Make royal icing.
6 Decorate cooled cookies with coloured icing. See pages 446 to 447 for some ideas.

ROYAL ICING Sift icing sugar through very fine sieve. Lightly beat egg white in small bowl with wooden spoon; add icing sugar, a heaped tablespoon at a time, beating well after each addition. When icing reaches the desired consistency, add juice; beat well. Cover surface of icing tightly with plastic wrap while not using to prevent crust developing. Colour royal icing by using liquid, paste or gel colourings; these can be bought from supermarkets, health-food stores and shops that supply to cake decorators.

Royal icing can be made soft enough to spread over cookies, or stiff enough to use for piping decorations – you simply need to adjust the amount of icing sugar you add.

☐ **PER COOKIE** 5.6g total fat (3.8g saturated); 435kj (104 cal); 11.3g carbohydrate; 1.2g protein; 0.4g fibre

☐ **PER TABLESPOON ICING** 0.0g total fat (0.0g saturated); 205kj (49 cal); 12.0g carbohydrate; 0.2g protein; 0.0g fibre

Christmas tree cookies

Make the cookies and icing on page 445, decorate as you wish and hang them on your Christmas tree.

SILVER ANGELS
Make cookies in a round or oval shape using cutters. Ice the cookies with white royal icing. Outline angel shapes before the icing sets using small round silver cachous.

CANDY CANES
Coarsely chop some candy canes; sprinkle on candy-cane-shaped cookies as soon as they are cooked (do not overcook). Return to the oven; bake a further 2 minutes or until the candy is melted slightly.

CHRISTMAS TREES
Cut out cookies using a Christmas tree cookie cutter; bake as instructed. Cool. Using coloured royal icing, decorate by piping with various Christmas tree themes.

CHRISTMAS COOKIE CANES
Divide the cookie dough in half; colour one half red. Roll the dough pieces into long sausages, twist the colours together. Shape into canes on oven trays; bake as instructed.

STAINED-GLASS COOKIES
Cut out the centres of cookies. Place on lined oven trays; bake for half the cooking time. Crush individually wrapped sugar-free fruit drops; unwrap and sprinkle into the centre of the cookies. Bake for remaining time.

CHRISTMAS BELLS
Colour a quarter of the cookie dough red. Cut bells from the remaining dough. Pipe red dough around the bells and bake as instructed.

SUGARED COOKIES
Using food colouring, colour caster sugar by massaging the colour through the sugar in a plastic bag. Ice cookies with coloured icing; sprinkle immediately with coloured sugars.

GINGERBREAD MEN
Make cookies using gingerbread men cutters; cool. Make a batch of royal icing. Use to pipe the face and clothes on gingerbread men. Decorate with brightly coloured ribbon; secure to the cookies with royal icing.

SNOW-FLAKES
Cut out cookies using a star-shaped cutter; bake as instructed. Melt some white chocolate Melts and use to cover the cooled stars. Sprinkle with flaked coconut before the chocolate sets.

HOLLY BAUBLES
Press rounds of cookie dough into a shallow round-based greased patty pan. Bake as instructed. Spread with white royal icing; when set, pipe holly with coloured royal icing.

CHRISTMAS COOKIE TREE
Using 5 different star cookie cutters, cut out shapes. Stack cookies, largest to smallest, on top of each other. Use melted white chocolate Melts to join the stars. Secure mini M&Ms with chocolate; dust with sifted icing sugar.

CHRISTMAS CHOCOLATE BAUBLES
Using a round cutter, cut out cookies; bake as instructed. Make a batch of royal icing; spread over the cookies and decorate with rainbow choc chips before the icing sets.

One quantity of this Christmas mix makes enough for all three of these Christmas recipes. It can be made a month before required and stored in a cool, dark place.

If you don't have time to soak the fruit mixture this way, place the fruit, juice and alcohol in a large saucepan, cover and gently heat, stirring occasionally, until the fruit has plumped up and the liquid has been absorbed. Alternatively, do this in the microwave on a low setting.

Three-in-one Christmas mix

PREPARATION TIME 45 MINUTES (PLUS STANDING TIME)

- 6 cups (1kg) sultanas
- 2½ cups (375g) dried currants
- 2¼ cups (425g) raisins, chopped
- 1½ cups (250g) seeded dried dates, chopped finely
- 1½ cups (250g) seeded prunes, chopped finely
- 1¼ cups (250g) glacé cherries, quartered
- ½ cup (125g) finely chopped glacé apricots
- ½ cup (115g) finely chopped glacé pineapple
- ½ cup (115g) finely chopped glacé ginger
- ¾ cup (120g) mixed peel
- 3 medium apples (450g), peeled, grated coarsely
- ⅔ cup (220g) marmalade or fig jam
- 2 tablespoons finely grated orange rind
- ¼ cup (60ml) lemon juice
- 2 cups (440g) firmly packed brown sugar
- 1 tablespoon mixed spice
- 1⅓ cups (330ml) orange liqueur, rum, brandy, whisky or sherry

1 Mix ingredients in large bowl; cover tightly with plastic wrap. Store mixture in cool, dark place for a month (or longer, if desired) before using; stir mixture every two or three days.

The safest way to flame a Christmas pudding is to warm brandy in a small saucepan or metal ladle, remove it from the heat, light it and then pour it over the pudding where it's being served.

You need a 60cm square of unbleached calico for the pudding cloth. If the calico has not been used before, soak it in cold water overnight; the next day, boil it for 20 minutes then rinse in cold water.

Christmas pudding

PREPARATION TIME 15 MINUTES **COOKING TIME** 4 HOURS (PLUS STANDING TIME) **SERVES** 12

- ¼ quantity three-in-one Christmas mix (see above)
- 250g butter, melted, cooled
- 3 eggs, beaten lightly
- 4 cups (280g) stale breadcrumbs
- ¼ cup (35g) plain flour

1 Place Christmas mix in large bowl. Stir in butter and egg then breadcrumbs and flour.
2 Fill large boiler three-quarters full of hot water, cover; bring to a boil. Have ready 2.5 metres of string and an extra ½ cup plain flour. Wearing thick rubber gloves, put pudding cloth in boiling water; boil 1 minute; squeeze out excess water. Spread hot cloth on bench, rub flour into centre of cloth to cover an area about 40cm in diameter, leaving flour a little thicker in centre of cloth where "skin" on the pudding needs to be thickest.
3 Place pudding mixture in centre of cloth. Gather cloth evenly around mixture, avoiding any deep pleats; then pat into round shape. Tie cloth tightly with string as close to mixture as possible. Pull ends of cloth tightly to ensure pudding is as round and firm as possible. Knot two pairs of corners together to make pudding easier to remove.
4 Lower pudding into boiling water; tie ends of string to handles of boiler to suspend pudding. Cover with tight-fitting lid; boil rapidly 4 hours, replenishing water as necessary.
5 Untie pudding from handles; place wooden spoon through knotted calico loops to lift pudding from water. Do not put pudding on bench; suspend from spoon by placing over rungs of upturned stool or wedging handle in a drawer. Pudding must be suspended freely.

Twist wet ends of cloth around string to prevent them touching pudding. If pudding has been cooked correctly, cloth will start to dry in patches within minutes; hang 10 minutes.
6 Place pudding on board; cut string, carefully peel back cloth. Turn pudding onto a plate then carefully peel cloth away completely; cool. Stand at least 20 minutes or until skin darkens and pudding becomes firm.

PER SERVING 19.5g total fat (11.9g saturated); 2203kj (527 cal); 74.7g carbohydrate; 6.6g protein; 4.0g fibre

---

Fruit mince slice

PREPARATION TIME 10 MINUTES **COOKING TIME** 25 MINUTES **SERVES** 30

Your hand is the best "utensil" for mixing cakes and puddings. Use just one hand to mix, and the other to steady the bowl.

- 2 sheets ready-rolled puff pastry
- ¼ quantity three-in-one Christmas mix (page 448)
- 1 egg white, beaten lightly
- 1 tablespoon caster sugar

1 Preheat oven to hot (220°C/200°C fan-forced). Grease 20cm x 30cm lamington pan.
2 Cut one pastry sheet large enough to cover base of pan. Using fork, prick pastry all over several times. Place 19cm x 29cm slice pan on top of pastry to prevent pastry rising during cooking. Bake pastry, uncovered, about 10 minutes or until pastry is browned lightly and crisp. Remove slice pan from lamington pan; spread Christmas mix evenly over pastry.
3 Cut remaining pastry sheet large enough to cover fruit mixture. Brush pastry with egg white, sprinkle with sugar; carefully score pastry in crosshatch pattern. Bake, uncovered, about 15 minutes or until pastry browns. Serve with custard, if desired.

PER SERVING 2.6g total fat (0.2g saturated); 623kj (149 cal); 27.4g carbohydrate; 1.3g protein; 1.3g fibre

---

Moist Christmas cake

PREPARATION TIME 15 MINUTES **COOKING TIME** 3 HOURS (PLUS COOLING TIME) **SERVES** 30

Orange liqueurs, such as Grand Marnier or Cointreau, marry well with the other citrus flavours in the basic fruit mixture. It is expensive, though, so rum, brandy, whisky or sherry all make great substitutes.

- ½ quantity three-in-one Christmas mix (page 448)
- 250g butter, melted, cooled
- 5 eggs, beaten lightly
- 2½ cups (375g) plain flour
- 2 tablespoons orange liqueur

1 Preheat oven to slow (150°C/130°C fan-forced). Line base and sides of deep 23cm-square cake pan with one thickness brown paper and two thicknesses baking paper, extending papers 5cm above sides of pan.
2 Place Christmas mix in large bowl. Mix in butter and egg then sifted flour in two batches. Spread mixture into pan; level top with spatula. Bake, uncovered, about 3 hours. Brush with liqueur; cover hot cake in pan with foil, cool overnight.

PER SERVING 8.1g total fat (4.8g saturated); 1392kj (333 cal); 55.4g carbohydrate; 3.6g protein; 2.8g fibre

This recipe was first published in The Australian Women's Weekly *in the 1980s and has since become one of our most asked-for recipes.*

We used Grand Marnier for this recipe, but you could use Cointreau.

Grand Marnier fruit cake

PREPARATION TIME 2 HOURS (PLUS STANDING TIME) **COOKING TIME** 3 HOURS 40 MINUTES (PLUS COOLING TIME) **SERVES** 20

3 cups (500g) sultanas

1½ cups (250g) mixed peel

¾ cup (120g) coarsely chopped raisins

¾ cup (110g) coarsely chopped seeded dried dates

⅔ cup (120g) coarsely chopped seeded prunes

½ cup (125g) coarsely chopped glacé apricots

⅔ cup (150g) coarsely chopped glacé pineapple

½ cup (70g) slivered almonds

½ cup (55g) coarsely chopped walnuts

1 tablespoon finely grated orange rind

½ cup (110g) caster sugar

¼ cup (60ml) orange juice

½ cup (125ml) orange liqueur

250g butter, softened

½ cup (110g) firmly packed brown sugar

5 eggs

2 cups (300g) plain flour

2 tablespoons orange liqueur, extra

1kg ready-made fondant

1 egg white, beaten lightly

½ cup (80g) pure icing sugar, sifted

25cm-round covered cake board

decorative ribbon

13g packet silver cachous

Check the cake halfway through the cooking time. If it is browning too quickly, cover it with foil for the rest of the cooking time.

1 Combine fruit, nuts and rind in large bowl. Heat caster sugar in medium frying pan over low heat, without stirring, until it begins to melt then stir until sugar is browned lightly. Remove from heat, slowly stir in juice; return to low heat, stir until toffee dissolves (do not boil). Add liqueur; pour over fruit mixture, cover tightly with plastic wrap. Store mixture in cool, dark place for 10 days, stirring every day.

2 Preheat oven to slow (150°C/130°C fan-forced). Line base and sides of deep 22cm-round or deep 19cm-square cake pan with one thickness of brown paper and two thicknesses of baking paper, extending papers 5cm above edge.

3 Beat butter and brown sugar in small bowl with electric mixer until just combined; beat in eggs, one at a time, until just combined between additions. Stir butter mixture into fruit mixture, mix in flour; spread mixture into pan. Tap pan firmly on bench to settle mixture into pan; level cake mixture with wet spatula.

4 Bake cake about 3½ hours. Remove cake from oven, brush with extra liqueur; cover hot cake with foil then turn upside down to cool overnight.

5 Trim top of cake with sharp knife to ensure it sits flat when turned upside down. Mix a little fondant and cold boiled water to a sticky paste. Spread about 2 tablespoons of this mixture into the centre of a sheet of baking paper about 5cm larger than the cake; position cake upside down on paper.

6 Using spatula and small pieces of fondant, patch any holes on cake.

7 Brush egg white evenly over cake. Knead fondant on surface dusted with icing sugar until smooth; roll to 7mm thickness. Lift fondant onto cake with rolling pin, smoothing fondant all over cake with hands dusted with icing sugar. Using sharp knife, cut excess fondant away from base of cake.

8 Mix scraps of fondant and cold boiled water to a sticky paste. Spread 2 tablespoons of paste in centre of board; centre cake on board. Move the cake to the correct position on board; using sharp craft knife or scalpel, carefully cut away excess baking paper extending around base of cake.

9 Secure ribbon around cake using pins (remove to a safe place before cutting cake). Push cachous gently into fondant in the design of your choice.

☐ **PER SERVING** 15.8g total fat (7.4g saturated); 2826kj (676 cal); 119g carbohydrate; 6.4g protein; 3.7g fibre

---

Frozen chocolate fruit cake pudding

PREPARATION TIME 40 MINUTES (PLUS STANDING, REFRIGERATION AND FREEZING TIME)
COOKING TIME 10 MINUTES **SERVES** 12

For a simpler version of this recipe, soften 1 litre good-quality chocolate ice-cream. Stir in the fruit mixture, spices, nuts and chopped chocolate. Spoon the mixture into the lined basin.

- ½ cup (100g) coarsely chopped dried figs
- ¾ cup (120g) mixed dried fruit
- 4 fresh dates (100g), seeded, chopped coarsely
- 2 teaspoons finely grated orange rind
- ½ cup (125ml) brandy
- 125g butter
- ½ cup (75g) plain flour
- ½ cup (110g) firmly packed brown sugar
- 1 cup (250ml) milk
- 600ml thickened cream
- ⅔ cup (220g) chocolate hazelnut spread
- 1 teaspoon ground nutmeg
- 1 teaspoon ground cinnamon
- 4 egg yolks
- ⅓ cup (45g) roasted hazelnuts, chopped coarsely
- 200g dark eating chocolate, chopped finely
- 200g dark eating chocolate, melted, extra

1 Combine fruit, rind and brandy in large bowl; mix well. Cover tightly with plastic wrap; store in a cool, dark place overnight or up to a week, stirring every day.

2 Line 17.5cm, 1.75-litre (7-cup) pudding basin with plastic wrap, extending plastic 5cm over edge of basin.

3 Melt butter in medium saucepan, add flour; stir over heat until bubbling. Remove from heat; stir in sugar then milk and half of the cream. Stir over medium heat until mixture boils and thickens. Transfer to large bowl; stir in spread, spices and egg yolks. Cover surface of mixture with plastic wrap; refrigerate 1 hour.

4 Stir in fruit mixture, nuts and chopped chocolate. Beat remaining cream in small bowl with electric mixer until soft peaks form, fold into pudding mixture. Spoon mixture into basin, tap basin lightly to remove air bubbles. Cover with foil; freeze 3 hours or overnight.

5 Turn pudding onto tray; remove plastic wrap, return pudding to freezer.

6 Cut a 35cm circle from a piece of paper to use as a guide; cover paper with plastic wrap. Spread melted chocolate over plastic wrap then quickly drape plastic, chocolate-side down, over pudding. Quickly smooth with hands, avoiding deep pleats in the plastic. Freeze until firm. Peel away plastic; trim away excess chocolate. Serve with a selection of fresh and frosted seasonal fruit, if desired.

This pudding is one of our favourites; the flavour is reminiscent of the delicious scrapings from the bowl in which a Christmas cake was made.

☐ **PER SERVING** 48.5g total fat (30.2g saturated); 3097kj (741 cal); 62g carbohydrate; 7.3g protein; 4.9g fibre

Gingerbread house

PREPARATION TIME 2 HOURS 30 MINUTES (PLUS REFRIGERATION TIME)
COOKING TIME 45 MINUTES (PLUS STANDING TIME)

Give the kids a Christmas surprise by filling the house with lollies before putting the roof on.

4½ cups (675g) self-raising flour
3 teaspoons ground ginger
2 teaspoons ground cinnamon
1½ teaspoons ground clove
1 teaspoon ground nutmeg
185g butter, chopped
1 cup (220g) firmly packed dark brown sugar
½ cup (180g) treacle
2 eggs, beaten lightly
35cm round or square board
assorted lollies

ROYAL ICING
2 egg whites
3 cups (480g) pure icing sugar

You need thin cardboard or thick paper to make the patterns for the house. The house can be assembled 3 days ahead.

1 Process flour, spices and butter until mixture is crumbly (you may have to process in two batches). Add sugar, treacle and enough egg for mixture to just combine. Turn dough onto floured surface; knead until smooth. Cover; refrigerate 1 hour.
2 Cut paper patterns for gingerbread house: cut two 12cm x 19cm rectangles for roof; two 10.5cm x 16cm rectangles for side walls of house; and two 16cm x 18cm rectangles for front and back walls of house. Trim front and back walls to form two 11cm-high gables.
3 Preheat oven to moderate (180°C/160°C fan-forced). Roll dough between sheets of baking paper until 5mm thick. Peel away top paper; use patterns to cut shapes from dough. Pull away excess dough; slide baking paper with shapes onto oven trays; bake, uncovered, about 12 minutes or until shapes are just firm (they become crisp after they cool). Re-roll dough scraps into one 5mm-thick piece; cut out tree and chimney.
4 While shapes are still warm and soft, use tip of sharp knife to cut out small windows from side walls of house, then cut out door from front wall; reserve cut-out door piece. Trim shapes to straighten sides; transfer all shapes to wire racks to cool.
5 Make royal icing. Cover board with foil or silver paper.
6 Secure two crossed skewers to back of each roof piece with icing. Allow to dry.
7 Assemble house, securing roof and walls together with icing. If possible, stand house several hours or overnight, supporting sides with four cans, so that it is thoroughly dry before decorating. Decorate board around house with remaining icing to resemble fallen snow. Secure door to house with icing; decorate house with lollies, securing with icing. Secure trees to board and chimney to roof with icing. Dust house with a little sifted icing sugar, if desired.

ROYAL ICING Beat egg whites in small bowl with electric mixer until frothy; gradually beat in sifted icing sugar. Cover icing with damp cloth while not using.

GINGERBREAD HOUSE

For mini Christmas pudding truffles, crumble left-over fruit cake; mix with brandy and melted dark eating chocolate. Roll into small balls; chill in the fridge for 30 minutes. Dip the tops of the balls into melted white chocolate, decorate with chopped pieces of red and green glacé cherries.

Last-minute fruit cake

PREPARATION TIME 20 MINUTES **COOKING TIME** 2 HOURS (PLUS COOLING TIME) **SERVES** 20

1½ cups (240g) sultanas
1 cup (150g) raisins, chopped coarsely
1 cup (160g) dried currants
½ cup (85g) mixed peel
⅓ cup (70g) glacé cherries, halved
2 tablespoons coarsely chopped glacé pineapple
2 tablespoons coarsely chopped glacé apricots
185g butter, chopped
¾ cup (165g) firmly packed brown sugar
⅓ cup (80ml) brandy
⅓ cup (80ml) water
2 teaspoons finely grated orange rind
1 teaspoon finely grated lemon rind
1 tablespoon treacle
3 eggs, beaten lightly
1¼ cups (185g) plain flour
¼ cup (35g) self-raising flour
½ teaspoon bicarbonate of soda
½ cup (80g) blanched almonds

1 Combine fruit, butter, sugar, brandy and the water in medium saucepan, stir over medium heat until butter is melted and sugar is dissolved; bring to a boil. Remove from heat; transfer to large bowl. Cool to room temperature.
2 Preheat oven to slow (150°C/130°C fan-forced). Line deep 20cm-round cake pan with three thicknesses of baking paper, extending paper 5cm above side.
3 Stir rinds, treacle and egg into fruit mixture then sifted dry ingredients. Spread mixture into pan; decorate with nuts.
4 Bake, uncovered, about 2 hours. Cover cake with foil; cool in pan overnight.

PER SERVING 10.9g total fat (5.4g saturated); 1267kj (303 cal); 44.1g carbohydrate; 3.8g protein; 2.3g fibre

Panettone, a traditional Italian Christmas bread, originated in Milan but is now found all over the world. Use any leftovers to make a delicious bread and butter pudding (see fig and brioche pudding, page 598) or french toast, with grilled bananas and maple syrup.

Panettone

PREPARATION TIME 30 MINUTES (PLUS STANDING TIME) **COOKING TIME** 45 MINUTES **SERVES** 16

½ cup (75g) raisins
¼ cup (40g) mixed peel
½ cup (80g) sultanas
⅓ cup (80ml) marsala
2 tablespoons dried yeast
1 teaspoon caster sugar
¼ cup (60ml) warm milk
5 cups (750g) plain flour
1 teaspoon salt
¼ cup (55g) caster sugar, extra
3 eggs, beaten lightly
3 egg yolks
2 teaspoons finely grated orange rind
1 teaspoon vanilla extract
100g butter, softened
1 cup (250ml) warm milk, extra
1 egg, beaten lightly, extra

1 Combine fruit with marsala in small bowl, cover; stand 30 minutes. Combine yeast, sugar and milk in small bowl; whisk until yeast dissolves. Cover; stand in warm place about 10 minutes or until mixture is frothy.

2 Sift flour, salt and extra sugar into large bowl; make well in centre. Add egg and egg yolks, then rind, extract, butter, extra milk, yeast mixture and undrained fruit mixture.
3 Beat dough vigorously with wooden spoon about 5 minutes. Cover bowl with greased plastic wrap, stand in warm place about 30 minutes or until dough has doubled in size.
4 Grease two deep 20cm-round cake pans. Using string, tie a collar of greased foil around outside of pans, bringing foil about 6cm above rims. Turn dough onto floured surface; knead until smooth. Cut dough in half; knead each half on a floured surface about 5 minutes or until the dough loses its stickiness. Press dough into pans, cover; stand in warm place about 30 minutes or until dough has doubled in size.
5 Preheat oven to moderately hot (200°C/180°C fan-forced). Brush panettone with extra egg; bake, uncovered, 15 minutes. Reduce oven tempertaure to moderate (180°C/160°C fan-forced); bake, uncovered, about 30 minutes.

Beating the dough is important to develop the protein (gluten) in the flour. Initially, the dough will be soft like a cake batter, but will become elastic as it is beaten and will leave the side of the bowl when it is ready.

☐ **PER SERVING** 9.0g total fat (4.7g saturated); 1346kj (322 cal); 48.3g carbohydrate; 8.9g protein; 2.7g fibre

---

Hot cross buns

Hot cross buns are enjoyed every Easter. Once you taste these wonderful buns, you will see that they are most definitely worth the time and effort!

PREPARATION TIME 30 MINUTES (PLUS STANDING TIME) **COOKING TIME** 30 MINUTES **MAKES** 16

1 tablespoon dried yeast
¼ cup (55g) caster sugar
1 cup (250ml) warm milk
4 cups (600g) plain flour
1 teaspoon ground cinnamon
60g butter
1 egg, beaten lightly
½ cup (125ml) warm water
¾ cup (120g) dried currants
¼ cup (40g) mixed peel
1 tablespoon apricot jam

FLOUR PASTE
½ cup (75g) plain flour
1 tablespoon caster sugar
⅓ cup (80ml) water

1 Combine yeast, sugar and milk in small bowl; whisk until yeast dissolves. Cover; stand in warm place about 10 minutes or until mixture is frothy. Sift flour and cinnamon into large bowl; rub in butter. Stir in yeast mixture, egg, the water and fruit, cover; stand in warm place about 1 hour or until mixture has doubled in size.
2 Grease deep 23cm-square cake pan. Turn dough onto floured surface; knead 5 minutes or until smooth and elastic. Divide dough into 16 portions; knead into balls. Place buns into pan; stand in warm place about 20 minutes or until dough has risen to top of pan.
3 Preheat oven to moderately hot (200°C/180°C fan-forced). Make flour paste.
4 Place flour paste into piping bag fitted with small plain tube, pipe crosses onto buns. Bake, uncovered, 10 minutes. Reduce temperature to moderate (180°C/160°C fan-forced); bake, uncovered, about 20 minutes. Turn onto wire rack; brush with warm sieved jam.

FLOUR PASTE Combine flour and sugar in small bowl, gradually blend in the water.

☐ **PER BUN** 4.6g total fat (2.6g saturated); 1024kj (245 cal); 43.2g carbohydrate; 6.1g protein; 2.3g fibre

You can replace the dried figs with chopped red glacé cherries, and sprinkle ¼ cup desiccated coconut over the branches before they set. Mix and match the fruit and nuts to suit your taste. A rocky road mix where the ingredients are chopped finely would make a great tree too.

Christmas nut tree

PREPARATION TIME 30 MINUTES (PLUS REFRIGERATION TIME)

24cm-round covered cake board

500g dark eating chocolate, melted

1 cup (140g) roasted slivered almonds, chopped finely

½ cup (100g) finely chopped dried figs

100g dark eating chocolate, melted, extra

1 brazil nut

2 teaspoons icing sugar

1 Grease four oven trays; line each with baking paper. Mark nine crosses, measuring 7cm, 9cm, 11cm, 13cm, 14cm, 15cm, 16cm, 17cm and 18cm on trays, leaving about 3cm space between each cross. Mark an 18cm cross on cake board.

2 Combine chocolate, almonds and figs in medium bowl. Drop teaspoonfuls of the chocolate mixture along all the marked crosses to make branches; refrigerate several hours or overnight.

3 Drop a teaspoon of the extra melted chocolate into the centre of the 18cm cross on cake board; position the 18cm branch on top, moving it around to find the best position.

4 Assemble the remaining eight branches in pairs, starting from the largest remaining branch and finishing with the smallest, using about a teaspoon of the extra melted chocolate in the centre of each crossed pair; refrigerate until set.

5 Secure each pair to the next with a little melted chocolate (if the branches look a little uneven, support them underneath with a match box). Secure brazil nut to centre of smallest branch with remaining melted chocolate; refrigerate until chocolate sets between branches. Store tree in refrigerator until required; dust with sifted icing sugar.

An alternative to rice flour is fine semolina. Try adding ¼ cup chopped glacé ginger or 1 tablespoon finely grated orange rind.

Scottish shortbread

PREPARATION TIME 20 MINUTES (PLUS REFRIGERATION TIME) **COOKING TIME** 40 MINUTES **MAKES** 16

250g butter, chopped

⅓ cup (75g) caster sugar

¼ cup (50g) rice flour

2¼ cups (335g) plain flour

2 tablespoons white sugar

1 Preheat oven to slow (150°C/130°C fan-forced). Lightly grease two oven trays.

2 Beat butter and caster sugar in medium bowl with electric mixer until light and fluffy; stir in sifted flours, in two batches. Knead on floured surface until smooth.

3 Divide mixture in half; shape into two 20cm rounds on trays. Mark each round into eight wedges, prick with fork, pinch edges with fingers. Sprinkle with white sugar.

4 Bake, uncovered, 40 minutes. Stand 5 minutes then cut into wedges; cool on trays.

PER SERVING 13.1g total fat (8.5g saturated); 949kj (227 cal); 24.5g carbohydrate; 2.5g protein; 0.9g fibre

CHRISTMAS NUT TREE

PRESERVING

Preserving

It's surprising who makes preserves. Capable countrywomen, yes, of course, but we've seen a restaurant manager, a rock singer, a designer – all male, as it happens – happily absorbed in the calm pleasures of transforming fresh produces into proud rows of jars filled with sweet or savoury pantry treasures.

Making your own preserves doesn't have to be a major project. A satisfying hour or two in the kitchen will produce enough to add charm to the breakfast toast, the lunch sandwiches, afternoon tea, cheese and more. Like their commercial cousins, preserves, once opened, must be stored in the fridge.

JAMS AND CONSERVES

Jam is made with small pieces of fruit, a conserve with whole fruit or large pieces. For both, fruit is cooked until tender, then sugar is added and the mixture is cooked until it will gel or, in the case of smooth jams, become spreadable.

WHAT MAKES JAM SET

The agent that makes jam set is pectin, a gelatinous substance present in fruits – but the pectin will only act to set a jam mixture to a consistency that will gel if the right balance of sugar, pectin and acid are present. Lemon or lime juice, high in both pectin and acid, may be added to the mixture to correct the balance, and pectin-rich lemon or lime pips are sometimes tied in a muslin bag and boiled with the fruits to boost the pectin level. The pectin test is easy to do if you are making a jelly; the amount of sugar needed is determined as a result of this test. After the fruit has been strained, put a teaspoon of the resulting liquid in a cup and stir in a teaspoon of methylated spirits. If the mixture clots, use 1 cup of sugar to each cup of the fruit liquid. If the mixtures results in a series of small clots, use ¾ cup of sugar to each cup of fruit liquid. If there are no clots at all, stir in the juice of a lemon or lime, then do the test again.

MARMALADES

Marmalades are clear jams made from citrus fruits, with fine or chunky rind or thin slices of fruit suspended in them.

JELLIES

For jelly, the cooked fruit is strained overnight through a jelly bag and the clear juice is boiled with sugar until it reaches a consistency that will gel.

MAKING A JELLY BAG Jelly bags are available from kitchen shops, or you can make your own from a square of damp, fine cloth (boiled unbleached calico, an old tea-towel, doubled muslin or sheeting), tied securely to the legs of an upturned stool, with enough slack to dip in the centre. Place a bowl underneath, pour in the fruit and leave to drip. Cover the fruit with greaseproof paper or a tea-towel to protect it from dust and insects. Don't stir or press down or the jelly will be cloudy.

TESTING FOR SET Jam or jelly is ready for testing when a candy thermometer, placed in the mixture, reads 105°C to 106°C. See page 626 for how to use a candy thermometer. If you don't have a thermometer, dip a wooden spoon into the jam or jelly, hold it horizontal above the pan and tilt the bowl of the spoon towards you. When the mixture will fall from the spoon in heavy drops, it is ready for testing. Remove the pan from the heat, allow the bubbles to subside and drop a teaspoon of mixture onto a plate that has been chilled in the freezer for a few minutes. Return the plate to the freezer briefly to cool the jam or jelly to room temperature. Smooth jam should be of a spreadable consistency; jam with pieces of fruit should form a skin and wrinkle when pushed with a finger; jelly should be a firm mass. If not, boil for a few minutes more and test again. Always take the jam or jelly off the heat and wait until it stops bubbling before testing.

JARS, SEALING AND STORING

Use super-clean, just-sterilised glass jars without chips or cracks. Sterilise jars and metal jam funnels (if using) by one of the following methods.

- Place in the dishwasher and run through the rinse cycle, without detergent, at the hottest temperature.
- Cover with cold water in a large saucepan, put the lid on, bring to a boil and boil for 20 minutes. Remove the jars, drain well and stand right-way up on a board. Their own heat will soon dry them.
- Stand the jars right-way up, not touching each other, on an oven tray in a cold oven. Heat the oven to very slow, and leave for 30 minutes.

JAM OR JELLY Pour hot jam or jelly through a funnel (or use a jug) into hot jars, filling right to the top. Seal immediately with special preserving lids or screw-on (not snap-on) plastic (not metal) lids. Wipe, label and date the jars; store in a cool, dark, dry place.

OTHER PRESERVES Fill hot through a funnel (or use a jug) into hot jars; cool, seal as above.

FRUIT BUTTERS Ideally, use unsalted butter, but ordinary butter will do.

FRUIT CHEESES OR PASTES So called because they have the consistency of soft cheese; these are superb with any cheese and keep in a baking-paper-lined airtight container more or less forever.

CHUTNEYS Chutneys are sweet and tangy. A little can make a sandwich sublime or give oomph to cold meat or a grilled chop. Mango chutney is a classic accompaniment to curries.

PICKLES Clear pickles are vegetables, usually a single kind such as cucumbers or onions, in vinegar flavoured with herbs, spices and other aromatics. Thickened pickles use a medley of vegetables and are assertive, sharp, spicy, usually mustardy.

RELISHES Relishes are usually based on a single vegetable such as corn or tomatoes, and are milder than pickles, being sweet/savoury and tangy rather than strong and sharp. These usually only keep for a few weeks; store in the fridge.

For best results in jam making, use small amounts of fruit; they will need a shorter cooking time and give better results in flavour, texture and appearance. Once the sugar is added to the fruit mixture you don't really want it to be more than 5cm deep.

Raspberry and peach jam

PREPARATION TIME 5 MINUTES (PLUS COOLING TIME) **COOKING TIME** 20 MINUTES **MAKES** 3 CUPS

500g raspberries

2 medium peaches (300g), peeled, chopped coarsely

1 ½ cups (330g) white sugar

2 teaspoons finely grated lemon rind

¼ cup (60ml) water

2 tablespoons port

1 Stir berries, peaches, sugar, rind and the water in large saucepan over heat, without boiling, until sugar dissolves; bring to a boil. Boil, uncovered, without stirring, about 15 minutes or until jam gels.

2 Stir in port. Pour into hot sterilised jars; seal.

PER TABLESPOON 0.1g total fat (0g saturated); 196kj (47 cal); 10.6g carbohydrate; 0.2g protein; 0.8g fibre

Sugar cubes have fewer impurities and are therefore more likely to result in a clearer jelly. Try adding ½ cup passionfruit pulp to this jelly just before bottling; it's delicious.

Apple jelly

PREPARATION TIME 5 MINUTES (PLUS COOLING TIME) **COOKING TIME** 1 HOUR 20 MINUTES **MAKES** 3 CUPS

5 medium apples (750g), chopped coarsely

1 ½ litres (6 cups) water

4 cups (880g) white sugar, approximately

1 Combine apples (seeds, skin, cores and all) and the water in large saucepan; bring to a boil. Simmer, covered, 1 hour. Strain mixture through fine cloth; discard pulp.

2 Measure liquid; pour into large saucepan. Add correct amount of sugar (according to pectin test; see page 460) to each cup of liquid. Stir over heat, without boiling, until sugar dissolves; bring to a boil. Boil, uncovered, 15 minutes or until jelly sets. Pour into hot sterilised jars; seal.

PER TABLESPOON 0g total fat (0g saturated); 447kj (107 cal); 26.2g carbohydrate; 0.1g protein; 0.3g fibre

Apricot and pineapple jam

PREPARATION TIME 10 MINUTES (PLUS COOLING TIME) **COOKING TIME** 40 MINUTES **MAKES** 4 CUPS

25 medium fresh apricots (1.25kg)

1 small pineapple (900g), chopped coarsely

½ cup (125ml) water

2 tablespoons lemon juice

3 cups (660g) white sugar

1 Quarter apricots; discard stones. Combine with pineapple, the water and juice in large saucepan; bring to a boil. Simmer, covered, about 15 minutes or until fruit is just soft.

2 Add sugar, stir over heat, without boiling, until dissolved; Boil, uncovered, without stirring, about 15 minutes or until jam gels. Pour into hot sterilised jars; seal immediately.

PER TABLESPOON 0.1g total fat (0g saturated); 284kj (68 cal); 18.1g carbohydrate; 0.3g protein; 0.7g fibre

Quince paste

PREPARATION TIME 25 MINUTES (PLUS STANDING TIME) **COOKING TIME** 1 HOUR **MAKES** 40 SLICES

4 large quinces (2kg)
¼ cup (60ml) lemon juice
5 cups (1.1kg) caster sugar, approximately
1¾ cups (430ml) water
¼ cup (35g) shelled pistachios, chopped coarsely

1 Oil 15cm x 25cm loaf pan. Peel, quarter and core quinces; chop coarsely. Place in large saucepan with juice and the water, simmer, covered, about 40 minutes or until soft; cool.
2 Push quince mixture through sieve into medium bowl. Measure puree, for each cup allow 1 cup sugar. Stir puree and sugar in medium saucepan over heat 20 minutes or until thick and red; stir in nuts. Spread into pan; smooth top. Stand, uncovered, 24 hours.

PER SLICE 0.5g total fat (0.1g saturated); 539kj (129 cal); 29.0g carbohydrate; 0.4g protein; 2.7g fibre

It is extremely important that the puree and sugar mixture is cooked until it turns a deep rose colour. The cooking times may vary, depending on the pectin content of the individual fruit. If you have a food processor, puree the cooked quinces in seconds, rather than using a sieve.

Strawberry conserve

PREPARATION TIME 10 MINUTES (PLUS COOLING TIME) **COOKING TIME** 1 HOUR **MAKES** 6 CUPS

1.5kg strawberries, hulled
5 cups (1.1kg) white sugar
1 cup (250ml) lemon juice

1 Place berries in large saucepan; heat gently, covered, 5 minutes to extract juice from berries. Carefully remove berries from pan with slotted spoon, place in large bowl; reserve.
2 Add sugar and lemon juice to berry juice in pan, stir over heat, without boiling, until sugar dissolves; bring to a boil. Boil, uncovered, without stirring, 20 minutes. Return berries to pan; simmer, uncovered, without stirring, about 25 minutes or until jam gels. Pour jam into hot sterilised jars; seal.

PER TABLESPOON 0g total fat (0g saturated); 280kj (67 cal); 15.9g carbohydrate; 0.4g protein; 0.5g fibre

Fruit for jam making should be barely ripe, as over-ripe fruit results in a jam or jelly that does not set well. Remove any bruised or damaged pieces before you start.

Tomato and passionfruit jam

PREPARATION TIME 30 MINUTES (PLUS COOLING TIME) **COOKING TIME** 1 HOUR **MAKES** 5 CUPS

10 medium tomatoes (1.5kg), peeled, chopped coarsely
2 large apples (400g), peeled, chopped coarsely
⅓ cup (80ml) lemon juice
2 cups (500ml) passionfruit pulp
4 cups (880g) white sugar

1 Cook tomato and apple in large saucepan over low heat about 25 minutes or until pulpy. Add remaining ingredients, stir over heat until sugar dissolves. Boil, uncovered, without stirring, 30 minutes or until jam gels. Pour into hot sterilised jars; seal.

PER TABLESPOON 0g total fat (0g saturated); 288kj (69 cal); 15.9g carbohydrate; 0.4g protein; 1.4g fibre

This is an old-fashioned Australian jam with a marvellous, not-too-sweet flavour.

The seeds and pith are reserved because they contain high levels of pectin, which will help the marmalade to set.

Sweet orange marmalade

PREPARATION TIME 25 MINUTES (PLUS STANDING AND COOLING TIME) **COOKING TIME** 1 HOUR **MAKES** 7 CUPS

5 large oranges (1.5kg)
1.25 litres (5 cups) water
2 teaspoons citric acid
2 tablespoons lemon juice
5 cups (1.1kg) white sugar

Seville oranges have a short season in winter, and they make a superb bitter-sweet marmalade. Follow the proportions of fruit to sugar and water for the sweet orange marmalade (at right). No need to add the citric acid or lemon juice; other than that, the recipe is the same.

1 Cut oranges into quarters. Using sharp knife, remove pith and rind from each quarter, reserve half of the pith, discard remaining pith. Cut orange flesh into thin slices, place into a large bowl, reserve seeds. Cut rind into very thin strips, place into bowl with orange flesh, add half of the water, cover; stand overnight.

2 Tie reserved seeds and pith in piece of muslin, place bag into separate bowl with citric acid and remaining water; cover; stand overnight.

3 Combine contents of bowls with juice in large saucepan; bring to a boil. Reduce heat; simmer, covered, about 40 minutes or until rind is soft. Discard muslin bag.

4 Add sugar, stir over heat, without boiling, until sugar dissolves; bring to a boil. Boil, uncovered, without stirring, about 15 minutes or until marmalade gels; stand 10 minutes. Pour into hot sterilised jars; seal.

PER TABLESPOON 0g total fat (0g saturated); 342kj (58 cal); 14.1g carbohydrate; 0.1g protein; 0.3g fibre

---

Spread this tangy fruit curd through the centre of a coconut cake, fold into ice-cream, spoon into little tart cases and top with fresh raspberries, spread over a baked cheesecake, or spoon onto scones. If you like, use all lemon juice instead of the lime juice. Replace the lime rind with lemon rind.

Lemon and lime butter

PREPARATION TIME 10 MINUTES (PLUS COOLING TIME) **COOKING TIME** 10 MINUTES **MAKES** 3 CUPS

185g butter, chopped
2 cups (440g) caster sugar
½ cup (125ml) lemon juice
1 teaspoon finely grated lime rind
⅓ cup (80ml) lime juice
4 eggs, beaten lightly, strained

1 Combine ingredients in top half of double saucepan or in large heatproof bowl placed over large saucepan of simmering water; stir until mixture thickly coats the back of a wooden spoon. Remove from heat and simmering water immediately.

2 Stand bowl in sink of cold water 10 minutes to stop cooking process. Pour into hot sterilised jars; seal.

PER TABLESPOON 4.8g total fat (3.0g saturated); 401kj (96 cal); 12.4g carbohydrate; 0.8g protein; 0g fibre

SWEET ORANGE MARMALADE

Spices

The tastes and aromas that bring thousands of dishes to life. Keep them dark, dry and airtight.

RAS EL HANOUT
The name means "top of the shop" and the mixture varies from one merchant to another, but is always subtly savoury with a touch of heat. Excellent with lamb or chicken.

STAR ANISE
The dried, star-shaped fruit of a small Asian tree with a pungent liquorice/clove/cinnamon flavour. Used whole or ground, it is the main spice in Chinese five-spice. Use sparingly with pork or duck or in a fruit compote.

SAFFRON
Expensive because it consists of the hand-gathered stigmas from a crocus flower. Buy it only from a reputable source. It colours food golden and has a bittersweet almondy taste.

BAHARAT
A spice blend used throughout the Middle East. It typically includes ground paprika, black pepper, cumin, coriander, cassia, cloves, cardamom and nutmeg. Rub on fish, beef or lamb before cooking.

ASAFOETIDA
The dried and ground resin of a giant fennel, notorious for its penetrating "rotten" smell but this is toned down in cooking. Its pungent flavour suggests fermented garlic. Use this spice sparingly with lentils and in fish and vegetable curries.

KALONJI
Also called nigella, these are the seeds of a plant related to buttercups. The flavour is sharp/metallic (reduced by cooking), nutty, peppery. Used in or on Turkish and Indian breads, and in the Indian spice mix, panch phora.

SUMAC
A purple-red spice ground from the berries of a small Mediterranean tree. Adds a tart, lemony flavour to dips and dressings and goes well with meat, chicken and fish, tomato and avocado.

ZA'ATAR
A blend of roasted dried oregano, marjoram, thyme, sumac and sesame seeds found in the Lebanese and Syrian kitchen. Traditionally sprinkled on toast spread with ricotta, it's great tossed with roasted potato wedges too.

HARISSA
A fiery Tunisian paste made by pounding chilli with spices, garlic and mint. Used to season meats such as kebabs and traditionally placed on the table as an all-purpose condiment.

FENUGREEK
The seeds of a herb of the pea family. Used in curry powder, good with seafood and in chutneys. The aroma of fenugreek is known for its characteristic of masking unpleasant odours.

SICHUAN PEPPERCORNS
No relation to other peppercorns, Sichuan (also spelt Szechuan) peppercorns are the dried berries of a small tree native to the Sichuan province of south-west China, where highly spiced foods are much appreciated. They smell and taste peppery/lemony.

GARAM MASALA
The name simply means "spice blend" and the mixture varies, but is always savoury with a touch of pepper bite. Used as a seasoning in Indian cooking and is sometimes sprinkled over the finished dish.

Jars must be made of glass, without chips or cracks, and should be thoroughly washed, then sterilised. For information on how to sterilise jars, see page 461.

Grapefruit and ginger marmalade

PREPARATION TIME 25 MINUTES (PLUS COOLING TIME) **COOKING TIME** 2 HOURS **MAKES** 8 CUPS

2 medium lemons (280g)
2 medium grapefruit (850g)
6cm piece fresh ginger (30g)
2.5 litres (10 cups) water
1 teaspoon tartaric acid
8 cups (1.75kg) white sugar
1 cup (180g) finely chopped glacé ginger

1 Peel lemons; chop rind coarsely. Chop flesh coarsely; reserve seeds and juice. Peel grapefruit, chop rind into fine strips, reserve. Chop flesh coarsely; reserve seeds and juice.
2 Combine lemon and grapefruit flesh with reserved juice in large saucepan. Tie reserved seeds, lemon rind and fresh peeled ginger in piece of muslin, add to pan. Add grapefruit rind with the water and acid; bring to a boil. Boil, uncovered, about 1½ hours or until rind is soft and mixture has reduced by half. Discard muslin bag.
3 Add sugar; stir, without boiling, until sugar dissolves. Boil, uncovered, without stirring, 15 minutes or until marmalade gels. Add glacé ginger; stand 10 minutes. Pour into hot sterilised jars; seal.

PER TABLESPOON 0g total fat (0g saturated); 343kj (82 cal); 20.1g carbohydrate; 0.1g protein; 0.1g fibre

---

When cooking jam, be sure to use a large wide-topped saucepan that allows for the necessary evaporation, otherwise you will end up with runny jam. Usually, about half the liquid has to evaporate before the jam will gel.

Dark plum jam

PREPARATION TIME 15 MINUTES (PLUS COOLING TIME) **COOKING TIME** 1 HOUR 30 MINUTES **MAKES** 8 CUPS

28 medium blood plums (2kg)
1 litre (4 cups) water
⅓ cup (80ml) lemon juice
6 cups (1.3kg) white sugar

1 Cut plums into quarters; remove stones. Combine plums and the water in large saucepan; bring to a boil. Reduce heat; simmer, covered, 1 hour.
2 Add juice and sugar, stir over heat, without boiling, until sugar dissolves. Boil, uncovered, without stirring, 20 minutes or until jam gels. Pour into hot sterilised jars; seal.

PER TABLESPOON 0g total fat (0g saturated); 255kj (61 cal); 14.7g carbohydrate; 0.1g protein; 0.4g fibre

---

The olives need to be marinated for 2 weeks before they are ready to eat.

Marinated olives

PREPARATION TIME 5 MINUTES (PLUS MARINATING TIME) **MAKES** 4 CUPS

1 clove garlic, sliced thinly
2 lemon wedges
1 sprig fresh dill
600g drained black or green olives
2 cups (500ml) olive oil

1 Combine ingredients in 1-litre (4-cup) hot sterilised jar; pour oil over top, seal jar.

PER ¼ CUP (UNDRAINED) 28.9g total fat (4.1g saturated); 1221kj (292 cal); 8.5g carbohydrate; 0.3g protein; 0.5g fibre

Spicy tomato chutney

PREPARATION TIME 20 MINUTES (PLUS COOLING TIME) **COOKING TIME** 1 HOUR 5 MINUTES
MAKES 6 CUPS

Tomato chutney makes a great addition to casseroles, rissoles, burgers and pot roasts.

- 10 medium ripe tomatoes (1.5kg), peeled, chopped coarsely
- 2 large apples (400g), peeled, chopped coarsely
- 2 medium brown onions (300g), chopped coarsely
- 1 cup (220g) firmly packed brown sugar
- 1½ cups (375ml) brown vinegar
- ¼ teaspoon chilli powder
- ½ teaspoon dry mustard
- ¾ cup (120g) sultanas
- 1 clove garlic, crushed
- 2 teaspoons curry powder
- 2 teaspoons ground allspice

1 Stir ingredients in large saucepan over heat, without boiling, until sugar dissolves; bring to a boil. Reduce heat; simmer, uncovered, stirring occasionally, about 1 hour or until mixture is thick. Pour into hot sterilised jars; seal.

PER TABLESPOON 0g total fat (0g saturated); 100kj (24 cal); 5.3g carbohydrate; 0.3g protein; 0.5g fibre

---

Spicy green tomato relish

PREPARATION TIME 25 MINUTES (PLUS STANDING TIME) **COOKING TIME** 1 HOUR **MAKES** 5 CUPS

Green tomatoes are simply unripened ordinary tomatoes, and gherkin cucumbers are just baby cucumbers. Use this relish in cheese or meat sandwiches or with cold meats, or put a spoonful in a stew to pep up the flavour.

- 10 medium green tomatoes (1.5kg), sliced thickly
- 1 medium brown onion (150g), sliced thickly
- 1kg gherkin cucumbers, chopped coarsely
- 1 medium green caspicum (200g), chopped coarsely
- ½ cup (145g) coarse cooking salt
- 2 cups (500ml) apple cider vinegar
- 1 cup (250ml) white vinegar
- 1 teaspoon dry mustard
- ½ teaspoon ground allspice
- ¼ teaspoon mixed spice
- ¼ teaspoon ground cinnamon
- ¼ teaspoon cracked black pepper
- 1 cup (220g) firmly packed brown sugar

1 Combine vegetables and salt in large bowl; stand 3 hours. Rinse under cold water; drain.
2 Place vegetables in large saucepan, stir in vinegars and spices; bring to a boil. Reduce heat; simmer, uncovered, stirring occasionally, about 45 minutes or until vegetables are pulpy. Add sugar, stir over heat, without boiling, until sugar dissolves; bring to a boil. Boil, uncovered, 10 minutes. Pour into hot sterilised jars; seal.

PER TABLESPOON 0.1g total fat (0g saturated); 159kj (38 cal); 8.5g carbohydrate; 0.4g protein; 0.7g fibre

This tart-sweet chutney partners hot or cold poultry and pork perfectly.

Rhubarb chutney

PREPARATION TIME 10 MINUTES (PLUS COOLING TIME) **COOKING TIME** 1 HOUR 20 MINUTES **MAKES** 5 CUPS

1kg rhubarb, chopped coarsely

2 medium brown onions (300g), chopped coarsely

3 cups (660g) firmly packed brown sugar

1½ cups (240g) sultanas

2½ cups (625ml) white vinegar

1 tablespoon mustard seeds

1 teaspoon mixed spice

1 teaspoon ground ginger

1 Combine ingredients in large saucepan; bring to a boil. Reduce heat; simmer, uncovered, stirring occasionally, about 1¼ hours or until mixture thickens.

2 Pour into hot sterilised jars; seal.

PER ¼ CUP 0.1g total fat (0g saturated); 259kj (62 cal); 14.2g carbohydrate; 0.5g protein; 0.8g fibre

---

For a delicious potato salad to serve 6 to 8, mix the corn relish with 2kg cooked, sliced pontiac potatoes, 6 finely sliced green onions and 250g cooked chopped bacon. Lighten the mix with a little french dressing or mayonnaise if you like.

Corn relish

PREPARATION TIME 15 MINUTES (PLUS COOLING TIME) **COOKING TIME** 1 HOUR **MAKES** 6 CUPS

3 x 440g cans corn kernels, drained

2 medium brown onions (300g), chopped coarsely

1 medium red capsicum (200g), chopped coarsely

1 medium green capsicum (200g), chopped coarsely

2 trimmed celery stalks (200g), chopped coarsely

2 cups (500ml) apple cider vinegar

1¾ cups (430ml) white vinegar

1 cup (220g) white sugar

1 tablespoon dry mustard

1 tablespoon mustard seeds

1 teaspoon ground turmeric

½ teaspoon ground clove

¼ cup (35g) cornflour

¼ cup (60ml) white vinegar, extra

1 Combine corn, onion, capsicums, celery, vinegars, sugar, mustards, turmeric and clove in large saucepan; bring to a boil. Reduce heat; simmer, uncovered, about 45 minutes or until mixture thickens slightly, stirring occasionally.

2 Stir in blended cornflour and extra vinegar; stir until mixture boils and thickens.

3 Pour into hot sterilised jars; seal.

PER ¼ CUP 0.1g total fat (0g saturated); 92kj (22 cal); 4.8g carbohydrate; 0.3g protein; 0.3g fibre

RHUBARB CHUTNEY

1

2

3

4

Green mango chutney

Mango chutney is a classic sambal to serve with curries and is excellent with cold meats.

PREPARATION TIME 25 MINUTES (PLUS STANDING AND COOLING TIME) **COOKING TIME** 1 HOUR
MAKES 8 CUPS

6 medium green mangoes (2kg), peeled, chopped coarsely
1 tablespoon coarse cooking salt
1¾ cups (385g) white sugar
2½ cups (625ml) brown vinegar
8cm piece fresh ginger (40g), grated
2 cloves garlic, crushed
¾ cup (110g) coarsely chopped dried dates
¾ cup (120g) coarsely chopped raisins
1 teaspoon chilli powder
1 teaspoon ground cinnamon
1 teaspoon ground cumin

1 Place mango and salt in large bowl. Barely cover with cold water, cover; stand overnight.
2 Drain mango; discard water. Stir sugar and vinegar in large saucepan over heat, without boiling, until sugar dissolves. Stir in mango and remaining ingredients; simmer, uncovered, stirring occasionally, 45 minutes or until mixture is thick. Pour into hot sterilised jars; seal.

PER TABLESPOON 0g total fat (0g saturated); 188kj (33 cal); 7.6g carbohydrate; 0.2g protein; 0.4g fibre

---

Spicy mustard pickles

An old-fashioned pickle that is splendid with cold roast lamb or cheddar cheese, or mix it with grated cheese, pile it on toast and grill.

PREPARATION TIME 25 MINUTES (PLUS STANDING AND COOLING TIME) **COOKING TIME** 25 MINUTES
MAKES 4 CUPS

¼ medium cauliflower (400g), chopped coarsely
250g green beans, trimmed, chopped coarsely
3 medium brown onions (450g), sliced thickly
1 medium red capsicum (200g), sliced thickly
¼ cup (70g) coarse cooking salt
2 teaspoons dry mustard
2 tablespoons wholegrain mustard
3 teaspoons curry powder
¼ teaspoon ground turmeric
2 cups (500ml) white vinegar
1 cup (220g) firmly packed brown sugar
2 tablespoons plain flour

1 Combine vegetables and salt in large bowl. Cover; stand overnight.
2 Rinse vegetables; drain. Stir vegetables, mustards, curry powder, turmeric, 1¾ cups of the vinegar and sugar in large saucepan over heat, without boiling, until sugar dissolves; bring to a boil. Simmer, uncovered, about 10 minutes or until vegetables are just tender.
3 Stir in blended flour and remaining vinegar; stir over heat until mixture boils and thickens. Pour into hot sterilised jars; seal.

PER TABLESPOON 0.1g total fat (0g saturated); 113kj (27 cal); 5.7g carbohydrate; 0.6g protein; 0.5g fibre

1 GREEN MANGO CHUTNEY **2** SPICY MUSTARD PICKLES
3 SUN-DRIED TOMATO AND OLIVE TAPENADE [P 474] **4** PESTO [P 474]

For a delicious canapé, spread ½ cup of this tapenade onto a sheet of ready-rolled puff pastry. Roll up like a swiss roll, encasing the tapenade; chill for 30 minutes. Cut into 1 cm slices, then place cut-side up on lightly oiled oven tray. Bake in a moderately hot oven for about 12 minutes or until browned lightly.

Sun-dried tomato and olive tapenade

PREPARATION TIME 15 MINUTES **MAKES** 1⅓ CUPS

1 cup (150g) drained sun-dried tomatoes

⅓ cup (80ml) olive oil

2 tablespoons red wine vinegar

1 tablespoon brown sugar

1 tablespoon coarsely chopped fresh oregano

1 tablespoon coarsely chopped fresh basil

½ teaspoon cracked black pepper

⅔ cup (80g) roasted pecans

⅓ cup (40g) seeded black olives

1 Blend or process ingredients until smooth.

PER TABLESPOON 8.6g total fat (1g saturated); 439kj (105 cal); 4.8g carbohydrate; 1.6g protein; 1.8g fibre

---

Pesto originates from Liguria in Italy, where it is traditionally served with linguine, green beans and boiled new potatoes.

Pesto

PREPARATION TIME 15 MINUTES **MAKES** 1¼ CUPS

2 cups firmly packed fresh basil leaves

½ cup (80g) roasted pine nuts

2 cloves garlic, quartered

½ cup (125ml) olive oil

⅓ cup (25g) finely grated parmesan

1 Process basil, nuts and garlic until chopped finely. With motor operating, add oil in thin, steady stream until combined. Add cheese; process until combined.

PER TABLESPOON 11.9g total fat (1.6g saturated); 472kj (113 cal); 0.3g carbohydrate; 1.4g protein; 0.5g fibre

---

Great for spreading on crusty bread or a pizza base, stirring into mashed potato, tossing through roasted Mediterranean vegetables, or combining with fresh mixed herbs to spread on fish as a crust

Traditional tapenade

PREPARATION TIME 10 MINUTES **MAKES** ½ CUP

1 tablespoon drained capers, rinsed

3 anchovy fillets, drained

½ cup (60g) seeded black olives

¼ cup (60ml) olive oil

1 Blend or process ingredients until tapenade is of desired consistency.

PER TABLESPOON 9.3g total fat (1.3g saturated); 385kj (92 cal); 2.0g carbohydrate; 0.5g protein; 0.1g fibre

Coriander pesto

PREPARATION TIME 5 MINUTES **MAKES** ⅔ CUP

2 tablespoons unsalted roasted peanuts

2 cloves garlic, quartered

½ cup firmly packed fresh coriander leaves

½ cup (125ml) peanut oil

1 Blend or process nuts, garlic and coriander until chopped finely. With motor operating, add oil in thin, steady stream until combined.

PER TABLESPOON 15.5g total fat (7.3g saturated); 143kj (59 cal); 0.4g carbohydrate; 0.8g protein; 0.4g fibre

Roasted cashews make a lovely alternative to roasted peanuts, and chilli is a nice addition to this recipe. Makes a great dressing for a pasta salad with roasted kumara and smoked chicken, or blend with avocado for a delicious dip.

Pickled onions

PREPARATION TIME 15 MINUTES (PLUS STANDING AND COOLING TIME) **COOKING TIME** 20 MINUTES **MAKES** 8 CUPS

1kg pickling onions, peeled

½ cup (145g) coarse cooking salt

1.25 litres (5 cups) water

1 litre (4 cups) white vinegar

½ cup (110g) white sugar

1 cinnamon stick

3cm piece fresh ginger (15g), peeled

1 fresh small red thai chilli, chopped coarsely

1 teaspoon cloves

1 teaspoon black peppercorns

1 Combine onions, salt and the water in large bowl, cover; stand overnight.

2 Drain onions; rinse well. Pack into large sterilised jar. Stir remaining ingredients in large saucepan over heat, without boiling, until sugar dissolves; bring to a boil. Reduce heat; simmer, uncovered, 10 minutes; cool 15 minutes. Strain vinegar mixture over onions; seal.

PER ¼ CUP (UNDRAINED) 0.1g total fat (0.0g saturated); 84kj (20 cal); 4.3g carbohydrate; 0.4g protein; 0.3g fibre

When peeling the onions, leave a tiny part of the root end of each onion intact; this will hold the onions together. For a more traditional pickled onion flavour, delete the chilli and ginger from this recipe.

Preserved lemons

PREPARATION TIME 10 MINUTES (PLUS STANDING TIME)

10 medium lemons (1.4kg), quartered

1 cup (250g) salt

1 bay leaf, torn

1 cinnamon stick, quartered

1 teaspoon coriander seeds, bruised

2 cups (500ml) lemon juice

1 Combine lemons and salt in large bowl.

2 Pack lemon mixture, bay leaf, cinnamon and seeds firmly into two 3-cup (750ml) sterilised jars. Pour in enough juice to cover lemons completely; seal jars tightly. Stand in cool, dry place at least a month.

You need approximately 8 lemons to make 2 cups of juice. We used fine sea salt, but coarse cooking salt or table salt can also be used. When recipes call for preserved lemon, use only the rind; scrape away and discard the lemon flesh.

BREADS & BUNS

Breads & Buns

Most people who try their hands at bread making enjoy it. Many become enthusiasts, not least because it is a vigorous job. Far from calling for a light hand, the dough needs plenty of energetic kneading to produce the chewy texture that characterises good bread. It is true that experience bestows a certain "feel" for when a dough seems right. If you are new to this, start with a recipe like onion focaccia, where you can get the feel of it all while the flavoursome ingredients will guarantee a good result.

THE BASICS

YEAST The yeast that interests cooks is one of a large family of microscopic plants that exist, invisibly, everywhere in nature. When they find warmth and moisture, they multiply – this is the process called fermentation. One yeast strain, baker's yeast, is the one that makes bread rise. As it grows in the warm, moist dough, it gives off thousands of tiny bubbles of the gas carbon dioxide, which inflate the dough so it swells and becomes light. Yeast is available in several forms.

- **Compressed or fresh yeast** comes in chunks that look rather like putty-coloured modelling clay and crumble easily. It should be pale and smell slightly and pleasantly of alcohol; dark patches and a strong smell mean it is stale and may not work. It will keep in an airtight jar in the fridge for about 2 weeks; it can be frozen, but sometimes seems a bit reluctant to work after thawing..
- **Dried yeast** is usually packed in boxes of sealed foil sachets containing 8g (3 teaspoons) each. Store in the fridge, where it will keep indefinitely.
- **Yeast compounds,** made from dried yeast and other ingredients designed to promote yeast activity and good flavour, are usually packed in large tins and are useful if you make bread often. They will keep for months if stored airtight in a cool place. Different brands vary slightly, so follow the instructions on the tin as to how and how much to use.

SUBSTITUTING TYPES OF YEAST Compressed and dried yeasts can be substituted for each other. One 8g sachet (3 teaspoons) of dried yeast is equivalent to 15g (3 teaspoons) of compressed or fresh yeast.

SOURDOUGH

Sourdough does not use commercial yeast, but a piece of dough from the last batch mixed into the new batch, to start fermentation. The sour tang comes from the continued action of the yeast, past the point where it would have been killed by baking, in the starter dough.

FLOUR

Flours contain a protein, gluten, which forms tiny elastic strands when it is moistened and agitated. Because the yeast in bread dough produces carbon dioxide slowly, the dough has to be strong and elastic enough to hold the gas for a long time. This is why bread dough is well beaten and then vigorously kneaded: these develop the gluten until it forms an elastic network strong enough to trap the gas.

Flours vary in their gluten content. Wheat flour contains more gluten than any other kind, so it nearly always forms part of the flour content for rye, barley and other non-wheat breads. Wheat flours vary according to the gluten content of the wheat from which they were made. Those used for breadmaking are high-gluten flours, known as bakers' flour, bread flour or strong flour. Lower-gluten flours are used for baked goods such as buns.

WATER

Yeast likes warmth, but it takes only 60°C heat to kill it. If you are using compressed yeast, the water should be lukewarm. If you use dried yeast, the water should be comfortably hand-warm. If in doubt, err on the cooler rather than the warmer side.

KNEADING

Kneading can be done by hand or with a dough hook in an electric mixer. To hand-knead, flour a work surface, place the dough on top (it will be sticky) and continuously fold the dough over towards you and push firmly away with the heel of your hand. Turn the dough a quarter turn after every second kneading. Sprinkle flour over as needed, but be sparing. The dough is sufficiently kneaded when it is smooth and elastic and the impression of a finger, pressed in, quickly disappears.

RISING

Put the dough in a lightly oiled bowl, turn to oil all over, then cover with greased plastic wrap and leave in a warm place until the dough doubles in bulk. You can slow down the rise, if it suits you, by leaving the bowl in a cooler place, even in the fridge overnight; many authorities say a slow rise gives better bread, having a finer crumb and better keeping quality. Bring the dough back to room temperature before proceeding. The dough is sufficiently risen when the impression of two fingers, quickly and lightly pressed in, remains.

SHAPING AND BAKING

Turn the risen dough onto a floured work surface, punch a couple a times to deflate it, then knead a few times and shape as required. Leave to partially rise again (follow recipe directions for the time); this last rise is called proving, and allows for the "oven spring" that takes place during the first 15 minutes or so of baking, when the yeast becomes more active before being killed by the heat, and the gas in the myriad pockets expands. Bake as the recipe directs. Bread is baked when it is brown and, when you tip it on to a cloth held in your hand, the bottom sounds hollow when you rap it with your knuckles.

BREAD MAKERS

Electric bread makers make bread making easy, although they produce only one small loaf at a time. Follow individual manufacturer's directions.

This pumperknickel is milder in flavour than the classic version, which uses rye flour only, but still has the characteristic sweet-sour tang of this popular German bread.

Pumpernickel bread

PREPARATION TIME 30 MINUTES (PLUS STANDING TIME) **COOKING TIME** 45 MINUTES **MAKES** 24 SLICES

2 teaspoons dried yeast
1 teaspoon caster sugar
1 cup (250ml) warm water
50g butter, melted
1 tablespoon molasses
1 tablespoon caraway seeds
½ cup (85g) polenta
1½ cups (185g) rye flour
1 cup (150g) plain flour
2 tablespoons cocoa powder
1 teaspoon salt

1 Whisk yeast, sugar and the water in large bowl until yeast dissolves, cover; stand in warm place about 10 minutes or until mixture is frothy.
2 Stir in butter and molasses, then seeds, polenta and sifted flours, cocoa and salt. Turn dough onto floured surface; knead about 10 minutes or until smooth. Place dough into large greased bowl, cover; stand in warm place about 2 hours or until dough has doubled in size.
3 Grease 8cm x 26cm bar cake pan; line sides of pan with baking paper, extending 5cm above edge. Turn dough onto floured surface; knead until smooth. Press dough into pan, cover loosely; stand in warm place about 45 minutes or until dough has risen to top of pan.
4 Preheat oven to moderate (180°C/160°C fan-forced). Cover pan with foil. Bake 15 minutes. Uncover; bake about 30 minutes. Turn onto wire rack to cool.

☐ **PER SLICE** 2.1g total fat (1.2g saturated); 334kj (80 cal); 12.3g carbohydrate; 2.2g protein; 1.4g fibre

Basic white bread

PREPARATION TIME 30 MINUTES (PLUS STANDING TIME) **COOKING TIME** 45 MINUTES **MAKES** 18 SLICES

3 teaspoons dried yeast
½ cup (125ml) warm water
2 teaspoons caster sugar
2½ cups (375g) plain flour
1 teaspoon salt
30g butter, melted
½ cup (125ml) warm milk

1 Whisk yeast, the water and sugar in small bowl until yeast dissolves, cover; stand in warm place about 10 minutes or until mixture is frothy.
2 Sift flour and salt into large bowl; stir in butter, milk and yeast mixture. Turn dough onto floured surface; knead about 10 minutes or until dough is elastic. Place dough into greased bowl, cover; stand in warm place 1 hour or until dough has doubled in size.
3 Preheat oven to moderately hot (200°C/180°C fan-forced). Grease oven tray.
4 Turn dough onto floured surface; knead until smooth. Roll dough to 18cm x 35cm rectangle; roll up from short side like a swiss roll. Place on tray; cut four diagonal slashes across top. Cover; stand in warm place 20 minutes or until risen. Bake, uncovered, 45 minutes. Turn onto wire rack to cool.

☐ **PER SLICE** 1.9g total fat (1.1g saturated); 393kj (94 cal); 15.9g carbohydrate; 2.7g protein; 0.9g fibre

Chapati

PREPARATION TIME 35 MINUTES (PLUS STANDING TIME) **COOKING TIME** 20 MINUTES **MAKES** 14

Chapatis are a classic accompaniment to curries. If made ahead, they can be wrapped in foil, then reheated in a moderate oven for 15 minutes.

1 ¼ cups (185g) white plain flour

1 cup (160g) wholemeal plain flour

1 teaspoon salt

1 tablespoon ghee

¾ cup (180ml) warm water, approximately

1 Sift 1 cup white flour, the wholemeal flour and salt into large bowl; rub in ghee. Add enough water to mix to a firm dough. Turn dough onto floured surface; knead 10 minutes, working in the remaining white flour. Cover dough with cloth; stand 1 hour. Divide dough into 14 portions; roll portions on floured surface into 20cm rounds. Cover with cloth; stand 10 minutes before cooking.

2 Heat griddle or heavy-based frying pan until very hot; cook, one round at a time, about 30 seconds on first side or until round just begins to colour. Remove from pan. Place uncooked side of chapati directly over medium flame, checking frequently until chapati begins to blister. Repeat with remaining rounds. Wrap cooked chapati in a cloth to keep warm or serve while warm.

PER CHAPATI 1.8g total fat (1.0g saturated); 4.0kj (98 cal); 16.6g carbohydrate; 2.8g protein; 1.8g fibre

---

Naan

PREPARATION TIME 20 MINUTES (PLUS STANDING TIME) **COOKING TIME** 15 MINUTES **MAKES** 6

Naan is that delicious puffy bread we associate with the tandoori dishes of northern India. This recipe is for a plain naan, but often naans are made with herbs, spices, onion, potatoes or even minced meat. One of the most popular varieties is garlic and coriander naan. Simply add 3 finely chopped garlic cloves and ¼ cup finely chopped fresh coriander to the dough mix. You can also make mini naans and serve them with dips.

⅔ cup (160ml) warm water

1 teaspoon dried yeast

1 teaspoon caster sugar

2 cups (300g) plain flour

1 teaspoon salt

2 tablespoons yogurt

4 tablespoons ghee, melted

2 teaspoons kalonji

1 Whisk the water, yeast and sugar in small bowl until yeast dissolves, cover; stand in warm place about 10 minutes or until mixture is frothy.

2 Sift flour and salt into large bowl, add yeast mixture, yogurt and half of the ghee; mix to a soft dough. Knead dough on floured surface about 5 minutes or until dough is smooth and elastic. Place dough in large greased bowl, cover; stand in warm place 1 ½ hours or until dough has doubled in size.

3 Turn dough onto floured surface; knead about 5 minutes or until smooth. Divide dough into six pieces; roll each piece into an oval about 20cm long.

4 Preheat grill to very hot. Cover oven tray with foil; grease foil. Cook ovals, one at a time, under grill about 2 minutes each side or until puffed and just browned. Brush naan with a little of the remaining ghee, sprinkle with a little of the kalonji; grill further 30 seconds. Keep naan warm while cooking remainder.

PER NAAN 12.4g total fat (7.9g saturated); 1204kj (288 cal); 37.1g carbohydrate; 5.9g protein; 2.0g fibre

Chelsea buns were created by a baker at the Chelsea bun house several hundred years ago. If you're not a fan of currants, swap them for chopped mixed nuts or other dried fruit, such as tropical fruit mix.

Chelsea buns

PREPARATION TIME 50 MINUTES (PLUS STANDING TIME) **COOKING TIME** 35 MINUTES **MAKES** 9

1 tablespoon dried yeast
1 tablespoon caster sugar
4 cups (600g) plain flour
1½ cups (375ml) warm milk
2 cups (320g) dried currants
1 teaspoon finely grated lemon rind
1 teaspoon ground cinnamon
1 egg
125g butter, melted
⅔ cup (150g) firmly packed brown sugar

ICING

1 cup (160g) icing sugar
1 tablespoon milk, approximately
pink food colouring

1 Combine yeast, 1 teaspoon of the caster sugar, 1 teaspoon of the flour and milk in small bowl, cover; stand in warm place about 10 minutes or until mixture is frothy.
2 Place currants in small saucepan, cover with water; bring to a boil. Remove from heat, cover; cool 15 minutes. Drain currants well; combine in small bowl with rind and cinnamon.
3 Whisk egg into yeast mixture. Sift remaining flour into large bowl; stir in yeast mixture, cover; stand in warm place about 40 minutes or until dough has doubled in size.
4 Knead dough on floured surface 3 minutes or until smooth. Roll dough ito 30cm x 40cm rectangle. Brush with a quarter of the butter; sprinkle with a third of the brown sugar.
5 Grease deep 23cm-square cake pan. Fold one end of the dough to come two-thirds of the way up dough, fold over top third to cover first fold. Turn dough halfway around to have open ends facing you.
6 Roll dough into 30cm x 40cm rectangle. Repeat folding as before, using same amount of butter and brown sugar. Turn dough halfway round; roll to 30cm x 40cm rectangle. Brush dough with half the remaining butter; sprinkle with remaining brown sugar and currant mixture.
7 Roll dough firmly from long side like a swiss roll. Cut dough evenly into nine pieces; place buns, cut-side up, in pan; sprinkle with remaining caster sugar. Stand, uncovered, in warm place about 20 minutes or until buns have risen slightly.
8 Preheat oven to moderately hot (200°C/180°C fan-forced).
9 Drizzle buns with remaining butter. Bake, uncovered, 5 minutes. Reduce temperature to moderate (180°C/160°C fan-forced); bake about 25 minutes or until golden brown.
10 Meanwhile, make icing.
11 Turn buns onto wire rack, drizzle a little icing onto each bun; cool.

ICING Sift icing sugar into small bowl; stir in enough milk to form a thin, smooth paste. Tint with pink colouring.

PER BUN 16.9g total fat (10.4g saturated); 2788kj (667 cal); 112.0g carbohydrate; 13.0g protein; 5.0g fibre

CHELSEA BUNS

G R
HARRISON BROS & HOWSON
SHEFFIELD ENGLAND
RUSTLESS

These rolls are made with bakers' flour (sometimes sold as bread flour), which has a higher gluten content than plain flour, so they have a particularly crisp crust. Bakers' flour can be found in most supermarkets and health-food stores. Plain flour can be used instead but the rolls won't be as crisp. Use scissors to snip small crosses in each roll.

Dinner rolls

PREPARATION TIME 30 MINUTES (PLUS STANDING TIME) **COOKING TIME** 15 MINUTES **MAKES** 20

2 cups (500ml) warm water
1 teaspoon caster sugar
2 teaspoons dried yeast
4 cups (640g) bakers' flour
2 teaspoons salt
cooking-oil spray

1 Whisk the water, sugar and yeast in small bowl until yeast dissolves, cover; stand in warm place about 15 minutes or until mixture is frothy.
2 Sift flour and salt into large bowl; stir in yeast mixture. Turn dough onto floured surface; knead about 15 minutes or until dough is smooth and elastic. Place dough in large greased bowl, turning dough once to coat, cover; stand in warm place about 1 hour or until dough has doubled in size.
3 Grease two oven trays. Turn dough onto floured surface; knead until smooth. Divide dough into quarters; divide each quarter into five pieces. Shape each into balls; place balls 5cm apart on trays. Cut small cross in top of each ball; spray lightly with oil. Cover loosely with plastic wrap; stand in warm place 20 minutes or until dough doubles in size.
4 Preheat oven to moderately hot (200°C/ 180°C fan-forced).
5 Bake rolls, uncovered, about 15 minutes. Turn onto wire racks to cool.

PER ROLL 0.5g total fat (0.1g saturated); 485kj (116 cal); 23.3g carbohydrate; 3.6g protein; 1.3g fibre

---

The popularity of Middle Eastern dips has created a surge in traditional accompaniments, especially different types of breads. Turkish bread (also known as pide) is also popular for sandwiches and makes a delicious pizza base.

Turkish bread

PREPARATION TIME 45 MINUTES (PLUS STANDING TIME) **COOKING TIME** 15 MINUTES **SERVES** 6

1 teaspoon dried yeast
1½ cups (375ml) warm water
1 teaspoon caster sugar
3 cups (450g) plain flour
1½ teaspoons salt
2 tablespoons olive oil
2 teaspoons kalonji

STARTER
½ teaspoon dried yeast
¼ cup (60ml) warm water
2 tablespoons warm milk
1 cup (150g) plain flour

1 Make starter. Turn onto floured surface; knead about 2 minutes or until smooth. Cut starter into 2cm pieces.
2 Whisk yeast, the water and sugar in small bowl until yeast dissolves; cover, stand in warm place about 10 minutes or until mixture is frothy.
3 Sift flour and salt into large bowl, add yeast mixture, starter pieces and oil; mix to a soft dough. Turn dough onto floured surface; knead about 2 minutes or until almost smooth. Place dough into large greased bowl, cover; stand in warm place 40 minutes or until dough has doubled in size.
4 Turn dough onto floured surface; knead until smooth. Halve dough; knead each half about 5 minutes or until smooth and elastic. Place each half in large greased bowl, cover; stand in warm place about 40 minutes or until dough has doubled in size.

5 Preheat oven to very hot (240°C/220°C fan-forced). Lightly grease two oven trays.
6 Roll each half of dough into an oval about 35cm long; make indents evenly over dough with your finger. Dust with a little flour; sprinkle with kalonji. Cover dough with greased plastic wrap to prevent drying out while oven trays are being heated. Place trays in very hot oven 3 minutes. Quickly remove plastic from dough and place dough onto hot trays. Bake, uncovered, about 12 minutes. Turn onto wire rack to cool.

STARTER Whisk yeast, the water and milk in small bowl until yeast dissolves; stir in flour. Cover, stand in warm place for at least 6 hours or overnight.

PER SERVING 7.6g total fat (1.2g saturated); 1747kj (418 cal); 73.1g carbohydrate; 11.3g protein; 4.0g fibre

---

Bagels

PREPARATION TIME 50 MINUTES (PLUS STANDING TIME) **COOKING TIME** 45 MINUTES **MAKES** 12

It is believed that bagels originated in the Jewish communities of eastern Europe and were introduced to the US by immigrants in the 1880s. They are now one of the most popular breads across the US and the world. Popular flavour additions to the dough are cinnamon, onion, currants, blueberries and rye flour. The classic filling for plain bagels is cream cheese and smoked salmon, topped with capers.

- 3 teaspoons dried yeast
- 1 tablespoon caster sugar
- ½ cup (125ml) warm water
- 1 cup (250ml) warm milk
- 3 cups (450g) plain flour
- 3 teaspoons salt
- 1 tablespoon caster sugar, extra
- 1 egg yolk
- 1 teaspoon water, extra
- 1 tablespoon poppy seeds
- 2 teaspoons sea salt

1 Whisk yeast, sugar, the water and milk in large bowl until yeast dissolves, cover; stand in warm place about 10 minutes or until mixture is frothy.
2 Stir sifted flour, salt and extra sugar into yeast mixture in two batches; mix to a firm dough. Turn dough onto floured surface; knead about 10 minutes or until dough is smooth and elastic. Place dough into large greased bowl, cover; stand in warm place about 1 hour or until dough has doubled in size.
3 Grease two oven trays. Turn dough onto floured surface; knead until smooth. Divide dough into 12 portions; knead each portion into a ball. Press finger in centre of each ball to make a hole; rotate ball with finger until the hole is a third of the size of the bagel. Place bagels about 3cm apart on trays, cover; stand in warm place about 15 minutes or until risen.
4 Preheat oven to moderately hot (200°C/180°C fan-forced).
5 Drop bagels individually into large saucepan of boiling water; they must not touch. Turn bagels after 1 minute; boil for a further 1 minute, remove with slotted spoon. Return bagels to trays; brush tops with combined egg yolk and extra water, sprinkle with combined seeds and sea salt. Bake, uncovered, about 20 minutes. Turn onto wire rack to cool.

PER BAGEL 2.2g total fat (0.8g saturated); 715kj (171 cal); 31.1g carbohydrate; 5.5g protein; 1.8g fibre

The traditional sourdough method uses no commercial yeast but adds a piece of dough from the last batch as a "starter" from which the yeast will spread through the new dough. However, it is difficult to keep a starter in good condition unless you bake every day. This loaf is a controlled version of sourdough, using commercial yeast but standing the yeast mixture for long enough to ferment and acquire the true sourdough flavour.

Crusty sourdough loaf

PREPARATION TIME 30 MINUTES (PLUS STANDING TIME) **COOKING TIME** 35 MINUTES **MAKES** 14 SLICES

1 teaspoon dried yeast

¾ cup (110g) white plain flour

¼ teaspoon ground cumin

1 cup (250ml) warm water

1⅔ cups (250g) white plain flour, extra

1⅔ cups (260g) wholemeal plain flour

2 teaspoons salt

1 tablespoon vegetable oil

½ cup (125ml) water, extra, approximately

1 Combine yeast, white flour, cumin and water in small bowl; mix well. Cover; stand in warm place 3 days.

2 Sift extra white flour, wholemeal flour and salt into large bowl; stir in oil, yeast mixture and enough extra water to mix to soft dough. Knead dough on floured surface about 10 minutes or until smooth. Place dough in large oiled bowl; cover stand in warm place about 1½ hours or until dough has doubled in size.

3 Knead dough on floured surface until smooth. Shape dough into 24cm loaf; place on greased oven tray. Cover; stand in warm place about 30 minutes or until dough has doubled in size.

4 Preheat oven to hot (220°C/200°C fan-forced).

5 Dust loaf with flour. Using sharp knife, make diagonal slashes on loaf, stand 5 minutes. Bake, uncovered, about 35 minutes or until browned and cooked. Using water sprayer, spray loaf lightly three times during first 10 minutes of baking to ensure a good crust and minimise cracking. Cool on wire rack.

PER SLICE 8.0g total fat (4.7g saturated); 1099kj (263 cal); 36.0g carbohydrate; 9.7g protein; 3.3g fibre

---

For a delicious sweet alternative, swap the potatoes for sweet potatoes, olives for sultanas, tomatoes for chopped pecans and mozzarella for 1 egg. Add 1 teaspoon of cinnamon to the mixture.

Potato, olive and sun-dried tomato bread

PREPARATION TIME 15 MINUTES **COOKING TIME** 1 HOUR **SERVES** 8

250g coliban potatoes, peeled, chopped coarsely

30g butter, melted

2 cups (300g) self-raising flour

1 cup (250ml) milk

½ cup (60g) seeded green olives, sliced thickly

½ cup (75g) drained sun-dried tomatoes, sliced thickly

1 cup (100g) coarsely grated mozzarella cheese

1 Preheat oven to moderately hot (200°C/180°C fan-forced). Grease 14cm x 21cm loaf pan; line base with baking paper.

2 Boil, steam or microwave potato until tender; drain. Mash potato in large bowl with butter until smooth.

3 Add flour, milk, olives, tomato and cheese to potato mixture; mix to combine. Spoon into pan; bake, uncovered, about 50 minutes or until cooked through.

PER SERVING 8.0g total fat (4.7g saturated); 1099kj (263 cal); 38.0g carbohydrate; 9.7g protein; 3.3g fibre

Napoletana pizza

PREPARATION TIME 20 MINUTES (PLUS STANDING TIME) **COOKING TIME** 30 MINUTES **SERVES** 6

300g mozzarella, sliced thinly

¼ cup loosely packed fresh basil leaves, torn

BASIC PIZZA DOUGH

2 teaspoons dried yeast

½ teaspoon salt

2½ cups (375g) plain flour

1 cup (250ml) warm water

1 tablespoon olive oil

BASIC TOMATO PIZZA SAUCE

1 tablespoon olive oil

1 small white onion (80g), chopped finely

2 cloves garlic, crushed

425g can crushed tomatoes

¼ cup (70g) tomato paste

1 teaspoon white sugar

1 tablespoon fresh oregano leaves

1 Make basic pizza dough and basic tomato pizza sauce.

2 Preheat oven to moderately hot (200°C/180°C fan-forced). Grease two oven trays.

3 Halve basic pizza dough; roll out each half on floured surface to form 30cm round. Place on trays; spread each with half of the basic tomato pizza sauce, top with cheese.

4 Bake, uncovered, about 15 minutes or until crust is golden and cheese is bubbling. Sprinkle each with basil before serving. See pages 488 to 489 for other topping ideas.

BASIC PIZZA DOUGH Combine yeast, salt and sifted flour in large bowl. Gradually stir in the water and oil. Turn dough onto floured surface; knead about 10 minutes or until smooth and elastic. Place dough in large greased bowl, cover; stand in warm place about 30 minutes or until dough has doubled in size. Turn dough onto floured surface; knead until smooth.

BASIC TOMATO PIZZA SAUCE Heat oil in medium frying pan; cook onion, stirring occasionally, over low heat until soft. Add garlic, undrained tomatoes, paste, sugar and oregano; bring to a boil. Reduce heat; simmer, uncovered, about 15 minutes or until mixture thickens.

PER SERVING 18.1g total fat (8.0g saturated); 1914kj (458 cal); 50.1g carbohydrate; 21.4g protein; 4.3g fibre

Official guidelines have been developed in Italy on how to make a traditional napoletana pizza. The reason for these guidelines is to try to protect the authenticity of this classic Neapolitan dish. The guidelines specify how the dough should be made and shaped, the ingredients and method for the tomato sauce and how the pizza should be cooked. This recipe is a close adaptation of the classic version.

Pizza toppings

Use any of the following ideas to top a home-made pizza base (see page 487 for the recipe).

POTATO AND ROSEMARY
Sprinkle a pizza base with grated parmesan; top with thinly sliced uncooked new potatoes, chopped fresh rosemary, thinly sliced garlic and a drizzle of olive oil.

BARBECUED CHICKEN
Spread a pizza base with a mixture of bottled tomato pasta sauce and barbecue sauce; sprinkle with grated cheddar. Top with shredded cooked chicken, thinly sliced mushrooms and more grated cheese.

SALAMI AND ROCKET
Spread a pizza base with bottled tomato pasta sauce; top with grated mozzarella and thinly sliced hot salami. Just before serving, top with baby rocket leaves.

FIG AND PROSCIUTTO
Spread a pizza base with bottled tomato pasta sauce; top with thickly sliced fresh figs, coarsely chopped prosciutto and crumbled blue cheese. Serve sprinkled with flat-leaf parsley leaves.

VEGETARIAN
Spread a pizza base with bottled tomato pasta sauce; sprinkle with grated mozzarella. Top with chopped drained char-grilled capsicum, chopped semi-dried tomatoes, sliced black olives and torn fresh basil leaves. Sprinkle with more grated cheese.

LAMB AND GOAT CHEESE
Spread a pizza base with bottled tomato pasta sauce; top with thinly sliced goat cheese, halved semi-dried tomatoes and sliced cooked lamb fillet. Serve with baby spinach leaves.

AUSSIE

Spread a pizza base with bottled tomato pasta sauce; sprinkle with grated cheddar. Top with thinly sliced bacon; gently crack eggs on top of bacon. Sprinkle with grated cheese.

ONION, ANCHOVY AND OLIVE

Cook sliced brown onions in butter in a large frying pan until caramelised. Spread a pizza base with tomato paste; top with the onion, chopped anchovy fillets and black olives. Top with fresh oregano leaves.

SPICY SAUSAGE AND BOCCONCINI

Spread a pizza base with bottled tomato pasta sauce; top with sliced cooked spicy Italian sausage, chopped chilli and sliced bocconcini. Serve topped with fresh basil leaves.

SUPREME

Spread a pizza base with bottled tomato pasta sauce; sprinkle with grated pizza cheese. Top with chopped cabanossi, sliced salami, chopped red capsicum and sliced mushrooms. Sprinkle with cheese.

MUSHROOM AND FETTA

Spread a pizza base with bottled tomato pasta sauce; sprinkle with grated pizza cheese. Top with thinly sliced flat mushrooms, crumbled fetta and chopped fresh thyme. Sprinkle with more grated cheese.

PEPPERONI AND OLIVE

Spread a pizza base with bottled tomato pasta sauce; sprinkle with grated mozzarella. Top with sliced pepperoni, black olives and sliced red onion. Sprinkle with mozzarella.

Brioche dough is enriched with a generous amount of butter and eggs. One of the most popular French breads, brioche can be made in the shape of a loaf or roll. The most recognisable shape, however, is the delightful "brioche à tête", or brioche with a head, formed by placing a small ball of dough on top of a larger one. Serve fresh brioche with jam, and toasted brioche with foie gras or pâté. It makes wonderful french toast or a luxurious bread pudding.

Brioche

PREPARATION TIME 40 MINUTES (PLUS STANDING TIME) **COOKING TIME** 15 MINUTES **MAKES** 12

2½ cups (375g) plain flour
1½ teaspoons dried yeast
¼ teaspoon salt
¼ cup (55g) caster sugar
¾ cup (180ml) warm milk
6 egg yolks
125g butter
2 teaspoons caster sugar, extra

1 Combine flour, yeast and salt in large bowl. Combine sugar and milk in small jug; stir until sugar dissolves. Add milk mixture to flour mixture, then stir in five of the egg yolks. Stir until mixture stiffens, then, using hand, mix until a firm dough forms.
2 Divide butter into 10 portions. Turn dough onto floured surface; work each portion of butter into dough, kneading well after each addition, until all of the butter is incorporated and the dough is smooth and glossy. Place dough in large greased bowl, cover; stand in warm place about 2 hours or until dough has doubled in size.
3 Grease 12 x ⅓-cup (80ml) fluted ovenproof moulds or 12-hole (⅓-cup/80ml) muffin pan. Divide dough into 12 portions; remove about a quarter of each portion. Roll both the small and the large portions into balls. Place large balls in moulds; make small indentation in top of each with fingertip, sit small round in each indentation. Brush each brioche with remaining egg yolk; sprinkle with extra sugar. Stand, uncovered, in warm place about 1 hour or until dough has doubled in size.
4 Preheat oven to moderate (180°C/160°C fan-forced).
5 Bake brioche, uncovered, about 15 minutes. Turn onto wire rack to cool.

PER BRIOCHE 2.3g total fat (6.9g saturated); 1049kj (251 cal); 28.7g carbohydrate; 5.7g protein; 1.3g fibre

This recipe is an all-time favourite on camping trips. Place the dough into a greased camp oven (a heavy metal pot with lid, used for baking over an open fire). Check the damper after 30 minutes. Alternatively divide the mixture into handfuls of dough and secure onto the end of sticks. Wrap foil around the dough and cook over the coals of a fire. Remove the stick, serve with butter, jam or honey pushed into the hole.

Damper

PREPARATION TIME 20 MINUTES **COOKING TIME** 45 MINUTES **SERVES** 6

3½ cups (525g) self-raising flour
1 teaspoon salt
2 teaspoons caster sugar
40g butter
½ cup (125ml) milk
1¼ cups (310ml) water, approximately

1 Preheat oven to moderately hot (200°C/180°C fan-forced). Grease oven tray.
2 Sift flour, salt and sugar into large bowl; rub in butter. Stir in milk and enough water to mix to a sticky dough.
3 Turn dough onto floured surface; knead until just smooth. Place dough on tray; press into 16cm round.
4 Cut a cross in the dough, about 1cm deep. Brush dough with a little extra milk; sprinkle with a little extra flour. Bake, uncovered, about 45 minutes. Lift onto wire rack to cool.

PER SERVING 7.3g total fat (4.3g saturated); 1547kj (370 cal); 64.2g carbohydrate; 9.3g protein; 3.3g fibre

For a New York-style deli sandwich, spread rye bread with mayonnaise, pile with thinly sliced corned beef, ham or pastrami, plus mustard, sauerkraut, thinly sliced Swiss cheese, or anything else you fancy. Top with a second slice of rye and serve with dill pickles.

Food processor rye bread

PREPARATION TIME 30 MINUTES (PLUS STANDING TIME) **COOKING TIME** 55 MINUTES **MAKES** 18 SLICES

- 2 teaspoons dried yeast
- ¼ cup (55g) caster sugar
- 1 cup (250ml) warm water
- 3 cups (450g) plain flour
- ½ cup (60g) rye flour
- 1½ teaspoons salt
- ¼ cup (25g) full-cream milk powder
- 2 tablespoons vegetable oil
- 1 egg
- ¼ cup (50g) kibbled rye
- 1 teaspoon milk

1 Whisk yeast, sugar and the water in small bowl until yeast dissolves, cover; stand in warm place about 10 minutes or until mixture is frothy. Place flours, salt and milk powder in bowl of processor; process few seconds.

2 With motor operating, add yeast mixture; process until combined. Add oil and egg; process few seconds. Scrape down sides of bowl; process further few seconds. Transfer mixture onto floured surface; knead into a ball. Place in greased bowl, cover; stand in warm place about 1 hour or until dough has doubled in size.

3 Grease 14cm x 21cm loaf pan; sprinkle base and sides with 2 tablespoons of the kibbled rye. Turn dough onto floured surface; knead into loaf shape. Place dough in pan; stand in warm place, uncovered, about 40 minutes or until dough has doubled in size.

4 Preheat oven to moderately hot (200°C/180°C fan-forced).

5 Brush top of dough with milk; sprinkle with remaining kibbled rye. Bake, uncovered, 15 minutes. Reduce oven temperature to moderate (180°C/160°C fan-forced); bake, uncovered, about 40 minutes. Turn onto wire rack to cool.

PER SLICE 1.3g total fat (0.4g saturated); 226kj (54 cal); 2.4g carbohydrate; 1.7g protein; 1.0g fibre

---

Before sprinkling the onion over the focaccia, press your fingers into the dough; this helps prevent the dough from rising, so the focaccia remains flat. Some alternative topping ideas are roasted garlic and pesto; rosemary and sea salt; cheese, semi-dried tomatoes and basil; olives; grapes, rosemary and walnuts; or fig and gorgonzola.

Onion focaccia

PREPARATION TIME 25 MINUTES (PLUS STANDING TIME) **COOKING TIME** 25 MINUTES **SERVES** 8

- 2 cups (300g) plain flour
- ½ teaspoon table salt
- 2 teaspoons dried yeast
- ¼ cup (20g) finely grated parmesan
- 1 tablespoon finely chopped fresh rosemary
- 1 tablespoon finely chopped fresh sage
- 2 teaspoons finely chopped fresh flat-leaf parsley
- 2 tablespoons olive oil
- 1 cup (250ml) warm water
- 1 small brown onion (80g), sliced thinly
- 1 tablespoon sea salt
- 1 tablespoon olive oil, extra

1 Sift flour and table salt into large bowl; stir in yeast, cheese and herbs, make a well in centre of flour mixture. Pour oil and the water into centre of bowl, gradually stir in flour mixture; mix to a soft dough.

2 Turn dough onto lightly floured surface; knead about 5 minutes or until dough is smooth and elastic.

3 Place dough on greased oven tray; press into 24cm round. Cover dough with greased plastic wrap; stand in warm place about 1 hour or until dough has doubled in size.
4 Preheat oven to hot (220°C/200°C fan-forced).
5 Remove plastic wrap; sprinkle dough with onion and sea salt, drizzle with extra oil. Bake, uncovered, about 25 minutes. Lift onto wire rack to cool.

PER SERVING 8.1g total fat (1.6g saturated); 878kj (210 cal); 27.8g carbohydrate; 5.5g protein; 1.8g fibre

---

Mixed-grain loaf

PREPARATION TIME 40 MINUTES (PLUS STANDING TIME) **COOKING TIME** 45 MINUTES **MAKES** 18 SLICES

- ¼ cup (45g) cracked buckwheat
- ½ cup (80g) burghul
- ¼ cup (50g) kibbled rye
- 3 teaspoons dried yeast
- 1 teaspoon caster sugar
- ¾ cup (180ml) warm milk
- ¼ cup (60ml) warm water
- 2¼ cups (335g) white plain flour
- ½ cup (80g) wholemeal plain flour
- 1 teaspoon salt
- 1 tablespoon linseeds
- 2 teaspoons olive oil
- 1 egg yolk
- 1 teaspoon milk, extra
- 2 teaspoons sesame seeds
- 2 teaspoons cracked buckwheat, extra

1 Place buckwheat, burghul and kibbled rye in small heatproof bowl; cover with boiling water. Cover; stand 30 minutes. Rinse well; drain.
2 Whisk yeast, sugar, milk and the water in small bowl until yeast dissolves, cover; stand in warm place about 10 minutes or until mixture is frothy.
3 Sift flours and salt into large bowl; add grain mixture and linseeds. Stir in oil and yeast mixture; mix to a soft dough. Turn dough onto floured surface; knead about 10 minutes or until dough is smooth and elastic. Place dough in large greased bowl, cover; stand in warm place about 1 hour or until dough has doubled in size.
4 Grease 14cm x 21cm loaf pan. Turn dough onto floured surface; knead until smooth. Divide dough into three pieces; shape each piece into a 30cm sausage. Plait sausages; place into pan. Cover; stand in warm place about 30 minutes or until risen.
5 Preheat oven to moderately hot (200°C/180°C fan-forced).
6 Brush dough with combined egg yolk and extra milk; sprinkle evenly with combined sesame seeds and extra buckwheat. Bake, uncovered, about 45 minutes. Turn onto wire rack to cool.

PER SLICE 2.0g total fat (0.5g saturated); 564kj (135 cal); 23.2g carbohydrate; 1.5g protein; 2.5g fibre

To check whether the dough has "proved" (risen sufficiently) gently press a couple of fingers into the dough. If it bounces back the dough isn't ready; if the imprints stay then it is ready. If the dough over-proves, the bread can collapse in the oven, the flavour can be very yeasty and the texture can be uneven with lots of burst air bubbles.

1

2

3

4

Chilli corn bread

PREPARATION TIME 10 MINUTES **COOKING TIME** 1 HOUR **MAKES** 27 SLICES

1 cup (150g) self-raising flour
1 teaspoon salt
1 cup (170g) polenta
½ cup (100g) kibbled rye
1 tablespoon brown sugar
1 teaspoon ground cumin
2 tablespoons finely chopped fresh flat-leaf parsley
1 teaspoon finely chopped fresh thyme
½ cup (60g) finely grated cheddar
310g can creamed corn
⅔ cup (110g) frozen corn kernels, thawed
⅔ cup (160ml) buttermilk
⅓ cup (80ml) milk
2 teaspoons sambal oelek
2 eggs, beaten lightly
50g butter, melted

1 Preheat oven to moderately hot (200°C/180°C fan-forced). Grease deep 19cm-square cake pan; line base with baking paper.
2 Sift flour and salt into large bowl; stir in polenta, rye, sugar, cumin, herbs and cheese.
3 Combine remaining ingredients in medium bowl; stir into dry ingredients.
4 Spread mixture into pan. Bake, uncovered, about 1 hour. Stand, covered, 10 minutes before turning onto wire rack to cool.

PER SLICE 3.6g total fat (1.8g saturated); 426kj (102 cal); 13.4g carbohydrate; 3.4g protein; 1.5g fibre

Corn (maize) was brought back to Europe from the US by Christopher Columbus. It has become an Italian staple in the form of polenta. In the US, corn bread may be served with butter and jam, or as an accompaniment to casseroles and other meat dishes.

Roti

PREPARATION TIME 30 MINUTES (PLUS REFRIGERATION TIME) **COOKING TIME** 30 MINUTES **MAKES** 16

1 cup (150g) white plain flour
1 cup (160g) wholemeal plain flour
1 teaspoon salt
1 teaspoon ground coriander
½ teaspoon ground turmeric
2 teaspoons cumin seeds
1 tablespoon vegetable oil
¾ cup (180ml) water, approximately
4 tablespoons ghee, approximately

1 Sift flours, salt and ground spices into large bowl. Make a well in centre of flour mixture; add seeds, oil and enough water to mix to a soft dough. Turn dough onto floured surface; knead 10 minutes. Wrap dough in plastic; refrigerate 30 minutes.
2 Divide dough into 16 portions; roll each portion on floured surface to 16cm round.
3 Heat heavy-based frying pan until very hot; add about 1 teaspoon of the ghee, quickly turn pan to coat base with ghee. Place one round into pan; cook about 1 minute or until round is puffed slightly and bubbles start to form. Turn; brown other side. Repeat with remaining ghee and rounds.

PER ROTI 7.1g total fat (3.9g saturated); 531kj (127 cal); 12.9g carbohydrate; 2.2g protein; 1.5g fibre

Roti and chapati are both made with a similar unleavened dough. The difference between them is that roti are fried in ghee and chapati are grilled or cooked over direct flame. Watch the ghee when making these; when it begins to burn and a few roti have been cooked, wipe the pan clean with absorbent paper.

1 CHILLI CORN BREAD **2** ROTI **3** ROSEMARY PUMPKIN BREAD [P 496] **4** FRUIT AND NUT LOAF [P 496]

A delicious variation to this recipe is to add 100g crumbled soft goat cheese or crumbled soft blue cheese to the pumpkin mixture.

Rosemary pumpkin bread

PREPARATION TIME 20 MINUTES (PLUS COOLING TIME) **COOKING TIME** 1 HOUR 40 MINUTES **MAKES** 8 SLICES

500g pumpkin, diced into 1cm pieces
1 tablespoon vegetable oil
1 tablespoon finely chopped fresh rosemary
1¾ cups (260g) self-raising flour
¾ cup (125g) polenta
½ cup (40g) finely grated parmesan
2 eggs
1¼ cups (300g) sour cream
⅓ cup (65g) pepitas

1 Preheat oven to moderately hot (200°C/180°C fan-forced). Grease 14cm x 21cm loaf pan; line base and long sides with baking paper.
2 Place combined pumpkin, oil and half of the rosemary, in single layer, on oven tray; roast, uncovered, about 20 minutes or until pumpkin is tender. Cool 10 minutes; mash mixture in medium bowl.
3 Reduce oven temperature to moderate (180°C/160°C fan-forced). Stir flour, polenta, cheese and remaining rosemary into pumpkin mixture. Whisk eggs and sour cream in medium jug; pour into mixture, stirring until just combined.
4 Spread mixture into pan; top with pepitas, pressing gently into surface. Cover with a piece of foil folded with a pleat; bake 1 hour. Uncover; bake a further 20 minutes. Stand in pan 5 minutes before turning onto wire rack to cool.

PER SLICE 23.7g total fat (11.8g saturated); 1718kj (411 cal); 38.1g carbohydrate; 10.0g protein; 3.1g fibre

Be careful to measure all the ingredients exactly, especially the salt and cinnamon which can retard the action of the yeast in making the bread rise. Measure dry ingredients by overfilling the cup or spoon, then levelling off with a knife.

Fruit and nut loaf

PREPARATION TIME 30 MINUTES (PLUS STANDING TIME) **COOKING TIME** 40 MINUTES **MAKES** 18 SLICES

2 teaspoons dried yeast
¼ cup (55g) caster sugar
2 tablespoons warm water
⅔ cup (160ml) warm milk
1 cup (150g) plain flour
1 egg, beaten lightly
2 teaspoons finely grated orange rind
2 cups (300g) plain flour, extra
1 teaspoon salt
½ teaspoon ground cinnamon
100g butter, softened
¼ cup (40g) sultanas
¼ cup (35g) raisins
¼ cup (40g) dried currants
¼ cup (25g) coarsely chopped roasted walnuts
1 egg yolk
1 tablespoon caster sugar, extra
½ teaspoon ground cinnamon, extra

1 Whisk yeast, 2 teaspoons of the sugar and the water in large bowl until yeast dissolves. Whisk in milk and sifted flour, cover; stand in warm place about 30 minutes or until mixture is frothy.

2 Stir in egg and rind, then sifted extra flour, salt, cinnamon and remaining sugar. Stir in butter, fruit and nuts.

3 Turn dough onto floured surface; knead until smooth. Place dough into large greased bowl, cover; stand in warm place about 1½ hours or until dough has doubled in size.

4 Grease 14cm x 21cm loaf pan; line base with baking paper. Turn dough onto floured surface; knead until smooth. Place into pan, cover loosely with greased plastic wrap; stand in warm place about 30 minutes or until risen slightly.

5 Preheat oven to moderately hot (200°C/180°C fan-forced).

6 Remove plastic wrap. Brush dough with egg yolk; sprinkle with combined extra sugar and extra cinnamon. Bake, uncovered, 10 minutes. Reduce oven temperature to moderate (180°C/160°C fan-forced); bake 30 minutes. Turn onto wire rack to cool.

▭ **PER SLICE** 6.8g total fat (3.5g saturated); 794kj (190 cal); 27.1g carbohydrate; 4.1g protein; 1.5g fibre

---

Gluten-free bread

PREPARATION TIME 20 MINUTES **COOKING TIME** 1 HOUR **MAKES** 18 SLICES

Gluten-free bread is more cake-like in texture than ordinary bread, but is the answer for people who are gluten-intolerant. The bread is best eaten the day it is baked, but will freeze well in individually wrapped slices.

3 cups (450g) gluten-free plain flour

1¼ cups (185g) buckwheat flour

2 teaspoons gluten-free baking powder

1½ teaspoons salt

1 cup (150g) sunflower seed kernels

70g butter, chopped

1½ cups (375ml) milk

2 eggs

1 teaspoon milk, extra

2 teaspoons poppy seeds

1 Preheat oven to moderate (180°C/160°C fan-forced). Grease 14cm x 21cm loaf pan.

2 Sift flours, baking powder and salt into large bowl; stir in kernels.

3 Rub in butter; stir in combined milk and eggs until just combined; do not overmix.

4 Press mixture into pan; do not smooth top. Brush with extra milk; sprinkle with seeds. Bake, uncovered, about 1 hour. Stand 10 minutes before turning onto wire rack to cool.

▭ **PER SLICE** 9.6g total fat (3.3g saturated); 3.3kj (228 cal); 26.8g carbohydrate; 7.4g protein; 2.2g fibre

MUFFINS, SCONES & FRIANDS

Muffins, Scones & Friands

Muffins and scones are the quickest and among the best-loved members of the cake family. You can run up a batch between the time that friends or family phone to say, "We're coming over" and the time that they arrive. You can freeze uncooked scones and bake them straight from the freezer; cooked scones and muffins also freeze well. Serve scones and muffins warm with butter.

Friands (which is French for small cakes) are perfect little somethings when you want a bite that is small and stylish but not too rich. One of their many charms is that they are very quickly put together. You can make them in muffin pans, but if you plan to make them often, elegant little oval or rectangular friand pans are a worthwhile investment. You can buy friand pans separately or in the form of 6-, 8-, 9- or 12-hole pans from good kitchen and cookware shops. Friands freeze well.

SCONES AND MUFFINS

MIXING SCONES AND MUFFINS

The reason scone and muffin recipes tell you to mix in the liquid quickly and lightly is that they contain a high proportion of flour to fat and liquid. Flour contains a protein called gluten, which forms tiny elastic strands (a process called developing) when it is moistened and agitated. You can do what you like with the flour while it is dry, even rubbing in the butter for scones by whizzing flour and butter in a food processor, but as soon as liquid is added and you start to mix, the gluten will start to develop. If you stir in the usual way, the gluten will develop enough to make the scones or muffins tough. The idea is to mix in a way that will disturb the flour as little as possible, and to handle the finished mixture gently.

FOR SCONES, use a round-ended table knife to "cut" the milk through the flour and butter mixture. The finished dough should be soft and sticky, just holding its shape when turned out, so add a little more milk if necessary. Turn the mixture onto a floured work surface, dust your hands with flour and shape the dough into a smooth ball by working it gently into a manageable, smooth shape. Sprinkle with a little more flour if necessary, but be sparing. Flatten the dough with your hand and pat it out to an even 2cm thickness, pressing from the centre outwards. Using a sharp metal cutter dipped in flour each time, cut scones close together, pushing the cutter sharply down and removing it without twisting. Lightly work the scraps together and press the dough out again, slightly thicker, to cut the remaining scones. The scones from the first cutting will be the lightest.

FOR MUFFINS, use a large metal spoon or fork and mix with the edge, in a cutting motion, in as few strokes as possible. Stop when the dry ingredients are just moistened – the mixture should still be coarse and lumpy. Spoon the mixture into each pan in one large spoonful, pushing it off with the spoon held low to avoid stretching the gluten strands.

BAKING SCONES

GLAZING is not necessary, but it removes excess flour from the tops of scones and encourages them to brown. Brush the tops of scones on the oven tray, using a brush dipped in water, milk or egg: water results in a light brown, egg in a golden brown, and milk is between the two. Milk and egg also give the tops a sheen. Brush the tops lightly – they should be just damp, not wet.

BAKING Preheat the oven to its hottest temperature and place a rack in the hottest part of the oven, usually the top shelf (scones need to rise quickly to be light). Reduce the heat to the temperature indicated in the recipe.

- Scones can be cooked on open, sideless oven trays, but they sometimes fall over. We prefer to cook them close together in shallow, aluminium cake pans. This will give you straight scones with crusty tops and bottoms and soft sides.They need to be cooked slightly longer than scones on open oven trays. Check them after 4 to 5 minutes and turn front to back if necessary to brown them evenly.
- Scones are cooked when they are browned and sound hollow when tapped firmly on top with your fingers. For crusty scones, turn them onto a wire rack to cool; for softer ones, wrap in a tea-towel while hot.
- Scones are best eaten the day they are made, ideally soon after they come out of the oven (not a big ask in most households).

FREEZING UNCOOKED SCONES

Leave scones in the pan, place in a freezer bag, press to expel the air, then seal and freeze for up to 2 months. Bake straight from freezer in a hot oven for about 20 minutes. To freeze scones individually, freeze well-separated and uncovered on an oven tray, then transfer to a freezer bag. Once frozen, they will stay separate and can be baked a few at a time, also for 20 minutes in a hot oven.

BAKING MUFFINS

Muffins are cooked when risen, browned, firm to touch and beginning to shrink from the sides of the pan. Turn onto a rack to cool. Muffins are best eaten the day they are made.

FRIANDS

You can use the frozen egg whites available in supermarkets for friands; thaw before using. If you are using fresh whites, freeze the left-over yolks individually, covered with a little water, in an ice-cube tray. When wanted, thaw and drain. Good ways to use them are for lemon curd, chocolate mousse, crème brûlée or ice-cream. If you are cooking with frozen berries, use them unthawed to minimise their colour "bleeding" into the mixture.

Friands are best eaten the day they are made, but can be stored in an airtight container for up to 2 days.

We use five different-sized muffin pans having hole capacities ranging from 1 tablespoon to the largest, ¾ cup. The latter is, appropriately enough, called the texas muffin pan, probably because it really is "bigger than...".

Blueberry muffins

PREPARATION TIME 10 MINUTES **COOKING TIME** 20 MINUTES **MAKES** 6

2 cups (300g) self-raising flour

¾ cup (165g) firmly packed brown sugar

1 cup (150g) fresh or frozen blueberries

1 egg, beaten lightly

¾ cup (180ml) buttermilk

½ cup (125ml) vegetable oil

1 Preheat oven to moderately hot (200°C/180°C fan-forced). Grease 6-hole texas (¾-cup/180ml) muffin pan.

2 Sift flour and sugar into large bowl; stir in remaining ingredients.

3 Spoon mixture into holes. Bake, uncovered, 20 minutes. Turn onto wire rack to cool.

PER MUFFIN 21.3g total fat (3.2g saturated); 2061kj (493 cal); 66.4g carbohydrate; 7.5g protein; 2.4g fibre

A delicious variation is to swap the white chocolate for dark eating chocolate and add ¼ cup finely chopped glacé ginger to the mixture.

White chocolate and macadamia muffins

PREPARATION TIME 10 MINUTES **COOKING TIME** 25 MINUTES **MAKES** 6

2 cups (300g) self-raising flour

⅔ cup (150g) caster sugar

60g butter, melted

¾ cup (180ml) milk

1 egg, beaten lightly

¾ cup (140g) white Choc Bits

½ cup (70g) coarsely chopped roasted macadamias

1 Preheat oven to moderately hot (200°C/180°C fan-forced). Grease 6-hole texas (¾-cup/180ml) muffin pan.

2 Sift flour and sugar into large bowl; stir in remaining ingredients.

3 Spoon mixture into holes. Bake, uncovered, 25 minutes. Turn onto wire rack to cool.

PER MUFFIN 27.5g total fat (12.6g saturated); 2475kj (592 cal); 75.1g carbohydrate; 9.6g protein; 2.6g fibre

Wholemeal fig muffins

PREPARATION TIME 10 MINUTES **COOKING TIME** 20 MINUTES (PLUS COOLING TIME) **MAKES** 12

2 cups (320g) wholemeal self-raising flour

1 cup (150g) self-raising flour

125g butter, chopped coarsely

½ cup (110g) raw sugar

1 cup (190g) coarsely chopped dried figs

2 eggs, beaten lightly

1 cup (250ml) milk

1 Preheat oven to moderately hot (200°C/180°C fan-forced). Grease 12-hole (⅓-cup/80ml) muffin pan.

2 Sift flours into large bowl, rub in butter; stir in remaining ingredients.

3 Spoon mixture into holes. Bake, uncovered, 20 minutes. Turn onto wire rack to cool.

PER MUFFIN 11.9g total fat (6.8g saturated); 1371kj (328 cal); 44.2g carbohydrate; 8.0g protein; 5.7g fibre

Ginger date muffins with caramel sauce

PREPARATION TIME 15 MINUTES **COOKING TIME** 25 MINUTES **MAKES** 12

Turn the humble muffin into a sensational dessert. Serve these warm with warm caramel sauce, cream, and maybe even some ice-cream. Freeze any left-over muffins for emergency desserts. To reheat them from frozen, wrap them in plastic wrap and place in a microwave oven for 30 seconds. The sauce will keep for several weeks in the fridge.

1 cup (140g) seeded coarsely chopped dates

⅓ cup (80ml) water

¼ teaspoon bicarbonate of soda

2 cups (300g) self-raising flour

1 cup (150g) plain flour

2 teaspoons ground ginger

½ teaspoon mixed spice

1 cup (220g) firmly packed brown sugar

1 egg, beaten lightly

1¼ cups (310ml) milk

¼ cup (60ml) vegetable oil

CARAMEL SAUCE

1 cup (220g) firmly packed brown sugar

1 cup (250ml) cream

40g butter

1 Preheat oven to moderately hot (200°C/180°C fan-forced). Grease 12-hole (⅓ cup/80ml) muffin pan.

2 Combine dates and the water in small saucepan; bring to a boil. Add soda; cool.

3 Sift dry ingredients into large bowl; stir in date mixture and remaining ingredients.

4 Spoon mixture into holes. Bake, uncovered, 20 minutes. Turn onto wire rack to cool.

5 Make caramel sauce. Serve with warm muffins.

CARAMEL SAUCE Stir ingredients in small saucepan over heat, without boiling, until sugar dissolves; bring to a boil. Simmer, without stirring, about 3 minutes or until sauce thickens.

PER MUFFIN 18.3g total fat (9.2g saturated); 2015kj (482 cal); 71.8g carbohydrate; 6.0g protein; 2.6g fibre

Muffins can be sweet or savoury and, although originally considered a breakfast bread, they are now eaten any time of the day. We used frozen mixed berries from the supermarket for this recipe.

Mixed-berry buttermilk muffins

PREPARATION TIME 5 MINUTES **COOKING TIME** 20 MINUTES **MAKES** 12

2½ cups (375g) self-raising flour
¾ cup (165g) caster sugar
1 egg, beaten lightly
1 teaspoon vanilla extract
⅔ cup (160ml) vegetable oil
¾ cup (180ml) buttermilk
200g frozen mixed berries

1 Preheat oven to moderately hot (200°C/180°C fan-forced). Grease 12-hole (⅓-cup/80ml) muffin pan.

2 Sift flour and sugar into large bowl; stir in remaining ingredients.

3 Spoon mixture into holes. Bake, uncovered, about 20 minutes. Turn onto wire rack to cool.

PER MUFFIN 13.4g total fat (1.9g saturated); 1233kj (295 cal); 38.1g carbohydrate; 4.4g protein; 1.8g fibre

---

Try replacing buttermilk with coconut milk, and when you make the lime syrup add a couple of bruised cardomom pods, a cinnamon stick and a star anise.

Lime syrup coconut muffins

PREPARATION TIME 15 MINUTES **COOKING TIME** 20 MINUTES **MAKES** 12

2½ cups (375g) self-raising flour
1 cup (80g) desiccated coconut
1 cup (220g) caster sugar
1 tablespoon finely grated lime rind
1 cup (250ml) buttermilk
125g butter, melted
2 eggs, beaten lightly

LIME SYRUP
½ cup (110g) caster sugar
¼ cup (60ml) water
2 teaspoons finely grated lime rind
⅓ cup (80ml) lime juice

Syrupy muffins are delicious on their own, or serve them as a dessert with a dollop of thick cream, rich creamy yogurt or mascarpone cheese.

1 Preheat oven to moderately hot (200°C/180°C fan-forced). Grease 12-hole (⅓ cup/80ml) muffin pan.

2 Sift flour into large bowl, add coconut and sugar; stir in remaining ingredients.

3 Spoon mixture into holes. Bake, uncovered, about 20 minutes. Turn onto wire rack.

4 Make lime syrup.

5 Place tray under wire rack; pour hot lime syrup over hot muffins. Drain syrup from tray and pour over muffins again.

LIME SYRUP Stir ingredients in small saucepan over heat, without boiling, until sugar dissolves; bring to a boil. Reduce heat; simmer, without stirring, 2 minutes.

PER MUFFIN 14.6g total fat (10.1g saturated); 1526kj (365 cal); 51.4g carbohydrate; 5.6g protein; 2.2g fibre

MIXED-BERRY BUTTERMILK MUFFINS

Butters & creams

The following butters and creams make enough to serve with a dozen freshly baked muffins or scones.

MAPLE AND PECAN BUTTER
Beat 100g softened butter with 2 tablespoons maple syrup in a small bowl with an electric mixer until light and fluffy; stir in ¼ cup finely chopped roasted pecans.

CITRUS BUTTER
Beat 100g softened butter with 1 teaspoon finely grated lime rind, 1 teaspoon finely grated lemon rind and 2 teaspoons icing sugar in a small bowl with an electric mixer until light and fluffy.

BRANDY BUTTER
Beat 100g softened butter with 2 tablespoons brown sugar, 1 tablespoon brandy and 1 teaspoon vanilla extract in a small bowl with an electric mixer until light and fluffy.

CHOC-HAZELNUT CREAM
Beat 100g melted cooled dark eating chocolate with ⅓ cup chocolate hazelnut spread and 50g butter in a small bowl with an electric mixer until thick and glossy.

COFFEE CREAM
Dissolve 1 teaspoon instant coffee granules in 1 teaspoon hot water. Beat the coffee mixture with ½ cup thickened cream, 1 tablespoon coffee liqueur and 2 teaspoons icing sugar in a small bowl with an electric mixer until soft peaks form.

MASCARPONE ORANGE CREAM
Whisk 125g mascarpone, ½ cup thickened cream, 1 tablespoon sifted icing sugar and ½ teaspoon finely grated orange rind in a small bowl until soft peaks form.

PASSIONFRUIT BUTTER
Beat 80g softened butter with ⅔ cup sifted icing sugar in a small bowl with an electric mixer until as white as possible. Stir in 1 tablespoon passionfruit pulp.

WHIPPED NUT BUTTER
Beat 100g softened butter in a small bowl with an electric mixer until light and fluffy; stir in 2 tablespoons finely chopped roasted walnuts and 2 tablespoons finely chopped roasted hazelnuts.

VANILLA BEAN CREAM
Split one vanilla bean in half lengthways, scrape the seeds into a bowl. Add ⅔ cup thickened cream and 1 tablespoon icing sugar; beat with an electric mixer until soft peaks form.

SPICED HONEY YOGURT
Combine 1 cup vanilla yogurt, 1 tablespoon honey, ½ teaspoon ground cinnamon and ¼ teaspoon ground nutmeg in a small bowl.

PRALINE CREAM
Dissolve ⅓ cup caster sugar in 2 tablespoons water in a saucepan over low heat. Boil until the mixture turns a toffee colour. Pour over ¼ cup roasted hazelnuts on a greased oven tray; leave to set. Chop the praline; fold into 300ml whipped thickened cream.

GINGER AND RICOTTA CREAM
Beat ⅓ cup thickened cream in a small bowl with an electric mixer until soft peaks form; fold in 150g ricotta and 2 tablespoons finely chopped crystallized or glacé ginger.

These muffins can be made and baked on the same day, but are actually much nicer if the mixture is made the day before and refrigerated overnight. Use any type of bran you like – wheat, rice or even wheatgerm.

Overnight date and muesli muffins

PREPARATION TIME 10 MINUTES (PLUS REFRIGERATION TIME) **COOKING TIME** 25 MINUTES **MAKES** 12

1¼ cups (185g) plain flour
1 teaspoon ground cinnamon
1 teaspoon bicarbonate of soda
1¼ cups (160g) toasted muesli
½ cup (110g) firmly packed brown sugar
½ cup (30g) bran
¾ cup (110g) coarsely chopped seeded dates
1½ cups (375ml) buttermilk
½ cup (125ml) vegetable oil
1 egg, beaten lightly

1 Sift flour, cinnamon and soda into large bowl; stir in remaining ingredients. Cover; refrigerate overnight.
2 Preheat oven to moderately hot (200°C/180°C fan-forced). Grease 12-hole (⅓ cup/80ml) muffin pan.
3 Spoon mixture into holes. Bake, uncovered, 25 minutes. Turn onto wire rack to cool.

PER MUFFIN 12.3g total fat (2.2g saturated); 1200kj (287 cal); 36.8g carbohydrate; 5.4g protein; 3.8g fibre

---

The flavour of pizza with the tenderness of muffins – a great, easy idea for brunch or Sunday-night dinner, or as an accompaniment to a bowl of soup. You can prepare the muffin pan, roast the capsicum and measure all the ingredients ahead of time, then mix and bake at the last minute.

Cheesy pizza muffins

PREPARATION TIME 20 MINUTES **COOKING TIME** 35 MINUTES **MAKES** 6

1 small red capsicum (150g)
2½ cups (375g) self-raising flour
1 egg, beaten lightly
1¼ cups (310ml) milk
⅓ cup (80ml) light olive oil
½ cup (60g) coarsely grated cheddar
¼ cup (20g) coarsely grated parmesan
½ cup (60g) seeded black olives, halved
¼ cup (35g) drained finely chopped sun-dried tomatoes
2 tablespoons finely chopped fresh basil
2 teaspoons finely chopped fresh rosemary
¼ cup (30g) coarsely grated cheddar, extra

1 Quarter capsicums; discard seeds and membrane. Roast under grill or in very hot oven, skin-side up, until skin blisters and blackens. Cover capsicum pieces with plastic or paper for 5 minutes; peel away skin, then slice capsicum thinly.
2 Preheat oven to moderately hot (200°C/180°C fan-forced). Grease 6-hole texas (¾-cup/180ml) muffin pan.
3 Sift flour into large bowl; stir in egg, milk, oil, cheeses, olives, tomato and herbs.
4 Spoon mixture into holes; top with capsicum strips, sprinkle with extra cheese. Bake, uncovered, about 25 minutes. Turn onto wire rack to cool.

PER MUFFIN 22.4g total fat (7.4g saturated); 1990kj (476 cal); 51.8g carbohydrate; 15.1g protein; 3.6g fibre

Bacon and herb muffins

PREPARATION TIME 15 MINUTES **COOKING TIME** 25 MINUTES (PLUS COOLING TIME) **MAKES** 12

Cooled muffins freeze well; wrap them individually in plastic wrap so you only need to defrost a certain number of them at any time. Place in freezer bags; press the bag gently or use a freezer pump to expel all the air. Muffins can be frozen for up to 3 months. Thaw at room temperature or in the microwave (still wrapped) for 30 seconds.

6 bacon rashers (420g), rind removed, chopped finely

3 cups (450g) self-raising flour

60g butter, chopped coarsely

1 tablespoon coarsely chopped fresh basil

2 tablespoons coarsely chopped fresh chives

2 teaspoons coarsely chopped fresh oregano

¾ cup (60g) finely grated parmesan

2 eggs

1 cup (250ml) milk

1 Preheat oven to moderately hot (200°C/180°C fan-forced). Grease 12-hole (⅓-cup/80ml) muffin pan.

2 Cook bacon in heated lightly oiled small frying pan, stirring, until crisp. Drain on absorbent paper; cool 10 minutes.

3 Sift flour into large bowl; rub in butter. Stir in bacon, herbs and cheese, then combined eggs and milk.

4 Spoon mixture into holes. Bake, uncovered, 20 minutes. Turn onto wire rack to cool.

PER MUFFIN 12.5g total fat (6.3g saturated); 1183kj (283 cal); 27.7g carbohydrate; 14.2g protein; 1.4g fibre

---

Choc-brownie muffins

PREPARATION TIME 10 MINUTES **COOKING TIME** 20 MINUTES **MAKES** 12

These muffins are just scrumptious, served with a citrus liqueur cream, as a simple dessert for a crowd. Place 300ml thickened cream, 2 tablespoons orange liqueur, 1 tablespoon sifted icing sugar and 1 teaspoon finely grated orange rind in a small bowl; beat with an electric mixer until soft peaks form.

2 cups (300g) self-raising flour

⅓ cup (35g) cocoa powder

⅓ cup (75g) caster sugar

60g butter, melted

½ cup (95g) dark Choc Bits

½ cup (70g) finely chopped shelled pistachios

½ cup (165ml) chocolate hazelnut spread

1 egg, beaten lightly

¾ cup (180ml) milk

½ cup (120g) sour cream

1 Preheat oven to moderately hot (200°C/180°C fan-forced). Grease 12-hole (⅓-cup/80ml) muffin pan.

2 Sift flour, cocoa and sugar into large bowl; stir in remaining ingredients.

3 Spoon mixture into holes. Bake, uncovered, 20 minutes. Turn onto wire rack to cool.

PER MUFFIN 19.5g total fat (10.0g saturated); 1505kj (360 cal); 38.5g carbohydrate; 6.6g protein; 2.1g fibre

It's important to use over-ripe bananas; the natural sugars in the fruit are a vital part of this recipe. You'll need two small bananas.

Banana maple muffins

PREPARATION TIME 10 MINUTES **COOKING TIME** 25 MINUTES **MAKES** 12

2 cups (300g) self-raising flour
1/3 cup (50g) plain flour
1/2 teaspoon bicarbonate of soda
1/2 cup (110g) firmly packed brown sugar
1/4 cup (60ml) pure maple syrup
2/3 cup mashed over-ripe banana
2 eggs, beaten lightly
1 cup (250ml) buttermilk
1/3 cup (80ml) vegetable oil

COCONUT TOPPING
20g butter
1 tablespoon pure maple syrup
2/3 cup (30g) flaked coconut

1 Preheat oven to moderately hot (200°C/180°C fan-forced). Grease 12-hole (1/3-cup/80ml) muffin pan. Make coconut topping.
2 Sift dry ingredients into large bowl; stir in remaining ingredients.
3 Spoon mixture into holes; sprinkle with coconut topping. Bake, uncovered, about 20 minutes. Turn onto wire rack to cool.

COCONUT TOPPING Melt butter in small frying pan; cook maple syrup and coconut, stirring, until coconut browns lightly.

PER MUFFIN 10.8g total fat (3.7g saturated); 1179kj (282 cal); 39.8g carbohydrate; 5.3g protein; 1.8g fibre

---

These muffins are more light and cakey than those made by other, more simple methods.

Citrus poppy seed muffins

PREPARATION TIME 15 MINUTES **COOKING TIME** 20 MINUTES **MAKES** 12

125g butter, softened
2 teaspoons finely grated lemon rind
2 teaspoons finely grated lime rind
2 teaspoons finely grated orange rind
2/3 cup (150g) caster sugar
2 eggs
2 cups (300g) self-raising flour
1 cup (500ml) milk
2 tablespoons poppy seeds

1 Preheat oven to moderately hot (200°C/180°C fan-forced). Grease 12-hole (1/3 cup/80ml) muffin pan.
2 Beat butter, rinds, sugar, eggs, flour and milk in medium bowl with electric mixer until combined; beat on medium speed until mixture changes to a lighter colour. Stir in seeds.
3 Spoon mixture into holes. Bake, uncovered, 20 minutes. Turn onto wire rack to cool.

PER MUFFIN 11.4g total fat (6.6g saturated); 1045kj (250 cal); 31.4g carbohydrate; 4.7g protein; 1.4g fibre

1 BANANA MAPPLE MUFFINS **2** CITRUS POPPY SEED MUFFINS
3 BASIC SCONES [P 512] **4** APRICOT SCONES [P 512]

1

2

3

4

The key to making perfect scones is working quickly, so that the butter doesn't soften too much. Always use butter straight from the fridge and use chilled milk as well. If you have a food processor process the flour, sugar, salt and cold butter until the mixture resembles breadcrumbs. Use a round-ended table knife to stir in the milk and water.

Basic scones

PREPARATION TIME 20 MINUTES **COOKING TIME** 15 MINUTES **MAKES** 16

2½ cups (375g) self-raising flour
1 tablespoon caster sugar
¼ teaspoon salt
30g butter
¾ cup (180ml) milk
½ cup (125ml) water, approximately
2 teaspoons milk, extra

1 Preheat oven to very hot (240°C/220°C fan-forced). Grease 23cm-square cake pan.
2 Sift flour, sugar and salt into large bowl; rub in butter. Stir in milk and enough water to mix to a soft, sticky dough.
3 Turn dough onto floured surface; knead quickly and lightly until just smooth. Use hand to press dough out evenly to 2cm thickness; using cutter, cut 5cm rounds from dough. Place rounds in pan; brush with extra milk. Bake, uncovered, about 15 minutes. Turn onto wire rack to cool.

PER SCONE 2.3g total fat (1.4g saturated); 447kj (107 cal); 18.2g carbohydrate; 2.7g protein; 0.9g fibre

---

Use your favourite dried fruit instead of apricots if you like, and change the spice to suit yourself. Finely chopped dried pear with ground ginger works well, as does finely chopped dates or prunes with ½ teaspoon ground cinnamon.

Apricot scones

PREPARATION TIME 20 MINUTES **COOKING TIME** 15 MINUTES **MAKES** 16

2½ cups (375g) self-raising flour
1 tablespoon caster sugar
1 teaspoon mixed spice
30g butter
1 cup (150g) finely chopped dried apricots
1¼ cups (310ml) milk, approximately

1 Preheat oven to very hot (240°C/220°C fan-forced). Grease 23cm-square cake pan.
2 Sift flour, sugar and spice into large bowl; rub in butter. Stir in apricots and enough milk to mix to a soft, sticky dough.
3 Turn dough onto floured surface; knead quickly and lightly until smooth. Use hand to press dough out evenly to 2cm thickness; using cutter, cut 5cm rounds from dough. Place rounds in pan. Bake, uncovered, about 15 minutes. Turn onto wire rack to cool.

PER SCONE 2.6g total fat (1.6g saturated); 548kj (131 cal); 22.5g carbohydrate; 3.4g protein; 1.7g fibre

Pumpkin scones

PREPARATION TIME 25 MINUTES **COOKING TIME** 15 MINUTES **MAKES** 16

These are one of the great specialities of Australian country cooks, using the natural sweetness and moistness of pumpkin to create a wonderful homely treat. Enjoy them straight from the oven. The amount of milk you need to make a soft sticky dough depends entirely on the moisture content of the pumpkin.

40g butter
¼ cup (55g) caster sugar
1 egg
¾ cup cooked mashed pumpkin
2½ cups (375g) self-raising flour
½ teaspoon ground nutmeg
⅓ cup (80ml) milk, approximately
2 teaspoons milk, extra

1 Preheat oven to very hot (240°C/220°C fan-forced). Lightly grease two 20cm-round sandwich pans.
2 Beat butter, sugar and egg in small bowl with electric mixer until combined (mixture will curdle at this stage, but that won't affect the finished scones). Transfer mixture to large bowl. Stir in pumpkin, then sifted dry ingredients and enough milk to make a soft, sticky dough.
3 Turn dough onto floured surface; knead quickly and lightly until just smooth. Press dough out evenly to 2cm thickness; using cutter, cut out 5cm rounds. Place rounds in pans; brush with extra milk. Bake, uncovered, 15 minutes. Turn onto wire rack to cool.

☐ **PER SCONE** 2.9g total fat (1.7g saturated); 531kj (127 cal); 21.1g carbohydrate; 3.2g protein; 1.1g fibre

---

Wholemeal date scones

PREPARATION TIME 20 MINUTES **COOKING TIME** 15 MINUTES **MAKES** 15

These scones are just delicious served with maple and pecan butter (see page 506).

1 cup (150g) white self-raising flour
1 cup (160g) wholemeal self-raising flour
1 cup (60g) unprocessed bran
¼ cup (25g) full-cream milk powder
60g butter
¾ cup (115g) finely chopped seeded dates
1 cup (250ml) water, approximately

1 Preheat oven to moderately hot (200°C/180°C fan-forced). Grease 19cm x 29cm slice cake pan.
2 Sift flours into large bowl; return husks from sifter to bowl. Stir in bran and milk powder; rub in butter, stir in dates. Make well in centre of dry ingredients; stir in enough water to make a soft, sticky dough.
3 Turn dough onto floured surface; knead quickly and lightly until just smooth. Press dough out evenly to 1cm thickness; using cutter, cut out 5cm rounds from dough. Place rounds into pan. Bake, uncovered, about 15 minutes. Turn onto wire rack to cool.

☐ **PER SCONE** 4.3g total fat (2.5g saturated); 589kj (141 cal); 19.9g carbohydrate; 3.6g protein; 4.1g fibre

How do you test if scones are cooked? Scones should be browned and sound hollow when tapped firmly on the bottom with your fingers. The scones in the middle are the ones to tap; they will take the longest to cook.

Buttermilk scones

PREPARATION TIME 20 MINUTES **COOKING TIME** 15 MINUTES **MAKES** 16

3 cups (450g) self-raising flour
¼ teaspoon salt
1 teaspoon icing sugar
60g butter
1¾ cups (430ml) buttermilk, approximately

1 Preheat oven to very hot (240°C/220°C fan-forced). Grease 23cm-square cake pan.
2 Sift flour, salt and sugar into large bowl; rub in butter. Stir in enough buttermilk to mix to a soft, sticky dough.
3 Turn dough onto floured surface; knead quickly and lightly until just smooth. Use hand to press dough out evenly to 2cm thickness; using cutter, cut 5cm rounds from dough. Place rounds into pan. Bake, uncovered, about 15 minutes. Turn onto wire rack to cool.

PER SCONE 4.0g total fat (2.4g saturated); 589kj (141 cal); 21.5g carbohydrate; 4.0g protein; 1.1g fibre

---

Be careful not to overmix the scone dough, the ingredients should just hold together. Over-mixing will result in tougher, heavier scones.

Spicy fruit scones

PREPARATION TIME 20 MINUTES (PLUS STANDING TIME) **COOKING TIME** 15 MINUTES **MAKES** 16

1¼ cups (310ml) hot strong strained black tea
¾ cup (120g) mixed dried fruit
3 cups (450g) self-raising flour
1 teaspoon ground cinnamon
1 teaspoon mixed spice
2 tablespoons caster sugar
20g butter
½ cup (120g) sour cream, approximately

1 Preheat oven to hot (220°C/200°C fan-forced). Grease 23cm-square cake pan.
2 Combine tea and fruit in small heatproof bowl, cover; stand 20 minutes or until cold.
3 Sift dry ingredients into large bowl; rub in butter. Stir in fruit mixture and enough sour cream to mix to a soft, sticky dough. Turn onto floured surface; knead until just smooth.
4 Press dough out evenly to 2cm thickness; cut out 5cm rounds. Place rounds into pan. Bake, uncovered, about 15 minutes. Turn onto wire rack to cool.

PER SCONE 4.4g total fat (2.7g saturated); 690kj (165 cal); 27.2g carbohydrate; 3.1g protein; 1.5g fibre

---

Friands are notorious for sticking to the pan, so make sure the pan is well greased, and turn the friands out of the pan while they are still warm.

Little lime friands

PREPARATION TIME 20 MINUTES **COOKING TIME** 15 MINUTES **MAKES** 30

6 egg whites
185g butter, melted
1 cup (120g) almond meal
1½ cups (240g) icing sugar
½ cup (75g) plain flour
1 tablespoon finely grated lime rind
1 tablespoon lime juice
30 whole blanched almonds (60g)

1 Preheat oven to moderately hot (200°C/180°C fan-forced). Lightly grease 30 mini (1-tablespoon/20ml) muffin pan holes.
2 Place egg whites in medium bowl; whisk lightly with a fork until combined. Add butter, almond meal, sifted icing sugar and flour, then rind and juice; using wooden spoon, stir until just combined.
3 Divide mixture among holes; top each friand with an almond. Bake, uncovered, about 15 minutes. Stand friands in pans 5 minutes before turning onto wire rack to cool.

PER FRIAND 8.4g total fat (3.6g saturated); 527kj (126 cal); 10.1g carbohydrate; 2.2g protein; 0.6g fibre

In France, friands are known as financiers, because they are baked in tiny gold-bar-shaped pans. The key to making perfect friands is to only just combine the egg whites. If possible, rest the mixture for at least 30 minutes before baking. This allows the mixture to settle, air bubbles to disappear, resulting in delicious, dense almond cakes.

Almond and strawberry friands

PREPARATION TIME 20 MINUTES **COOKING TIME** 25 MINUTES **MAKES** 12

6 egg whites
185g butter, melted
1 cup (120g) almond meal
1½ cups (240g) icing sugar
½ cup (75g) plain flour
100g strawberries, sliced thinly

1 Preheat oven to moderately hot (200°C/180°C fan-forced). Grease 12 (½-cup/125ml) rectangular or oval friand pans, stand on oven tray.
2 Place egg whites in medium bowl; whisk lightly with a fork until combined. Add butter, almond meal, sifted icing sugar and flour; using wooden spoon, stir until just combined.
3 Divide mixture among pans; top with strawberry slices. Bake, uncovered, about 25 minutes. Stand friands in pans 5 minutes before turning onto wire rack to cool.

PER FRIAND 18.2g total fat (8.7g saturated); 1191kj (285 cal); 25.3g carbohydrate; 4.7g protein; 1.3g fibre

---

Cherry friands

PREPARATION TIME 15 MINUTES **COOKING TIME** 25 MINUTES **MAKES** 12

1½ cups (240g) icing sugar
½ cup (75g) plain flour
185g butter, melted
6 egg whites, beaten lightly
1 cup (120g) almond meal
250g fresh cherries, halved, seeded

Seeded cherries can be frozen for up to 18 months. Freeze them in batches, when they are in season. Use them unthawed – this will minimise the "bleeding" of colour into the mixture.

1 Preheat oven to moderately hot (200°C/180°C fan-forced). Grease 12 small rectangular or oval friand pans (stand on oven tray) or 12-hole (⅓-cup/80ml) muffin pan.
2 Sift icing sugar and flour into medium bowl. Add butter, egg whites and almond meal; using wooden spoon, stir until just combined.
3 Divide mixture among pans; top with cherries. Bake, uncovered, about 25 minutes. Stand 5 minutes; turn onto wire rack to cool.

PER FRIAND 18.3g total fat (8.7g saturated); 1216kj (291 cal); 26.5g carbohydrate; 4.7g protein; 1.4g fibre

BISCUITS & SLICES

Biscuits & Slices

A jar of homemade biscuits speaks of pleasant family life and a welcome to the visitor. Many of the best recipes are the legacy of cooks who may never have char-grilled asparagus or run up a beurre blanc, but who bowed to no one in their ability to bake a tray of irresistible biscuits.

Slices were our mothers' pride at morning and afternoon tea, and as lunch-box treats. They still perform beautifully in both roles or, cut small, as delicious mouthfuls to have with after-dinner coffee.

MIXING

- For best results, have butter and eggs at room temperature.
- Don't overbeat butter and sugar – stop when they are well combined but the mixture is still firm. Overbeating makes the mixture too soft, causing biscuits to spread.
- Usually dry ingredients are mixed in by hand in two batches.

THE RIGHT PANS

The shape of a baking pan or oven tray affects the way biscuits and slices will bake. For biscuits, we use either flat oven trays or aluminium pans with shallow sides (swiss roll pans) so that the heat "skims" over the top and ensures proper circulation and browning. For slices, we use aluminium slice or lamington pans (rectangular, with sides about 2.5cm high).

POSITION IN THE OVEN

- Two or more trays or pans of biscuits or slices can be baked in an oven at the same time, provided the pans don't touch the oven sides or the door when it is closed, and that each tray has 2cm space around it to allow for proper heat circulation.
- For even baking, swap the positions of the pans halfway through the baking time. You may also need to turn pans front-to-back to brown biscuits evenly.
- As a general rule, the top half of a gas oven is best for baking biscuits, but in an electric oven, the lower half is usually best.
- Fan-forced ovens maintain even heat throughout the oven, so you should not have to change the trays around – however, check them once or twice.

BAKING AND COOLING

- Position the oven racks as required and preheat the oven to the correct temperature.
- Check biscuits during baking; opening the oven door briefly will not affect them.

- To test if a biscuit is cooked, push it gently with your finger. If it can be moved on the tray without breaking, it can be removed from the oven. It will become firm on cooling.
- Bases for layered slices should be golden. They will feel soft in the oven, but will become firm as they cool.
- Follow recipes regarding whether to cool biscuits on trays or on wire racks.

STORING AND FREEZING

- Cool biscuits and slices before storing – if you store them warm, they will become soft. Store in an airtight container, leaving minimal air space. Biscuits with fillings should be stored unfilled and assembled just before serving; if the filling is baked in, they are best eaten the same day. Don't store biscuits with cake or bread as it will soften them.
- If unfilled and un-iced biscuits do become soft, they can be re-crisped by arranging in a single layer on oven trays and heating in a moderate oven for 5 to 10 minutes – check often as they will over-brown quickly. Transfer to wire racks to cool.
- Don't store biscuits and slices for too long – even in airtight containers, they gradually become "tired" after about a week. To keep them longer, freeze in rigid containers. Some icings and cream fillings may crack or change in appearance on thawing.

SPECIAL TECHNIQUES

MELTING CHOCOLATE Place chopped chocolate in a heatproof bowl over a saucepan of simmering water; the base of the bowl should not touch the water. Remove the bowl when the chocolate feels soft and stir until it is smooth.

ROASTING NUTS AND COCONUT Spread nuts or coconut evenly on an oven tray and roast in a moderate oven, checking and stirring to ensure even browning. Remove from the oven when almost brown enough and tip onto a plate to stop their own heat from over-browning them. You can also roast nuts or coconut in a dry frying pan by stirring constantly over low to medium heat. Remove from the pan to cool.

WHAT WENT WRONG?

Biscuits are fairly forgiving: even if they are not perfect, they are usually good to eat. Partly for that reason, they are often the first thing that children learn to cook. However, it's the nature of cooks to strive for perfection, so here are clues to making them better.

- If biscuits are **too hard**, the ingredients may have been measured incorrectly or the biscuits may have been baked at too high a temperature or for too long.
- If biscuits are **too soft**, the ingredients may have been measured incorrectly or the biscuits may have been baked at too low a temperature or for not long enough. If biscuits are not cooled as directed or are stacked on top of each other to cool, they may be softened because the moist heat they give off cannot disperse.
- If biscuits **spread too much** while baking, the mixture may have been too soft because of overbeating (see "mixing", above), or the ingredients may have been measured incorrectly, or the wrong type of flour may have been used, or the oven may not have been hot enough to set the mixture quickly.
- If biscuits are **too brown underneath**, the trays may have been over-greased; excess greasing will burn and, in turn, burn the biscuits. Incorrect oven position and/or temperature can also cause over-browning; so can over-measuring sweet ingredients.

Hazelnut pinwheels

PREPARATION TIME 20 MINUTES (PLUS REFRIGERATION TIME) **BAKING TIME** 20 MINUTES **MAKES** 30

1 ¼ cups (185g) plain flour
100g butter, chopped
½ cup (110g) caster sugar
1 egg yolk
1 tablespoon milk, approximately
⅓ cup (110g) chocolate hazelnut spread
2 tablespoons hazelnut meal

1 Process flour, butter and sugar until crumbly. Add egg yolk; process with enough milk until mixture forms a ball. Knead dough on lightly floured surface until smooth; cover, refrigerate 1 hour.

2 Roll dough between sheets of baking paper to form 20cm x 30cm rectangle; remove top sheet of paper. Spread dough evenly with hazelnut spread; sprinkle with hazelnut meal. Using paper as a guide, roll dough tightly from long side to enclose filling. Enclose roll in plastic wrap; refrigerate 30 minutes.

3 Preheat oven to moderate (180°C/160°C fan-forced). Grease oven trays; line with baking paper.

4 Remove plastic; cut roll into 1cm slices. Place slices on trays 2cm apart. Bake about 20 minutes. Stand pinwheels on trays 5 minutes; transfer to wire racks to cool.

PER PINWHEEL 4.6g total fat (2.3g saturated); 301kj (72 cal); 6.6g carbohydrate; 1.1g protein; 0.3g fibre

If you don't have hazelnut meal in your pantry, it's easy enough to grind the nuts yourself for the small amount required here. Roast the nuts briefly in a small frying pan, stirring constantly to ensure they don't burn. Cool then wrap in a tea-towel and rub off their skins. Process in a coffee- or spice-grinder (or mini food processor) to a coarse meal consistency: take care – if you process for too long they'll turn into an oily paste.

Almond jam cookies

PREPARATION TIME 30 MINUTES **COOKING TIME** 25MINUTES **MAKES** 30

185g butter, chopped
1 teaspoon vanilla extract
¾ cup (165g) caster sugar
2 egg yolks
½ cup (60g) almond meal
1 ½ cups (225g) plain flour
½ teaspoon baking powder
2 tablespoons apricot jam
1 teaspoon finely grated lemon rind
2 tablespoons raspberry jam

1 Preheat oven to moderately slow (170°C/150°C fan-forced).

2 Beat butter, extract, sugar and yolks in medium bowl with electric mixer until just combined. Stir in almond meal, sifted flour and baking powderl. Roll level tablespoons of mixture into balls, place 5cm apart on ungreased oven trays. Press a hollow in each ball about 1cm deep and 1.5cm wide with the handle end of a floured wooden spoon.

3 Combine apricot jam with half of the rind. Combine raspberry jam with remaining rind. Carefully spoon a little apricot jam into half of the cookies; spoon raspberry jam into remaining cookies. Bake, uncovered, about 25 minutes or until cookies are browned lightly; cool on trays.

PER COOKIE 6.6g total fat (3.5g saturated); 493kj (118 cal); 12.8g carbohydrate; 1.5g protein; 0.5g fibre

This recipe gives you a chance to experiment with some different flavour combinations. For example, use hazelnut meal instead of almond, and use plum and fig jams instead of apricot and raspberry. The lemon rind is optional – the choice is yours.

HAZELNUT PINWHEELS

These soft chewy biscuits are Italian in origin and were originally made with ground almonds, with coconut becoming an equally popular adaptation. You could use ground almonds or even ground hazelnuts instead of the coconut.

Coconut macaroons

PREPARATION TIME 20 MINUTES **COOKING TIME** 40 MINUTES **MAKES** 24

2 egg whites

½ cup (110g) caster sugar

1 teaspoon vanilla extract

2 tablespoons plain flour

1½ cups (120g) desiccated coconut

6 glacé cherries, quartered

1 Preheat oven to slow (150°C/130°C fan-forced). Line oven trays with baking paper.

2 Beat egg whites in small bowl with electric mixer until soft peaks form. Gradually add sugar, beating until dissolved after each addition. Stir in extract, sifted flour and coconut, in two batches.

3 Drop level tablespoons of the mixture 5cm apart onto trays. Place a cherry quarter on top of each macaroon. Bake, uncovered, about 40 minutes or until browned lightly; cool on trays.

PER MACAROON 3.3g total fat (2.9g saturated); 251kj (60 cal); 6.6g carbohydrate; 0.7g protein; 0.8g fibre

---

Originally called toll house cookies, these American biscuits were invented by the owner of the Toll House Inn, Ruth Graves Wakefield, in the 1930s in Massachusetts. Ruth added bits of dark chocolate to her favourite cookie dough, expecting them to melt during baking. Instead, the chocolate held its shape but became delicate and creamy – and the classic chocolate chip cookie was born.

Chocolate chip cookies

PREPARATION TIME 40 MINUTES (PLUS REFRIGERATION TIME) **COOKING TIME** 15 MINUTES **MAKES** 40

250g butter, softened

1 teaspoon vanilla extract

¾ cup (165g) caster sugar

¾ cup (165g) firmly packed brown sugar

1 egg

2¼ cups (335g) plain flour

1 teaspoon bicarbonate of soda

2 cups (300g) dark chocolate Melts, chopped coarsely

1 Beat butter, extract, sugars and egg in small bowl with electric mixer until light and fluffy. Transfer to large bowl. Stir combined sifted flour and soda into egg mixture, in two batches. Stir in chocolate, cover; refrigerate 1 hour.

2 Preheat oven to moderate (180°C/160°C fan-forced). Grease oven trays.

3 Roll level tablespoons of the dough into balls; place 3cm apart on trays. Bake, uncovered, about 12 minutes. Cool on trays.

PER COOKIE 7.6g total fat (5.5g saturated); 623kj (149 cal); 18.5g carbohydrate; 1.4g protein; 0.7g fibre

Coconut tuiles

PREPARATION TIME 20 MINUTES **COOKING TIME** 5 MINUTES **MAKES** 15

Tuile is French for tile, and these biscuits are named for their similarity to the shape of curved roofing tiles. These tuiles are a perfect accompaniment to creamy desserts, such as ice-cream, mousse or panna cotta.

1 egg white
¼ cup (55g) caster sugar
2 tablespoons plain flour
30g butter, melted
¼ teaspoon coconut essence
2 tablespoons shredded coconut

1 Preheat oven to moderate (180°C/160°C fan-forced). Grease oven trays.
2 Beat egg white in small bowl with electric mixer until soft peaks form. Gradually add sugar, beating until sugar dissolves between additions. Fold in flour, butter and essence.
3 Drop rounded teaspoons of mixture onto trays; allow four tuiles per tray. Spread into 7cm rounds; sprinkle with coconut. Bake, uncovered, 5 minutes or until browned lightly.
4 Slide a metal spatula under each hot tuile, then quickly shape over a rolling pin; cool.

PER TUILE 2.2g total fat (1.6g saturated); 171kj (41 cal); 4.8g carbohydrate; 0.5g protein; 0.2g fibre

---

Crunchy muesli cookies

PREPARATION TIME 15 MINUTES **COOKING TIME** 25 MINUTES **MAKES** 36

Mix and match the fruit and nuts to suit your own tastes. Honey (not the pouring variety), treacle, or even more strongly flavoured molasses could be subsituted for the golden syrup.

1 cup (90g) rolled oats
1 cup (150g) plain flour
1 cup (220g) caster sugar
2 teaspoons ground cinnamon
¼ cup (35g) craisins
⅓ cup (55g) finely chopped dried apricots
½ cup (70g) slivered almonds
125g butter
2 tablespoons golden syrup
½ teaspoon bicarbonate of soda
1 tablespoon boiling water

1 Preheat oven to slow (150°C/130°C fan-forced). Grease oven trays; line with baking paper.
2 Combine oats, flour, sugar, cinnamon, dried fruit and nuts in large bowl.
3 Melt butter with golden syrup in small saucepan over low heat; add combined soda and the boiling water. Stir warm butter mixture into dry ingredients.
4 Roll level tablespoons of mixture into balls, place on trays 5cm apart; flatten with hand. Bake about 20 minutes; cool cookies on trays.

PER COOKIE 4.2g total fat (2.0g saturated); 405kj (97 cal); 13.2g carbohydrate; 1.2g protein; 0.7g fibre

Gingernuts are great for desserts. Try layering stewed strawberries and rhubarb into tumblers, followed by cinnamon yogurt and a topping of lightly crushed gingernuts. For an easy dessert terrine, line a loaf pan with plastic wrap; brush gingernuts with a coffee liqueur, then arrange alternate layers of gingernuts and vanilla-flavoured whipped thickened cream to the top of the loaf pan. Chill in the fridge for 1 hour before turning out and slicing.

Gingernuts

PREPARATION TIME 15 MINUTES (PLUS STANDING TIME) **COOKING TIME** 15 MINUTES **MAKES** 35

90g butter
⅓ cup (75g) firmly packed brown sugar
⅓ cup (115g) golden syrup
1⅓ cups (200g) plain flour
¾ teaspoon bicarbonate of soda
1 teaspoon ground cinnamon
1 tablespoon ground ginger
¼ teaspoon ground clove

1 Preheat oven to moderate (180°C/160°C fan-forced). Grease oven trays.
2 Stir butter, sugar and golden syrup in medium saucepan over heat until butter is melted. Remove from heat; stir in sifted dry ingredients. Stand until mixture feels warm to the touch.
3 Roll rounded teaspoons of the mixture into balls, place 3cm apart on trays; flatten slightly. Bake, uncovered, about 12 minutes or until browned lightly. Loosen biscuits; cool on trays.

PER GINGERNUT 2.2g total fat (1.4g saturated); 238kj (57 cal); 8.7g carbohydrate; 0.6g protein; 0.2g fibre

Greek shortbread

PREPARATION TIME 45 MINUTES **COOKING TIME** 15 MINUTES **MAKES** 50

250g butter, softened
1 teaspoon vanilla extract
1 cup (220g) caster sugar
1 egg
¼ cup (60ml) brandy
¾ cup (120g) roasted blanched almonds, chopped finely
1½ cups (225g) self-raising flour
2½ cups (375g) plain flour
½ teaspoon ground nutmeg
¼ cup (60ml) rosewater
½ cup (125ml) water
3 cups (480g) icing sugar

These are an adaptation of traditional Greek kourabiethes, which are celebratory biscuits often served for Christmas, weddings and christenings.

1 Preheat oven to moderate (180°C/160°C fan-forced). Grease oven trays.
2 Beat butter, extract and caster sugar in small bowl with electric mixer until light and fluffy. Beat in egg and brandy; transfer mixture to large bowl. Stir in nuts and sifted flours and nutmeg, in two batches.
3 Turn dough onto floured surface; knead gently until smooth. Shape level tablespoons of the dough into crescent shapes; place about 3cm apart on trays. Bake, uncovered, about 15 minutes or until browned lightly.
4 Lift shortbread onto wire racks; brush hot shortbread with combined rosewater and the water. Coat thickly with sifted icing sugar; cool to room temperature.

PER PIECE 5.7g total fat (2.8g saturated); 644kj (154 cal); 22.7g carbohydrate; 1.9g protein; 0.7g fibre

Bran and apricot cookies

PREPARATION TIME 20 MINUTES **COOKING TIME** 10 MINUTES **MAKES** 25

1 cup (70g) bran

1 cup (150g) self-raising flour

1 cup (80g) desiccated coconut

½ cup (110g) firmly packed brown sugar

½ cup (125g) finely chopped glacé apricots

125g butter, melted

1 egg, beaten lightly

1 Preheat oven to moderately hot (200°C/180°C fan-forced). Grease oven trays.

2 Combine ingredients in large bowl.

3 Place level tablespoons of the mixture about 5cm apart on trays. Bake, uncovered, about 10 minutes or until browned lightly; cool on trays.

PER COOKIE 2.5g total fat (0.1g saturated); 343kj (82 cal); 12.3g carbohydrate; 1.5g protein; 2.0g fibre

These are a healthy idea for children's lunchboxes to give them an energy boost. To make them more appealing, drizzle melted white chocolate in zig zags over them.

Passionfruit butter yoyo bites

PREPARATION TIME 20 MINUTES **COOKING TIME** 15 MINUTES **MAKES** 35

250g butter, chopped

1 teaspoon vanilla extract

½ cup (80g) icing sugar

1½ cups (225g) plain flour

½ cup (75g) cornflour

PASSIONFRUIT BUTTER

80g butter

⅔ cup (110g) icing sugar

1 tablespoon passionfruit pulp

1 Preheat oven to moderately slow (170°C/150°C fan-forced). Line two oven trays with baking paper.

2 Beat butter, extract and sifted sugar in medium bowl with electric mixer until light and fluffy; stir in sifted flours, in two batches.

3 Roll rounded teaspoons of mixture into balls; place 3cm apart on trays. Using floured fork, press tines gently onto each biscuit to flatten slightly. Bake, uncovered, 12 minutes. Stand biscuits 5 minutes; transfer to wire racks to cool.

4 Make passionfruit butter. Sandwich cold biscuits with passionfruit butter.

PASSIONFRUIT BUTTER Beat butter and sifted sugar in small bowl with electric mixer until light and fluffy; stir in passionfruit pulp.

PER BITE 7.8g total fat (5.1g saturated); 510kj (122 cal); 12.1g carbohydrate; 0.8g protein; 0.3g fibre

Yoyos are one of the oldest known toys and stone yoyos have been found in Greece dating back more than 3000 years. These biscuits are named after this classic toy. For different flavoured butters try vanilla, cinnamon and honey, maple syrup, citrus rind or raspberries.

Teas & coffees

These stylish recipes show you some clever ways to literally spice up a cup of tea or coffee.

MOROCCAN MINT TEA
Combine 3 teabags, 1 cup fresh mint leaves, 4 cups boiling water and 2 tablespoons sugar in a large jug. Stand 10 minutes; strain. Serve chilled with extra mint and ice.

CARDAMOM COFFEE
Combine 2 tablespoons coarsely ground roasted coffee beans, 3 bruised cardamom pods, 1 teaspoon sugar and 1 cup water in a small saucepan; bring to a boil. Stand 3 minutes; strain into espresso cups.

CINNAMON AND ORANGE TEA
Combine 2 tablespoons loose-leaf tea, 2 cinnamon sticks, 10cm strip orange rind, 1 tablespoon honey and 4 cups water in a medium saucepan. Simmer 5 minutes, then strain.

LEMON ICED TEA
Combine 3 plain teabags, 3 lemon teabags, 6 cups boiling water, ⅓ cup sugar and two strips lemon rind in a jug. Stand 10 minutes; strain. Serve chilled with ice cubes and strips of lemon rind.

LEMON GRASS AND KAFFIR LIME TEA
Combine 2 tablespoons loose-leaf tea, 2 tablespoons finely chopped fresh lemon grass, 4 shredded kaffir lime leaves and 4 cups water in a small saucepan; bring to a boil. Simmer 5 minutes, then strain.

CARDAMOM AND CHAMOMILE TEA
Combine 2 tablespoons loose-leaf chamomile tea, 4 bruised cardamom pods and 4 cups water in a medium saucepan; bring to a boil. Simmer 5 minutes, then strain.

GINGER TEA
Combine 2 tablespoons loose-leaf tea, a 4cm piece fresh ginger, grated, and 4 cups water in a medium saucepan; bring to a boil. Simmer 5 minutes, then strain. Serve with lemon.

AFFOGATO
Combine 2 tablespoons ground espresso coffee and ⅔ cup boiling water in a coffee plunger; stand 2 minutes before plunging. Divide vanilla ice-cream among glasses; top with Irish cream liqueur and coffee .

ICED MOCHA
Dissolve 2 tablespoons instant coffee granules in 2 tablespoons boiling water; add ¼ cup chocolate topping and 3 cups milk. Pour into glasses; top with ice-cream and drinking chocolate.

SPICED ICED COFFEE MILKSHAKE
Place ¼ cup ground coffee and ¾ cup boiling water in a plunger; stand before plunging. Add 2 bruised cardamom pods, ¼ teaspoon ground cinnamon and 1 tablespoon brown sugar. Strain; blend with ice-cream and milk.

IRISH COFFEE
Combine 2 tablespoons ground espresso coffee and ⅔ cup boiling water in a coffee plunger; stand 2 minutes before plunging. Divide 1 tablespoon brown sugar among glasses; add ⅓ cup whisky then the coffee. Float thickened cream on each coffee.

CHAI TEA
Combine 2 teaspoons honey, 1 teaspoon ground cardamom, ½ teaspoon each ground cinnamon and clove, and 395g can sweetened condensed milk; refrigerate 3 hours. Use to flavour black tea.

No one really knows the true origins of the name for these biscuits. Some think they were made by Australian women to send to their men fighting in the first world war and were originally called soldiers' biscuits. Others believe that they were not named until after the war, when they were made and sold as fund-raisers for returned soldiers. It is best to use traditional (not quick cook) oats in our version.

Anzac biscuits

PREPARATION TIME 20 MINUTES **COOKING TIME** 25 MINUTES **MAKES** 30

1 cup (90g) rolled oats
1 cup (150g) plain flour
1 cup (220g) caster sugar
¾ cup (60g) desiccated coconut
125g butter
1 tablespoon golden syrup
1 teaspoon bicarbonate of soda
2 tablespoons boiling water

1 Preheat oven to slow (150°C/130°C fan-forced). Grease oven trays.
2 Combine oats, sifted flour, sugar and coconut in large bowl.
3 Stir butter and golden syrup in small saucepan over low heat until butter is melted. Combine soda and the water, add to butter mixture; stir into dry ingredients while mixture is warm.
4 Place heaped teaspoons of the mixture about 4cm apart on trays; flatten slightly. Bake, uncovered, about 20 minutes or until golden brown. Loosen biscuits while warm; cool on trays.

☐ **PER BISCUIT** 5.0g total fat (3.5g saturated); 439kj (105 cal); 13.7g carbohydrate; 1.0g protein; 0.7g fibre

---

Shortbread is the national biscuit of Scotland and shortbread making for some has become a serious competition, featuring as a category at the annual Scottish highland games.

Glazed lemon shortbreads

PREPARATION TIME 20 MINUTES (PLUS COOLING TIME) **COOKING TIME** 40 MINUTES **MAKES** 30

2 tablespoons rice flour
⅓ cup (55g) icing sugar
2 cups (300g) plain flour
250g butter
1 teaspoon finely grated lemon rind
2 teaspoons lemon juice

LEMON GLAZE
1 cup (160g) icing sugar
½ teaspoon finely grated lemon rind
¼ cup (60ml) lemon juice

1 Preheat oven to moderately slow (170°C/150°C fan-forced). Grease 20cm x 30cm lamington pan.
2 Sift dry ingredients into medium bowl; rub in butter. Stir in rind and juice. Turn dough onto floured surface; knead lightly until smooth. Press into pan; mark into finger lengths. Bake, uncovered, 40 minutes. Cut shortbread in pan; stand 10 minutes. Cool on wire rack.
3 Make lemon glaze. Dip one end of shortbreads in glaze, place on foil-lined tray to set.

LEMON GLAZE Stir sifted icing sugar, rind and juice in small bowl until smooth.

☐ **PER PIECE** 7.0g total fat (4.5g saturated); 543kj (130 cal); 15.2g carbohydrate; 1.2g protein; 0.4g fibre

Amaretti

PREPARATION TIME 15 MINUTES **COOKING TIME** 15 MINUTES **MAKES** 20

In Italy, these traditional almond biscuits are served with coffee at any time of the day. They are delicious plain or try them sandwiched together with melted chocolate.

- 1 cup (120g) almond meal
- 1 cup (220g) caster sugar
- 2 large egg whites
- ½ teaspoon vanilla extract
- 2 drops almond essence
- 20 blanched almonds

1 Preheat oven to moderate (180°C/160°C fan-forced). Line oven trays with baking paper.

2 Beat almond meal, sugar, egg whites, extract and essence in medium bowl with electric mixer, on medium speed, 3 minutes; stand 5 minutes.

3 Spoon mixture into piping bag fitted with 1cm plain tube; pipe onto trays in circular motion from centre, to make biscuits about 4cm in diameter leaving 2cm between each. Top with nuts. Bake, uncovered, 12 minutes or until tops are browned lightly. Stand on trays 5 minutes before removing with metal spatula. Cool on wire rack.

PER BISCUIT 4.0g total fat (0.3g saturated); 376kj (90 cal); 11.3g carbohydrate; 1.8g protein; 0.6g fibre

---

Lemon and pistachio biscotti

PREPARATION TIME 20 MINUTES (PLUS REFRIGERATION TIME)
COOKING TIME 40 MINUTES (PLUS COOLING TIME) **MAKES** 60

Serve these biscuits with fruit tea or at the end of dinner with a tiny glass of limoncello. For a change, use orange rind instead of lemon rind, and slivered almonds instead of pistachios.

- 60g butter, chopped coarsely
- 1 cup (220g) caster sugar
- 1 teaspoon vanilla extract
- 1 tablespoon finely grated lemon rind
- 4 eggs
- 2¼ cups (335g) plain flour
- 1 teaspoon baking powder
- ½ teaspoon bicarbonate of soda
- 1 cup (140g) shelled pistachios, chopped coarsely
- 1 tablespoon water
- 2 tablespoons caster sugar, extra

1 Preheat oven to moderate (180°C/160°C fan-forced). Grease oven trays.

2 Beat butter, sugar, extract and rind in medium bowl until just combined. Add three of the eggs, one at a time, beating until combined between each addition. Stir in sifted flour, baking powder and soda, then nuts. Cover; refrigerate 1 hour.

3 Knead dough on lightly floured surface until smooth but still sticky. Halve dough; shape each half into 30cm log. Place logs on oven trays. Combine remaining egg with the water in small bowl. Brush egg mixture over logs; sprinkle thickly with extra sugar. Bake, uncovered, about 20 minutes or until firm; cool on trays. Reduce oven temperature to moderately slow (170°C/150°C fan-forced).

4 Using serrated knife, cut logs, diagonally, into 1cm slices. Place slices on ungreased oven trays. Bake, uncovered, about 15 minutes or until dry and crisp, turning halfway through; cool on wire racks.

PER PIECE 2.4g total fat (0.8g saturated); 268kj (64 cal); 8.7g carbohydrate; 1.5g protein; 0.4g fibre

Biscotti make lovely home-made presents. For a gift idea place biscotti in a large white coffee cup and wrap the whole thing in clear cellophane; tie with dark brown and bronze ribbons.

Coffee and hazelnut biscotti

PREPARATION TIME 35 MINUTES (PLUS STANDING TIME)
COOKING TIME 40 MINUTES (PLUS COOLING TIME) **MAKES** 20

½ cup (110g) caster sugar
1 egg, beaten lightly
¾ cup (110g) plain flour
½ teaspoon baking powder
1 tablespoon instant coffee granules
1 cup (140g) roasted hazelnuts, chopped coarsely
100g dark eating chocolate, melted

1 Preheat oven to moderate (180°C/160°C fan-forced). Grease oven tray.
2 Whisk sugar and egg in medium bowl; stir in sifted flour and baking powder and the coffee. Stir in nuts. Roll dough into 20cm log. Place on tray. Bake, uncovered, 25 minutes; cool on tray. Reduce oven temperature to moderately slow (170°C/150°C fan-forced).
3 Cut log, diagonally, into 1cm slices. Place slices on ungreased oven trays. Bake, uncovered, 15 minutes or until crisp, turning halfway through cooking; cool on wire racks.
4 Spread chocolate over one cut side of each biscotti. Allow to set at room temperature.

☐ **PER PIECE** 29.1g total fat (7.9g saturated); 1990kj (476 cal); 43.7g carbohydrate; 7.9g protein; 4.8g fibre

---

The word biscotti is plural for biscotto, which is Italian for biscuit and means twice-baked. Biscotti are first baked as a loaf of dough, then cut into thin slices and baked again to dry them to a crisp texture. Traditionally, biscotti are dunked into coffee or vin santo, a delicious Italian dessert wine.

Swirled choc-almond biscotti

PREPARATION TIME 25 MINUTES (PLUS REFRIGERATION TIME)
COOKING TIME 45 MINUTES (PLUS COOLING TIME) **MAKES** 25

30g butter
½ cup (110g) caster sugar
½ teaspoon almond essence
3 eggs
1 cup (150g) plain flour
½ teaspoon baking powder
¾ cup (120g) blanched almonds, chopped coarsely
2 tablespoons cocoa powder
2 tablespoons plain flour, extra

1 Beat butter, sugar and essence in medium bowl until just combined. Add eggs, beat until combined (mixture will curdle at this stage, but will reconstitute later). Stir in sifted flour and baking powder and then nuts. Cover; refrigerate about 1 hour.
2 Preheat oven to moderate (180°C/160°C fan-forced). Grease oven tray.
3 Halve dough. Knead cocoa into one half of dough; shape into a 25cm log. Knead extra flour into remaining dough; shape into a 25cm log. Gently twist cocoa log and plain log together; place on tray. Bake, uncovered, about 30 minutes or until firm; cool on tray. Reduce oven temperature to moderately slow (170°C/150°C fan-forced).
4 Using serrated knife cut log, diagonally, into 1cm slices. Place slices on ungreased oven trays. Bake, uncovered, about 15 minutes or until dry and crisp, turning halfway through cooking; cool on wire racks.

☐ **PER PIECE** 4.4g total fat (1.1g saturated); 380kj (91 cal); 9.8g carbohydrate; 2.6g protein; 0.7g fibre

Triple-choc brownies

PREPARATION TIME 15 MINUTES **COOKING TIME** 40 MINUTES **MAKES** 18

These brownies are the most popular item ordered from our test kitchen catering service. In a single year nearly 30,000 brownies are consumed by the staff at the Sydney office of Australian Consolidated Press.

- 125g butter, melted
- 200g dark eating chocolate, melted
- ½ cup (110g) caster sugar
- 2 eggs, beaten lightly
- 1 ¼ cups (185g) plain flour
- 150g white eating chocolate, chopped coarsely
- 100g milk eating chocolate, chopped coarsely

1 Preheat oven to moderate (180°C/160°C fan-forced). Lightly grease and line deep 19cm-square cake pan with baking paper.

2 Combine ingredients in large bowl. Spread mixture into pan; bake about 35 minutes or until mixture is firm to touch. Cool in pan.

☐ **PER BROWNIE** 14.3g total fat (9.9g saturated); 1062kj (254 cal); 27.5g carbohydrate; 3.3g protein; 1g fibre

---

Apple and rhubarb streusel slice

PREPARATION TIME 20 MINUTES (PLUS COOLING AND FREEZING TIME)
COOKING TIME 45 MINUTES **MAKES** 15

Streusel is the German word for "sprinkle". For a great dessert, line a 22cm pie plate with ready-made shortcrust pastry; blind bake following instructions for lemon meringue pie on page 588. Spread the apple and rhubarb filling into the pastry case, top with streusel and bake for 15 minutes.

- 100g butter, softened
- ½ cup (110g) caster sugar
- 1 egg yolk
- ⅔ cup (100g) plain flour
- ¼ cup (35g) self-raising flour
- 1 tablespoon custard powder
- 4 cups (440g) coarsely chopped rhubarb
- 2 large granny smith apples (400g), sliced thinly
- 2 tablespoons honey
- 1 ½ teaspoons finely grated orange rind

STREUSEL

- ½ cup (75g) plain flour
- ¼ cup (35g) self-raising flour
- ⅓ cup (75g) firmly packed brown sugar
- ½ teaspoon ground cinnamon
- 80g butter, chopped

1 Make streusel by blending or processing ingredients until just combined. Enclose in plastic wrap; freeze about 1 hour or until firm.

2 Preheat oven to moderate (180°C/160°C fan-forced). Line 20cm x 30cm lamington pan with baking paper, extending paper 3cm over long sides of pan.

3 Beat butter, sugar and egg yolk in small bowl with electric mixer until light and fluffy. Stir in sifted flours and custard powder; press mixture into pan. Bake 20 minutes. Cool 15 minutes. Increase oven temperature to moderately hot (200°C/180°C fan-forced).

4 Meanwhile, cook rhubarb, apple, honey and rind in medium saucepan about 5 minutes or until apples are just tender; cool 15 minutes. Spread over slice base; coarsely grate streusel over fruit. Bake, uncovered, about 15 minutes. Cool in pan before cutting.

☐ **PER PIECE** 10.5g total fat (6.6g saturated); 924kj (221 cal); 28.4g carbohydrate; 2.5g protein; 1.6g fibre

1

2

3

4

Chocolate rum and raisin slice

Cut these treats into fingers to serve with a creamy or fruity dessert, or into small squares to serve with after-dinner coffee.

PREPARATION TIME 10 MINUTES **COOKING TIME** 35 MINUTES **MAKES** 15

125g butter, chopped

200g dark eating chocolate, chopped coarsely

1 cup (160g) coarsely chopped raisins

½ cup (110g) caster sugar

2 eggs, beaten lightly

1 ½ cups (225g) plain flour

1 tablespoon dark rum

1 Preheat oven to moderately slow (170°C/150°C fan-forced). Grease 20cm x 30cm lamington pan.

2 Stir butter, chocolate, raisins and sugar in medium saucepan over low heat until chocolate melts. Cool to room temperature. Stir in remaining ingredients, mix well; spread into pan. Bake, uncovered, 30 minutes; cool in pan. Dust with icing sugar, if desired.

PER PIECE 11.9g total fat (8.5g saturated); 1087kj (260 cal); 33.4g carbohydrate; 3.3g protein; 1.7g fibre

---

Hazelnut caramel slice

Slices and bases for layered slices usually feel slightly soft in the oven but will become firm when cold.

PREPARATION TIME 20 MINUTES (PLUS REFRIGERATION TIME) **COOKING TIME** 30 MINUTES **MAKES** 20

200g butter, chopped

½ cup (50g) cocoa powder

2 cups (440g) firmly packed brown sugar

1 teaspoon vanilla extract

2 eggs, beaten lightly

1 ½ cups (225g) plain flour

200g dark eating chocolate, melted, cooled

1 tablespoon vegetable oil

CARAMEL FILLING

185g butter, chopped

½ cup (110g) caster sugar

2 tablespoons golden syrup

¾ cup (180ml) sweetened condensed milk

1 ¼ cups (175g) roasted hazelnuts

1 Preheat oven to moderately slow (170°C/150°C fan-forced). Grease 20cm x 30cm lamington pan; line base and two long sides with baking paper.

2 Stir butter with sifted cocoa in medium saucepan over low heat until smooth. Add sugar; stir until dissolved. Remove from heat; add extract, egg and sifted flour, mix well. Spread mixture into pan; bake, uncovered, 20 minutes; cool 10 minutes.

3 Meanwhile, make caramel filling by stirring butter, sugar, syrup and condensed milk in medium saucepan over low heat until butter is melted. Increase heat to medium; simmer, stirring, 10 minutes or until mixture is a dark caramel colour. Remove from heat; stir in nuts.

4 Spread caramel filling evenly over base; refrigerate at least 30 minutes or until firm. Combine chocolate and oil in small bowl, spread over caramel filling; refrigerate until set.

PER PIECE 26.6g total fat (14.2g saturated); 1981kj (474 cal); 52.6g carbohydrate; 5.3g protein; 1.9g fibre

1 CHOCOLATE RUM AND RAISIN SLICE **2** HAZELNUT CARAMEL SLICE
3 APRICOT MUESLI SLICE (P 534) **4** TANGY LEMON SQUARES (P 534)

Any warmed jam can be used in this recipe. Alternative fillings are stewed apple, a mashed banana or ½ cup of chocolate hazelnut spread.

Apricot muesli slice

PREPARATION TIME 25 MINUTES **COOKING TIME** 30 MINUTES **MAKES** 20

100g butter
½ cup (110g) caster sugar
1 egg yolk
⅔ cup (100g) plain flour
¼ cup (35g) self-raising flour
1 tablespoon custard powder
½ cup (160g) apricot jam, warmed

MUESLI TOPPING
¼ cup (90g) honey
50g butter
1½ cups (135g) rolled oats
1 cup (40g) corn flakes
½ cup (40g) shredded coconut
½ cup (80g) finely chopped dried apricots

1 Preheat oven to moderate (180°C/160°C fan-forced). Grease and line 20cm x 30cm lamington pan with baking paper.
2 Beat butter, sugar and egg yolk in small bowl with electric mixer until light and fluffy. Stir in sifted flours and custard powder. Press mixture over base of pan. Bake, uncovered, about 15 minutes or until browned lightly.
3 Meanwhile, make muesli topping.
4 Remove slice from oven; spread with jam. Sprinkle muesli topping over jam, pressing gently with fingers. Bake, uncovered, about 15 minutes. Cool slice in pan before cutting.

MUESLI TOPPING Heat honey and butter in small saucepan until butter melts; transfer to large bowl. Stir in remaining ingredients.

☐ **PER PIECE** 8.4g total fat (5.4g saturated); 823kj (197 cal); 27.3g carbohydrate; 2.1g protein; 1.5g fibre

---

Wonderful for an afternoon tea with a pot of earl grey. These squares are also delicious made with orange or mandarin rind and juice.

Tangy lemon squares

PREPARATION TIME 15 MINUTES **COOKING TIME** 35 MINUTES **MAKES** 16

125g butter
¼ cup (40g) icing sugar
1¼ cups (185g) plain flour
3 eggs
1 cup (220g) caster sugar
2 teaspoons finely grated lemon rind
½ cup (125ml) lemon juice

1 Preheat oven to moderate (180°C/160°C fan-forced). Grease 23cm-square pan; line base and two opposite sides of pan with baking paper.
2 Beat butter and sifted icing sugar in small bowl with electric mixer until smooth. Stir in 1 cup of the sifted flour. Press mixture over base of pan. Bake, uncovered, about 15 minutes or until browned lightly.
3 Place eggs, caster sugar, remaining sifted flour, rind and juice in medium bowl; whisk until combined. Pour egg mixture over hot base. Bake, uncovered, about 20 minutes or until firm. Cool in pan on wire rack. Lift slice from pan before cutting. Dust with extra sifted icing sugar, if desired.

☐ **PER SQUARE** 7.5g total fat (4.5g saturated); 748kj (179 cal); 24.9g carbohydrate; 2.6g protein; 0.5g fibre

No-bake slices

PREPARATION TIME 10 MINUTES (PLUS REFRIGERATION TIME) **COOKING TIME** 10 MINUTES **MAKES** 24

Children can make these with only a little supervision for processing the biscuits and making the topping.

CHOC-PEPPERMINT

250g plain sweet biscuits

100g butter, chopped

½ cup (125ml) sweetened condensed milk

2 x 35g crispy peppermint chocolate bars, chopped coarsely

CHOCOLATE TOPPING

200g milk eating chocolate, chopped coarsely

2 teaspoons vegetable oil

1 Grease 19cm x 29cm slice pan; line base and two long sides with baking paper.

2 Process 200g of the biscuits until crushed finely. Chop remaining biscuits coarsely.

3 Stir butter and milk in small saucepan over low heat until smooth. Combine processed and chopped biscuits with chocolate bar in medium bowl; stir in butter mixture.

4 Press mixture firmly into pan; refrigerate, covered, about 20 minutes or until set.

5 Make chocolate topping. Spread over slice; refrigerate until firm. Cut into squares.

CHOCOLATE TOPPING Stir chocolate and oil in medium heatproof bowl over medium saucepan of simmering water until smooth;

PER PIECE 8.9g total fat (5.4g saturated); 669kj (160 cal); 17.9g carbohydrate; 1.9g protein; 0.3g fibre

LEMON

Replace peppermint bars with 1 teaspoon finely grated lemon rind and 1 tablespoon lemon juice in the biscuit mixture. Press mixture firmly into pan; refrigerate, covered, about 20 minutes or until set. Top with lemon icing made by stirring 1 ¼ cups icing sugar with 10g butter and 1 tablespoon lemon juice in medium heatproof bowl over saucepan of simmering water until smooth.

PER PIECE 8.8g total fat (5.2g saturated); 748kj (179 cal); 23.1g carbohydrate; 1.9g protein; 0.3g fibre

APRICOT AND COCONUT

Replace peppermint bars with ½ cup roasted shredded coconut and ½ cup finely chopped dried apricots in the biscuit mixture. Press mixture firmly into pan; refrigerate, covered, about 20 minutes or until set. Top with icing made by stirring 200g coarsely chopped white eating chocolate and 2 teaspoons vegetable oil in medium heatproof bowl over saucepan of simmering water until smooth.

PER PIECE 12.6g total fat (7.7g saturated); 886kj (212 cal); 21.7g carbohydrate; 2.7g protein; 0.8g fibre

COFFEE AND MACADAMIA

Replace peppermint bars with ½ cup coarsely chopped macadamias in the biscuit mixture. Press mixture firmly into pan; refrigerate, covered, about 20 minutes or until set. Top with icing made by dissolving 2 teaspoons instant coffee granules in 2 tablespoons boiling water in medium heatproof bowl over saucepan of simmering water; add 1 ¼ cups icing sugar and 10g butter, stir until smooth.

PER PIECE 11.0g total fat (5.5g saturated); 840kj (201 cal); 23.2g carbohydrate; 2.1g protein; 0.5g fibre

CAKES

Cakes

The cakes you make yourself, whether family favourites or gorgeous creations, always say it best – happy birthday, welcome, thank you or simply, with love. Cake making takes care and attention rather than great skill. The recipes in this chapter, all champions from the famed AWW Test Kitchen, are perfect for beginner and expert alike. Whatever you decide to make, read the recipe right through, well ahead of when you plan to start, so that you will have time to let the butter and eggs come to room temperature and to check that you have the right pan and all the ingredients. Then turn your full attention to your creation.

MEASURING INGREDIENTS

- Measure ingredients accurately: a little more or less than the correct amounts will affect the way the cake turns out.
- Measure dry ingredients by gently shaking the ingredient into the measuring cup, then using a knife or spatula to level it off with the top of the cup. Level off spoonfuls in the same way. Alternatively, you may weigh these ingredients: see recipes for equivalents.
- When measuring liquids, stand the measuring cup or jug on a flat surface at eye level for accuracy. Before measuring honey, golden syrup or treacle, warm the spoon or cup or spray lightly with cooking-oil spray and they will run off easily.

CAKE PANS

We tested these recipes using plain aluminium cake pans. Cake pans with a non-stick coating work well provided the surface is unscratched. Pans made from tin or stainless steel do not conduct heat as evenly as aluminium. If you are using pans with a non-stick coating or anodised, stainless steel or tin pans, lower the oven temperature by 10°C.

PREPARING CAKE PANS

- To grease a cake pan, use either a light, even coating of cooking-oil spray or a pastry brush to brush melted butter lightly and evenly over the base and sides.
- To grease and flour a cake pan, grease with melted butter and allow it to set before sprinkling with a little flour. Tap the pan to knock out excess flour.
- To line the base of a cake pan, stand the pan on baking paper, use a pencil to trace around the base and cut out slightly inside the pencil mark. Grease the sides of the pan and fit the paper; in most cases, it is not necessary to grease baking paper.
- Cakes requiring 1 hour or more to bake should have a baking-paper collar extending about 5cm above the top of the pan, to stop the top of the cake from over-browning.

Cut three baking-paper strips long enough to fit round the inside and 8cm wider than the depth of the pan. Stack the strips, fold lengthways about 2cm from the edge, then open out and use scissors to make short diagonal cuts across the narrow side, up to the fold mark and about 2cm apart, from one end of the paper to the other. This makes it easier to ease the paper round the curves or corners of the pan, with the cut section fitting round the base. If the base is to be lined, follow the earlier instructions for making a base lining, but use three thicknesses of paper. Fit the base lining after the side lining.

- Cakes that are high in sugar, or that contain honey, golden syrup or treacle, have a tendency to stick, so line the base and/or sides as the recipe instructs.
- Pans for long-cooking, heavy fruit cakes are lined with a combination of brown paper and greaseproof or baking paper.

MIXING CAKES

- Have butter and eggs at room temperature
- Don't mix cakes in a blender or food processor unless specified in the recipe. Beat butter and sugar together with a wooden spoon or an electric beater. Beating (also known as creaming) butter, sugar and eggs is the method used for most cakes. The best way to do this is to beat the butter until it is as pale as possible, add the sugar and beat until light and fluffy. Do not try to dissolve the sugar. Then add one egg, and beat only until the egg is absorbed. The faster you can add the eggs, the less chance there is of the mixture curdling; more beating will only cause the mixture to curdle more. If the eggs are too large, causing the mixture to curdle, don't worry; just proceed with the recipe.
- Mix in flour and liquid by hand, unless the recipe says otherwise. Folding means cutting down through the mixture, lifting some of the underneath mixture up and over onto the top, and repeating until the ingredients are just mixed in.

BAKING CAKES

The best position for a cake is usually where the top is closest to the centre of the oven. More than one cake can be cooked at the same time, provided the pans do not touch one another, the oven walls or the closed door. Swap the positions of cakes halfway through cooking and, if necessary, turn them front to back to brown evenly. Temperatures for both fan-forced and convection ovens are included in all recipes.

TESTING WHETHER A CAKE IS COOKED Check shortly before the end of the suggested baking time. The cake is cooked if it is browned, feels firm to the touch and is starting to shrink, and if a thin metal skewer, inserted into the centre, comes out clean. Do not use a skewer when testing sponges; the other indications are fine.

COOLING A CAKE Stand the cake in the pan for the time the recipe directs, then shake gently to loosen the cake, turn upside-down onto a wire rack and then turn right-way up, using another rack. To avoid marking a delicate cake, cover the rack with baking paper.

STORING A CAKE Cool the cake completely before storing in an airtight container, ideally a close-fitting one. Cakes, particularly un-iced and unfilled, freeze well for several months. Most cakes will keep for 2 or 3 days. Recipes that are high in fat (butter, cream, eggs etc) keep better than those that are low in fat. Rich fruit cakes will keep for months or even longer; light fruit cakes about 2 weeks. Filled or frosted cakes need to be refrigerated.

It is believed that lamingtons were invented in the kitchens of Government House, Brisbane, when Lord Lamington was Governor of Queensland, as a creative use for sponge cake. It is true that day-old cake is ideal. Lamingtons have become such an institution in Australia that they are a popular means of raising money for community groups. These fund raisers are known as lamington drives.

Lamingtons

PREPARATION TIME 1 HOUR **COOKING TIME** 30 MINUTES (PLUS COOLING TIME) **MAKES** 16

6 eggs
⅔ cup (150g) caster sugar
⅓ cup (50g) cornflour
½ cup (75g) plain flour
⅓ cup (50g) self-raising flour
2 cups (160g) desiccated coconut, approximately

ICING
4 cups (640g) icing sugar
½ cup (50g) cocoa powder
20g butter, melted
⅔ cup (160ml) milk

1 Preheat oven to moderate (180°C/160°C fan-forced). Grease 23cm-square cake pan.
2 Beat eggs in medium bowl with electric mixer about 10 minutes or until thick and creamy. Gradually beat in sugar, 1 tablespoon at a time, until sugar dissolves after each addition. Fold in triple-sifted flours.
3 Spread mixture into pan. Bake, uncovered, about 30 minutes. Turn cake onto wire rack to cool.
4 Make icing.
5 Cut cake into 16 squares, dip squares in icing; drain off excess icing, toss squares in coconut. Place lamingtons on wire rack to set.

ICING Sift icing sugar and cocoa into medium heatproof bowl; stir in butter and milk. Stir icing over medium saucepan of simmering water until it is of a coating consistency.

PER LAMINGTON 10.4g total fat (7.6g saturated); 1342kj (321 cal); 50.5g carbohydrate; 5g protein; 1.9g fibre

---

The divine combination of apple, cinnamon, custard and cake evokes memories of childhood comfort food for many, making this a well-loved treat for afternoon tea.

Apple custard tea cake

PREPARATION TIME 25 MINUTES **COOKING TIME** 1 HOUR 20 MINUTES **SERVES** 8

200g butter, softened
½ cup (110g) caster sugar
2 eggs
1¼ cups (185g) self-raising flour
⅓ cup (40g) custard powder
2 medium green apples (300g), peeled, sliced thinly
1 tablespoon butter, melted
2 teaspoons caster sugar, extra
½ teaspoon ground cinnamon

CUSTARD
2 tablespoons custard powder
¼ cup (55g) caster sugar
1 cup (250ml) milk
20g butter
1 teaspoon vanilla extract

1 Preheat oven to moderate (180°C/160°C fan-forced). Grease deep 22cm-round cake pan; line base with baking paper.
2 Make custard.
3 Beat butter and sugar in small bowl with electric mixer until light and fluffy. Add eggs, one at a time, beating well between additions. Stir in sifted flour and custard powder.

4 Spread half of the cake mixture into pan; top with custard. Top custard with spoonfuls of the remaining cake mixture; gently spread with spatula to completely cover custard. Arrange apples on top, brush with melted butter then sprinkle with combined extra sugar and cinnamon. Bake, uncovered, 1 ¼ hours; cool in pan.

CUSTARD Combine custard powder and sugar in small saucepan; gradually add milk, stir over heat until mixture thickens. Remove from heat; stir in butter and extract. Press plastic wrap over surface of custard; cool. Whisk until smooth just before using.

PER SERVING 27.5g total fat (17.5g saturated); 1952kj (467 cal); 49.3g carbohydrate; 5.3g protein; 1.4g fibre

---

Carrot cake with lemon cream cheese frosting

PREPARATION TIME 35 MINUTES **COOKING TIME** 1 HOUR 15 MINUTES **SERVES** 12

1 cup (250ml) vegetable oil

1 ⅓ cups (300g) firmly packed brown sugar

3 eggs

3 cups firmly packed, coarsely grated carrot

1 cup (110g) coarsely chopped walnuts

2½ cups (375g) self-raising flour

½ teaspoon bicarbonate of soda

2 teaspoons mixed spice

LEMON CREAM CHEESE FROSTING

30g butter, softened

80g cream cheese, softened

1 teaspoon finely grated lemon rind

1 ½ cups (240g) icing sugar

1 Preheat oven to moderate (180°C/160°C fan-forced). Grease deep 22cm-round cake pan; line base with baking paper.

2 Beat oil, sugar and eggs in small bowl with electric mixer until thick and creamy. Transfer mixture to large bowl; using wooden spoon, stir in carrot and nuts then sifted dry ingredients.

3 Pour mixture into pan. Bake, uncovered, about 1 ¼ hours. Stand cake 5 minutes then turn onto wire rack; turn cake top-side up to cool.

4 Make lemon cream cheese frosting.

5 Spread cold cake with lemon cream cheese frosting.

LEMON CREAM CHEESE FROSTING Beat butter, cream cheese and rind in small bowl with electric mixer until light and fluffy; gradually beat in sifted icing sugar until frosting is of a spreadable consistency.

PER SERVING 31.5g total fat (6.0g saturated); 2458kj (588 cal); 68.2g carbohydrate; 6.9g protein; 2.6g fibre

Carrots are often used in cooking to add sweetness to dishes. It is believed that carrot cakes are an adaptation of carrot pudding, which was popular in the UK in the 18th and 19th centuries. Remember to use a light blended vegetable oil, such as corn, sunflower or canola, to allow the carrot flavour to shine through.

Pecans can be used instead of walnuts.

You need about seven large stalks of rhubarb for this recipe. Cut off and discard all the leaves, as they are poisonous. The tart flavour of rhubarb balances beautifully with others, such as strawberry, orange, vanilla or ginger.

Rhubarb and coconut cake

PREPARATION TIME 25 MINUTES **COOKING TIME** 1 HOUR 30 MINUTES **SERVES** 8

1 ½ cups (225g) self-raising flour
1 ¼ cups (275g) caster sugar
1 ¼ cups (100g) desiccated coconut
125g butter, melted
3 eggs, beaten lightly
½ cup (125ml) milk
½ teaspoon vanilla extract
1 cup (110g) finely chopped rhubarb
5 trimmed rhubarb stalks (300g)
2 tablespoons demerara sugar

1 Preheat oven to slow (150°C/130°C fan-forced). Grease 14cm x 21cm loaf pan; line base with baking paper.
2 Combine flour, caster sugar and coconut in medium bowl; stir in butter, eggs, milk and extract.
3 Spread half of the cake mixture into pan; sprinkle evenly with chopped rhubarb, spread remaining cake mixture over rhubarb.
4 Cut rhubarb stalks into 12cm lengths. Arrange rhubarb pieces over top of cake; sprinkle with demerara sugar. Bake, uncovered, about 1 ½ hours. Stand cake 5 minutes then turn onto wire rack; turn cake top-side up to cool.

PER SERVING 24.0g total fat (16.7g saturated); 2082kj (498 cal); 60.9g carbohydrate; 7.4g protein; 4.5g fibre

---

This cake is so moist and dense that it can be difficult to determine if it is cooked. The baking times given are your best guide, and when cooked, the cake should have a thick, sugary crust. If you like, cut the crust off the cake, although the frosting will soften it.

Caramel mud cake

PREPARATION TIME 30 MINUTES (PLUS COOLING TIME) **COOKING TIME** 2 HOURS 10 MINUTES **SERVES** 12

250g unsalted butter, chopped
200g white eating chocolate, chopped coarsely
2 ¼ cups (495g) firmly packed brown sugar
1 ½ cups (375ml) water
2 cups (300g) plain flour
⅔ cup (100g) self-raising flour
1 teaspoon vanilla extract
3 eggs, beaten lightly

CARAMEL FROSTING
125g butter, chopped
1 cup (220g) firmly packed brown sugar
⅓ cup (80ml) milk
1 ½ cups (240g) icing sugar

1 Preheat oven to slow (150°C/130°C fan-forced). Grease deep 22cm-round cake pan; line base and side with baking paper, extending paper 5cm above edge of pan.
2 Stir butter, chocolate, sugar and the water in medium saucepan over low heat until mixture is smooth. Transfer mixture to large bowl; cool 15 minutes. Whisk in sifted flours, then extract and eggs.
3 Pour mixture into pan. Bake, uncovered, about 2 hours. Stand cake 10 minutes then turn onto wire rack to cool.
4 Make caramel frosting. Place cake, top-side up, on serving plate, spread with frosting.

CARAMEL FROSTING Melt butter in small saucepan. Stir in brown sugar and milk; bring to a boil. Reduce heat; simmer, uncovered, 3 minutes, cool 10 minutes. Gradually stir in sifted icing sugar until frosting is of a spreadable consistency.

☐ **PER SERVING** 33.4g total fat (21.1g saturated); 3248kj (777 cal); 111.2g carbohydrate; 6.9g protein; 1.3g fibre

---

Genoise sponge

PREPARATION TIME 35 MINUTES (PLUS REFRIGERATION TIME)
COOKING TIME 30 MINUTES (PLUS COOLING TIME) **SERVES** 8

Genoise is the Italian sponge cake, named after its place of origin, Genoa. This cake has no raising agent except air, which is trapped in thousands of tiny bubbles in the egg and sugar mixture. For this reason, it is important to whisk the eggs and sugar for long enough and to fold the dry ingredients in carefully, so you don't knock out the air.

- 4 eggs
- ½ cup (110g) caster sugar
- ⅔ cup (100g) plain flour
- 60g butter, melted
- 300ml thickened cream
- 1 tablespoon icing sugar
- ¼ cup (80g) strawberry jam, warmed
- 500g strawberries, sliced thinly
- 1 tablespoon icing sugar, extra

1 Preheat oven to moderate (180°C/160°C fan-forced). Grease deep 20cm-round cake pan; line base with baking paper.
2 Combine eggs and sugar in large heatproof bowl; place over large saucepan of simmering water. Do not allow water to touch base of bowl. Using electric mixer, beat 10 minutes or until mixture is thick and creamy. Remove bowl from saucepan; beat mixture until it returns to room temperature.
3 Double-sift half of the flour over egg mixture, carefully fold in flour; then fold in remaining sifted flour.
4 Quickly and carefully fold in cooled melted butter; pour mixture into pan. Bake, uncovered, about 20 minutes or until sponge feels elastic to the touch. Turn immediately onto wire rack to cool.
5 Beat cream and sifted icing sugar in small bowl with electric mixer until soft peaks form. Split sponge in half; place one half, cut-side up, on serving plate. Spread with jam and cream; top with strawberries, then remaining sponge half. Decorate cake with extra sifted icing sugar and strawberries, if desired.

☐ **PER SERVING** 22.9g total fat (14.0g saturated); 1342kj (321 cal); 21.5g carbohydrate; 6.6g protein; 2.0g fibre

Sacher torte

PREPARATION TIME 30 MINUTES (PLUS STANDING TIME)
COOKING TIME 40 MINUTES (PLUS COOLING TIME) **SERVES** 10

This famous Viennese cake was originally made in 1832 by the grandfather of Eduard Sacher, founder of the Hotel Sacher, for the court of the empire's Prince Metternich. Today people visiting Austria flock to the Sacher Hotels to sample the "secret" recipe that was handed down to Eduard, who is responsible for popularising it in the hotel and around the world.

150g dark eating chocolate, chopped

1 tablespoon water

150g unsalted butter, softened

½ cup (110g) caster sugar

3 eggs, separated

1 cup (150g) plain flour

2 tablespoons caster sugar, extra

1 cup (320g) apricot jam

CHOCOLATE ICING

125g dark eating chocolate, chopped

125g unsalted butter

1 Preheat oven to moderate (180°C/160°C fan-forced). Grease deep 22cm-round cake pan, line base with baking paper.

2 Make chocolate icing.

3 Melt chocolate in heatproof bowl over hot water. Stir in the water; cool to room temperature.

4 Beat butter and sugar in small bowl with electric mixer until light and fluffy. Beat in egg yolks one at a time, beat until combined. Transfer mixture to large bowl, stir in chocolate mixture, then sifted flour. Beat egg whites in small bowl with electric mixer until soft peaks form, gradually add extra sugar, beat until dissolved between each addition; fold lightly into chocolate mixture. Spread into pan. Bake, uncovered, about 30 minutes. Stand 5 minutes, turn onto wire rack to cool; leave cake upside down.

5 Split cold cake in half; place one half, cut-side up, on serving plate. Heat and strain jam; brush half of the jam over cake half. Top with remaining cake half, cut-side down; brush cake all over with remaining jam. Stand about 1 hour at room temperature to allow jam to set. Spread top and side of cake with icing, set at room temperature.

CHOCOLATE ICING Melt chocolate and butter in bowl over hot water, stir until smooth. Cool at room temperature until spreadable, stirring occasionally; this can take up to 2 hours.

PER SERVING 32.6g total fat (23.0g saturated); 2358kj (564 cal); 61.9g carbohydrate; 5.0g protein; 2.1g fibre

SACHER TORTE

Serve this heavenly cake warm, as a dessert with cinnamon ice-cream. See page 622 for a basic vanilla ice-cream and add 3 cinnamon sticks at stage one. Alternatively, stir some ground cinnamon through good-quality commercial vanilla ice-cream.

Upside-down toffee banana cake

PREPARATION TIME 15 MINUTES **COOKING TIME** 55 MINUTES **SERVES** 8

1 cup (220g) caster sugar

1 cup (250ml) water

2 medium bananas (400g), sliced thinly

2 eggs, beaten lightly

⅔ cup (160ml) vegetable oil

¾ cup (165g) firmly packed brown sugar

1 teaspoon vanilla extract

⅔ cup (100g) plain flour

⅓ cup (50g) wholemeal self-raising flour

2 teaspoons mixed spice

1 teaspoon bicarbonate of soda

1 cup mashed over-ripe banana

You will need 2 large over-ripe bananas to make 1 cup of mashed banana.

1 Preheat oven to moderate (180°C/160°C fan-forced). Grease deep 22cm-round cake pan; line base with baking paper.

2 Stir caster sugar and the water in medium saucepan over heat, without boiling, until sugar dissolves; bring to a boil. Boil, uncovered, without stirring, about 10 minutes or until caramel in colour. Pour toffee into pan; top with sliced banana.

3 Combine egg, oil, brown sugar and extract in medium bowl. Stir in sifted dry ingredients, then mashed banana; pour mixture into pan. Bake, uncovered, about 40 minutes. Turn onto wire rack, peel off baking paper. Serve cake warm or at room temperature with thick cream, if desired.

PER SERVING 20.1g total fat (2.8g saturated); 2082kj (498 cal); 72.9g carbohydrate; 4.9g protein; 2.6g fibre

---

Dating back to Victorian times, these soft little fruit and spice cakes are perfect for a tea break. Try 2 tablespoons orange marmalade as an alternative to honey and ½ cup quartered glacé cherries instead of apricots. Rock cakes are cooked when they still feel soft in the oven. When they look firm, push one with your finger. If it moves easily on the tray, the cakes are cooked; they will become firmer on cooling.

Apricot and honey rock cakes

PREPARATION TIME 20 MINUTES **COOKING TIME** 15 MINUTES **MAKES** 15

1 cup (160g) wholemeal self-raising flour

1 cup (150g) white self-raising flour

¼ cup (55g) caster sugar

¼ teaspoon ground cinnamon

90g butter, chopped

½ cup (80g) finely chopped dried apricots

2 tablespoons sultanas

1 egg

2 tablespoons honey

⅓ cup (80ml) milk

1 Preheat oven to moderately hot (200°C/180°C fan-forced). Grease two oven trays.

2 Sift dry ingredients into large bowl; rub in butter. Stir in apricots and sultanas. Combine egg and honey in small bowl; stir into mixture with milk.

3 Drop tablespoonfuls of the mixture in rough heaps onto trays. Bake, uncovered, about 15 minutes. Cool on trays.

PER CAKE 5.8g total fat (3.5g saturated); 702kj (168 cal); 24.3g carbohydrate; 3.2g protein; 2.1g fibre

1 UPSIDE-DOWN TOFFEE BANANA CAKE **2** APRICOT AND HONEY ROCK CAKES
3 WENDY'S SPONGE CAKE [P 548] **4** FAMILY CHOCOLATE CAKE [P 548]

1

2

3

4

This prize-winning sponge cake recipe has been a family secret, passed down through the generations for years. It is a real treat that Wendy was prepared to share her secrets with us.

Wendy's sponge cake

PREPARATION TIME 20 MINUTES **COOKING TIME** 20 MINUTES **SERVES** 10

4 eggs
¾ cup (165g) caster sugar
⅔ cup (100g) wheaten cornflour
¼ cup (30g) custard powder
1 teaspoon cream of tartar
½ teaspoon bicarbonate of soda
300ml thickened cream
1 tablespoon icing sugar
½ teaspoon vanilla extract
¼ cup (80g) strawberry jam, warmed
250g strawberries, sliced thinly

1 Preheat oven to moderate (180°C/160°C fan-forced). Grease and flour two deep 22cm-round cake pans.
2 Beat eggs and caster sugar in small bowl with electric mixer about 5 minutes or until thick and creamy; transfer to large bowl.
3 Sift dry ingredients twice onto paper, sift over egg mixture; fold ingredients together.
4 Divide mixture evenly between pans. Bake, uncovered, about 20 minutes. Turn sponges immediately onto baking-paper-lined wire rack; turn sponges top-side up to cool.
5 Beat cream, icing sugar and extract in small bowl with electric mixer until firm peaks form. Place one sponge on serving plate; spread with jam, then cream mixture. Top with strawberries, then remaining sponge. Dust with sifted icing sugar, if desired.

PER SERVING 13.3g total fat (8.0g saturated); 1179kj (282 cal); 36.2g carbohydrate; 3.8g protein; 0.7g fibre

---

Choose a perfectly level-bottomed baking dish; one made from cast aluminium is the best choice, but almost any type will work. If the cake appears to be cooking too quickly in the corners of the pan, reduce the oven temperature to moderately slow; this will increase the cooking time by up to 15 minutes.

Family chocolate cake

PREPARATION TIME 20 MINUTES (PLUS COOLING TIME) **COOKING TIME** 1 HOUR 15 MINUTES **SERVES** 20

2 cups (500ml) water
3 cups (660g) caster sugar
250g butter, chopped
⅓ cup (35g) cocoa powder
1 teaspoon bicarbonate of soda
3 cups (450g) self-raising flour
4 eggs

FUDGE FROSTING
90g butter
⅓ cup (80ml) water
½ cup (110g) caster sugar
1½ cups (240g) icing sugar
⅓ cup (35g) cocoa powder

1 Preheat oven to moderate (180°C/160°C fan-forced). Grease deep 26.5cm x 33cm 3.5-litre (14-cup) baking dish; line base with baking paper.
2 Stir the water, sugar, butter and sifted cocoa and soda in medium saucepan over heat, without boiling, until sugar dissolves; simmer 5 minutes. Transfer to large bowl; cool.
3 Sift flour over cocoa mixture, add eggs; beat with electric mixer until a paler colour. Pour into dish. Bake, uncovered, 50 minutes. Stand 10 minutes; cool cake, top-side up.
4 Make fudge frosting by stirring butter, the water and caster sugar in small saucepan over heat until sugar dissolves. Sift icing sugar and cocoa into small bowl then gradually stir in butter mixture. Refrigerate 20 minutes or until thickened. Beat; spread over cake.

PER SERVING 15.8g total fat (9.8g saturated); 1806kj (432 cal); 67.3g carbohydrate; 4.3g protein; 1.0g fibre

Honey yogurt cake

PREPARATION TIME 20 MINUTES **COOKING TIME** 45 MINUTES **SERVES** 12

Yogurt makes a great alternative to sour cream.

200g unsalted butter, chopped
¾ cup (210g) yogurt
½ cup (175g) honey
1 teaspoon ground cinnamon
2 eggs
¼ cup (55g) caster sugar
1¾ cups (260g) self-raising flour
½ teaspoon baking powder
1 tablespoon icing sugar

1 Preheat oven to moderate (180°C/160°C). Grease 15cm x 25cm loaf pan; line base with baking paper.

2 Beat butter, yogurt, honey and half the cinnamon in small bowl with electric mixer until just combined and smooth. Transfer mixture to large bowl.

3 Beat eggs and caster sugar in small bowl with electric mixer until thick and creamy.

4 Stir egg mixture into yogurt mixture; fold in sifted flour and baking powder. Spread mixture into pan. Bake, uncovered, about 45 minutes. Stand cake 10 minutes then turn onto wire rack; turn cake top-side up to cool. Dust with sifted icing sugar and remaining cinnamon to serve.

PER SERVING 15.6g total fat (9.8g saturated); 1229kj (294 cal); 33.8g carbohydrate; 4.2g protein; 0.8g fibre

---

Patty cakes with vanilla butter cream

PREPARATION TIME 30 MINUTES **COOKING TIME** 20 MINUTES **MAKES** 24

Patty cakes are a big hit at children's parties if they are iced and decorated with sweets. Buy an assortment and make animal or clown faces, bugs, spiders, ghosts, fish and so on.

125g butter, softened
1 teaspoon vanilla extract
⅔ cup (150g) caster sugar
3 eggs
1½ cups (225g) self-raising flour
¼ cup (60ml) milk

VANILLA BUTTER CREAM
125g butter, softened
1 teaspoon vanilla extract
1½ cups (240g) icing sugar
2 tablespoons milk

1 Preheat oven to moderate (180°C/160°C fan-forced). Line two deep 12-hole patty pans with paper cases.

2 Combine ingredients in small bowl of electric mixer; beat on low speed until ingredients are just combined. Increase speed to medium; beat about 3 minutes or until mixture is smooth and changed to a paler colour.

3 Drop slightly rounded tablespoons of mixture into paper cases. Bake, uncovered, 20 minutes. Turn cakes onto wire rack; turn top-side up to cool.

4 Make vanilla butter cream. Decorate cakes as desired.

VANILLA BUTTER CREAM Beat butter and extract in small bowl with electric mixer until as white as possible. Gradually beat in half the sifted icing sugar, milk, then remaining icing sugar. Tint with food colouring, if desired.

PER CAKE 9.5g total fat (6.0g saturated); 777kj (186 cal); 23.1g carbohydrate; 2.0g protein; 0.4g fibre

Cupcakes

Decorate the patty cakes on page 549; see pages 549 and 558 for the recipes for butter cream and ganache.

SUGARED BERRY CAKE
Spread the top of the cake with vanilla butter cream. Brush fresh berries sparingly with lightly beaten egg white; gently roll the wet fruit in caster sugar. Position on the cake.

DAISY CAKES
Spread the top of the cake with butter cream. Cut the marshmallows in half horizontally; squeeze the ends together to form petals. Decorate the cake with petals; position a smartie in the centre of each daisy.

NEOPOLITAN ICE-CREAM CAKE
Divide butter cream into three bowls. Tint one mixture with pink colouring; stir sifted cocoa powder into another. Spread the cake with coloured butter creams to make three stripes.

ROCKY ROAD
Spread the top of the cake with soft white chocolate ganache (replace dark chocolate with white). Dip halved marshmallows, craisins and pistachios in the ganache and arrange on top of the cake.

FAIRY FLOSS
Spread the top of the cake with pale pink butter cream. Pile the cake high with pink fairy floss; serve immediately. Don't attempt this cake if the weather is hot or humid, as the fairy floss will deflate quickly.

STARFRUIT CHRISTMAS TREE
Spread the top of the cake with butter cream. Cut starfruit into 5mm thick slices; layer the slices on top of the cake to represent a Christmas tree.

STRAWBERRY CREAMCAKE
Spread the top of the cake with butter cream. Remove the green top from strawberries, slice thinly and arrange on top of the cake to make a flower. Brush with warmed, strained strawberry jam.

SNOWBALL
Refrigerate white chocolate ganache (replace dark chocolate with white) for 30 minutes; beat in a small bowl with an electric mixer until fluffy. Spread the whipped ganache over the cake; top with flaked coconut.

AFTER DINNER MINT
Spread the top of the cake with firm dark chocolate ganache. Cut thin dinner mints into strips; stack on top of the cake, pushing slightly into the ganache to secure.

CHOCOLATE ON CHOCOLATE
Spread the top of the cake with firm dark chocolate ganache. Spread melted chocolate onto a cold surface; when set, drag a melon baller over the chocolate to make curls. Arrange on top of the cake.

MALTED CHOCOLATE
Spread the top of the cake with chocolate butter cream (sift 1 tablespoon cocoa powder with the icing sugar used in the butter cream recipe). Cut chocolate-covered malt balls in half with a sharp knife. Pile generously over the butter cream.

PEANUT CHOCOLATE CRUNCH
Spread the top of the cake with dark chocolate ganache. Sprinkle with finely chopped unsalted roasted peanuts (or use crushed nuts).

Banana cake with passionfruit icing

PREPARATION TIME 35 MINUTES **COOKING TIME** 50 MINUTES **SERVES** 10

125g butter, softened

¾ cup (165g) firmly packed brown sugar

2 eggs

1 ½ cups (225g) self-raising flour

½ teaspoon bicarbonate of soda

1 teaspoon mixed spice

1 cup mashed banana

½ cup (120g) sour cream

¼ cup (60ml) milk

PASSIONFRUIT ICING

1 ½ cups (240g) icing sugar

1 teaspoon soft butter

2 tablespoons passionfruit pulp, approximately

1 Preheat oven to moderate (180°C/160°C fan-forced). Grease 15cm x 25cm loaf pan; line base with baking paper.

2 Beat butter and sugar in small bowl with electric mixer until light and fluffy. Beat in eggs, one at a time, until combined.

3 Transfer mixture to large bowl; using wooden spoon, stir in sifted dry ingredients, banana, cream and milk. Spread mixture into pan. Bake, uncovered, about 50 minutes. Stand cake 5 minutes then turn onto wire rack; turn cake top-side up to cool.

4 Make passionfruit icing.

5 Spread cold cake with passionfruit icing.

PASSIONFRUIT ICING Place icing sugar in small heatproof bowl; stir in butter and enough pulp to give a firm paste. Stir over hot water until icing is of a spreadable consistency, taking care not to overheat; use immediately.

PER SERVING 17.0g total fat (10.7g saturated); 1768kj (423 cal); 61.5g carbohydrate; 4.7g protein; 1.9g fibre

You will need 2 large ripe bananas to make 1 cup of mashed banana. It is important that the bananas are over-ripe: not only do they mash easily but, if they are underripe, the cake will be too heavy. A banana's natural starch is converted to sugar during the ripening process, and it's this natural sugar that contributes to the correct balance of ingredients. The cake develops a crusty edge due to this sugar content.

BANANA CAKE WITH PASSIONFRUIT ICING

This cake keeps well for several days because of its high butter content. Store it in an airtight container.

Buttery orange cake

PREPARATION TIME 20 MINUTES **COOKING TIME** 1 HOUR 20 MINUTES **SERVES** 12

250g butter, softened

2 tablespoons finely grated orange rind

1 ½ cups (330g) caster sugar

4 eggs

1 ½ cups (225g) self-raising flour

½ cup (75g) plain flour

¾ cup (180ml) orange juice

GLACE ICING

1 ½ cups (240g) icing sugar

1 teaspoon butter

2 tablespoons orange juice

1 Preheat oven to moderately slow (170°C/150°C fan-forced). Grease deep 22cm-round cake pan; line base and side with baking paper, extending paper 5cm above edge of pan.

2 Beat butter, rind and sugar in medium bowl with electric mixer until light and fluffy. Add eggs, one at a time, beating until just combined between additions. Fold in sifted flours and juice, in two batches.

3 Pour mixture into pan; bake, uncovered, 1 hour 10 minutes. Stand in pan 10 minutes then turn onto wire rack; turn top-side up to cool.

4 Make glacé icing.

5 Place cake, top-side up, on serving plate; spread cold cake with glacé icing.

GLACE ICING Place icing sugar in small heatproof bowl; stir in butter and juice. Place bowl over small saucepan of simmering water; stir until icing is of a spreadable consistency. Use immediately.

PER SERVING 19.5g total fat (12.1g saturated); 1952kj (467 cal); 67.0g carbohydrate; 5.0g protein; 1.0g fibre

---

You can also melt the milk chocolate with the cream in a microwave oven; heat on high (100%) for about 1 ½ minutes, pausing to stir every 30 seconds.

Double-decker mud cake

PREPARATION TIME 30 MINUTES (PLUS REFRIGERATION AND STANDING TIME)
COOKING TIME 1 HOUR **SERVES** 10

250g butter, chopped

150g white eating chocolate, chopped coarsely

2 cups (440g) caster sugar

1 cup (250ml) milk

1 ½ cups (225g) plain flour

½ cup (75g) self-raising flour

1 teaspoon vanilla extract

2 eggs, beaten lightly

2 tablespoons cocoa powder

600g milk eating chocolate, chopped coarsely

1 cup (250ml) cream

1 Preheat oven to slow (150°C/130°C fan-forced). Grease two deep 20cm-round cake pans; line bases and sides with baking paper.

2 Stir butter, white chocolate, sugar and milk in medium saucepan over low heat, without boiling, until smooth. Transfer mixture to large bowl; cool 15 minutes.

3 Whisk sifted flours into white chocolate mixture then whisk in extract and egg; pour half of the mixture into one of the pans. Whisk sifted cocoa into remaining mixture; pour into other pan. Bake cakes, uncovered, about 50 minutes. Stand cakes 5 minutes then turn onto wire racks; turn cakes top-side up to cool.

4 Stir milk chocolate and cream in medium saucepan over low heat until smooth. Transfer to medium bowl, cover; refrigerate, stirring occasionally, until chocolate mixture is of a spreadable consistency. Reserve 1 cup of the chocolate mixture for spreading over cake.

5 Split each cooled cake in half. Centre one layer of cake on serving plate; spread with ½ cup of the remaining milk chocolate mixture. Repeat layering, alternating colours. Cover top and sides of cake with reserved chocolate mixture.

PER SERVING 58.3g total fat (36.9g saturated); 4213kj (1008 cal); 109.4g carbohydrate; 11.0g protein; 1.7g fibre

---

Mocha buttercake

PREPARATION TIME 30 MINUTES (PLUS COOLING TIME) **COOKING TIME** 45 MINUTES **SERVES** 12

Coffee and chocolate marry divinely in this cake. The flavour is more coffee than chocolate, so if you want to serve it as a dessert, and be really wicked, think about serving it with a hot chocolate sauce (see page 424). This is the type of cake that will freeze perfectly – frosting and all – for about 3 months.

- ½ cup (125ml) warm water
- 1 tablespoon instant coffee granules
- 1½ cups (225g) self-raising flour
- ¾ cup (165g) caster sugar
- 2 tablespoons cocoa powder
- 125g butter, softened
- 2 eggs
- 1 teaspoon vanilla extract
- ½ cup (60g) finely chopped walnuts

MOCHA FROSTING

- 1 teaspoon cocoa powder
- 1 teaspoon instant coffee granules
- 1 tablespoon boiling water
- 60g butter
- 1½ cups (240g) icing sugar

1 Preheat oven to moderate (180°C/160°C fan-forced). Grease 20cm ring pan; line base and sides with baking paper.

2 Stir the water and coffee in small bowl until coffee dissolves; cool to room temperature.

3 Sift dry ingredients into medium bowl; add butter, eggs, extract and coffee mixture.

4 Beat on low speed with electric mixer until combined. Increase speed to medium; beat 3 minutes or until ingredients are smooth and mixture has changed to a paler colour. Stir in nuts; spread into pan. Bake, uncovered, 40 minutes. Stand cake 5 minutes then turn onto wire rack; turn cake top-side up to cool.

5 Make mocha frosting.

6 Serve cake topped with mocha frosting and extra walnuts, if desired.

MOCHA FROSTING Stir cocoa, coffee and the water in small bowl until coffee dissolves; cool. Beat butter in small bowl with electric mixer until creamy; beat in sifted icing sugar and coffee mixture.

PER SERVING 17.2g total fat (8.9g saturated); 1534kj (367 cal); 47.9g carbohydrate; 4.3g protein; 1.1g fibre

If you like, decorate the cake with mini chocolate curls. To do this, pull a vegetable peeler down the side of a bar of dark chocolate.

Black forest cake will keep for up to 3 days if stored, covered, in the fridge.

Black forest cake

PREPARATION TIME 35 MINUTES **COOKING TIME** 1 HOUR 50 MINUTES (PLUS COOLING TIME) **SERVES** 12

- 250g butter, chopped
- 1 tablespoon instant coffee granules
- 1½ cups (375ml) hot water
- 200g dark eating chocolate, chopped
- 2 cups (440g) caster sugar
- 1½ cups (225g) self-raising flour
- 1 cup (150g) plain flour
- ¼ cup (25g) cocoa powder
- 2 eggs
- 2 teaspoons vanilla extract
- 600ml thickened cream
- ¼ cup (60ml) kirsch
- 2 x 425g cans cherries, drained, halved

1 Preheat oven to slow (150°C/130°C fan-forced). Grease deep 22cm-round cake pan, line base and side with baking paper.
2 Melt butter in medium saucepan over low heat, stir in combined coffee and the water, then chocolate and sugar; stir over low heat, without boiling, until smooth. Transfer to medium bowl, cool to warm. Beat mixture on low speed with electric mixer; beat in sifted dry ingredients, in three batches. Beat in eggs, one at a time, then extract. Pour into pan. Bake about 1¾ hours. Stand 5 minutes before turning onto wire rack to cool.
3 Beat cream until firm peaks form. Trim top of cake to make it flat. Split cake into three even layers. Place one layer on serving plate, brush with a third of the kirsch, top with a third of the cream and half the cherries. Repeat layering once more, then top with final layer of cake. Brush top of cake with remaining kirsch; spread with remaining cream. Decorate with grated chocolate and fresh cherries, if desired.

PER SERVING 42.3g total fat (28.6g saturated); 3085kj (738 cal); 78.5g carbohydrate; 6.9g protein; 2.5g fibre

BLACK FOREST CAKE

This rich, moist and tangy fruit cake is a beautiful alternative to a traditional Christmas cake.

Fig, walnut and ginger cake

PREPARATION TIME 20 MINUTES **COOKING TIME** 1 HOUR 15 MINUTES **SERVES** 12

185g butter, softened

¾ cup (165g) caster sugar

3 eggs

½ cup (150g) finely chopped glacé figs

⅓ cup (60g) finely chopped glacé ginger

½ cup (60g) finely chopped walnuts

½ cup (75g) plain flour

½ cup (75g) self-raising flour

⅓ cup (80g) sour cream

1 Preheat oven to moderately slow (170°C/150°C fan-forced). Grease 14cm x 21cm loaf pan; line base with baking paper.

2 Beat butter and sugar in small bowl with electric mixer until light and fluffy. Beat in eggs, one at a time, until combined. Transfer mixture to large bowl; stir in figs, ginger and nuts, then sifted flours and sour cream.

3 Spread mixture into pan. Bake, uncovered, about 1¼ hours. Stand cake 5 minutes then turn onto wire rack; turn cake top-side up to cool.

PER SERVING 20.3g total fat (10.7g saturated); 1425kj (341 cal); 34g carbohydrate; 4.4g protein; 2.6g fibre

Vienna almonds are whole almonds coated in toffee and are available from selected supermarkets, nut shops and gourmet food and specialty confectionery stores.

Dark chocolate and almond torte

PREPARATION TIME 20 MINUTES (PLUS STANDING TIME) **COOKING TIME** 55 MINUTES **SERVES** 14

160g dark eating chocolate, chopped coarsely

160g unsalted butter

5 eggs, separated

¾ cup (165g) caster sugar

1 cup (120g) almond meal

⅔ cup (50g) roasted flaked almonds, chopped coarsely

⅓ cup (35g) coarsely grated dark eating chocolate

1 cup (150g) vienna almonds

DARK CHOCOLATE GANACHE

125g dark eating chocolate, chopped coarsely

⅓ cup (80ml) thickened cream

1 Preheat oven to moderate (180°C/160°C fan-forced). Grease deep 22cm-round cake pan; line base and side with baking paper.

2 Stir chopped chocolate and butter in small saucepan over low heat until smooth; cool to room temperature.

3 Beat egg yolks and sugar in small bowl with electric mixer until thick and creamy. Place in large bowl; fold in chocolate mixture, almond meal, flaked almonds and grated chocolate.

4 Beat egg whites in small bowl with electric mixer until soft peaks form; fold into chocolate mixture, in two batches. Pour mixture into pan. Bake, uncovered, 45 minutes. Stand cake 15 minutes then turn onto wire rack; turn cake top-side up to cool.

5 Make dark chocolate ganache.
6 Spread ganache over cake, decorate cake with vienna almonds.

DARK CHOCOLATE GANACHE Stir ingredients in small saucepan over low heat until smooth. Cool to spreading consistency.

☐ **PER SERVING** 31.0g total fat (15.3g saturated); 1793kj (429 cal); 29.6g carbohydrate; 7.3g protein; 2.8g fibre

---

Mixed-berry cake with vanilla bean syrup

Sugar syrups last for ages in the fridge. You could make a large batch of vanilla bean syrup and have it to hand for adding to fruit salads, cocktails and milkshakes.

PREPARATION TIME 20 MINUTES **COOKING TIME** 40 MINUTES **SERVES** 8

125g butter, softened
1 cup (220g) caster sugar
3 eggs
½ cup (75g) plain flour
¼ cup (35g) self-raising flour
½ cup (60g) almond meal
⅓ cup (80g) sour cream
1 ½ cups (225g) frozen mixed berries
½ cup (100g) drained canned seeded black cherries

VANILLA BEAN SYRUP
½ cup (125ml) water
½ cup (110g) caster sugar
2 vanilla beans

1 Preheat oven to moderate (180°C/160°C fan-forced). Grease 20cm baba pan well.
2 Beat butter and sugar in small bowl with electric mixer until light and fluffy. Add eggs, one at a time, beating until just combined between additions. Mixture will curdle at this stage, but will come together later.
3 Transfer mixture to large bowl; stir in sifted flours, almond meal, sour cream, berries and cherries. Pour mixture into pan. Bake, uncovered, about 40 minutes.
4 Make vanilla bean syrup.
5 Stand cake 5 minutes then turn onto wire rack placed over a large tray. Pour hot vanilla bean syrup over hot cake.

VANILLA BEAN SYRUP Combine the water and sugar in small saucepan. Split vanilla beans in half lengthways; scrape seeds into pan then place pods in pan. Stir over heat, without boiling, until sugar dissolves. Simmer, uncovered, without stirring, 5 minutes. Remove pods from syrup.

☐ **PER SERVING** 23.1g total fat (12.0g saturated); 1935kj (463 cal); 56.3g carbohydrate; 6.1g protein; 2.4g fibre

This cake is the perfect dessert when you're feeding a crowd. Serve with vanilla ice-cream or Greek-style yogurt with a little brown sugar and vanilla extract mixed in.

Pear and polenta syrup cake

PREPARATION TIME 30 MINUTES (PLUS STANDING TIME) **COOKING TIME** 1 HOUR 5 MINUTES **SERVES** 12

125g butter, softened

2 teaspoons finely grated orange rind

1 teaspoon finely grated lemon rind

1 cup (220g) caster sugar

3 eggs

1 ⅓ cups (200g) self-raising flour

½ cup (85g) polenta

⅓ cup (95g) yogurt

2 medium pears (460g), peeled, chopped coarsely

CITRUS SYRUP

½ cup (110g) caster sugar

¼ cup (60ml) water

¼ cup (60ml) orange juice

2 tablespoons lemon juice

½ vanilla bean, split lengthways

1 Preheat oven to moderately slow (170°C/150°C fan-forced). Grease deep 19cm-square cake pan; line base and sides with baking paper.

2 Beat butter, rinds and sugar in medium bowl with electric mixer until light and fluffy. Add eggs, one at a time, beating until just combined between additions.

3 Fold in sifted flour, polenta and yogurt in two batches. Gently fold in pears. Spread mixture into pan. Bake, uncovered, about 1 hour 5 minutes.

4 Make citrus syrup.

5 Pour hot syrup over hot cake. Stand in pan 15 minutes before turning onto wire rack.

CITRUS SYRUP Stir ingredients in small saucepan over low heat until sugar dissolves; bring to a boil. Reduce heat; simmer, uncovered, without stirring, about 5 minutes or until thickened slightly. Remove vanilla bean from syrup.

PER SERVING 10.5g total fat (6.3g saturated fat); 1292kJ (309 cal); 48g carbohydrate; 4.5g protein; 1.4g fibre

---

Known as a jelly roll in the US, this filled and rolled sponge cake has long been a favourite there and in the UK. Quick and easy to make, yet very impressive-looking, slices of the roll are good served warm or at room temperature with a dollop of whipped cream.

Jam roll

PREPARATION TIME 20 MINUTES **COOKING TIME** 10 MINUTES **SERVES** 10

3 eggs, separated

½ cup (110g) caster sugar

¾ cup (110g) self-raising flour

2 tablespoons hot milk

¼ cup (55g) caster sugar, extra

½ cup (160g) jam, warmed

1 Preheat oven to moderately hot (200°C/180°C fan-forced). Grease 25cm x 30cm swiss roll pan; line base and short sides of pan with a strip of baking paper, bringing paper 5cm over edges.

2 Beat egg whites in small bowl with electric mixer until soft peaks form; gradually add sugar, 1 tablespoon at a time, beating until dissolved between additions.

3 With motor operating, add egg yolks, one at a time, beating until mixture is pale and thick; this will take about 10 minutes.

4 Meanwhile, sift flour three times onto baking paper.

5 Pour hot milk down side of bowl; add triple-sifted flour. Working quickly, use plastic spatula to fold milk and flour through egg mixture. Pour mixture into pan, gently spreading mixture evenly into corners. Bake, uncovered, about 8 minutes or until top of cake feels soft and springy when touched lightly with fingertips.

6 Meanwhile, place a piece of baking paper cut the same size as cake on board or bench; sprinkle evenly with extra sugar.

7 Turn cake onto sugared paper, quickly peeling away the lining paper. Working rapidly, use serrated knife to cut away crisp edges from all sides of cake.

8 Using hands, gently roll cake loosely from one of the short sides; unroll, spread evenly with jam. Roll cake again, from same short side, by lifting paper and using it to guide the roll into shape. Either serve immediately with cream, or place onto wire rack to cool.

▭ **PER SERVING** 1.9g total fat (0.6g saturated); 723kj (173 cal); 35.0g carbohydrate; 3.3g protein; 0.6g fibre

---

Maple pecan cake

PREPARATION TIME 15 MINUTES **COOKING TIME** 1 HOUR **SERVES** 10

This cake can be baked in two 8cm x 26cm bar cake pans. Bake in a moderate oven for about 45 minutes. Sultanas or finely chopped seeded dates or prunes can be used instead of the raisins, and walnuts instead of the pecans.

cooking-oil spray

1 cup (120g) pecans

⅓ cup (80ml) pure maple syrup

1 ¼ cups (310ml) boiling water

1 ¼ cups (235g) coarsely chopped dried figs

1 teaspoon bicarbonate of soda

60g butter, chopped

¾ cup (165g) firmly packed brown sugar

2 eggs

1 cup (150g) self-raising flour

MAPLE BUTTERSCOTCH SAUCE

1 cup (250ml) pure maple syrup

½ cup (125ml) cream

100g butter, chopped

1 Preheat oven to moderate (180°C/160°C fan-forced). Grease deep 20cm-round cake pan; line base with baking paper. Spray paper with oil.

2 Arrange nuts over base of pan; drizzle with maple syrup.

3 Combine the water, figs and soda in bowl of food processor. Cover with lid; stand 5 minutes. Add butter and sugar; process until almost smooth. Add eggs and flour; process until just combined.

4 Pour mixture into pan. Bake, uncovered, about 55 minutes. Stand cake 5 minutes then turn onto wire rack; turn cake top-side up to cool.

5 Make maple butterscotch sauce.

6 Serve cake with maple butterscotch sauce and, if desired, vanilla ice-cream.

MAPLE BUTTERSCOTCH SAUCE Stir ingredients in small saucepan over low heat until smooth; bring to a boil. Boil, uncovered, about 2 minutes or until mixture thickens slightly.

▭ **PER SERVING** 28.6g total fat (13.1g saturated); 2374kj (568 cal); 70.0g carbohydrate; 5.2g protein; 4.9g fibre

This moist, luscious cake was created in the American south, where ladies' lunches and afternoon teas were once a way of life. It will keep for several days in an airtight container.

You will need 2 large over-ripe bananas to make 1 cup of mashed banana.

Hummingbird cake

PREPARATION TIME 35 MINUTES **COOKING TIME** 40 MINUTES **SERVES** 12

450g can crushed pineapple in syrup

1 cup (150g) plain flour

½ cup (75g) self-raising flour

½ teaspoon bicarbonate of soda

½ teaspoon ground cinnamon

½ teaspoon ground ginger

1 cup (220g) firmly packed brown sugar

½ cup (40g) desiccated coconut

1 cup mashed banana

2 eggs, beaten lightly

¾ cup (180ml) vegetable oil

CREAM CHEESE FROSTING

30g butter, softened

60g packaged cream cheese, softened

1 teaspoon vanilla extract

1½ cups (240g) icing sugar

1 Preheat oven to moderate (180°C/160°C fan-forced). Grease deep 23cm-square cake pan; line base with baking paper.

2 Drain pineapple over medium bowl, pressing with spoon to extract as much syrup as possible. Reserve ¼ cup syrup.

3 Sift flours, soda, spices and sugar into large bowl. Stir in pineapple, reserved syrup, coconut, banana, egg and oil; pour into pan. Bake, uncovered, about 40 minutes. Stand cake 5 minutes then turn onto wire rack; turn cake top-side up to cool.

4 Make cream cheese frosting.

5 Spread cold cake with cream cheese frosting.

CREAM CHEESE FROSTING Beat butter, cream cheese and extract in small bowl with electric mixer until light and fluffy; gradually beat in sifted icing sugar.

☐ **PER SERVING** 20.8g total fat (6.4g saturated); 1935kj (463 cal); 63.3g carbohydrate; 4.3g protein; 2.1g fibre

HUMMINGBIRD CAKE

With increasing numbers of people being diagnosed as gluten intolerant, it is worth having some recipes up your sleeve for when you find yourself having to accommodate these needs. This cake makes a delicious dessert that the whole family can enjoy.

Gluten-free orange syrup cake

PREPARATION TIME 25 MINUTES **COOKING TIME** 1 HOUR **SERVES** 8

185g butter, softened
1 tablespoon finely grated orange rind
1¼ cups (275g) caster sugar
6 eggs
3 cups (360g) almond meal
¾ cup (60g) desiccated coconut
¾ cup (150g) rice flour
1 teaspoon gluten-free baking powder

ORANGE SYRUP
1 large orange (300g)
⅓ cup (75g) caster sugar
⅓ cup (80ml) water

1 Preheat oven to moderate (180°C/160°C fan-forced). Grease 21cm baba pan.
2 Beat butter, rind and sugar in medium bowl with electric mixer until light and fluffy. Add eggs, one at a time, beating until just combined between additions. Mixture will curdle at this stage, but will come together later.
3 Stir in almond meal, coconut and sifted flour and baking powder; spread cake mixture into pan. Bake, uncovered, about 1 hour.
4 Make orange syrup.
5 Stand cake in pan about 5 minutes; turn onto wire rack over tray. Pour hot syrup over hot cake.

ORANGE SYRUP Using vegetable peeler; slice rind thinly from orange; cut rind into thin strips. Squeeze juice from orange (you need ⅓ cup) into small saucepan; stir in rind, sugar and the water. Stir over heat, without boiling, until sugar dissolves; bring to a boil. Reduce heat; simmer, uncovered, without stirring, 5 minutes.

PER SERVING 52.9g total fat (19.7g saturated); 3382kj (809 cal); 65g carbohydrate; 16g protein; 6.2g fibre

An old favourite that was very popular in our early books. You may like to experiment with other flavoured jellies, such as passionfruit, lime, raspberry or cherry.

Strawberry jelly cakes

PREPARATION TIME 45 MINUTES **COOKING TIME** 25 MINUTES (PLUS REFRIGERATION TIME) **MAKES** 36

125g butter, softened
½ teaspoon vanilla extract
½ cup (110g) caster sugar
2 eggs
1½ cups (225g) self-raising flour
⅓ cup (80ml) milk
80g packet strawberry jelly
3 cups (150g) flaked coconut
½ cup (125ml) thickened cream

1 Preheat oven to moderate (180°C/160°C fan-forced). Grease deep 23cm-square cake pan; line base with baking paper.
2 Beat butter, extract and sugar in small bowl with electric mixer until light and fluffy. Beat in eggs, one at a time. Stir in sifted flour and milk; spread mixture into pan. Bake, uncovered, about 25 minutes. Stand cake 5 minutes then cool, top-side up on wire rack.
3 Meanwhile, make jelly. Refrigerate until set to the consistency of unbeaten egg white.

4 Cut cake into 36 squares; dip each into jelly then coconut. Refrigerate 30 minutes.
5 Beat cream in small bowl with electric mixer until firm peaks form. Serve with cakes.

PER CAKE 7.3g total fat (5.3g saturated fat); 460kJ (110 cal); 10g carbohydrate; 1.6g protein; 0.9g fibre

---

Eggless date and nut cake

This cake was developed for those who are intolerant to eggs. Try serving warmed slices with hot butterscotch sauce (see page 423) for something really indulgent.

PREPARATION TIME 20 MINUTES **COOKING TIME** 45 MINUTES **SERVES** 9

1 cup (350g) honey

1 cup (250ml) water

30g butter

2¼ cups (360g) wholemeal self-raising flour

2 teaspoons mixed spice

1½ cups (210g) coarsely chopped seeded dried dates

¾ cup (90g) coarsely chopped walnuts

¼ cup (35g) slivered almonds, chopped coarsely

1 Preheat oven to moderate (180°C/160°C fan-forced). Grease deep 19cm-square cake pan; line base with baking paper.
2 Stir honey, the water and butter in medium saucepan over low heat until butter melts.
3 Combine sifted flour and spice, dates and nuts in medium bowl; stir in warm honey mixture. Spread cake mixture into pan. Bake, uncovered, about 40 minutes. Stand cake 5 minutes then turn onto wire rack; turn cake top-side up to cool.

PER SERVING 12.7g total fat (2.5g saturated); 1894kj (453 cal); 72.7g carbohydrate; 7.7g protein; 7.7g fibre

---

Wholemeal fruit and coconut loaf

If you prefer not to bake with wholemeal flour, use the same quantities of white self-raising and plain flour.

PREPARATION TIME 15 MINUTES (PLUS STANDING TIME) **COOKING TIME** 50 MINUTES **SERVES** 12

⅔ cup (100g) finely chopped seeded dried dates

⅓ cup (55g) finely chopped dried apricots

¼ cup (20g) desiccated coconut

2 tablespoons brandy

⅔ cup (150g) firmly packed brown sugar

125g butter, chopped

½ teaspoon bicarbonate of soda

¾ cup (180ml) boiling water

2 eggs, beaten lightly

¾ cup (120g) wholemeal self-raising flour

¾ cup (120g) wholemeal plain flour

1 teaspoon mixed spice

1 Combine dates, apricots, coconut and brandy in medium bowl; stand overnight.
2 Preheat oven to moderate (180°C/160°C fan-forced). Grease 15cm x 25cm loaf pan; line base with baking paper.
3 Add sugar, butter and soda to date mixture, stir in the boiling water; cool 10 minutes.
4 Stir in eggs, then sifted dry ingredients. Pour into pan. Bake, uncovered, about 50 minutes. Stand cake 5 minutes before turning onto wire rack to cool.

PER SERVING 10.9g total fat (6.9g saturated); 1078kj (258 cal); 32.1g carbohydrate; 4.1g protein; 3.7g fibre

For best results, use butter and eggs at room temperature. There is no need to sift the dry ingredients; however, if the bicarbonate of soda is lumpy, push it through a small sieve.

Cut 'n' keep butter cake

PREPARATION TIME 15 MINUTES **COOKING TIME** 1 HOUR 15 MINUTES **SERVES** 22

125g butter, softened
1 teaspoon vanilla extract
1¼ cups (275g) caster sugar
3 eggs
1 cup (150g) plain flour
½ cup (75g) self-raising flour
¼ teaspoon bicarbonate of soda
½ cup (125ml) milk

1 Preheat oven to moderately slow (170°C/150°C fan-forced). Grease deep 20cm-round cake pan; line base with baking paper.
2 Beat ingredients in medium bowl on low speed with electric mixer until just combined.
3 Beat on medium speed until mixture is smooth and changed to a paler colour. Pour mixture into pan. Bake, uncovered, about 1¼ hours. Stand cake 5 minutes then turn onto wire rack; turn cake top-side up to cool.

☐ **PER SERVING** 5.7g total fat (3.5g saturated); 594kj (142 cal); 20.1g carbohydrate; 2.2g protein; 0.4g fibre

---

Cover the cake loosely with foil during baking if it starts to overbrown; and give the cake quarter turns several times during baking if it is browning unevenly. This cake can be made up to 3 months ahead. Store in an airtight container in a cool, dry place, or refrigerate if the weather is humid.

Best-ever boiled fruit cake

PREPARATION TIME 30 MINUTES (PLUS COOLING TIME) **COOKING TIME** 2 HOURS 45 MINUTES **SERVES** 20

2¼ cups (360g) sultanas
2 cups (320g) coarsely chopped raisins
1½ cups (240g) currants
½ cup (85g) mixed peel
¾ cup (150g) halved red glacé cherries
250g butter, chopped
1 cup (220g) firmly packed brown sugar
½ cup (125ml) brandy
½ cup (125ml) water
5 eggs, beaten lightly
2 tablespoons apricot jam
2 teaspoons finely grated orange rind
1 teaspoon finely grated lemon rind
1¾ cups (260g) plain flour
⅓ cup (50g) self-raising flour
½ teaspoon bicarbonate of soda
½ cup (80g) blanched almonds
¼ cup (60ml) brandy, extra

1 Stir fruit, butter, sugar, brandy and the water in large saucepan over heat, without boiling, until sugar dissolves; bring to a boil. Reduce heat; simmer, covered, 10 minutes. Transfer mixture to large bowl; cool to room temperature.
2 Preheat oven to slow (150°C/130°C fan-forced). Grease deep 19cm-square cake pan or a deep 22cm-round cake pan; line base and sides with two layers of brown paper and two layers of baking paper, bringing paper 5cm above edge of pan.
3 Add egg, jam and rinds to fruit mixture; stir until combined. Stir in sifted dry ingredients. Spread mixture evenly into pan; arrange almonds on top. Bake, uncovered, about 2½ hours.
4 Brush extra brandy over top of hot cake; cover tightly with foil, cool cake in pan.

☐ **PER SERVING** 14.2g total fat (7.4g saturated); 1806kj (432 cal); 63.7g carbohydrate; 5.5g protein; 3.4g fibre

Butterfly cakes

PREPARATION TIME 30 MINUTES **BAKING TIME** 20 MINUTES **MAKES** 24

These are at their best the day they are made. Once filled with cream, these cakes should be refrigerated if made more than an hour ahead of time. You can fill them with mousse, lemon butter (see page 464) or ice-cream for something a little different.

125g butter, softened
1 teaspoon vanilla extract
⅔ cup (150g) caster sugar
3 eggs
1 ½ cups (225g) self-raising flour
¼ cup (60ml) milk
½ cup (160g) jam
300ml thickened cream

1 Preheat oven to moderate (180°C/160°C fan-forced). Line two deep 12-hole patty pans with paper cases.
2 Combine butter, extract, sugar, eggs, flour and milk in small bowl of electric mixer; beat on low speed until ingredients are just combined. Increase speed to medium, beat about 3 minutes, or until mixture is smooth and changed to a paler colour. Drop slightly rounded tablespoons of mixture into paper cases. Bake 20 minutes. Cool, top-side up, on wire racks.
3 Cut circle from top of each cake; cut circle in half to make two "wings". Fill cavities with jam and whipped cream. Put wings in position.

PER SERVING 9.8g total fat (6.2g saturated); 702kj (168 cal); 17.8g carbohydrate; 2.2g protein; 0.4g fibre

---

Devil's food cake

PREPARATION TIME 20 MINUTES **COOKING TIME** 50 MINUTES **SERVES** 8

Devil's food cake was so-named for its reddish-brown colour, which originally came from the reaction of the bicarbonate of soda with the cocoa. To enhance this colour, red food colouring is often added, as it is in this recipe.

185g butter, softened
1 ¾ cups (385g) caster sugar
3 eggs
1 ½ cups (225g) self-raising flour
½ cup (75g) plain flour
½ teaspoon bicarbonate of soda
⅔ cup (70g) cocoa powder
3 teaspoons instant coffee granules
½ teaspoon red food colouring
½ cup (125ml) water
½ cup (125ml) milk
60g dark eating chocolate, chopped
60g butter, chopped, extra
300ml thickened cream, whipped

1 Preheat oven to moderate (180°C/160°C fan-forced). Grease two deep 20cm-round cake pans; line bases with baking paper.
2 Beat butter and sugar in small bowl with electric mixer until light and fluffy; add eggs, one at a time, beating well after each addition.
3 Transfer mixture to large bowl; fold in sifted flours, soda and cocoa with combined coffee, colouring, the water and milk, in two batches. Pour mixture into pans.
4 Bake about 45 minutes. Turn cakes onto wire racks to cool.
5 Melt chocolate and extra butter in small heatproof bowl over small saucepan of simmering water. Cool until spreadable, stirring occasionally.
6 Join cold cakes with whipped cream. Spread cake with frosting.

PER SERVING 45.6g total fat (29.6g saturated); 3281kj (785 cal); 83.3g carbohydrate; 9.8g protein; 2.2g fibre

PIES & TARTS

Pies & Tarts

With just three easy pastries at your command, a world of possibilities opens up. Plain and sweet shortcrust pastry make savoury pies, gorgeous desserts, cafe-style pastries, open tarts and much more. Choux pastry makes profiteroles, eclairs, little savoury puffs and party pieces that look marvellous but are surprisingly simple. There are also good commercial pastries available now: crisp layers of fillo and puff pastry make splendid treats, both sweet and savoury.

SHORTCRUST PASTRY

MIXING

There is nothing hard about making shortcrust pastry, but it helps to understand what you are aiming for.

First, you want to mix flour and butter (or other fat, as the recipe specifies) so that they coat each other evenly, but with the butter particles still firm and not melting into the flour. Second, you want to mix in enough water (and egg yolk, if using) to make the mixture cling together, but without unduly working the protein (gluten) in the flour, which develops (forms tiny elastic strands) when it is moistened and agitated.

To achieve the first, use finely diced, chilled butter and rub it into the flour with your fingertips (not the warm palms of your hands), and use chilled water to mix together.

Try to make pastry when the kitchen is cool; dice the butter ahead of time and return it to the fridge until you are ready to rub it in; have water chilled, measured and waiting in the fridge, plus an egg yolk if using; if you are interrupted while you are making pastry, put the bowl in the fridge until you return.

To achieve the second, add the egg yolk, if using, and nearly all the water at once, use a round-ended table knife to "cut" the water through the flour mixture just until the mixture starts to cling together, then gather it up with your fingers; if any dry mixture is left in the bowl, sprinkle with just enough water to dampen it and use the ball of dough to gather it up. The dough should leave the bowl clean.

MIXING WITH A FOOD PROCESSOR You can make good shortcrust pastry in a food processor as long as you are fast on the pulse button. Place the flour and diced butter in the container, combine with short bursts of power, then add the water and egg yolk, if using, and mix with just a few very short bursts, stopping immediately the mixture starts to form a ball.

RESTING

The dough is wrapped and refrigerated for 30 minutes (or as the recipe states) so that its moisture content will even out and the gluten will have time to relax, to minimise shrinkage during baking. No harm is done by longer resting (provided you give the dough time to become pliable before you roll it out); in fact, many cooks think their pastry is more tender if it has had a long rest. After rolling and shaping, rest the pastry again before baking.

ROLLING

Pastry is best rolled on a cool surface; marble is ideal. Roll on a lightly floured surface or between two sheets of baking paper, greaseproof paper or plastic wrap. If rolling directly on the work surface, keep turning the pastry to ensure that it is not sticking. Use short, light strokes, starting from the centre each time to roll the pastry towards you or away from you. Roll to the edge of the pastry, not over the edge.

LINING

Roll pastry loosely around the rolling pin and unroll it over a tart plate or flan tin etc. Gently ease the pastry in, taking care not to stretch it and pressing gently to prevent air pockets, to line the sides and base. Hold the plate flat on one hand and trim away surplus pastry with a knife held at a slight outward angle, using short, downward strokes. If using a metal flan tin, run the rolling pin over the top to cut off the surplus pastry.

BAKING

Follow recipe directions for temperatures and times. Check once or twice to ensure that the pastry is not puffing up – if it does, press down gently with a tea-towel folded into a pad; press tartlet cases down with the back of a spoon.

BAKING BLIND This means baking or partially baking a pastry case without the filling. Place a circle of baking paper, about 5cm larger than the base, over the pastry and fill with dried beans or uncooked rice, to weigh down the pastry so that it will not rise. Bake as directed. Pastry cases, especially small tartlets, are sometimes pricked all over with a fork to help prevent rising, instead of being baked blind.

CHOUX PASTRY

Choux pastry is really just a panada (a sauce so thick as to be solid) with eggs beaten into it. The only special care it takes is to be sure that puffs or eclairs are cooked and dry right through so that they will not collapse after coming out of the oven. This simply means removing them when they are cooked, making a slit in the sides of eclairs or a slit or a hole with the point of a knife in round puffs to allow any steam to escape, and returning them to the turned-off oven, with the door propped open, to dry out thoroughly as they cool.

STORING PASTRIES

Cool pastries completely before storing. They keep well in airtight containers, but after a week or so they gradually become "tired", so it is best to freeze them if you want to keep them for longer.

Beef bourguignon pies

PREPARATION TIME 30 MINUTES **COOKING TIME** 2 HOURS **MAKES** 6

- 12 pickling onions (480g)
- 6 bacon rashers (420g), rind removed, sliced thinly
- 2 tablespoons olive oil
- 400g mushrooms
- 1kg gravy beef, trimmed, cut into 2cm pieces
- ¼ cup (35g) plain flour
- 1 tablespoon tomato paste
- 2 teaspoons fresh thyme leaves
- 1 cup (250ml) dry red wine
- 2 cups (500ml) beef stock
- 2 sheets ready-rolled butter puff pastry
- cooking-oil spray
- ½ cup finely chopped fresh flat-leaf parsley

1 Peel onions, leaving roots intact; halve lengthways.

2 Cook bacon in heated large heavy-based saucepan, stirring, until crisp; drain on absorbent paper. Reheat same pan; cook onion, stirring, until browned all over, remove from pan. Heat 2 teaspoons of the oil in same pan; cook mushrooms, stirring, until just browned, remove from pan.

3 Coat beef in flour; shake off excess. Heat remaining oil in same pan; cook beef, in batches, until browned all over. Return beef and any juices to pan, add bacon and onion with tomato paste and thyme; cook, stirring, 2 minutes. Add wine and stock; bring to a boil. Reduce heat; simmer, covered, 1 hour. Add mushrooms; simmer, uncovered, about 40 minutes or until beef is tender, stirring occasionally.

4 Meanwhile, preheat oven to hot (220°C/200°C fan-forced).

5 Place pastry sheets on board; using 1¼-cup (310ml) ovenproof dish as a guide, cut lid for one pie by tracing around upper-rim of dish with tip of sharp knife. Repeat process until you have six lids. Place lids on oiled oven tray, spray with cooking-oil spray; bake, uncovered, about 5 minutes or until lids are browned lightly.

6 Meanwhile, stir parsley into beef bourguignon then divide among six 1¼-cup (310ml) ovenproof dishes; top each with pastry lid. Serve pies with hot chips, if desired.

PER PIE 36.4g total fat (8.5g saturated); 2817kj (674 cal); 23.5g carbohydrate; 55.0g protein; 3.4g fibre

Beef bourguignon is a French beef stew from the region of Burgundy, using red wine as part of the liquid for cooking. This dish is perfect for a cold winter's day, and the stew part is even better made a day in advance.

BEEF BOURGUIGNON PIES

Make these pies in advance for a dinner party, but do not grill. When your guests arrive, place the pies in a moderate oven for 20 to 25 minutes until heated through and lightly browned.

Trevally mornay pies

PREPARATION TIME 25 MINUTES **COOKING TIME** 35 MINUTES **MAKES** 4

- 2½ cups (625ml) milk
- ½ small brown onion (40g)
- 1 bay leaf
- 6 black peppercorns
- 4 x 170g trevally fillets, skinned
- 3 large potatoes (900g), chopped coarsely
- 600g celeriac, chopped coarsely
- 1 egg yolk
- ½ cup (40g) finely grated parmesan
- ¾ cup (180ml) cream
- 60g butter
- ¼ cup (35g) plain flour
- 2 tablespoons coarsely chopped fresh flat-leaf parsley

1 Place milk, onion, bay leaf and peppercorns in large saucepan; bring to a boil. Add fish, reduce heat; simmer, covered, 5 minutes. Remove fish, chop coarsely; divide among four 1½-cup (375ml) ovenproof dishes. Strain milk into medium jug. Discard solids; reserve milk.
2 Boil, steam or microwave potato and celeriac, separately, until tender; drain. Push potato and celeriac through sieve into large bowl; stir in egg yolk, cheese, ¼ cup of the cream and half of the butter until smooth. Cover to keep warm.
3 Meanwhile, melt remaining butter in medium saucepan; add flour, cook, stirring, about 3 minutes or until mixture bubbles and thickens slightly. Gradually stir in reserved milk and remaining cream; cook, stirring, until mixture boils and thickens. Stir in parsley.
4 Preheat grill. Divide mornay mixture among dishes; cover each with potato mixture. Place pies on oven tray; place under hot grill until browned lightly.

PER PIE 47.8g total fat (29g saturated); 3520kj (842 cal); 45.4g carbohydrate; 53.9g protein; 8.7g fibre

---

The Australian meat pie is a national icon; there is even an official "Great Aussie Pie Competition" held annually, with thousands of entries. Australians consume the greatest number of pies per head of population anywhere in the world.

Aussie meat pies

PREPARATION TIME 35 MINUTES (PLUS REFRIGERATION TIME)
COOKING TIME 1 HOUR (PLUS COOLING TIME) **MAKES** 6

- 1½ cups (225g) plain flour
- 90g butter, chopped
- 1 egg
- 1 tablespoon iced water, approximately
- 2 sheets ready-rolled puff pastry
- 1 egg, beaten lightly, extra

BEEF FILLING

- 1 tablespoon vegetable oil
- 1 medium (150g) onion, chopped
- 700g beef mince
- 425g can tomatoes
- 2 tablespoons tomato paste
- ¼ cup (60ml) worcestershire sauce
- 1 cup (250ml) beef stock
- 2 tablespoons cornflour
- 2 tablespoons water

1 Lightly oil six ½-cup (125ml) pie tins. Process flour and butter until crumbly. Add egg and enough water to make ingredients just cling together; knead dough on floured surface until smooth. Roll into a ball; cover with plastic wrap, refrigerate 30 minutes.

2 Turn a pie tin upside down on puff pastry, cut around tin. Repeat to make six pastry tops; cover and refrigerate. Wrap pastry scraps in plastic and refrigerate; use for decoration.
3 Divide dough into six portions; roll between sheets of baking paper until large enough to line tins. Lift pastry into tins, ease into sides, trim edges. Lightly prick bases with fork; refrigerate 30 minutes. Preheat oven to moderately hot (200°C/ 180°C fan-forced).
4 Place cases on oven trays, line each with baking paper; fill with dried beans. Blind-bake 10 minutes. Remove paper and beans; bake 7 minutes or until cases are browned. Cool.
5 Make beef filling. Spoon into pastry cases, brushing edges with a little extra egg; top with puff pastry lids, gently press edges to seal. Decorate with pastry scraps, if desired. Brush pies with a little more egg; bake about 20 minutes or until browned.

BEEF FILLING Heat oil in medium saucepan, cook onion, stirring, until soft. Add mince; cook until browned. Add undrained crushed tomatoes, paste, sauce and stock; simmer, uncovered, 20 minutes. Add blended cornflour and water, stir over heat until mixture boils and thickens; cool.

PER PIE 37.4g total fat (13.0g saturated); 2989kj (715 cal); 56.9g carbohydrate; 36.0g protein; 3.7g fibre

---

Little chicken and leek pies

PREPARATION TIME 30 MINUTES **COOKING TIME** 40 MINUTES (PLUS COOLING TIME) **MAKES** 36

These make substantial finger food for the party season. You can freeze the uncooked pies in advance. Bake from frozen in a hot oven for 5 minutes, then lower the temperature to moderate for the rest of the cooking time. The total baking time will be about 5 to10 minutes longer than cooking them unfrozen.

- ¾ cup (180ml) chicken stock
- ½ cup (125ml) dry white wine
- 2 chicken breast fillets (400g)
- 20g butter
- 1 medium leek (350g), chopped finely
- 1 trimmed celery stalk (100g), chopped finely
- 1 tablespoon plain flour
- 2 teaspoons fresh lemon thyme leaves
- ½ cup (125ml) cream
- 1 teaspoon dijon mustard
- 4 sheets ready-rolled shortcrust pastry
- 3 sheets ready-rolled puff pastry
- 1 egg yolk
- lemon thyme leaves, extra

1 Preheat oven to hot (220°C/200°C fan-forced). Grease three 12-hole patty pans.
2 Combine stock and wine in medium saucepan; bring to a boil. Add chicken, return to a boil, cover; reduce heat, simmer about 10 minutes or until chicken is just cooked through. Remove from heat, stand chicken 10 minutes; remove chicken, reserve ¾ cup (180ml) cooking liquid; chop chicken finely.
3 Meanwhile, melt butter in medium saucepan; cook leek and celery, stirring, until soft. Add flour and thyme, stir until bubbling. Gradually stir in reserved liquid and cream; cook, stirring, until mixture boils and thickens. Stir in chicken and mustard. Remove from heat, cool 10 minutes.
4 Using 7cm cutter, cut 36 rounds from shortcrust pastry. Press into pans. Spoon 1 tablespoon of chicken mixture into each pastry case. Using 6cm cutter, cut 36 rounds from puff pastry. Top chicken mixture with pastry lids, brush with egg yolk and sprinkle with extra thyme leaves. Bake about 15 minutes or until browned.

PER PIE 10.6g total fat (4.2g saturated); 711kj (170 cal); 13.4g carbohydrate; 4.6g protein; 0.7g fibre

The ingredients in worcestershire sauce include anchovies, tamarind, chilli peppers, molasses and cloves.

Cottage pie

PREPARATION TIME 20 MINUTES **COOKING TIME** 1 HOUR 35 MINUTES **SERVES** 8

1 tablespoon vegetable oil

2 cloves garlic, crushed

1 large brown onion (200g), chopped finely

2 medium carrots (240g), chopped finely

1kg beef mince

1 tablespoon worcestershire sauce

2 tablespoons tomato paste

2 x 425g cans crushed tomatoes

1 teaspoon dried mixed herbs

200g mushrooms, chopped coarsely

1 cup (120g) frozen peas

1kg potatoes, chopped coarsely

¾ cup (180ml) hot milk

40g butter, softened

½ cup (50g) coarsely grated pizza cheese

You can make the pie up to 2 days in advance; keep, covered, in the fridge. Reheat, covered, in a moderately slow oven for about 40 minutes. The pie can also be frozen for up to 3 months; thaw overnight in the fridge before reheating as above.

1 Heat oil in large saucepan; cook garlic, onion and carrot, stirring, until onion softens. Add beef; cook, stirring, about 10 minutes or until changed in colour.

2 Add sauce, paste, undrained tomatoes and herbs; bring to a boil. Reduce heat; simmer, uncovered, 30 minutes or until mixture thickens slightly. Stir in mushrooms and peas.

3 Meanwhile, preheat oven to moderate (180°C/160°C fan-forced). Boil, steam or microwave potato until tender; drain. Mash potato in large bowl with milk and butter.

4 Pour beef mixture into deep 3-litre (12-cup) ovenproof dish; top with mashed potato; sprinkle with cheese. Bake, uncovered, about 45 minutes or until pie is heated through and top is browned lightly.

PER SERVING 15.7g total fat (7.0g saturated); 1634kj (391 cal); 24.6g carbohydrate; 34.8g protein; 6.2g fibre

This anchovy and onion tart is a speciality of Nice in southern France. It takes its name from pissalat, a traditional Niçois condiment of pureed anchovies, cloves and thyme. Most recipes today use salted anchovies as a replacement. For a quick version try using ready-rolled puff pastry or a store-bought pizza base instead of the dough.

Pissaladière

PREPARATION TIME 25 MINUTES **COOKING TIME** 1 HOUR 10 MINUTES **SERVES** 8

50g butter

1 tablespoon olive oil

3 large (600g) brown onions, sliced thinly

2 cloves garlic, crushed

1 bay leaf

1 sprig fresh thyme

1 tablespoon drained baby capers, rinsed

¾ cup (110g) self-raising flour

¾ cup (110g) plain flour

30g butter, extra

¾ cup (180ml) buttermilk

20 dried anchovy fillets, halved lengthways

½ cup (90g) small black olives

1 Heat butter and oil in large saucepan; cook onion, garlic, bay leaf and thyme, covered, stirring occasionally, about 30 minutes or until onions are very soft but not browned. Cook, uncovered, a further 10 minutes. Discard bay leaf and thyme, then stir in capers.

2 Preheat oven to moderately hot (200°C/180°C fan-forced). Grease an oven tray.

3 Meanwhile, sift flours into large bowl. Rub in extra butter; stir in buttermilk to form a soft dough. Turn dough onto floured surface; knead until smooth.

4 Roll out dough to form rough rectangular shape, about 25cm x 35cm. Place on tray.

5 Spread onion mixture over dough, spreading it to edges. Top with anchovies and olives in diamond pattern. Bake about 30 minutes or until the base is browned and crisp.

PER SERVING 11.9g total fat (6.2g saturated); 1049kj (251 cal); 27.7g carbohydrate; 7.1g protein; 2.3g fibre

---

100g crumbled soft goat cheese sprinkled over the onion and beetroot makes a delicious addition to this tart. Chopped fresh mint leaves scattered just before serving is also a nice touch.

Caramelised onion and beetroot tart

PREPARATION TIME 20 MINUTES **COOKING TIME** 45 MINUTES **SERVES** 6

50g butter

4 medium red onions (680g), halved, sliced thinly

1 tablespoon red wine vinegar

1 teaspoon fresh thyme leaves

3 medium beetroot (500g), trimmed

1 sheet ready-rolled butter puff pastry

cooking-oil spray

120g baby rocket leaves

CHIVE OIL

½ cup coarsely chopped fresh chives

¾ cup (180ml) olive oil

1 ice cube

HORSERADISH CREAM

¾ cup (180ml) cream

1 tablespoon horseradish cream

1 Melt butter in medium frying pan; cook onion, stirring occasionally, over medium heat about 30 minutes or until caramelised. Stir in vinegar and thyme.

2 Meanwhile, boil, steam or microwave unpeeled beetroot until just tender; drain. When cool enough to handle, peel beetroot then slice thinly.

3 Preheat oven to hot (220°C/200°C fan-forced). Oil oven tray.

4 Place pastry sheet on flat surface; cut a 24cm circle out of pastry. Place on oven tray, prick all over with fork; freeze 10 minutes. Bake, uncovered, about 5 minutes or until browned lightly.
5 Make chive oil. Make horseradish cream.
6 Spread onion mixture over pastry; top with slightly overlapping beetroot slices. Spray tart lightly with oil; bake, uncovered, in hot oven 10 minutes.
7 Meanwhile, combine rocket in medium bowl with half of the chive oil; divide among serving plates.
8 Cut tart into six wedges. Place each wedge on rocket, drizzle with remaining chive oil; serve with horseradish cream.

CHIVE OIL Blend or process ingredients until smooth.

HORSERADISH CREAM Beat cream in small bowl with electric mixer until soft peaks form; fold in horseradish cream.

PER SERVING 54.5g total fat (20.6g saturated); 2558kj (612 cal); 24.2g carbohydrate; 5.8g protein; 4.6g fibre

Large rounds of wholemeal Lebanese bread, pitta, or pre-baked pizza bases can be used instead of the puff pastry for the base of this tart if you like. Skip over step 4 at left if using either of these alternatives.

Roasted vegetable fillo tart

PREPARATION TIME 20 MINUTES **COOKING TIME** 45 MINUTES (PLUS COOLING TIME) **SERVES** 6

6 medium egg tomatoes (450g), quartered
1 small red onion (100g), sliced thickly
2 small yellow capsicums (300g)
2 small red capsicums (300g)
100g fetta cheese, crumbled
1 tablespoon finely shredded fresh basil
9 sheets fillo pastry
cooking-oil spray

1 Preheat oven to hot (220°C/200°C fan-forced).
2 Combine tomato and onion in baking dish; roast, uncovered, 30 minutes or until onion softens. Remove from oven; cool. Reduce oven temperature to moderately hot (200°C/180°C fan-forced).
3 Meanwhile, quarter capsicums; discard seeds and membranes. Roast under grill or in very hot oven, skin-side up, until skin blisters and blackens; cover capsicum pieces with plastic or paper 5 minutes. Peel away skin; slice capsicum thinly. Cool. Place capsicum, cheese and basil in baking dish with tomato mixture; stir gently to combine.
4 Stack all nine sheets of fillo on an oven tray, spraying every third sheet with cooking-oil spray. Fold all four sides of fillo stack in slightly to form a18cm x 30cm tart "shell". Fill shell with vegetable mixture, gently spreading it out to an even thickness. Bake tart, uncovered, about 15 minutes or until pasty is browned lightly.

PER SERVING 3.7g total fat (1.7g saturated); 656kj (157 cal); 20.1g carbohydrate; 9.3g protein; 2.6g fibre

The delightful Mediterranean flavours of roasted vegetables, fetta and fillo make for a tasty light lunch served with dressed salad leaves. This tart is also delicious with the addition of pesto or tapenade.

Quick puff pastry recipes

Take some puff pastry sheets from the freezer and make these speedy meals, snacks and desserts in no time.

SOUP DIPPERS
Brush the pastry with melted butter; sprinkle with poppy seeds. Cut into triangles; bake, between two oven trays, in a moderately hot oven about 10 minutes. Serve with soup.

BARBECUED DUCK TARTLETS
Cut 4cm rounds from the pastry; press into the holes of a mini muffin tray. Prick the base with a fork; bake in a hot oven about 8 minutes. Fill the tart cases with shredded barbecued duck; top with hoisin sauce and sliced green onion.

TAPENADE PASTRIES
Cut 8cm rounds from the pastry; bake, between two oven trays, in a moderately hot oven 10 minutes. Top the pastry rounds with bottled tapenade, sliced tomato, crumbled goat cheese and oregano leaves.

BANANA TARTE TATIN
Line a 23cm pie dish with thinly sliced banana; sprinkle with brown sugar and melted butter. Top with a 24cm round of pastry; bake in a hot oven 15 minutes. Stand 10 minutes; turn onto a plate.

FIG GALETTES
Cut 10cm rounds from the pastry; sprinkle with almond meal. Top each with sliced figs; brush with a mixture of melted butter and pure maple syrup. Turn the edges of the pastry up; bake in a moderate oven 20 minutes.

ROASTED PEAR TART
Cut the pastry in half; brush with egg. Place three well-drained canned pear halves on each pastry half; brush with melted butter. Sprinkle with brown sugar; bake in a moderately hot oven 20 minutes.

CHEESY PASTRY TWISTS

Brush a pastry sheet with egg; sprinkle with pizza cheese. Top with another pastry sheet; brush with egg and sprinkle with grated parmesan. Cut into 24 strips; twist each. Bake in a hot oven about 10 minutes.

BACON AND TOMATO PINWHEELS

Brush a pastry sheet with sun-dried tomato pesto; top with a mixture of finely chopped bacon, sliced green onions and grated parmesan. Roll the pastry tightly to enclose the filling; cut into 1.5cm slices and bake in a hot oven about 10 minutes.

VEGETABLE FREE-FORM TARTS

Cut the pastry in half, place on an over tray; top with coarsely chopped drained char-grilled vegetables, tomatoes and crumbled fetta cheese. Turn the edges of the pastry up; bake in a moderate oven 30 minutes.

PISTACHIO ROSEWATER PINWHEELS

Combine a few drops of rosewater with melted butter; brush over the pastry. Sprinkle with finely chopped pistachios, caster sugar and cinnamon. Roll up tightly; cut into 1.5cm slices and bake in a hot oven 10 minutes.

CHOC-MARMALADE CROISSANTS

Cut a pastry sheet into four triangles; brush each with warmed marmalade. Sprinkle generously with grated white eating chocolate. Roll the triangles to enclose the filling; curve the ends to form a crescent shape. Bake in hot oven about 12 minutes.

APPLE TURNOVERS

Cut the pastry into four triangles; brush with egg. Combine canned pie apple with cinnamon, caster sugar and sultanas. Top half of each triangle with apple; fold over to enclose the filling. Bake in a moderate oven 20 minutes.

From the simplest cream puff to the elaborate tower of a caramel-glazed croquembouche, the choux pastry profiterole is a French baking classic loved by cooks around the world.

Profiteroles

PREPARATION TIME 10 MINUTES **COOKING TIME** 30 MINUTES (PLUS COOLING TIME) **MAKES** 24

20g butter
¼ cup (60ml) water
¼ cup (35g) plain flour
1 egg

PASTRY CREAM
1 cup (250ml) milk
½ vanilla bean, split
3 egg yolks
⅓ cup (75g) caster sugar
2 tablespoons cornflour

TOFFEE
1 cup (220g) caster sugar
½ cup (125ml) water

1 Preheat oven to hot (220°C/200°C fan-forced). Lightly grease two oven trays.
2 Place butter and the water in small saucepan; bring to a boil. Add flour; beat with wooden spoon over heat until mixture comes away from base and side of saucepan and forms a smooth ball. Transfer to small bowl; beat in egg with electric mixer until glossy. Spoon mixture into piping bag fitted with 1cm plain tube.
3 Pipe small dollops of pastry 5cm apart onto trays; bake, uncovered, 7 minutes. Reduce oven temperature to moderate (180°C/160°C fan-forced); bake, uncovered, 10 minutes or until profiteroles are crisp. Cut small opening in side of each profiterole; bake further 5 minutes or until dried out. Cool.
4 Make pastry cream. Make toffee.
5 Spoon pastry cream into piping bag fitted with 1cm plain tube; pipe cream through cuts into profiteroles. Place profiteroles on foil-covered tray; drizzle with toffee.

PASTRY CREAM Combine milk and vanilla bean in small saucepan; bring to a boil. Discard vanilla bean. Beat egg yolks, sugar and cornflour in small bowl with electric mixer until thick. With motor operating, gradually beat in hot milk mixture. Return custard to saucepan; stir over heat until mixture boils and thickens. Cover, cool to room temperature.

TOFFEE Combine sugar with the water in medium heavy-based frying pan. Stir over heat, without boiling, until sugar dissolves; bring to a boil. Reduce heat; simmer, uncovered, without stirring, until mixture is golden brown in colour.

PER PROFITEROLE 2g total fat (1g saturated); 343kj (82 cal); 14.6g carbohydrate; 1.2g protein; 0.1g fibre

Paris-brest, which looks more like a puffy doughnut than a bicycle wheel, was created by a French chef in honour of the famous annual bicycle race run between the two cities of Paris and Brest.

PARIS-BREST

MAKES 16

Follows steps 1–2 in profiteroles to make choux pastry. Line trays with baking paper then draw eight 4cm-circles on each tray. Pipe choux pastry around edge of each circle; bake, uncovered, 7 minutes. Reduce oven temperature to moderate (180°C/160°C fan-forced); bake, uncovered, 10 minutes or until browned lightly. Cut each in half horizontally; bake further 5 minutes or until rings are dried out. Cool. Spoon pastry cream into piping bag fitted with 1cm plain tube; pipe cream into 16 ring halves; top with remaining halves. Place paris-brest on foil-covered tray. Drizzle with toffee; top with ¼ cup flaked almonds.

PER PIECE 3.8g total fat (1.6g saturated); 552kj (132 cal); 22.0g carbohydrate; 2.1g protein; 0.2g fibre

MINI CHOCOLATE ECLAIRS

MAKES 16

Follows steps 1–2 in profiteroles to make choux pastry. Pipe 5cm lengths of choux pastry mixture 3cm apart onto trays; bake, uncovered, 7 minutes. Reduce oven temperature to moderate (180°C/160°C fan-forced); bake, uncovered, 10 minutes or until eclairs are browned lightly and crisp. Carefully cut eclairs in half, remove any soft centre; bake further 5 minutes or until eclairs are dried out. Cool. Spoon pastry cream into piping bag fitted with 1cm plain tube; pipe cream onto 16 eclair halves; top with remaining halves. Place eclairs on foil-covered tray; spread with about 60g of melted dark chocolate.

PER ECLAIR 4.2g total fat (2.5g saturated); 364kj (87 cal); 10.3g carbohydrate; 1.9g protein; 0.3g fibre

An eclair is a small, delicate, log-shaped pastry, filled with either pastry cream (crème pâtissière) or fresh whipped cream, and topped with chocolate, toffee, or glacé icing.

Apple pie

PREPARATION TIME 45 MINUTES (PLUS REFRIGERATION TIME)
COOKING TIME 50 MINUTES (PLUS COOLING TIME) **SERVES** 8

- 1 cup (150g) plain flour
- ½ cup (75g) self-raising flour
- ¼ cup (35g) cornflour
- ¼ cup (30g) custard powder
- 1 tablespoon caster sugar
- 100g cold butter, chopped
- 1 egg, separated
- ⅓ cup (80ml) cold water, approximately
- 1 tablespoon caster sugar, extra

FILLING

- 10 medium apples (1.5kg)
- ½ cup (125ml) water
- ¼ cup (55g) caster sugar
- 1 teaspoon grated lemon rind
- ¼ teaspoon ground cinnamon

1 Process flours, custard powder, sugar and butter until mixture resembles breadcrumbs. Add egg yolk and enough water to make ingredients just come together. Press dough into a ball, knead on floured surface until smooth; cover and refrigerate 30 minutes.

2 Make filling; cool. Preheat oven to hot (220°C/200°C fan-forced).

3 Divide dough into two portions. Roll one portion between sheets of baking paper until large enough to line base and side of deep 25cm pie plate. Lift pastry into pie plate. Spoon filling into pastry case, brush edge with egg white.

4 Roll remaining pastry until large enough to cover filling. Press edges together; trim edge. Brush pastry with egg white. Decorate with pastry scraps, if desired; brush with a little more egg white, sprinkle with extra sugar. Bake 20 minutes; reduce temperature to moderate (180°C/160°C fan-forced), bake 25 minutes or until pastry is browned.

FILLING Peel, quarter, core and slice apples. Combine apples in large saucepan with the water, cover; simmer about 5 minutes or until apples are tender. Drain apples, discard liquid. Transfer apples to large bowl; stir in sugar, rind and cinnamon, cool.

PER SERVING 11.4g total fat (7.0g saturated); 1442kj (345 cal); 54.2g carbohydrate; 4.3g protein; 3.7g fibre

It is believed that apple pie was introduced to the UK by William the Conqueror and taken to the US with the pilgrims. You can make this pie ahead and freeze it un-baked. Bake the frozen pie in a hot oven for 15 to 20 minutes, then lower the temperature to moderate for the remainder of the cooking time. The total baking time from frozen will be about 20 minutes longer than if unfrozen.

Granny smith or golden delicious apples work well in this recipe.

1

2

3

4

Rhubarb galette

PREPARATION TIME 10 MINUTES **COOKING TIME** 20 MINUTES **SERVES** 4

20g butter, melted

2½ cups (275g) coarsely chopped rhubarb

⅓ cup (75g) firmly packed brown sugar

1 teaspoon finely grated orange rind

1 sheet ready-rolled puff pastry

2 tablespoons hazelnut meal

10g butter, melted, extra

1 Preheat oven to hot (220°C/200°C fan-forced). Line oven tray with baking paper.

2 Combine butter, rhubarb, sugar and rind in medium bowl.

3 Cut 24cm round from pastry, place on tray; sprinkle with hazelnut meal. Spread rhubarb mixture over pastry, leaving a 4cm border. Fold 2cm of pastry edge up and around filling. Brush edge with extra butter. Bake, uncovered, 20 minutes or until browned lightly.

☐ **PER SERVING** 18.2g total fat (4.8g saturated); 1354kj (324 cal); 34.6g carbohydrate; 4.0g protein; 3.2g fibre

Galettes are another delight from France. For a delicious addition place an 18cm round of marzipan, 5mm thick, in the centre of the pastry and then top with rhubarb. Also delicious with plums and apricots.

Gourmet chocolate tart

PREPARATION TIME 40 MINUTES (PLUS REFRIGERATION TIME) **COOKING TIME** 30 MINUTES **SERVES** 8

2 eggs

2 egg yolks

¼ cup (55g) caster sugar

250g dark eating chocolate, melted

200g unsalted butter, melted

PASTRY

1½ cups (225g) plain flour

½ cup (110g) caster sugar

140g cold butter, chopped

1 egg, beaten lightly

1 Make pastry. Preheat oven to moderately hot (200°C/180°C fan-forced).

2 Place flant tin on oven tray; cover pastry with baking paper, fill with dried beans or uncooked rice. Bake 10 minutes. Remove paper and beans; bake 5 minutes or until shell is browned lightly. Cool. Reduce oven temperature to moderate (180°C/200°C fan-forced)

3 Whisk eggs, egg yolks and sugar in medium heatproof bowl over medium saucepan of simmering water about 15 minutes or until light and fluffy. Whisk in chocolate and butter.

4 Pour mixture into pastry case. Bake, uncovered, 10 minutes or until filling is set; cool 10 minutes. Refrigerate 1 hour. Serve dusted with sifted cocoa powder, if desired.

PASTRY Blend or process flour, sugar and butter until crumbly; add egg, process until ingredients just come together. Enclose in plastic wrap; refrigerate 30 minutes. Grease 24cm round loose-based flan tin. Roll dough between sheets of baking paper until large enough to line tin. Lift dough into tin; press into side, trim edge, prick base with fork. Cover; refrigerate 30 minutes.

☐ **PER SERVING** 48.0g total fat (32.7g saturated); 2930kj (701 cal); 59g carbohydrate; 7.8g protein; 2.5g fibre

1 RHUBARB GALETTE **2** GOURMET CHOCOLATE TART **3** MILLE-FEUILLE WITH ALMONDS AND RASPBERRIES [P 586] **4** RHUBARB AND ALMOND JALOUSIE [P 586]

Mille-feuille, pronounced meal-fwee, translates as "thousand leaves", and refers to the many fine layers in cooked puff pastry. We've adapted the idea here by layering fillo pastry with almonds and honey.

Mille-feuille with almonds and raspberries

PREPARATION TIME 25 MINUTES **COOKING TIME** 15 MINUTES (PLUS REFRIGERATION AND COOLING TIME) **SERVES** 8

1⅓ cups (330ml) milk
4 egg yolks
½ cup (110g) caster sugar
2 tablespoons plain flour
1 tablespoon cornflour
1 teaspoon vanilla extract
50g butter
1 tablespoon honey
2 sheets fillo pastry
⅓ cup (55g) roasted blanched almonds, chopped finely
¾ cup (180ml) thickened cream
300g raspberries

1 Bring milk to a boil in medium saucepan. Combine egg yolks, sugar, flours and extract in medium bowl; gradually whisk in hot milk. Return custard mixture to same pan; stir, over heat, until mixture boils and thickens. Return custard to same bowl, cover; refrigerate about 1 hour or until cold.
2 Combine butter and honey in same cleaned pan; stir over low heat, until smooth.
3 Preheat oven to moderately hot (200°C/180°C fan-forced). Grease two oven trays.
4 Brush one fillo sheet with half of the honey mixture; sprinkle with nuts. Top with remaining fillo sheet; brush with remaining honey mixture. Cut fillo stack into 7cm-squares; place squares on trays. Bake, uncovered, about 5 minutes or until browned lightly. Cool 10 minutes.
5 Meanwhile, beat cream in small bowl with electric mixer until soft peaks form; fold into cold custard mixture. Place one pastry square on each serving plate; top with one heaped tablespoon of the custard mixture and a few raspberries. Place second pastry square on top; repeat with another layer of custard and raspberries then top with third pastry square. Serve mille-feuilles with remaining raspberries; dust with icing sugar, if desired.

PER SERVING 22.0g total fat (11.1g saturated); 1409kj (337 cal); 27.6g carbohydrate; 6.1g protein; 2.9g fibre

In the 16th century an Italian nobleman, Marquis Muzio Frangipani, created a perfume for scenting gloves. It was popular in Paris, and pastry cooks decided to replicate the scent in a dessert; they started flavouring pastry cream with almonds and called it "frangipane".

Rhubarb and almond jalousie

PREPARATION TIME 20 MINUTES **COOKING TIME** 40 MINUTES **SERVES** 8

2 cups (220g) chopped rhubarb
⅓ cup (75g) caster sugar
2 sheets ready-rolled puff pastry
1 tablespoon apricot jam
1 egg white
1 tablespoon caster sugar, extra

FRANGIPANE FILLING
30g butter
¼ teaspoon vanilla extract
¼ cup (55g) caster sugar
1 egg
1 tablespoon plain flour
⅔ cup (80g) almond meal

1 Preheat oven to moderately hot (200°C/180°C fan-forced). Grease oven tray.
2 Cook rhubarb and sugar in medium saucepan, over low heat, until rhubarb softens.
3 Make frangipane filling.

4 Cut one pastry sheet into 14cm x 24cm rectangle; cut remaining pastry sheet into 16cm x 24cm rectangle. Leaving 2cm border around all sides, make about eight evenly spaced slits across width of larger pastry piece.
5 Place smaller pastry sheet on tray; spread with jam. Place filling on pastry, leaving 2cm border around the edges; top filling evenly with rhubarb mixture. Brush around border with egg white. Place remaining pastry sheet over filling; press edges of pastry together.
6 Brush jalousie with remaining egg white; sprinkle with extra sugar. Bake, uncovered, 35 minutes or until browned lightly and cooked through. Serve warm or cold.

FRANGIPANE FILLING Beat butter, extract and sugar in small bowl with electric mixer until thick and creamy. Add egg; beat until combined. Stir in flour and almond meal.

PER SERVING 18.8g total fat (3.3g saturated); 1446kj (346 cal); 37.0g carbohydrate; 6.2g protein; 2.4g fibre

---

Banana caramel tart

The combination of banana and caramel is heavenly. There are many desserts and cakes that use this classic combination. In the UK there is the famous banoffee pie made with a biscuit base, caramel filling, bananas and whipped cream. The classic tarte tatin is sublime with bananas, or try our gorgeous upside-down toffee banana cake on page 546.

PREPARATION TIME 25 MINUTES (PLUS REFRIGERATION TIME)
COOKING TIME 30 MINUTES (PLUS COOLING TIME) **SERVES** 8

- 1 cup (150g) plain flour
- 60g cold butter, chopped
- 2 tablespoons caster sugar
- 1 egg yolk
- 1 tablespoon cold water
- 2 medium bananas (400g),
- 300ml thickened cream
- 1 tablespoon desiccated coconut, roasted

CARAMEL FILLING

- 1 cup (220g) firmly packed brown sugar
- 125g butter, chopped
- 1 tablespoon water
- ¼ cup (35g) cornflour
- 1 cup (250ml) milk
- 2 egg yolks
- 1 teaspoon vanilla extract

1 Grease 24cm loose-based flan tin.
2 Sift flour into medium bowl, rub in butter. Add sugar, egg yolk and enough of the water to mix to a soft dough. Knead dough on floured surface until smooth, wrap in plastic; refrigerate 30 minutes. Preheat oven to moderately hot (200°C/180°C fan-forced).
3 Roll pastry between sheets of baking paper until large enough to line tin. Lift pastry into tin; press into side, trim edge, prick base with fork. Cover pastry with baking paper then fill with dried beans or uncooked rice. Bake 10 minutes; remove paper and beans, bake, uncovered, 10 minutes. Cool.
4 Make caramel filling. Spread into pastry case, top with sliced banana then whipped cream; sprinkle with coconut. Refrigerate 1 hour before serving.

CARAMEL FILLING Combine sugar, butter and the water in medium saucepan; stir over low heat until sugar is dissolved. Add blended cornflour and milk; stir over heat until mixture boils and thickens. Remove from heat; whisk in egg yolks and extract. Cover; cool.

PER SERVING 37g total fat (23.6g saturated); 2466kj (590 cal); 58.2g carbohydrate; 5.9g protein; 1.6g fibre

These little tarts known as pasteis de nata are made all over Portugal, but their origin apparently lies with the kitchen monks in Lisbon's Jeronimos monastery. It is believed by many that the original, secret recipe is now closely guarded by the famous bakery Antiga Confeitaria de Belem, where they produce 35,000 custard tarts each day, with around 12,000 sold on the premises alone.

Portuguese custard tarts

PREPARATION TIME 25 MINUTES (PLUS THAWING TIME)

COOKING TIME 30 MINUTES (PLUS COOLING TIME) **MAKES** 12

4 egg yolks

½ cup (110g) caster sugar

2 tablespoons cornflour

1 cup (250ml) cream

½ cup (125ml) water

strip of lemon rind

2 teaspoons vanilla extract

1 sheet ready-rolled butter puff pastry

1 Preheat oven to hot (220°C/200°C fan-forced). Grease 12-hole (⅓-cup/80ml) muffin pan. Whisk egg yolks, sugar, cornflour, cream and the water in medium saucepan.

2 Add rind; stir over medium heat until mixture just comes to a boil. Remove from heat immediately. Remove rind; stir in extract.

3 Cut pastry sheet in half; stack halves on top of each other. Stand about 5 minutes or until thawed. Roll pastry up tightly, from the short side; cut log into 12 x 1cm rounds.

4 Lay pastry, cut-side up, on lightly floured board; roll each round out to about 10cm. Push rounds into muffin pans. Spoon custard into pastry cases.

5 Bake tarts about 20 minutes or until well browned. Transfer to wire rack to cool.

PER TART 14.1g total fat (8.2g saturated); 836kj (200 cal); 16.3g carbohydrate; 2.2g protein; 0.2g fibre

---

It is thought that the meringue was invented by a Swiss pastry-cook called Gasparini in 1720. It quickly became a favourite of the French court, and Marie Antoinette apparently used to make it with her own regal hands! To get maximum juice from the lemons, keep them at room temperature and roll them under your palm against the kitchen counter before cutting.

Lemon meringue pie

PREPARATION TIME 40 MINUTES (PLUS REFRIGERATION TIME)

COOKING TIME 30 MINUTES (PLUS COOLING TIME) **SERVES** 8

1½ cups (225g) plain flour

3 teaspoons icing sugar

140g cold butter, chopped

1 egg yolk

2 tablespoons water, approximately

FILLING

½ cup (75g) cornflour

1 cup (220g) caster sugar

½ cup (125ml) lemon juice

1¼ cups (310 ml) water

2 teaspoons finely grated lemon rind

3 egg yolks

60g butter

MERINGUE

3 egg whites

½ cup (110g) caster sugar

1 Sift flour and icing sugar into medium bowl, rub in butter. Add yolk and enough water to make ingredients cling together. Press dough into ball, knead gently on floured surface until smooth; cover, refrigerate 30 minutes.

2 Preheat oven to moderately hot (200°C/180°C fan-forced). Lightly grease 24cm flan tin.

3 Roll dough on floured surface until large enough to line tin. Lift pastry into tin, ease into side; trim edge.

4 Place tin on oven tray, line pastry with baking paper, then fill with dried beans or uncooked rice. Bake 10 minutes. Remove paper and beans; bake, uncovered, 10 minutes or until pastry case is browned lightly. Cool. Reduce oven temperature to moderate (180°C/160°C fan-forced).
5 Make filling and meringue. Spread filling into pastry case, top with meringue. Bake 5 minutes or until meringue is browned lightly. Stand 5 minutes before serving.

FILLING Combine cornflour and sugar in medium saucepan, gradually stir in juice and water. Stir over heat until mixture boils and thickens (mixture should be very thick). Reduce heat; simmer, stirring, 30 seconds. Remove from heat, quickly stir in rind, egg yolks and butter, stir until smooth; cover, cool to room temperature.

MERINGUE Beat egg whites in small bowl with electric mixer until soft peaks form; gradually add sugar, beating until dissolved after each addition.

PER SERVING 23.7g total fat (14.4g saturated); 2211kj (529 cal); 71.7g carbohydrate; 6.2g protein; 1.1g fibre

Be sure to spread the meringue up to the edge of the pastry so that the lemon filling is completely sealed underneath. This protects the filling from overheating and thinning.

Mini macadamia, pecan and walnut pies

PREPARATION TIME 20 MINUTES (PLUS REFRIGERATION TIME) **COOKING TIME** 25 MINUTES **MAKES** 4

- 1 ¼ cups (185g) plain flour
- ⅓ cup (55g) icing sugar
- ¼ cup (30g) almond meal
- 125g cold butter, chopped
- 1 egg yolk

FILLING

- ⅓ cup (45g) macadamias, roasted
- ⅓ cup (40g) pecans, roasted
- ⅓ cup (35g) walnuts, roasted
- 2 tablespoons brown sugar
- 1 tablespoon plain flour
- 40g butter, melted
- 2 eggs, beaten lightly
- ¾ cup (180ml) pure maple syrup

1 Blend or process flour, sugar and almond meal with butter until crumbly. Add egg yolk; process until ingredients just come together. Knead pastry on floured surface until smooth. Cover with plastic wrap; refrigerate 30 minutes.
2 Grease four 10cm-round loose-based flan tins. Divide pastry into quarters. Roll each piece, between sheets of baking paper, into rounds large enough to line tins; lift pastry into each tin. Press into sides; trim edges. Cover; refrigerate 1 hour.
3 Preheat oven to moderately hot (200°C/180°C fan-forced). Place tins on oven tray; line each tin with baking paper then fill with dried beans or uncooked rice. Bake 10 minutes; remove paper and beans. Bake, uncovered, about 7 minutes or until cases are browned lightly; cool. Reduce oven temperature to moderate (180°C/160°C fan-forced).
4 Make filling; divide among pastry cases. Bake about 25 minutes or until set; cool.

FILLING Combine ingredients in medium bowl.

PER PIE 64.5g total fat (25.9g saturated); 4318kj (1033 cal); 97.5g carbohydrate; 14.3g protein; 4.6g fibre

Macadamia nuts are one of the few plant foods native to Australia that are produced and exported in significant quantities. The tree does not begin to produce commercially usable nuts until it is 5 to 7 years old.

For a bit of crunch, sprinkle with ½ cup halved, roasted hazelnuts. Other fruits that work well on this tart are berries (strawberries, raspberries, blueberries, blackberries), cherries, plums and peaches.

Roasted nectarine tart

PREPARATION TIME 40 MINUTES (PLUS REFRIGERATION TIME) **COOKING TIME** 45 MINUTES **SERVES** 8

8 nectarines (1.3kg), halved, stones removed

¼ cup (60ml) orange juice

½ cup (110g) firmly packed brown sugar

PASTRY

1 ⅔ cups (250g) plain flour

⅔ cup (110g) icing sugar

125g cold butter, chopped

1 egg yolk

1 ½ tablespoons cold water, approximately

CREME PATISSIERE

300ml thickened cream

1 cup (250ml) milk

½ cup (110g) caster sugar

1 vanilla bean

3 egg yolks

2 tablespoons cornflour

90g unsalted butter, chopped

1 Grease 19cm x 27cm loose-based flan tin. Make pastry. Preheat oven to moderate (180°C/160°C fan-forced).

2 Place tin on oven tray. Line pastry case with baking paper, then fill with dried beans or uncooked rice. Bake 10 minutes. Remove paper and beans; bake, uncovered, about 10 minutes or until pastry case is browned lightly. Cool.

3 Meanwhile, make crème pâtissière.

4 Increase oven temperature to hot (220°C/200°C fan-forced). Place nectarines, in single layer, in large shallow baking dish; sprinkle with juice and sugar. Roast, uncovered, about 20 minutes or until nectarines are soft. Cool.

5 Meanwhile, spoon crème pâtissière into pastry case, cover; refrigerate 30 minutes or until firm. Top with nectarines; drizzle with pan juices.

PASTRY Blend or process flour, sugar and butter until crumbly. Add egg yolk and enough of the water to make ingredients just come together. Knead dough on floured surface until smooth. Cover; refrigerate 30 minutes. Roll dough between sheets of baking paper until large enough to line tin. Ease dough into tin, press into sides; trim edges. Cover; refrigerate 30 minutes.

CREME PATISSIERE Combine cream, milk and sugar in medium saucepan. Split vanilla bean in half lengthways, scrape seeds into pan, then add pod; bring to a boil. Remove from heat; discard pod. Beat egg yolks in small bowl with electric mixer until thick and creamy; beat in cornflour. Gradually beat in hot cream mixture. Strain mixture into same cleaned saucepan; stir over heat until mixture boils and thickens. Remove from heat; whisk in butter. Cover surface of custard with plastic wrap; cool to room temperature.

PER SERVING 40.7g total fat (25.5g saturated); 3043kj (728 cal); 80.0g carbohydrate; 8.6g protein; 4.6g fibre

The key lime flourishes in Florida, where it is used in many dishes. There are many variations of this famous American recipe, but this is our favourite. During mixing, a reaction occurs between the condensed milk and the lime juice, which causes the filling to thicken. Many early recipes were actually uncooked, relying on this reaction to create the right consistency. Today, however, in the interest of safety regarding raw eggs, these pies are almost always cooked.

Key lime pie

PREPARATION TIME 20 MINUTES (PLUS REFRIGERATION TIME) **COOKING TIME** 35 MINUTES **SERVES** 8

1 cup (150g) plain flour

2 teaspoons icing sugar

60g butter

2 teaspoons lemon juice

1 tablespoon water, approximately

FILLING

¾ cup (185 ml) sweetened condensed milk

1 cup (200g) ricotta cheese

3 eggs, separated

2 teaspoons finely grated lemon rind

⅓ cup (80ml) lime juice

1 Sift flour and icing sugar into bowl, rub in butter. Stir in lemon juice and enough water to mix to a soft dough. Knead dough gently on floured surface until smooth; cover, refrigerate 30 minutes. Preheat oven to moderately hot (200°C/180°C fan-forced).
2 Roll dough between sheets of baking paper until large enough to fit 23cm pie plate. Lift pastry into pie plate, ease into side of plate; trim edge.
3 Place pie plate on oven tray, line pastry with baking paper, then fill with dried beans or uncooked rice. Bake 10 minutes. Remove paper and beans; bake, uncovered, 7 minutes or until browned lightly. Cool.
4 Make filling. Pour into pastry case; bake about 25 minutes or until filling is set. Cool.
5 Refrigerate pie until cold; dust with sifted icing sugar before serving, if desired.

FILLING Blend or process milk, cheese, egg yolks, rind and juice until smooth; transfer to large bowl. Beat egg whites in small bowl until soft peaks form, fold into lime mixture in two batches.

PER SERVING 12.4g total fat (7.2g saturated); 1179kj (282 cal); 32.0g carbohydrate; 10.1g protein; 0.8g fibre

---

Some people draw breath at the long cooking times for quince, but the result is worth the wait. The fact that this yellow nondescript-looking fruit can, with a few hours' cooking, transform itself into a deep-pink delectable treat explains why its other name is "honey apple".

Quince tarte tatin

PREPARATION TIME 20 MINUTES (PLUS REFRIGERATION TIME) **COOKING TIME** 3 HOURS **SERVES** 6

4 medium quinces (1.4kg)

1 cup (220g) caster sugar

1 litre (4 cups) water

¼ cup (60ml) orange juice

1 teaspoon finely grated orange rind

40g butter

PASTRY

1 cup (150g) plain flour

¼ cup (40g) icing sugar

100g butter, chopped

1 egg yolk

1 tablespoon cold water, approximately

1 Peel and core quinces; quarter lengthways.
2 Place quince in large saucepan with sugar, the water, juice and rind; bring to a boil. Reduce heat; simmer, covered, about 2½ hours or until quince is rosy in colour. Using slotted spoon, remove quinces from syrup; bring syrup to a boil. Boil, uncovered, until syrup reduces to ¾ cup. Stir in butter.
3 Meanwhile, make pastry.

4 Preheat oven to moderately hot (200°C/180°C fan-forced). Line base of deep 22cm-round cake pan with baking paper.
5 Place quince, rounded-sides down, in pan; pour syrup over quince.
6 Roll pastry between sheets of baking paper until large enough to cover quince completely. Lift pastry into pan, tucking pastry down side of pan. Bake, uncovered, about 30 minutes or until pastry is browned lightly. Cool 5 minutes; turn tart onto serving plate, fruit-side up. Serve with vanilla ice-cream, if desired.

PASTRY Blend or process flour, sugar and butter until crumbly. Add egg yolk and enough of the water to make the ingredients just come together. Shape dough into ball, enclose in plastic wrap; refrigerate 30 minutes.

☐ **PER SERVING** 20.7g total fat (12.9g saturated); 2299kj (550 cal); 80.0g carbohydrate; 4.2g protein; 13.1g fibre

---

Lemon tart

PREPARATION TIME 20 MINUTES (PLUS REFRIGERATION TIME)
COOKING TIME 1 HOUR 10 MINUTES (PLUS COOLING TIME) **SERVES** 8

Once they have been used for blind-baking, dried beans and rice are too dried out to be suitable for cooking. Keep them in an airtight jar for baking use only.

1¼ cups (185g) plain flour
⅓ cup (55g) icing sugar
¼ cup (30g) almond meal
125g cold butter, chopped
1 egg yolk

LEMON FILLING
1 tablespoon finely grated lemon rind
½ cup (125ml) lemon juice
5 eggs
¾ cup (165g) caster sugar
300ml thickened cream

1 Process flour, icing sugar, almond meal and butter until crumbly. Add egg yolk; process until ingredients just come together. Knead dough on floured surface until smooth. Enclose in plastic wrap; refrigerate 30 minutes.
2 Lightly grease 24cm loose-based flan tin. Roll pastry between sheets of baking paper until large enough to line tin. Ease pastry into tin; trim edges. Cover; refrigerate about 30 minutes. Preheat oven to moderately hot (200°C/180°C fan-forced).
3 Line pastry with baking paper, then fill with dried beans or uncooked rice; place tin on oven tray. Bake 10 minutes. Remove paper and beans; bake, uncovered, 10 minutes or until tart shell is browned lightly. Remove from oven; reduce oven temperature to moderately slow (170°C/150°C fan-forced). Refrigerate cooled pastry case until cold.
4 Make lemon filling. Pour into pastry case; bake, uncovered, about 40 minutes or until filling just sets. Stand 10 minutes; refrigerate lemon tart until cold.

LEMON FILLING Whisk ingredients in medium bowl. Stand 5 minutes; strain.

☐ **PER SERVING** 33.1g total fat (19.0g saturated); 2165kj (518 cal); 46.1g carbohydrate; 8.8g protein; 1.3g fibre

DESSERTS

Desserts

For most of us today, desserts are treats to be relished when we're eating out, have guests or are having a special family meal, rather than something we eat every day. All the more applause for the cook, then, when something sweet and beautiful appears to crown the meal. The recipes in this chapter are beloved classics and other all-time favourites we've published over the years. Some are simple and quick to put together, others are more time-consuming, but worth it.

MERINGUE DESSERTS

Pavlova and meringue roll are desserts of this type. The main point to watch when making meringue is that all utensils are dry and free of grease and that egg whites are completely free of yolk, as even a hint of grease or a speck of yolk will prevent the whites from beating up properly. See also "To separate eggs" and "To whisk egg whites" on page 326. The meringue case for pavlova can be made up to 4 days ahead and stored in an airtight container at room temperature. Fill with cream and fruit about an hour before serving.

GELATINE DESSERTS

Panna cotta and berry jelly are desserts of this type. Gelatine comes in two forms and you can substitute one for the other. Powdered gelatine, from supermarkets, comes in a box of sealed sachets each containing 7g (3 teaspoons) of gelatine. Leaf gelatine, from specialty food stores, is usually packed in bags of 12 or more sheets or leaves. It is more expensive than powdered, but is the choice of most professionals because it gives a clearer jelly.

Follow recipes for quantities, but as a general guide, one sachet of powdered gelatine is approximately equivalent to four gelatine leaves and each will set 2 cups (500ml) of liquid to a soft jelly. If the jelly is to be unmoulded, use a little more gelatine to make it firmer. To use powdered gelatine, sprinkle it over cold liquid (whatever quantity is in the recipe) in a small bowl, leave until the liquid is absorbed then place the bowl in a pan of simmering water, stirring the gelatine mixture until it is completely dissolved. Add the dissolved gelatine to the remaining liquid for the recipe; stir, cool and refrigerate as directed. Setting takes 4 to 6 hours or overnight.

To use leaf gelatine, soak the sheets in cold water until softened, then squeeze out any excess water, add to the warm liquid specified in the recipe and stir until dissolved. Cool before refrigerating. Gelatine products do not freeze successfully unless their fat content is very high, as in some ice-creams. Store, covered, in the fridge and serve within 24 hours of setting.

CHOCOLATE DESSERTS

To melt chocolate, see "Special techniques" on page 519.

TOFFEE, BRITTLE AND PRALINE

Toffee is a plain, clear confection made by boiling sugar (usually with a little water) to a caramel, then pouring out as a thin sheet to cool and harden. Brittle is toffee poured over nuts. Praline is brittle crushed to a powder.

FROZEN DESSERTS

Ice-cream can be made by hand, freezing the mixture in a shallow pan (preferably aluminium or stainless steel rather than plastic) and taking it out twice during the process to beat it and break up too-large ice crystals. Ice-cream makers, electric or hand-turned, churn the mixture constantly to keep the ice crystals very small, so the ice-cream is smooth and creamy; follow the manufacturer's instructions. Home-made ice-cream should be stored in the freezer to allow it to develop (let the flavours become stronger and texture firmer) for at least an hour after it is made. It is at its best eaten within 48 hours of being made. Note that home-made ice-cream is harder than commercial ice-cream and should be transferred from the freezer to the fridge about half an hour before serving, to soften.

Gelato is like ice-cream, but denser and more intensely flavoured. Granitas and sorbets are water ices, made with fruit juice, coffee or other flavours. Sorbets are smooth, granitas are more granular. Semi-freddo is a custard-like mixture frozen without beating or churning.

ACCOMPANIMENTS

Most desserts are served with an accompaniment such as cream or ice-cream. Except for family meals where you know everyone's taste, it is best to pass accompaniments separately so that everyone can choose whether to have them, and how much.

- **Cream** may be thickened or thin (pouring), whipped or plain. Thickened cream is the best for whipping; serve plain or sweetened with a dash of sugar and vanilla to make crème chantilly.
- **Sour cream and yoghurt** are good plain for very sweet desserts, or sweetened with brown sugar for fruits.
- **Crème fraîche,** with a slight tang, can be bought or made by mixing 1 ½ tablespoons of yogurt into 1 cup cream (do not use thickened cream) in a jar and and leaving, with the lid on and wrapped in a tea-towel, in a warm place such as a stovetop over (not in) a very slow oven, for 8 hours or overnight.
- **Custard** can be the everyday version made with eggs, sugar and milk or even using packaged custard powder, or the richer version, crème anglaise, on page 424. Place plastic wrap or a circle of greaseproof or baking paper directly on the surface of the custard to prevent a skin forming.

Today, "coulis" usually means a thick puree or sauce made from soft fruits or vegetables, such as berries or tomatoes. However, the original French culinary use of the word referred to the juices that flow into the pan from meat as it cooks. For tips on making soufflés, see page 336.

Chocolate soufflé with raspberry coulis

PREPARATION TIME 15 MINUTES **COOKING TIME** 20 MINUTES **SERVES** 4

1 tablespoon caster sugar
50g butter
1 tablespoon plain flour
200g dark eating chocolate, melted
2 egg yolks
4 egg whites
¼ cup (55g) caster sugar, extra

RASPBERRY COULIS
150g frozen raspberries, thawed
2 tablespoons caster sugar
4 cloves
½ cup (125ml) dry red wine

1 Preheat oven to moderately hot (200°C/180°C fan-forced). Grease four ¾-cup (180ml) soufflé dishes. Sprinkle insides of dishes evenly with sugar; shake away excess. Place dishes on oven tray.
2 Melt butter in small saucepan, add flour; cook, stirring, until mixture thickens and bubbles. Remove from heat; stir in chocolate and egg yolks. Transfer to large bowl.
3 Beat egg whites in small bowl with electric mixer until soft peaks form. Gradually add extra sugar, 1 tablespoon at a time, beating until sugar dissolves between additions. Fold egg white mixture into chocolate mixture, in two batches.
4 Divide soufflé mixture among dishes; bake, uncovered, about 15 minutes or until soufflés are puffed.
5 Meanwhile, make raspberry coulis.
6 Serve soufflés with coulis.

RASPBERRY COULIS Combine raspberries and sugar in small saucepan; cook, without boiling, until sugar dissolves. Add cloves and wine; bring to a boil. Reduce heat; simmer, uncovered, about 5 minutes or until coulis thickens. Strain coulis into medium jug.

PER SERVING 28.4g total fat (21.5g saturated); 2328kj (557 cal); 60.3g carbohydrate; 8g protein; 4.4g fibre

Figs are one of the sweetest fruits, with a 55% sugar content. The flowers of the fig are inside the fruit, so there are no blossoms on fig trees.

Fig and brioche pudding

PREPARATION TIME 15 MINUTES **COOKING TIME** 1 HOUR 15 MINUTES **SERVES** 6

1½ cups (375ml) milk
600ml cream
1 cinnamon stick
1 vanilla bean
¼ cup (90g) honey
4 eggs
2 small brioche (200g)
3 medium fresh figs (180g)
1 tablespoon demerara sugar

1 Stir milk, cream, cinnamon, vanilla bean and honey in medium saucepan until hot; strain into large heatproof jug.
2 Whisk eggs in large bowl; whisking constantly, pour hot milk mixture into egg mixture.
3 Preheat oven to moderate (180°C/160°C fan-forced). Lightly grease shallow 2-litre (8-cup) ovenproof dish

4 Cut each brioche into six slices and each fig into five slices. Layer brioche and figs, overlapping slightly, in dish. Pour hot milk mixture over brioche and figs; sprinkle evenly with sugar.

5 Place pudding dish in large baking dish; add enough boiling water to come halfway up sides of pudding dish; bake, uncovered, about 40 minutes or until pudding sets. Remove pudding dish from baking dish; stand 5 minutes before serving.

☐ **PER SERVING** 53.2g total fat (33.0g saturated); 2847kj (681 cal); 39.4g carbohydrate; 11.7g protein; 1.4g fibre

---

Chocolate mocha dacquoise terrine

PREPARATION TIME 20 MINUTES (PLUS REFRIGERATION TIME) **COOKING TIME** 45 MINUTES **SERVES** 12

A classic dacquoise is two meringue layers sandwiched with a butter-cream filling; it originated in the French town of Dax, whose residents are called Dacquois. It is served cold, often with a complementary seasonal fruit, or with nuts mixed into the butter cream. This makes an elegant dessert for a dinner party.

- 4 egg whites
- 1 cup (220g) caster sugar
- 2 tablespoons cocoa powder
- 200g dark eating chocolate, chopped coarsely
- ¾ cup (180ml) cream
- 2 teaspoons cocoa powder, extra

MOCHA BUTTER CREAM

- 1 tablespoon instant coffee granules
- 2 tablespoons boiling water
- 100g unsalted butter, softened
- 2¼ cups (360g) icing sugar

1 Preheat oven to slow (150°C/130°C fan-forced). Line three oven trays with baking paper; draw a 10cm x 25cm rectangle on each tray.

2 Beat egg whites in small bowl with electric mixer until soft peaks form. Gradually add sugar, 1 tablespoon at a time; beat until sugar dissolves between each addition. Fold in sifted cocoa.

3 Spread meringue mixture evenly over drawn rectangles; bake, uncovered, about 45 minutes or until meringue is dry. Turn off oven; cool meringues in oven with door ajar.

4 Meanwhile, stir chocolate and cream in small saucepan over low heat until smooth, transfer to small bowl; refrigerate until firm. Beat chocolate mixture with electric mixer about 20 seconds or until just changed in colour.

5 Make mocha butter cream.

6 Place one meringue layer on serving plate; spread with half of the chocolate mixture, then top with half of the butter cream. Top with another meringue layer; spread with remaining chocolate mixture, then with remaining butter cream. Top with last meringue layer, cover; refrigerate 3 hours or overnight. Dust with sifted extra cocoa powder just before serving.

MOCHA BUTTER CREAM Dissolve coffee granules in the boiling water in small bowl; cool. Beat butter in small bowl with electric mixer until pale in colour; gradually beat in sifted sugar. Beat in coffee mixture.

☐ **PER SERVING** 18.7g total fat (13.6g saturated); 1735kj (415 cal); 58.6g carbohydrate; 2.5g protein; 0.9g fibre

Wild blackberry is classified as a noxious weed in Australia, with the exception of the Northern Territory. Over the summer months it may be tempting to go blackberry picking, but this should only be attempted if you know for sure that the bushes have not been sprayed with weed-killer. We used cultivated blackberries, closely related to the wild ones, but not a pest.

Blackberry pudding

PREPARATION TIME 20 MINUTES

COOKING TIME 30 MINUTES (PLUS COOLING AND REFRIGERATION TIME) **SERVES** 6

3 eggs
½ cup (110g) caster sugar
1 tablespoon cornflour
¾ cup (110g) self-raising flour
1 teaspoon butter
¼ cup (60ml) boiling water
⅓ cup (75g) caster sugar, extra
½ cup (125ml) water
300g frozen blackberries
500g frozen mixed berries
¼ cup (80g) blackberry jam

1 Preheat oven to moderate (180°C/160°C fan-forced). Grease 25cm x 30cm swiss roll pan; line with baking paper.

2 Beat eggs in small bowl with electric mixer until thick and creamy. Gradually add sugar, 1 tablespoon at a time, beating until sugar dissolves between each addition. Transfer to large bowl.

3 Fold triple-sifted flours into egg mixture. Pour combined butter and the boiling water down side of bowl; fold into egg mixture. Pour mixture into pan. Bake, uncovered, about 15 minutes. Turn onto wire rack to cool.

4 Meanwhile, place extra sugar and the water in medium saucepan; bring to a boil. Stir in fruit; return to a boil. Reduce heat; simmer, uncovered, about 3 minutes or until fruit thaws. Strain over medium bowl; reserve syrup and berries separately.

5 Line 1-litre (4-cup) pudding basin with plastic wrap, extending wrap 10cm over side of basin. Cut circle slightly smaller than top edge of basin. Cut another circle from cake, the same size of base of basin. Cut remaining cake into 10cm pieces; place small cake circle in base of basin and use pieces to line side of basin. Pour ⅔ cup of the reserved syrup into small jug; reserve. Fill basin with berries; cover with remaining syrup, top with large cake circle. Cover pudding with overhanging plastic wrap, weight pudding with saucer; refrigerate 3 hours or overnight.

6 Stir jam and 2 tablespoons of the reserved syrup in small saucepan until heated through. Turn pudding onto serving plate; brush with remaining reserved syrup then jam mixture. Serve with whipped cream, if desired.

PER SERVING 3.9g total fat (1.3g saturated); 1421kj (340 cal); 65.3g carbohydrate; 6.6g protein; 7.0g fibre

BLACKBERRY PUDDING

If you'd like to add an extra flavour to this mousse try a teaspoon finely grated orange rind or 1 tablespoon of your favourite coffee, orange, raspberry or hazelnut liqueur.

Chocolate mousse

PREPARATION TIME 15 MINUTES (PLUS REFRIGERATION TIME)
COOKING TIME 5 MINUTES (PLUS COOLING TIME) **SERVES** 4

- 200g dark eating chocolate
- 300ml thickened cream
- 3 eggs, separated
- 2 tablespoons caster sugar

1 Break off and reserve a long piece of the chocolate, weighing about 25g, for making decorative chocolate shavings.
2 Chop remaining chocolate coarsely. Combine with half of the cream in large heatproof bowl. Place bowl over saucepan of simmering water; stir until chocolate melts. Cool chocolate mixture for 5 minutes then stir in egg yolks, one at a time.
3 Beat egg whites in small bowl with electric mixer until soft peaks form. Add sugar; beat until dissolved. Fold whites into chocolate mixture, in two batches; pour mixture into four ⅔-cup (160ml) serving glasses. Cover; refrigerate 3 hours or overnight.
4 Beat remaining cream in small bowl with electric mixer until soft peaks form. Using vegetable peeler, make chocolate curls from reserved chocolate. Dollop cream and sprinkle chocolate curls over each mousse.

PER SERVING 47g total fat (33.4g saturated); 2579kj (617 cal); 40g carbohydrate; 8.6g protein; 2.3g fibre

Crème brûlée literally translates from French as "burnt cream", which describes the final step of sprinkling with sugar and then caramelising. Try swapping half the cream for coconut cream and adding a couple of crushed cardamom pods at stage 2.

Ginger and lime crème brûlée

PREPARATION TIME 20 MINUTES (PLUS REFRIGERATION TIME) **COOKING TIME** 30 MINUTES **SERVES** 6

- 600ml thickened cream
- 1 tablespoon finely grated lime rind
- 4cm piece fresh ginger (20g), grated
- 2 eggs
- 4 egg yolks
- ¼ cup (55g) caster sugar
- 2 tablespoons grated palm sugar

1 Preheat oven to moderately slow (170°C/150°C fan-forced).
2 Combine cream, rind and ginger in medium saucepan, heat to just below boiling; cool 10 minutes. Strain into medium jug.
3 Whisk eggs, egg yolks and caster sugar in medium heatproof bowl; gradually whisk in cream mixture. Place bowl over medium saucepan of simmering water; stir over heat about 10 minutes or until mixture thickens slightly and coats the back of a spoon.
4 Place six ¾-cup (180ml) ovenproof dishes in large baking dish; pour cream mixture into ovenproof dishes. Add enough boiling water to come halfway up sides of dishes. Bake, uncovered, about 15 minutes or until custard is set. Remove dishes from water; cool to room temperature. Cover; refrigerate 3 hours or overnight.
5 Just before serving, sprinkle each evenly with 2 teaspoons of the palm sugar. Use a small blow torch to caramelise the sugar or place under a hot grill until browned lightly.

PER SERVING 42.7g total fat (26.1g saturated); 1973kj (472 cal); 16.8g carbohydrate; 6.5g protein; 0.2g fibre

Banana fritters

PREPARATION TIME 15 MINUTES **COOKING TIME** 20 MINUTES **SERVES** 8

- 8 small bananas (1kg)
- ¼ cup (35g) plain flour
- ⅓ cup (50g) cornflour
- 1½ teaspoons baking powder
- ½ cup (125ml) milk
- 1 egg white
- vegetable oil, for deep-frying
- ½ cup (110g) caster sugar

1 Peel bananas; cut in half crossways. Sift flour, cornflour and baking powder into medium bowl. Gradually stir in milk until smooth.

2 Beat egg white in small bowl with electric mixer until soft peaks form; fold into batter. Drop banana pieces into batter. Heat oil in wok or large saucepan; deep-fry banana, in batches, until browned lightly. Drain on absorbent paper. Toss in sugar, serve hot.

PER SERVING 5.4g total fat (1.0g saturated); 949kj (227 cal); 40.3g carbohydrate; 2.9g protein; 2.0g fibre

The word fritter comes from the Latin word "frictura", meaning fried. You can serve these fritters drizzled with pure maple syrup, sprinkled with chopped roasted pecans and topped with a scoop of vanilla ice-cream. They are also delicious drizzled with coconut liqueur and sprinkled with roasted shredded coconut.

Crème caramel

PREPARATION TIME 20 MINUTES **COOKING TIME** 50 MINUTES (PLUS COOLING TIME) **SERVES** 8

- ¾ cup (165g) caster sugar
- ¾ cup (180ml) water
- 6 eggs
- 1 teaspoon vanilla extract
- ⅓ cup (75g) caster sugar, extra
- 1¾ cups (430ml) milk
- 300ml thickened cream

1 Preheat oven to moderately slow (170°C/150°C fan-forced).

2 Stir sugar and the water in medium heavy-based saucepan using wooden spoon over medium heat, without boiling, until sugar dissolves. Use pastry brush dipped in water to brush any sugar crystals down from side of pan before mixture boils.

3 Bring sugar mixture to a boil. Boil, uncovered, without stirring, about 5 minutes or until mixture turns a light golden brown.

4 Pour caramel into deep 20cm-round cake pan; hold pan with cloth. Quickly tilt pan to coat base evenly with caramel. There is no need to spread caramel up side of pan. It is correct for caramel to set at this stage.

5 Lightly whisk eggs, extract and extra sugar in medium bowl. Do not overwhisk. Combine milk and cream in medium saucepan; bring to a boil. Remove from heat. Gradually whisk milk mixture into egg mixture; strain into cake pan over caramel.

6 Place pan in baking dish; add enough boiling water to come halfway up side of pan. Bake, uncovered, 40 minutes or until custard is just set; it will set further on cooling. Remove from water; stand about 3 hours to cool to room temperature. Cover; refrigerate overnight. This will ensure the caramel will coat the custard when it is turned out.

7 Use fingers to pull the top of custard from around side of pan. It shouldn't stick to pan but, if you're in doubt, carefully run a knife or spatula around edge of custard. Invert onto serving dish; serve with whipped cream and fresh fruit, if desired.

PER SERVING 22.3g total fat (13.3g saturated); 1526kj (365 cal); 33.8g carbohydrate; 7.5g protein; 0g fibre

Also known in France as crème renversee, crème caramel is a custard that has been baked in a caramel-coated mould. When the chilled custard is turned out onto a serving plate it is automatically glazed and sauced with the caramel in the mould. In Italy it's known as crema caramella, and in Spain as flan. You can flavour it with orange, cinnamon or coffee. This recipe must be made a day ahead, and will keep for up to 4 days, covered and refrigerated.

1

2

3

4

Vanilla panna cotta with berry jelly

PREPARATION TIME 20 MINUTES (PLUS REFRIGERATION TIME) **COOKING TIME** 15 MINUTES **SERVES** 4

Panna cotta is gorgeous made with Greek-style yogurt instead of thickened cream. Try using cinnamon, passionfruit or other flavoured yogurts and reduce the sugar, depending on how sweet they are. Dissolve the gelatine and sugar with milk; allow to cool slightly before adding to the yogurt.

120g raspberries
½ teaspoon gelatine
1 ½ tablespoons caster sugar
1 tablespoon lemon juice
⅓ cup (80ml) cranberry juice

VANILLA PANNA COTTA
2 teaspoons gelatine
¼ cup (55g) caster sugar
⅔ cup (160ml) milk
300ml thickened cream
½ teaspoon vanilla extract

1 Grease four ⅔-cup (160ml) metal moulds. Place four raspberries in each mould.
2 Sprinkle gelatine and sugar over combined juices in small heatproof jug; stand jug in small saucepan of simmering water, stir until gelatine and sugar dissolve. Divide gelatine mixture among moulds, cover; refrigerate about 2 hours or until set.
3 Make vanilla panna cotta. Pour into moulds, cover; refrigerate 3 hours or overnight.
4 Turn panna cotta onto serving plates; serve with remaining raspberries.

VANILLA PANNA COTTA Sprinkle gelatine and sugar over combined milk and cream in small saucepan. Stir over low heat, without boiling, until gelatine and sugar dissolve; stir in extract. Strain into medium jug; cool to room temperature.

PER SERVING 34.1g total fat (22.5g saturated); 1839kj (440 cal); 28.2g carbohydrate; 5g protein; 1.7g fibre

---

Baked lemon cheesecake

PREPARATION TIME 20 MINUTES (PLUS REFRIGERATION TIME) **COOKING TIME** 1 HOUR **SERVES** 10

This is one of the most loved desserts around the world. Gingernuts are a lovely alternative for the base, and fresh passionfruit pulp or raspberries are delicious served on top.

250g packet plain sweet biscuits
125g butter, melted
3 eggs
½ cup (110g) caster sugar
3 x 250g packets cream cheese, softened
1 tablespoon finely grated lemon rind
¼ cup (60ml) lemon juice

1 Preheat oven to moderate (180°C/160°C fan-forced). Line base of 22cm springform tin with foil.
2 Process biscuits until crushed finely. Add butter; process until just combined. Press biscuit mixture evenly over base and side of tin, cover; refrigerate 1 hour.
3 Beat eggs and sugar in medium bowl with electric mixer until thick and creamy; add cheese, rind and juice; beat until smooth. Place tin on oven tray; pour cheese mixture into tin. Bake, uncovered, about 1 hour or until firm. Cool in oven with the door ajar. Cover cheesecake; refrigerate 3 hours or overnight.

PER SERVING 40.7g total fat (25g saturated); 2203kj (527 cal); 30.9g carbohydrate; 10g protein; 0.5g fibre

1 VANILLA PANNA COTTA WITH BERRY JELLY **2** BAKED LEMON CHEESECAKE **3** CHOCOLATE, PEAR AND HAZELNUT SELF-SAUCING PUDDING [P 606] **4** TIRAMISU CAKE [P 606]

Self-saucing puddings are loved by Australians as a quick, easy dessert. Tinned self-saucing puddings have become popular treats for camping trips. One such pudding has actually been travelling around Australia by motorcycle (with members of the Western Australian BMW motorcycle club) for the last 30 years, after gaining a reputation for "just going along for the ride". What started as a joke has become a renowned story.

Chocolate, pear and hazelnut self-saucing pudding

PREPARATION TIME 30 MINUTES **COOKING TIME** 1 HOUR 10 MINUTES **SERVES** 6

100g dark eating chocolate, chopped coarsely

50g butter

⅔ cup (160ml) milk

¼ cup (25g) hazelnut meal

⅔ cup (100g) roasted hazelnuts, chopped coarsely

1 cup (220g) firmly packed brown sugar

1 cup (150g) self-raising flour

1 egg, beaten lightly

2 medium pears (460g)

FUDGE SAUCE

1¾ cups (430ml) water

100g butter

1 cup (220g) firmly packed brown sugar

½ cup (50g) cocoa powder, sifted

1 Preheat oven to moderate (180°C/160°C fan-forced). Lightly grease shallow 3-litre (12-cup) baking dish.

2 Stir chocolate, butter and milk in small saucepan over low heat until smooth. Transfer to large bowl; stir in hazelnut meal, nuts and brown sugar then sifted flour and egg.

3 Peel and core pears; slice thinly. Place pear slices, slightly overlapping, in dish; top with chocolate mixture.

4 Make fudge sauce.

5 Pour sauce over chocolate mixture. Bake pudding, uncovered, about 1 hour. Stand 10 minutes before serving. Serve with whipped cream or ice-cream, if desired.

FUDGE SAUCE Stir ingredients in small saucepan over low heat until smooth.

PER SERVING 41.9g total fat (20.4g saturated); 3624kj (867 cal); 109g carbohydrate; 10.4g protein; 5.5g fibre

---

Tiramisu literally means "pick-me-up". In order for the flavours to really develop this cake is best made a day ahead and kept refrigerated in an airtight container.

Tiramisu cake

PREPARATION TIME 45 MINUTES (PLUS REFRIGERATION TIME) **COOKING TIME** 25 MINUTES **SERVES** 12

6 eggs

1½ cups (330g) caster sugar

1 cup (150g) self-raising flour

½ cup (75g) cornflour

1 cup (250ml) boiling water

1½ tablespoons instant coffee granules

¾ cup (180ml) marsala

4 egg yolks

2 cups (500g) mascarpone cheese

¼ cup (25g) finely grated dark eating chocolate

300ml thickened cream

75g dark eating chocolate, extra

1 Preheat oven to moderate (180°C/160°C fan-forced). Grease two deep 19cm-square cake pans; line bases with baking paper.

2 Beat eggs in medium bowl with electric mixer about 10 minutes or until thick and creamy. Add 1 cup of the sugar, 1 tablespoon at a time, beating until sugar dissolves between each addition. Gently fold in triple-sifted flours, then ¼ cup of the boiling water; divide mixture evenly between pans. Bake, uncovered, about 25 minutes. Turn cakes immediately onto wire racks to cool.
3 Meanwhile, combine remaining boiling water, coffee and ½ cup of the marsala in small bowl; cool to room temperature.
4 Beat egg yolks and remaining sugar in small bowl with electric mixer until thick and creamy. Add remaining marsala and mascarpone; beat until combined.
5 Line deep 19cm-square cake pan with plastic wrap. Split cakes in half horizontally; place one layer of cake in pan, brush with ⅓ cup of the coffee mixture. Spread with 1 cup of the mascarpone mixture; sprinkle with 1 tablespoon of the grated chocolate. Repeat layering, finishing with layer of cake, cover; refrigerate 3 hours or overnight.
6 Beat cream in small bowl with electric mixer until soft peaks form. Turn cake onto serving plate; spread top and sides with cream. Using vegetable peeler, make chocolate curls from extra chocolate; sprinkle over cake.

PER SERVING 40.0g total fat (26.0g saturated); 2508kj (600 cal); 50.1g carbohydrate; 6g protein; 0.9g fibre

---

Lemon delicious puddings

PREPARATION TIME 20 MINUTES **COOKING TIME** 45 MINUTES **MAKES** 6

This is the all-time best lemon delicious pudding. It needs to be served straight from the oven or the pudding will sink and absorb all the sauce.

- 125g butter, melted
- 2 teaspoons finely grated lemon rind
- 1 ½ cups (330g) caster sugar
- 3 eggs, separated
- 75g (½ cup) self raising flour
- ⅓ cup (80ml) lemon juice
- 1 ⅓ cups (330ml) milk

1 Preheat oven to 180°C/160°C fan-forced. Grease six 1-cup (250ml) ovenproof dishes.
2 Combine butter, rind, sugar and yolks in large bowl. Stir in sifted flour and juice. Gradually stir in milk to give a smooth, runny mixture.
3 Beat egg whites in small bowl with electric mixer until soft peaks form; Fold into lemon mixture in two batches.
4 Place dishes in a baking dish, pour lemon mixture evenly into dishes. Add enough boiling water to come halfway up sides of dishes. Bake about 45 minutes or until puddings are set. Dust with sifted icing sugar before serving, if desired.

PER PUDDING 21.4g total fat (13.0g saturated); 2044kj (489 cal); 67.1g carbohydrate; 6.6g protein; 0.5g fibre

Tropical fruits

Most kinds of tropical fruits are now grown in this country, making them an everyday luxury.

RAMBUTAN
A relative of the lychee, with similar luscious, perfumed, grape-like flesh. To remove the leathery, tendril-covered shell, break open with a fingernail and peel like an egg.

GOLDEN BANANA
These are small, golden-skinned bananas from Asia. The flesh is sweet and creamy. These bananas are usually sold in bunches in Asian food shops. Do not store in the fridge as the skin will turn black.

STARFRUIT
Also called carombola and belimbing (a smaller variety). Some ripen to yellow or pinky yellow, most to a yellow-green. Very crisp and juicy, with a mild sweet flavour.

LYCHEE
Its juicy, translucent flesh tastes like a more luscious, perfumed grape. Will keep, unshelled, for weeks in the fridge. Ambrosial alone, in fruit salads or as a touch of delicate sweetness in a duck salad.

JACKFRUIT
A huge fruit containing numerous seeds surrounded by golden, richly flavoured, sharp-sweet flesh. Used in fruit salads, ice-cream, milk drinks and soups. The seeds are edible boiled, then roasted in a pan with a little oil.

DRAGON FRUIT
The fruit of a pitaya cactus. The flesh, eaten raw, is tasty and mildly sweet, a little like the flavour of kiwifruit. Scoop the flesh and seeds out of the chilled fruit with a teaspoon.

GREEN MANGO
This is the unripe fruit of the mango tree. The flesh is deliciously tart. Used raw in many Asian salads or as a vegetable; it can also be bought pickled or dried.

MANGO
Paradise flavour, texture and fragrance – wonderful alone, in desserts and also with curries. Buy fully coloured but not oversoft, or with a touch of green, then ripen at room temperature.

PAPAYA
The papaya family includes both the yellow-fleshed fruit called pawpaw and the pink-fleshed fruit called papaya. Their mild, sweet flavour is best with a squeeze of lime.

PANAMA PASSIONFRUIT
A member of the berry family, this fruit is filled with tart-sweet pulp with small black seeds. It is not as tart as the more common purple variety of passionfruit.

MANGOSTEEN
The shiny, purple-brown skin peels to reveal segments of white flesh whose refreshing, sweet-sour flavour is reminiscent of pineapple. Delicious eaten out of hand, like an orange, or chilled and mixed with other tropical fruits.

DURIAN
Famous as the fruit which "smells like hell and tastes like heaven". One recommendation for enjoying the taste without the smell is to cut the sweet, aromatic flesh into pieces and soak for a day in coconut milk.

Clafoutis is originally from the Limousin region of central France where, in the local dialect, it translates as "brimming over". It is one of the world's easiest desserts to make: a sweet batter is poured into a baking dish "brimming" with cherries, prunes or the fresh fruit of your choice, and baked. Traditionally, cherries native to the region were used, but our version uses golden delicious apples, caramelised then topped with batter.

Caramelised apple clafoutis

PREPARATION TIME 15 MINUTES **COOKING TIME** 50 MINUTES (PLUS COOLING TIME) **SERVES** 6

- 6 medium apples (900g)
- 50g unsalted butter
- ½ cup (110g) firmly packed brown sugar
- ⅓ cup (75g) caster sugar
- ⅓ cup (50g) plain flour
- ⅓ cup (50g) self-raising flour
- 4 eggs, beaten lightly
- ⅔ cup (160ml) milk
- ⅔ cup (160ml) cream
- 80g unsalted butter, melted, extra
- 1 teaspoon vanilla extract

1 Preheat oven to moderately hot (200°C/180°C fan-forced). Grease shallow 2.5-litre (10-cup) ovenproof dish. Peel, core and halve apples; cut each half into four wedges.

2 Melt butter in large frying pan; cook apple, stirring, 5 minutes or until browned lightly. Add brown sugar; cook 5 minutes or until mixture thickens. Place into dish; cool 5 minutes.

3 Combine caster sugar and sifted flours in medium bowl. Gradually whisk in combined remaining ingredients until smooth; pour over apple mixture. Bake, uncovered, 40 minutes.

4 Serve hot with whipped cream, dust with sifted icing sugar, if desired.

PER SERVING 34.4g total fat (21.3g saturated); 2404kj (575 cal); 57.2g carbohydrate; 8g protein; 2.9g fibre

---

Italian for "half cold", semi-freddo culinarily refers to any partially frozen dessert, including cake, ice-cream, fruit and custard or whipped cream. Serve with a glass of your favourite dessert wine.

Poached figs with semi-freddo

PREPARATION TIME 15 MINUTES (PLUS FREEZING TIME) **COOKING TIME** 35 MINUTES **SERVES** 8

- 300ml thickened cream
- 2 tablespoons icing sugar
- 75g dark eating chocolate, chopped finely
- ⅓ cup (45g) roasted shelled pistachios, chopped coarsely

POACHED FIGS

- 1½ cups (375ml) vin santo
- 1½ cups (375ml) water
- ¾ cup (165g) caster sugar
- 1 vanilla bean, halved lengthways
- 16 medium figs (950g)

1 Line base and sides of an 8cm x 26cm bar cake pan with baking paper. Beat cream and sifted sugar with an electric mixer until soft peaks form. Stir in chocolate and nuts. Spread mixture into pan. Cover, freeze until firm.

2 Make poached figs. An hour before serving, transfer the semi-freddo from freezer to fridge. Turn onto a board and cut into 16 slices. Serve figs and syrup with semi-freddo.

POACHED FIGS Stir wine, the water, sugar and vanilla bean in medium saucepan over medium heat until sugar dissolves; bring to a boil. Reduce heat; simmer, uncovered, 3 minutes. Add figs; simmer, uncovered, 10 minutes or until tender. Gently remove figs. Boil remaining liquid, uncovered, about 10 minutes or until syrup reduces to 1½ cups.

PER SERVING 22.3g total fat (13.6g saturated); 1923kj (460 cal); 46.1g carbohydrate; 4g protein; 3.9g fibre

CARAMELISED APPLE CLAFOUTIS

Sorbet is a great dessert for people who are allergic to dairy products. The French traditionally serve sorbet between the starter and main course, as a palate cleanser.

Raspberry sorbet

PREPARATION TIME 15 MINUTES (PLUS FREEZING TIME) **COOKING TIME** 10 MINUTES **SERVES** 6

1 cup (250ml) water
1 cup (220g) caster sugar
600g frozen raspberries
1 tablespoon lemon juice
2 egg whites

1 Stir the water and sugar in small saucepan over heat, without boiling, until sugar dissolves; bring to a boil. Reduce heat, simmer, uncovered, without stirring, 5 minutes.
2 Blend or process raspberries, juice and hot sugar syrup mixture until smooth.
3 Push mixture through fine sieve into 20cm x 30cm lamington pan; discard seeds. Cover pan with foil; freeze until firm.
4 Chop frozen berry mixture coarsely. Blend or process with egg whites until smooth and paler in colour. Return mixture to pan, cover; freeze until firm.

PER SERVING 0.4g total fat (0g saturated); 823kj (197 cal); 42.8g carbohydrate; 2.4g protein; 5.4g fibre

---

The word granita comes from the Italian word "granire" which means to make grainy. What makes granita different from sorbet is that the sugar syrup content is far lower, allowing larger ice crystals to form, which gives granita its rough texture.

Coffee granita with walnut crisps

PREPARATION TIME 25 MINUTES (PLUS FREEZING TIME) **COOKING TIME** 10 MINUTES **SERVES** 4

2 cups (500ml) boiling water
¼ cup (30g) ground coffee beans
⅓ cup (75g) caster sugar
10g butter
1 tablespoon honey
1 tablespoon plain flour
1 tablespoon icing sugar
2 tablespoons finely chopped roasted walnuts

1 Pour the water over coffee in plunger; stand 5 minutes before plunging and pouring into medium jug. Add caster sugar; stir until sugar dissolves. Pour coffee into 20cm x 30cm lamington pan, cover with foil; freeze about 3 hours or until almost set.
2 Using fork, scrape granita from bottom and sides of pan, cover; return to freezer. Repeat process every hour for about 4 hours or until large ice crystals form and granita has a dry, shard-like appearance.
3 Meanwhile, melt butter with honey in small saucepan over low heat; stir in flour, icing sugar and nuts. Place walnut crisp mixture in small bowl, cover; refrigerate 1 hour.
4 Preheat oven to hot (220°C/200°C fan-forced). Line oven trays with baking paper.
5 Drop level teaspoons of the crisp mixture on trays about 10cm apart; bake, uncovered, about 3 minutes or until crisps are browned lightly. Remove from oven; cool 1 minute. Using spatula, lift crisps carefully and place over rolling pin to curve while cooling.
6 Serve granita with walnut crisps.

PER SERVING 5.2g total fat (1.6g saturated); 757kj (181 cal); 30.3g carbohydrate; 2.0g protein; 1.6g fibre

Lemon gelato

Gelato is an Italian ice-cream made from a base of water, juice, milk, soy milk or cream. This is then combined with flavourings and sweeteners. Unlike ice-cream, gelato is is not light and airy, but has a much denser texture and more intense flavour.

PREPARATION TIME 15 MINUTES (PLUS FREEZING TIME)
COOKING TIME 15 MINUTES (PLUS COOLING TIME) **SERVES** 2

½ cup (110g) caster sugar
½ cup (125ml) water
½ cup (125ml) dry white wine
½ cup (125ml) lemon juice, strained
1 egg white

1 Stir sugar, the water and wine in small saucepan over low heat, without boiling, until sugar dissolves; bring to a boil. Reduce heat; simmer, uncovered, 10 minutes; cool.
2 Stir juice into wine mixture. Pour mixture into medium shallow pan; cover with foil, freeze about 1 hour or until mixture is just firm.
3 Remove from freezer. Turn mixture into medium bowl; using fork, beat until smooth. Beat egg white in small bowl with electric mixer until firm; fold into lemon mixture. Return to pan; cover, freeze until firm.

PER SERVING 0.1g total fat (0g saturated); 1179kj (282 cal); 57.0g carbohydrate; 2.4g protein; 0.1g fibre

---

Mango bombe alaska

This dessert is also known as baked Alaska, glacé au four and omelette á la norvégienne. Earlier versions used pastry crust or crumbs over the ice-cream, but the use of meringue was introduced in 1804 by the physicist Benjamin Thompson after investigating the heat resistance of beaten egg whites. If mango ice-cream is unavailable, puree canned mangoes, fold them into softened vanilla ice-cream and re-freeze.

PREPARATION TIME 20 MINUTES (PLUS FREEZING TIME) **COOKING TIME** 5 MINUTES **SERVES** 6

2 litres mango ice-cream, softened
¼ cup (60ml) orange juice
2 tablespoons orange liqueur
16cm-round unfilled packaged sponge cake
1 large mango (600g), sliced thinly
4 egg whites
1 cup (220g) caster sugar

1 Line 15cm 1.375-litre (5½-cup) pudding basin or bowl with plastic wrap, extending plastic 5cm over edge of basin.
2 Pack ice-cream into basin, cover with foil; freeze about 2 hours or until firm.
3 Preheat oven to very hot (240°C/220°C fan-forced).
4 Combine juice and liqueur in small jug. Trim top of cake to flatten; split cake in half horizontally. Place bottom layer of cake on oven tray; brush with half of the juice mixture. Top with mango, then with remaining cake half; brush with remaining juice mixture.
5 Invert ice-cream from basin onto cake; working quickly, trim cake to exact size of ice-cream. Cover, return to freezer.
6 Beat egg whites in small bowl with electric mixer until soft peaks form. Gradually add sugar, 1 tablespoon at a time, beating until sugar dissolves between each addition.
7 Remove bombe from freezer; spread meringue over to enclose bombe completely. Bake, uncovered, about 3 minutes or until browned lightly. Lift onto serving plate; serve immediately.

PER SERVING 22.1g total fat (13.7g saturated); 2913kj (697 cal); 108.4g carbohydrate; 12.6g protein; 1.6g fibre

Both the pudding and sauce can be made a day ahead and stored, separately, covered, in the fridge. You can freeze the pudding for up to 3 months. Defrost and warm in a microwave oven while making the butterscotch sauce. Or, freeze wedges of the pudding, thaw in a microwave oven for about 30 seconds – an instant dessert to have with cream or ice-cream, with or without the sauce.

Sticky date pudding with butterscotch sauce

PREPARATION TIME 10 MINUTES (PLUS STANDING TIME)
COOKING TIME 1 HOUR (PLUS STANDING TIME) **SERVES** 6

- 1 ¼ cups (275g) seeded dried dates
- 1 ¼ cups (310ml) boiling water
- 1 teaspoon bicarbonate of soda
- 50g butter, chopped
- ½ cup (110g) firmly packed brown sugar
- 2 eggs
- 1 cup (150g) self-raising flour

BUTTERSCOTCH SAUCE

- ¾ cup (165g) firmly packed brown sugar
- 300ml cream
- 80g butter

1 Preheat oven to moderate (180°C/160°C fan-forced). Grease deep 20cm-round cake pan; line base with baking paper.

2 Combine dates and the water in food processor. Stir in soda; cover with lid, stand 5 minutes.

3 Process date mixture with butter and sugar until pureed. Add eggs and flour; process until just combined. Pour mixture into pan. Bake, uncovered, about 1 hour.

4 Make butterscotch sauce.

5 Stand cake10 minutes; turn onto serving plate. Serve warm with butterscotch sauce.

BUTTERSCOTCH SAUCE Stir ingredients in small saucepan over low heat until sauce is smooth and thickened slightly.

PER SERVING 41.5g total fat (26.6g saturated); 2993kj (716 cal); 77g carbohydrate; 6.7g protein; 5.4g fibre

---

The first recorded mention of cheesecake dates all the way back to ancient Greece but it gained wide popularity in the Jewish delis of New York. Our version takes its flavour from the much-loved cookies and cream ice-cream variety. Place the melted chocolate in a small plastic bag and snip off a corner, then squeeze to drizzle the chocolate evenly over the cheesecake.

Cookies and cream cheesecake

PREPARATION TIME 20 MINUTES (PLUS REFRIGERATION TIME) **COOKING TIME** 5 MINUTES **SERVES** 12

- 250g plain chocolate biscuits
- 150g butter, melted
- 2 teaspoons gelatine
- ¼ cup (60ml) water
- 1 ½ cups (360g) packaged cream cheese, softened
- 300ml thickened cream
- 1 teaspoon vanilla extract
- ½ cup (110g) caster sugar
- 180g white eating chocolate, melted
- 150g cream-filled chocolate biscuits, quartered
- 50g dark eating chocolate, melted

1 Line base of 23cm springform tin with baking paper.

2 Blend or process plain chocolate biscuits until fine. Add butter; process until combined. Press biscuit mixture evenly over base and 3cm up side of tin, cover; refrigerate about 20 minutes.

3 Sprinkle gelatine over the water in small heatproof jug; stand jug in small saucepan of simmering water. Stir until gelatine dissolves; cool 5 minutes.

4 Beat cheese, cream, extract and sugar in medium bowl with electric mixer until smooth. Stir in gelatine mixture and white chocolate; fold in quartered biscuits. Pour cheesecake mixture over biscuit mixture in tin, cover; refrigerate about 3 hours or until set. Drizzle with dark chocolate to serve.

PER SERVING 42g total fat (26.7g saturated); 2399kj (574 cal); 42.8g carbohydrate; 6.8g protein; 0.8g fibre

---

Rice pudding with raspberries

PREPARATION TIME 10 MINUTES **COOKING TIME** 1 HOUR 20 MINUTES **SERVES** 4

½ cup (100g) white medium-grain rice
2 cups (500ml) milk
1 cup (250ml) skim milk
1 teaspoon vanilla extract
¼ cup (55g) caster sugar

RASPBERRY COMPOTE
300g frozen raspberries
1 tablespoon caster sugar

1 Preheat oven to moderately slow (170°C/150°C fan-forced).
2 Rinse rice under cold water; drain. Spread rice into shallow 1-litre (4-cup) baking dish.
3 Combine milks, extract and sugar in medium saucepan; bring to a boil. Pour hot milk mixture over rice in baking dish; mix gently with fork. Cover dish tightly with foil. Bake 1 ¼ hours or until rice is softened and almost all liquid is absorbed.
4 Meanwhile, make raspberry compote.
5 Serve pudding with compote.

RASPBERRY COMPOTE Stir ingredients in small saucepan over low heat until sugar dissolves. Cool 10 minutes.

PER SERVING 5.4g total fat (3.3g saturated); 1267kj (303 cal); 51.8g carbohydrate; 9.1g protein; 4.3g fibre

In Denmark at Christmas, children leave a bowl of rice pudding in the attic as an offering to the attic-dwelling elves called Nisse, to ensure they help the gift-bringer Julemanden to deliver their presents. To make this pudding recklessly rich, stir in 100g roughly chopped white chocolate just before serving.

Black sticky rice

PREPARATION TIME 10 MINUTES (PLUS STANDING TIME) **COOKING TIME** 30 MINUTES **SERVES** 6

1 cup (200g) black glutinous rice
2 cups (500ml) coconut milk
⅓ cup (90g) grated palm sugar

1 Place rice in bowl; cover with water. Cover; stand overnight. Drain.
2 Add rice to medium saucepan of boiling water; simmer, uncovered, about 15 minutes or until tender. Drain.
3 Combine rice, coconut milk and sugar in same cleaned pan; simmer, uncovered, stirring occasionally, about 15 minutes or until thickened to porridge-like consistency. Serve drizzled with a little coconut cream, if desired.

PER SERVING 17.4g total fat (15.2g saturated); 1471kj (352 cal); 44.0g carbohydrate; 3.8g protein; 1.7g fibre

To cut through the richness of this dish, serve with slices of mango, banana or papaya with a squeeze of lime, or spoon on a little passionfruit pulp.

Pavlova

PREPARATION TIME 15 MINUTES **COOKING TIME** 1 HOUR 15 MINUTES (PLUS COOLING TIME) **SERVES** 8

Pavlova is said to have been invented by Perth chef Bert Sachse in the 1930s. It was so named because it was considered to be as light as the dancer Anna Pavlova. This super recipe was introduced to the Test Kitchen in 1968 by Peggy Frizell; originally her mother's recipe, it has been known fondly ever since as Peg's pav.

4 egg whites
1 cup (220g) caster sugar
1 tablespoon cornflour
1 teaspoon white vinegar
300ml thickened cream
1 teaspoon vanilla extract
1 tablespoon icing sugar

1 Preheat oven to very slow (120°C/100°C fan-forced). Line oven tray with baking paper; mark 18cm circle on baking paper.
2 Beat egg whites in small bowl with electric mixer until soft peaks form; gradually add caster sugar, beating until sugar dissolves between additions. Fold in cornflour and vinegar.
3 Spread meringue inside circle on tray. For best results, do not squash or flatten mixture but shape side up and in towards the centre, like a mound. Make furrows up side of meringue using spatula, level top. Bake, uncovered, about 1¼ hours or until dry. Turn oven off; leave meringue to cool in oven with door ajar.
4 An hour before serving, beat cream, extract and sifted icing sugar in small bowl with electric mixer until soft peaks form. Fill pavlova with cream and fruit of your choice.

PER SERVING 13.9g total fat (9.2g saturated); 1070kj (256 cal); 30.1g carbohydrate; 2.6g protein; 0.0g fibre

---

Meringue roll

PREPARATION TIME 25 MINUTES (PLUS REFRIGERATION TIME) **COOKING TIME** 10 MINUTES **SERVES** 6

Meringues are temperamental creatures and can be affected by silly things such as the weather (particularly the wet or humid variety) and the chickens' diet. This recipe is a little fiddly but the end result is a glorious light dessert, perfect for a summer lunch.

4 egg whites
½ cup (110g) caster sugar
2 tablespoons caster sugar, extra
2 cups (500ml) thickened cream
250g strawberries, halved
1 medium kiwifruit (85g), sliced thinly
2 tablespoons passionfruit pulp

1 Preheat oven to moderately hot (200°C/180°C fan-forced). Grease 26cm x 32cm swiss roll pan, line base with baking paper, extending 5cm over edge of long sides of pan.
2 Beat egg whites in small bowl with electric mixer until soft peaks form. Add sugar, 1 tablespoon at a time, beating until sugar dissolves between additions. Spread mixture into pan. Bake, uncovered, about 10 minutes or until browned lightly. Turn meringue onto baking paper sprinkled with extra sugar. Gently peel away lining paper; stand 2 minutes.
3 Beat cream in small bowl with electric mixer until soft peaks form. Spread a third of the cream over slightly warm meringue. Place half of the strawberries lengthways along centre of the meringue; roll firmly from long side, using paper as a guide. Cover; refrigerate about 30 minutes. Trim ends; cover roll with remaining cream. Cover; refrigerate until ready to serve. Serve meringue roll with remaining fruit.

PER SERVING 31.1g total fat (20.4g saturated); 1760kj (421 cal); 29.7g carbohydrate; 5g protein; 2.2g fibre

Roasting fruit is an unusual idea, but it gives a wonderful, concentrated flavour to the fruit and lovely caramelised juices to serve with it. You can roast apples and pears in the same way, varying the flavouring with cinnamon, ginger or star anise.

Roasted stone fruit with lemon grass

PREPARATION TIME 5 MINUTES **COOKING TIME** 25 MINUTES **SERVES** 4

- 2 x 10cm sticks (40g) fresh lemon grass
- 4 small plums (300g)
- 4 small apricots (200g)
- 4 medium nectarines (680g), halved, seeded
- ½ cup (125ml) water
- ¼ cup (55g) caster sugar

1 Preheat oven to moderately hot (200°C/180°C fan-forced).

2 Cut each stick of lemon grass in half lengthways. Place lemon grass in large baking dish with fruit and the water; sprinkle with sugar. Roast, uncovered, about 25 minutes or until fruit softens and begins to brown. Discard lemon grass.

3 Serve fruit warm or cold with pan juices and a dollop of yogurt, if desired.

PER SERVING 0.3g total fat (0.0g saturated); 644kj (154 cal); 32.2g carbohydrate; 2.3g protein; 5.8g fibre

---

Palm sugar, also known as jaggery and coconut sugar, is made by boiling down the sap of various kinds of palm tree. Generally brown in colour, it has a coarse, sticky texture and is used in Asian dishes. Logs, tubs, or cans of palm sugar are sold in Asian markets and larger supermarkets. If you can't find palm sugar, use light brown sugar.

Asian fruit salad

PREPARATION TIME 20 MINUTES **COOKING TIME** 15 MINUTES (PLUS COOLING AND REFRIGERATION TIME) **SERVES** 8

- 1 litre (4 cups) water
- 1 cup (270g) grated palm sugar
- 1 vanilla bean
- 2cm piece fresh ginger (10g), chopped finely
- 3 star anise
- 1 tablespoon finely grated lime rind
- ⅓ cup (80ml) lime juice
- ½ cup coarsely chopped fresh vietnamese mint
- 2 large mangoes (1.2kg), chopped coarsely
- 3 starfruit (480g), sliced thinly
- 2 large oranges (600g), segmented
- 1 large pineapple (2kg), chopped coarsely
- 1 medium papaya (1kg), chopped coarsely
- ½ cup (125ml) passionfruit pulp
- 12 rambutans (500g), halved
- 12 lychees (300g), halved

1 Stir the water and sugar in medium saucepan over high heat until sugar dissolves; bring to a boil. Reduce heat; simmer, uncovered, without stirring, 5 minutes. Split vanilla bean in half lengthways; scrape seeds into pan. Add vanilla pod, ginger and star anise; simmer, uncovered, 10 minutes or until syrup thickens. Discard pod; cool to room temperature. Stir in rind, juice and mint.

2 Combine remaining ingredients in large bowl. Pour syrup over fruit; stir gently to combine. Refrigerate fruit salad, covered, until cold.

PER SERVING 1.0g total fat (0.0g saturated); 1680kj (402 cal); 85.5g carbohydrate; 5.3g protein; 12.9g fibre

Plum and rhubarb crumble

PREPARATION TIME 15 MINUTES **COOKING TIME** 25 MINUTES **SERVES** 4

2 ½ cups (275g) coarsely chopped rhubarb

⅓ cup (75g) brown sugar

¼ cup (60ml) water

825g can dark plums in syrup, drained, halved, seeded

2 teaspoons finely grated lemon rind

CRUMBLE TOPPING

2 tablespoons brown sugar

2 tablespoons plain flour

30g butter, chopped coarsely

½ cup (45g) rolled oats

½ cup (70g) roasted hazelnuts, chopped coarsely

1 Preheat oven to moderate (180°C/160°C fan-forced). Make crumble topping.

2 Combine rhubarb, ¼ cup of the sugar and the water in medium saucepan. Bring to a boil then reduce heat; simmer, covered, 5 minutes or until rhubarb is just soft.

3 Combine plums, rhubarb, rind and remaining sugar in 1-litre (4-cup) ovenproof dish; sprinkle with crumple topping. Bake, uncovered, 25 minutes or until topping is browned lightly. Serve crumble dusted with sifted icing sugar, if desired.

CRUMBLE TOPPING Combine sugar and flour in medium bowl; rub in butter. Add oats and nuts; mix well.

☐ **PER SERVING** 18.2g total fat (4.7g saturated); 1902kj (455 cal); 62.9g carbohydrate; 6.0g protein; 7.4g fibre

For a spicy touch, add 2 teaspoons grated fresh ginger to the plums and rhubarb, and ½ teaspoon ground cinnamon to the crumble topping. Serve the crumble with crème anglaise (see page 424).

Raspberry and chocolate mousse trifle

PREPARATION TIME 30 MINUTES (PLUS REFRIGERATION TIME) **SERVES** 6

150g dark eating chocolate, chopped coarsely

½ cup (125ml) thickened cream

1 egg, separated

2 teaspoons caster sugar

85g packet raspberry jelly crystals

200g packaged sponge fingers (approximately 6)

¼ cup (60ml) coffee liqueur

1 cup (135g) raspberries

300ml thickened cream, extra

1 Stir chocolate and cream in small saucepan over low heat, without boiling, until smooth. Remove from heat; whisk in egg yolk. Transfer to medium bowl.

2 Place egg white and sugar in small bowl; beat with electric mixer until sugar dissolves. Fold egg white mixture into chocolate mixture. Refrigerate mousse 3 hours or overnight.

3 Meanwhile, make jelly according to manufacturer's instructions. Refrigerate until set to the consistency of unbeaten egg white.

4 Cut sponge fingers into 1.5cm slices. Place slices over base and around side of deep 2-litre (8-cup) large serving bowl; drizzle with liqueur. Pour jelly over sponge fingers; refrigerate until jelly sets.

5 Sprinkle half of the raspberries over jelly; spread evenly with mousse. Top with whipped extra cream and remaining raspberries. Sprinkle with chocolate shavings, if desired.

☐ **PER SERVING** 36.4g total fat (25g saturated); 2537kj (607 cal); 57g carbohydrate; 7.6g protein; 2.7g fibre

For easy service, make individual trifles in tall dessert glasses. Try making the mousse using white chocolate and ½ cup desiccated coconut.

For a really easy frozen yogurt, freeze 4 large bananas and process them in a food processor with 2 cups yogurt and 1–2 tablespoons pure maple syrup. Serve immediately or freeze for 30 minutes.

Frozen passionfruit yogurt

PREPARATION TIME 10 MINUTES (PLUS FREEZING TIME) **COOKING TIME** 5 MINUTES **SERVES** 4

½ cup (110g) caster sugar
¼ cup (60ml) water
1 teaspoon gelatine
2 cups (560g) yogurt
½ cup (125ml) passionfruit pulp

1 Stir sugar and the water in small saucepan over low heat until sugar dissolves; transfer to medium jug.
2 Sprinkle gelatine over sugar syrup; stir until gelatine dissolves.
3 Combine yogurt and pulp in jug with syrup. Pour yogurt mixture into loaf pan, cover tightly with foil; freeze 3 hours or until almost set. Scrape yogurt from bottom and sides of pan with fork; cover, return to freezer until firm.

PER SERVING 0.4g total fat (0.1g saturated); 853kj (204 cal); 37.4g carbohydrate; 9.9g protein; 4.3g fibre

---

We like the method of setting the cake in jelly as a base, but some people prefer to place the cake in the bowl, sprinkle it with orange juice or sherry, then add jelly and custard, nuts and fruit, according to the texture and flavour required. The custard can be made over direct heat (not over water) because it contains custard powder and can withstand boiling. However, a custard using eggs as a thickening agent should be made in a double saucepan or in a bowl over a saucepan of simmering water.

Classic trifle

PREPARATION TIME 25 MINUTES (PLUS REFRIGERATION AND STANDING TIME)
COOKING TIME 10 MINUTES **SERVES** 4

150g unfilled sponge cake
2 tablespoons sweet sherry
85g packet raspberry jelly crystals
1 cup (250ml) boiling water
½ cup (125ml) cold water
425g can sliced peaches, drained
½ cup (125ml) thickened cream
2 teaspoons icing sugar

CUSTARD
1¾ cups (430ml) milk
¼ cup (30g) custard powder
2 tablespoons caster sugar
¼ cup (60ml) milk, extra
1 tablespoon sweet sherry

1 Cut cake into even-sized pieces. Place in large serving dish; drizzle evenly with sherry.
2 Combine jelly crystals and the boiling water in medium jug; stir until jelly is dissolved. Stir in the cold water. Gently pour jelly over back of spoon onto cake to prevent cake breaking up. Refrigerate until set.
3 Make custard.
4 Place peaches over jelly; top with custard. Refrigerate until set. Beat cream and sugar with electric mixer in small bowl until soft peaks form; spread over trifle.

CUSTARD Place milk in medium saucepan; bring to a boil. Reduce heat. Blend custard powder and sugar with extra milk in small bowl. Gradually stir into milk in saucepan; stir over medium heat until mixture boils and thickens. Stir in sherry. Cover; stand 10 minutes.

PER SERVING 18.1g total fat (11.3g saturated); 2161kj (517 cal); 73.4g carbohydrate; 10.1g protein; 1.7g fibre

FROZEN PASSIONFRUIT YOGURT

A tip taught at technical college to aspiring chefs, which may contradict many ice-cream maker manuals, is not to chill the maker ahead of churning. Instead pour the chilled mixture into the ice-cream maker and then turn it on. This gives a much more even result, as the mixture doesn't prematurely stick to the sides of the ice-cream maker.

Vanilla ice-cream

PREPARATION TIME 15 MINUTES (PLUS REFRIGERATION AND CHURNING TIME)
COOKING TIME 10 MINUTES **SERVES** 8

2 vanilla beans, halved lengthways

1⅔ cups (410ml) milk

600ml thickened cream

8 egg yolks

¾ cup (165g) caster sugar

1 Scrape seeds from beans into medium saucepan. Add pods with milk and cream; bring just to a boil.

2 Meanwhile, whisk egg yolks and sugar in medium bowl until creamy. Gradually whisk into hot milk mixture; stir over low heat, without boiling, until mixture thickens slightly.

3 Strain mixture into large jug or bowl; press plastic wrap over surface of custard; cool, then refrigerate 1 hour or until cold.

4 Pour mixture into an ice-cream maker, then churn according to the manufacturer's instructions. Or, transfer the mixture to a shallow cake pan, cover with foil and freeze until almost firm. Place ice-cream in large bowl; chop coarsely. Beat ice-cream with an electric mixer until smooth. Pour into deep cake pan; freeze until firm. Repeat twice.

PER SERVING 35.5g total fat (21.4g saturated); 1856kj (444 cal); 25.5g carbohydrate; 6.5g protein; 0g fibre

It's best to freeze ice-cream as quickly as possible. To do this use, use a metal cake pan or two (plastic will not freeze ice-cream quickly) and cover the pans with foil.

STRAWBERRY Blend or process 250g strawberries until smooth. Stir in at the end of step 3.

PER SERVING 35.6g total fat (21.4g saturated); 1885kj (451 cal); 26.3g carbohydrate; 7g protein; 0.7g fibre

CHOCOLATE MALT Open a small section of one end of 165g packet of chocolate-covered malt balls; use a rolling pin to crush coarsely. Stir in at the end of step 3 with ¼ cup malted milk powder.

PER SERVING 40.4g total fat (24.3g saturated); 2278kj (545 cal); 38.6g carbohydrate; 8g protein; 0.2g fibre

BANANA, MAPLE AND MACADAMIA Stir in 1 cup roasted coarsely chopped macadamias, 2 coarsely chopped medium bananas and ¼ cup pure maple syrup at the end of step 3.

PER SERVING 48.9g total fat (23.2g saturated); 2617kj (626 cal); 38.7g carbohydrate; 8.2g protein; 1.7g fibre

All the topping recipes will serve four people.

PISTACHIO PRALINE TOPPING

Preheat oven to hot (220°C/200°C fan-forced). Sprinkle ¼ cup caster sugar evenly over baking-paper-lined oven tray, then place in oven about 8 minutes or until sugar just becomes a light golden-brown toffee. Remove from oven; sprinkle 1 tablespoon roasted coarsely chopped shelled pistachios over hot toffee. Cool completely, then break the praline into bits. Blend or process until praline pieces resemble breadcrumbs. Serve spooned over vanilla ice-cream.

PER SERVING 36.2g total fat (21.4g saturated); 2002kj (479 cal); 32.6g carbohydrate; 6.7g protein; 0.1g fibre

MIXED BERRY SAUCE TOPPING

Stir ½ cup cream and ¼ cup firmly packed brown sugar in medium saucepan over heat until sugar dissolves. Add 1 cup frozen mixed berries; cook, stirring, 2 minutes. Cool 10 minutes before spooning over vanilla ice-cream.

PER SERVING 42.4g total fat (25.8g saturated); 2253kj (539 cal); 33g carbohydrate; 7g protein; 1.1g fibre

ROCKY ROAD TOPPING

Combine 2 coarsely chopped 55g Cherry Ripe bars in medium bowl with 50g baby marshmallows and 2 tablespoons crushed roasted peanuts. Serve spooned over vanilla ice-cream; drizzle with ¼ cup chocolate Ice Magic.

PER SERVING 6.2g total fat (3.4g saturated); 451kj (108 cal); 11.5g carbohydrate; 1.7g protein; 0.5g fibre

---

Lemon curd crepe cake

Crepes are the thin, delicate French version of the pancake. They are exquisite simply sprinkled with sugar and lemon juice and rolled up, or folded around stewed fruit and other sweet fillings, or savoury fillings such as creamed seafood or mushrooms.

PREPARATION TIME 30 MINUTES (PLUS REFRIGERATION AND STANDING TIME)
COOKING TIME 40 MINUTES **SERVES** 10

- ¾ cup (110g) plain flour
- 3 eggs
- 1 tablespoon vegetable oil
- 1 ⅓ cups (330ml) milk
- 2 teaspoons finely grated lemon rind
- ¾ cup (180ml) lemon juice
- 1 ½ cups (330g) caster sugar
- 6 eggs, beaten lightly, extra
- 125g butter, chopped
- 2 teaspoons gelatine
- 2 tablespoons water

1 Line base and side of deep 20cm-round cake pan with plastic wrap.

2 Sift flour into medium bowl; make well in centre. Gradually whisk in combined eggs, oil and milk; strain batter into large jug. Cover; stand crepe batter 30 minutes.

3 Heat greased crepe pan or small heavy-based frying pan over high heat; pour about 2 tablespoons of the batter into pan, tilting pan so batter coats base evenly. Cook, over low heat, loosening edge with spatula until crepe is browned lightly. Turn crepe; brown other side. Remove from pan; repeat with remaining batter to make 12 crepes.

4 Combine rind, juice, sugar, strained extra egg and butter in large heatproof bowl. Place bowl over large saucepan of simmering water; cook, stirring, about 15 minutes or until lemon curd coats the back of a spoon.

5 Sprinkle gelatine over the water in small heatproof jug. Stand jug in small saucepan of simmering water; stir until gelatine dissolves. Stir gelatine mixture into warm lemon curd.

6 Place one crepe in pan; spread with ¼ cup of the lemon curd. Continue layering with remaining crepes and curd, finishing with crepe. Cover; refrigerate overnight or until firm.

PER SERVING 18.3g total fat (9.3g saturated); 1568kj (375 cal); 43.3g carbohydrate; 9.1g protein; 0.5g fibre

AFTER-DINNER TREATS

After-dinner Treats

Confections like these are best made when you are feeling unhurried enough to take care over their decorative looks – shaping truffles and piping meringues just so, and cutting nougat, fudge, caramel chews or coconut ice into clean, precise squares. You can schedule this at any time up to a week before they are needed, then store them in airtight containers with baking paper between the layers. Be sure that they are all completely cool before storing.

SUGAR

- If boiling sugar with other ingredients, you need a candy thermometer to ensure the mixture reaches the right temperature to give the firm, fine-grained texture required. Choose a thermometer that is easy to handle when dealing with hot mixtures. It should have a stainless steel body and an adjustable clip or hook enabling it to be attached to your pan. The most accurate ones hold the bulb securely up and away from the pan's base. Test your thermometer first by placing it in a small saucepan of cold water; bring the water to the boil – an accurate thermometer will display 100°C. If the reading is higher or lower, take this difference into account when testing whatever you're cooking. Read the temperature with your eyes at the same level as the mercury; looking from a different angle can result in an inaccurate reading. Watch the temperature closely once it reaches 90°C as it can escalate quite quickly. Don't allow the thermometer to sit in the mixture after it has reached the desired temperature; take it out, put it in a saucepan of boiling water, remove from the heat and leave the water to cool with the thermometer in it. Wash and dry the cold thermometer carefully, wrap in a cloth and keep it in a safe place where it won't be bumped or broken.
- If making a caramel, start with sugar mixed with a little water, or with just sugar. The purpose of the water is to melt the sugar so that it is smooth by the time the water evaporates and the sugar starts to turn into caramel. The sugar-only method is faster, the sugar-and-water method is a little more relaxing.
- **Sugar-only method:** Spread sugar fairly evenly over the base of a heavy-based frying pan and place over high heat. Do not stir, but turn the pan gently as needed to swirl the sugar for even melting and browning until it is a rich golden brown.
- **Sugar-and-water method:** Put the sugar and water specified in the recipe into a medium heavy-based saucepan and use a wooden spoon to stir constantly over high

heat, without boiling, until the sugar is completely dissolved. If any grains cling to the side of the pan or the spoon, wash them down into the syrup with a wet pastry brush. Once the sugar is dissolved, stop stirring, bring to the boil and boil rapidly, turning, until it is a rich golden brown.

- If making toffees, pour the toffee into paper patty cases in patty pans. If making nut brittle, have the nuts evenly spread on a lightly oiled oven tray, pour the toffee over the top and leave to set and cool, then break into pieces with your hands. If making praline, grind the nut brittle to a powder in a blender or food processor. When completely cooled, store in airtight screwtop jars. Do not refrigerate.

CHOCOLATE

- Use good-quality eating chocolate, not cooking chocolate or chocolate compounds unless specified. The best, from specialist chocolate or food shops, is called couverture and is expensive, though not always more so, weight for weight, than a good-quality chocolate bar.
- To melt chocolate, please see "Special techniques" on page 519.

PRESENTATION

Delicious confections deserve to be presented with flair. Crisp little paper or foil cases in petit-four size, available from specialist kitchen shops, give instant presence – the look of creations from an expensive patisserie. You might wrap coconut ice, nougat or fudge in cellophane, twisting the ends like bonbons or, if you are neat-fingered, enclose them in smooth silverfoil. Look in gift-wrap departments for silver, gold or other wraps that could make your creations look glamorous. Beautiful papers that are not suitable for wrapping because they might stick can be cut into circles or diamonds on which to place each treat.

To serve petits-fours with coffee, present them on your most elegant plate or tray – a footed, flat cake plate or a silver tray are perfect. Arrange the sweetmeats, each in its case, geometrically in rows like the treasures they are.

OTHER IDEAS

Even if you are not the neat-fingered type who delights in precision and detail, you can still make petits-fours that will be greeted with acclaim. The key is to think of everyday cakes and biscuits and take the size down. Some, such as slices, brownies and shortbreads, can be cut into petit-four-sized squares. For others, make the usual mixture but think small when you are putting them out for baking. Miniature florentines, gingernuts, chocolate chip cookies and anzacs are fun and delicious with coffee. You might make miniature lamingtons, too, by cutting day-old sponge-cake into bite-sized cubes and dipping them in thin chocolate icing, then rolling in desiccated coconut.

Easy ideas that don't call for skill or cooking include dipping perfect strawberries with their green hulls still on, cherries with their stems still on, orange or mandarin segments or strips of candied citrus peel into melted chocolate. Dip them about halfway in, place on a tray lined with aluminium foil and refrigerate until wanted. Serve in petit-four cases. Bite-sized pieces of glacé fruit such as apricot, pineapple, peach or pear also look elegant in petit-four cases.

For gifts, cut the rocky road into squares and place in small lined boxes or in clear cellophane bags with rose and pale green ribbons to complement the colour of the turkish delight and pistachios.

Gourmet rocky road

PREPARATION TIME 20 MINUTES (PLUS REFRIGERATION TIME) **SERVES** 30

300g marshmallows with roasted coconut, chopped coarsely

400g turkish delight, chopped coarsely

¼ cup (40g) roasted blanched almonds, chopped coarsely

½ cup (70g) roasted shelled pistachios

450g white eating chocolate, melted

1 Grease two 8cm x 26cm bar cake pans; line base and sides with baking paper, extending paper 5cm above long sides.

2 Combine marshmallow, turkish delight and nuts in large bowl. Working quickly, stir in chocolate; spread mixture into pans, push mixture down firmly to flatten top. Refrigerate until set.

PER PIECE 6.9g total fat (3.3g saturated); 744kj (178 cal); 26.5g carbohydrate; 2.3g protein; 0.3g fibre

---

These are perfect for summer parties as they are lovely and light. If you want to make them ahead and store them, leave the meringues unfilled, then sandwich them together just before they're needed.

Meringue kisses with passionfruit cream

PREPARATION TIME 25 MINUTES (PLUS COOLING TIME) **COOKING TIME** 30 MINUTES **MAKES** 35

1 egg white

½ teaspoon white vinegar

⅓ cup (75g) caster sugar

1 teaspoon icing sugar

¼ cup (60ml) thickened cream

1 tablespoon icing sugar, extra

1 tablespoon passionfruit pulp

1 Preheat oven to very slow (120°C/100°C fan-forced). Grease oven trays; dust with cornflour, shake off excess.

2 Beat egg white, vinegar and caster sugar in small bowl with electric mixer 10 minutes or until sugar is dissolved; fold in sifted icing sugar.

3 Place meringue mixture in piping bag fitted with small plain tube; pipe 1.5cm rounds 3cm apart on trays. Bake, uncovered, about 30 minutes or until crisp and dry. Cool meringues on trays.

4 Beat cream with 2 teaspoons of the extra sifted icing sugar in small bowl with electric mixer until firm peaks form. Stir in passionfruit.

5 Sandwich meringues with passionfruit cream; dust with remaining sifted icing sugar.

PER KISS 0.6g total fat (0.4g saturated); 71kj (17 cal); 2.6g carbohydrate; 0.2g protein; 0.1g fibre

Chocolate peppermint squares

PREPARATION TIME 20 MINUTES (PLUS REFRIGERATION TIME) **COOKING TIME** 15 MINUTES **MAKES** 30

These little squares are perfect with a cup of freshly brewed coffee.

- 2⅓ cups (350g) milk chocolate Melts
- 2 teaspoons vegetable oil
- ¼ cup (60ml) cream
- 2 x 35g crispy peppermint chocolate bars, chopped finely

1 Grease and line 8cm x 26cm bar cake pan with baking paper.
2 Combine ⅔ cup of the chocolate Melts and half of the oil in small heatproof bowl; place bowl over small saucepan of simmering water, stirring until chocolate melts. Using metal spatula, spread chocolate mixture over base of pan. Refrigerate until set.
3 Place cream and 1 cup of the remaining chocolate Melts in small saucepan; stir over low heat until smooth. Cool 5 minutes, then stir chocolate bar into chocolate cream mixture. Using metal spatula, spread peppermint chocolate mixture over the set chocolate base; refrigerate 20 minutes.
4 Place remaining chocolate Melts and remaining oil in small heatproof bowl; place bowl over small saucepan of simmering water, stirring until chocolate melts. Using metal spatula, spread chocolate mixture smoothly over the set peppermint chocolate; refrigerate 1 hour or overnight.
5 Dip small sharp knife in hot water, wipe dry; while knife is still warm, cut chocolate peppermint into 2.5cm squares.

PER SQUARE 5.3g total fat (3.3g saturated); 351kj (84 cal); 8.2g carbohydrate; 0.8g protein; 0.1g fibre

---

Hazelnut and pine nut brittle

PREPARATION TIME 10 MINUTES (PLUS COOLING TIME) **COOKING TIME** 15 MINUTES **SERVES** 16

Nut brittle is great broken into shards and stuck into an ice-cream dessert as a jaunty garnish. It can also be pulverised in a food processor to make praline to sprinkle over custards and other creamy desserts. Keep brittle or praline in an airtight jar.

- 2 sheets rice paper, optional
- 2 cups (440g) caster sugar
- ¼ teaspoon cream of tartar
- ½ cup (125ml) water
- 2 tablespoons golden syrup
- 60g butter, chopped
- ⅓ cup (50g) roasted pine nuts
- 1 cup (140g) roasted hazelnuts
- ¼ cup (35g) roasted sesame seeds
- ½ teaspoon bicarbonate of soda

1 Line tray with baking paper, cover with rice paper.
2 Stir sugar, cream of tartar and the water in medium saucepan over low heat, without boiling, until sugar dissolves; bring to a boil. Boil, uncovered, without stirring, about 10 minutes or until mixture turns golden brown.
3 Remove from heat; stir in golden syrup and butter. Return pan to heat; bring to a boil. Boil, uncovered, 1 minute. Remove from heat; stir in nuts, sesame seeds and soda.
4 Pour mixture onto rice paper; cool. Break into pieces.

PER SERVING 11.9g total fat (2.5g saturated); 1012kj (242 cal); 30.8g carbohydrate; 2.2g protein; 1.3g fibre

Mini florentines are the perfect home-made gift to contribute to a dinner party. People love them for their chewy, crunchy topping and chocolate bottoms as a sweet treat after dinner.

Mini florentines

PREPARATION TIME 10 MINUTES **COOKING TIME** 5 MINUTES **MAKES** 45

¾ cup (120g) sultanas
2 cups (80g) corn flakes
¾ cup (60g) flaked almonds, roasted
½ cup (100g) red glacé cherries, quartered
⅔ cup (160ml) sweetened condensed milk
60g white eating chocolate, melted
60g dark eating chocolate, melted

1 Preheat oven to moderate (180°C/160°C fan-forced). Line two oven trays with baking paper.
2 Combine sultanas, corn flakes, nuts, cherries and milk in medium bowl. Drop heaped teaspoons of the mixture 5cm apart onto trays. Bake, uncovered, about 5 minutes or until browned lightly. Cool on trays.
3 Spread half of the bases with white chocolate and remaining half with dark chocolate; run fork through chocolate to make waves. Allow chocolate to set at room temperature.

PER FLORENTINE 1.8g total fat (0.8g saturated); 242kj (58 cal); 9.2g carbohydrate; 1.1g protein; 0.4g fibre

---

For the best results use a candy thermometer to get the correct consistency. It is important to cool the nougat at room temperature – refrigeration causes it to soften.

Almond nougat

PREPARATION TIME 10 MINUTES (PLUS STANDING TIME) **COOKING TIME** 30 MINUTES **MAKES** 50

2 sheets rice paper
½ cup (175g) honey
1 ⅓ cups (300g) caster sugar
2 tablespoons water
1 egg white
2 cups (320g) roasted blanched almonds

1 Lightly grease deep 15cm-square cake pan. Trim one sheet of rice paper into 15cm square; line base of pan.
2 Stir honey, sugar and the water in small saucepan over heat, without boiling, until sugar dissolves. Using pastry brush dipped in hot water, brush down side of pan to dissolve any sugar crystals; bring to a boil. Boil, uncovered, without stirring, about 10 minutes or until syrup reaches 164°C on candy thermometer; remove pan immediately from heat. Place thermometer in pan of boiling water; remove from heat to allow thermometer to gradually decrease in temperature.
3 Beat egg white in small heatproof bowl with electric mixer until soft peaks form. With motor operating, add hot syrup to egg white in thin, steady stream.
4 Stir almonds into egg white mixture; spoon into pan. Press mixture firmly into pan. Cut remaining sheet of rice paper large enough to cover top of nougat; press lightly onto nougat. Stand about 2 hours or until cool; cut into 2cm squares.

PER PIECE 3.6g total fat (0.2g saturated); 322kj (77 cal); 9.3g carbohydrate; 1.4g protein; 0.6g fibre

MINI FLORENTINES

Truffles

Use good-quality chocolate, and roll rounded teaspoons of mixture to make even-sized truffles. Each recipe makes 30.

WHITE CHOCOLATE AND PISTACHIO
Melt 300g white chocolate and ⅓ cup cream in a saucepan; stir over low heat until smooth. Refrigerate overnight. Roll the mixture into balls; roll in ¾ cup chopped pistachios.

WHITE CHOCOLATE AND ALMOND
Melt 250g white chocolate and ¼ cup cream in a saucepan. Stir in ½ cup slivered almonds and 1 tablespoon almond liqueur; refrigerate overnight. Roll the mixture into balls; roll in 250g melted white chocolate Melts.

DARK CHOCOLATE AND GINGER
Melt 200g dark chocolate and ¼ cup cream in a saucepan. Stir in ½ cup chopped glacé ginger; refrigerate overnight. Roll the mixture into balls; roll in cocoa powder.

CRAISIN, PORT AND CHOCOLATE
Melt 200g dark chocolate and ¼ cup cream in a small saucepan. Stir in 2 tablespoons port and ⅓ cup chopped craisins; refrigerate overnight. Roll into balls; roll in 300g melted dark chocolate.

WHITE CHOCOLATE AND PINEAPPLE
Melt 250g white chocolate and ¼ cup cream in a small saucepan. Stir in ⅓ cup chopped glacé pineapple and 1 tablespoon Malibu; refrigerate overnight. Roll into balls; roll in 250g melted white chocolate Melts and then in 1 cup roasted desiccated coconut.

WHITE CHOC, LEMON AND LIME
Melt 360g white chocolate, ½ cup coconut cream and 2 teaspoons each finely grated lemon and lime rind in a small saucepan. Refrigerate overnight. Roll the mixture into balls; roll in 1 cup shredded coconut.

RUM AND RAISIN
Melt 200g dark chocolate and ¼ cup cream in a saucepan. Stir in 1 tablespoon rum and ⅓ cup chopped raisins; refrigerate overnight. Roll into balls; roll in melted dark chocolate.

CHOCOLATE AND PEPPERMINT
Melt 200g milk chocolate and ¼ cup cream in a small saucepan. Stir in two chopped crispy peppermint chocolate bars; refrigerate overnight. Roll the mixture into balls; roll in 300g melted milk chocolate.

APRICOT AND WHITE CHOCOLATE
Combine 1 cup chopped dried apricots, 1 cup desiccated coconut and ⅓ cup condensed milk in a bowl; refrigerate 1 hour. Roll into balls; drizzle with melted white chocolate Melts.

ORANGE AND ALMOND
Melt 250g dark chocolate and ⅓ cup cream in a small saucepan. Stir in 2 teaspoons finely grated orange rind and 1 tablespoon orange liqueur; refrigerate overnight. Roll into balls; roll in 1 cup chopped vienna almonds.

COFFEE AND MILK CHOCOLATE
Melt 250g milk chocolate and ⅓ cup cream in a small saucepan; stir over low heat until smooth. Stir in 2 tablespoons coffee liqueur; refrigerate overnight. Roll the mixture into balls; roll in ¼ cup cocoa powder.

PEANUT AND MILK CHOCOLATE
Melt 200g milk chocolate and ¼ cup cream in a small saucepan. Stir in ¼ cup unsalted crunchy peanut butter; refrigerate overnight. Roll into balls; roll in ¾ cup crushed nuts.

1

2

3

4

Caramel chews

PREPARATION TIME 10 MINUTES **COOKING TIME** 15 MINUTES **MAKES** 50

You'll know that the caramel is ready to be removed from the heat when the mixture starts to come away from the base and side of the saucepan.

125g butter, chopped

395g can sweetened condensed milk

2 tablespoons honey

¾ cup (165g) firmly packed brown sugar

100g dark eating chocolate, melted

¼ cup (35g) roasted hazelnuts, chopped coarsely

1 Grease deep 15cm-square cake pan; line base and sides with baking paper.

2 Stir butter, milk, honey and sugar in medium saucepan over low heat, without boiling, until sugar dissolves. Increase heat; cook, stirring, about 10 minutes or until glossy and caramel in colour.

3 Pour caramel into pan; cool. Remove caramel from pan. Spread with chocolate; top with nuts. Allow chocolate to set at room temperature; cut into small squares to serve.

☐ **PER CHEW** 3.4g total fat (2.1g saturated); 309kj (74 cal); 9.9g carbohydrate; 1.0g protein; 0.2g fibre

Chocolate nut clusters

PREPARATION TIME 20 MINUTES (PLUS REFRIGERATION TIME) **COOKING TIME** 10 MINUTES **MAKES** 24

For a festive twist, use white chocolate instead of milk, halved red glacé cherries instead of sultanas, and sprinkle the clusters with desiccated coconut.

¼ cup (35g) shelled unsalted pistachios

¼ cup (35g) slivered almonds

1 cup (150g) milk chocolate Melts

½ cup (80g) sultanas

1 Line oven tray with baking paper.

2 Heat small heavy-based frying pan; roast nuts, stirring constantly, until browned lightly (take care not to scorch nuts because they burn easily). Remove nuts from pan.

3 Place chocolate in small heatproof bowl; place bowl over small saucepan of simmering water, stirring until chocolate melts. Stir nuts and sultanas into chocolate.

4 Drop heaped teaspoons of the chocolate mixture; drop onto tray. Refrigerate, uncovered, until chocolate sets.

☐ **PER CLUSTER** 3.6g total fat (1.4g saturated); 259kj (62 cal); 6.2g carbohydrate; 1.1g protein; 0.5g fibre

1 CARAMEL CHEWS **2** CHOCOLATE NUT CLUSTERS **3** BRANDY SNAPS [P 636] **4** CHOCOLATE CREAM FUDGE [P 636]

Make a couple of snaps first to establish a precise cooking time, then proceed with the remaining mixture, cooking about four snaps on a tray at a time. Once you become confident, you can bake several trays at staggered times.

Brandy snaps

PREPARATION TIME 25 MINUTES **COOKING TIME** 15 MINUTES **MAKES** 20

60g butter

⅓ cup (75g) firmly packed brown sugar

2 tablespoons golden syrup

½ teaspoon ground ginger

½ cup (75g) plain flour

½ teaspoon lemon juice

300ml thickened cream, whipped

1 Preheat oven to moderate (180°C/160°C fan-forced). Grease oven trays.

2 Stir butter, sugar, syrup and ginger in medium saucepan over low heat, without boiling, until butter is melted. Remove from heat; stir in sifted flour and juice.

3 Drop rounded teaspoons of mixture 6cm apart onto trays. Bake, uncovered, about 7 minutes or until snaps are bubbling and golden brown; remove from oven.

4 Slide a spatula under each snap, then quickly shape into a cone. Place snaps on wire rack to cool. Fill with whipped cream just before serving.

PER BRANDY SNAP 10.6g total fat (7.0g saturated); 560kj (134 cal); 9.1g carbohydrate; 0.8g protein; 0.1g fibre

---

It is important to use a candy thermometer when making the fudge in order to get the correct consistency. Glucose syrup, also known as liquid glucose, is made from wheat starch. It is mostly used in confectionery and is available at health-food shops and supermarkets.

Chocolate cream fudge

PREPARATION TIME 5 MINUTES (PLUS STANDING TIME) **COOKING TIME** 40 MINUTES **MAKES** 50

1½ cups (330g) caster sugar

½ cup (110g) firmly packed brown sugar

60g dark eating chocolate, chopped coarsely

2 tablespoons glucose syrup

½ cup (125ml) cream

¼ cup (60ml) milk

40g butter

1 Grease deep 15cm-square cake pan.

2 Stir sugars, chocolate, syrup, cream and milk in small saucepan over low heat, without boiling, until sugar dissolves. Using pastry brush dipped in hot water, brush down side of pan to dissolve any sugar crystals; bring to a boil. Boil, uncovered, without stirring, about 10 minutes or until syrup reaches 116°C on candy thermometer. Remove pan immediately from heat, leaving candy thermometer in syrup; add butter, do not stir. Cool fudge, about 20 minutes or until syrup drops to 40°C on candy thermometer. Remove thermometer.

3 Stir fudge with wooden spoon about 10 minutes or until a small amount dropped from the spoon holds its shape. Spread fudge into pan; cover with foil. Stand at room temperature about 3 hours or until fudge sets. Turn fudge out of pan; trim edges. Cut into 2cm squares.

PER PIECE 2.2g total fat (1.5g saturated); 259kj (62 cal); 10.4g carbohydrate; 0.1g protein; 0.1g fibre

Coconut ice

PREPARATION TIME 10 MINUTES (PLUS REFRIGERATION TIME) **MAKES** 36

One of Australia's favourite sweets, it is quick and easy, and needs no cooking – perfect for children to make.

5¼ cups (840g) icing sugar
2½ cups (200g) desiccated coconut
395g can sweetened condensed milk
1 egg white, beaten lightly
pink food colouring

1 Line deep 19cm-square cake pan with baking paper.
2 Sift icing sugar into large bowl. Add coconut, then milk and egg white; stir to combine.
3 Press half of the mixture into pan. Tint remaining mixture pink; press evenly over first layer. Cover; refrigerate several hours before cutting into squares.

PER PIECE 4.0g total fat (3.5g saturated); 690kj (165 cal); 29.9g carbohydrate; 1.5g protein; 0.8g fibre

---

Toasted marshmallows

PREPARATION TIME 20 MINUTES (PLUS COOLING AND REFRIGERATION TIME)
COOKING TIME 30 MINUTES **MAKES** 36

Boiling the gelatine for this recipe is probably the only time you would ever be asked to do so; this technique is usually considered a culinary no-no. Be prepared to beat the mixture for at least 10 minutes, until it holds its own shape and is at room temperature. The marshmallow works well cut into different shapes: try using heart-shaped cutters for Valentines or star-shaped cutters for Christmas. Spray the cutters with vegetable oil before using.

⅓ cup (55g) gelatine
1 cup (250ml) cold water
4 cups (880g) caster sugar
2 cups (500ml) boiling water
2 teaspoons vanilla extract
2 teaspoons lemon juice
3⅓ cups (250g) shredded coconut

1 Combine gelatine and the cold water in small jug.
2 Stir sugar and the boiling water in large saucepan over low heat until sugar dissolves; bring to a boil. Stir in gelatine mixture; boil, uncovered, 20 minutes. Cool 20 minutes; pour into large bowl.
3 Beat sugar mixture, extract and juice with electric mixer until very thick and white. Pour into two deep 19cm-square cake pans which have been rinsed out with cold water. Refrigerate until set.
4 Stir coconut in large heavy-based frying pan over heat until browned lightly. Remove from pan immediately; cool. Cut marshmallow into squares with wet knife while still in the pan. Lift out with small spatula; toss in toasted coconut.

PER PIECE 4.5g total fat (4.0g saturated); 627kj (150 cal); 24.9g carbohydrate; 1.7g protein; 1.0g fibre

This traditional rich Italian Christmas cake originates in the Tuscan city of Siena. Panforte was originally a white cake; the cocoa and chocolate were a later addition. The classic way to serve it is in thin slices or small fingers, with a glass of vin santo.

Chocolate panforte

PREPARATION TIME 15 MINUTES **COOKING TIME** 55 MINUTES **SERVES** 30

- 2 sheets rice paper
- ¾ cup (110g) plain flour
- 2 tablespoons cocoa powder
- ½ teaspoon ground cinnamon
- ½ teaspoon ground ginger
- ½ cup (150g) coarsely chopped glacé figs
- ½ cup (70g) dates, halved
- ½ cup (125g) coarsely chopped glacé peaches
- ¼ cup (50g) red glacé cherries, halved
- ¼ cup (50g) green glacé cherries, halved
- ½ cup (80g) roasted blanched almonds
- ½ cup (75g) roasted unsalted cashews,
- ½ cup (70g) roasted hazelnuts
- ½ cup (70g) roasted macadamias
- ⅓ cup (115g) honey
- ⅓ cup (75g) caster sugar
- ⅓ cup (75g) firmly packed brown sugar
- 2 tablespoons water
- 100g dark eating chocolate, melted

1 Preheat oven to moderately slow (170°C/150°C fan-forced). Grease 20cm sandwich pan; line base with rice paper sheets.

2 Sift flour, cocoa and spices into large bowl; stir in fruit and nuts. Stir honey, sugars and the water in small saucepan over low heat, without boiling, until sugar dissolves. Simmer; uncovered, without stirring, 5 minutes. Pour hot syrup then chocolate into nut mixture; stir until well combined. Press mixture firmly into pan. Bake, uncovered, 45 minutes; cool in pan.

3 Remove panforte from pan; wrap in foil. Stand overnight; cut into thin wedges to serve.

PER PIECE 7.1g total fat (1.6g saturated); 694kj (166 cal); 21.6g carbohydrate; 2.6g protein; 2.4g fibre

---

The toffee will start to liquidise if it sits too long on the cream-cheese filling, so add it no more than an hour ahead. If this is inconvenient, make all chocolate-drizzled dates or simply omit the toppings – the dates will be delicious anyway.

Cream cheese-filled brandied dates

PREPARATION TIME 30 MINUTES (PLUS STANDING TIME) **COOKING TIME** 15 MINUTES **MAKES** 24

- 24 fresh dates (600g)
- ¼ cup (60ml) brandy
- 125g packaged cream cheese, softened
- 1 tablespoon icing sugar
- ¼ cup (35g) roasted hazelnuts, chopped finely
- ½ cup (110g) caster sugar
- ¼ cup (60ml) water
- 50g dark eating chocolate, melted

1 Make a shallow cut lengthways in each date (do not cut through); discard seeds. Combine dates in medium bowl with brandy; stand 15 minutes.

2 Meanwhile, beat cheese and icing sugar in small bowl with wooden spoon; stir in nuts.

3 Drain brandy from dates into cheese mixture; stir until filling is smooth.

4 Spoon filling into piping bag fitted with small plain tube; pipe filling into date cavities.

5 Stir caster sugar and the water in small saucepan over low heat, without boiling, until sugar dissolves; bring to a boil. Reduce heat; simmer, uncovered, without stirring, until mixture is golden in colour. Remove from heat; stand until bubbles subside.
6 Drizzle half of the dates with toffee and remaining dates with chocolate; allow to set at room temperature.

☐ **PER DATE** 3.3g total fat (1.7g saturated); 368kj (88 cal); 11.9g carbohydrate; 0.9g protein; 1.0g fibre

---

Turkish delight

PREPARATION TIME 25 MINUTES (PLUS STANDING TIME) **COOKING TIME** 30 MINUTES **MAKES** 36

- 2 tablespoons gelatine
- ¼ cup (60ml) water
- ¾ cup (180ml) water, extra
- 3 cups (660g) white sugar
- ⅔ cup (100g) cornflour
- ¼ cup (60ml) rosewater
- red food colouring
- 2 cups (320g) icing sugar

1 Lightly oil deep 19cm-square cake pan.
2 Sprinkle gelatine over the water in small heatproof bowl; stand bowl in small saucepan of simmering water, stir until gelatine dissolves.
3 Reserve 1 tablespoon from the extra water. Stir remaining extra water and sugar in medium saucepan over low heat, without boiling, until sugar dissolves. Using pastry brush dipped in hot water, brush down side of pan to dissolve any sugar crystals; bring to a boil. Boil, uncovered, until temperature reaches 116°C on candy thermometer. Reduce heat; simmer, uncovered, 5 minutes, without stirring, regulating heat to maintain temperature at 116°C. Remove from heat.
4 Blend cornflour with the reserved 1 tablespoon water, gelatine mixture, rosewater and a few drops of food colouring until smooth. Stir into sugar syrup off heat (if mixture begins to set, stand bowl over pan of simmering water until softened). Return to heat; simmer, stirring, about 3 minutes or until mixture is opaque. Strain mixture into pan, skim any scum from surface; stand overnight at room temperature.
5 Turn turkish delight onto board dusted heavily with sifted icing sugar, cut into squares with a knife dipped in icing sugar. Roll shapes in sifted icing sugar.

☐ **PER PIECE** 0.0g total fat (0.0g saturated); 518kj (124 cal); 29.7g carbohydrate; 0.6g protein; 0.0g fibre

ORANGE VARIATION Use plain water in place of the rosewater and orange food colouring instead of red. Just before straining sugar syrup and cornflour mixture into pan, stir in orange essence to taste.

☐ **PER PIECE** 0.0g total fat (0.0g saturated); 514kj (123 cal); 29.7g carbohydrate; 0.6g protein; 0.0g fibre

MINT VARIATION Use plain water in place of the rosewater and green food colouring instead of red. Just before straining sugar syrup and cornflour mixture into pan, stir in peppermint essence to taste.

☐ **PER PIECE** 0.0g total fat (0.0g saturated); 514kj (123 cal); 29.7g carbohydrate; 0.6g protein; 0.0g fibre

Do not try this recipe without a candy thermometer (available from specialty cookware stores); it's just too hard. Make sure you use a cornflour based on corn, not wheat. Rosewater is available from health-food shops and some supermarkets. This recipe can be made 4 days ahead; store well coated with icing sugar in an airtight container at room temperature.

To Weigh 4 lbs. by ½ oz.
CULINARY
Persinware

Glossary

ACIDULATED WATER cold water into which white vinegar or lemon juice/pulp has been added, at about a proportion of 1 tablespoon acid per litre water, to prevent the cut surfaces of foods, such as artichokes, apples, pears and bananas from discolouring.

AIOLI home-made garlic mayonnaise from the south of France served traditionally with seafood stews, like bouillabaisse, or crudités. Aïoli is a love-it or hate-it food, and has enflamed the passions of so many people around the world that they hold annual aïoli festivals at garlic harvest time.

ALLSPICE also known as pimento or jamaican pepper; so-named because it tastes like a combination of nutmeg, cumin, clove and cinnamon. Available whole (a dark-brown berry the size of a pea) or ground, and used in both sweet and savoury dishes.

ALMONDS flat, pointy-tipped nuts having a pitted brown shell enclosing a creamy white kernel which is covered by a brown skin; there are two types, sweet and bitter, with the former being the most readily available and most used in cooking.

blanched brown skins removed.

essence made with almond oil and alcohol or another agent. *see essence/extract*

flaked paper-thin slices.

meal also known as ground almonds; nuts are powdered to a coarse flour texture for use in baking or as a thickening agent.

slivered small pieces cut lengthways.

vienna toffee-coated almonds.

ANGOSTURA AROMATIC BITTERS brand-name of a type of aromatic bitters, used mainly in drinks, from aperitifs and cocktails to digestifs, but also desserts and savoury dishes. Named after the Venezuelan town where it originated, it is a blend of a reported forty herbs and spices, and is arguably the most widely distributed bar item in the world.

APPLE CIDER, SPARKLING unfermented non-alcoholic type of apple juice with sugar added to make it effervesce.

ARROWROOT a starch made from the rhizome of a Central American plant, used mostly as a thickening agent. *Cornflour* can be substituted but does not make as clear a glaze and imparts its own taste.

ARTICHOKES

globe large flower-bud of a member of the thistle family; it has tough petal-like leaves, and is edible in part when cooked.

hearts tender centre of the globe artichoke; can be harvested from the plant after the prickly choke is removed. Cooked hearts can be bought from delicatessens or canned in brine.

jerusalem neither from Jerusalem nor an artichoke, this crunchy brown-skinned tuber tastes a bit like a water chestnut and belongs to the sunflower family. Eat raw in salads or cooked like potatoes.

BACON RASHERS also known as bacon slices; made from cured and smoked pork side. *Middle rashers* are thin strips of belly pork having a lean, rather round piece of loin at one end; *streaky bacon* is the same cut minus the round loin section.

BAGEL small ring-shaped bread roll; yeast-based but egg-less, with a dense, chewy texture and shiny crust. A true bagel is boiled in water before it's baked.

BAKE BLIND a cooking term to describe baking a pie shell or pastry case before filling is added. If a filling does not need to be baked or is very wet, it may be necessary to "blind bake" the unfilled shell. To bake blind, ease the pastry into a pan or dish, place on an oven tray; line the pastry with baking paper then fill with dried beans, uncooked rice or "baking beans" (also called pie weights). Bake according to the recipe's directions then cool before adding the filling.

BAKING PAPER also known as parchment, silicon paper or non-stick baking paper; not to be confused with greaseproof or waxed paper. Used to line pans before cooking and baking; also to make piping bags.

BAKING POWDER a raising agent consisting mainly of two parts cream of tartar to one part bicarbonate of soda (baking soda). The acid and alkaline combination, when moistened and heated, gives off carbon dioxide which aerates and lightens a mixture during baking.

BAMBOO SHOOTS tender, pale yellow, edible first-growth of the bamboo plant; add crunch and fibre as well as a certain distinctive sweetness to a dish. Available fresh in Asian greengrocers, in season, but usually purchased canned; these must be drained and rinsed before use. There are many different types and sizes of bamboo shoots but the largest is most commonly canned, sliced and used in stir-fries.

BAMBOO SKEWERS used for cocktail food and satay instead of metal skewers; should be soaked in water for 1 hour before use to help prevent splintering or scorching during cooking. Available in several different lengths.

BAMBOO STEAMERS lattice-woven, multi-layered steamers with tight-fitting lids. Inexpensive and available in various sizes from Asian and specialty cookware shops, they can be used for steaming anything from dim sum and vegetables to elaborate fish and meat dishes.

BANANA LEAVES used to line steamers and cook food "en papillote" (enclosed, wrapped); sold in bundles in Asian food shops, greengrocers and supermarkets. Leaves are cut, on both sides of the centre stem, into the required sized pieces then immersed in hot water or held over a flame until pliable enough to wrap around or fold over food; they are secured with kitchen string, toothpicks or bamboo skewers before barbecuing or steaming.

BARBECUE SAUCE spicy, tomato-based sauce used to marinate, baste or as an accompaniment.

BARLEY a nutritious grain used in soups and stews. Hulled barley, the least processed form of barley, is high in fibre. Pearl barley has had the husk removed then been steamed and polished so that only the"pearl" of the original grain remains, much the same as white rice.

BASIL

holy also known as kra pao or hot basil; different from thai and sweet basil, having an almost hot, spicy flavour similar to clove. Used in many Thai dishes, especially curries; distinguished from thai basil by tiny "hairs" on its leaves and stems.

opal has large purple leaves and a sweet, almost gingery flavour. Can replace thai but not holy basil in recipes.

sweet the most common type of basil; used extensively in Italian dishes and one of the main ingredients in pesto.

thai also known as horapa; different from holy basil and sweet basil in both look and taste, having smaller leaves and purplish stems. It has a slight aniseed taste and is one of the identifying flavours of Thai food.

BAY LEAVES aromatic leaves from the bay tree available fresh or dried; used to add a strong, slightly peppery flavour to soups, stocks and casseroles.

BEAN SPROUTS also known as bean shoots; tender new growths of assorted beans and seeds germinated for consumption as sprouts. The most readily available are mung bean, soybean, alfalfa and snow pea sprouts. Sprout mixtures or tendrils are also available.

BEANS

black also known as turtle beans or black kidney beans; an earthy-flavoured dried bean completely different from the better-known Chinese black beans (which are fermented soybeans). Used mostly in Mexican, South American and Caribbean cooking, especially soups and stews.

black-eyed also known as black-eyed peas or cowpea; the dried seed of a variant of the snake or yard-long bean. Not too dissimilar to white beans in flavour; good cooked and used cold in salads.

borlotti also known as roman beans or pink beans, can be eaten fresh or dried. Interchangeable with pinto beans because of the similarity in appearance – pale pink or beige with dark red streaks. The bean of choice for frijoles refritos (refried beans).

broad also known as fava, windsor and horse beans; available dried, fresh, canned and frozen. Fresh should be peeled twice (discarding both the outer long green pod and the beige-green tough inner shell); the frozen beans have had their pods removed but the beige shell still needs removal. Good eaten raw or cooked in salads, tossed through pasta or pureed; often used in Mediterranean soups and dips.

butter also known as lima beans; large, flat, kidney-shaped bean, off-white in colour, with a mealy texture and mild taste. Available canned and dried; best used in soups or salads.

cannellini small white bean similar in appearance and flavour to other *phaseolus vulgaris* varieties (great northern, navy or haricot). Available dried or canned; used in baked beans and traditional ham and bean soup.

green also known as french or string beans (although the tough string they once had has generally been bred out of them), this long thin fresh bean is consumed in its entirety once cooked.

kidney medium-size red bean, slightly floury in texture yet sweet in flavour; sold dried or canned, it's found in bean mixes and is the bean used in chilli con carne.

pinto similar to borlotti, a plump, kidney-shaped, pinky-beige bean speckled with brown to red streaks; available canned or dried and used in Mexican cooking.

refried pinto or borlotti beans, cooked twice: first soaked and boiled, then mashed and fried (traditionally in lard). A Mexican staple, frijoles refritos (refried beans) are sold canned in supermarkets.

snake long (about 40cm), thin, round, fresh green beans, Asian in origin, with a taste similar to green or french beans. Used most frequently in stir-fries, they are also known as yard-long beans because of their (pre-metric) length.

soybean the most nutritious of all legumes; only recently embraced by the West but a staple in Asia for centuries. High in protein and low in carbohydrates, and the source of products such as tofu, soy milk, soy sauce, tamari and miso. Sometimes sold fresh as edamame; also available dried and canned.

white beans in this book, some recipes may simply call for "white beans", a generic term we use for canned or dried cannellini, haricot, navy or great northern beans which are all of the same family, *phaseolus vulgaris*.

BEEF

baby back ribs shorter and wider than spareribs; quite lean and meaty.

cheeks boneless inexpensive cut that benefits from slow cooking.

chuck inexpensive cut from the neck and shoulder area; good minced and slow-cooked.

corned beef also known as corned silverside; little fat, cut from the upper leg and cured. Sold cryovac-packed in brine.

eye-fillet tenderloin, fillet; fine texture, most expensive and extremely tender.

gravy boneless stewing beef cut from shin; slow-cooked, imbues stocks, soups and casseroles with a gelatine richness. Cut crossways, with bone in, is osso buco.

minced also known as ground beef.

new-york cut boneless striploin steak.

oxtail a flavourful cut originally from the ox but today more likely to be from any beef cattle; requires long, slow cooking so it is perfect for curries and stews.

porterhouse striploin steak, bone in.

round steak boneless cut from the tender muscle running from rump to ankle; used for stir-fries, minute steaks and pot-roasts.

rump boneless tender cut taken from the upper part of the round (hindquarter). Cut into steaks, good for barbecuing; in the piece, great as a roast.

scotch fillet cut from the muscle running behind the shoulder along the spine. Also known as cube roll, cuts include standing rib roast and rib-eye.

silverside also known as topside roast; this is the actual cut used for making corned beef.

skirt steak lean, flavourful coarse-grained cut from the inner thigh. Needs slow-cooking; good for stews or casseroles.

t-bone sirloin steak with bone in and fillet eye attached; good barbecued or grilled.

BEETROOT also known as red beets; firm, round root vegetable. Can be grated or finely chopped; boiled or steamed then diced or sliced; or roasted then mashed.

BELGIAN-STYLE WAFFLES true belgian waffles are made from a yeast dough; each waffle is sprinkled with sugar, resulting in a crisp, rich product with a slightly caramelised flavour. Available from large supermarket or delicatessens.

BESAN *see flour*

BICARBONATE OF SODA also known as baking soda; a mild alkali used as a leavening agent in baking.

BISCUITS also known as cookies; almost always an "eat-in-your-hand"-sized soft or crisp sweet cake.

BLACK BEAN SAUCE an Asian cooking sauce made from salted and fermented soybeans, spices and wheat flour; used most often in stir-fries.

BLANCHING a cooking term to describe the act of plunging an ingredient, usually vegetable, briefly into boiling water, draining then placing it into a bowl of iced water, or rinsing under cold water, to immediately halt the cooking process. Blanching is used when the cooking time is to be minimal; when it is to precede another cooking process, as with certain hard vegetables before stir-frying; or to loosen the skin on fruit before peeling.

BLINI also known as blintzes; yeast-risen buckwheat pancakes. Originally from Russia where they are traditionally served with sour cream and caviar or smoked salmon; fillings can be either sweet or savoury and are perfect in mini version for canapés.

BLOOD ORANGE a virtually seedless citrus fruit with blood-red-streaked rind and flesh; sweet, non-acidic, salmon-coloured pulp and juice having slight strawberry or raspberry overtones. Thought to have occurred in nature by accident in 17th-century Sicily. The juice can be drunk straight or used in cocktails, sauces, sorbets and jellies; can be frozen for use in cooking when the growing season finishes. The rind is not as bitter as that of an ordinary orange; grated or finely sliced, it can be strewn over salads, puddings or cakes.

BRAISING a cooking term to describe the method of slow-cooking food with fat in a covered saucepan or casserole dish over low heat. This process helps tenderise and bring out the flavour in many meats with little added moisture.

BRAN the outer casing (the husk of various cereal grains such as wheat or oats) made up of several layers to protect the inner kernel; rich in vitamin B and carbohydrates and a valuable source of fibre. Usually removed when a grain is milled for flour, but is added to many breakfast cereals or eaten sprinkled over food as a dietary supplement.

BRANDY short for brandywine, the translation of the Dutch "brandwijn", burnt wine. A general term for a liqueur distilled from wine grapes (usually white), it is used as the basis for many sweet-to-dry spirits made with fruits. Cognac and Armagnac are two of the finest aged brandies available.

BRAZIL NUT native to South America, a triangular-shelled oily nut with an unusually tender white flesh and a mild, rich flavour. Good for eating as well as cooking, the nuts can be eaten raw or cooked, or can be ground into meal for baking.

BREADCRUMBS

fresh bread, usually white, processed into crumbs; good for poultry stuffings and as a thickening agent in some soups and cold sauces.

packaged prepared fine-textured but crunchy white breadcrumbs; good for coating or crumbing foods that are to be fried.

stale crumbs made by grating, blending or processing 1- or 2-day-old bread.

BRIOCHE French in origin; a rich, yeast-leavened, cake-like bread made with butter and eggs. Most common form is the *brioche à tête*, a round fluted roll topped with a much smaller ball of dough. Eaten freshly baked or toasted; available from cake or specialty bread shops.

BROCCOLINI a cross between broccoli and Chinese kale; long asparagus-like stems with a long loose floret, both completely edible. Resembles broccoli in look but is milder and sweeter in taste.

BRUISE a cooking term to describe the slight crushing given to aromatic ingredients, particularly herbs, with the flat side of a heavy knife or cleaver to release flavour and aroma.

BRUSCHETTA pronounced broo-skeh-tah, this traditional Italian snack is fresh white bread, usually ciabatta, rubbed with garlic-infused olive oil, toasted and served with various toppings such as tomato and basil.

BUCKWHEAT a herb in the same plant family as rhubarb; not a cereal so it is gluten-free. Available as flour (used for blini, pancakes and soba); ground (cracked) into coarse, medium or fine granules which are called *kasha* and used similarly to polenta; or groats, the whole kernel sold roasted as a cereal product which, like rice or couscous, forms the basis for a grain-and-vegetable main dish.

BUK CHOY also known as bok choy, pak choi, Chinese white cabbage or Chinese chard; has a fresh, mild mustard taste. Use both stems and leaves, stir-fried or braised. Baby buk choy, also known as pak kat farang or shanghai bok choy, is much smaller and more tender than buk choy.

Its mildly acrid, distinctively appealing taste has made it one of the most commonly used Asian greens.

BURGHUL also known as bulghur wheat; hulled steamed wheat kernels that, once dried, are crushed into various size grains. Used in Middle Eastern dishes such as felafel, kibbeh and tabbouleh. Burghul is not the same thing as cracked wheat, the untreated whole wheat berry broken during milling into a cereal product of varying degrees of coarseness used in bread making.

BUTTER this book uses salted butter unless stated otherwise; 125g is equal to 1 stick (4 ounces) in other recipes. Butter is basically churned pasteurised cream with salted being the highest percentage sold in supermarkets; made from pure cream with a minimum 80 per cent fat and about 3 per cent salt added after churning with the buttermilk poured away. Unsalted or "sweet" butter has no salt added to the churned cream and is perhaps the most popular butter among pastry-chefs.

BUTTERMILK *see milk*

CACHOUS also called dragées in some countries; minuscule (3mm to 5mm) metallic-looking-but-edible confectionery balls used in cake decorating; available in silver, gold or various colours.

CAPERBERRIES olive-sized fruit formed after the buds of the caper bush have flowered; they are usually sold pickled in a vinegar brine with stalks intact.

CAPERS the grey-green buds of a warm climate (usually Mediterranean) shrub, sold either dried and salted or pickled in a vinegar brine; tiny young ones, called baby capers, are also available both in brine or dried in salt. Their pungent taste adds piquancy to a classic steak tartare, tapenade, sauces and condiments.

CAPSICUM also known as pepper or bell pepper. Native to central and South America; found in red, green, yellow, orange or purplish-black varieties. Discard seeds and membranes before use.

CARAWAY SEEDS the small, half-moon-shaped dried seed from a member of the parsley family; adds a sharp anise flavour when used in both sweet and savoury dishes. Used widely, in such different foods as rye bread, harissa and the classic Hungarian fresh cheese, liptauer.

CARDAMOM a spice native to India and used extensively in its cuisine; can be purchased in pod, seed or ground form. Has a distinctive aromatic, sweetly rich flavour and is one of the world's most expensive spices. Used to flavour curries, rice dishes, sweet desserts and cakes.

CASHEWS plump, kidney-shaped, golden-brown nuts having a distinctive sweet, buttery flavour and containing about 48 per cent fat. Because of this high fat content, they should be kept, sealed tightly, under refrigeration to avoid becoming rancid. We use roasted unsalted cashews in this book, available from health-food stores and most supermarkets; as with most nuts intended to be eaten as snacks, roasting cashews brings out their intense nutty flavour.

CAYENNE PEPPER *see chilli*

CELERIAC tuberous root with knobbly brown skin, white flesh and a celery-like flavour. Keep peeled celeriac in acidulated water to keep it from discolouring. It can be grated and eaten raw in remoulade or salads; used in soups and stews; boiled and mashed like potatoes; or sliced thinly and deep-fried as chips.

CHAMPAGNE we use sweet sparkling wine in this book rather than the more expensive French original.

CHAPATI a popular unleavened Indian bread, similar in appearance to pitta, chapati accompany saucy curries, often serving as cutlery to scoop up the food. Made from whole-wheat flour, salt and water, and dry-fried on a "tawa" (a cast-iron griddle). Available from Indian food shops and on the bread shelf in most supermarkets.

CHAR SIU also called Chinese barbecue sauce; a paste-like ingredient dark-red-brown in colour with a sharp sweet and spicy flavour. Made with fermented soybeans, honey and various spices, char siu can be diluted and used as a marinade or brushed directly onto grilling meat.

CHEESE

blue mould-treated cheeses mottled with blue veining. Varieties include firm and crumbly stilton types and mild, creamy brie-like cheeses.

bocconcini from the diminutive of "boccone", meaning mouthful in Italian; walnut-sized, baby mozzarella, a delicate, semi-soft, white cheese traditionally made from buffalo milk. Sold fresh, it spoils rapidly so will only keep, refrigerated in brine, for 1 or 2 days at the most.

brie often referred in France as the queen of cheeses; soft-ripened cow-milk cheese with a delicate, creamy texture and a rich, sweet taste that varies from buttery to mushroomy. Best served at room temperature after a brief period of ageing, brie should have a bloomy white rind and creamy, voluptuous centre which becomes runny with ripening.

cheddar the most common cow-milk tasty cheese; should be aged, hard and have a pronounced bite. We use a version having no more than 20 per cent fat when calling for low-fat cheese.

cottage fresh, white, unripened curd cheese with a lumpy consistency and mild, sweet flavour. Fat content ranges between 15 per cent to 55 per cent, determined by whether it is made from whole, low-fat or fat-free cow milk.

cream commonly known as philadelphia or philly; a soft cow-milk cheese with a fat content ranging from 14 per cent to 33 per cent.

fetta Greek in origin; a crumbly textured goat- or sheep-milk cheese having a sharp, salty taste. Ripened and stored in salted whey; particularly good cubed and tossed into salads. We use a version having no more than 15 per cent fat when calling for low-fat cheese.

fontina a smooth, firm Italian cow-milk cheese with a creamy, nutty taste and brown or red rind; an ideal melting or grilling cheese.

goat made from goat milk, has an earthy, strong taste. Available in soft, crumbly and firm textures, in various shapes and sizes, and sometimes rolled in ash or herbs.

gorgonzola a creamy Italian blue cheese having a mild, sweet taste; good as an accompaniment to fruit or used to flavour sauces (especially pasta).

gruyère a hard-rind Swiss cheese with small holes and a nutty, slightly salty flavour. A popular cheese for soufflés.

haloumi a Greek Cypriot cheese having a semi-firm, spongy texture and very salty yet sweet flavour. Ripened and stored in salted whey; it's best grilled or fried, and holds its shape well on being heated. Should be eaten while still warm as it becomes tough and rubbery on cooling.

jarlsberg brand-name of a popular Norwegian cheese made from cow milk; has large holes and a mild, nutty taste.

mascarpone an Italian fresh cultured-cream product made in much the same way as yogurt. Whiteish to creamy yellow in colour, with a buttery-rich, luscious texture. Soft, creamy and spreadable, it is used in many Italian desserts and as an accompaniment to a dessert of fresh fruit.

mozzarella soft, spun-curd cheese; originating in southern Italy where it was traditionally made from water-buffalo milk. Now generally manufactured from cow milk, it is the most popular pizza cheese because of its low melting point and elasticity when heated (used for texture rather than flavour). We use a version having no more than 17.5 per cent fat when calling for low-fat cheese.

parmesan also known as parmigiano, parmesan is a hard, grainy cow-milk cheese which originated in the Parma region of Italy. The curd for this cheese is salted in brine for a month before being aged for up to 2 years, preferably in humid conditions. Parmesan is grated or flaked and used for pasta, salads and soups; it is also eaten on its own with fruit. Reggiano is the best parmesan, aged for a minimum 2 years and made only in the Italian region of Emilia-Romagna.

pecorino the Italian generic name for cheeses made from sheep milk. This family of hard, white to pale-yellow cheeses, traditionally made in the Italian winter and spring when sheep graze on natural pastures, have been matured for 8 to 12 months. They are classified according to the area in which they were produced – romano from Rome, sardo from Sardinia, siciliano from Sicily and toscano from Tuscany. If you can't find it, use parmesan.

pizza cheese a commercial blend of varying proportions of processed grated mozzarella, cheddar and parmesan.

provolone a mild stretched-curd cheese similar to mozzarella when young, becoming hard, spicy and grainy the longer it's aged. Golden yellow in colour, with a smooth waxy rind, provolone is a good all-purpose cheese used in cooking, for dessert with cheese, and shredded or flaked.

raclette a Swiss cow-milk cheese with a hard, rosy-brown rind and semi-soft interior dotted with small holes. Used in Switzerland and Alsace to make a dish of the same name: the cheese is melted on a special raclette grill and poured over steamed or boiled baby potatoes. Heating releases the cheese's unique fruity and nutty flavour and intensifies its aroma. It can be used to replace gruyère in a recipe.

roquefort considered the "king of cheeses", this is a blue cheese with a singularly pungent taste; made only from the milk of specially bred sheep and ripened in the damp limestone caves found under the village of Roquefort-sur-Soulzon in France. Has a sticky, bone-coloured rind and, when ripe, the sharp, almost metallic-tasting interior is creamy and almost shiny. Most famously used in the self-named salad dressing and for being one of the world's best eating cheeses.

ricotta a soft, sweet, moist, white cow-milk cheese with a low fat content (about 8.5 per cent) and a slightly grainy texture. The name roughly translates as "cooked again" and refers to ricotta's manufacture from a whey that is itself a by-product of other cheese making.

soft blue vein also known as a light blue cheese because it has the creamy, moist texture of a brie but is veined and mildly acidic like typical blues. A double-cream blue cheese; blue castello is an example.

swiss generic name for a variety of slightly firm to hard Swiss cheeses, among them emmentaler and gruyère.

tasty generic name for a variety of processed and naturally made cheddar-like table cheeses.

CHERMOULLA a Moroccan blend of fresh herbs, spices and condiments traditionally used for preserving or seasoning meat and fish, for flavouring stews and tagines, or for use as a baste or marinade. You can keep freshly made chermoulla in the fridge, covered with a thin layer of olive oil to help preserve it, for up to a month. Available ready-made in Middle Eastern food shops, delicatessens and specialty food stores.

CHERRY small, soft stone fruit varying in colour from yellow to dark red. Sweet cherries are eaten whole and in desserts while sour cherries such as the morello variety are used for jams, preserves, pies and savoury dishes (particularly good with game birds and meats).

glacé also known as candied cherries; boiled in heavy sugar syrup and then dried. Used in cakes, breads and sweets.

maraschino pronounced mahr-uh-skee-no. Any variety of cherry can be used; maraschino are macerated in a flavoured and coloured sugar syrup then preserved. Originally an Italian confection, these are most often found in cocktails or as a colourful garnish, but they can be used in baked items and fruit salads.

CHERVIL also known as cicily; mildly fennel-flavoured member of the parsley family with curly dark-green leaves. Available both fresh and dried but, like all herbs, is best used fresh; like coriander and parsley, its delicate flavour diminishes the longer it is cooked. It's one of the herbs usually included in the French staple *fines herbes* (along with chives, parsley and tarragon) used in the seasoning of omelettes and poached fish dishes.

CHICKEN

barbecued we use already-cooked whole barbecued chickens weighing about 900g apiece in our recipes. Skin discarded and bones removed, this size chicken provides 4 cups (400g) shredded meat or about 3 cups (400g) coarsely chopped meat.

breast fillet breast halved, skinned and boned.

drumette small fleshy part of the wing between shoulder and elbow, trimmed to resemble a drumstick.

drumstick leg with skin and bone intact.

maryland leg and thigh still connected in a single piece; bones and skin intact.

smoked chicken ready-to-eat, available as whole small bird or breasts sold cryovac-packed in supermarkets.

tenderloin thin strip of meat lying just under the breast, especially good for stir-frying.

thigh skin and bone intact.

thigh cutlet thigh with skin and centre bone intact; sometimes found skinned with bone intact.

thigh fillet thigh with skin and centre bone removed; makes flavoursome mince.

wing the whole wing, bone and skin intact.

CHICKPEAS also called garbanzos, hummus or channa; an irregularly round, sandy-coloured legume used extensively in Mediterranean, Indian and Hispanic cooking. Firm texture even after cooking, a floury mouth-feel and robust nutty flavour; available canned or dried (the latter need several hours reconstituting in cold water before being used).

CHILLI always use rubber gloves when seeding and chopping fresh chillies as they can burn your skin. We use unseeded chillies in our recipes because the seeds contain the heat; use fewer chillies rather than seeding the lot. Excess chillies are easily kept, submerged in oil or vinegar, in clean glass containers with tight-fitting lids in the fridge for up to 3 months. Whole chillies freeze well: wrap 2 or 3 together in plastic bundles and keep in the freezer until required. Chillies can also be dried: for hundred of years, Mexicans have been stringing them into "ristras", long garlands hung at room temperature in a dry spot that make an interesting kitchen decoration as well as an excellent drying method. Dried chiles can be ground and stored in airtight glass bottles.

cayenne also known as cayenne pepper; a thin-fleshed, long, extremely hot, dried red chilli native to South America, usually purchased ground.

chipotle pronounced cheh-pote-lay. The name used for jalapeño chillies once they've been dried and smoked. Having a deep, intensely smokey flavour, rather than a searing heat, chipotles are dark brown, almost black in colour and wrinkled in appearance.

flakes also sold as crushed chilli; dehydrated deep-red extremely fine slices and whole seeds; good in cooking or for sprinkling over a dish as one does with salt and pepper.

green any unripened chilli; also some particular varieties that are ripe when green, such as jalapeño, habanero, poblano or serrano.

hot sauce we use a hot Asian variety made from bird's-eye chillies, salt and vinegar. Use sparingly, increasing the quantity to suit your taste.

jalapeño pronounced hah-lah-pain-yo. Fairly hot, medium-sized, plump, dark green chilli; available pickled, sold canned or bottled, and fresh, from greengrocers.

long red available both fresh and dried; a generic term used for any moderately hot, long, thin chilli (about 6cm to 8cm long).

pasilla pronounced pah-see-yah. Also known as "chile negro" because of its almost black skin; medium-hot, smokey and pungent dried chilli measuring about 15cm to 20cm in length. Many commercial chilli powders are made with pasillas and can replace this chilli in some instances: use sparingly until you discover the right amount for your palate.

paste every Asian cuisine has its own chilli paste, and each is different from the next: Vietnamese chilli paste is quite hot; Indonesian sambal oelek (chilli with ginger, oil and garlic) has medium heat; or, for more sweetness than fire, mild sweet thai chilli sauce, made with vinegar and sugar.

powder the Asian variety is the hottest, made from dried ground thai chillies; can be used instead of fresh chillies in the proportion of ½ teaspoon chilli powder to 1 medium chopped fresh red chilli.

sauce, sweet comparatively mild, fairly sticky and runny bottled sauce made from red chillies, sugar, garlic and white vinegar; used in Thai cooking and as a condiment.

thai also known as "scuds"; tiny, very hot and bright red in colour.

CHINESE BARBECUED DUCK *see duck*

CHINESE BARBECUED PORK *see pork*

CHINESE BROCCOLI *see gai lan*

CHINESE CABBAGE also known as wombok, peking or napa cabbage; elongated in shape with pale green, crinkly leaves, this is the most common cabbage in South-East Asia, forming the basis of the pickled Korean condiment, kim chi. Can be shredded or chopped and eaten raw or braised, steamed or stir-fried.

CHINESE COOKING WINE also known as hao hsing or chinese rice wine; made from fermented rice, wheat, sugar and salt with a 13.5 per cent alcohol content. Inexpensive and found in Asian food shops; if you can't find it, replace with mirin or sherry.

CHIVES related to the onion and leek; has a subtle onion flavour. Used more for flavour than as an ingredient; chopped finely, they're good in sauces, dressings, omelettes or as a garnish. Chinese (or garlic) chives have rougher, flatter leaves than simple chives, and possess a pink-tinged teardrop-shaped flowering bud at the end; used as a salad green, or steamed and eaten as a vegetable.

CHOCOLATE

cherry ripe dark chocolate bar made with coconut and cherries; standard size bar weighs 55g.

choc Bits also known as chocolate chips or chocolate morsels; available in milk, white and dark chocolate. Made of cocoa liquor, cocoa butter, sugar and an emulsifier, these hold their shape in baking and are ideal for decorating.

chocolate Melts small discs of compounded milk, white or dark chocolate ideal for melting and moulding.

cocoa *see cocoa powder*

couverture a term used to describe a fine quality, very rich chocolate high in both cocoa butter and cocoa liquor. Requires tempering when used to coat but not if used in baking, mousses or fillings.

dark cooking also known as compounded chocolate; good for cooking as it doesn't require tempering and sets at room temperature. Made with vegetable fat instead of cocoa butter so it lacks the rich, buttery flavour of eating chocolate. Cocoa butter is the most expensive component in chocolate, so the substitution of a vegetable fat means that compounded chocolate is much cheaper to produce.

dark eating also known as semi-sweet or luxury chocolate; made of a high percentage of cocoa liquor and cocoa butter, and little added sugar. Unless stated otherwise, we use dark eating chocolate in this book as it's ideal for use in desserts and cakes.

milk most popular eating chocolate, mild and very sweet; similar in make-up to dark with the difference being the addition of milk solids.

white contains no cocoa solids but derives its sweet flavour from cocoa butter. Very sensitive to heat.

CHORIZO sausage of Spanish origin, made of coarsely ground pork and highly seasoned with garlic and chilli.

CHOY SUM also known as pakaukeo or flowering cabbage, a member of the buk choy family; easy to identify with its long stems, light green leaves and yellow flowers. Stems and leaves are both edible, steamed or stir-fried.

CIABATTA in Italian, the word means slipper, the traditional shape of this popular crisp-crusted, open-textured white sourdough bread. A good bread to use for bruschetta.

CINNAMON available both in the piece (called sticks or quills) and ground into powder; one of the world's most common spices, used universally as a sweet, fragrant flavouring for both sweet and savoury foods. The dried inner bark of the shoots of the Sri Lankan native cinnamon tree; much of what is sold as the real thing is in fact cassia, Chinese cinnamon, from the bark of the cassia tree. Less expensive to process than true cinnamon, it is often blended with Sri Lankan cinnamon to produce the type of "cinnamon" most commonly found in supermarkets.

CITRIC ACID commonly found in most fruits, especially limes and lemons. Commercial citric acid helps to accentuate the acid flavour of fruit; it does not act as a preservative.

CLOVES dried flower buds of a tropical tree; can be used whole or in ground form. They have a strong scent and taste so should be used sparingly.

COCOA POWDER also known as unsweetened cocoa; cocoa beans (cacao seeds) that have been fermented, roasted, shelled, ground into powder then cleared of most of the fat content. Unsweetened cocoa is used in hot chocolate drink mixtures; milk powder and sugar are added to the ground product.

COCONUT

cream obtained commercially from the first pressing of the coconut flesh alone, without the addition of water; the second pressing (less rich) is sold as coconut milk. Available in cans and cartons at most supermarkets.

desiccated concentrated, dried, unsweetened and finely shredded coconut flesh.

essence synthetically produced from flavouring, oil and alcohol. *see essence/extract*

flaked dried flaked coconut flesh.

milk not the liquid found inside the fruit, which is called coconut water, but the diluted liquid from the second pressing of the white flesh of a mature coconut (the first pressing produces coconut cream). Available in cans and cartons at most supermarkets.

shredded unsweetened thin strips of dried coconut flesh.

COOKING-OIL SPRAY we use a cholesterol-free cooking spray made from canola oil.

CORIANDER also known as cilantro, pak chee or chinese parsley; bright-green-leafed herb having both pungent aroma and taste. Used as an ingredient in a wide variety of cuisines from Mexican to South-East Asian. Often stirred into or sprinkled over a dish just before serving for maximum impact as, like other leafy herbs, its characteristics diminish with cooking. Both the stems and roots of coriander are used in Thai cooking: wash well before chopping. Coriander seeds are dried and sold either whole or ground, and neither form tastes remotely like the fresh leaf but rather like an acrid combination of sage and caraway. Seeds and ground are both used in garam masala, mixed spice, Indian and Thai curry pastes and sauces, sausages, and some breads and desserts.

CORNFLAKES commercially manufactured cereal made of dehydrated then baked crisp flakes of corn. Also available is a prepared finely ground mixture used for coating or crumbing food before frying or baking, sold as "crushed corn flakes" in 300g packages in most supermarkets.

CORNFLOUR also known as cornstarch. Available made from corn or wheat (wheaten cornflour, gluten-free, gives a lighter texture in cakes); used as a thickening agent in cooking.

CORNICHON French for gherkin, a very small variety of cucumber. Pickled, they are a traditional accompaniment to pâté; the Swiss always serve them with fondue (or raclette).

COUSCOUS a fine, grain-like cereal product made from semolina; from the countries of North Africa. A semolina flour and water dough is sieved then dehydrated to produce minuscule even-sized pellets of couscous; it is rehydrated by steaming or with the addition of a warm liquid and swells to three or four times its original size; eaten like rice with a tagine, as a side dish or salad ingredient.

CRAISINS dried sweetened cranberries; used in cooking sweet or savoury dishes. Can usually be substituted for or with other dried fruit in most recipes.

CRANBERRY SAUCE a manufactured product made of cranberries cooked in sugar syrup; the astringent flavour goes beautifully with roast poultry and barbecued meats.

CREAM OF TARTAR the acid ingredient in baking powder; added to confectionery mixtures to help prevent sugar from crystallising. Keeps frostings creamy and improves volume when beating egg whites.

CREME FRAICHE a mature, naturally fermented cream (minimum fat content 35 per cent) having a velvety texture and slightly tangy, nutty flavour. Crème fraîche, a French variation of sour cream, can boil without curdling and can be used in both sweet and savoury dishes.

CUCUMBER one of the oldest and most universally cultivated vegetables; about a third of the world's crop is pickled, with the rest consumed raw. Most are cylindrical in shape and green-skinned, have an extremely high water content, crisp texture, and mildly acidic flavour.

apple round, with pale-green thick skin and very large seeds; very mild and juicy. Must be peeled before use.

gherkin short and broad with a rough, thick skin; most used variety for pickling. . A mini version is pickled and sold as the French cornichon.

lebanese short, slender and thin-skinned. Probably the most popular variety because of its tender, edible skin, tiny, yielding seeds, and sweet, fresh and flavoursome taste.

telegraph also known as the european or burpless cucumber; slender and long (35cm and more), its thin dark-green skin has shallow ridges running down its length.

CUMIN also known as zeera or comino; resembling caraway in size, cumin is the dried seed of a plant related to the parsley family. Its spicy, almost curry-like flavour is essential to the traditional foods of Mexico, India, North Africa and the Middle East. Available dried as seeds or ground. Black cumin seeds are smaller than standard cumin, and dark brown rather than true black; they are mistakenly confused with kalonji.

CURLY ENDIVE also known as frisée; a prickly-looking, curly-leafed green vegetable with an edible white heart. Fairly bitter in flavour (like chicory, with which it is often confused), it is used mainly in salads.

CURRANTS dried tiny, almost black raisins so-named from the grape type native to Corinth, Greece; most often used in jams, jellies and sauces (the best-known of which is the English cumberland sauce). These are not the same as fresh currants, which are the fruit of a plant in the gooseberry family.

CURRY PASTES make your own with the recipes found in this book or purchase the ready-made pastes from the supermarket.

balti taking its name from Baltistan, a mountainous region in northern Pakistan, and sharing it with the wok-shaped pot the curry is cooked in (similarly to tagine); a medium-hot, aromatic paste containing coriander, fenugreek and mint, which gives it its distinctive mild "green" flavour.

green hottest of the traditional thai pastes; particularly good in chicken and vegetable curries, and a great addition to stir-fry and noodle dishes.

korma a classic north Indian sauce with a rich yet delicate coconut flavour and hints of garlic, ginger and coriander.

massaman rich, spicy flavour reminiscent of Middle Eastern cooking; favoured by southern Thai cooks for use in hot and sour stew-like curries and satay sauces.

panang based on the curries of Penang, an island off the north-west coast of Malaysia, close to the Thai border. A complex, sweet and milder variation of red curry paste; good with seafood and for adding to soups and salad dressings.

red probably the most popular thai curry paste; a hot blend of different flavours that complements the richness of pork, duck and seafood. Also works well stirred into marinades and sauces.

rogan josh a paste of medium heat, from the Kashmir region of India, made from fresh chillies or paprika, tomato and spices, especially cardamom. It sometimes has beetroot added to make it a dark red.

tikka in Indian cooking, the word "masala" loosely translates as paste and the word "tikka" means a bite-sized piece of meat, poultry or fish, or sometimes a cutlet. Tikka paste is any maker's choice of spices and oils, mixed into a mild paste, frequently coloured red. Used for marinating or for brushing over meat, seafood or poultry, before or during cooking instead of as an ingredient.

vindaloo a Goan combination of vinegar, tomatoes, pepper and other spices that exemplies the Portuguese influence on this part of India's west coast.

yellow one of the mildest thai pastes; similar in appearance to Indian curries as they both include yellow chilli and fresh turmeric. Good blended with coconut in vegetable, rice and noodle dishes.

CURRY POWDER a blend of ground spices used for making Indian and some South-East Asian dishes. Consists of some of the following spices: dried chilli, cinnamon, coriander, cumin, fennel, fenugreek, mace, cardamom and turmeric. Available in mild or hot varieties.

CUSTARD POWDER instant mixture used to make pouring custard; similar to North American instant pudding mixes.

DAIKON *see white radish*

DAMPER originally, a simple unleavened bread cooked in the coals of a campfire; today, available commercially in loaf and mini sizes enriched with butter and milk.

DASHI the basic fish and seaweed stock that accounts for the distinctive flavour of many Japanese dishes, such as soups and various casserole dishes. Made from dried bonito (a type of tuna) flakes and kombu (kelp); instant dashi (dashi-no-moto) is available in powder, granules and liquid concentrate from Asian food shops.

DATES fruit of the date palm tree, eaten fresh or dried, on their own or in prepared dishes. About 4cm to 6cm in length, oval and plump, thin-skinned, with a honey-sweet flavour and sticky texture. Best known, perhaps, for its inclusion in sticky toffee pudding; also found in muesli and other cereals; muffins, scones and cakes; compotes and stewed fruit desserts.

DEGLAZE a cooking term to describe making the base for a sauce by heating a small amount of wine, stock or water in a pan in which meat or poultry has been cooked (with most of the excess fat removed) then stirring to loosen the browned bits of food adhering to the bottom. After a pan has been "deglazed", the mixture is used as part of the sauce accompanying that food cooked earlier in the pan.

DHAL an Indian food term used to describe both a whole spectrum of lentils, dried peas and beans, and the range of spicy stew-like dishes containing them.

DIJONNAISE a commercial blend of mayonnaise and dijon mustard, available in most supermarkets; used in sauces and salad dressings, and as a sandwich spread or condiment.

DILL also known as dill weed; used fresh or dried, in seed form or ground. Its anise/celery sweetness flavours the food of the Scandinavian countries, and Germany and Greece. Distinctive feathery, frond-like fresh leaves are grassier and more subtle than the dried version or the seeds (which slightly resemble caraway in flavour). Use dill leaves with smoked salmon and sour cream, poached fish or roast chicken; use the seeds with simply cooked vegetables, or home-baked dark breads.

DISGORGING (or degorging) describes how to rid an uncooked eggplant of its bitter juices. Slice or chop the eggplant as required, place the pieces in a colander or on a sloping surface and sprinkle them, both sides, with enough salt to cover the surface of each piece. Stand for at least half an hour; the salt will turn slightly brown as it absorbs the bitter liquid. Rinse the eggplant well under cold running water then pat dry with absorbent paper before using. This process also helps reduce the amount of oil eggplant will absorb when being fried.

DRIED MIXED HERBS a commercial blend of dried crushed thyme, rosemary, marjoram, basil, oregano and sage; available in supermarkets.

DRIED PEAS also known a blue boilers, cowpeas or field peas; the classic pea for a pie floater. Hard, round, blueish-green pea grown specifically for drying; once dried, they are split along a natural seam. Whole and split boilers are available packaged in supermarkets and in bulk in health-food stores, and are great, among other things, for soup making.

DUCK we use whole ducks in some recipes; available from specialty chicken shops, open-air markets and some supermarkets.

breast fillets boneless whole breasts, with the skin on.

Chinese barbecued traditionally cooked in special ovens in China; dipped into and brushed during roasting with a sticky sweet coating made from soy sauce, sherry, ginger, five-spice, star anise and hoisin sauce. Available from Asian food shops as well as dedicated Chinese barbecued meat shops.

maryland thigh and drumstick still connected, skin on.

EGGPLANT also called aubergine; often thought of as a vegetable but actually a fruit and belongs to the same family as the tomato, chilli and potato. Ranging in size from tiny to very large and in colour from pale green to deep purple. Can be purchased char-grilled, packed in oil, in jars.

baby also known as finger or japanese eggplant; very small and slender so can be used without disgorging.

pea tiny, about the size of peas; sometimes known by their thai name, "makeua puang". Sold in clusters of 10 to 15 eggplants, similar to vine-ripened cherry tomatoes; very bitter in flavour, a quality suited to balance rich, sweet coconut-sauced thai curries. Available in Asian greengrocers and food shops, fresh or pickled.

thai found in a variety of different sizes and colours, from a long, thin, purplish-green one to a hard, round, golf-ball size having a white-streaked pale-green skin. This last looks like a small unripe tomato and is the most popular eggplant used in Thai and Vietnamese curries and stir-fries.

EGGS we use large chicken eggs having an average weigh of 60g in our recipes unless stated otherwise. Shell colour is determined by the breed of hen and what it has been fed on; it has nothing to do with quality. As far as the differences between cage, barn-laid and free-range eggs is concerned, nutrient content, value for money and taste have all got to be factored into the equation; in the end, the decision is left to individual preference. Store eggs, in the carton they come in, under refrigeration as soon as you bring them home to slow down deterioration. This helps reduce water loss and protects them from absorbing flavour from other fridge items. Most eggs can be kept, in their carton, in the fridge, for up to 4 weeks. Some recipes in this book call for raw or barely cooked eggs; exercise caution if there is a salmonella problem in your community, particularly in food eaten by children and pregnant women.

EGGWASH beaten egg (white, yolk or both) and milk or water; often brushed over pastry or bread to impart colour or gloss.

ENGLISH MUFFIN a round teacake made from yeast, flour, milk, some semolina and salt; often confused with crumpets. Pre-baked and sold packaged in supermarkets, muffins should be split open and toasted before eating.

ESSENCE/EXTRACT an essence is either a distilled concentration of a food quality or an artificial creation of it. Coconut and almond essences are synthetically produced substances used in small amounts to impart their respective flavours to foods. An extract is made by actually extracting the flavour from a food product. In the case of vanilla, pods are soaked, usually in alcohol, to capture the authentic flavour. Both extracts and essences will keep indefinitely if stored in a cool dark place.

ESCHALOTS *see onion*

FENNEL also known as finocchio or anise; a crunchy green vegetable slightly resembling celery that's eaten raw in salads; fried as an accompaniment; or used as an ingredient in pasta sauces, soups and sauce. Also the name given to the dried seeds of the plant which have a stronger licorice flavour.

FIGS originally from the countries that border the eastern Mediterranean; are best eaten in peak season, at the height of summer. Vary in skin and flesh colour according to type not ripeness: the purple-black mission or black mission fig, with pink flesh, is a rich-flavoured, good all-rounder; the thick-skinned, pale green kadota, another all-purpose fruit, is good canned or dried as well as fresh; the yellow smyrna has nutty-tasting flesh; and the pale olive, golden-skinned adriatic has honey-sweet, light pink flesh. When ripe, figs should be unblemished and bursting with flesh; nectar beads at the base indicate when a fig is at its best. Figs are also glacéd (candied), dried or canned in sugar syrup; these are usually sold at health-food stores, Middle Eastern food shops or specialty cheese counters.

FISH SAUCE called naam pla on the label if Thai-made, nuoc naam if Vietnamese; the two are almost identical. Made from pulverised salted fermented fish (most often anchovies); has a pungent smell and strong taste. Available in varying degrees of intensity, so use according to your taste.

FIVE-SPICE although the ingredients vary from country to country, five-spice is usually a fragrant mixture of ground cinnamon, cloves, star anise, sichuan pepper and fennel seeds. Used in Chinese and other Asian cooking; available from most supermarkets or Asian food shops.

FLORET the small flower that tops the stalks of a much larger composite cauliflower or broccoli head; good eaten raw or lightly steamed.

FLOUR

besan also known as chickpea flour or gram; made from ground chickpeas so is gluten-free and high in protein. Used in Indian cooking to make dumplings, noodles and chapati; for a batter coating for deep-frying; and as a sauce thickener.

buckwheat *see buckwheat*

cornflour *see cornflour*

maize milled from maize (corn); finely ground polenta (cornmeal) can be substituted in some instances.

plain also known as all-purpose; unbleached wheat flour is the best for baking: the gluten content ensures a strong dough, which produces a light result. Also used as a thickening agent in sauces and gravies.

rice very fine, almost powdery, gluten-free flour; made from ground white rice. Used in baking, as a thickener, and in some Asian noodles and desserts. Another variety, made from glutinous sweet rice, is used for chinese dumplings and rice paper.

rye milled from the cereal grain rye; contains less gluten than plain or wholemeal flour. Produces a dense, heavy bread.

self-raising all-purpose plain or wholemeal flour with baking powder and salt added; can be made at home with plain or wholemeal flour sifted with baking powder in the proportion of 1 cup flour to 2 teaspoons baking powder.

semolina coarsely ground flour milled from durum wheat; the flour used in making gnocchi, pasta and couscous.

strong also known as gluten-enriched, baker's or bread-mix flour. Produced from a variety of wheat that has a high gluten (protein) content and is best suited for pizza and bread making: the expansion caused by the yeast and the stretchiness imposed by kneading require a flour that is "strong" enough to handle these stresses. Since domestic breadmakers entered the marketplace, it has become easier to find strong flour; look for it at your supermarket or a health-food store.

wholemeal also known as wholewheat flour; milled with the wheat germ so is higher in fibre and more nutritional than plain flour.

GAI LAN also known as gai larn, chinese broccoli and chinese kale; green vegetable appreciated more for its stems than its coarse leaves. Can be served steamed and stir-fried, in soups and noodle dishes. One of the most popular Asian greens, best known for its appearance on a yum cha trolley, where it's steamed then sprinkled with a mixture of oyster sauce and sesame oil.

GALANGAL also known as ka or lengkaus if fresh and laos if dried and powdered; a root, similar to ginger in its use. It has a hot-sour ginger-citrusy flavour; used in fish curries and soups.

GANACHE pronounced gah-nash, a creamy chocolate filling or frosting for cakes. Depending on its intended use, it is made from varying proportions of good-quality chocolate and pouring cream. Other ingredients can be added for flavour, or to increase its richness or gloss. Ganache can be whipped, piped or poured like a glaze, and can be frozen for up to 3 months.

GARAM MASALA literally meaning blended spices in its northern Indian place of origin; based on varying proportions of cardamom, cinnamon, cloves, coriander, fennel and cumin, roasted and ground together. Black pepper and chilli can be added for a hotter version.

GARLIC like onion, a member of the lily family with the edible bulb growning underground. Each bulb is made up of many cloves which, uncooked, can be crushed, sliced, chopped, or used whole, peeled or unpeeled. Garlic powder is the ground product made from dehydrated garlic flakes and is used mostly for convenience purposes.

GELATI Italian for ice-cream but within that name are several different types. One, gelato, is most similar in taste and make-up to what we call ice-cream. Two more types, granita (ice) and sorbetto (sorbet in French or sherbet in English), are similar with the essential distinction being that a sorbet is usually more solidly frozen and made only with fruit or fruit juice and egg whites, while granita is an icy slush made from sugar syrup and one of a myriad flavourings, from fruit to coffee to liqueur. Two other frozen sweets that relate to this entry are semifreddo (loosely translated, "a bit cold"), a partially frozen custard-like mixture made of cream and eggs poured directly into a mould without the use of an ice-cream maker, and cassata, two or more flavours of gelati frozen solid in a mould around a candied-fruit and ricotta or whipped-cream centre.

GELATINE we use dried (powdered) gelatine in the recipes in this book; it's also available in sheet form known as leaf gelatine. A thickening agent made from either collagen, a protein found in animal connective tissue and bones, or certain algae (agar-agar). Three teaspoons of dried gelatine (8g or one sachet) is roughly equivalent to four gelatine leaves. Professionals use leaf gelatine because it generally results in a smoother, clearer consistency; it is also most commonly used throughout Europe. The two types are interchangable but leaf gelatine gives a much clearer mixture than dried gelatine; it's perfect in dishes where appearance really counts.

GHEE clarified butter; with the milk solids removed, this fat has a high smoking point so can be heated to a high temperature without burning. Used as a cooking medium in most Indian recipes.

GINGER

fresh also known as green or root ginger; the thick gnarled root of a tropical plant. Can be kept, peeled, covered with dry sherry in a jar and refrigerated, or frozen in an airtight container.

glacé fresh ginger root preserved in sugar syrup; crystallised ginger (sweetened with cane sugar) can be substituted if rinsed with warm water and dried before using.

ground also known as powdered ginger; used as a flavouring in baking but cannot be substituted for fresh ginger.

pickled pink or red coloured; available, packaged, from Asian food shops. Pickled paper-thin shavings of ginger in a mixture of vinegar, sugar and natural colouring; most used in Japanese cooking.

GLUCOSE SYRUP also known as liquid glucose, made from wheat starch; used in jam and confectionery making. Available at health-food stores and supermarkets.

GLUTEN one of the proteins in wheat and most other cereal flours that helps act as a levening agent. *see flour*

GLUTEN-FREE BAKING POWDER used as a leavening agent in bread, cake, pastry or pudding mixtures. Suitable for people having an allergic response to glutens or seeking an alternative to everyday baking powder. *see baking powder*

GOLDEN SYRUP a by-product of refined sugarcane; pure maple syrup or honey can be substituted. Golden syrup and treacle (a thicker, darker syrup not unlike molasses), also known as flavour syrups, are similar sugar products made by partly breaking down sugar into its component parts and adding water. Treacle is more viscous, and has a stronger flavour and aroma than golden syrup (which has been refined further and contains fewer impurities, so is lighter in colour and more fluid). Both can be use in baking and for making certain confectionery items.

GOW GEE PASTRY *see wonton wrappers*

GRAND MARNIER orange liqueur based on cognac-brandy.

GRAPEFRUIT one of the largest citrus fruits, grapefruit is available both seedless or with seeds; the seeded variety has more flavour. There are pink seedless and ruby or ruby red varieties in addition to the ordinary yellow fruit. Eat on its own or in salads, sorbets and granitas.

GRAPEVINE LEAVES from early spring, fresh grapevine leaves can be found in most specialist greengrocers. Alternatively, cryovac-packages containing about 60 leaves in brine can be found in Middle Eastern food shops and some delicatessens; these must be well rinsed and dried before using. Used as wrappers for a large of number of savoury fillings in Mediterranean cuisines.

GREASING PANS use butter, margarine, oil or cooking-oil spray to grease baking pans; over-greasing pans can cause food to overbrown. Use absorbent paper or a pastry brush to spread the oil or butter over the pan. Try covering your hand with a small plastic bag then swiping it into the butter or margarine.

GREMOLATA an aromatic garnish usually made of minced parsley, lemon peel and garlic, but can also include breadcrumbs. Can be sprinkled over dishes just before serving (the classic finish to osso buco) or used as a coating for meat.

HARISSA a North African paste made from dried red chillies, garlic, olive oil and caraway seeds; can be used as a rub for meat, an ingredient in sauces and dressings, or eaten as a condiment. It is available from Middle Eastern food shops and some supermarkets.

HAZELNUTS also known as filberts; plump, grape-sized, rich, sweet nut having a brown skin that is removed by rubbing heated nuts together vigorously in a tea-towel. Hazelnut meal is made by grounding the hazelnuts to a coarse flour texture for use in baking or as a thickening agent.

HERBS we specify when to use fresh or dried herbs in this book. Dried (not ground) herbs can be used in the proportion of one to four, ie, use 1 teaspoon dried herbs instead of 4 teaspoons (1 tablespoon) chopped fresh herbs.

HOISIN a thick, sweet and spicy Chinese barbecue sauce made from salted fermented soybeans, onions and garlic; used as a marinade or baste, or to accent stir-fries and barbecued or roasted foods. From Asian food shops and supermarkets.

HOLLANDAISE a classic sauce based on a béchamel, made with butter and egg yolks, usually with the addition of a little lemon juice or vinegar.

HONEYDEW MELON a heavy oval fruit with a pale-green to yellow skin, delicate taste and pale green flesh.

HORSERADISH a vegetable having edible green leaves but mainly grown for its long, pungent white root. Occasionally found fresh in specialty greengrocers and some Asian food shops, but commonly purchased in bottles at the supermarket in two forms: prepared horseradish and horseradish cream. These cannot be substituted one for the other in cooking but both can be used as table condiments. Horseradish cream is a commercially prepared creamy paste consisting of grated horseradish, vinegar, oil and sugar, while prepared horseradish is the preserved grated root.

HUMMUS a Middle Eastern salad or dip made from softened dried chickpeas, garlic, lemon juice and tahini; can be purchased ready-made from most delicatessens and supermarkets. Also the Arabic word for chickpeas.

ICE-CREAM we use a good quality ice-cream having 5g of fat per 100ml for the recipes in this book.

ICING SUGAR *see sugar*

JAM also known as preserve or conserve; a thickened mixture of a fruit (and occasionally, a vegetable) and sugar. Usually eaten on toast for breakfast, it's also used as a filling or icing for sweet biscuits and cakes.

KAFFIR LIME also known as magrood, leech lime or jeruk purut. The wrinkled, bumpy-skinned green fruit of a small citrus tree originally grown in South Africa and South-East Asia. As a rule, only the rind or leaves are used.

KAFFIR LIME LEAVES, also known as bai magrood, look like they are two glossy dark green leaves joined end to end, forming a rounded hourglass shape. Used fresh or dried in many South-East Asian dishes, they are used like bay leaves or curry leaves, especially in Thai cooking. Sold fresh, dried or frozen, the dried leaves are less potent so double the number if using them as a substitute for fresh; a strip of fresh lime peei may be substituted for each kaffir lime leaf.

KALONJI also known as nigella or black onion seeds. Tiny, angular seeds, black on the outside and creamy within, with a sharp nutty flavour that can be enhanced by frying briefly in a dry hot pan before use. Typically sprinkled over Turkish bread immediately after baking or as an important spice in Indian cooking, kalonji can be found in most Asian and Middle Eastern food shops. Often erroneously called black cumin seeds.

KASHA *see buckwheat*

KECAP MANIS a dark, thick sweet soy sauce used in most South-East Asian cuisines. Depending on the manufacturer, the sauces's sweetness is derived from the addition of either molasses or palm sugar when brewed. Use as a condiment, dipping sauce, ingredient or marinade.

KITCHEN STRING made from a natural product such as cotton or hemp that will neither melt nor affect the flavour of the food during cooking as would a string made from synthetic materials.

KIWIFRUIT also known as Chinese gooseberry; having a brown, somewhat hairy skin and bright-green flesh with a unique sweet-tart flavour. Used in fruit salads, desserts and eaten (peeled) as is.

KUMARA the polynesian name of an orange-fleshed sweet potato often confused with yam; good baked, boiled, mashed or fried similarly to other potatoes.

LAMB

backstrap also known as eye of loin; the larger fillet from a row of loin chops or cutlets. Tender, best cooked rapidly: barbecued or pan-fried.

chump cut from just above the hind legs to the mid-loin section; can be used as a piece for roasting or cut into chops.

cutlet small, tender rib chop; sometimes sold french-trimmed, with all the fat and gristle at the narrow end of the bone removed.

diced cubed lean meat.

fillets fine texture, most expensive and extremely tender.

leg cut from the hindquarter; can be boned, butterflied, rolled and tied, or cut into dice.

minced ground lamb.

rack row of 4, 6 or 8 cutlets still attached.

rolled shoulder boneless section of the forequarter, rolled and secured with string or netting.

shank forequarter leg; sometimes sold as drumsticks or frenched shanks if the gristle and narrow end of the bone are discarded and the remaining meat trimmed.

shoulder large, tasty piece having much connective tissue so is best pot-roasted or braised. Makes the best mince.

LAMINGTON PAN 20cm x 30cm slab cake pan, 3cm deep.

LAVASH flat, unleavened bread of Mediterranean origin; good used as a wrapper or torn and used for dips.

LEEKS a member of the onion family, the leek resembles a green onion but is much larger and more subtle in flavour. Tender baby or pencil leeks can be eaten whole with minimal cooking but adult leeks are usually trimmed of most of the green tops then chopped or sliced and cooked as an ingredient in stews, casseroles and soups.

LEMON GRASS also known as takrai, serai or serah. A tall, clumping, lemon-smelling and tasting, sharp-edged aromatic tropical grass; the white lower part of the stem is used, finely chopped, in much of the cooking of South-East Asia. Can be found, fresh, dried, powdered and frozen, in supermarkets and greengrocers as well as Asian food shops.

LEMON PEPPER SEASONING a commercially made blend of crushed black pepper, lemon, herbs and spices; found on supermarket shelves.

LEMON THYME *see thyme*

LENTILS (red, brown, yellow) dried pulses often identified by and named after their colour. Eaten by cultures all over the world, most famously perhaps in the dhals of India, lentils have high food value.

french green lentils are a local cousin to the famous (and very expensive) French lentils du puy, green-blue, tiny lentils with a nutty, earthy flavour and a hardy nature that allows them to be rapidly cooked without disintegrating.

LETTUCE

butter small, round, loosely formed heads with a sweet flavour; soft, buttery-textured leaves range from pale green on the outer leaves to pale yellow-green inner leaves.

coral very curly and tightly furled leaves that do look like coral; comes in distinctive tasting red and green leaves.

cos also known as romaine lettuce; the traditional caesar salad lettuce. Long, with leaves ranging from dark green on the outside to almost white near the core; the leaves have a stiff centre rib giving a slight cupping effect to the leaf on either side.

iceberg a heavy, firm round lettuce with tightly packed leaves and crisp texture; the most common "family" lettuce used on sandwiches and in salads.

mesclun pronounced mess-kluhn; also known as mixed greens or spring salad mix. A commercial blend of assorted young lettuce and other green leaves, including baby spinach leaves, mizuna and curly endive.

mixed baby lettuce leaves very similar to mesclun with the exception that only the very youngest, smallest leaves are used in the mix.

mizuna Japanese in origin; the frizzy green salad leaves have a delicate mustard flavour.

oak-leaf also known as feuille de chene; curly-leafed but not as frizzy as the coral lettuce. Found in both red and green varieties.

radicchio Italian in origin; a member of the chicory family. The dark burgundy leaves and strong, bitter flavour can be cooked or eaten raw in salads.

LYCHEES a small fruit from China with a hard shell and sweet, juicy flesh. The white flesh has a gelatinous texture and musky, perfumed taste. Discard the rough skin and seed before using in salads or as a dessert fruit. Also available canned in a sugar syrup.

MACADAMIAS native to Australia; fairly large, slightly soft, buttery rich nut. Used to make oil and macadamia butter; equally good in salads or cakes and pastries; delicious eaten on their own. Should always be stored in the fridge to prevent their high oil content turning them rancid.

MANDARIN also known as tangerine; a small, loose-skinned, easy-to-peel, sweet and juicy citrus fruit, prized for its eating qualities more than for juicing. Segments in a light syrup are available canned.

MANDOLINE a hand-operated implement with adjustable blades for thick to very thin slicing, shredding, dicing and cutting into match- or straw-sized sticks with speed and precision; ideal for shredding carrot and making french fries. Similar results can be achieved with a food processor or V-slicer and, as a last resort, the coarse side of a grater. Take care as this is an extremely sharp instrument.

MANGO tropical fruit originally from India and South-East Asia. With skin colour ranging from green to yellow and deep red; fragrant, deep yellow flesh surrounds a large flat seed. Slicing off the cheeks, cross-hatching them with a knife then turning them inside out shows the sweet, juicy flesh at its best. Mangoes can also be used in curries and salsas, or pureed for ice-cream, smoothies or mousse. Mango cheeks in light syrup are available canned. Sour and crunchy, green mangoes are just the immature fruit that is used as a vegetable in salads, salsas and curries.

MAPLE SYRUP distilled from the sap of sugar maple trees found only in Canada and about ten states in the USA. Most often eaten with pancakes or waffles, but also used as an ingredient in baking or in preparing desserts. Maple-flavoured syrup or pancake syrup is not an adequate substitute for the real thing.

MAPLE-FLAVOURED SYRUP is made from sugar cane and is also known as golden or pancake syrup. It is not a substitute for pure maple syrup.

MARINADE a mixture of ingredients blended together in which food (usually meat, poultry or seafood) is immersed for a minimum 3 hours in order to impart as much flavour as possible into the marinating food. It is also used as a method of tenderising food, usually meat.

MARJORAM an aromatic herb that is a member of the mint family; has long, thin, oval-shaped, pale-green leaves and a sweet taste similar to oregano. Used fresh or dried with lamb, seafood, vegetables and eggs. Usually added at the end of cooking so as not to lose its mild and delicate flavour.

MARMALADE a preserve, usually based on citrus fruit and its rind, cooked with sugar until the mixture has an intense flavour and thick consistency. Orange, lemon and lime are some of the commercially prepared varieties available.

MARSALA a fortified Italian wine produced in the region surrounding the Sicilian city of Marsala; recognisable by its intense amber colour and complex aroma. Often used in cooking, especially in sauces, risottos and desserts.

MARZIPAN a paste made from ground almonds, sugar and water. Similar to almond paste but sweeter, more pliable and finer in texture. Easily coloured and rolled into thin sheets to cover cakes, or sculpted into shapes for confectionery.

MAYONNAISE we use whole-egg mayonnaise. *see whole-egg mayonnaise*

MERGUEZ a small, spicy sausage believed to have originated in Tunisia but eaten throughout North Africa, France and Spain; is traditionally made with lamb meat and is easily recognised because of its chilli-red colour. Can be fried, grilled or roasted; available from many butchers, delicatessens and specialty sausage stores.

MILK we use full-cream homogenised milk unless otherwise specified.

buttermilk in spite of its name, buttermilk is actually low in fat, varying between 0.6 per cent and 2.0 per cent per 100 ml. Originally the term given to the slightly sour liquid left after butter was churned from cream, today it is intentionally made from no-fat or low-fat milk to which specific bacterial cultures have been added during the manufacturing process. It is readily available from the dairy department in supermarkets. Because it is low in fat, it's a good substitute for dairy products such as cream or sour cream in some baking and salad dressings.

evaporated unsweetened canned milk from which water has been extracted by evaporation. Evaporated skim or low-fat milk has 0.3 per cent fat content.

full-cream powder instant powder milk made from whole cow milk with liquid removed and emulsifiers added.

skim sometimes labelled *no-fat*; both have 0.1 per cent fat content.

skim-milk powder dried milk powder with 1 per cent fat content when dry and 0.1 per cent when reconstituted with water.

sweetened condensed a canned milk product consisting of milk with more than half the water content removed and sugar added to the remaining milk.

MINCED MEAT also known as ground meat, as in beef, pork, lamb and veal.

MINT

spearmint the most commonly used variety of mint; has pointed, bright green leaves and a fresh flavour. Common garden mint has rounder, coarser leaves.

thai (saranae) also known as marsh mint; similar to spearmint. Its somewhat thick, round leaves are usually used raw, as a flavouring sprinkled over soups and salads before serving.

vietnamese not a mint at all, but a pungent and peppery narrow-leafed member of the buckwheat family. Not confined to Vietnam, it is also known as Cambodian mint, pak pai (Thailand), laksa leaf (Indonesia), daun kesom (Singapore) and rau ram in Vietnam. It is a common ingredient in Thai foods, particularly soups, salads and stir-fries.

MIRIN a Japanese champagne-coloured cooking wine, made of glutinous rice and alcohol. It is used expressly for cooking and should not be confused with sake. A seasoned sweet mirin, manjo mirin, made of water, rice, corn syrup and alcohol, is used in various Japanese dipping sauces.

MISO fermented soybean paste. There are many types of miso, each with its own aroma, flavour, colour and texture; it can be kept, airtight, for up to a year in the fridge. Generally, the darker the miso, the saltier the taste and denser the texture. Salt-reduced miso is available. Buy in tubs or plastic packs.

MIXED DRIED FRUIT a combination of sultanas, raisins, currants, mixed peel and cherries.

MIXED PEEL candied citrus peel.

MIXED SPICE a classic mixture generally containing caraway, allspice, coriander, cumin, nutmeg and ginger, although cinnamon and other spices can be added. It is used with fruit and in cakes.

MOLASSES a thick, dark brown syrup, the residue from the refining of sugar; available in light, dark and blackstrap varieties. Its slightly bitter taste is an essential ingredient in American cooking, found in foods such as gingerbread, shoofly pie and boston baked beans.

MORTAR AND PESTLE a cooking tool whose design has remained the same over the centuries: the mortar is a bowl-shaped container and the pestle a rounded, bat-shaped tool. Together, they grind and pulverise spices, herbs and other foods. The pestle is pressed against the mortar and rotated, grinding the ingredient between the two surfaces until the desired consistency is obtained. Essential for making curry pastes and crushing spices.

MOULI also known as food mill; an essential kitchen tool in terms of versatility, ease of use and multi-task function. It's a rotary grater large enough to fit over a saucepan or bowl which comes with variety of interchangeable plates for processing different textures; it strains, pulps, rices, mashes, purees and even dices. Unlike a blender or processor, it separates the peel, seeds, cores, etc, from the puree and allows the cook a degree of control over the final texture.

MUESLI also known as granola; a combination of grains (mainly oats), nuts and dried fruits. Some manufacturers toast their product in oil and honey, adding crispness and kilojoules.

MUSCAT also known as muscatel; refers to both the grape variety and the sweet dessert wine made from them. The grape is superb eaten fresh; when dried, its distinctively musty flavour goes well with cheese, chocolate, pork and game. In winemaking, the grape is used for Italian Asti Spumante, a range of Australian fortifieds, Metaxa from Greece and so on.

MUSHROOMS

button small, cultivated white mushrooms with a mild flavour. When a recipe in this book calls for an unspecified type of mushroom, use button.

dried porcini the richest-flavoured mushrooms, also known as cèpes. Expensive but, because they are so strongly flavoured, only a small amount is required for any particular dish. Use in risottos and stews.

dried shiitake also called donko or dried Chinese mushrooms; have a unique meaty flavour. Sold dried; rehydrate before use.

flat large, flat mushrooms with a rich earthy flavour, ideal for filling and barbecuing. They are sometimes misnamed field mushrooms which are wild mushrooms.

oyster also known as abalone; grey-white mushrooms shaped like a fan. Prized for their smooth texture and subtle, oyster-like flavour.

shiitake fresh, are also known as Chinese black, forest or golden oak mushrooms. Although cultivated, they have the earthiness and taste of wild mushrooms. Large and meaty, they can be used as a substitute for meat in some Asian vegetarian dishes. *see dried shiitake*

swiss brown also known as roman or cremini. Light to dark brown mushrooms with full-bodied flavour; suited for use in casseroles or being stuffed and baked.

MUSLIN inexpensive, undyed, finely woven cotton fabric called for in cooking to strain stocks and sauces; if unavailable, use disposable coffee filter papers.

MUSTARD

american-style bright yellow in colour, a sweet mustard containing mustard seeds, sugar, salt, spices and garlic. Serve with hot dogs and hamburgers.

dijon also known as french. Pale brown, creamy, distinctively flavoured, fairly mild French mustard.

english the traditional hot, pungent, deep yellow mustard. Serve with roast beef and ham; wonderful with hard cheeses.

wholegrain also known as seeded. A French-style coarse-grain mustard made from crushed mustard seeds and dijon-style french mustard. Works well with cold meats and sausages.

MUSTARD SEEDS

black also known as brown mustard seeds; more pungent than the white variety; used frequently in curries.

white also known as yellow mustard seeds; used ground for mustard powder and in most prepared mustards.

NAAN the rather thick, leavened bread associated with the tandoori dishes of northern India, where it is baked pressed against the inside wall of a heated tandoor (clay oven). Now available prepared by commercial bakeries and sold in most supermarkets.

NAN JIM generic term for a Thai dipping sauce; most versions include fish sauce and chillies, but the remaining ingredients are up to the individual cook's discretion. Used as a dressing and dipping sauce.

NASHI a member of the pear family but resembling an apple with its pale-yellow-green, tennis-ball-sized appearance; more commonly known as the Asian pear to much of the world. The nashi is different from other pears in that it is crisp, juicy and ready to eat as soon as it is picked and for several months thereafter, unlike its European cousins. These very qualities are more apple- than pear-like, which probably accounts for the widespread misconception that the nashi is a cross between an apple and a pear. Its distinctive texture and mildly sweet taste make it perfect for use raw in salads, or as part of a cheese platter.

NECTAR thick, undiluted fruit juice or a mixture of fruit juices (most commonly apricot, peaches and pears); found in cans in supermarkets.

NECTARINES smooth-skinned, slightly smaller cousin to the peach; juicy, with a rich and rather spicy flavour. Good for desserts peeled and sliced with a little cinnamon sugar and lemon.

NOODLES

dried rice noodles also known as rice stick noodles. Made from rice flour and water, available flat and wide or very thin (vermicelli). Must be soaked in boiling water to soften.

fresh egg also known as ba mee or yellow noodles; made from wheat flour and eggs, sold fresh or dried. Range in size from very fine strands to wide, spaghetti-like pieces as thick as a shoelace.

fresh rice also known as ho fun, khao pun, sen yau, pho or kway tiau, depending on the country of manufacture; the most common form of noodle used in Thailand. Can be purchased in strands of various widths or large sheets weighing about 500g which are to be cut into the desired noodle size. Chewy and pure white, they do not need pre-cooking before use.

fried crispy egg noodles that have been deep-fried then packaged for sale on supermarket shelves.

hokkien also known as stir-fry noodles; fresh wheat noodles resembling thick, yellow-brown spaghetti needing no pre-cooking before use.

rice stick also known assen lek, ho fun or kway teow; especially popular South-East Asian dried rice noodles. They come in different widths (thin used in soups, wide in stir-fries), but all should be soaked in hot water to soften. The traditional noodle used in pad thai which, before soaking, measures about 5mm in width.

rice vermicelli also known as sen mee, mei fun or bee hoon. Used throughout Asia in spring rolls and cold salads; similar to bean threads, only longer and made with rice flour instead of mung bean starch. Before using, soak the dried noodles in hot water until softened, boil them briefly then rinse with hot water. Vermicelli can also be deep-fried until crunchy and then used in Chinese chicken salad, or as a garnish or bed for sauces.

singapore pre-cooked wheat noodles best described as a thinner version of hokkien; sold, packaged, in the refrigerated section of supermarkets.

soba thin, pale-brown noodle originally from Japan; made from buckwheat and varying proportions of wheat flour. Available dried and fresh, and in flavoured (for instance, green tea) varieties; eaten in soups, stir-fries and, chilled, on their own.

udon available fresh and dried, these broad, white, wheat Japanese noodles are similar to the ones in home-made chicken noodle soup.

NORI a type of dried seaweed used in Japanese cooking as a flavouring, garnish or for sushi. Sold in thin sheets, plain or toasted (yaki-nori).

NUTMEG a strong and pungent spice ground from the dried nut of an evergreen tree native to Indonesia. Usually found ground but the flavour is more intense from a whole nut, available from spice shops, so it's best to grate your own. Used most often in baking and milk-based desserts, but also works nicely in savoury dishes. Found in mixed spice mixtures.

OIL

cooking spray we use a cholesterol-free cooking spray made from canola oil.

macadamia oil *see macadamias*

olive made from ripened olives. Extra virgin and virgin are the first and second press, respectively, of the olives and are therefore considered the best; the "extra light" or "light" name on other types refers to taste not fat levels.

peanut pressed from ground peanuts; the most commonly used oil in Asian cooking because of its high smoke point (capacity to handle high heat without burning).

sesame made from roasted, crushed, white sesame seeds; a flavouring rather than a cooking medium.

vegetable any of a number of oils sourced from plant rather than animal fats.

OKRA also known as bamia or lady fingers. A green, ridged, oblong pod with a furry skin. Native to Africa, this vegetable is used in Indian, Middle Eastern and South American cooking. Can be eaten on its own; as part of a casserole, curry or gumbo; used to thicken stews or gravies.

ONIONS

baby also known as cocktail or pickling onions. These small brown onions have an average weight of 25g. Pickled in a vinegar brine or cooked whole in stews and casseroles.

flakes packaged (usually in 55g packets) chopped and dehydrated white onion pieces; used more often for garnish than as an ingredient.

fried onion/shallot served as a condiment on Asian tables to be sprinkled over just-cooked food. Found in cellophane bags or jars at all Asian grocery shops; once opened, they will keep for months if stored tightly seeled. Make your own by frying thinly sliced peeled shallots or baby onions until golden brown and crisp.

green also known as scallion or (incorrectly) shallot; an immature onion picked before the bulb has formed, having a long, bright-green edible stalk.

leek *see leek*

purple shallots also known as Asian shallots; related to the onion but resembling garlic (they grow in bulbs of multiple cloves). Thin-layered and intensely flavoured, they are used in cooking throughout South-East Asia.

red also known as spanish, red spanish or bermuda onion; a sweet-flavoured, large, purple-red onion.

shallots also called french shallots, golden shallots or eschalots. Small and elongated, with a brown-skin, they grow in tight clusters similar to garlic.

spring crisp, narrow green-leafed tops and a round sweet white bulb larger than green onions.

OXTAIL *see beef*

OYSTER SAUCE Asian in origin, this thick, richly flavoured brown sauce is made from oysters and their brine, cooked with salt and soy sauce, and thickened with starches. Use as a condiment.

PAK CHOY also known as rosette, tat soi and chinese flat cabbage; a member of the same family as buk choy, it has the same mild flavour. Its dark-green leaves are usually eaten in salads, but are also good in soups, curries and stir-fries.

PANCETTA an Italian unsmoked bacon, pork belly cured in salt and spices then rolled into a sausage shape and dried for several weeks. Used, sliced or chopped, as an ingredient rather than eaten on its own; can also be used to add taste and moisture to tough or dry cuts of meat. Hot pancetta is lean pork belly first salted and cured then spiced and rolled into a fat loaf; used in pasta sauces and meat dishes except in its place of origin, Corsica, where it is eaten on its own.

PAPPADUMS dried cracker-like wafers made from a combination of lentil and rice flours, oil and spices. Pappadums need to be reconstituted to make them edible: they are usually deep-fried briefly until they puff and double in size, but they can also be cooked in a low-fat manner in a microwave oven. Unless otherwise stated, we use large plain pappadums in our recipes, however, there are many different size and flavouring combinations.

PAPRIKA ground dried sweet red capsicum (bell pepper); there are many grades and types available, including sweet, hot, mild and smoked.

PARSLEY a versatile herb with a fresh, earthy flavour. There are about 30 varieties of curly parsley; the flat-leaf variety (also called continental or Italian parsley) is stronger in flavour and darker in colour.

PASTA

ditali, or ditalini, are tiny, very short tubes of macaroni, often used in minestrone.

farfalle bow-tie shaped short pasta; sometimes known as butterfly pasta.

fettuccine ribbon pasta made from durum wheat, semolina and egg. Available fresh or dried, plain or flavoured.

fresh lasagne sheets thinly rolled wide sheets of plain or flavoured pasta; they do not requiring par-boiling prior to being used in cooking.

gnocchi Italian 'dumplings' made of potatoes, semolina or flour; can be cooked in boiling water or baked with sauce.

macaroni tube-shaped pasta available in various sizes; made from semolina and water, and does not contain eggs.

orecchiette small disc-shaped pasta, translates literally as "little ears".

risoni small rice-shape pasta; very similar to another small pasta, orzo.

shell pasta shell-shaped pasta ranging from tiny to very large in size.

spaghetti long, thin solid strands of pasta.

spiral pasta corkscrew-shaped pasta available in various flavours and sizes.

tagliatelle long, flat strips of wheat pasta, slightly narrower and thinner than fettuccine.

tortellini circles of fresh plain pasta that are stuffed with a meat or cheese filling, and then folded into little hats.

PASTA SAUCE a prepared tomato-based sauce (sometimes called ragu or sugo on the label); comes in varying degrees of thickness and with different flavourings.

PATTY-PAN SQUASH also known as crookneck or custard marrow pumpkins; a round, slightly flat summer squash being yellow to pale green in colour and having a scalloped edge. Harvested young, it has firm white flesh and a distinct flavour.

PEANUTS, also known as groundnut, not in fact a nut but the pod of a legume. We mainly use raw (unroasted) or unsalted roasted peanuts.

PEARL BARLEY *see barley*

PECANS native to the US and now grown locally; pecans are golden brown, buttery and rich. Good in savoury as well as sweet dishes; walnuts are a good substitute.

PECTIN is a carbohydrate present in certain fruits and vegetables which, when combined with sugar, helps a jam, jelly or marmalade to set or jell. Commercial pectin can be bought from health-food stores; it can be used to set jams and jellies made with fruit low in pectin.

PEPITAS are the pale green kernels of dried pumpkin seeds; they can be bought plain or salted.

PESTO a classic uncooked sauce made from basil, garlic, pine nuts, parmesan and olive oil; often served over pasta.

PIDE also known as Turkish bread. Sold in long (about 45cm) flat loaves as well as individual rounds; made from wheat flour and sprinkled with black onion seeds.

PINE NUTS also known as pignoli; not in fact a nut but a small, cream-coloured kernel from pine cones. They are best roasted before use to bring out the flavour.

PISTACHIO green, delicately flavoured nuts inside hard off-white shells. Available salted or unsalted in their shells; you can also get them shelled.

PITTA also known as lebanese bread; wheat-flour pocket bread sold in large, flat pieces that separate into two thin rounds. Also available in small thick pieces called pocket pitta.

PLUM SAUCE a thick, sweet and sour dipping sauce made from plums, vinegar, sugar, chillies and spices.

POACH a cooking term to describe gentle simmering of food in liquid (generally water or stock); spices or herbs can be added to impart their flavour.

POLENTA also known as cornmeal; a flour-like cereal made of dried corn (maize). also the name of the dish made from it.

POMEGRANATE dark-red, leathery-skinned fresh fruit about the size of an orange filled with hundreds of seeds, each wrapped in an edible lucent-crimson pulp having a unique tangy sweet-sour flavour.

POMEGRANATE MOLASSES not to be confused with pomegranate syrup or grenadine (used in cocktails); pomegranate molasses is thicker, browner, and more concentrated in flavour – tart and sharp, slightly sweet and fruity. Brush over grilling or roasting meat, seafood or poultry, add to salad dressings or sauces. Buy from Middle Eastern food stores or specialty food shops.

POMELO similar to grapefruit but sweeter, somewhat more conical in shape and slightly larger, about the size of a small coconut. The firm rind peels away easily and neatly, like a mandarin, and the segments are easy to separate.

POPPY SEEDS

black small, dried, bluish-grey seeds of the poppy plant, with a crunchy texture and a nutty flavour. Can be purchased whole or ground in delicatessens and most supermarkets.

white also known as kas kas. Quite dissimilar to the black variety, these seeds from the white poppy are used, ground, as a thickening agent in sauces. Toasted, they take on a nutty flavour so are also used as a substitute for ground almonds.

PORK

american-style spareribs well-trimmed mid-loin ribs.

belly fatty cut sold in rashers or in a piece, with or without rind or bone.

butterfly skinless, boneless mid-loin chop, split in half and flattened.

Chinese barbecued pork roasted pork fillet with a sweet, sticky coating. Available from Asian food shops or specialty stores.

cutlets cut from ribs.

fat selvedge fat from pork loin.

fillet skinless, boneless eye-fillet cut from the loin.

minced ground lean pork.

neck sometimes called pork scotch, boneless cut from the foreloin.

pancetta *see pancetta*

prosciutto *see prosciutto*

rack of pork joined row of trimmed cutlets.

shoulder joint sold with bone in or out.

steak schnitzel is usually cut from the leg or rump.

POTATOES

bintje oval, creamy skin, yellow flesh; good all-purpose potato, great baked and fried, good in salads.

coliban round, smooth white skin and flesh; good for baking and mashing.

congo purple flesh, small, elongated, sweet, mealy; good boiled and in salads.

desiree oval, smooth and pink-skinned, waxy yellow flesh; good in salads, boiled and roasted.

idaho also known as russet burbank; russet in colour, fabulous baked.

king edward slightly plump and rosy; great mashed.

kipfler small, finger-shaped, nutty flavour; great baked and in salads.

lasoda round, red skin with deep eyes, white flesh; good for mashing or roasting.

new potatoes also known as chats; not a separate variety but an early harvest with very thin skin. Good unpeeled steamed, eaten hot or cold in salads.

nicola medium-sized, oval, beige skin, yellow flesh; good for mashing.

pink-eye small, off-white skin, purple eyes; good steamed and boiled, great baked.

pink fir apple elongated, rosy skin, waxy; good boiled, baked and in salads.

pontiac large, red skin, deep eyes, white flesh; good grated, boiled and baked.

russet burbank long and oval, rough white skin with shallow eyes, white flesh; good for baking and frying.

sebago white skin, oval; good fried, mashed and baked.

spunta large, long, yellow flesh, floury; great mashed and fried.

PRESERVED LEMON an indispensable ingredient in Moroccan cooking and used as a flavouring by many modern chefs; has a silken texture and distinctive flavour. Preserved in salt, oil or lemon juice and occasionally spices such as cinnamon, clove and coriander for about 30 days, the lemon must be rinsed well before being either chopped and stirred into yogurt or a salad dressing without being cooked, or added to a casserole or tagine to add salty-sour piquancy to the finished dish.

PRESERVED TURNIP also known as hua chai po or cu cai muoi, or dried radish because of its similarity to daikon. Sold packaged whole or sliced, it is very salty and must be rinsed and dried before use.

PROSCIUTTO a kind of unsmoked Italian ham; salted, air-cured and aged, it is usually eaten uncooked. There are many styles of prosciutto, one of the best being Parma ham, from Italy's Emilia Romagna region, traditionally lightly salted, dried then eaten raw.

PRUNES commercially or sun-dried plums; store in the fridge.

PUMPKIN often used interchangeably with the word squash, the pumpkin is a member of the gourd family and comes in a variety of sizes, shapes and colours. Used in sweet and savoury dishes, pumpkin can be boiled, steamed, mashed or roasted.

QUAIL related to the pheasant and partridge; a small, delicate-flavoured farmed game bird ranging in weight from 250g to 300g.

QUINCE yellow-skinned fruit with hard texture and astringent, tart taste; eaten cooked or as a preserve. Long, slow cooking makes the flesh a deep rose pink.

QUINOA pronounced keen-wa. The seed of a leafy plant similar to spinach. Like corn, rice, buckwheat and millet, quinoa is gluten-free and thought to be safe for consumption by people with coeliac disease. Its cooking qualities are similar to rice, and its delicate, slightly nutty taste and chewy texture make it a good partner for rich or spicy foods. You can buy it in most health-food stores and some delicatessens; keep quinoa sealed in a glass jar under refrigeration because, like nuts and nut oils, it spoils easily.

RAISINS dried sweet grapes (traditionally muscatel grapes).

RAITA yogurt that is whipped and seasoned with salt, pepper and one or two piquant spices; often has mint stirred in. Served as a condiment, it possesses cooling properties to help temper the heat of a curry.

READY-ROLLED PUFF PASTRY packaged sheets of frozen puff pastry, available from supermarkets.

REDCURRANT JELLY a preserve made from redcurrants used as a glaze for desserts and meats or in sauces.

REMOULADE a French mayonnaise-like mixture traditionally containing capers, dijon mustard and parsley.

RICE

arborio small, round grain rice well-suited to absorb a large amount of liquid; the high level of starch makes it especially suitable for risottos, giving the dish its classic creaminess.

basmati a white, fragrant long-grained rice; the grains fluff up beautifully when cooked. It should be washed several times before cooking.

black also known as purple rice because, although a deep charcoal in colour when raw, after cooking it turns a purplish-black colour. A medium-grain unmilled rice, with a white kernel under the black bran, it has a nutty, whole-grain flavour and is crunchy to the bite like wild rice.

calrose a medium-grain rice that is extremely versatile; can be substituted for short- or long-grain rices if necessary.

glutinous also known as sweet rice or sticky rice; a short, fat grain having a chalky white centre. When cooked it becomes soft and sticky, hence the name; requires long soaking and steaming.

jasmine or Thai jasmine, is a long-grained white rice recognised around the world as having a perfumed aromatic quality; moist in texture, it clings together after cooking. Sometimes substituted for basmati rice.

long-grain elongated grains that remain separate when cooked; this is the most popular steaming rice in Asia.

medium-grain *see calrose*

short-grain fat, almost round grain with a high starch content; tends to clump together when cooked.

white is hulled and polished rice, can be short-or long-grained.

wild not a true member of the rice family but a very dark brown seed of a North American aquatic grass having a distinctively nutty flavour and crunchy, resilient texture. Sold on its own or in a blend with basmati or long-grain white rice.

RICE PAPER there are two products sold as rice paper. Banh trang is made from rice flour and water then stamped into rounds; is quite brittle and breaks easily Dipped briefly in water, they become pliable wrappers for food. The other, edible, translucent glossy rice paper is made from a dough made of water combined with the pith of an Asian shrub called the rice-paper plant (or rice-paper tree). Resembling a grainy sheet of paper and whiter than banh trang, it is imported from Holland. Use in confectionery making and baking; never eat it uncooked.

RIGANI also known as greek oregano; a stronger, sharper version of the familiar herb used in Italian cooking.

ROASTING nuts and dried coconut can be roasted in the oven to restore their fresh flavour and release their aromatic essential oils. Spread them evenly onto an oven tray then roast in a moderate oven for about 5 minutes. Desiccated coconut, pine nuts and sesame seeds roast more evenly if stirred over low heat in a heavy-base frying pan; their natural oils will help turn them golden brown.

ROCKET also known as arugula, rugula and rucola; peppery green leaf eaten raw in salads or used in cooking. Baby rocket leaves are smaller and less peppery.

ROLLED OATS flattened oat grain rolled into flakes and traditionally used for porridge. Instant oats are also available, but use traditional oats for baking.

ROLLED RICE flattened rice grain rolled into flakes; looks similar to rolled oats.

ROLLED RYE flattened rye grain rolled into flakes and similar in appearance to rolled oats.

ROSEMARY pungent herb with long, thin pointy leaves; use large and small sprigs, and the leaves are usually chopped finely.

ROSEWATER extract made from crushed rose petals, called gulab in India; used for its aromatic quality in many sweetmeats and desserts.

ROUILLE French for rust; is a capsicum and chilli-flavoured mayonnaise-like sauce used to garnish seafood stews, particularly the French classic, bouillabaisse.

RUM we use a dark underproof rum (not overproof) for a more subtle flavour in cooking. White rum is almost colourless, sweet and used mostly in mixed drinks.

SAFFRON stigma of a member of the crocus family, available ground or in strands; imparts a yellow-orange colour to food once infused. The quality can vary greatly; the best is the most expensive spice in the world.

SAGE pungent herb with narrow, grey-green leaves; slightly bitter with a slightly musty mint aroma. Dried sage comes whole, crumbled or ground.

SAKE Japan's favourite wine, made from fermented rice, is used for marinating, cooking and as part of dipping sauces. If sake is unavailable, dry sherry, vermouth or brandy can be substituted. If drinking sake, stand it first in a container in hot water for 20 minutes to warm it through.

SALSA the Spanish word for sauce but generally used in cooking to describe any raw or cooked Mexican sauce served also as a salad or dip, Raw, it is called "salsa cruda" or "salsa fresca"; there are a myriad cooked salsas and most are named after their colour or content.

SALSA VERDE while we generally associate the word "salsa" with Mexican salads, sauces or dips, this zesty fresh herb sauce is in fact an Italian classic that adds tang to poached or steamed fish dishes and is a part of a traditional bollito misto, the famous Piedmontese version of a boiled dinner. The herbs used in salsa verde can vary with the single common denominator being parsley.

SALT unless specified otherwise, we use normal iodised table salt. Because we believe cooks salt as they like or not at all, the vast majority of our recipes do not list it as one of the ingredients.

SAMBAL OELEK also ulek or olek; Indonesian in origin, this is a salty paste made from ground chillies and vinegar.

SAVOIARDI also known as savoy biscuits, lady's fingers or sponge fingers, they are Italian-style crisp fingers made from sponge cake mixture.

SCORE a cooking term to describe making shallow cuts, usually in criss-cross pattern, over meat, vegetables or seafood; often used on squid.

SEAFOOD

balmain bug also known as slipper or shovelnose lobster, or southern bay lobster; crustacean, a type of crayfish. Substitute with moreton bay bugs, king prawns or scampi.

barramundi an Aboriginal word, barramundi means "river fish with large scales". Wild barramundi, found in both coastal and fresh waters in the tropical northern half of Australia, weigh an average 4kg; farmed barramundi are an average 400g in weight. "Baby" barramundi (often referred to as "plate-size"), also farmed commercially, are a firm, moist white fish best served whole. Substitute with nile perch.

blue swimmer crab also known as sand crab, blue manna crab, bluey, sand crab or sandy. Substitute with lobster, balmain or moreton bay bugs.

blue-eye also known as deep sea trevalla or trevally and blue-eye cod; thick, moist white-fleshed fish.

bream (yellowfin) also known as silver or black bream, seabream or surf bream; soft, moist white flesh. Substitute with snapper or ocean perch.

calamari a mollusc, a type of squid; substitute with baby octopus.

clams also called vongole; we use a small ridge-shelled variety of this bivalve mollusc.

cod, smoked substitute with smoked haddock.

crab meat flesh of fresh crabs; frozen uncooked flesh is also available. Use canned if neither is available.

dhufish also known as WA pearl perch and jewfish; caught off the West Australian coast, popular with recreational fisherman. Substitute with jewfish, snapper or bream.

dried shrimp also known as goong hang, salted sun-dried prawns ranging in size from not much larger than a rice seed to big ones measuring about 1cm in length. They are sold packaged, shelled as a rule, in all Asian grocery stores.

fish fillet use your favourite firm-fleshed white fish fillet.

flathead many varieties, most commonly dusky flathead, which is also the largest. Mostly fished from river mouths and estuaries; substitute with whiting or your favourite white fish.

kingfish (yellowtail) also known as southern yellowfish, kingie, Tasmanian yellowtail. Substitute with jewfish.

lobster (rock lobster) also known as cray, spiny lobster, eastern, southern or western lobster. Substitute with balmain or moreton bay bugs.

mahi mahi also known as dolphin fish, dorado. Substitute with swordfish, mako shark or striped marlin.

mud crab also known as mangrove crab, green or black. Native to the tropical regions of the Bay of Bengal and the Pacific and Indian oceans. Substitute with scampi, lobster or balmain bugs.

mussels should only be bought from a reliable fish market: they must be tightly closed when bought, indicating they are alive. Before cooking, scrub shells with a strong brush and remove the beards; do not eat any that do not open after cooking. Varieties include black and green-lip.

ocean perch also known as coral, red or sea perch, or coral cod; white flesh with a delicate flavour. Substitute with snapper.

ocean trout a farmed fish with pink, soft flesh. It is from the same family as the atlantic salmon; one can be substituted for the other.

octopus usually tenderised before you buy them; both octopus and squid require either long slow cooking (usually for the large molluscs) or quick cooking over high heat (usually for the small molluscs) – anything in between will make the octopus tough and rubbery.

oysters available in many varieties, including pacific, bay/blacklip, and Sydney or New Zealand rock oyster.

pipis small smooth-shelled triangular shaped bivalve mollusc; substitute with clams or vongole.

prawns also known as shrimp. Varieties include, school, king, royal red, Sydney harbour, tiger. Can be bought uncooked (green) or cooked, with or without shells.

salmon red-pink firm flesh with few bones; moist delicate flavour.

sardines also known as pilchards; small silvery fish with soft, oily flesh. Substitute with garfish.

scallops a bivalve mollusc with fluted shell valve; we use scallops that have the coral (roe) attached.

squid also known as calamari; a type of mollusc. Buy squid hoods to make preparation and cooking faster.

swordfish also known as broadbill. Substitute with yellowfin or bluefin tuna or mahi mahi.

trevally (silver trevally) also known as skippy; firm, slightly oily pink flesh. Substitute with warehou or yellow jack.

tuna reddish, firm flesh; slightly dry. Varieties available include bluefin, yellowfin, skipjack or albacore; substitute with swordfish.

white fish means non-oily fish. This category includes bream, flathead, whiting, snapper, dhufish, redfish and ling.

whiting (sand whiting), also called silver whiting, summer whiting, king george whiting or trumpeter. Substitute with bream.

SEAWEED sheet (yaki-nori) *see nori*

SEGMENTING a cooking term to describe cutting citrus fruits in such a way that the pieces contain no pith, seed or membrane. The peeled fruit is cut towards the centre inside each membrane, forming wedges.

SESAME SEEDS black and white are the most common of this small oval seed, however there are also red and brown varieties. The seeds are used in cuisines the world over as an ingredient and as a condiment. Roast the seeds in a heavy-based frying pan over low heat.

SEVEN-SPICE MIX (shichimi togarashi) a Japanese blend of seven ground spices, seeds and seaweed. The mixture varies but will include some hot and aromatic flavours. Used as a seasoning with noodles and cooked meats and fish.

SHERRY fortified wine consumed as an aperitif or used in cooking. Sherries differ in colour and flavour; sold as fino (light, dry), amontillado (medium sweet, dark) and oloroso (full-bodied, very dark).

SHRIMP PASTE also known as kapi, trasi and blanchan; a strong-scented, very firm preserved paste made of salted dried shrimp. Used sparingly as a pungent flavouring in many South-East Asian soups, sauces and rice dishes. It should be chopped or sliced thinly then wrapped in foil and roasted before use.

SICHUAN PEPPERCORNS also known as szechuan or Chinese pepper, native to the Sichuan province of China. A mildly hot spice that comes from the prickly ash tree. Although it is not related to the peppercorn family, small, red-brown aromatic sichuan berries look like black peppercorns and have a distinctive peppery-lemon flavour and aroma.

SILVERBEET also known as Swiss chard and incorrectly, spinach; has fleshy stalks and large leaves, both of which can be prepared as for spinach.

SKEWERS metal or bamboo skewers can be used. Rub oil onto metal skewers to stop meat sticking; soak bamboo skewers in water for at least 1 hour or overnight to stop them burning.

SNOW PEAS also called mangetout; a variety of garden pea, eaten pod and all (although you may need to string them). Used in stir-fries or eaten raw in salads. Snow pea sprouts are available from supermarkets or greengrocers and are usually eaten raw in salads or sandwiches.

SOY SAUCE also known as sieu; made from fermented soybeans. Several variations are available in supermarkets and Asian food stores; we use Japanese soy sauce unless indicated otherwise.

dark deep brown, almost black in colour; rich, with a thicker consistency than other types. Pungent but not particularly salty, it is good for marinating.

japanese an all-purpose low-sodium soy sauce made with more wheat content than its Chinese counterparts; fermented in barrels and aged. Possibly the best table soy and the one to choose if you only want one variety.

light fairly thin in consistency and, while paler than the others, the saltiest tasting; used in dishes in which the natural colour of the ingredients is to be maintained. Not to be confused with salt-reduced or low-sodium soy sauces.

tamari similar to but thicker than japanese soy; very dark in colour with a distinctively mellow flavour. Good used as a dipping sauce or for basting.

SPATCHCOCK a small chicken (poussin), no more than 6 weeks old, weighing a maximum of 500g. Also, a cooking term to describe splitting a small chicken open, then flattening and grilling.

SPECK smoked pork.

SPINACH also known as english spinach and incorrectly, silverbeet. Baby spinach leaves are best eaten raw in salads; the larger leaves should be added last to soups, stews and stir-fries, and should be cooked until barely wilted.

SPRING ROLL WRAPPERS also known as egg roll wrappers; they come in various sizes and can be purchased fresh or frozen. Made from a delicate wheat-based pastry, they can be used for making gow gee and samosas as well as spring rolls.

SQUASH *see patty-pan squash*

STAR ANISE a dried star-shaped pod whose seeds have an astringent aniseed flavour; commonly used to flavour stocks and marinades.

STARFRUIT also known as carambola, five-corner fruit or Chinese star fruit; pale green or yellow colour, it has a clean, crisp texture. Flavour may be either sweet or sour, depending on the variety and when it was picked. There is no need to peel or seed it and they're slow to discolour.

STOCK These recipes can be made up to 4 days ahead and kept, covered, in the fridge. Remove any fat from the surface after the stock has been refrigerated overnight. All the recipes below make approximately 2.5 litres (10 cups).

beef stock

2kg meaty beef bones
2 medium onions (300g)
2 celery stalks (300g), chopped
2 medium carrots (240g), chopped
3 bay leaves
2 teaspoons black peppercorns
5 litres (20 cups) water
3 litres (12 cups) water, extra

Place the beef bones and unpeeled chopped onions in a baking dish. Bake in a hot oven (220°C/200°C fan-forced) for about 1 hour or until well browned. Transfer the bones and onion to a large saucepan, add the celery, carrots, bay leaves, peppercorns and the water; bring to a boil, then simmer, uncovered, for 3 hours. Add the extra water, then simmer, uncovered, for about 1 hour; strain.

chicken stock

2kg chicken bones
2 medium onions (300g), chopped
2 celery stalks (300g), chopped
2 medium carrots (240g), chopped
3 bay leaves
2 teaspoons black peppercorns
5 litres (20 cups) water

Combine all the ingredients in a large saucepan, simmer, uncovered, for about 2 hours; strain.

fish stock

1.5kg fish bones
3 litres (12 cups) water
1 medium onion (150g), chopped
2 celery stalks (300g), chopped
2 bay leaves
1 teaspoon black peppercorns

Combine all the ingredients in a large saucepan, simmer, uncovered, for about 20 minutes; strain.

vegetable stock

2 large carrots (360g), chopped
2 large parsnips (700g), chopped
4 medium onions (600g), chopped
10 celery stalks (1.5kg), chopped
4 bay leaves
2 teaspoons black peppercorns
6 litres (24 cups) water

Combine all the ingredients in a large saucepan, simmer, uncovered, for about 1 ½ hours; strain.

SUGAR we use coarse, granulated table sugar, also known as crystal sugar, unless otherwise specified.

brown an extremely soft, fine granulated sugar retaining molasses for its characteristic colour and flavour.

caster also known as superfine or finely granulated table sugar. The fine crystals dissolve easily so it is perfect for cakes, meringues and desserts.

cinnamon combination of ground cinnamon and caster sugar. Most commonly sprinkled over buttered toast.

demerara small-grained golden-coloured crystal sugar.

icing also known as confectioners' sugar or powdered sugar; pulverised granulated sugar crushed together with a small amount (about 3 per cent) of cornflour.

palm also known as nam tan pip, jaggery, jawa or gula melaka; made from the sap of the sugar palm tree. Light brown to black in colour and usually sold in rock-hard cakes; substitute with brown sugar if unavailable.

pure icing also known as confectioners' sugar or powdered sugar.

raw natural brown granulated sugar.

SUGAR SNAP PEAS also known as honey snap peas; fresh small pea which can be eaten whole, pod and all.

SUMAC a purple-red, astringent spice ground from berries growing on shrubs that flourish wild around the Mediterranean; adds a tart, lemony flavour to dips and dressings and goes well with barbecued meat. Can be found in Middle Eastern food stores.

SUNFLOWER SEED KERNELS grey-green, slightly soft, oily kernels; a nutritious snack.

SWEET CHILLI SAUCE *see chilli*

SWEETBREADS the thymus glands from veal, lamb and pork; they perish quickly so cook within a day of purchase.

SWISS ROLL PAN (also known as a jelly-roll pan) measures 26cm x 32cm; its slightly raised sides help contain the mixture being baked, preventing the Swiss roll, sponge, roulade, jam roll, slice, pizza base, etc from rising. Often the baked item is removed from the pan and rolled while still hot and malleable, then later unrolled, spread with sweet or savoury fillings, and rolled again before slicing.

TABASCO brand-name of an extremely fiery sauce made from vinegar, hot red peppers and salt.

TACO SEASONING MIX a packaged seasoning meant to duplicate the Mexican sauce made from oregano, cumin, chillies and other spices.

TAGINE a stew of Moroccan origin; also the name of the dish in which the stew is cooked.

TAHINI sesame seed paste available from Middle Eastern food stores; most often used in hummus and baba ghanoush.

TAMARIND the tamarind tree produces clusters of hairy brown pods, each of which is filled with seeds and a viscous pulp, that are dried and pressed into the blocks of tamarind found in Asian food shops. Gives a sweet-sour, slightly astringent taste to marinades, pastes, sauces and dressings.

TAMARIND CONCENTRATE (or paste) the commercial result of the distillation of tamarind juice into a condensed, compacted paste.

TAPENADE a thick paste made from black or green olives, capers, anchovies, olive oil and lemon juice.

TARRAGON often called the king of herbs by the French, it is used as the essential flavouring for many of their classic sauces (bêarnaise, tartare, etc). It is one of the herbs blended with parsley, chives and chervil to make *fines herbes*, and is the unique taste giving singularity to so many French egg, fish and chicken dishes.

TARTARIC ACID used in making sweets and preserves; prevents the crystallisation of the sugar.

TEMPERING the process by which chocolate is melted at a specific temperature that enables it to set with a glossy finish.

TEQUILA colourless alcoholic liquor of Mexican origin made from the fermented sap of the agave, a succulent desert plant.

TERIYAKI either home-made or commercially bottled, this Japanese sauce, made from soy sauce, mirin, sugar, ginger and other spices, imparts a distinctive glaze when brushed over grilled meat or poultry.

THYME a member of the mint family; there are many types of this herb but two that we use most. The "household" variety, simply called thyme in most shops, is French thyme; it has tiny grey-green leaves that give off a pungent minty, light-lemon aroma. Dried thyme comes in both leaf and powdered form. Lemon thyme's scent is due to the high level of citral in its leaves, an oil also found in lemon, orange, verbena and lemon grass. The citrus scent is enhanced by crushing the leaves in your hands before using the herb.

TOFU also known as soybean curd or bean curd; an off-white, custard-like product made from the "milk" of crushed soybeans. Comes fresh as soft or firm, and processed as fried or pressed dried sheets. Fresh tofu can be refrigerated in water (changed daily) for up to 4 days.

firm made by compressing bean curd to remove most of the water. Good used in stir-fries as it can be tossed without disintegrating. Can also be flavoured, preserved in rice wine or brine.

fried packaged pieces of deep-fried soft bean curd; the surface is brown and crunchy and the inside quite dry. Add to soups and stir-fries at the last minute so they don't soak up too much liquid.

sheets also known as dried bean curd skins or yuba. Manufactured product made from the sweet, stiffened skin that forms on warm soybean liquid as it cools. Must be reconstituted before being used as a wrapper. Also good, cut into strips, as a garnish.

silken not a type of tofu but reference to the manufacturing process of straining soybean liquid through silk; this denotes best quality.

soft delicate texture; does not hold its shape when overhandled. Can also be used as a dairy substitute in ice-cream or cheesecakes.

TOMATOES

canned whole peeled tomatoes in natural juices; available crushed, chopped or diced, sometimes unsalted or reduced salt. Use in recipes undrained.

cherry also known as tiny tim or tom thumb tomatoes; small and round.

egg also called plum or roma, these are smallish, oval-shaped tomatoes much used in Italian cooking or salads.

grape small, long oval-shaped tomatoes with a good tomato flavour.

green simply, underripe tomatoes.

paste triple-concentrated tomato puree used to flavour soups, stews, sauces and casseroles.

puree canned pureed tomatoes (not tomato paste); substitute with fresh peeled and pureed tomatoes.

semi-dried partially dried tomato pieces in olive oil; softer and juicier than sun-dried, these are not a preserve thus do not keep as long as sun-dried.

sun-dried tomato pieces that have been dried with salt; this dehydrates the tomato and concentrates the flavour. We use sun-dried tomatoes packaged in oil, unless otherwise specified. Also available in flavoured oil, such as chilli or herbs.

truss small vine-ripened tomatoes with vine still attached.

TOMATO SAUCE also known as ketchup or catsup; a flavoured condiment made from tomatoes, vinegar and spices.

TORTILLA thin, round unleavened bread originating in Mexico; can be made at home or purchased frozen, fresh or vacuum-packed. Wheat and corn flour varieties are available.

TREACLE thick, dark syrup not unlike molasses. *see golden syrup*

TURMERIC also known as kamin; is a rhizome related to galangal and ginger. Must be grated or pounded to release its somewhat acrid aroma and pungent flavour. Known for the golden colour it imparts, fresh turmeric can be substituted with the more commonly found dried powder.

VANILLA

bean dried, long, thin pod from a tropical golden orchid grown in central and South America and Tahiti; the minuscule black seeds inside the bean are used to impart a luscious vanilla flavour in baking and desserts. Place a whole bean in a jar of sugar to make the vanilla sugar often called for in recipes; a bean can be used three or four times.

essence obtained from vanilla beans infused in alcohol and water.

extract obtained from vanilla beans infused in water; a non-alcoholic version of essence.

VEAL

osso buco another name butchers use for veal shin, usually cut into 3cm to 5cm thick slices and used in the famous Italian slow-cooked casserole of the same name.

rack row of small chops or cutlets.

scaloppine a piece of lean steak hammered with a meat mallet until almost see-through; should be cooked over high heat for as little time as possible.

schnitzel thinly sliced steak.

VERMOUTH a wine flavoured with a number of different herbs, mostly used as an aperitif and for cocktails.

VINEGAR

balsamic originally from Modena, Italy, there are now many balsamic vinegars on the market ranging in pungency and quality depending on how, and for how long, they have been aged. Quality can be determined up to a point by price; use the most expensive sparingly.

brown malt made from fermented malt and beech shavings.

cider made from fermented apples.

raspberry made from fresh raspberries steeped in a white wine vinegar.

red wine made from red wine.

rice a colourless vinegar made from fermented rice and flavoured with sugar and salt. Also known as seasoned rice vinegar; sherry can be substituted.

sherry natural vinegar aged in oak according to the traditional Spanish system; a mellow wine vinegar named for its colour.

white made from distilled grain alcohol.

white wine made from white wine.

VIN SANTO translates as "holy wine" or "wine from heaven", alluding to its ethereal quality. A traditional Italian sweet dessert wine originally produced only in Tuscany. The high sugar content is obtained by drying the grapes for months before they are crushed to yield an intense liquid which is then barrel-aged for several years.

V-SLICER is a classic German kitchen tool used for slicing, shredding, dicing and julienning fresh vegetables and fruits; prized for its speed and precision. Caution is advised when hand-operating this extremely sharp instrument. A mandoline, the generic Italian slicer, or the various cutting discs of a food processor, perform various kitchen tasks similarly.

WALNUTS as well as being a good source of fibre and healthy oils, nuts contain a range of vitamins, minerals and other beneficial plant components called phytochemicals. Each type of nut has a special make-up and walnuts contain the beneficial omega-3 fatty acids, which is terrific news for people who dislike the taste of fish.

WASABI also known as wasabe; an Asian horseradish used to make the pungent, green-coloured sauce traditionally served with Japanese raw fish dishes; sold in powdered or paste form.

WATER CHESTNUTS resemble true chestnuts in appearance, hence the English name. Small brown tubers with a crisp, white, nutty-tasting flesh. Their crunchy texture is best experienced fresh; however, canned water chestnuts are more easily obtained and can be kept for about a month in the fridge, once opened. Used, rinsed and drained, in salads and stir-fries.

WATERCRESS one of the cress family, a large group of peppery greens used raw in salads, dips and sandwiches, or cooked in soups. Highly perishable, so it must be used as soon as possible after purchase.

WHEAT BRAN *see bran*

WHITE RADISH also known as daikon; an everyday fixture at the Japanese table, this long, white horseradish has a wonderful, sweet flavour. After peeling, eat it raw in salads or shredded as a garnish; also great when sliced or cubed and cooked in stir-fries and casseroles. The flesh is white but the skin can be either white or black; buy those that are firm and unwrinkled from Asian food shops.

WHOLE-EGG MAYONNAISE commercial mayonnaise of high quality made with whole eggs and labelled as such; some prepared mayonnaises substitute emulsifiers such as food starch, cellulose gel or other thickeners to achieve the same thick and creamy consistency but never achieve the same rich flavour. Must be refrigerated once opened.

WILD RICE *see rice*

WINE the adage that you should never cook with wine you wouldn't drink holds true in this book; unless specified otherwise, we use good-quality dry white and red wines in our recipes.

WITLOF also known as belgian endive; related to and confused with chicory. A versatile vegetable, it tastes as good cooked as it does eaten raw. Grown in darkness like white asparagus to prevent it becoming green; looks somewhat like a tightly furled, cream to very light-green cigar. The leaves can be removed and used to hold a canapé filling; the whole vegetable can be opened up, stuffed then baked or casseroled; and the leaves can be tossed in a salad with other vegetables.

WOMBOK *see Chinese cabbage*

WONTON small parcels of a filling encased in a thin noodle or pastry wrapper then steamed or fried.

WONTON WRAPPERS and gow gee or spring roll pastry sheets, made of flour, egg and water, are found in the refrigerated or freezer section of Asian food shops and many supermarkets. These come in different thicknesses and shapes. Thin wrappers work best in soups, while the thicker ones are best for frying; and the choice of round or square, small or large is dependent on the recipe.

WORCESTERSHIRE thin, dark-brown spicy sauce developed by the British when in India; used as a seasoning for meat, gravies and cocktails, and as a condiment.

YAKI-NORI *see nori*

YEAST (dried and fresh), a raising agent used in dough making. A microscopic living organism that grows best in warm, moist conditions; over-hot conditions or dissolving liquid will kill yeast and keep the dough from rising. Granular (7g sachets) and fresh compressed (20g blocks) yeast can almost always be substituted one for the other when yeast is called for.

YOGURT we use plain full-cream yogurt in our recipes unless specificially noted otherwise. If a recipe in this book calls for low-fat yogurt, we use one with a fat content of less than 0.2 per cent.

ZA'ATAR a blend of whole roasted sesame seeds, sumac and crushed dried herbs such as wild marjoram and thyme, its content is largely determined by the individual maker. Used to flavour many familiar Middle Eastern dishes, pizza and savoury pastries; available in delicatessens and specialty food stores.

ZUCCHINI also known as courgette; small, pale- or dark-green, yellow or white vegetable belonging to the squash family. Good cored and stuffed with various meat or rice fillings; in Italian vegetable dishes and pasta sauces; and as one of the vegetables that make ratatouille. Harvested when young, its edible flowers can be stuffed with a mild cheese or other similarly delicate ingredients then deep-fried or oven-baked to make a delicious appetiser.

Index

A

acidulated water 641
adzuki beans 394, 402
affogato 527
aïoli 422, 641
  bouillabaisse with aïoli and rouille 102
  tomato aïoli and prawn canapés 78
  vegetable tempura with wasabi aïoli 130
allspice 641
almonds 420, 641
  amaretti 529
  blanched 641
  chocolate nut clusters 635
  cookies, almond jam 521
  couscous, almond coriander 406
  dark chocolate and almond torte 558
  eggless date and nut cake 565
  essence 641
  flaked 641
  friands, almond and strawberry 515
  gourmet rocky road 628
  meal 641
  mille-feuille with almonds and raspberries 586
  nougat 630
  rhubarb and almond jalousie 586
  slivered 641
  swirled choc-almond biscotti 530
  vienna 641
anchovy 212
  onion, anchovy and olive pizza 489
  toasts 97
angostura aromatic bitters 641
antipasto topping 38
apple
  asian pork and apple salad 136
  butterflied pork steaks with pear and apple salsa 264
  caramelised apple clafoutis 610
  cider, sparking 641
  compote, apple and pear 32
  cucumber, celery, apple and spinach juice 57
  fruit scrolls with spiced yogurt 35
  jelly 462
  lassi, apple and melon 52
  mandarin apple juice with passionfruit ice 59
  pie 583
  pork cutlet with stuffed apple and peppercorn cider sauce 263
  streusel slice, apple and rhubarb 531
(*apple* continued)
  tea cake, apple custard 540
  turnovers 581
apricot
  bran and apricot cookies 525
  jam, apricot and pineapple 462
  muesli slice 534
  roasted stone fruit with lemon grass 618
  rock cakes, apricot and honey 546
  scones 512
  slice, apricot and coconut 535
  wholemeal fruit and coconut loaf 565
arancini 386
arrowroot 641
artichokes 322, 641
  cooking 322
  globe 641
  hearts 641
  jerusalem 641
  orecchiette with ham, artichokes and sun-dried tomatoes 356
  salad, artichoke and broad bean 322
asafoetida 466
asiago 335
asian greens 312
  stir-fried, in black bean sauce 306
asian-spiced barbecued turkey 438
asparagus
  grilled, with chilli butter 235
  haloumi, asparagus and rocket salad 136
  prawn and asparagus risotto 382
  salad, asparagus and tomato 118
avocado
  buying and storing 135
  caprese salad 140
  chicken and avocado sandwich 203
  fajitas with salsa cruda and avocado mash 237
  salmon, avocado on cucumber 78
  smoked salmon with avocado salsa and prawns 116
  tuna and avocado topping 38

B

baba ghanoush 125
bacon
  and eggs 32
  blt on mini toasts 79
  cheese, tomato and bacon topping 39
(*bacon* continued)
  fettuccine carbonara 349
  florentine eggs with bacon and pecorino 333
  muffins, bacon and herb 509
  oysters with tomato, bacon and basil 172
  pancetta see pancetta
  pinwheels, bacon and tomato 581
  rashers 641
  roast bacon-wrapped quail with muscat sauce 194
  toasts 96
bagels 485, 641
baharat 466
bain-marie 8
baked alaska 613
baked beans with fried eggs 42
baking blind 8, 571, 641
baking paper 641
baking powder 641
  gluten-free 651
balmain bugs 659
  citrus salad with 160
  preparing 157
balsamic vinegar 662
  dressing 149
  herb and balsamic marinade 276
  mustard balsamic marinade 288
balti 648
  biryani 384
bamboo shoots 641
bamboo skewers 641
bamboo steamers 641
banana
  cake with passionfruit icing 553
  caramelised banana and pecan waffles 40
  chocolate banana bread 41
  chocolate bananas 235
  fritters 603
  golden 608
  grilled prawns with tropical fruits 162
  hummingbird cake 562
  ice-cream, banana, maple and macadamia 622
  muffins, banana maple 510
  smoothie, banana-passionfruit soy 60
  tart, banana caramel 587
  tarte tatin 580
  topping, banana and hazelnut 39
  upside-down toffee banana cake 546

banana leaves 641
hot and sour fish steamed in 179
steamed chicken in 215
bar equipment 21, 48
barbecue glaze 238
barbecue ideas 234
barbecue sauce 257, 642
barley 395, 642
leek and saffron 409
swiss brown mushroom and barley soup 107
barramundi 659
kipflers and roasted capsicum with 184
basil 169, 642
chicken and thai basil fried rice 376
holy 642
opal 642
oysters with tomato, bacon and basil 172
risotto cakes with basil sauce and pancetta 389
sweet 642
thai 169, 642
basting 8
bay leaves 642
bean sprouts 642
bean thread noodles 345, 352
beans 394, 402, 642
adzuki 394, 402
artichoke and broad bean salad 322
baked beans with fried eggs 42
beef, bean and chorizo stew 221
black see black beans
black-eyed 394, 402, 642
black-eyed beans, okra and kumara gumbo 408
borlotti 394, 642
broad 200, 394, 403, 642
burritos 241
butter 642
buying and storing 395
cannellini 394, 403, 642
chile con carne 227
green 642
haricot 394, 402
kidney 394, 642
lamb shanks with white bean puree 285
mexican broad bean burgers 405
mixed pea, broad bean and turkey salad 200
panang pork curry with pickled snake beans 256
pinto 642
quartet of beans in chilli lime sauce 397
refried 642
snake 642
soaking 395
soybeans 394, 642
(*beans* continued)
three-bean salad 152
tuscan white bean salad 137
types 394, 402, 642
vegetable cassoulet 318
white 642
white bean, leek and garlic sausage soup 106
white bean puree 285
béarnaise sauce 412, 415
beating 11
béchamel sauce 414
beef 218, 642
aussie meat pies 574
baby back ribs 642
balti biryani 384
barbecue-glazed meatloaf 238
beef, bean and chorizo stew 221
black bean sauce, with buk choy and 245
bourguignon 242
bourguignon pies 573
braised beef cheeks in red wine 243
braised oxtails with orange gremolata 224
burritos 241
buying, storing and handling 218, 248
carpaccio with fennel salad 241
char-grilled thai beef salad 141
cheeks 642
chile con carne 227
chuck 219, 642
corned 219, 642
corned beef hash with poached eggs 331
cottage pie 576
cuts 219, 642
eye-fillet 642
fajitas with salsa cruda and avocado mash 237
gravy beef 219, 642
grilling or barbecuing 219
hamburger with a twist 236
judging when cooked 219
massaman curry 222
minced 642
new york cut 219, 642
new york steaks with grilled cheesy polenta triangles 401
new york steaks with lemon-thyme butter 232
ox kidney 219
oxtail 642
porterhouse 219, 642
pot-roasting 219
rendang 236
rissoles with cabbage mash 246
roast beef and horseradish cream blini 84
(*beef* continued)
roast beef with yorkshire puddings 228
roasted eye fillet with red wine risotto 378
roasting 219
round steak 643
rump 219, 643
satay sticks 121
scotch fillet 219, 643
silverside 219, 643
sirloin 219
skirt steak 237, 643
spaghetti bolognese 357
spareribs 229
standing rib roast with lemon and garlic 244
steak diane 245
steak sandwich revisited 233
steak tartare 248
stew, beef and horseradish, with kumara potato mash 220
stock 661
t-bone 219, 643
t-bones with blue-cheese butter and pear salad 224
thai red curry beef skewers 234
traditional beef pot roast 221
twice-fried sichuan beef 230
vietnamese beef, chicken and tofu soup 92
beetroot 643
baby beetroot with caper vinaigrette 320
barbecued vegetarian pizzas 311
beetroot, carrot and spinach juice 62
borscht 95
buying and storing 135
caramelised onion and beetroot tart 578
pan-fried tofu with beetroot hummus 322
bell pepper see capsicum
berry see also specific berry types
compote 29
French toast with berry compote 29
fresh berry frappé 57
mixed-berry buttermilk muffins 504
mixed-berry cake with vanilla bean syrup 559
mixed-berry punch 52
mixed-berry sauce topping 623
mixed-berry smoothie 60
mixed-berry topping 39
sugared berry cake 550
vanilla panna cotta with berry jelly 605
besan flour 214, 650
betel leaves 313

beurre blanc 290, 416
lamb backstraps with vegetable crisps and 290
bicarbonate of soda 643
binding 8
Bircher muesli 26, 40
biscotti 530
coffee and hazelnut 530
lemon and pistachio 529
swirled choc-almond 530
biscuits 518, 643
almond jam cookies 521
amaretti 529
anzac biscuits 528
baking 518
bran and apricot cookies 525
brandy snaps 636
chocolate chip cookies 522
Christmas cookies 445
Christmas tree 446
coconut macaroons 522
coconut tuiles 523
crunchy muesli cookies 523
florentines, mini 630
gingernuts 524
glazed lemon shortbreads 528
greek shortbread 524
hazelnut pinwheels 521
mixing 518
passionfruit butter yoyo bites 525
presentation 627
storing and freezing 519
black beans 394, 402, 642
cuban black bean soup 99
sauce 245, 643
stir-fried asian greens in black bean sauce 306
black rice 381, 658
black sticky rice 615
blackberry pudding 600
blanching 9, 643
blini 84, 643
buckwheat 84
crème fraîche and salmon roe 84
roast beef and horseradish cream 84
smoked chicken and mustard 84
spinach and horseradish 84
blood orange see orange
bloody mary 59
oyster shots 69
blt
italian 259
on mini toasts 79
blueberry
hotcakes with walnuts and maple syrup 30
muffins 502
blue-eye 659
curried, with lentils and raita 174
bocconcini 335, 644
avocado caprese salad 140
italian blt 259
pancetta and bocconcini topping 38
spicy sausage and bocconcini pizza 489
boiling vegetables 303
bok choy see buk choy
bombe alaska, mango 613
borscht 95
bouillabaisse with aïoli and rouille 102
bowls 16
brains, lamb 275
crumbed, with celeriac remoulade 296
braising 9, 643
vegetables 303
bran 643
bran and apricot cookies 525
brandy 643
butter 506
snaps 636
brazil nuts 420, 643
bread and buns 478
bagels 485, 641
baking 479
basic white 480
brioche 490, 643
chapati 481, 644
checking if dough proved 493
chelsea buns 482
chilli corn 495
crusty sourdough loaf 486
damper 490, 648
dinner rolls 484
food processor rye 492
fruit and nut loaf 496
gluten-free 497
lavash 652
making 479
mixed-grain loaf 493
naan 481, 655
onion focaccia 492
pide 484, 656
pitta 657
potato, olive and sun-dried tomato 486
pumpernickel 480
rosemary pumpkin 496
roti 495
sourdough 478
turkish 484
breadcrumbs 643
breadknife 14
breakfast 26
cereal 26
fry up 29
in a glass 26
(*breakfast* continued)
quick 26
slow 27
bream 659
citrus-ginger steamed 185
brie 335, 644
caramelised onion and brie tart 120
turkey, brie and cranberry 78
brioche 490, 643
fig and brioche pudding 598
broad beans see beans
broccolini 643
polonaise 323
brown malt vinegar 662
brown sauce 412
brown sugar 661
brownies
choc-brownie muffins 509
triple-choc 531
bruising 9, 643
bruschetta 643
haloumi and tapenade 79
olive and tomato 119
white bean puree 285
buckwheat 395, 643
blini 84
mushrooms with buckwheat kernels 408
buffalo wings, classic 205
buk choy 312, 643
beef with black bean sauce and 245
burgers
asian chicken, with pickled cucumber and wasabi mayonnaise 213
chicken schnitzel 206
hamburger with a twist 236
mexican broad bean 405
pork, with caramelised pears 264
thai fish, with sour and sweet green salad 163
burghul 395, 402, 644
burghul and wild rice salad 406
salad with chickpeas 400
burritos, beef 241
butter 644
clarified 9
creaming 11
flavoured see butters and creams
butter beans 642
butter chicken 198
butterflying 9
buttermilk 37, 653
mixed-berry buttermilk muffins 504
pancakes with glazed strawberries 37
scones 514
butters and creams 506
blue-cheese butter 224
brandy butter 506
burnt butter 350

(*butters and creams* continued)
chilli butter 235
choc-hazelnut cream 506
cinnamon cream 96
citrus butter 506
citrus liqueur cream 509
coffee cream 506
dill cream 97
garlic and fennel cream 172
ginger and ricotta cream 507
harissa butter 288
horseradish cream 84, 578
lemon and lime butter 464
lemon-thyme butter 232
maple and pecan butter 506
mascarpone orange cream 506
mocha butter cream 599
mustard and rosemary cream 289
mustard and walnut butter 311
paprika butter 96
passionfruit butter 507, 525
pesto butter 289
praline cream 507
saffron cream sauce 161
sage butter 129
vanilla bean cream 507
vanilla butter cream 549
whipped nut butter 41, 507
butterscotch sauce 423, 614
maple butterscotch sauce 561
sticky date pudding with 614

C

cabbage
chinese 313, 646
crunchy fried noodle coleslaw 148
mixed cabbage coleslaw with chinese barbecued pork 270
pork cabbage rolls 254
pork fillet with mash and wilted cabbage 259
rissoles with cabbage mash 246
wombok 313
cachous 644
caesar salad 144
chicken 203
caipiroska 50
cakes 538
after dinner mint 551
apple custard tea 540
apricot and honey rock 546
baked lemon cheesecake 605
baking 539
banana, with passionfruit icing 553
black forest 556
butter 566
butterfly 567

(*cakes* continued)
buttery orange 554
caramel mud cake 542
carrot, with lemon cream cheese frosting 541
chocolate, family 548
chocolate, malted 551
chocolate on chocolate 551
Christmas cake 449
cookies and cream cheesecake 614
cupcakes 550
cut 'n' keep butter 566
daisy 550
dark chocolate and almond torte 558
devil's food 567
double-decker mud 554
eggless date and nut 565
fairy floss 550
fig, walnut and ginger 558
fruit cake, best ever boiled 566
fruit cake, last minute 454
genoise sponge 543
glacé icing 554
gluten-free orange syrup 564
Grand Marnier fruit cake 450
honey yogurt 549
hummingbird 562
jam roll 560
lamingtons 540
malted chocolate 551
maple pecan 561
mixed-berry, with vanilla bean syrup 559
mixing 539
mocha buttercake 555
neopolitan ice-cream 550
orange syrup, gluten-free 564
pans 538
patty cakes with vanilla butter cream 549
peanut chocolate crunch 551
pear and polenta syrup 560
presentation 627
rhubarb and coconut 542
rocky road 550
sacher torte 545
snowball 551
starfruit Christmas tree 550
storing 539
strawberry creamcake 551
strawberry jelly 564
sugared berry 550
testing whether cooked 539
tiramisu 606
upside-down toffee banana 546
Wendy's sponge 548
wholemeal fruit and coconut loaf 565

calamari 127, 659
preparing 157
stuffed with fetta and chilli 127
california handrolls 376
calzones, ricotta and herb 321
canapés
fig and fetta 80
smoked salmon and dill 79
sun-dried tomato and olive tapenade 474
tomato aïoli and prawn 78
candy canes 446
candy thermometer 21, 636, 639
cannellini beans 394, 403, 642
cannelloni, chicken and prosciutto 361
caperberries 644
capers 644
baby beetroot with caper vinaigrette 320
caper and roasted capsicum salsa 431
smoked salmon caper and dill frittata 341
capsicum 644
barramundi with kipflers and roasted 184
buying and storing 135
caper and roasted capsicum salsa 431
eggplant, fetta and capsicum stack with mesclun salad 315
gazpacho 92
grilled vegetable salad 149
mash 309
prosciutto and roast capsicum rösti stacks 43
roasted vegetable filo tart 579
roasted vegetable salad 119
rouille 658
spicy mustard pickles 473
tomato, carrot and red capsicum juice 62
caramel
banana caramel tart 587
boiling sugar 626
chews 635
crème caramel 603
filling 587
frosting 543
ginger date muffins with caramel sauce 503
hazelnut caramel slice 533
mud cake 542
sauce 503
caramelising 9
caraway seeds 644
cardamom 644
blood plums with honey and cardamom yogurt 44
cardamom-crumbed cutlets 289

(*cardamom* continued)
coffee 526
tea, cardamom and chamomile 526
carpaccio
beef, with fennel salad 241
tuna, kingfish and salmon 177
carrot
beetroot, carrot and spinach juice 62
braised root vegetables with gremolata 310
buying and storing 135
cake with lemon cream cheese frosting 541
middle-eastern roasted pumpkin, carrot and parsnip 323
tomato, carrot and red capsicum juice 62
vegetable cassoulet 318
carving
ham 435
turkey 435
carving knife 21, 435
cashews 421, 644
coriander pesto 475
cassata 650
casserole
dish 17
lamb for casseroling 275
pork for casseroling 253
udon casseroles 351
cassoulet
pork 254
vegetable 318
caster sugar 661
cauliflower
cheese 367
floret 650
mornay 286
pickled 124
spicy mustard pickles 473
cayenne pepper 646
celeriac 644
mash 309
remoulade, crumbed brains with 296
celery
buying and storing 135
cucumber, celery, apple and spinach juice 57
garnishes for drinks 55
cereal 26
ceviche, lime and ginger 181
champagne 49, 644
cocktail 51
chapati 481, 644
char-grilling 9
stovetop char-grill 21
vegetables 303
char kway teow 346
char sui 644
marinade, char sui and honey 289
cheese see also specific cheese types
blue 644
blue cheese and green onion mini pizzas 69
cheddar 644
cheese and chive souffléd oysters 173
cheese, tomato and bacon topping 39
cheesy pastry twists 581
cheesy rice croquettes 385
grater 18, 21
plane 21
sauce, basic 414
soft blue vein 645
swiss 645
tasty 645
tomato, spinach and cheese topping 38
twice-cooked cheese soufflés 338
types 334, 644
cheesecake
baked lemon 605
cookies and cream 614
chef's knife 14
chef's salad 147
chelsea buns 482
chermoulla 159, 645
sardines in, with tomato salsa 159
cherry 645
black forest cake 556
cucumber, celery, apple and spinach juice 57
friands 515
garnishes for drinks 54
glacé 645
jelly cakes 564
maraschino 645
chervil 168, 645
creamy chervil dressing 339
chiang mai noodles 352
chicken 188, 645
asian chicken burger with pickled cucumber and wasabi mayonnaise 213
barbecued 645
barbecued chicken pizza 488
breast fillet 646
buffalo wings 205
butter chicken 198
buying, storing and handling 188
cacciatore 212
caesar salad 203
cajun chicken with pineapple salsa 214
cannelloni, chicken and prosciutto 361
chicken, caramelised onion and fig pizza 199
chilli pizza 202
(*chicken* continued)
chow mein 195
coconut chicken salad in crisp wonton cups 82
coronation chicken 194
crisp-skinned soy, with spiced salt 190
cuts 188
drumette 646
drumettes in crisp spicy batter 214
drumstick 646
enchiladas with corn salsa 191
fettuccine boscaiola with 364
fried rice 203
fried rice, chicken and thai basil 376
green curry 209
jambalaya 373
judging when cooked 189
larb chicken salad 151
little chicken and leek pies 575
liver salad with polenta croutons 193
maryland 646
nachos 202
peanut and chicken gow gees 77
pecan chicken open sandwich 202
pesto and chicken gnocchi 202
pesto chicken 235
poached, with ruby grapefruit salad 197
roasted, with 40 cloves of garlic 205
salad, old-fashioned 141
sandwich, chicken and avocado 203
sandwich, italian-style toasted 203
satay sticks 121
schnitzel burgers 206
smoked 646
smoked chicken and mustard blini 84
smoked chicken and pear salad 119
smoked chicken wonton crisps 79
soup, chicken and corn 107
soup, chicken and zucchini 203
spatchcock see spatchcock
spicy chicken legs with mango salad 210
steamed chicken in banana leaf 215
stir-fry, chicken and mixed mushroom 195
stock 661
tagine with olives and preserved lemon 197
tandoori pockets with raita 190
tenderloin 646
teriyaki rice paper rolls 202
thigh cutlet 646
thigh fillet 646
tikka drumettes 234
trussing 13
udon casseroles 351
vietnamese beef, chicken and tofu soup 92
wing 646

(*chicken* continued)
wraps 202
yakitori with sesame dipping sauce 206
chickpeas 394, 403, 646
burghul salad with 400
chickpea, pumpkin and eggplant curry 304
cooking 395
felafel 396
hummus 125
hummus bi tahini 397
pan-fried tofu with beetroot hummus 322
soaking 395
za'atar lamb with warm chickpea salad 297
chicory 143
chilli 646
butter 235, 277
calamari stuffed with fetta and 127
cayenne 646
chile con carne 227
chilli and paprika rub 288
chipotle 260, 646
corn bread 495
flakes 646
green 646
grilled asparagus with chilli butter 235
honey chilli sauce 423
hot sauce 646
jalapeño 646
jalapeño corn muffins 227
kaffir lime marinade 276
lamb cutlets with chilli lemon grass marinade 289
lamb cutlets with grilled corn and garlic 277
lime and chilli yogurt topping 311
lime dressing 166, 179, 427
lime vinaigrette 182
long red 646
octopus, chilli garlic 234
parmesan crisps 96
pasilla 646
paste 646
powder 646
quartet of beans in chilli lime sauce 397
singapore chilli crab 178
sweet chilli dipping sauce 81
sweet chilli sauce 646
thai 646
tomato jam 233
chinese barbecued duck see duck
chinese barbecued pork see pork
chinese broccoli 313, 650
chinese cabbage 313, 646
chinese cooking wine 646
chinese noodles 345
chipotle 260, 646
chive oil 579
chives 646
garlic 168
chocolate 627, 646
after dinner mint cake 551
banana bread 41
bananas 235
black forest cake 556
cherry ripe 646
choc Bits 646
choc-brownie muffins 509
choc-hazelnut cream 506
choc-marmalade croissants 581
choc-peppermint no-bake slice 535
chocolate chip cookies 522
chocolate malt ice-cream 622
chocolate on chocolate cake 551
chocolate, pear and hazelnut self-saucing pudding 606
chocolate peppermint squares 629
couverture 647
cream fudge 636
dark chocolate and almond torte 558
dark cooking 647
dark eating 647
double-decker mud cake 554
family chocolate cake 548
florentines, mini 630
ganache 650
gourmet chocolate tart 585
gourmet rocky road 628
hazelnut croissants 42
malted chocolate cake 551
melting 519
Melts 647
milk 647
mini chocolate eclairs 583
mocha buttercake 555
mocha dacquoise terrine 599
mousse 602
nut clusters 635
panforte 638
peanut chocolate crunch cake 551
raspberry and chocolate mousse trifle 619
rum and raisin slice 533
sauce 424
slice, no-bake 535
snowball cake 551
swirled choc-almond biscotti 530
white 647
white chocolate and macadamia muffins 502
chopping board 16
chorizo 260, 647
beef, bean and chorizo stew 221
chorizo and kumara frittata 329
chowder, smoked cod 103
choy sum 312, 647
Christmas 434
Christmas cake 449
Christmas nut tree 456
Christmas pudding 442, 448
Christmas tree cookies 446
cookies 445
gingerbread house 453
steamed Christmas pudding 442
stollen 444
three-in-one Christmas mix 448
chutney 280
green mango 473
rhubarb 470
spicy tomato 469
ciabatta 647
cider vinegar 662
cinnamon 647
cream 96
tea, cinnamon and orange 526
cinnamon sugar 661
porridge topping 32
toast topping 39
cioppino 181
citric acid 647
citrus butter 506
citrus salad 161
citrus syrup 560
clafoutis, caramelised apple 610
clams 659
cioppino 181
paella 379
preparing 157
spaghetti alla vongole 360
cloves 647
cocktail party drinks 48
bar equipment 21, 48
garnishes 54
cocoa powder 647
coconut 647
apricot and coconut no-bake slice 535
chicken salad in crisp wonton cups 82
coconut ice 637
cream 647
desiccated 647
essence 647
flaked 647
garnishes for drinks 54
lime syrup coconut muffins 504
macaroons 522
milk 647
pipis stir-fried in coconut milk 185
rhubarb and coconut cake 542
roasting 519
shredded 647
thai coconut prawns 76
tuiles 523

(*coconut* continued)
wholemeal fruit and coconut loaf 565
yellow coconut rice 375
cod see smoked cod
coffee 27
affogato 527
cardamom 526
chocolate mocha dacquoise terrine 599
coffee and hazelnut biscotti 530
coffee and macadamia no-bake slice 535
cream 506
granita with walnut crisps 612
iced mocha 527
irish 527
mocha butter cream 599
mocha buttercake 555
spiced iced coffee milkshake 63, 527
coleslaw
crunchy fried noodle 148
mixed cabbage, with chinese barbecued pork 270
confit 10
duck, with pan-fried kipflers and pear and watercress salad 212
conserve see jams, jellies and conserves
conversion charts 23
cookies see biscuits
cooking oil spray 647, 655
coral lettuce 142, 652
coriander 168, 647
almond coriander couscous 406
garlic and coriander naan 481
pesto 475
corn
chicken and corn soup 107
chicken enchiladas with corn salsa 191
chilli corn bread 495
chilli lamb cutlets with grilled corn and garlic 277
grilled corn and zucchini salsa 431
grilled mahi mahi with roasted corn and chilli salad 160
jalapeño corn muffins 227
polenta and corn fritters 36
relish 470
saffron scrambled eggs on corn cakes 330
salsa 191
corned beef 219, 642
hash with poached eggs 331
cornflakes 647
cornflour 647
cornichons 647
potted pork with witlof and 268
coronation chicken 194
cos lettuce 142, 652
cosmopolitan 50
cottage cheese 644
cottage pie 576
coulis 598
raspberry 424, 598
courgette see zucchini
couscous 395, 403, 647
almond coriander 406
lamb and quince tagine with pistachio 283
lemon 308
pistachio 283
crab
blue swimmer 659
california handrolls 376
cioppino 181
crab fried rice in omelette 331
meat 659
mud crab 659
preparing 157
radicchio with thai crab salad 129
singapore chilli 178
craisins 648
pork chops with kumara craisin salad 266
cranberry sauce 648
pork chops with kumara craisin salad and 266
cream
dessert accompaniment 597
flavoured see butters and creams
cream cheese 644
carrot cake with lemon cream cheese frosting 541
cream cheese and pesto potato topping 310
cream cheese-filled brandied dates 638
frosting 562
smoked salmon and cream cheese topping 38
cream of tartar 648
creaming 11
crème anglaise 424
crème brûlée, ginger and lime 602
crème caramel 603
crème fraîche 597, 648
blini with salmon roe and 84
rösti with smoked trout and 82
crème patissiere 590
crepes 623
crepe pan 21
lemon curd crepe cake 623
smoked salmon and sour cream 85
vegetarian 85
croissants 36
choc-marmalade 581
chocolate hazelnut 42
prosciutto and fontina 36
croquettes, cheesy rice 385
crostini 76
duck and hoisin 76
crumbing 10
crumble, plum and rhubarb 619
cucumber 648
apple 648
buying and storing 135
cucumber, celery, apple and spinach juice 57
garnishes for drinks 55
gherkin 648
lebanese 648
pickled 213
salmon and avocado on 78
salsa, cucumber and onion 97
telegraph 648
tuna and cucumber mini maki 383
cumberland sauce 417
cumin 648
curly endive 142, 648
currants 648
curry
balti 648
balti biryani 384
beef massaman 222
beef rendang 236
blue-eye with lentils and raita 174
chicken green 209
chickpea, pumpkin and eggplant 304
curried eggs 332
green curry paste 209, 648
korma 648
malaysian swordfish 173
massaman curry paste 222, 320, 648
panang 648
panang pork, with pickled snake beans 256
pastes 649
pork vindaloo 262
powder 648
red 648
rogan josh 276, 648
thai red curry beef skewers 234
tikka 648
tikka drumettes 234
tofu and thai eggplant massaman 320
vindaloo 648
yellow 307, 648
curry puffs with sweet chilli sauce 81
custard 597, 620
apple custard tea cake 540
classic trifle 620
portuguese custard tarts 588
powder 648
vanilla 444
cutting in 12
cuttlefish, preparing 157

D

daikon 663
daiquiri 51
damper 490, 648
    mini muffin dampers 33
dashi 648
dates 648
    cream cheese-filled brandied 638
    eggless date and nut cake 565
    ginger date muffins with caramel sauce 503
    lamb cutlets with tamarind and date chutney 288
    maple creamed rice with pecans and 44
    overnight date and muesli muffins 508
    sticky date pudding with butterscotch sauce 614
    wholemeal date scones 513
    wholemeal fruit and coconut loaf 565
deep-frying 11
    vegetables 303
deglazing 10, 649
degorging 10
degreasing 10
demerara sugar 661
deveining 10
devil's food cake 567
dhal 649
    egg and eggplant, with 340
    mixed 396
dhufish 659
dijonnaise 649
dill 168, 649
    cream 97
    scrambled eggs with smoked salmon and 43
    smoked salmon and dill canapés 79
    smoked salmon caper and dill frittata 341
disgorging 649
dolmades 375
dragées (cachous) 644
dragon fruit 608
dressings 413
dried mixed herbs 649
dry-frying 11
dry martini 51
duck 188, 649
    barbecued duck tartlets 580
    breast fillets 649
    breasts with fig sauce and spinach risoni 198
    buying, storing and handling 188
    chinese barbecued 649
    confit with pan-fried kipflers and pear and watercress salad 212
    cuts 189, 649

(*duck* continued)
    duck and hoisin crostini 76
    judging when cooked 189
    liver parfait with red onion jam 114
    maryland 649
    peking duck 204
    peking duck pancakes 120, 204
    ravioli in asian broth 127
dumplings
    gyoza with soy vinegar sauce 70
    irish stew with herb dumplings 290
    peanut and chicken gow gees 77
    prawn 70
    steamed spinach, with fresh tomato and herb sauce 306
durian 609
dusting 10
duxelles, sweetbreads with herb salad and 249

E

éclairs, mini chocolate 583
egg noodles 345, 353, 655
eggplant 649
    baba ghanoush 125
    baby 649
    chickpea, pumpkin and eggplant curry 304
    dhal with egg and eggplant 340
    eggplant, fetta and capsicum stack with mesclun salad 315
    grilled vegetable salad 149
    moussaka 291
    pea eggplant 261, 649
    roasted vegetable salad 119
    thai 649
    tofu and thai eggplant massaman curry 320
    veal and eggplant parmigiana 230
eggs 326, 649
    bacon and eggs 32
    baked 327
    baked beans with fried eggs 42
    baked, with pancetta 330
    benedict 333
    boiled 41, 327
    braised leek and witlof salad with poached eggs and roasted kipflers 339
    breakfast fry up 29
    breakfast with the lot topping 39
    buying and storing 326
    chorizo and kumara frittata 329
    cooking 327
    corned beef hash with poached eggs 331
    crab fried rice in omelette 331

(*eggs* continued)
    creamy egg and lettuce finger sandwiches 341
    creamy stuffed 336
    curried 332
    denver omelette 338
    dhal with egg and eggplant 340
    egg flip 26
    eggwash 649
    egg-white omelette 332
    fettuccine carbonara 349
    florentine eggs with bacon and pecorino 333
    french toast with berry compote 29
    fried 327
    frittata 229
    meringue see meringue
    omelettes 327
    poached 327
    ranchero-style 329
    saffron scrambled eggs on corn cakes 330
    scrambled 327
    scrambled, with dill and smoked salmon 43
    separating 326
    smoked salmon caper and dill frittata 341
    smoked salmon omelette 28
    soufflé see soufflé
    spanish tortilla 33
    spinach, speck and poached egg salad 270
    tortilla pizza 329
    whisking whites 326
eggwash 649
emulsion 10
enchiladas with corn salsa, chicken 191
endive
    belgian 143
    curly 142
essence/extract 649

F

fajitas with salsa cruda and avocado mash 237
fattoush 140
felafel 396
fennel 649
    barbecued fennel, orange and red onion with quinoa 316
    beef carpaccio with fennel salad 241
    garlic and fennel cream oysters 172
    lamb cutlets with olive salsa, polenta and 284
    mash 309
fenugreek 467

fetta 334, 644
calamari stuffed with chilli and 127
eggplant, fetta and capsicum stack with mesclun salad 315
fig and fetta canapés 80
grilled 118
marinated 71
mushroom and fetta pizza 489
tomato, leek and marinated fetta tartlets 71
fettuccine 656
boscaiola with chicken 364
carbonara 349
fig 650
chicken, caramelised onion and fig pizza 199
duck breasts with fig sauce and spinach risoni 198
fig and brioche pudding 598
fig and fetta canapés 80
fig and prosciutto pizza 488
fig, walnut and ginger cake 558
galettes 580
poached, with semifreddo 610
quail, fig and orange salad 126
wholemeal fig muffins 502
finger food 66
fish see also specific fish types
barramundi 659
barramundi with kipflers and roasted capsicum 184
blue-eye 659
bream 659
carpaccio 177
cioppino 181
citrus-ginger steamed bream 185
cleaning and filleting 156
cooking 156
curried blue-eye with lentils and raita 174
deep-fried perch with chilli lime dressing 166
dhufish 659
fillet 659
fish cakes with mirin dipping sauce 74
fish in beer batter with chips 162
flathead 659
grilled mahi mahi with roasted corn and chilli salad 160
hot and sour fish steamed in banana leaves 179
kingfish 659
lime and ginger ceviche 181
mahi mahi 659
ocean perch 659
salmon see salmon; smoked salmon
sardines 660
(*fish* continued)
sardines in chermoulla with tomato salsa 159
smoked cod 659
smoked cod chowder 103
stock 661
swordfish 660
swordfish curry, malaysian 173
thai fish burgers with sour and sweet green salad 163
trevally 660
trevally mornay pies 574
trout see trout
tuna see tuna
white fish 660
whiting 660
whiting parcels with porcini and sun-dried tomatoes on soft polenta 183
fish sauce 650
five-spice 650
lamb shanks in five-spice, tamarind and ginger 284
flame/flambe 10
florentines, mini 630
floret 650
flour 650
focaccia, onion 492
folding 11
fontina 335, 644
baked three-cheese pasta 367
gnocchi al quattro formaggi 362
frangipane filling 586
frappé 49
alcoholic 59
fresh berry 57
kiwifruit, orange and mint 59
pineapple-orange 60
french dressing 427
french onion soup 94
french toast with berry compote 29
friands 501
almond and strawberry 515
cherry 515
little lime 514
frittata 229
chorizo and kumara 329
smoked salmon caper and dill 341
frozen chocolate fruit cake pudding 451
frozen desserts 597
fruit and nut loaf 496
fruit and vegetable juices 49
fruit and vegetable knife 14
fruit cake
boiled 566
frozen chocolate fruit cake pudding 451
Grand Marnier 450
last minute 454
fruit mince slice 449
fruit salad
asian 618
minted 37
fruit scrolls with spiced yogurt 35
fudge, chocolate cream 636

G

gado gado 138
gai lan 313, 650
galangal 260, 650
galettes 585
fig 580
rhubarb 585
ganache 650
garam masala 467, 650
garlic 650
aïoli see aïoli
chilli garlic octopus 234
chilli lamb cutlets with grilled corn and 277
lemon garlic dressing 140
lemon garlic marinade 288
mongolian garlic lamb 294
naan, garlic and coriander 481
oysters, garlic and fennel cream 172
prawns 117
roast rack of pork with lemon and 268
roasted chicken with 40 cloves of 205
roasted parsnip and garlic soup 101
standing rib roast with lemon and 244
garlic chives 168
garnishes
drinks 54
soups 89, 96
gazpacho 92
gelati 650
lemon gelato 613
gelatine 651
desserts 596
ghee 9, 651
ginger 651
citrus-ginger steamed bream 185
cream, ginger and ricotta 507
crème brûlée, ginger and lime 602
dressing 176
fig, walnut and ginger cake 558
fresh 651
gingernuts 524
glacé 651
ground 651
lamb shanks in five-spice, tamarind and 284
lime and ginger ceviche 181
muffins, ginger date, with caramel sauce 503
pickled 651

(*ginger* continued)
tea 527
tea, minted lemon grass and ginger iced 58
tuna tartare 176
gingerbread house 453
gingerbread men 447
glacé au four 613
glacé fruit 627
glasses and bar equipment 48
glazed ham 439
glucose syrup 651
gluten 651
gluten-free
baking powder 651
bread 497
orange syrup cake 564
gnocchi 656
al quattro formaggi 362
burnt butter and tomato, with 350
pesto and chicken 202
spinach and ricotta, with sage butter 129
goat cheese 334, 644
lamb and goat cheese pizza 488
potato puffs 79
soufflé with creamed spinach sauce 336
golden syrup 651
gorgonzola 645
baked three-cheese pasta 367
cheese and spinach tortellini with gorgonzola sauce 366
gnocchi al quattro formaggi 362
gow gee see wontons
grains 395
Grand Manier 651
fruit cake 450
granita 612, 651
coffee, with walnut crisps 612
grapefruit 651
citrus salad 161
juice, grapefruit and blood orange 62
poached chicken with ruby grapefruit salad 197
grapevine leaves see vine leaves
gratin dish 17
gratin, pumpkin and potato 367
gravlax 176
gravy 413, 417
greasing pans 651
greek lamb, slow-roasted 280
greek salad 145
greek shortbread 524
green beans 642
buying and storing 135
panang pork curry with pickled snake beans 256
spicy mustard pickles 473
green onion 656
blue cheese and green onion mini pizzas 69
buying and storing 135
gremolata 96, 225, 310, 651
braised oxtails with orange gremolata 224
braised root vegetables with 310
lamb pasta salad 153
orange 224
osso buco 225
grill pan 21
grilled vegetable salad 149
gruyère 645
toasts 97
gumbo, black-eyed beans, okra and kumara 408
gyoza with soy vinegar sauce 70

H

haloumi 334, 645
asparagus and rocket salad 136
bruschetta, haloumi and tapenade 79
pan-fried, with green salad 304
ham
breakfast fry up 29
breakfast with the lot topping 39
carving 435
glazed 439
mascarpone and ham mini pizzas 69
orecchiette with ham, artichokes and sun-dried tomatoes 356
pea and ham soup 100
prosciutto see prosciutto
traditional glazed 439
hard sauce 442
haricot beans 394, 402
harira 100
harissa 467, 651
butter on cutlets 288
hazelnuts 421, 651
banana and hazelnut topping 39
choc-hazelnut cream 506
chocolate hazelnut croissants 42
chocolate, pear and hazelnut self-saucing pudding 606
coffee and hazelnut biscotti 530
hazelnut and pine nut brittle 629
hazelnut caramel slice 533
pinwheels 521
whipped nut butter 507
herb and balsamic marinade 276
herb sauce 162
herbs 168, 651
hoisin 651
duck and hoisin crostini 76
peanut and hoisin sauce 204
hokkien noodles 345, 352, 655
mee noodles 363
hollandaise sauce 333, 412, 415, 651
eggs benedict 333
honey
apricot and honey rock cakes 546
char sui and honey marinade 289
honey chilli sauce 423
honey soy marinade 276
honey yogurt cake 549
mustard and honey-glazed roasted kumara 315
porridge topping, honey and yogurt 32
prawns 182
ricotta, pear and honey topping 38
spiced honey yogurt 507
honeydew melon 651
horseradish 261, 651
beef and horseradish stew with kumara potato mash 220
cream 84, 578
spinach and horseradish blini 84
roast beef and horseradish cream blini 84
hot and sweet glaze 267
hot cross buns 455
hummingbird cake 562
hummus 125, 277, 652
bi tahini 397
lamb kofta with 277
pan-fried tofu with beetroot hummus 322

I

ice-cream 652
banana, maple and macadamia 622
chocolate malt 622
gelati 650
lemon gelato 613
mango bombe alaska 613
mixed-berry sauce topping 623
neopolitan ice-cream cake 550
pistachio praline topping 622
rocky road topping 623
strawberry 622
vanilla 622
icing sugar 661
infusing 11
irish stew with herb dumplings 290
italian blt 259
italian dressing 427

J

jackfruit 608
jalapeño 646
corn muffins 227

jam roll 560
jambalaya, chicken 373
jams, jellies and conserves
- apple jelly 462
- apricot and pineapple jam 462
- jam 652
- jars, sealing and storing 461
- jellies 460
- jelly cakes 564
- marmalade 460
- quince paste 463
- raspberry and peach jam 462
- redcurrant jelly 658
- strawberry conserve 463
- sweet orange marmalade 464
- tomato and passionfruit jam 463

japanese noodles 345, 352
jarlsberg 645

K

kaffir lime 652
- chilli and kaffir lime marinade 276
- leaves 313, 652
- lemon grass and kaffir lime tea 526

kalonji 466, 652
kang kong 313
kecap manis 261, 652
kidneys
- lamb 275
- ox 219

kingfish 659
- tuna, kingfish and salmon carpaccio 177

kitchen utensils 18
kiwifruit 652
- frappé, kiwifruit, orange and mint 59

kneading 11
knives 14
kumara 652
- beef and horseradish stew with kumara potato mash 220
- black-eyed beans, okra and kumara gumbo 408
- chorizo and kumara frittata 329
- kumara craisin salad 266
- mustard and honey-glazed roasted 315
- pork chops with cranberry sauce and kumara craisin salad 266
- potato mash 220
- roasted 315

L

labne 125
lahma bi ajeen 124
laksa, prawn 104
lamb 274, 652
- asian mini lamb roasts 278
- backstrap 652
- backstraps with vegetable crisps and beurre blanc 290
- barbecued chops with three marinades 276
- brains 275
- brains, crumbed, with celeriac remoulade 296
- braised shanks with white bean puree 285
- buying, storing and handling 274
- cardamom-crumbed cutlets 289
- casseroling 275
- char sui and honey marinade 289
- chilli and paprika rub for cutlets 288
- chilli cutlets with grilled corn and garlic 277
- chilli lemon grass marinade 289
- chump 274, 652
- cooking 275
- cutlets 274, 288, 652
- cutlets with olive salsa, polenta and fennel 284
- cuts 274, 652
- diced 652
- fillets 652
- greek lamb salad 298
- gremolata lamb pasta salad 153
- grilling or barbecuing 274
- harissa butter on cutlets 288
- herb-crusted lamb racks with kipfler potatoes and leek 295
- irish stew with herb dumplings 290
- judging when cooked 275
- kidneys 275
- kofta with hummus 277
- lahma bi ajeen 124
- leg 274, 652
- lemon and garlic marinade for cutlets 288
- liver 275
- minced 652
- minced lamb in vine leaves 117
- mini lamb pies 124
- mongolian garlic lamb 294
- morrocan lamb cutlets 119
- moussaka 291
- mustard and rosemary cream on cutlets 289
- mustard balsamic marinade 288
- pan-frying 275
- parmesan-breaded lamb cutlets 296
- pesto butter on cutlets 289
- pilaf 372
- pizza, lamb and goat cheese 488

(*lamb* continued)
- pizzas, lamb and rocket mini 69
- pot-roasting 275
- raan with lemon pilau 293
- rack 274, 652
- roasting 274
- rogan josh 276
- rolled shoulder 274, 652
- rosemary and lamb kebabs 234
- shank 274, 652
- shank soup 90
- shanks in five-spice, tamarind and ginger 284
- shepherd's pie 281
- shoulder 652
- slow-roasted greek 280
- spiced lamb topping 124
- tagine, lamb and quince, with pistachio couscous 283
- tamarind and date chutney with cutlets 288
- tandoori cutlets with chutney 280
- tandoori lamb cutlets 289
- traditional roast dinner 286
- turkish herbed lamb pizza 294
- wrap, lamb and tabbouleh 278
- za'atar crusted cutlets 288
- za'atar lamb with warm chickpea salad 297

lamb's fry 275
lamb's lettuce 142
lamington pan 652
lamingtons 540
larb chicken salad 151
larb dressing 151
large serrated knife 14
lasagne
- bolognese 347
- fresh sheets 656
- roasted vegetable 316

lassi 49
- apple and melon 52

lavash 652
leeks 652
- braised leek and witlof salad with poached eggs and roasted kipflers 339
- caramelised 233
- herb-crusted lamb racks with kipfler potatoes and leek 295
- leek and saffron barley 409
- little chicken and leek pies 575
- pork rissoles on potato rösti with leek puree 255
- tomato, leek and marinated fetta tartlets 71
- white bean, leek and garlic sausage soup 106

lemon
baked lemon cheesecake 605
biscotti, lemon and pistachio 529
butter, lemon and lime 464
chicken tagine with olives and preserved lemon 197
citrus butter 506
citrus-ginger steamed bream 185
citrus salad 161
delicious pudding 607
dipping sauce 131
dressing, lemon dijon 304
dressing, lemon garlic 140
dressing, lemon mustard 200
garnishes for drinks 54
gelato 613
glazed lemon shortbreads 528
iced tea 526
lemon curd crepe cake 623
marinade, lemon garlic 288
meringue pie 588
new york steaks with lemon-thyme butter 232
pilau, raan with 293
preserved 197, 475, 657
roast rack of pork with garlic and 268
skewered lemon prawns 234
soybean patties with lemon and herb yogurt 399
spaetzle 248
squeezer 18
standing rib roast with garlic and 244
tangy lemon squares 534
tart 593
wiener schnitzel with lemon spaetzle 248
zucchini flowers, lemon ricotta 118
lemon grass 312, 652
dressing 166
lamb cutlets with chilli lemon grass marinade 289
lemon grass and kaffir lime tea 526
lobster with flavoured butter and lemon grass mash 167
minted lemon grass and ginger iced tea 58
roasted stone fruit with 618
salmon lemon grass skewers 235
lemon myrtle 260
lemon pepper seasoning 652
lemon thyme 662
butter 232
lentils 394, 652
buying and storing 395
curried blue-eye with raita and 174
dhal 649
dhal with egg and eggplant 340
french green 652
(*lentils* continued)
megadarra 400
mixed dhal 396
puy 394, 402
soaking 395
types 394
lettuce 142, 652
blt on mini toasts 79
braised spatchcock with peas and 207
butter 652
buying and storing 134
coral 142, 652
cos 142, 652
creamy egg and lettuce finger sandwiches 341
iceberg 653
mesclun 143, 653
mignonette 143
mixed leaves 653
mizuna 142, 653
oak-leaf 143, 653
radicchio 143, 653
types 142, 652
lime
chilli and kaffir lime marinade 276
chilli lime dressing 166, 179, 427
chilli lime vinaigrette 182
citrus butter 506
daiquiri 51
friands 514
garnishes for drinks 54
ginger and lime crème brûlée 602
jelly cakes 564
kaffir lime leaves 313
key lime pie 592
lemon and lime butter 464
lemon grass and kaffir lime tea 526
lime and chilli yogurt potato topping 311
lime and ginger ceviche 181
lime and mustard dressing 391
lime syrup coconut muffins 504
quartet of beans in chilli lime sauce 397
sugared lime and mango cheeks 235
syrup 504
tarragon and lime scallops 68
liver
chicken liver salad with polenta croutons 193
duck liver parfait with red onion jam 114
lamb 275
seared calves, with persillade and parsnip mash 242
lobster 659
flavoured butter and lemon grass mash with 167
preparing 157
long island iced tea 50
lychee 608, 653
asian fruit salad 618

M

macadamias 421, 589, 653
banana, maple and macadamia ice-cream 622
coffee and macadamia no-bake slice 535
mini macadamia, pecan and walnut pies 589
prawn cakes 171
white chocolate and macadamia muffins 502
macaroons, coconut 522
mache 142
mahi mahi 659
grilled, with roasted corn and chilli salad 160
mandarin 653
apple juice with passionfruit ice 59
mandoline 21, 653
mango 609, 653
asian fruit salad 618
barbecued seafood and green mango salad 166
bombe alaska 613
green 609
green mango chutney 473
grilled prawns with tropical fruits 162
mango and avocado salsa 428
spicy chicken legs with mango salad 210
sugared lime and mango cheeks 235
mangosteen 609
maple syrup 44, 653
banana, maple and macadamia ice-cream 622
banana maple muffins 510
blueberry hotcakes with walnuts and 30
maple and pecan butter 506
maple creamed rice with pecans and dates 44
maple-flavoured syrup 653
maple pecan cake 561
margarita 52
marinade 653
char sui and honey 289
chilli and kaffir lime 276
chilli lemon grass 289
herb and balsamic 276
honey soy 276
kaffir lime 276
lemon garlic 288
mustard balsamic 288
marinating 12

marjoram 169, 653
dressing 298
marmalade 460, 653
choc-marmalade croissants 581
sweet orange 464
marron 157
marsala 653
marshmallows
gourmet rocky road 628
toasted 637
marzipan 653
mascarpone 335, 645
and ham mini pizzas 69
gnocchi al quattro formaggi 362
mascarpone orange cream 506
massaman curry see curry
mayonnaise 653
aïoli see aïoli
basic 425
dijonnaise 649
thousand island dressing 425
wasabi 213
whole-egg 663
measurement conversion charts 23
measuring utensils 16
meat thermometer 21
meatloaf, barbecue-glazed 238
megadarra 400
melon
apple and melon lassi 52
garnishes for drinks 55
merguez 653
white bean, leek and garlic sausage soup 106
meringue 588, 617
desserts 596
kisses, with passionfruit cream 628
lemon meringue pie 588
pavlova 617
roll 617
mesclun 143, 653
eggplant, fetta and capsicum stack with mesclun salad 315
mexican broad bean burgers 405
mexican-style fried oysters 172
mezze platter 124
middle-eastern roasted pumpkin, carrot and parsnip 323
mignonette lettuce 143
milk 63, 653
buttermilk see buttermilk
evaporated 653
full-cream powder 653
skim 653
smoothies see smoothies
spiced iced coffee milkshake 63, 527
sweetened condensed 654
minced meat 654
minestrone 91
mint see also peppermint
garnishes for drinks 55
kiwifruit, orange and mint frappé 59
minted fruit salad 37
minted lemon grass and ginger iced tea 58
moroccan mint tea 526
sauce 417
spearmint 654
thai 654
vietnamese 168, 654
mirin 654
fish cakes with mirin dipping sauce 74
oysters with 118
miso 654
mixed dried fruit 654
mixed peel 654
mixed spice 654
mizuna 142, 653
molasses 654
pomegranate 657
mongolian garlic lamb 294
morrocan lamb cutlets 119
mortar and pestle 654
mouli 654
moussaka 291
mousse
chocolate 602
raspberry and chocolate mousse trifle 619
mozzarella 645
muesli 26, 654
apricot muesli slice 534
Bircher 26, 40
crunchy muesli cookies 523
overnight date and muesli muffins 508
roasted, with dried fruit and honey 30
muffins
bacon and herb 509
baking 501
banana maple 510
blueberry 502
cheesy pizza 508
choc-brownie 509
citrus poppy seed 510
english 649
ginger date, with caramel sauce 503
jalapeño corn 227
lime syrup coconut 504
mixed-berry buttermilk 504
mixing 500
overnight date and muesli 508
white chocolate and macadamia 502
wholemeal fig 502
muscat 654
roast bacon-wrapped quail with muscat sauce 194
mushrooms 654
breakfast fry up 29
buckwheat kernels, with 408
button 654
buying and storing 135
chicken and mixed mushroom stir-fry 195
creamy tarragon and mushroom sauce 418
dried porcini 654
flat 654
japanese oysters with shiitake mushrooms 172
microwave mushroom risotto 372
mixed mushroom ragout with soft polenta 317
mushroom and fetta pizza 489
oyster 312, 654
risotto primavera on grilled 113
sausages with caramelised onions, kipflers and 229
sauteed mushroom topping 39
shiitake 313, 654
swiss brown 654
swiss brown mushroom and barley soup 107
muslin 654
mussels 659
in fragrant thai broth 126
paella 379
preparing 157
steamed belgian 178
steamed, with saffron 119
mustard 654
american-style 654
dijon 654
dijonnaise 649
english 654
lamb cutlets with mustard and rosemary cream 289
lemon dijon dressing 304
lemon mustard dressing 200
lime and mustard dressing 391
mustard and honey-glazed roasted kumara 315
mustard and walnut butter topping 311
mustard balsamic marinade 288
seeds 655
smoked chicken and mustard blini 84
spicy mustard pickles 473
wholegrain 654

N

naan 481, 655
garlic and coriander 481
nachos, chicken 202
nan jim 655

nashi 655
witlof and nashi salad 148
nectar 655
nectarine 655
roasted necartine tart 590
roasted stone fruit with lemon grass 618
niçoise salad 145
noodles see also pasta
bean thread 345, 352
char kway teow 346
chiang mai 352
chilled soba 360
chinese 345, 352
dried rice 655
egg 345, 353, 655
fried 352, 655
hokkien 345, 352, 655
hokkien mee 363
japanese 345, 352
pad thai 349
ramen 345, 352
rice 345, 353, 655
rice stick 353, 655
rice vermicelli 353, 655
singapore 354, 655
soba 345, 352, 655
somen 345, 353
storing 345
sweet soy fried 366
thai fried stick 349
types 345, 353
udon 345, 353, 655
wheat 345
nori 655
nougat, almond 630
nutmeg 655
nuts and seeds 420
chocolate nut clusters 635
nut brittle 629
roasting 519

O

oak-leaf lettuce 143, 653
octopus 659
barbecued seafood and green mango salad 166
braised in red wine 164
chilli garlic 234
preparing 157
oil 655
okra 655
black-eyed beans, okra and kumara gumbo 408
olive oil 655
olives
chicken tagine with olives and preserved lemon 197
(*olives* continued)
haloumi and tapenade bruschetta 79
kalamata olives on pizza 311
lamb cutlets with olive salsa, polenta and fennel 284
marinated 468
olive and tomato bruschetta 119
onion, anchovy and olive pizza 489
pepperoni and olive pizza 489
potato, olive and sun-dried tomato bread 486
sun-dried tomato and olive tapenade 474
tapenade pastries 580
omelette see eggs
onion
baby 655
blue cheese and green onion mini pizzas 69
caramelised 199, 400
caramelised onion and beetroot tart 578
caramelised onion and brie tart 120
chicken, caramelised onion and fig pizza 199
flakes 655
focaccia 492
fried 656
green 656
megadarra 400
onion, anchovy and olive pizza 489
pickled 475
potato and onion hash 234
purple shallots 260, 656
red 656
roasted vegetable filo tart 579
sausages with caramelised onions, kipflers and mushrooms 229
spicy mustard pickles 473
spring 656
orange
asian fruit salad 618
barbecued fennel, orange and red onion with quinoa 316
blood orange 643
braised oxtails with orange gremolata 224
buttery orange cake 554
citrus-ginger steamed bream 185
citrus salad 161
gluten-free orange syrup cake 564
grapefruit and blood orange juice 62
kiwifruit, orange and mint frappé 59
mascarpone orange cream 506
pineapple-orange frappé 60
quail, fig and orange salad 126
stewed prunes with 44
sweet orange marmalade 464
(*orange* continued)
syrup 564
turkish delight 639
oregano 168
osso buco 225, 662
oven dishes 17
oven temperatures 22
oven thermometer 21
oxtails, braised, with orange gremolata 224
oyster mushrooms 312, 654
oyster sauce 656
oysters 172, 659
bloody mary oyster shots 69
cheese and chive souffléd 173
garlic and fennel cream 172
japanese, with shiitake mushrooms 172
mexican-style fried 172
preparing 157
with mirin 118
with salsa verde 172
with tomato, bacon and basil 172

P

paella 379
pak choy 656
palette knife 21
palm sugar 618, 661
pancakes see also crepes
blueberry, with walnuts and maple syrup 30
buttermilk, with glazed strawberries 37
peking duck 120, 204
pancetta 656
baked eggs with 330
italian blt 259
pancetta and bocconcini topping 38
risotto cakes with basil sauce and 389
panforte, chocolate 638
pan-frying 11
vegetables 303
panna cotta, vanilla, with berry jelly 605
panettone 454
panzanella 147
papaya 609
asian fruit salad 618
green 312
pappadums 656
paprika 656
butter 96
par-cooking/par-boiling 12
paring knife 14
parmesan 334, 645
baby rocket and parmesan salad 137
baked three-cheese pasta 367
crisps 96
gnocchi al quattro formaggi 362
parmesan-breaded lamb cutlets 296

parsley 169, 656
parsnip
braised root vegetables with gremolata 310
middle-eastern roasted pumpkin, carrot and parsnip 323
roasted parsnip and garlic soup 101
seared calves liver with persillade and parsnip mash 242
passionfruit
asian fruit salad 618
banana cake with passionfruit icing 553
banana-passionfruit soy smoothie 60
butter 507, 525
frozen passionfruit yogurt 620
icing 553
jelly cakes 564
mandarin apple juice with passionfruit ice 59
meringue kisses with passionfruit cream 628
panama 609
pineapple with 235
tomato and passionfruit jam 463
yoyo bites 525
pasta 344, 656
baked three-cheese 367
buying and storing 345
cheese and spinach tortellini with gorgonzola sauce 366
chicken and prosciutto cannelloni 361
cooking 345
ditali 656
farfalle 656
farfalle with fried zucchini, creamy 367
fettuccine 656
fettuccine boscaiola with chicken 364
fettuccine carbonara 349
gnocchi see gnocchi
lasagne bolognese 347
macaroni 656
orecchiette 356, 656
orecchiette with ham, artichokes and sun-dried tomatoes 356
pastitsio 359
primavera 350
ricotta and spinach stuffed pasta shells 364
risoni see risoni
roasted vegetable lasagne 316
saganaki prawn ravioli 356
shapes 344
shells 656
spaghetti see spaghetti
spiral 656
tagliatelle 656
tagliatelle puttanesca 357
(*pasta* continued)
tortellini 656
types 344, 656
pasta salad 153
chicken 203
gremolata lamb 153
tuna 152
pastitsio 359
pastry
apple turnovers 581
bacon and tomato pinwheels 581
baking 570
baking blind 571, 641
cheesy twists 581
choux 571
croissants see croissants
fig galettes 580
mille-feuille with almonds and raspberries 586
mini chocolate eclairs 583
mixing 570
paris-brest 582
pies see pies and tarts
pistachio rosewater pinwheels 581
profiteroles 582
quick puff pastry recipes 580
ready-rolled puff 658
rhubarb and almond jalousie 586
shortcrust 570
soup dippers 580
tapenade pastries 580
tarts see pies and tarts
pastry brush 18
patty-pan squash 656
pavlova 617
pea eggplant 261, 649
peach
iced tea 58
raspberry and peach jam 462
peanut 656
coriander pesto 475
gow gees, peanut and chicken 77
oil 655
peanut and hoisin sauce 204
peanut chocolate crunch cake 551
sauce 138
pear
apple and pear compote 32
butterflied pork steaks with pear and apple salsa 264
chocolate, pear and hazelnut self-saucing pudding 606
duck confit with pan-fried kipflers and pear and watercress salad 212
garnishes for drinks 55
nashi 655
pear and polenta syrup cake 560
(*pear* continued)
pork burgers with caramelised pears 264
ricotta, pear and honey topping 38
roasted pear tart 580
scones 512
smoked chicken and pear salad 119
t-bones with blue-cheese butter and pear salad 224
witlof and nashi salad 148
peas
black-eyed 394, 402
blue boilers 394
braised spatchcock with lettuce and 207
buying and storing 135, 395
dried 394, 649
mash 309
mixed pea, broad bean and turkey salad 200
pea and ham soup 100
snow peas 660
split 394, 403
sugar snap 661
types 394
pecans 420, 656
caramelised banana and pecan waffles 40
maple and pecan butter 506
maple butterscotch sauce 561
maple creamed rice with pecans and dates 44
maple pecan cake 561
mini macadamia, pecan and walnut pies 589
pecan chicken open sandwich 202
pecorino 645
florentine eggs with bacon and 333
pectin 656
peking duck see duck
pepitas 421, 656
pepper
bell see capsicum
cayenne 646
sichuan peppercorns 467, 660
peppermint
choc-peppermint slice 535
chocolate peppermint squares 629
turkish delight 639
perch
deep-fried, with chilli lime dressing 166
ocean perch 659
persillade 242
seared calves liver with parsnip mash and 242
pesto 474, 656
chicken 235
coriander 475

(*pesto* continued)
cream cheese and pesto potato topping 310
lamb cutlets with pesto butter 289
mini muffin dampers 33
pesto and chicken gnocchi 202
veal rack with rosemary and rocket pesto 232
pickles
cauliflower 124
gherkin 648
ginger 651
onion 475
spicy mustard 473
pide 484, 656
pies and tarts
apple pie 583
aussie meat pies 574
baking pastry 570
banana caramel tart 587
banana tarte tatin 580
barbecued duck tartlets 580
beef bourguignon pies 573
caramelised onion and beetroot tart 578
caramelised onion and brie tart 120
choux pastry 571
cottage pie 576
gourmet chocolate tart 585
key lime pie 592
lemon meringue pie 588
lemon tart 593
little chicken and leek pies 575
mille-feuille with almonds and raspberries 586
mini macadamia, pecan and walnut pies 589
mixing pastry 570
portuguese custard tarts 588
quince tarte tatin 592
rhubarb galette 585
roasted nectarine tart 590
roasted pear tart 580
roasted vegetable filo tart 579
shortcrust pastry 570
tapenade pastries 580
tomato, leek and marinated fetta tartlets 71
trevally mornay pies 574
vegetable free-form tarts 581
pilaf
lamb 372
tunisian spicy nut 372
piña colada 51
pine nuts 420, 656
hazelnut and pine nut brittle 629
pineapple
apricot and pineapple jam 462
(*pineapple* continued)
asian fruit salad 618
barbecued, with passionfruit 235
cajun chicken with pineapple salsa 214
garnishes for drinks 54
grilled prawns with tropical fruits 162
hummingbird cake 562
pineapple-orange frappé 60
salsa 214
pinwheels
bacon and tomato 581
hazelnut 521
pistachio rosewater 581
pipis 659
preparing 157
stir-fried in coconut milk 185
pistachio 420, 657
chocolate nut clusters 635
couscous 283
gourmet rocky road 628
lemon and pistachio biscotti 529
pistachio praline topping 622
pistachio rosewater pinwheels 581
pistou 97
pitta 657
pizza
aussie 489
barbecued chicken 488
barbecued vegetarian 311
basic pizza dough 487
basic tomato pizza sauce 487
blue cheese and green onion mini 69
char-grilled vegetable mini 69
cheese 645
cheesy pizza muffins 508
chicken, caramelised onion and fig 199
dough 199, 487
fig and prosciutto 488
greek mini pizzas 78
lamb and goat cheese 488
lamb and rocket mini 69
mascarpone and ham mini 69
mini pizzas 69, 78
mushroom and fetta 489
napoletana 487
onion, anchovy and olive 489
pepperoni and olive 489
potato and rosemary 488
salami and rocket 488
spicy sausage and bocconcini 489
supreme 489
toppings 488
turkish herbed lamb 294
vegetarian 488
vegetarian, barbecued 311
plum sauce 657
plums
blood plums 35, 44
(*plums* continued)
blood plums with honey and cardamom yogurt 44
plum and rhubarb crumble 619
roasted stone fruit with lemon grass 618
spiced, with yogurt 35
poached eggs see eggs
poaching 12, 657
polenta 395, 403, 657
cheesy 243
chicken liver salad with polenta croutons 193
fritters, polenta and corn 36
lamb cutlets with olive salsa, fennel and 284
mixed mushroom ragout with soft polenta 317
new york steaks with grilled cheesy polenta triangles 401
pear and polenta syrup cake 560
soft 183, 409
whiting parcels with porcini and sun-dried tomatoes on 183
polonaise, broccolini 323
pomegranate 260, 657
pomegranate molasses 657
pomelo 657
poppy seeds 657
citrus poppy seed muffins 510
soup dippers 580
pork 252, 657
american-style spareribs 257, 657
asian pork and apple salad 136
asian-spiced roasted pork belly 266
belly 253, 266, 657
burgers with caramelised pears 264
butterflied steaks with pear and apple salsa 264
butterfly 657
buying, storing and handling 252
caramelised barbecued pork neck 267
casseroling 253
cassoulet 254
chinese barbecued 657
chinese-style spareribs 253
chops with cranberry sauce and kumara craisin salad 266
cooking 253
cutlet 657
cutlet with stuffed apple and peppercorn cider sauce 263
cuts 252, 657
fillet 252, 657
fillet with mash and wilted cabbage 259
grilling or barbecuing 252
loin with spinach and pancetta stuffing 438

(*pork* continued)
minced 657
mixed cabbage coleslaw with chinese barbecued 270
neck 252, 267, 657
panang pork curry with pickled snake beans 256
pancetta see pancetta
pork cabbage rolls 254
pot-roasting 252
potted pork with witlof and cornichons 268
rack 657
rissoles on potato rösti with leek puree 255
roast rack, with lemon and garlic 268
roasting 252
sang choy bow 113
satay sticks 121
schnitzel 252, 657
shoulder 657
spareribs 253, 657
spinach, speck and poached egg salad 270
steamed pork buns 269
sweet and sour 262
vindaloo 262
porridge 32
portuguese custard tarts 588
potatoes 657
baked 310
barramundi with kipflers and roasted capsicum 184
beef and horseradish stew with kumara potato mash 220
bintje 657
braised leek and witlof salad with poached eggs and roasted kipflers 339
cabbage mash 246
cakes see rösti
capsicum mash 309
celeriac mash 309
chips 303
coliban 657
congo 657
cottage pie 576
cream cheese and pesto topping 310
desiree 657
duck confit with pan-fried kipflers and pear and watercress salad 212
fennel mash 309
fish and chips 162
german hot potato salad 144
gnocchi with burnt butter and tomato 350
gratin 367
hash, potato and onion 234
(*potatoes* continued)
herb-crusted lamb racks with kipflers and leek 295
idaho 657
king edward 657
kipfler 657
kumara potato mash 220
lasoda 657
lime and chilli yogurt topping 311
lobster with flavoured butter and lemon grass mash 167
masher 21
mashes 309
mustard and walnut butter topping 311
pea mash 309
pink-eye 657
pink fir apple 657
pontiac 657
pork fillet with mash and wilted cabbage 259
potato and goat cheese puffs 79
potato and rosemary pizza 488
potato, olive and sun-dried tomato bread 486
pumpkin mash 309
rissoles with cabbage mash 246
roasted 205
rösti see rösti
salad 144, 149
sausages with caramelised onions, kipflers and mushrooms 229
seared tuna with kipfler smash and salsa verde 159
sebago 657
shepherd's pie 281
skordalia 298, 423
spinach mash 309
spunta 657
pots and pans 16
praline 597
cream 507
pistachio praline topping 622
prawns 659
barbecued seafood and green mango salad 166
cioppino 181
deveining 10
dried shrimp 659
dumplings 70
grilled, with tropical fruits 162
honey prawns 182
laksa 104
macadamia prawn cakes 171
mango salsa with 118
mini prawn cocktail 78
paella 379
prawn and asparagus risotto 382
(*prawns* continued)
prawn, snow pea and wild rice salad 390
preparing 157
saganaki prawn ravioli 356
salt and pepper butterflied 130
skewered lemon 234
smoked salmon with avocado salsa and 116
spicy sour prawn soup 94
stir-fried garlic 117
thai coconut 76
tomato aïoli and prawn canapés 78
profiteroles 582
mini chocolate eclairs 583
paris-brest 582
prosciutto 657
chicken and prosciutto cannelloni 361
croissants, prosciutto and fontina 36
fig and prosciutto pizza 488
raclette parcels in vine leaves and 85
rösti stacks, prosciutto and roast capsicum 43
wild rocket with 118
provolone 335, 645
prunes 658
scones 512
stewed, with orange 44
pudding
blackberry 600
chocolate, pear and hazelnut self-saucing 606
Christmas pudding 442, 448
fig and brioche 598
frozen chocolate fruit cake pudding 451
lemon delicious 607
rice, with raspberries 615
sticky date, with butterscotch sauce 614
yorkshire 228
pulses see beans; lentils; peas
pumpernickel bread 480
pumpkin 658
chickpea, pumpkin and eggplant curry 304
gratin 367
mash 309
middle-eastern roasted pumpkin, carrot and parsnip 323
roasted vegetable salad 119
rosemary pumpkin bread 496
scones 513
soup 91
punch
mixed-berry 52
party 63
purple shallot 260, 656

Q

quail 658
  buying, storing and handling 188
  cuts 189
  quail, fig and orange salad 126
  roast bacon-wrapped, with muscat sauce 194
quince 592, 658
  lamb and quince tagine with pistachio couscous 283
  paste 463
  tarte tatin 592
quinoa 316, 658
  barbecued fennel, orange and red onion with 316

R

raan with lemon pilau 293
raclette 334, 645
  parcels in vine leaves and prosciutto 85
radicchio 143, 653
  thai crab salad with 129
raisins 658
raita 174, 422, 658
  chicken tandoori pockets with 190
  curried blue-eye with lentils and 174
  tandoori lamb cutlets with 280
rambutan 608
  asian fruit salad 618
ramen noodles 345, 352
ranch dressing 428
ras el hanout 466
raspberry
  chocolate soufflé with raspberry coulis 598
  coulis 424, 598
  jelly cakes 564
  mille-feuille with almonds and raspberries 586
  raspberry and chocolate mousse trifle 619
  raspberry and peach jam 462
  rice pudding with 615
  sorbet 612
  vinegar 662
ravioli
  duck, in asian broth 127
  saganaki prawn 356
raw sugar 661
red onion 656
  barbecued fennel, orange and red onion with quinoa 316
  jam, duck liver parfait with 114
red wine
  basic red wine sauce 416
  braised beef cheeks in 243

(*red wine* continued)
  octopus braised in 164
  risotto, roasted eye fillet with 378
  vinaigrette 147
  vinegar 663
redcurrant jelly 658
  cumberland sauce 417
relish
  corn 470
  spicy green tomato 469
remoulade 422, 658
  crumbed brains with celeriac 296
rendering 12
resting (meat) 12
rhubarb
  apple and rhubarb streusel slice 531
  chutney 470
  galette 585
  plum and rhubarb crumble 619
  rhubarb and almond jalousie 586
  rhubarb and coconut cake 542
rice 658
  arancini 386
  arborio 380, 658
  basmati 380, 658
  black 381, 658
  black sticky rice 615
  brown 381
  burghul and wild rice salad 406
  buying and storing 370
  california handrolls 376
  calrose 381, 658
  cheesy rice croquettes 385
  chicken and thai basil fried rice 376
  chicken fried rice 203
  chicken jambalaya 373
  combination fried rice 378
  cooking methods 12, 370
  cooking times 371
  dolmades 375
  glutinous 380, 658
  italian brown rice salad 391
  jasmine 380, 658
  koskihikari 381
  lemon pilau 293
  long-grain 381, 658
  maple creamed rice with pecans and dates 44
  nishiki 380
  paella 379
  prawn, snow pea and wild rice salad 390
  pudding with raspberries 615
  raan with lemon pilau 293
  risotto see risotto
  rolled 658
  short-grain 658
  sushi rice 382
  tuna and cucumber mini maki 383

(*rice* continued)
  tunisian spicy nut pilaf 372
  types 370, 380, 658
  vinegar 663
  white 658
  wild 381, 658
  wild blend 380
  yellow coconut rice 375
rice flour 650
rice noodles 345, 353, 655
  sweet soy fried noodles 366
rice paper 658
rice paper rolls
  teriyaki chicken 202
  vietnamese 68
ricotta 334, 645
  baked, with tomato 28
  ginger and ricotta cream 507
  lemon ricotta zucchini flowers 118
  ricotta and herb calzones 321
  ricotta and spinach stuffed pasta shells 364
  ricotta, pear and honey topping 38
  spinach and ricotta gnocchi with sage butter 129
rigani 658
risoni 656
  duck breasts with fig sauce and spinach risoni 198
  salmon, risoni and pea salad 119
  spinach and semi-dried tomatoes, with 354
risotto
  cakes with basil sauce and pancetta 389
  microwave mushroom 372
  milanese 390
  oven-baked, with italian sausages 373
  prawn and asparagus 382
  primavera, on grilled flat mushrooms 113
  roasted eye fillet with red wine 378
  zucchini flowers filled with 384
rissoles
  cabbage mash with 246
  pork, on potato rösti with leek puree 255
roasted stone fruit with lemon grass 618
roasting 658
  vegetables 303
roasting pan 17
rocket 143, 658
  baby rocket and parmesan salad 137
  haloumi, asparagus and rocket salad 136
  italian blt 259
  lamb and rocket mini pizzas 69
  prosciutto with wild 118
  salad 401
  salami and rocket pizza 488
  veal rack with rosemary and rocket pesto 232

rocky road
cake 550
gourmet 628
ice-cream topping 623
rogan josh 276, 648
rolled oats 658
porridge 32
roquefort 645
rosemary 658
lamb cutlets with mustard and rosemary cream 289
lamb kebabs with 234
potato and rosemary pizza 488
rosemary pumpkin bread 496
veal rack with rocket pesto and 232
rosewater 639, 658
pistachio rosewater pinwheels 581
turkish delight 639
rösti 82
pork rissoles on, with leek puree 255
prosciutto and roast capsicum 43
smoked trout and crème fraîche 82
roti 495
rouille 658
bouillabaisse with aïoli and 102
rubbing in 12
rum 658
chocolate rum and raisin slice 533
rye
flour 650
food processor rye bread 492
rolled 658

S

sacher torte 545
saffron 466, 659
cream sauce 161
leek and saffron barley 409
saffron scrambled eggs on corn cakes 330
salt-baked whole ocean trout in saffron cream sauce 161
steamed mussels with 119
sage 169, 659
butter 129
sake 659
salad leaves 134, 142
salad spinner 21
salads 134
artichoke and broad bean 322
asian pork and apple 136
asparagus and tomato 118
avocado caprese salad 140
baby rocket and parmesan 137
burghul and wild rice 406
burghul, with chickpeas 400
caesar 144
(*salads* continued)
char-grilled thai beef 141
chef's 147
chicken caesar 203
chicken, old-fashioned 141
chicken pasta 203
citrus 161
crunchy fried noodle coleslaw 148
fattoush 140
gado gado 138
german hot potato 144
greek 145
greek lamb 298
green mango 166
gremolata lamb pasta 153
grilled vegetable 149
haloumi, asparagus and rocket 136
herb 311
hot-smoked trout and vermicelli 184
italian brown rice 391
kumara craisin 266
larb chicken 151
mixed pea, broad bean and turkey 200
niçoise 145
panzanella 147
pasta, simple 153
pear and watercress 213
potato 144, 149
prawn, snow pea and wild rice 390
quail, fig and orange 126
roasted vegetable 119
rocket 401
salmon, risoni and pea 119
smoked chicken and pear 119
sour and sweet green 163
spinach, speck and poached egg 270
tabbouleh 125
three-bean 152
tuna pasta 152
tuscan white bean 137
white radish and snow pea 182
witlof and nashi 148
salami and rocket pizza 488
salmon 660
crème fraîche and salmon roe on blini 84
gravlax 176
salmon and avocado on cucumber 78
salmon lemon grass skewers 235
salmon, risoni and pea salad 119
salt and pepper salmon cutlets with white radish and snow pea salad 182
smoked see smoked salmon
teriyaki 164
tuna, kingfish and salmon carpaccio 177
salsa 413, 659
caper and roasted capsicum 431
corn 191
(*salsa* continued)
cruda 237
grilled corn and zucchini 431
mango and avocado 428
salsa verde 159, 428, 659
oysters with 172
seared tuna with kipfler smash and 159
salt 659
sambal oelek 659
samosas with tamarind sauce 80
sandwiches
chicken and avocado 203
creamy egg and lettuce fingers 341
italian-style toasted 203
New York deli style 492
pecan chicken open 202
steak sandwich revisited 233
sang choy bow 113
sangria 57
sardines 660
in chermoulla with tomato salsa 159
satay sauce 121, 307, 418
satay sticks, mixed 121
sausage
beef, bean and chorizo stew 221
caramelised onions, kipflers and mushrooms with 229
chorizo 260, 647
chorizo and kumara frittata 329
frittata 229
oven-baked risotto with italian sausages 373
spicy sausage and bocconcini pizza 489
white bean, leek and garlic sausage soup 106
sausage rolls 74
sauté 11
savoiardi 659
scalding 12
scales 16
scallops 660
Asian 79
cioppino 181
lime and ginger ceviche 181
preparing 157
steamed, with asian flavours 177
tarragon and lime 68
scampi, preparing 157
scones
apricot 512
baking 501
basic 512
buttermilk 514
date/prune and cinnamon 512
freezing 501
mixing 500
pear and ginger 512

(*scones* continued)
pumpkin 513
spicy fruit 514
wholemeal date 513
score 659
scottish shortbread 456
seafood see also specific types
barbecued seafood and green mango salad 166
buying and storing 156
cold seafood platter with dipping sauces 441
cooking 156
hot seafood platter 170
paella 379
spaghetti marinara 346
seasoning 13
segmenting 660
self-raising flour 650
semifreddo 610, 650
poached figs with 610
semolina 650
sesame oil 655
sesame seeds 421, 660
seven-spice mix 660
shallots 656
dressing 193
purple 260, 656
shallow-frying 11
shellfish see also specific types
cooking 156
preparing 157
shepherd's pie 281
vegetarian 318
sherry 660
sherry vinegar 663
shiitake mushrooms 313, 654
dried 654
japanese oysters with 172
shortbread
glazed lemon 528
greek 524
presentation 627
scottish 456
shrimp see also prawns
dried 659
paste 660
sichuan beef, twice-fried 230
sichuan peppercorns 467, 660
silverbeet 660
silverside 219, 643
simmering 12
singapore noodles 354, 655
skewers 18, 660
skordalia 298, 423
slices
apple and rhubarb streusel 531
apricot and coconut no-bake 535

(*slices* continued)
apricot muesli 534
baking 518
choc-peppermint no-bake 535
chocolate no-bake 535
chocolate rum and raisin 533
coffee and macadamia no-bake 535
fruit mince slice 449
hazelnut caramel 533
lemon no-bake 535
mixing 518
no-bake slices 535
storing and freezing 519
tangy lemon squares 534
triple-choc brownies 531
smoked cod 659
chowder 103
smoked salmon
avocado salsa and prawns with 116
canapés 79
cream cheese topping 38
crepe cakes, smoked salmon and sour cream 85
omelette 28
scrambled eggs with dill and 43
smoked salmon caper and dill frittata 341
smoked trout see trout
smoothies 49
banana-passionfruit soy 60
low-fat mocha 63
mixed-berry 60
snow peas 660
buying and storing 135
prawn, snow pea and wild rice salad 390
white radish and snow pea salad 182
soba noodles 345, 352, 655
chilled soba 360
somen noodles 345, 353
sorbet 650
raspberry 612
soufflé
cheese and chive souffléd oysters 173
chocolate, with raspberry coulis 598
goat cheese, with creamed spinach sauce 336
spinach, with fresh tomato sauce 123
twice-cooked cheese 338
soup 88
accompaniments 89, 96
borscht 95
bouillabaisse with aïoli and rouille 102
chicken and corn 107
chicken and zucchini 203
cuban black bean 99
french onion 94
garnishes 89
gazpacho 92

(*soup* continued)
harira 100
lamb shank 90
minestrone 91
pastry soup dippers 580
pea and ham 100
prawn laksa 104
pumpkin 91
roasted parsnip and garlic 101
smoked cod chowder 103
spicy sour prawn 94
stocks 88
swiss brown mushroom and barley 107
tomato 90
vichyssoise 99
vietnamese beef, chicken and tofu 92
watercress, creamy 106
white bean, leek and garlic sausage 106
sour cream
dessert accompaniment 597
smoked salmon and sour cream crepes 85
sourdough 478
crusty sourdough loaf 486
soy sauce 660
crisp-skinned soy chicken with spiced salt 190
dark 660
gyoza with soy vinegar sauce 70
honey soy marinade 276
japanese 660
light 660
soy vinegar sauce 70
sweet soy dressing 270
sweet soy fried noodles 366
tamari 660
soybeans 394, 642
patties with lemon and herb yogurt 399
spaghetti 656
alla vongole 360
bolognese 357
marinara 346
napoletana 363
spanish tortilla 33
spareribs 229
american-style 257, 657
chinese-style 253
spatchcock 189, 660
braised, with peas and lettuce 207
portuguese-style grilled 210
spearmint 654
speck 660
spinach, speck and poached egg salad 270
spices 466

spinach 660
beetroot, carrot and spinach juice 62
blini, spinach and horseradish 84
cheese and spinach tortellini with gorgonzola sauce 366
cucumber, celery, apple and spinach juice 57
duck breasts with fig sauce and spinach risoni 198
filo triangles 124
goat cheese soufflé with creamed spinach sauce 336
kang kong 313
mash 309
ricotta and spinach stuffed pasta shells 364
risoni with spinach and semi-dried tomatoes 354
soufflé with fresh tomato sauce 123
spinach and ricotta gnocchi with sage butter 129
spinach, speck and poached egg salad 270
steamed spinach dumplings with fresh tomato and herb sauce 306
tomato, spinach and cheese topping 38
water spinach 313
spoons 18
spring rolls 73
wrappers 660
sprouts and shoots 134
squid 660 see also calamari
barbecued seafood and green mango salad 166
preparing 157
salt and pepper 170
star anise 466, 660
starfruit 608, 660
asian fruit salad 618
Christmas tree cake 550
starters 110
fast 118
steak see beef
steamed Christmas pudding 442
steaming vegetables 303
steel 16
stir-frying 11
vegetables 303
stirring 11
stirring implements 18
stock 88, 660
beef 661
chicken 661
fish 661
vegetable 661
stollen 444
strawberry
almond and strawberry friands 515
buttermilk pancakes with glazed 37
conserve 463
creamcake 551
garnishes for drinks 55
ice-cream 622
jelly cakes 564
sugar 626, 661
sugar snap peas 661
sugar syrup 48
sumac 278, 467, 661
dressing 297, 400
sunflower seeds 421, 661
sushi rice 382
sushi vinegar 382
sweating 13
sweet and sour pork 262
sweet chilli sauce 81, 646
sweet soy dressing 270
sweetbreads 661
swiss cheese 645
swiss roll pan 661
swordfish 660
malaysian swordfish curry 173

T

tabasco 661
tabbouleh 125
lamb and tabbouleh wrap 278
taco seasoning mix 661
tagine 661
chicken, with olives and preserved lemon 197
lamb and quince, with pistachio couscous 283
vegetable 308
tahini 661
hummus bi tahini 397
tamari 661
tamarind 261, 349, 661
concentrate 661
lamb cutlets with tamarind and date chutney 288
lamb shanks in five-spice, tamarind and ginger 284
pad thai 349
samosas with tamarind sauce 80
tandoori
chicken pockets with raita 190
lamb cutlets 289
lamb cutlets with chutney 280
tapenade 661
haloumi and tapenade bruschetta 79
pastries 580
sun-dried tomato and olive 474
tarragon 169, 661
creamy tarragon and mushroom sauce 418
tarragon and lime scallops 68
tartare sauce 163, 425
tartaric acid 661
tarts see pies and tarts
tat soi 312
tea 27, 49
cardamom and chamomile 526
chai 527
cinnamon and orange 526
ginger 527
lemon grass and kaffir lime 526
lemon iced 526
minted lemon grass and ginger iced 58
moroccan mint 526
peach iced 58
tempering 661
tempura 130
vegetable tempura with wasabi aïoli 130
tequila 662
teriyaki 77, 662
rice paper rolls 202
salmon 164
tuna 77
thai
basil 169, 642
chillies 646
coconut prawns 76
dressing 215
eggplant 649
fish burgers with sour and sweet green salad 163
fried stick noodles 349
mint 654
pad thai 349
red curry beef skewers 234
thousand island dressing 425
thyme 662
new york steaks with lemon-thyme butter 232
tiramisu cake 606
toast toppings 38
toffee 582, 597
boiling sugar 626
brittle 597
hazelnut and pine nut brittle 629
nut brittle 629
pistachio praline topping 622
praline 597
praline cream 507
upside-down toffee banana cake 546
tofu 662
firm 662
fried 662
pan-fried, with beetroot hummus 322
sheets 662

(*tofu* continued)
silken 662
soft 662
tofu and thai eggplant massaman curry 320
vietnamese beef, chicken and tofu soup 92
tom collins 62
tomato
asparagus and tomato salad 118
avocado caprese salad 140
baked ricotta with 28
blt on mini toasts 79
breakfast fry up 29
buying and storing 134
canned 662
cheese, tomato and bacon topping 39
cherry 662
chilli tomato jam 233
chutney, spicy 469
egg/roma 662
gnocchi with burnt butter and tomato 350
grape 662
green 469, 662
jam, chilli tomato 233
jam, tomato and passionfruit 463
juice see tomato juice
olive and tomato bruschetta 119
orecchiette with ham, artichokes and sun-dried tomatoes 356
oysters with tomato, bacon and basil 172
paste 662
potato, olive and sun-dried tomato bread 486
puree 662
risoni with spinach and semi-dried tomatoes 354
roasted vegetable filo tart 579
roma 662
salsa 405
sauce see tomato sauce
semi-dried 662
soup 90
spicy green tomato relish 469
sun-dried 662
sun-dried tomato and olive tapenade 474
tomato, leek and marinated fetta tartlets 71
tomato, spinach and cheese topping 38
truss 662
tomato juice
bloody mary 59
gazpacho 92
tomato, carrot and red capsicum juice 62
tomato sauce 662
basic 416
basic pizza sauce 487
fresh 123
fresh tomato and herb sauce 306
spinach soufflé with fresh 123
steamed spinach dumplings with 306
tortellini 656
cheese and spinach, with gorgonzola sauce 366
tortilla 662
crisps 96
spanish 33
treacle 651, 662
trevally 660
mornay pies 574
trifle
classic 620
raspberry and chocolate mousse 619
tropical fruits 608
trout
hot-smoked trout and vermicelli salad 184
ocean trout 659
rösti with smoked trout and crème fraîche 82
salt-baked whole ocean trout in saffron cream sauce 161
sashimi rolls with lemon dipping sauce 131
trussing 13
tuna 660
carpaccio 177
niçoise salad 145
pasta salad 152
salad on pitta crisps 78
seared, with kipfler smash and salsa verde 159
spicy teriaki tuna 77
tartare 176
tuna and avocado topping 38
tuna and cucumber mini maki 383
turkey
asian-spiced barbecued 438
buying, storing and handling 188
carving 435
cuts 189
forcemeat stuffing, with 436
judging when cooked 189
mixed pea, broad bean and turkey salad 200
preparing for roasting 13
traditional, with forcemeat stuffing 436
turkey, brie and cranberry 78
turkish bread 484
turkish delight 639
gourmet rocky road 628
turmeric 261, 662
turnip
braised root vegetables with gremolata 310
preserved 657
turtle beans see black beans

U

udon noodles 345, 353, 655
casseroles 351

V

v-slicer 21, 663
vanilla 662
bean 662
bean cream 507
bean syrup 559
butter cream 549
custard 444
essence 662
extract 662
ice-cream 622
panna cotta with berry jelly 605
veal 218, 662
and eggplant parmigiana 230
buying, storing and handling 218
cooking 219
cuts 219
marsala 244
osso buco 225, 662
rack 662
rack with rosemary and rocket pesto 232
scaloppine 662
schnitzel 662
sweetbreads with duxelles and herb salad 249
wiener schnitzel with lemon spaetzle 248
vegetable oil 655
vegetable stock 661
vegetables see also specific vegetables
barbecued vegetarian pizzas 311
braised root vegetables with gremolata 310
buying, storing and handling 302
cassoulet 318
char-grilled vegetable mini pizzas 69
cooking 303
crisps, lamb backstraps with 290
free-form tarts 581
fritters 303
judging when cooked 302
potato and vegetable mashes 309
roasted vegetable filo tart 579
roasted vegetable lasagne 316
roasted vegetable salad 119

(*vegetables* continued)
tagine 308
tempura with wasabi aïoli 130
yellow curry 307
velouté sauce 414
vermouth 662
vichyssoise 99
vietnamese beef, chicken and tofu soup 92
vietnamese mint 168, 654
vietnamese rice paper rolls 68
vin santo 663
vinaigrette 176
chilli and lime 182
red wine 147
white wine 147
vine leaves 85, 651
dolmades 375
minced lamb in 117
raclette parcels in prosciutto and 85
vinegar 662
vodka
bloody mary 59
caipiroska 50
cosmopolitan 50
gazpacho 92
long island iced tea 50

W

waffles
belgian-style 643
caramelised banana and pecan 40
walnuts 420, 663
coffee granita with walnut crisps 612
eggless date and nut cake 565
fig, walnut and ginger cake 558
mini macadamia, pecan and walnut pies 589
mustard and walnut butter potato topping 311
whipped nut butter 41, 507
wasabi 261, 663
mayonnaise 213
vegetable tempura with wasabi aïoli 130
water chestnuts 663
watercress 142, 663
duck confit with pan-fried kipflers and pear and watercress salad 212
soup, creamy 106
wheat noodles 345
whipped nut butter 41, 507
whipping/whisking 11
white bean 642
puree 285
soup, white bean, leek and garlic sausage 106
tuscan white bean salad 137
white chocolate see chocolate
white radish (daikon) 663
salmon cutlets with white radish and snow pea salad 182
white sauce 291, 316, 412
white vinegar 663
white wine
vinaigrette 147
vinegar 663
whiting 660
parcels with porcini and sun-dried tomatoes on soft polenta 183
wholemeal flour 650
date scones 513
fig muffins 502
fruit and coconut loaf 565
wiener schnitzel with lemon spaetzle 248
wine 49, 663
chinese cooking 646
red see red wine
vin santo 663
white wine vinaigrette 147
witlof 143, 663
braised leek and witlof salad with poached eggs and roasted kipflers 339
potted pork with cornichons and 268
salad, witlof and nashi 148
wombok 313
wontons 77, 663
coconut chicken salad in crisp wonton cups 82
peanut and chicken gow gees 77
smoked chicken wonton crisps 79
wrappers 663
wooden spoons 18
worcestershire sauce 663

Y

yakitori with sesame dipping sauce 206
yeast 478, 663
yogurt 663
apple and melon lassi 52
blood plums with honey and cardamom 44
dessert accompaniment 597
frozen passionfruit 620
fruit scrolls with spiced 35
honey and yogurt topping 32
honey yogurt cake 549
labne 125
lassi 49
lime and chilli yogurt potato topping 311
raita see raita
soybean patties with lemon and herb yogurt 399
spiced 97
(*yogurt* continued)
spiced honey 507
spiced plums with 35
yorkshire puddings 228

Z

za'atar 297, 467, 663
crusted cutlets 288
lamb with warm chickpea salad 297
zucchini 663
buying and storing 135
chicken and zucchini soup 203
creamy farfalle with fried zucchini 367
grilled corn and zucchini salsa 431
grilled vegetable salad 149
vegetable cassoulet 318
zucchini flowers
lemon ricotta 118
risotto-filled 384

Editorial director *Susan Tomnay*
Creative director *Hieu Chi Nguyen*
Project manager *Rachel Carter*
Feature writers *Meg Thomason, Fiona Roberts, Karen Hammial*
Designer *Karen Grant*
Food director *Pamela Clark*
Food editor *Cathie Lonnie*
Nutritional information *Rebecca Squadrito*

Sales director *Brian Cearnes*
Marketing manager *Bridget Cody*
Production manager *Cedric Taylor*
Business analyst *Ashley Davies*
Chief executive officer *Ian Law*
Group publisher *Pat Ingram*
General manager *Christine Whiston*
Editorial director (AWW) *Deborah Thomas*

The publishers would like to thank the following for props used in photography *Bodum, Bondi Junction; Top 3 by Design, Bondi Junction; Simon Johnson, Woollahra; Cambodia House, Paddington; The Essential Ingredient, Crows Nest; New Age Veneers Pty Ltd, Sydney.*

Photographers *Alan Benson; Russell Brooks; Steve Brown; Scott Cameron; Chris Chen; Paul Clarke; Gerry Colley; Brett Danton; Joshua Dasey; Ben Dearnley; Joe Filshie; Rowan Fotheringham; Chris Jones; Louise Lister; Ashley Mackevicius; Andre Martin; Mark O'Meara; Con Poulos; Tim Robinson; Prue Ruscoe; Stuart Scott; Brett Stevens; Robert Taylor; John Paul Urizar; Ian Wallace; Andrew Young.*
Stylists *Myles Beaufort; Wendy Berecry; Julz Beresford; Janelle Bloom; Margot Braddon; Kate Brown; Kirsty Cassidy; Marie-Helene Clauzon; Jane Collins; Kay Francis; Jane Hann; Trish Heagerty; Jacqui Hing; Katy Holder; Amber Keller; Cherise Koch; Michaela Le Compte; Michelle Noerianto; Sarah O'Brien; Louise Pickford; Suzie Smith; Sophia Young.*

Chapter openers and special features:
Photographer *Joshua Dasey*
Stylist *Margot Braddon*
Food preparation *Nicole Jennings*

Produced by ACP Books, published by ACP Books, a division of ACP Magazines Ltd.
54 Park St, Sydney NSW 2000 Australia; GPO Box 4088, Sydney, NSW 2001.
Phone +61 2 9282 8618 Fax +61 2 9267 9438
acpbooks@acpmagazines.com.au www.acpbooks.com.au
To order books, phone 136 116. Send recipe enquiries to recipeenquiries@acpmagazines.com.au
Printed by C&C Offset Printing, 4/F C&C Building, 36 Ting Lai Road, Tai Po, China.

Rights enquiries Laura Bamford, Director ACP Books. lbamford@acpuk.com

Australia Distributed by Network Services, GPO Box 4088, Sydney, NSW 2001.
Phone +61 2 9282 8777 Fax +61 2 9264 3278 networkweb@networkservicescompany.com.au
United Kingdom Distributed by Australian Consolidated Press (UK),
10 Scirocco Close, Moulton Park Office Village, Northampton, NN3 6AP.
Phone +44 1604 642 200 Fax +44 1604 642 300
books@acpuk.com www.acpuk.com
New Zealand Distributed by Netlink Distribution Company, ACP Media Centre, Cnr Fanshawe and Beaumont Streets, Westhaven, Auckland. PO Box 47906, Ponsonby, Auckland, NZ.
Phone +64 9 366 9966 Fax 0800 277 412 ask@ndc.co.nz
South Africa Distributed by PSD Promotions, 30 Diesel Road Isando, Gauteng Johannesburg.
PO Box 1175, Isando 1600, Gauteng Johannesburg.
Phone +27 11 392 6065/6/7 Fax +27 11 392 6079/80 orders@psdprom.co.za

Clark, Pamela.
The Australian women's weekly cook.
Includes index.
ISBN 978-1-86396-427-2
1. Cookery.
641.5

ABN 18 053 273 546

First published 2006. Reprinted 2006, 2007 (three times).